Artificial Intelligence

Rajendra Akerkar

Artificial Intelligence

Transcending Traditional Paradigms

 Springer

Rajendra Akerkar
Big Data and Emerging Technologies
Vestlandsforsking
Sogndal, Norway

ISBN 978-3-031-91083-8   ISBN 978-3-031-91084-5 (eBook)
https://doi.org/10.1007/978-3-031-91084-5

To
To those who will inherit both the promise
and responsibility of intelligent machines.

Preface

What we want is a machine that can learn from experience.—Alan Turing, 1947

There are more things in heaven and earth, Horatio, than are dreamt of in your philosophy.—William Shakespeare, Hamlet

The history of artificial intelligence (AI) spans more than seventy years, marked by pivotal milestones and transformative breakthroughs. Over the past two decades, the field has expanded rapidly, with a proliferation of tools and techniques that have significantly reshaped its scope. From its early beginnings, characterized by simple rule-based systems, AI has evolved into a sophisticated discipline capable of addressing complex, real-world challenges. As illustrated in Fig. 1, this progression reflects a steady increase in both capability and complexity. Today, AI is poised to transform nearly every sector, bridging the gap between digital intelligence and physical interaction and enabling more seamless collaboration between humans and machines.

Since its formal inception at the Dartmouth Conference in 1956, AI has undergone several paradigm shifts. The early era was dominated by symbolic AI, which relied on logical reasoning and rule-based systems. While effective in structured environments, these approaches struggled with ambiguity and real-world variability. This limitation led to the rise of connectionist models, particularly neural networks and deep learning, which revolutionized pattern recognition and natural language processing. Probabilistic models, such as Bayesian networks, introduced reasoning under uncertainty, while evolutionary algorithms enabled optimization in complex problem spaces. Advances in hardware, especially the use of GPUs, further accelerated progress, culminating in the development of transformer architectures that now underpin many state-of-the-art AI systems.

In recent years, AI has moved beyond traditional rule-based and statistical models toward more integrated and adaptive architectures. Modern systems increasingly combine symbolic reasoning with neural computation, incorporate cognitive features such as self-reflection, and exhibit emergent behaviours not explicitly programmed.

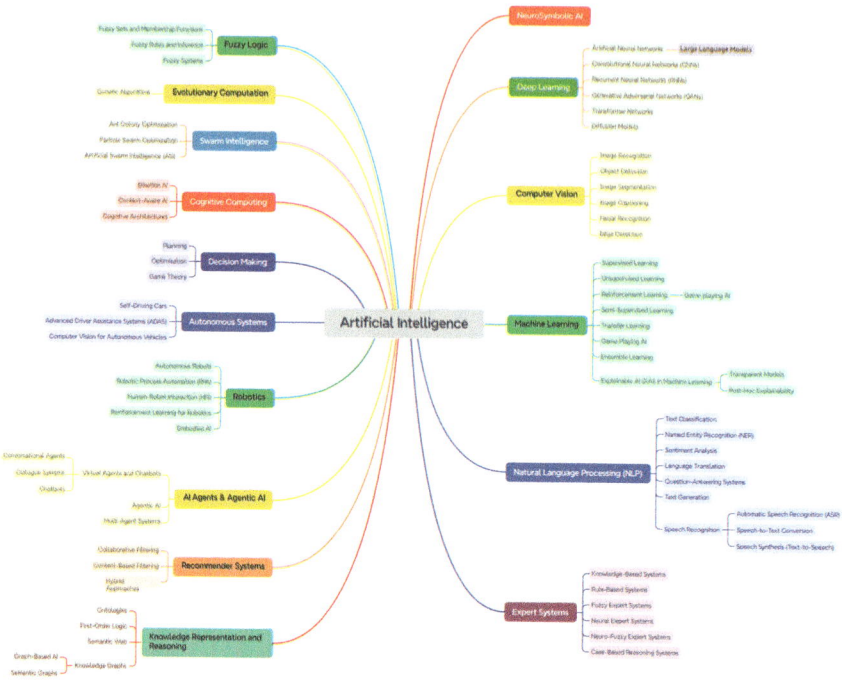

Fig. 1 Various branches of artificial intelligence

These systems can reason across domains, interpret nuanced inputs, and manage complex, multi-step tasks with a level of generalization that approaches human-like flexibility.

Key developments include the rise of foundation models, neuro-symbolic systems, self-supervised learning, and multi-agent frameworks, all of which enable AI to learn continuously, adapt dynamically, and operate autonomously across diverse contexts. Innovations such as neuromorphic computing, processing-in-memory, and on-device AI have enhanced efficiency, privacy, and responsiveness. Meanwhile, domain-specific models and federated learning have extended AI's reach into specialized and privacy-sensitive applications.

The ongoing convergence of diverse AI methodologies marks not merely a technical evolution but a fundamental reimagining of artificial intelligence itself. This synthesis enables systems that integrate perception, reasoning, and action within unified frameworks, moving beyond the limitations of earlier models that were narrowly focused or domain-specific. As AI transcends its traditional boundaries, it is increasingly positioned to interact more deeply with human cognition and society, offering the potential for more adaptive, generalizable, and context-aware intelligence.

This shift toward holistic AI architectures represents a transformative moment in the field. By combining multiple forms of reasoning, contextual understanding, and adaptive learning, modern AI systems are capable of addressing complex, real-world problems that span diverse domains. These systems can deliver more nuanced, personalized, and effective solutions, basically reshaping how organizations operate and make decisions. Moreover, they exhibit emergent behaviours and human-like flexibility, allowing them to engage with open-ended challenges and maintain coherence across multi-step processes.

Such advancements demand new approaches to leadership, ethics, and interdisciplinary collaboration. As AI becomes more autonomous and embedded in everyday life, its role evolves from that of a tool for automation to a collaborative partner—one that supports innovation, enhances well-being, and aligns with human values. Ensuring that this integration is responsible and trustworthy is essential for realizing AI's full potential in service of society.

Specific Features and Target Audience

This book offers a broad yet accessible overview of artificial intelligence, covering both traditional approaches and the latest advancements in the field. Rather than focusing on mathematical formalism, it presents key AI concepts and techniques in a concise and comprehensible manner, making it a valuable resource for readers seeking a well-rounded understanding. It is designed to inspire innovation among students and researchers while also providing developers and practitioners with adaptable methods for building AI-driven solutions.

The book assumes a foundational knowledge of computer science, particularly in algorithms and data structures at a second-year undergraduate level. Familiarity with statistics and basic calculus will further support comprehension.

Intended primarily as a textbook for advanced undergraduate students in computer science, AI, and related disciplines (including engineering, psychology, and linguistics) it also serves as a follow-up to introductory AI courses.

Overview of the Book

This book offers a comprehensive journey through the evolving landscape of artificial intelligence, covering both foundational and cutting-edge topics. It emphasizes practical methods and current practices, drawing on recent research to highlight the challenges and opportunities shaping the field today. Rather than focusing on mathematical formalism, the book presents key AI concepts in a clear and accessible way, aiming to provide readers with a solid conceptual understanding.

The material is technical in nature but does not require an advanced mathematical background. Core AI principles are explored alongside essential skills and knowledge that a practical AI scientist needs. Some topics are the central focus of dedicated chapters, while others are introduced more organically through discussion.

Each chapter is self-contained and includes a section on further reading, guiding readers to additional resources for deeper exploration. Supplementary materials, including Python code, are available at: https://github.com/ArtificialIntelligence-Book.

This book is organized into six parts, each offering a structured exploration of artificial intelligence, from its foundational principles to advanced and responsible applications. Drawing on over three decades of experience as an AI educator and researcher, the content reflects both the historical depth and the evolving complexity of the field.

Part I: Foundations of Artificial Intelligence

This part traces the historical and conceptual roots of AI. Chapter 1 explores the origins of the field, from early philosophical ideas to the formal establishment of AI at the Dartmouth Conference, and the rise of symbolic AI. It examines core concepts such as reasoning, learning, and the interdisciplinary nature of AI, while also addressing recent trends and applications. Chapter 2 focuses on foundational techniques, including search algorithms, knowledge representation, reasoning methods like logic and semantic networks, and automated planning. It also highlights early applications in computer vision, natural language processing, and expert systems.

Part II: The Learning Revolution—Data-Driven Intelligence

This part introduces the shift toward learning-based AI. Chapter 3 presents soft computing approaches—neural networks, genetic algorithms, and fuzzy logic—as tools for handling complexity and uncertainty. Chapter 4 offers a comprehensive overview of machine learning, covering the full pipeline from data handling to deployment, including supervised and unsupervised learning, model evaluation, and advanced topics like causal reasoning and meta-learning. Chapter 5 delves into deep learning, exploring neural architectures and training techniques. Chapter 6 introduces reinforcement learning, discussing learning through interaction and the integration of deep learning methods.

Part III: AI Odyssey—Exploring Language and Intelligent Agents

Focusing on specific application areas, this part begins with Chap. 7, which examines large language models, their training, adaptation, and the role of prompt engineering.

It also addresses challenges and the rise of multimodal AI. Chapter 8 explores intelligent agents, their architectures, and the dynamics of multi-agent systems, including ethical considerations in autonomous decision-making.

Part IV: Expanding the Frontiers of AI

This part explores hybrid and emerging approaches. Chapter 9 introduces neuro-symbolic AI, combining neural networks with symbolic reasoning, and discusses applications such as visual question-answering and knowledge graphs. Chapter 10 focuses on cognitive AI, covering topics like commonsense reasoning, meta-cognition, and embodied perception. Chapter 11 explores embodied intelligence, emphasizing the role of physical interaction in cognition, learning, and communication, including theory of mind and multi-agent collaboration.

Part V: Building Advanced and Responsible AI

This part addresses the practical and ethical dimensions of AI development. Chapter 12 provides guidance on building robust AI systems, covering project planning, data management, model development, deployment, monitoring, and ethical workflows. Chapter 13 discusses continual learning, enabling systems to adapt over time without forgetting. Chapter 14 emphasizes explainability, exploring techniques for transparency, bias detection, human-centred design, and the broader societal and regulatory context of responsible AI.

Part VI: Epilogue—AI at the Threshold

The final chapter (Chap. 15) reflects on the current state of AI and its future trajectory, offering insights into the transformative potential and ongoing challenges of the field.

Acknowledgments

I would like to express my sincere appreciation to everyone who provided feedback on this book. I am especially grateful to the many authors of books and research articles whose work laid the foundation for this text. My thanks go to Helen Desmond and the entire team at Springer for their continued professionalism and support. I am also indebted to Long Nguyễn Hoàng for his assistance with several figures in the book.

I extend my deep gratitude to my colleagues at Western Norway Research Institute for their ongoing encouragement and support throughout this project. Most importantly, I offer my heartfelt thanks and love to my wife and son, whose patience and understanding have been invaluable as I pursued the many ideas and reflections that shaped this work.

I hope readers find the field of artificial intelligence as fascinating and rewarding as I do.

May 2025   Rajendra Akerkar

Contents

Part IV   Expanding the Frontiers of AI

Part VI Conclusion and Future Outlook

Part I
Foundations of Artificial Intelligence

Chapter 1
The Genesis of Artificial Intelligence: Origins and Evolution

*The machine does not isolate man from the great problems of
nature but plunges him more deeply into them.*
—Antoine de Saint-Exupéry

Conceptual Origins

We trace the genesis of artificial intelligence (AI) back to foundational concepts
exploring the mechanization of thought and reasoning. Early efforts in the mid-
twentieth century focused on symbolic AI, aiming to replicate human intelligence
through logical rules and knowledge representation. The field subsequently evolved,
embracing connectionist approaches and the power of data-driven learning, leading
to significant advancements. The more recent emergence of Large Language Model
(LLM) has triggered a remarkable surge in AI capabilities, demonstrating unprecedented success in complex tasks. This historical trajectory underscores that AI is not
a static invention but rather a continuously evolving scientific endeavour.

Turing Test

One of the foundational papers to address the question of *machine intelligence* specifically in relation to the modern digital computer was written in 1950 by the British
mathematician Alan Turing. Computing machinery and intelligence remain timely in
both its assessment of the arguments against the possibility of creating an intelligent
computing machine and its answers to those arguments.

Turing, known primarily for his contributions to the theory of computability,
considered the question of whether a machine could actually be made to think. Stating
the underlying ambiguities in the question itself precluded any rational answer, he
proposed that the question of intelligence be replaced by a more clearly defined
empirical test.

R. Akerkar, *Artificial Intelligence*, https://doi.org/10.1007/978-3-031-91084-5_1

The Turing test is a test of a machine's ability to exhibit intelligent behaviour equivalent to, or indistinguishable from, that of a human. A human evaluator engages in natural language conversations with both a human and a machine, without knowing which is which. If the evaluator cannot reliably tell the machine apart from the human, the machine is said to have passed the test.

The Turing test, which Turing himself termed the "imitation game," evaluates a machine's purported intelligence by comparing its performance to that of a human, considered by some to be the ultimate standard for intelligent behaviour. In this test, the machine and a human participant are placed in separate rooms, isolated from a second human participant known as the "interrogator." The interrogator, unable to see or speak directly to either the machine or the human, communicates with them solely through a textual medium, such as a terminal. The interrogator's task is to distinguish the computer from the human based solely on their responses to questions posed via this device. Turing posited that if the interrogator cannot differentiate the machine from the human, the machine can be considered intelligent.

By isolating the interrogator from direct contact with both the machine and the human, the test aims to prevent any bias due to the machine's appearance or the mechanical properties of its voice. The interrogator is free to employ any questioning strategy, including devious or indirect inquiries, to determine the computer's identity. For instance, the interrogator might ask both subjects to perform a complex arithmetic calculation, assuming the computer is more likely to provide a correct answer. To counter this, the computer would need to strategically provide incorrect answers at times to mimic human fallibility. Similarly, to probe the human's emotional nature, the interrogator could ask for responses to a poem or artwork, requiring the computer to possess knowledge of human emotional responses.

The Turing test offers several key advantages: it provides an objective measure of intelligence, defining it as the behaviour of a known intelligent being in response to a specific set of questions. This approach establishes a standard for determining intelligence that avoids debates about its "true" nature. It also sidesteps potentially confusing and currently unanswerable questions, such as whether the computer employs appropriate internal processes or is conscious of its actions. Furthermore, the test eliminates bias in favour of living organisms by compelling the interrogator to focus solely on the content of the answers. These advantages have led to the Turing test serving as a foundation for many modern AI program evaluation methods. A program demonstrating potential intelligence in a specific domain may be evaluated by comparing its performance on a set of problems to that of a human expert. This evaluation technique represents a variation of the Turing test, where a group of humans compares the performance of a computer and a human on a given set of problems without knowing which is which. This methodology has become a vital tool in both the development and validation of contemporary expert systems.

Despite its intuitive appeal, the Turing test is subject to several valid criticisms. A primary concern is its bias toward purely symbolic problem-solving tasks. It does not assess abilities that involve perceptual skill or manual dexterity, both of which are important aspects of human intelligence. Conversely, some argue that the Turing test unnecessarily restricts machine intelligence to a human model. It is possible that machine intelligence differs fundamentally from human intelligence and evaluating it in human terms is a mistake. Should a machine be expected to perform mathematics with the slowness and inaccuracy of a human? It might be more appropriate for an intelligent machine to leverage its inherent strengths, such as a large, fast, and reliable memory, rather than attempting to replicate human cognition. Indeed, some AI practitioners view striving to pass the full Turing test as a misdirection, diverting attention from the more crucial task of developing general theories to explain intelligence in humans and machines, and applying these theories to create tools for solving specific, practical problems. While acknowledging these concerns, the Turing test remains a valuable element in the verification and validation of modern AI software.

Turing also explored the feasibility of creating an intelligent program on a digital computer. By considering a specific model of computation—an electronic discrete state computing machine—he made informed predictions about the storage capacity, program complexity, and fundamental design principles necessary for such a system. Additionally, he addressed various moral, philosophical, and scientific objections to the possibility of constructing such a program using available technology. It's also common to see a reciprocal relationship: observing how humans perform a task can inform the creation of a program to mimic that behaviour, and the program (particularly a learning program) can potentially lead to improvements in human performance. The DENDRAL system, which identifies chemical structures from mass spectrograms and has derived rules not previously known to human experts, exemplifies this. DENDRAL is a highly successful program and is considered the world's leading expert in this type of analysis. This raises the question of what constitutes machine intelligence, a problem Turing considered in the 1950s, leading to the development of his test.

A very early attempt to create a program capable of passing the Turing test was Joseph Weizenbaum's ELIZA, developed at MIT in 1966. This program aimed to simulate a conversation with a psychologist. While initially appearing effective, its limitations become apparent after a short period of interaction, revealing the underlying mechanics. Clearly, a system must possess natural language understanding to succeed in the Turing test, a formidable challenge. Humans rely on a wide range of assumptions and inferences to comprehend sentences and utterances. It is generally believed that achieving human-level natural language processing requires a system to incorporate commonsense reasoning and possess a breadth of general knowledge comparable to that of a human.

The Turing test is among the earliest proposed methods for assessing machine intelligence. Success in this test indicates a level of artificial intelligence that mirrors human conversational and thought processes. Although groundbreaking, the Turing test has been superseded by modern AI research. Current AI systems are evaluated based on their performance in specialized tasks such as language understanding, image recognition, and problem-solving, which may not necessitate passing the

Turing test. Nevertheless, the concept continues to represent a symbolic objective for AI systems striving for artificial general intelligence (AGI).

Dartmouth Conference (1956)—AI's Formal Inception

In the summer of 1956, a pivotal event occurred that would forever change the landscape of computer science and human technological advancement. The Dartmouth Summer Research Project on Artificial Intelligence, now known simply as the Dartmouth Conference, marked the formal inception of artificial intelligence as a new academic discipline. This watershed moment brought together leading minds who would shape the future of computing and cognitive science for decades to come. The conference originated from a proposal drafted by John McCarthy, Marvin Minsky, Nathaniel Rochester, and Claude Shannon in 1955. Their ambitious proposal stated that "every aspect of learning or any other feature of intelligence can in principle be so precisely described that a machine can be made to simulate it." This assertion, revolutionary for its time, set the stage for what would become a two-month exploration of machine intelligence.

The organizers secured funding from the Rockefeller Foundation, demonstrating early institutional recognition of AI's potential significance. The proposal outlined several key areas of investigation, including natural language processing, neural networks, computation theory, abstraction, and creativity. These topics continue to resonate in contemporary AI research, highlighting the prescience of the conference's scope. The Dartmouth Conference's influence extended far beyond its immediate proceedings. It established artificial intelligence as a legitimate field of academic inquiry and set research agendas that would guide the discipline for decades.

The conference attracted an extraordinary assemblage of talent. Beyond the organizers, participants included:

Herbert Simon and Allen Newell, who would soon create the Logic Theorist, considered the first artificial intelligence program. Ray Solomonoff, a pioneer in algorithmic probability theory. Oliver Selfridge, who would later develop influential pattern recognition work. Trenchard More, who contributed to mathematical logic applications. Arthur Samuel, who developed early machine learning programs for checkers. These researchers, though relatively young at the time, would go on to become foundational figures in computer science and artificial intelligence.

The conference discussions were marked by both optimism and rigorous scientific inquiry. Participants explored fundamental questions about the nature of intelligence, computation, and learning.

The term "artificial intelligence" itself was coined by McCarthy during the conference, providing a unified identity for the field. He defined the field as:

Definition Artificial intelligence is the science and engineering of making intelligent machines, especially intelligent computer programs. It is related to the similar task of using computers to understand human intelligence, but AI does not have to confine itself to methods that are biologically observable.

This terminology choice proved influential, though not without subsequent controversy regarding its implications.

The Dartmouth Conference's historical importance is clear, though its initial optimism was too early. Predictions of human-level AI within a generation didn't materialize, leading to "AI winters" with funding cuts. However, this initial enthusiasm should be understood historically. As AI reshapes society, the Dartmouth Conference stands as both a historical landmark and ongoing inspiration.

Early Symbolic AI by Newell and Simon

The foundations of AI were greatly shaped by the pioneering work of Allen Newell and Herbert Simon during the 1950s and 1960s. Their landmark research established symbolic processing as a fundamental paradigm for understanding both human cognition and machine intelligence. This analysis examines their seminal contributions and lasting impact on the field of artificial intelligence. Newell and Simon's work was anchored in their physical symbol system hypothesis (PSSH), which proposed that symbolic manipulation constitutes the necessary and sufficient condition for intelligent action. They argued that intelligence emerges from the ability to process and manipulate symbols according to systematic rules. This hypothesis became a cornerstone of classical artificial intelligence. The PSSH suggested that human cognition could be understood as a form of information processing, where thinking involves manipulating symbolic representations through explicit rules and procedures. This marked a significant departure from behaviourist approaches dominant at the time, which focused solely on observable behaviours rather than internal mental processes.

In 1956, Newell and Simon created the Logic Theorist, widely recognized as the first artificial intelligence program. This system demonstrated that machines could engage in sophisticated problem-solving through symbolic manipulation. The program was specifically designed to prove mathematical theorems from Whitehead and Russell's Principia Mathematica.

The *Logic Theorist* operated by:

1. Representing mathematical expressions as symbolic structures.
2. Applying transformation rules to these structures.
3. Searching through possible proof paths.

4. Constructing formal proofs of mathematical theorems.

The system successfully proved 38 of the 52 theorems it attempted from the Principia Mathematica, in some cases finding more elegant proofs than those originally published. This achievement demonstrated that machines could perform tasks previously thought to require human intelligence.

Building on the success of the Logic Theorist, Newell and Simon developed the General Problem Solver (GPS) in 1957. This more ambitious program aimed to solve a wider range of problems through general-purpose reasoning strategies. GPS introduced several revolutionary concepts such as *means-ends analysis*, a problem-solving approach that identified differences between current and goal states, selected operators to reduce these differences and recursively applied this strategy to achieve goals.

Moreover, Newell and Simon's work extended beyond artificial intelligence into cognitive psychology. They developed information processing in psychology, a theoretical framework that viewed human cognition as a form of information processing similar to computer operations. This approach yielded valuable insights into human cognition and demonstrated the potential of using computational models to understand psychological processes. Their legacy serves as a reminder that breakthrough innovations often emerge from combining rigorous theoretical frameworks with practical implementation and empirical validation.

Searle's Chinese Room Argument

The quest to understand and replicate human intelligence has long captivated thinkers, from philosophers to computer scientists. At the heart of this pursuit lies the field of artificial intelligence (AI), striving to create machines capable of performing tasks that typically require human intelligence. However, as AI capabilities advance, fundamental questions about the nature of mind, consciousness, and understanding emerge. One of the most provocative and enduring challenges to the strong AI thesis—the idea that sufficiently programmed computers can genuinely *think* and possess consciousness—is John Searle's Chinese Room Argument (CRA). Introduced in his 1980 paper "Minds, Brains, and Programs," the CRA remains a potent thought experiment, forcing us to confront the distinction between mere symbol manipulation and genuine understanding, and ultimately questioning whether computation alone can ever give rise to consciousness.

Searle's Chinese Room Argument is not a direct attack on the practical applications of AI, often termed "Weak AI," which focuses on creating useful AI tools without claiming genuine understanding. Instead, it directly targets "Strong AI," the philosophical position that asserts that a properly programmed computer *is* a mind, capable of understanding, consciousness, and other cognitive states in the same way humans are. To illustrate his point, Searle constructs a vivid and easily graspable thought experiment.

Imagine yourself, Searle proposes, a person who understands no Chinese, locked in a room. Slips of paper with Chinese writing are passed into the room. You, inside the room, possess a rule book written in English, detailing how to manipulate these Chinese symbols based purely on their shape and form. The rule book is incredibly detailed and comprehensive, allowing you to correlate certain Chinese symbols as "inputs" with other Chinese symbols as "outputs." For example, the rules might dictate that when you receive a paper with symbol set "X," you should consult rule "Y" and then output paper with symbol set "Z." The slips of paper passed into the room are questions in Chinese, and the papers you output, following the rule book, are perfectly sensible and contextually appropriate answers in Chinese. From the perspective of someone outside the room who *does* understand Chinese, the room appears to be a fluent Chinese speaker. It passes the Turing test for understanding Chinese.

However, Searle's crucial point is this: despite the room's perfect performance in responding to Chinese questions, *you* inside the room, the actual executor of the rules, understand absolutely nothing about Chinese. You are merely manipulating meaningless symbols according to syntactical rules, devoid of any semantic understanding of what those symbols represent. You don't grasp the meaning of the questions or the answers. You are simply a symbol processor, expertly following instructions.

Searle then draws the analogy: he argues that the person in the Chinese Room is analogous to the central processing unit (CPU) of a computer. The rule book is analogous to the computer program, and the Chinese symbols are analogous to the data that the computer processes. Just as the person in the room, following the rules, can produce seemingly intelligent Chinese outputs without understanding Chinese, Searle contends that a computer, running a program, can manipulate symbols and produce seemingly intelligent outputs without genuinely understanding anything. The computer, like the person in the room, is merely manipulating syntax (the structure and rules of symbols) without grasping semantics (the meaning and understanding of those symbols).

The core of Searle's argument can be distilled into a few key claims:

1. **Programs are purely syntactical**: Computer programs are defined by their formal, syntactical structure, and the rules for manipulating symbols. They are sequences of instructions that operate on data based on their form, not their meaning.
2. **Understanding involves semantics**: True understanding, however, is not merely syntactical manipulation. It requires grasping the *meaning* of symbols and their relationship to the world. This is the semantics, of content, of intentionality—the "aboutness" of mental states, their directedness toward objects and propositions.
3. **Syntax is not sufficient for semantics**: Simply manipulating symbols according to rules, no matter how complex or sophisticated, cannot, in itself, generate genuine understanding or intentionality. Syntax alone can never give rise to semantics.

4. **Therefore, running a program, no matter how sophisticated, is not sufficient for understanding or consciousness**: If a computer is essentially just a symbol-manipulating machine following syntactical rules, and syntax is not sufficient for semantics, then running a program cannot create a genuinely understanding or conscious mind. Strong AI, in its claim that programs can create minds, is therefore fundamentally flawed.

Searle's argument is not denying that computers can be incredibly useful tools, capable of performing complex calculations and simulations. He acknowledges the success of "Weak AI" in building machines that can perform specific tasks intelligently *as if* they understood. His argument specifically targets the philosophical claim of "Strong AI," which posits that computers can be more than just tools; they can become genuine minds.

The Chinese Room Argument has generated a vast and complex debate within philosophy of mind and AI. It has been met with numerous counterarguments, each seeking to dismantle its logic or offer alternative perspectives. Some of the most prominent replies include:

- **The Systems Reply**: This is perhaps the most common and influential counterargument. It concedes that the person *inside* the room may not understand Chinese, but argues that the *entire system*—the room, the rule book, the person, and the paper exchanges—*does* understand Chinese. The understanding is not localized to the individual person but emerges from the complex interaction of all the components working together as a system. Searle's rebuttal to this reply is to imagine internalizing the entire system. He asks us to imagine him memorizing the rule book and performing all the operations internally, still without understanding Chinese. He argues that even if the entire system is considered, there is still no genuine understanding present, only complex symbol manipulation.

- **The Robot Reply**: This argument suggests that if we were to embody the Chinese Room in a robot, equipping it with sensory and motor capacities to interact with the real world, then it might genuinely understand Chinese. By grounding the symbol manipulation in real-world experience and interaction, the robot would move beyond mere syntax and begin to acquire semantics. Searle counters that even with robotic embodiment, the core issue remains. The robot's CPU, like the person in the room, is still just manipulating symbols. Adding sensors and actuators does not magically instil symbol manipulation with meaning or consciousness. The robot, like the room, might behave *as if* it understands, but there is no guarantee of genuine internal understanding.

- **The Brain Simulator Reply**: This reply argues that if we could create a computer program that precisely simulated the neuron-level firings of a human brain that understands Chinese, then such a simulation *would* understand Chinese. By simulating the actual causal processes of the brain, we would be replicating the very mechanism that gives rise to understanding. Searle's response is that even a perfect simulation of brain processes is still just a simulation. It is still manipulating symbols according to rules, even if those rules are incredibly complex and mimic neural activity. Simulation, he argues, is not duplication. Simulating digestion doesn't digest a pizza, and simulating understanding doesn't create understanding.

Despite these and other counterarguments, the Chinese Room Argument continues to resonate and provoke debate. It highlights a fundamental challenge in AI: the difficulty of bridging the gap between syntax and semantics, between computation and genuine understanding. It forces us to confront the question of what it truly means for a machine to "understand," and whether simply passing behavioural tests like the Turing test is sufficient evidence of genuine intelligence and consciousness.

While the CRA doesn't necessarily preclude the possibility of creating truly intelligent machines in the future, it does cast serious doubt on the idea that current computational approaches, based solely on symbol manipulation, are sufficient. It suggests that understanding and consciousness may require something more than just running the right program, something perhaps tied to the biological and physical nature of the brain itself. Whether this "something more" is essential or whether future AI paradigms can overcome the limitations identified by Searle remains a central question in the ongoing exploration of artificial intelligence and the very nature of the mind. The Chinese Room Argument, therefore, stands as a crucial philosophical touchstone, constantly reminding us to critically examine our assumptions about AI and the elusive nature of genuine understanding in both machines and us.

Understanding Intelligence in AI

"Intelligence" in AI

While we all possess an instinctive understanding of intelligence, a precise definition remains elusive. We often attempt to define it through survival-related functionalities: perceiving the environment, securing sustenance, seeking shelter, sensing danger, and reacting accordingly. These behaviours, indicative of intelligent action, are evident in many living creatures. However, intelligence, as we typically conceive it, encompasses more than mere survival instincts.

Beyond basic survival, we associate intelligence with the ability to reason, perform calculations, and engage in strategic activities like chess. While computers excel in these areas, these capabilities alone do not fully capture our notion of intelligence. The ability to use language and learn from experience are equally essential components.

Given that artificial intelligence (AI) deals with the creation of "intelligent machines," it's crucial to define what we expect from such machines. Naturally, we expect them to be intelligent. But what does intelligence truly mean? According to dictionary definitions:

- **Intelligence**: The faculty of understanding.
- **Understanding**: To comprehend something or recognize its significance.

This leads us to the question of how to measure and replicate this "faculty of understanding" in machines.

Intelligence, in essence, reflects an individual's capacity to comprehend the objective world and apply knowledge to solve problems. This encompasses a range of capabilities, including: perceiving and understanding both external reality and oneself; acquiring knowledge through learning; applying knowledge and experience to problem analysis and resolution; engaging in association, reasoning, judgement, and decision-making; utilizing linguistic abstraction and generalization; fostering discovery, invention, creativity, and innovation; responding effectively to complex environments; and predicting future developments and changes. Given our social nature, intelligence is also inherently intertwined with social contexts.

A fundamental insight from early AI research is that "intelligence requires knowledge." However, knowledge, while indispensable, presents challenges: it is voluminous, difficult to accurately characterize, constantly evolving, and distinguished from mere data by its organized structure. Importantly, knowledge and intelligence are distinct concepts. A machine may store knowledge without possessing intelligence, but an intelligent machine devoid of knowledge is inconceivable. The core question for AI is how, to what extent, and in what sense knowledge can be imparted to a machine.

In practical terms, knowledge is crucial for intelligence, both human and artificial. It enables AI agents or systems to exhibit intelligent behaviour, acting accurately on input based on accumulated knowledge or experience.

Rather than get bogged down in debates about the nature of human intelligence, AI practitioners have adopted a pragmatic approach. They define an intelligent machine as one capable of tasks that, if performed by a human, would be considered intelligent. This bypasses the need for a precise definition of intelligence, relying instead on our ability to recognize intelligent behaviour.

However, this approach is not without its critics. The argument that a machine replicating a human intelligent function is itself intelligent is countered by the assertion that once a machine performs a task, it is deemed mechanical. If we can explain the machine's operation, we effectively demystify its apparent intelligence.

Even if we admit that a machine is behaving intelligently, may it not be that the intelligence we see is a property of the people who programmed the computer and not of the machine itself? Also, can a distinction be drawn between intelligent behaviour and behaviour which merely appears to be intelligent?

Certainly, since we do not know what goes on in our brain, acceptance of this argument implies that our own intelligence may be in some fashion illusory perhaps we only think we are intelligent. In the case of a machine, we can establish the nature of the internal processes. If a machine and person display similar behaviour, are the internal processes in some way comparable?

If knowledge amounted to no more than an accumulation of data, even a comparatively modest computer would be rated more highly than the most intelligent human beings. It is indisputable that, in terms of sheer capacity computer memories have far outstripped our own. This is precisely why computers are so useful; within microseconds they can tell a booking clerk whether there is a seat left on tomorrow's flight to Oslo. The enormous memory is only accessible because there is a human being operating the terminal, asking exactly the right questions, in exactly the right way, and in exactly the right order.

Definition Knowledge manipulation occurs primarily through inference and deduction and the often search-oriented control strategy or inference engine which determines the items of knowledge to be accessed, the deductions to be made, and order of steps to be used.

Definition Knowledge representation involves structuring information in a form that a computer can understand. A way to do this is by using ontologies or knowledge graphs, which allows for relationships and hierarchies within your data to be represented.

Definition Knowledge acquisition is the transfer and transformation of potential problem-solving expertise from some knowledge source to a program.

The knowledge acquisition process can also be defined as the task of identifying and eliciting relevant domain knowledge in sufficient quantities to provide the power to solve complex problems. The process often referred to as expertise transfer involves the extraction of knowledge from a variety of sources and its representation in a suitable format.

Deductive Reasoning

Deductive reasoning uses a basis of known facts, applying logic or other systematic methods to draw conclusions. This approach includes several techniques, such as search and logic-based methods, and finds application in areas like theorem proving and game playing. While inductive and deductive methods often address different types of problems, some problems can be approached with either. Deductive reasoning is frequently employed for problems with clearly defined tasks that involve logical inferences from known facts, those requiring substantial amounts of known domain knowledge, or those demanding impractical amounts of data or computational power for inductive learning. However, as computational power and data availability have increased, some problems previously solved with deductive reasoning methods have shifted into the sphere of inductive learning. In recent years, inductive learning methods have increasingly been applied to problem types that were once the domain of deductive reasoning, largely due to the growth in computational power that enables the use of ever-larger datasets.

Deductive reasoning, while powerful, possesses inherent limitations that mirror its strengths. Its effectiveness hinges on the ability to translate expert knowledge into a structured knowledge base, a process that necessitates human comprehension and interpretation. This leads to systems that are highly transparent, a clearly beneficial attribute. However, this very interpretability presents a challenge in achieving truly human-like behaviour, as many human decisions are rooted in complex levels of understanding that are not easily codified or explained. A significant benefit of deductive reasoning lies in its capacity to integrate existing knowledge, offering an efficient route to incorporating established facts without the need for repetitive inductive learning. It is particularly well-suited for focused areas where a limited amount of information is sufficient for drawing meaningful inferences, or when the foundational knowledge is well-defined and undisputed. In contemporary applications, deductive methods are frequently integrated into inductive learning frameworks to lessen the reliance on extensive datasets by complementing them with smaller knowledge bases. This integrated approach aligns with biological principles, as human cognition itself appears to be a blend of both deductive and inductive processes.

Inductive Learning

Contrasting deductive reasoning, which proceeds from general principles to specific conclusions, inductive learning generates broader conceptualizations from limited empirical data. This approach forms the basis of machine learning methodologies, allowing intelligent systems to extract meaningful insights and predictive models from complex datasets.

The concept of inductive learning finds its intellectual origins in epistemological investigations that date back to the Enlightenment period. Philosophers like David Hume primarily challenged traditional approaches to knowledge acquisition by questioning the logical foundations of generalization. Hume's critical insight was that universal principles cannot be definitively proven through finite observations, introducing what became known as the "problem of induction." Inductive learning represents a profound intellectual process of moving from particular instances to broader, more comprehensive theoretical frameworks. Consider a simple analogy: if a researcher observes multiple white swans across different geographical locations, traditional inductive reasoning might lead to the generalization that "all swans are white." This process encapsulates the basic challenge and potential of inductive reasoning—extracting universal principles from limited empirical evidence.

In artificial intelligence, this philosophical concept transforms into sophisticated computational mechanisms. Machine learning algorithms essentially perform a technologically advanced version of inductive reasoning by:

1. Analysing Finite Datasets Computational systems receive a limited set of training data, representing specific instances or observations. Unlike traditional computational approaches that require exhaustive rule specification, inductive learning algorithms can extract underlying patterns from these finite datasets.
2. Pattern Abstraction Through advanced statistical and mathematical techniques, these algorithms identify recurring structural relationships that transcend individual data points. This process involves sophisticated feature extraction, where complex multidimensional representations are constructed to capture nuanced interconnections.
3. Generalization Capability The critical achievement of inductive learning lies in its ability to generate predictive models that perform effectively on novel, unseen data. This means the computational system can make intelligent predictions or classifications beyond its original training instances.

Inductive learning algorithms must be balanced between:

- Overfitting: Creating models too closely aligned with training data.
- Underfitting: Developing models too simplistic to capture meaningful patterns.

This balance represents a modern computational interpretation of the classic philosophical problem of generalization.

Inductive learning in AI represents more than a technological tool. It embodies a profound philosophical approach to knowledge construction. It mirrors human cognitive processes of pattern recognition and generalization, challenging traditional distinctions between empirical observation and theoretical understanding.

Does AI Learn to Reason?

Reasoning is a fundamental aspect of human intelligence. Since the earliest days of humanity, abductive reasoning has been used to anticipate potential threats, while inductive reasoning has enabled the discovery of patterns and regularities in the natural world. In Ancient Greece, deductive reasoning emerged as a method for deriving logical conclusions based on premises assumed to be true. The development of reasoning methods with guaranteed logical validity played a crucial role in the progress of modern science, mathematics, and engineering. Philosophers like Charles Sanders Peirce emphasized that the interplay between abduction, deduction, and induction forms the foundation of the scientific method, which underpins all modern scientific inquiry.

Efforts to mechanize logical reasoning date back to the thirteenth-century philosopher Ramon Lull and are closely tied to the concept of computation. Probabilistic reasoning also significantly influenced this domain, relying on principles such as Bayes' theorem on inverse probability, which now serves as a cornerstone for many approaches in machine learning and statistics. Furthermore, evaluating correct reasoning is central to most quantitative measures of human cognition.

Given its importance, reasoning has been a central focus of AI research since its inception. Early AI studies, beginning with programs like Logic Theorist, concentrated heavily on reasoning processes. By the 1960s, AI began incorporating probabilistic reasoning models, initially applied in medical diagnosis. Over time, AI research expanded to address diverse reasoning tasks, including planning, temporal reasoning, diagnosis, and explanation. Early efforts in AI explored both plausible reasoning methods such as case-based or analogical reasoning and formal reasoning techniques with logical guarantees such as probabilistic and constraint-based approaches. However, as AI evolved, there was a shift toward prioritizing formal reasoning methods with guarantees due to their ability to address human limitations in performing rigorous logical analysis.

This focus on formal reasoning has led to impactful applications in AI systems. Examples include SAT solvers, SMT solvers, and constraint-solving techniques used for verifying computer hardware and software correctness, ensuring communication protocol safety, designing new proteins, and assessing neural network robustness against adversarial attacks. Probabilistic graphical models have also emerged as powerful tools for modelling and inference across various domains such as medicine and robotics.

Reasoning, in the human context, involves a variety of cognitive processes, including:

- Deduction: Drawing certain conclusions from given premises.
- Induction: Generalizing from specific observations to broader principles.
- Abduction: Inferring the most likely explanation for a given observation.
- Analogy: Reasoning based on similarities between different situations.
- Commonsense reasoning: Using general knowledge about the world to make inferences.

Modern AI, especially deep learning, excels at tasks that involve recognizing patterns in large amounts of data. For example, an AI can be trained to identify cats in images with high accuracy. However, this is not the same as understanding the concept of "cat" in a way that a human does. The AI doesn't know that cats are mammals, that they meow, or that they like to chase mice.

Examples Let's consider a few examples to illustrate the difference:
Deduction
Human:
Premise 1: All men are mortal.
Premise 2: Socrates is a man.
Conclusion: Therefore, Socrates is mortal.
AI: A classical AI system with a knowledge base could be programmed with these premises and use a logical inference engine to arrive at the same conclusion. However, this requires explicit programming of the rules and facts.

Modern AI systems might struggle with this unless trained on a massive dataset of similar logical problems.

Commonsense Reasoning

Human: If you put a cup on a table and then knock the table, the cup will fall.

AI: This kind of reasoning, which requires understanding cause and effect and the physical properties of objects, is very challenging for AI. While some progress has been made in this area, AI still struggles with the nuances of commonsense.

Analogy

Human: "The brain is like a computer, processing information."

AI: AI can be trained to recognize analogies in text, but understanding the deeper meaning and implications of an analogy requires a level of conceptual understanding that is still beyond the reach of most AI systems.

Recently, large language models (LLMs) have demonstrated remarkable capabilities in plausible reasoning by leveraging patterns learned from extensive training on massive datasets. However, this type of reasoning lacks formal guarantees. Despite these advancements in plausible reasoning through LLMs, formal reasoning techniques remain essential for critical applications involving hardware and software verification, real-world planning challenges, and resource allocation problems. Formal methods are increasingly recognized as vital for ensuring the robustness of machine learning systems like neural networks against adversarial threats.

Active research continues to focus on enhancing various types of reasoning algorithms, particularly in terms of computational efficiency, and integrating learning into formal reasoning processes. Efforts are also being made to combine learning-based approaches with sound formal reasoning techniques to address complex challenges across diverse fields. This ongoing work emphasizes the importance of both plausible and formal reasoning in advancing cutting-edge AI technologies while ensuring their reliability and practical impact.

Reasoning with Uncertainty

Reasoning with uncertainty is crucial for AI and decision-making systems operating in complex, ambiguous environments with incomplete information. Unlike classical logic, uncertainty reasoning accepts that real-world knowledge is often incomplete, imprecise, or varies in confidence.

Reasoning with uncertainty involves making inferences, predictions, and decisions while explicitly representing and manipulating the doubt inherent in our knowledge. Most reasoning tasks in practical settings involve some level of uncertainty—whether from measurement errors, incomplete observations, conflicting evidence, inherent randomness, or the limitations of available knowledge.

Several mathematical frameworks have been developed to formalize uncertainty reasoning. Probability theory serves as the foundation, providing a rigorous mathematical basis for quantifying uncertainty through probability distributions. Bayesian networks extend this approach by representing conditional dependencies between random variables in directed acyclic graphs, allowing for efficient reasoning about complex probability distributions through local computations. These networks excel at updating beliefs when new evidence arrives, implementing Bayes' theorem to revise probability assessments in the light of observations.

Fuzzy logic offers an alternative perspective on uncertainty by addressing vagueness rather than randomness. While probability theory deals with uncertainty about which crisp state is true, fuzzy logic handles concepts that inherently lack sharp boundaries, like "tall" or "hot", by allowing partial membership in sets. This approach is particularly valuable when dealing with linguistic variables and imprecise human knowledge.

Dempster–Shafer theory provides yet another framework, distinguishing between uncertainty and ignorance. It allows for assigning belief to sets of possibilities rather than individual outcomes, making it useful when evidence supports a proposition without necessarily contradicting its negation. This nuanced view of uncertainty can represent situations where "I don't know" differs meaningfully from equal probabilities.

Markov Decision Processes incorporate uncertainty into sequential decision-making, modelling stochastic environments where actions have probabilistic outcomes. By computing expected utilities over possible future states, these frameworks enable optimal policies even when action effects cannot be predicted with certainty.

In practical applications, reasoning with uncertainty enables robust system behaviour across numerous domains. Medical diagnosis systems use probabilistic reasoning to interpret symptoms and test results, accounting for test sensitivity and specificity. Autonomous vehicles must constantly reason about uncertain sensor readings and the unpredictable behaviour of other road users. Financial models incorporate uncertainty about market movements to manage risk appropriately. Weather forecasting systems express prediction confidence through probability distributions rather than single-point forecasts.

The challenge of uncertainty reasoning extends beyond the mathematical frameworks to implementation issues. Acquiring accurate probability assessments remains difficult, whether from statistical data or expert judgement. Computational tractability presents another obstacle, as exact inference in complex models often proves intractable, necessitating approximate methods like Monte Carlo sampling or variational inference.

Recent advances in machine learning have transformed uncertainty reasoning by enabling data-driven approaches to probability estimation and inference. Bayesian deep learning attempts to combine the representational power of neural networks with principled uncertainty quantification. Meanwhile, reinforcement learning directly addresses sequential decision-making under uncertainty, learning policies through experience in stochastic environments.

As AI systems increasingly participate in critical decision-making contexts, proper uncertainty representation becomes not just a technical concern but an ethical imperative. Systems that express appropriate confidence in their conclusions can better support human decision-makers, avoid overconfident errors, and operate more safely in unfamiliar situations. The ability to recognize when knowledge is limited, to know what one doesn't know, remains a hallmark of intelligence, whether human or artificial.

AI in the Twentieth Century

Since its inception in the early 1950s, artificial intelligence (AI) has been defined in various ways. One definition highlights AI as technology that empowers computers and machines to function intelligently. Another perspective focuses on AI's capacity to replace human labour, boosting efficiency and speed. Still others define AI by its ability to accurately analyse data, learn from it, and utilize these insights to reach specific objectives through flexible methods. AI's ability to alleviate workload has led to its widespread integration into everyday life. Fundamentally, AI can be seen as an attempt to replicate human cognitive abilities in computers, enabling them to perform tasks that typically require human intelligence and to behave in a more intelligent manner. Despite the range of definitions, the dominant understanding of AI revolves around machines and computers designed to support humanity by solving problems and making work more efficient. In essence, AI is intelligence crafted by humans and exhibited through machines.

While knowledge of the history of AI is not essential to understand the subject, it presents a context by which we can interpret current developments and appreciate the progress that AI has made till date. In the history of AI research, different types of thought are studied from different views of *Symbolisms*, *Connectionism*, and *Behaviourism*.

Symbolisms is also known as logicism or traditional AI. It is based on the physical symbol system hypothesis proposed by Alan Newell and Herbert Simon, which states that a physical symbol system has the necessary and sufficient means for general intelligent action. A physical symbol system consists of a set of entities, called symbols, which are physical patterns that can occur as components of another type of entity called an expression. *Connectionism*, also known as neural computing or bionics or physiology school, focuses on the essentials and capabilities for non-programmable, adaptative, and brain-like information processing. Researchers in the connectionist tradition would frequently point out the disconnection between symbolic cognition and how the brain works. The research field developed with a great number of neural network mechanisms, models, and algorithms emerging unceasingly. By the late 80s, the future seemed bright for connectionist models. Even so, they would rapidly collide with the limitations of data availability and computational power. It turned out that training large neural networks to learn anything resembling human-level intelligence, required large amounts of data and computation, which were scarce and expensive at the time. *Behaviourism*, also known as behaviour-based AI or evolutionism or cybernetics, in many respects reflects the behaviour physiological views in AI. These three research categories investigate different aspects of human natural intelligence corresponding to different layers in the model of human thought. There were attempts to introduce models of attentional control of executive functioning combining symbolic-like planning and connectionist-like pattern recognition. This line of thinking has widened until today, with many researchers bidding to take advantage of the strengths of both approaches. Briefly, Symbolisms focuses on abstract thought, Connectionism focuses on imagery thought, while Behaviourism focuses on perceptual thought.

Core Components of AI

Four Core Capabilities

Four core capabilities form the heart of AI.

Learning, the ability of AI to improve its performance over time, relies on various machine learning models. In supervised learning, algorithms learn from labelled data to perform tasks like classification and regression, employing models such as linear regression, logistic regression, decision trees, support vector machines, and deep neural networks with architectures like convolutional neural networks for image tasks and recurrent neural networks or transformers for sequential data. Unsupervised learning enables AI to discover hidden patterns in unlabelled data through techniques like clustering, dimensionality reduction, and association rule mining. Reinforcement learning allows agents to learn optimal behaviours by interacting with the environment and receiving feedback in the form of rewards and penalties, utilizing algorithms like Q-learning, Deep Q-Networks, and policy gradient methods.

Reasoning and *decision-making* empower AI to derive conclusions and make informed judgements. Symbolic reasoning employs formal logic, rule-based systems, and knowledge representation techniques like ontologies to perform logical inference. Probabilistic reasoning utilizes probabilistic models such as Bayesian networks and Hidden Markov Models to handle uncertainty and make decisions based on probabilities. AI also employs various algorithms for decision-making, including search algorithms, game theory algorithms, and planning algorithms. Ensuring consistent and sound reasoning often involves techniques for verifying and validating AI models, and the field of explainable AI focuses on making these reasoning processes transparent.

Perception is the capability of AI to interpret its surroundings through a variety of sensors. These sensors can include cameras, microphones, lidar, radar, tactile sensors, and more. Processing this sensory data often involves specialized techniques. For instance, image recognition and object detection heavily rely on CNNs, while video analysis might involve temporal extensions of CNNs or recurrent architectures. Audio processing utilizes techniques like feature extraction and models like RNNs and transformers. Natural language processing, which can be considered a form of perception for textual data, employs techniques like tokenization, embedding, and deep learning models. Sensor fusion techniques are used to integrate information from multiple sensors.

Problem-solving is the culmination of these abilities, where AI systems integrate learning, reasoning, and perception to address specific challenges. This can involve analysing complex datasets, processing intricate information, and devising solutions through various approaches. Examples include state-space search, constraint satisfaction, and planning under uncertainty. Effective problem-solving often requires a well-defined problem representation, the application of appropriate algorithms, and the iterative refinement of solutions.

Information Creation, Autonomy, and Situatedness

Contemporary AI research and development is broadly structured around three core themes: **Information Creation, Autonomy, and Situatedness**. The utility of vast datasets is limited by conventional retrieval methods. AI offers advanced techniques to extract relevant information by formulating insightful queries and establishing meaningful data connections. Data mining, a commercially significant field largely enabled by AI, exemplifies this capability, utilizing methods ranging from statistical analysis to neural networks and machine learning algorithms to process diverse data types.

The **information generated** is not created from nothing; it is a condensed and explicit form of knowledge already implicit within the data. This aspect, alongside the methodologies employed, renders data mining a compelling area of inquiry for AI research. While machine learning is often considered a model for human learning, this perspective is overly narrow. Cognitive science underscores the role of statistical processes in human learning, suggesting a complex interplay of diverse methods. This complexity is mirrored in the multifaceted approaches within data mining.

However, current data mining practices often employ these diverse methods in isolation. A critical future research direction involves integrating these methods into a cohesive information creation process. Such integration promises to enhance data mining efficiency and offer cognitive insights, potentially simulating the human process of abstracting expert knowledge from extensive experiential data. This abstraction, occurring both consciously and unconsciously and guided by background and domain-specific knowledge, could be replicated through advanced data mining techniques, enabling automated expert knowledge generation.

Parallel to these developments, computer science has witnessed the rise of distributed systems, augmented problem-solving capabilities, and expanding application domains. AI's contribution to distributed systems lies in imbuing system components with **autonomy**. Traditionally viewed as computational and storage utilities for decision support, computer systems are evolving toward autonomy, demonstrated by their increasing control in technical domains, albeit with human oversight.

Multi-agent systems, a key AI contribution to distributed computing, foreground **autonomy**. Agency, a defining characteristic of system components, is predicated on autonomy, manifested through proactivity (action selection, including strategic inaction), goal maintenance (goal setting and adaptation), and active communication and cooperation (proactive inter-agent communication). This paradigm shift fosters a novel partnership between human operators and autonomous agents, moving beyond a mere tool-user relationship to one of collaborative co-existence within increasingly complex systems. This necessitates interdisciplinary investigation by AI researchers and sociologists to address the emergent societal implications.

Situatedness, a critical attribute particularly for agents in multi-agent systems and adaptable mobile robots, emphasizes the capacity to operate and respond within complex, dynamic environments. Intrinsically linked to autonomy, situatedness necessitates that systems effectively locate, orient, and act within environments characterized by partially unpredictable influences. Situation sensing, ranging from straightforward for software agents in controlled environments to highly complex for agents in dynamic environments like the Internet or embodied robots, is a central challenge. Sensor fusion, the integration of multi-source sensory data into a coherent situation description, represents a key area for AI methodologies. Cognitive science insights underscore the complexity of situation understanding in humans, involving extensive background knowledge and neural processing. AI-driven simulations hold promise for elucidating this process and enabling artificial situated systems to construct effective situation descriptions.

For situated systems, situation descriptions are primarily instrumental, serving to inform action selection rather than representing exhaustive or perfectly consistent environmental models. "Situated knowledge bases," characterized by broad background knowledge and contextually relevant knowledge chunks—potentially inconsistent and represented at varying granularities—are required. Developing methods for knowledge chunk selection, combination, and transformation is essential. Furthermore, situated systems necessitate planning capabilities for action sequencing and learning mechanisms to adapt to the inherent unpredictability of environmental influences. Learning, through the detection and classification of similar situations, is crucial for improving situated system behaviour.

Briefly, Information Creation, Autonomy, and Situatedness represent the dominant research and development foci within AI. Addressing these multifaceted challenges necessitates the integration of diverse methodologies into comprehensive

systems. The overarching trajectory of AI research and development is thus characterized by the creation of sophisticated, integrated systems capable of meeting these
tripartite requirements.

Let us take a look at a few prominent sub-disciplines of AI in twentieth century.

Early Applications of AI

Natural Language Processing

Human communication is incredibly complex, even though we do it effortlessly.
Making computers understand and generate even simple parts of human language
has proven to be very difficult. Language works so well for humans because it relies
on a vast amount of shared knowledge and context between speakers. This shared
context allows us to communicate concisely, but it's a major hurdle for computers
trying to decode and generate language. Natural language understanding is, therefore,
a very complex problem of encoding and decoding meaning.

Creating programs that can understand and produce human language has been a
long-held goal in AI. This ability is not only central to human intelligence but would
also revolutionize how we interact with computers. While AI has made progress in
natural language processing within limited situations, achieving the flexibility and
broad understanding of human language remains beyond current AI capabilities.

Understanding natural language requires much more than just knowing grammar
and vocabulary. It demands deep knowledge of the subject matter, familiarity with
common expressions, and the ability to use general world knowledge to fill in missing
information and resolve ambiguities inherent in human speech. Building truly
capable natural language systems necessitates capturing this contextual knowledge
and developing effective reasoning processes. This remains a key and captivating
area of AI research.

Intelligent Retrieval from Databases

Database systems are large bodies of facts about some subjects, which are used to
answer users' queries about that subject. For example, consider a player database.
For each player listed in the database, there could be entities representing his age,
height, weight, number of caps, total earnings, etc. With these facts stored in an
orderly form, one can obtain answers to queries like "List all players who are over
6 feet tall." or "What is the average yearly salary of player X?", etc. The design
of database systems is a very active field in computer science even today. From the
point of view of AI, the field becomes even more interesting if the answers require
deductive reasoning with the facts in the database.

There are numerous problems that confront an individual trying to build such an intelligent retrieval system. First, the problem of understanding queries stated in a natural language like English. Second, if the system has fully understood the query, how should it deduce the answer from the facts in the database? Third, for the given facts there are some queries which require common knowledge. For example, if player P is the captain of a side, then the system should be able to know that P leads the team always on the field and he is a part of the core group which has chosen the team. Such facts may not be explicitly stated during the development of the database.

Expert Systems

Think of expert systems as AI's way of creating automatic consultants—computer programs that offer expert-level conclusions in niche areas. These systems aren't just theoretical; they've been practically applied to diagnose faults in complex machinery like military radars, classify biological species, propose chemical structures, evaluate ore deposits, and even diagnose medical diseases often matching the performance of human experts.

The design of every expert system hinges on two crucial elements: knowledge representation and knowledge utilization (inference). Representing expert knowledge is a significant challenge because it's often characterized by imprecision and uncertainty. Common approaches involve encoding knowledge as a large collection of simple rules or in more structured formats like frames and scripts. Expert systems typically derive conclusions using rule-based deduction, but researchers are actively investigating other reasoning methods like probabilistic deduction to handle uncertainty more effectively.

DENDRAL, a pioneering system from the late 1960s at Stanford, was among the first to truly leverage domain-specific knowledge for problem-solving. DENDRAL's task was to deduce the structure of organic molecules based on their chemical formulas and mass spectra, which reveal information about molecular bonds. The challenge was immense: the potential number of molecular structures is astronomical, especially for large organic molecules. DENDRAL tackled this vast "search space" by incorporating the specialized, heuristic knowledge of expert chemists to guide the structure determination process. DENDRAL's approach was revolutionary, consistently identifying the correct molecular structure from millions of possibilities in very few attempts. Its success was so profound that systems based on DENDRAL are still used in chemical and pharmaceutical labs worldwide.

While DENDRAL showcased the power of domain knowledge for expert-level performance, MYCIN, developed at Stanford in the mid-1970s, established the foundational methodology for contemporary expert systems. MYCIN focused on medical expertise, diagnosing and recommending treatments for spinal meningitis and bacterial blood infections. MYCIN was particularly innovative because it addressed the crucial challenge of reasoning with uncertain and incomplete medical information. Furthermore, MYCIN provided clear, understandable explanations of its reasoning, employed a control structure specifically tailored to the diagnostic domain, and importantly, defined reliable criteria for objectively evaluating its performance, setting a new standard for expert system development.

Game Playing

Much of the early research in state-space search was done using common board games such as checkers, chess, and the 15-puzzle. In addition to their inherent intellectual appeal, board games have certain properties that made them ideal subjects for this early work. Most games are played using a well-defined set of rules: this makes it easy to generate the search space and frees the researcher from many of the ambiguities and complexities inherent in less structured problems. The board configurations used in playing these games are easily represented on a computer, requiring none of the complex formalisms needed to capture the semantic subtleties of more complex problem domains. Games can generate extremely large search spaces. These are large and complex enough to require powerful techniques for determining what alternatives to explore in the problem space. These techniques are called *heuristics* and constitute a major area of AI research. Much of what we commonly call intelligence seems to reside in the heuristics used by humans to solve problems.

Theorem Proving

The process of proving or disproving mathematical theorems constitutes a rigorous intellectual undertaking. Its inherent difficulty arises from the dual requirement of deductive reasoning from hypotheses and the application of expert judgement. This critical judgement is predicated upon a substantial body of specialized knowledge, enabling the accurate identification of prior theorems pertinent to the current proof effort. Such discernment is instrumental in decomposing overarching problems into tractable subproblems suitable for independent investigation. While automated theorem-proving programs have achieved partial success in replicating this faculty, the formalization of deductive methodologies through predicate logic provides a valuable framework for elucidating the fundamental elements of reasoning. Consequently, numerous seemingly informal tasks, such as medical diagnosis, can be effectively modelled as theorem-proving problems.

The main appeal of automated theorem proving lies in the rigour and generality of logical systems. Logic, as a formal system, is particularly amenable to automation. This characteristic permits the application of automated theorem proving to a wide spectrum of problems, wherein problem descriptions and relevant background knowledge are encoded as logical axioms, and problem instances are treated as theorems requiring formal proof. The sustained interest in automated theorem provers is motivated by the recognition that these systems need not operate autonomously in solving highly intricate problems. Instead, contemporary theorem provers frequently serve as intelligent assistive tools, empowering human researchers to execute the more cognitively demanding stages of decomposing complex problems into manageable components and formulating heuristics for navigating the proof search space. Subsequently, the theorem prover undertakes the relatively less strategic, but nonetheless demanding, tasks of proving lemmas, validating minor conjectures, and completing the formalization of proof structures delineated by human collaborators. Thus, theorem proving occupies a significant position as a subdiscipline within the broader field of artificial intelligence.

Goal-Based Agents

An AI agent is a system or program capable of autonomously performing tasks on behalf of a user or another system by designing its workflow and utilizing available tools. AI agents can perform a wide range of functions beyond natural language processing, including decision-making, problem-solving, interacting with external environments, and executing actions. Although AI agents make autonomous decisions, they require goals and environments defined by humans. There are three main influences on autonomous agent behaviour: the team of developers who design and train the AI system, the team that deploys the agent and provides user access, and the user who sets specific goals and establishes the tools available to the AI agent.

Given the user's goals and the agent's available tools, the AI agent performs task decomposition to improve performance. Essentially, the agent creates a plan of specific tasks and subtasks to accomplish the complex goal. For simple tasks, planning is not always necessary. Instead, an agent can iteratively reflect on its responses and improve them without planning its next steps. This involves describing a situation we want to achieve and defining a set of properties that should be held when the agent succeeds at its goal. This requires defining a goal test that captures what it means to have achieved or satisfied the goal. While specifying the goal test is straightforward in some domains, like chess, it can be more complex in others and requires considerable thought.

The cognitive processes related to goal selection and specification in humans and animals are not well understood. Consequently, designing autonomous systems that select, prioritize, and update their goals remains largely an unsolved problem in AI. Typically, the system designer or user specifies the goal to be achieved. It is necessary to precisely define all primitive actions, including their preconditions and expected effects on the environment, which are sufficient to achieve the goal. Early AI systems assumed that given an action and a description of the current state of the world, the action completely specifies the conditions under which it can be applied and the exact state of the world after the action is executed. Actions were viewed as atomic, discrete events occurring at an instant in time, with the world transitioning to a different state once the action is executed.

Early AI systems also assumed that all information necessary for choosing an action is available in each percept, making each state a complete description of the current world. The knowledge representation problem involves deciding what information from raw perceptual or sensory data is relevant to keep and how to represent this data to make explicit the most important features for solving the goal. This process is crucial for the effective functioning of AI agents in achieving their specified goals.

Robotics

We humans take for granted our ability to move around and interact with the world, walking through a room, reaching for a light switch, or stacking blocks. These actions, which we do automatically, are incredibly intricate when you try to program a machine to do them. When we attempt to build robots that can perform these everyday tasks, we quickly realize they require many of the same sophisticated AI techniques needed for high-level intellectual problems.

For robots to be truly useful and adaptable, they need to be able to plan. Planning is the process of figuring out a sequence of actions to achieve a goal. Imagine a robot that has a set of basic moves it can perform (like moving forward, turning, etc.). Planning is about finding the *right* sequence of these simple moves to accomplish a more complex objective, like navigating from one side of a room to the other while avoiding obstacles.

One of the biggest challenges in robot planning is the sheer number of possibilities. Even for a robot with a limited set of actions, the number of possible sequences of movements can be enormous. Consider a simple robot that can just move forward, backward, left, or right in a room with furniture. Think about all the different paths it could take! Programming a robot to intelligently choose the *best* path, avoiding obstacles efficiently, requires incredibly sophisticated techniques. We need ways to represent the robot's understanding of space and clever algorithms to search through the vast landscape of possible moves without getting completely lost.

The field of robotics has been a driving force in the development of AI. Robotics research has contributed significantly to our understanding of how to model the state of the world in AI and how actions can transform those states. These insights are fundamental to building intelligent systems that can plan and act effectively in real-world environments.

Combinatorial and Scheduling Problems

One type of challenging problem involves finding the best schedule or sequence from many possibilities. A classic example is the traveling salesperson problem (TSP):

imagine a salesperson who needs to visit multiple cities, starting and ending at the same city, while finding the shortest possible route that visits each city exactly once.

These scheduling problems often involve finding the "cheapest" path across a network of locations, ensuring each location is visited at most once. The difficulty lies in the sheer number of possible routes or combinations, which explodes rapidly as the number of cities or locations increases. Trying to check every single route (brute force) quickly becomes impossible, even for powerful computers. Problems like these are known as NP-complete problems, signifying their computational hardness.

AI researchers have developed clever methods to tackle these combinatorial challenges. The key to success is using knowledge about the specific problem. The techniques created for these tough problems have also proven useful for solving simpler problems that are less computationally demanding.

Perception Problems

Giving computers the ability to "see" with cameras and "hear" with microphones has been a long-standing goal, but initial results were disappointing. The reason? Just like humans, computers need more than just raw sensory input. They need *understanding* to process complex information effectively. And understanding, in turn, comes from a vast reservoir of knowledge about the world.

In AI, we study perception as a series of operations, like building understanding layer by layer. Imagine a visual scene being captured by a camera as a giant grid of numbers representing light intensity. The first step is to find simple building blocks—like lines, curves, and corners—using specialized detectors. Then, these basic shapes are used to figure out what objects are present. The aim is to distil this massive input into a concise, high-level description, a simplified "model" of the scene, for example, recognizing "a hill with a tree on top."

However, the sheer amount of raw visual or auditory data creates a problem. There are countless ways to interpret and describe any given scene. How does the computer choose the right one? One approach is to make intelligent "guesses" or hypotheses about what's being perceived. The system tries out different interpretations and checks if they fit the sensory data. But to make *good* guesses, the system needs a substantial amount of knowledge about what kinds of things it's likely to encounter.

Exercises

1. What is artificial intelligence (AI)?
2. Who is considered the father of AI and why?
3. What was the significance of the Dartmouth Conference in 1956?
4. Describe the Turing test and its importance in AI.

5. Research and write a brief essay on the history of AI, highlighting key milestones.
6. Create a timeline of significant events in AI history, including major breakthroughs and setbacks.
7. Design a simple Turing test scenario and explain how it would be conducted.
8. Identify and discuss three current AI technologies and their applications in various industries.
9. Debate the potential benefits and risks of AI in a group setting or through a written argument.
10. Interview a professional working in the AI field and summarize their insights on the future of AI.
11. Analyse the relationship between Alan Turing's concept of computation and human intelligence. How does the Turing test reflect early assumptions about machine intelligence? Consider writing a detailed response comparing human and machine approaches to solving a specific problem, like language translation.
12. Examine Searle's Chinese Room argument. Design your own thought experiment that either supports or challenges Searle's conclusions about understanding versus symbol manipulation. What does your experiment reveal about the nature of intelligence?
13. Compare and contrast the symbolic AI approach of the 1950s–1970s with modern neural networks. Choose a specific cognitive task and analyse how each paradigm would approach solving it. What are the philosophical implications of these different approaches?
14. Analyse the concept of representation in AI systems. Choose three different AI applications and break down how they represent knowledge internally. What does this tell us about the relationship between representation and intelligence?
15. Consider the concept of intelligence augmentation (IA) versus artificial intelligence (AI). Develop a detailed scenario that explores how these approaches might lead to different societal outcomes. What criteria would you use to evaluate which approach is more beneficial?
16. Analyse the relationship between consciousness and intelligence. Design a series of tests that might help distinguish between intelligent behaviour and conscious experience. What would these tests reveal about our assumptions about machine consciousness?
17. Design a small experiment testing a specific aspect of machine intelligence (like analogical reasoning). Document your methodology and reflect on what the results suggest about the nature of intelligence.

Further Reading

Akerkar R, Sajja P (2010) Knowledge based systems. Jones & Bartlett Publisher, USA. ISBN 9780763776473

Boden MA (ed) (1990) The philosophy of artificial intelligence. Oxford University Press, Oxford

Brachman RJ, Levesque HJ (2004) Knowledge representation and reasoning. The MIT Press

Buchanan BG, Shortliffe EH (eds) (1984) Rule-based expert systems: the MYCIN experiments of the Stanford heuristic programming project. Addison-Wesley, Reading, Massachusetts

Daniel Crevier AI (1993) The tumultuous history of the search for artificial intelligence. Basic Books, New York

Davis R, Lenat DB (1982) Knowledge-based systems in artificial intelligence. McGraw-Hill, New York

Feigenbaum EA, Feldman J (eds) (1963) Computers and thought. McGraw-Hill, New York

Haugeland J (1985) Artificial intelligence: the very idea. MIT Press, Cambridge, MA

McCarthy J (1959) Programs with common sense. In: Proceedings of the Teddington conference on the mechanization of thought processes, pp 75–91

McCarthy J (1963) Formal requirements for mathematical reasoning. In: Feigenbaum, Feldman (eds) Computers and thought

McCarthy J, Hayes PJ (1969) Some philosophical problems from the standpoint of artificial intelligence. Mach Intell 4:463–502

McCarthy J, Minsky M, Rochester N, Shannon C (1955) A proposal for the Dartmouth summer research project on artificial intelligence

McCorduck P (1979) Machines who think: a personal inquiry into the history and prospects of artificial intelligence. W.H. Freeman, San Francisco

McCulloch WS, Pitts W (1943) A logical calculus of the ideas immanent in nervous activity. Bull Math Biophys 5:115–133

Minsky M (1961) Steps toward artificial intelligence. Proc IRE 49(1):8–30

Minsky M (1968) Semantic information processing. MIT Press, Cambridge, MA

Minsky M (1986) The society of mind. Simon & Schuster, New York

Newell A, Simon HA (1956) The logic theory machine: a complex information processing system. IRE Trans Inf Theory 2(3):61–79

Russell S, Norvig P (1995) Artificial intelligence: a modern approach. Prentice Hall, Englewood Cliffs, NJ

Schalkoff RJ (1990) Artificial intelligence: an engineering approach. McGraw-Hill, New York

Searle J (1980) Minds, brains and programs. Behav Brain Sci 3:417–457

Searle JR (1984) Minds, brains and science. Harvard University Press, Cambridge, Massachusetts

Searle J (1999) The Chinese room. In: Wilson RA, Keil F (eds) The MIT encyclopedia of the cognitive sciences. MIT Press, Cambridge, MA

Shannon CE (1950) Programming a computer for playing chess. Philos Mag 41(314):256–275

Smolensky P (1987) Connectionist AI, symbolic AI, and the brain. Artif Intell Rev 1(2):95–109

Turing AM (1950) Computing machinery and intelligence. Mind 59:433–460

Turing AM, Strachey C, Bates MA, Bowden BV (1953) Digital computers applied to games. In: Bowden BV (ed) Faster than thought. Pitman, London, pp 286–310

Wade SS (2021) A brief history of artificial intelligence: unravelling the threads of machine intelligence. Independently published

Weizenbaum J (1966) ELIZA—a computer program for the study of natural language communication between man and machine. Commun ACM 9(1):36–45

Wiener N (1948) Cybernetics: or control and communication in the animal and the machine. MIT Press, Cambridge, MA

Winograd T, Flores F (1986) Understanding computers and cognition. Ablex, Norwood, New Jersey

Wooldridge M (2021) A brief history of artificial Intelligence: what it is, where we are, and where we are going. Flatiron Books, New York

Chapter 2
The Dawn of AI: Early Innovations and Discoveries

Artificial intelligence... I've been following that since I was in high school.
—*Paul Allen*

The dawn of AI was characterized by ambitious aspirations to replicate human-level intelligence in machines. This period saw the birth of foundational concepts, including symbolic reasoning and the development of early algorithms designed to solve logical problems. Landmark achievements like the creation of programs that could play checkers and prove mathematical theorems demonstrated the initial feasibility of these ideas. These early innovations, though limited by computational power, established the core principles of knowledge representation and problem-solving that would shape the future of AI research. This initial burst of creativity and discovery laid the crucial groundwork for the sophisticated AI systems we observe today.

This *Good Old-Fashioned AI* (GOFAI), emerged in the mid-twentieth century, was characterized using symbolic reasoning and rule-based systems. It is effective at handling narrowly defined problems, and it is proven to be useful in various applications such as scheduling logistics, automating tax software, and virtual board games. This type of AI technology works through all possible outputs to generate the best recommendations for a given problem. The early years of AI were characterized by high hopes and ambitious goals. Researchers focused on creating systems that could perform tasks requiring human-like reasoning, such as playing chess, proving mathematical theorems, and understanding natural language. These systems, known as "symbolic AI," relied on explicitly programmed rules and logic. Notable achievements of this era include the development of the General Problem Solver by Allen Newell and Herbert A. Simon and the creation of ELIZA, an early natural language processing program by Joseph Weizenbaum.

Search techniques and logic from the symbolic AI paradigm are useful also in the current AI era. While modern AI has seen significant advancements with neural networks and deep learning, symbolic AI techniques continue to play a crucial role, especially in areas requiring explainability, reasoning, and knowledge representation. Symbolic AI techniques, such as logic-based reasoning, provide clear and

© The Author(s), under exclusive license to Springer Nature Switzerland AG 2026
R. Akerkar, *Artificial Intelligence*, https://doi.org/10.1007/978-3-031-91084-5_2

interpretable decision-making processes. This is essential for applications where understanding the rationale behind AI decisions is critical, such as in healthcare and legal domains. The field of neuro-symbolic AI combines the strengths of symbolic AI (reasoning and knowledge representation) with the learning capabilities of neural networks. This integration aims to create more robust and intelligent systems. Search algorithms like A* and heuristic search are still widely used in various applications, including pathfinding, game playing, and optimization problems. These techniques are effective for exploring large search spaces and finding optimal or near-optimal solutions. Moreover, symbolic AI excels in representing structured knowledge and rules, which is beneficial for tasks that require a deep understanding of relationships and constraints within data. Overall, the combination of symbolic and subsymbolic (neural network-based) approaches is seen as a promising direction for advancing AI, leveraging the strengths of both paradigms to address complex challenges in a more comprehensive manner.

Search Methods

The objective of any search technique is to apply a suitable sequence of operators to an initial task domain (state) to reach the desired goal. There are two primary methods to achieve this: forward reasoning and backward reasoning. Forward reasoning involves applying operators to structures in the database that describe the task domain, resulting in a modified state. This approach is also known as bottom-up or data-driven reasoning, where the goal is to progress from the initial state to one that meets the goal condition. For instance, in a game of chess, the initial situation is the placement of chess pieces on the board at the start of the game, the goal is any board configuration that results in checkmate, and the operators are the rules for legal moves in chess.

Backward reasoning, also referred to as top-down or goal-directed reasoning, involves breaking down the goal (problem) statement into subgoals (problems) that are hopefully easier to solve and whose solutions collectively address the original problem. For example, consider the problem of integration.

$$\int \frac{1}{\cos^2 x} \, dx.$$

If the operator permits

$$\frac{1}{\cos^2 x} = \sec x,$$

then we can restate our problem as

$$\int \sec^2 x \, dx = \tan x + c.$$

It's fascinating to observe that a significant portion of our reasoning tends to be backward. This means we often start with a goal or desired outcome and work our way back to determine the steps needed to achieve it.

The Search Space: Defining the Problem

To find a solution, we first need to define the "search space," which is all possible states or arrangements relevant to the problem. For example, in chess, the search space is all possible chess positions, and in route planning, it's all possible routes. Each point in this space represents a "state." Our task is to move from the "initial state" to a "goal state" (the desired outcome). This movement happens through "operators," which are the possible actions or moves within the problem.

Definition A *graph* is a data object. A graph, G, consists of two sets called *vertices* (nodes) V and *edges* E. V is a finite non-empty set of nodes and E is a finite set of pairs of nodes. Each pair in E is an edge in G. If the pairs of vertices are ordered, that is (i, j) is different from (j, i), then G is said to be directed. Otherwise, it is undirected.

Definition A *tree* is a finite set of one or more nodes such that (i) there is a specially designated node called the *root*; (ii) the remaining nodes are partitioned into $n \geq 0$ disjoint sets $T_1 \ldots T_n$ where each of these sets is a tree. $T_1 \ldots T_n$ are called the *subtrees* of the root.

Tree structures are frequently employed to represent control strategies in search processes. In state-space representation, a tree can illustrate the set of problem states generated by applying operators. Here, the root node signifies the initial problem state or situation. Each new state, produced by applying a single operator to the root, is depicted as a successor node. Further applications of operators create successors to these nodes, and so forth. Each operator application is represented by a directed edge in the tree.

However, in practice, states are often represented by a graph rather than a tree, as multiple paths may lead from the root to a given node. In addition to trees and graphs, other representation schemes include AND/OR graphs, which are used in problem-solving methods involving problem reduction. These graphs facilitate the identification of subgoals, whose combination is sufficient to achieve the desired goal.

Figure 2.1 is a depiction of a tree that illustrates various states along with their transitions. Additionally, Fig. 2.2 provides an example of a transition from one state to another, which occurs when an operator is applied to a branch of the tree.

To find a path from the start node, S, to the goal node, G, search procedures traverse trees like these, discovering connections and distances along the way. As the search progresses, it gathers information about the various paths and their respective costs, ultimately aiming to identify the most efficient route from S to G.

We can visualize this as a "state-space graph" or "tree," where states are "nodes" and the transitions between them (caused by operators) are "edges." Searching for a solution then exploring this graph to find a path from the start to the goal.

"Uninformed search" (or "blind search") is a basic approach that, while inefficient for complex problems, is crucial for understanding more advanced search methods. It works with minimal information, exploring the search space systematically based only on the problem's definition.

Fig. 2.1 Basic search problem

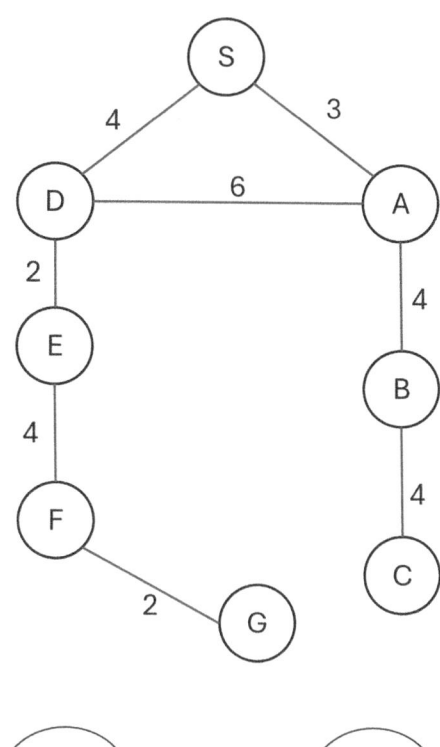

Fig. 2.2 State change for A to B on the application of an operator O_p

Search algorithms typically rely on these assumptions:

- We can "expand" a state to find its possible next states.
- The state space is treated as a "tree," implying a single starting point and unique paths between states (this is often a simplification).
- When a state is expanded, "back-pointers" are created to its parent state. This allows us to reconstruct the solution path after finding a goal.

Blind Search

Blind search techniques (also called *uninformed search techniques*) are search strategies that explore the problem space without any domain-specific knowledge or *heuristics*.

These techniques do not have information about the goal's location or the best way to reach it; they only know the structure of the problem (e.g., the set of possible states and actions). Blind search techniques are typically used in scenarios where there is no prior knowledge or heuristic information about the goal state. They are contrasted with *informed search techniques*, which use heuristics to guide the search process.

Common blind search techniques are as follows:

Breadth-First Search (BFS) explores the search space layer by layer. It starts at the initial state and expands all its neighbours. Then, it expands the neighbours of those neighbours, and so on. In short, in order to decide which is the best solution to our travel problem, it is necessary to consider all possibilities. BFS guarantees finding the shortest path to the goal if one exists; however, it is memory intensive by the fact that all information about all paths must be stored until we reach the goal, when the final comparison can be made.

Example Breadth-First Search (BFS) is a systematic search algorithm used to explore all possible paths in a graph or tree structure without using any heuristics or prior knowledge about the problem.

Here's how BFS works:

1. **Initialization**: Start at the root node (or initial state) and place it in a queue.
2. **Exploration**: Remove the node from the front of the queue and examine it. If it's the goal node, the search is complete.
3. **Expansion**: If the node is not the goal, add all its unvisited neighbouring nodes to the back of the queue.

4. **Iteration**: Repeat the exploration and expansion steps until the goal node
    is found or the queue is empty.

BFS explores all nodes at the current depth level before moving on to nodes
at the next depth level. This ensures that the shortest path to the goal is found
if one exists, but it can be memory intensive as it stores all nodes at each level.

For instance, in a maze-solving problem, BFS would start at the entrance
and explore all possible paths level by level until it finds the exit. It doesn't
prioritize any path over another, making it a blind search method.

Depth-First Search (DFS) explores the search space by going as deep as possible
along a single path. It backtracks when it reaches a dead end. That means, one
complete path is tried initially from the start point to finish at the goal and then a
different path is tried from start to finish. DFS is less memory-intensive than BFS
but doesn't guarantee finding the shortest path and can get stuck in infinite loops if
the search space is infinite.

Depth-Limited Search (DLS)

Depth-limited search (DLS) where DFS with a depth limit is to prevent infinite
searching. DLS addresses the potential infinite loop problem of DFS by imposing a
depth limit. It explores only up to a specified depth. While it avoids infinite loops, it
might miss the goal if it lies beyond the depth limit. Undoubtedly, there is an amount
of commonsense and, where viable, knowledge of the particular problem needs to
be applied with a depth-limited search.

Selecting the appropriate depth parameter is crucial. If the parameter is set too
deep, it can lead to unnecessary expenditure of time and space. Conversely, if the
depth parameter is set too shallow, it may prevent the search from ever reaching a
goal state.

Iterative Deepening Search (IDS)

Iterative deepening search (IDS) is a search algorithm designed to find solutions
within a state space by intelligently integrating the strengths of both Depth-First
Search (DFS) and Breadth-First Search (BFS), resulting in an efficient search process.
The core principle of IDS involves repeatedly executing depth-limited searches, with
the allowed search depth increasing incrementally in each iteration until the desired
goal state is discovered. This method ensures systematic exploration of the search
space, effectively sidestepping the common limitations associated with standard DFS
and BFS approaches.

In each cycle, IDS performs a depth-first exploration of the search space, but
only down to a predefined depth. If the target solution is not found within this depth
constraint, the algorithm proceeds to the next iteration, where the maximum search
depth is increased. This new search begins again from the initial state. This process
of incrementally deepening the search limit continues until the goal state is reached.
By gradually expanding the search horizon, IDS ensures that all nodes at a particular

depth are examined before the search moves to the next level, mirroring the behaviour of BFS. Simultaneously, it preserves the memory advantages of DFS because it only needs to keep track of a single path from the starting point to the currently explored node at any given time.

A significant benefit of employing IDS is its optimal performance with respect to both time and memory usage. The algorithm guarantees that the first solution it finds will be the one located at the shallowest depth in the search space, as it systematically explores all possibilities at each depth level before progressing further. Moreover, IDS has a linear space complexity, meaning the amount of memory it requires grows proportionally to the depth of the solution. This is a considerable advantage over BFS, which often needs to store a vast number of nodes in memory simultaneously, especially in large search spaces.

To illustrate, consider the task of finding a route between two points in a tree-like structure. IDS would first attempt a DFS with a maximum depth of one. If the destination is not reached, the algorithm would then restart the search with a depth limit of two, again using DFS. This process of increasing the allowed depth by one and repeating the DFS continues until the target destination is found.

In summary, iterative deepening search stands out as a robust and effective algorithm for tackling search problems. It cleverly combines the exhaustive nature of Breadth-First Search, which guarantees finding the shortest path, with the efficient memory utilization characteristic of Depth-First Search.

Uniform-Cost Search (UCS)

Uniform-Cost Search (UCS) is a search algorithm used to find the least-cost path from a start node to a goal node in a weighted graph. Unlike other search algorithms that prioritize depth or breadth, UCS focuses on minimizing the total cost of the path. Working of the algorithm is as follows:

1. *Priority Queue*: UCS uses a priority queue to keep track of nodes to be explored. The priority is determined by the cumulative cost from the start node to the current node.
2. *Cost-Based Expansion*: Nodes are expanded based on their cumulative cost. The node with the lowest cost is expanded first, ensuring that the search progresses along the least-cost path.
3. *Pathfinding*: UCS is particularly useful in scenarios where the path costs vary and finding the optimal path is crucial. It guarantees finding the least-cost path if one exists.
4. *Optimality*: UCS is optimal and complete, meaning it will always find the least-cost path if there is one, and it will explore all possible paths if necessary.

UCS is commonly used in pathfinding problems, such as route planning, network routing, and puzzle solving, where the cost of each step or move varies. Consider a graph where nodes represent cities and edges represent roads with different travel costs. UCS would start at the initial city and explore the roads, always choosing the road with the lowest cumulative travel cost until it reaches the destination city.

Bidirectional Search

Bidirectional search runs two simultaneous searches—one forward from the initial state and one backward from the goal state—until the two searches meet. The big advantage of this technique is that it can save a lot of time in finding a solution; however, it can require significant memory.

Heuristic Search

Blind searches are normally very inefficient. By adding domain knowledge, we can improve the search process. Unlike blind search techniques, which explore the problem space without any guidance, heuristic search techniques guide the search by prioritizing nodes based on their estimated distance or cost to the goal.

> **Heuristic search** in AI refers to a search strategy that uses heuristics, or rules of thumb, to improve the efficiency of finding solutions to problems. Heuristics are techniques that guide the search process by prioritizing certain paths or choices based on their likelihood of leading to a solution. This approach is particularly useful in complex problem-solving scenarios where exhaustive search methods would be too time-consuming.

The idea behind a heuristic search is that we explore the node that is most likely to be nearest to a goal state. To do this we use a heuristic function which tells us how close we are to a goal state. There is no guarantee that the heuristic function will return a value that ensures that a particular node is closer to a goal state than any other node. If we could do that, we would not be carrying out a search. We would simply be moving through the various states in order to reach the goal state.

Key aspects of heuristic search include:

1. **Guidance**: Heuristics provide direction to the search process, helping to focus on more promising paths and avoid less likely ones.
2. **Efficiency**: By using heuristics, the search can be performed more quickly and with fewer resources compared to brute-force methods.
3. **Approximation**: Heuristic search often involves making educated guesses, which may not always lead to the optimal solution but can find satisfactory solutions faster.

To implement a heuristic function, we need to have some knowledge of the domain. That is, the heuristic function has to know something about the problem so that it can judge how close the current state is to the goal state.

When we looked at blind searches, we have already seen one type of evaluation function, where we expanded the node with the lowest path cost (for the Uniform-Cost Search). Using this type of evaluation function, we are calculating the cheapest cost so far. Heuristic searches are different in that we are trying to estimate how close we are from a goal state; not how cheap the solution is so far.

Common heuristic search techniques are as follows:

Best-First Search (BFS) expands the most promising node according to a heuristic evaluation function, usually denoted as $f(n)$, where n is a node. The heuristic function $h(n)$ estimates the cost from node n to the goal. This algorithm is flexible and can use various heuristics to prioritize nodes, and it can lead to optimal or suboptimal solutions depending on the heuristic. When specific domain knowledge can help guide the search toward the goal.

$A*$ **Search** is a combination of Uniform-Cost Search and Best-First Search. $A*$ uses a heuristic function $f(n) = g(n) + h(n)$, where $g(n)$ is the cost to reach node n from the start, and $h(n)$ is the estimated cost from n to the goal. This means, it combines the cost to reach a node and the estimated cost to reach the goal from that node. This algorithm is widely used in pathfinding, like in navigation systems, games, and robotic movement.

Greedy Best-First Search is a type of Best-First Search that only uses the heuristic function $f(n) = h(n)$, where $h(n)$ is the estimated cost from the current node to the goal. This search prioritizes nodes based on a heuristic estimate of the cost to reach the goal. This strategy expands the node that is closest to the goal according to the heuristic function. It's like taking the most promising path based on immediate estimates. However, greedy search can get stuck in local optima and might not find the optimal path. In other words, heuristic function tries to minimize the estimated cost to reach the goal without considering the path cost so far. When speed is more important than guaranteed optimality, it is suitable in some real-time systems.

Example Greedy Best-First Search algorithm uses a heuristic to prioritize which node to explore next, aiming to find the shortest path to the goal quickly. Here's how it works:

1. **Initialization**: Start at the initial node and add it to a priority queue.
2. **Exploration**: Remove the node with the lowest heuristic value from the queue and examine it. If it's the goal node, the search is complete.
3. **Expansion**: If the node is not the goal, add its neighbouring nodes to the priority queue, prioritizing them based on their heuristic values.
4. **Iteration**: Repeat the exploration and expansion steps until the goal node is found or the queue is empty.

In a pathfinding problem on a grid, the heuristic could be the straight-line distance (Euclidean distance) to the goal. The algorithm would prioritize nodes that are closer to the goal, making the search more efficient than exploring all possible paths blindly.

Local Search

Local search algorithms are useful for optimization problems where finding the exact path is less important than finding a good solution. They start with a candidate solution and iteratively improve it by making small changes.

Hill climbing is a local search technique that iteratively moves toward a neighbour node with a better heuristic value (higher or lower depending on the problem) than the current node, hoping to reach the goal.

> **Hill climbing** continuously moves toward the direction of increasing value (or decreasing cost) based on heuristics.

The hill climbing works well for optimization problems with smooth search spaces. There are different variants of this method such as:

- **Simple Hill Climbing**: Evaluates only one neighbour and moves to it if it's better.
- **Steepest-Ascent Hill Climbing**: Evaluates all neighbours and moves to the one with the best improvement.
- **Stochastic Hill Climbing**: Randomly selects one of the better neighbours instead of always choosing the best.

One of the main problems of hill climbing is that it ends up climbing false foothills. This means that it gets stuck in local maxima. So, it is better to check out the whole space before we make any climbing decisions. In order to achieve this, the whole space is initially explored to see what it is like. This helps us avoid getting stuck in a plateau or local maxima.

Simulated annealing is very similar to hill climbing but occasionally allows "downhill" moves (worse solutions) to escape local optima. It is a type of local search as well as a stochastic search technique. We reformulate the problem and solve it for minimization, as opposed to maximization. So, we are now descending into valleys as opposed to climbing hills. We are pretty much doing the same thing, but in a different way. We use an objective function to guide the search. This objective function serves as our heuristic. Here heuristic function includes a probability function that determines whether to accept a worse move based on a temperature parameter that decreases over time. The reason it is called simulated annealing is because it is derived from the metallurgical process. We first heat metals up and then let them cool until they reach the optimal energy state. It is usually used in complex optimization problems such as scheduling, traveling salesman problem, and VLSI design.

Heuristic search techniques are more efficient than blind search techniques because they use additional knowledge about the problem domain to guide the search. The choice of heuristic and technique depends on the problem's characteristics, including whether optimality, completeness, or speed is the priority.

Adversary Search

Adversary search is a type of search algorithm used in competitive situations, like games (chess, tic-tac-toe, Go), where multiple agents or players are in direct conflict. The goal is to maximize one's own advantage while minimizing the opponent's, acknowledging that the opponent has the same objective.

Adversary search is commonly used in two-player, zero-sum games, where one player's gain equals the other's loss. The primary technique is the minimax algorithm, often improved with alpha-beta pruning for efficiency.

Here's a breakdown of key concepts:

- **Minimax Algorithm**: This decision-making algorithm is used in games where one player (the maximizing player) aims to maximize their score, while the other (the minimizing player) tries to minimize it. The game is represented as a game tree, where nodes are game states, and edges are moves. Leaf nodes (terminal states) have evaluations indicating who is winning. The maximizing player tries to maximize this evaluation (e.g., probability of winning), while the minimizing player tries to minimize it. The algorithm explores all possible moves, assuming the opponent will play optimally, and alternates between minimizing and maximizing at each tree level to determine the best move.

- **Alpha-Beta Pruning**: This optimization technique enhances the minimax algorithm by reducing the number of nodes evaluated in the game tree, without affecting the outcome. It uses two values: alpha (the best value the maximizing player can guarantee) and beta (the best value the minimizing player can guarantee). If a branch cannot influence the final decision, it is "pruned" (skipped). This pruning improves efficiency, especially in games with deep trees like chess, and doesn't compromise correctness.

- **Evaluation Function**: In games with large search spaces (e.g., chess), searching the entire game tree is often impossible. Therefore, minimax and alpha-beta pruning use an evaluation function to estimate the value of non-terminal states. This function assigns a score to a game state, indicating a player's relative advantage, often based on factors like material, position, or other game-specific heuristics.

- **Horizon Effect**: This occurs when the algorithm fails to see beyond a certain search depth and misses critical future consequences. A move might seem good in the short term but lead to a disadvantage later.

- **Quiescence Search**: To mitigate the horizon effect, techniques like quiescence search are used. This extends the search in unstable positions (e.g., captures in chess) to avoid overlooking significant consequences just beyond the search depth.

- **Iterative Deepening**: In practice, adversary search algorithms often employ iterative deepening. The search runs to increasing depths until a time limit is reached. This ensures a reasonable move is always available, even if the search can't be completed to the maximum depth.

Knowledge Representation and Reasoning

Knowledge representation and reasoning (KRR) is a field in artificial intelligence that focuses on how to represent information in a way that a computer system can use to make decisions with human-like reasoning. Knowledge representation involves structuring information in a form that a computer can understand. Knowledge representation is a study of how the beliefs, intentions, and judgments of an intelligent agent can be expressed suitably for automated reasoning. One of the primary purposes of knowledge representation includes modelling intelligent behaviour for an agent. It focuses on how information about the world can be structured so that computer systems can effectively solve complex problems.

> **Definition Knowledge representation (KR)** involves creating models of the world that a computer can understand. It's about encoding real-world information in a way that facilitates computational processing. Using these models, AI systems can then make decisions, perform tasks, or infer new information.

> **Definition** Reasoning allows the system to apply knowledge in practical scenarios.

Knowledge representation provides a framework for representing, organizing, and manipulating knowledge that can be used to solve complex problems, make decisions, and learn from data.

Representation is how computers translate their knowledge into something useful. It's like turning knowledge into language computers understand. This includes things like:

- **Object**: The AI needs to know all the facts about the objects in our world domain. For example, a keyboard has keys, a guitar has strings, etc.
- **Events**: The actions which occur in our world are called events.
- **Performance**: It describes a behaviour involving knowledge about how to do things.
- **Meta-knowledge**: The knowledge about what we know is called meta-knowledge.
- **Facts**: The things in the real world that are known and proven true.
- **Knowledge Base**: A knowledge base in artificial intelligence aims to capture human expert knowledge to support decision-making, problem-solving, and more.

Figure 2.3 depicts how an AI system interacts with the real world, highlighting the key components working in concert to exhibit intelligence.

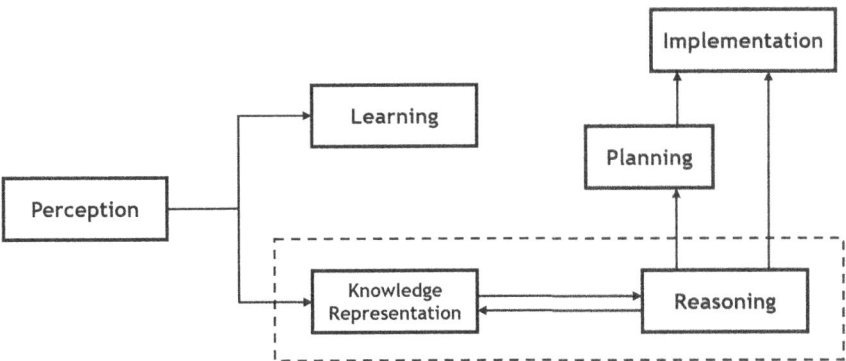

Fig. 2.3 Components of AI system

The **perception component** functions as the system's sensory apparatus, collecting data from its surroundings. Its role includes environmental data acquisition, noise source identification, damage assessment, and defining initial reactions to sensed inputs.

The **learning component** then takes centre stage, processing the data gathered through perception. A core objective of AI is to develop systems capable of learning from experience, minimizing the need for explicit programming. Learning within AI involves continuous self-improvement through mechanisms like knowledge acquisition, inferential reasoning, heuristic development, and optimized search processes.

The **knowledge representation and reasoning component** is pivotal, embodying the system's human-like intelligence. It focuses on the fundamental challenge of representing and manipulating knowledge to achieve intelligent behaviour. Adopting a top-down approach, it seeks to understand the essential knowledge required for intelligent agency, rather than replicating brain structure. Furthermore, it establishes how automated reasoning mechanisms can effectively access and deploy this knowledge.

Planning and implementation components are subsequent stages, driven by the outputs of knowledge representation and reasoning. Planning entails defining initial conditions, required prerequisites, and intended effects, ultimately generating a sequence of actions to reach a desired state. Execution, the final component, involves carrying out the planned sequence, completing the intelligent action cycle.

These interconnected elements represent the fundamental components of knowledge representation within an AI system.

There are several common methods for reasoning with knowledge in the field of knowledge representation and reasoning (KRR):

1. Logical Reasoning: This method involves using formal logic systems, such as first-order or modal logics, to represent and reason about knowledge. Rules and

constraints can be encoded as logical statements, and various inference techniques like resolution or unification are used to draw conclusions from the given information.

2. Constraint Satisfaction: In this approach, problems are modelled as sets of constraints that must be satisfied by potential solutions. Reasoning involves finding an assignment of values to variables such that all constraints are met. Common techniques for solving constraint satisfaction problems include search algorithms and local consistency methods.

3. Probabilistic Reasoning: This method is used when dealing with uncertain or imprecise information. Knowledge is represented as probabilistic distributions over possible outcomes, and reasoning involves updating these distributions based on new evidence using Bayesian inference or other probability update rules.

4. Rule-Based Systems: In rule-based systems, knowledge is represented as a set of production rules that can be fired to draw conclusions from given facts. Reasoning involves applying these rules in a forward (data-driven) or backward (goal-driven) manner to arrive at the desired outcome.

5. Case-Based Reasoning: This method involves storing and retrieving past experiences (cases) to solve new problems. Knowledge is represented as case descriptions, and reasoning involves finding similar cases in memory and adapting their solutions to match the current problem context.

6. Default Reasoning: In some situations, it may be necessary to make assumptions when information is incomplete or contradictory. Default reasoning involves using default rules that can be retracted if new conflicting information is discovered, allowing for more flexible and adaptive reasoning processes.

7. Spatial and Temporal Reasoning: These methods are used to reason about the spatial and temporal aspects of knowledge. Knowledge is represented as geometric or topological structures (for spatial reasoning) or event sequences (for temporal reasoning), and reasoning involves applying various inference techniques based on these structures.

These methods, along with others, provide a rich set of tools for representing and reasoning with knowledge in KRR applications ranging from expert systems and natural language processing to robotics and autonomous agents.

To sum up, KRR is the field dedicated to translating real-world information into a format machine can understand and use. The goal of KRR extends far beyond data storage; it seeks to empower machines to learn from this knowledge and apply it to solve intricate, real-life challenges, such as natural language interaction. Tracing its roots back to philosophical inquiries into logic and reasoning, KRR has become a fundamental area of AI research, developing alongside our deepening understanding of computational models of human cognition.

Now we briefly overview common approaches for representing knowledge in the following section.

Logic

Logic is a formal method of reasoning. Many concepts which can be verbalized can be translated into symbolic representations which closely approximate the meaning of these concepts, and these symbolic structures can be manipulated in programs to deduce various facts to carry out a form of automatic reasoning.

Predicate logic and propositional logic are two fundamental forms of logic used in AI for knowledge representation, reasoning, and problem-solving. They provide the formal framework for AI systems to model knowledge, infer conclusions, and solve logical problems.

In propositional logic, we are interested in declarative sentences that can be either true or false, but not both. Any such declarative sentence is called a proposition or statement.

> **Definition** A "proposition" is a declarative sentence that is either true or false, but, not both.

Predicate calculus, also known as first-order predicate logic (FOPL), is one of the oldest and most significant knowledge representation frameworks in artificial intelligence. Predicate logic serves as a high-level, human-oriented language for articulating problems and problem-solving strategies. Developed by logicians for formal reasoning, particularly in mathematics, it is crucial for AI students to understand FOPL for several reasons:

- It provides the only formal reasoning approach with a solid theoretical foundation.
- The structure of predicate logic is sufficiently flexible to accurately represent natural language statements.
- It is widely recognized in the AI community as one of the most valuable representation methods.

There are various views about the definition of "logic." But in our context, "Logic is the Art of Correct Reasoning."

There are two main issues with reasoning. Suppose we are given a set of statements. The issues are:

(a) Can we get all the correct facts through reasoning (also known as *inferencing*), over the given set of statements? This issue refers to the *completeness* of reasoning.

(b) Will we derive a *wrong* fact through reasoning? This issue refers to the *soundness* of reasoning.

Hence when our reasoning possesses the above two properties over the given set of statements, also known as the *domain of knowledge*, we call the reasoning to be *correct*. This art of correct reasoning is "logic."

But here we are talking about "symbolic logic." The purpose of this symbolic logic is to symbolize reasoning encountered not only in mathematics but also in daily life.

In propositional logic, this symbolization is done by using *declarative statements* that can be either true or false, but not both. Hence, *propositional logic* refers to the style of reasoning which reasons over a given set of declarative statements. Any such declarative statement is known as a *proposition*.

Predicate logic consists of a predicate that gives further information about a sentence's subject. It can be referred to as an attribute that determines the properties of the subject in a sentence. In short, propositional logic consists of a declarative statement with a truth value, i.e., true or false, and predicate logic consists of a predicate that gives further information about a sentence's subject.

In the context of AI, predicate logic is a formal framework for deducing relationships between objects and their qualities. It is a mathematical language that enables knowledge to be expressed precisely and unambiguously, making it perfect for usage in AI systems. It is used as a foundational framework for the representation of knowledge and reasoning.

Quantifiers are another crucial aspect of predicate logic. They express the extent to which a predicate is true over a range of elements. There are two types of quantifiers: the universal quantifier, denoted as "$\forall$", and the existential quantifier, denoted as "$\exists$". The universal quantifier $\forall x\, P(x)$ means that for all x, $P(x)$ is true. The existential quantifier $\exists x\, P(x)$ means that there exists at least one x for which $P(x)$ is true.

In AI, logical expressions in predicate logic are assertions made up of predicates, variables, quantifiers, and logical connectives. They are used to represent relationships between things and their properties and infer and deduce information.

For example, consider the predicate $P(x, y) : x + 2 = y$. The statement $\forall x\, \exists y\, P(x, y) = T$ means that for any x, there exists a y such that $x + 2 = y$ is true. This kind of logical expression can be used in AI to represent and reason about relationships between different entities or concepts.

First-order logic predicates apply to individual subjects, such as "Tom is a mechanic," while higher-order logic allows predicates to apply to other predicates, enabling propositions like "is a mechanic who wears glasses."

Horn clauses, a subset of first-order logic clauses, are structured for efficiency with a single positive literal at most, facilitating easier computation. General first-order clauses, without such restrictions, can be more complex and variable-rich, making them harder to process. The most general form of a Horn clause is a conjunction of literals with at most one being positive, and without any positive literals, it becomes a Horn formula or sentence. Conversely, the least general form is a ground clause with a single, variable-free literal representing an absolute fact.

Horn clauses efficiently encode both factual and procedural knowledge, allowing for inference—deriving new facts from existing clauses and facts—and non-monotonic reasoning, which adapts to new information over time. This adaptability is crucial for dynamic environments like stock markets or weather forecasting, making Horn clauses a robust tool for knowledge representation in AI.

Substitution

Substitution in first-order logic is a fundamental concept used to replace variables in logical expressions with terms. A term can be a constant, a variable, or a function applied to other terms. The process of substitution involves taking a logical formula and systematically replacing its variables with specific terms to create a new formula. This is particularly useful in logical proofs and automated reasoning, where it helps in deriving conclusions from given premises.

For example, consider a logical formula $P(x)$, where x is a variable. If we substitute x with a constant a, the formula becomes $P(a)$. Similarly, if we substitute x with another variable y, the formula becomes $P(y)$. Substitution can also involve more complex terms, such as functions. If we have a function $f(y)$ and we substitute x with $f(y)$, the formula becomes $P(f(y))$.

Substitution is governed by certain rules to ensure consistency and avoid conflicts, such as avoiding the substitution of a variable with a term that contains the same variable, which could lead to circular definitions. This process is crucial in unification, where two logical expressions are made identical by finding a suitable substitution for their variables. Overall, substitution is a key mechanism in first-order logic that enables the manipulation and transformation of logical expressions to facilitate reasoning and proof construction.

Conjunctive Normal Form

Conjunctive Normal Form (CNF) is a way of structuring logical expressions in Boolean algebra. In CNF, a formula is expressed as a conjunction (AND) of one or more clauses, where each clause is a disjunction (OR) of literals. A literal is either a variable or its negation.

For example, the formula $(A \lor B) \land (\neg C \lor D)(A \lor B) \land (\neg C \lor D)$ is in CNF. Here, $(A \lor B)(A \lor B)$ and $(\neg C \lor D)(\neg C \lor D)$ are clauses, and the entire expression is a conjunction of these clauses.

CNF is particularly useful in various areas of computer science, such as in algorithms for satisfiability problems (SAT), where determining if there exists an assignment of truth values to variables that makes the entire formula true is a key task.

Disjunctive Normal Form

Disjunctive Normal Form (DNF) is a way of structuring logical expressions in Boolean algebra. In DNF, a formula is expressed as a disjunction (OR) of one or more conjunctions (AND) of literals. A literal is either a variable or its negation.

For example, the formula $(A \land B) \lor (\neg C \land D)(A \land B) \lor (\neg C \land D)$ is in DNF. Here, $(A \land B)(A \land B)$ and $(\neg C \land D)(\neg C \land D)$ are conjunctions, and the entire expression is a disjunction of these conjunctions.

DNF is useful in various areas of computer science, such as in simplifying logical expressions and in certain types of decision-making algorithms.

First-Order Logic Inference Through Unification

First-order logic inference through unification is a process used to determine if two logical expressions can be made identical by finding a suitable substitution for their variables. Unification is essential in automated reasoning and logic programming, as it allows for the systematic combination of different logical statements to derive new conclusions.

Unification works by identifying a set of substitutions that, when applied to the variables in the expressions, make the expressions identical. This process involves comparing the structure of the expressions and recursively finding substitutions for their components.

For example, consider the two logical expressions $P(x, f(y))$ and $P(a, f(b))$. To unify these expressions, we need to find substitutions for the variables x and y that make the expressions identical. In this case, the substitution $\{x \mapsto a, y \mapsto b\}$ achieves this, resulting in both expressions becoming $P(a, f(b))$.

Unification is particularly useful in inference rules such as modus ponens. For instance, if we have the implication $P(x) \rightarrow Q(x)$ and the fact $P(a)$, we can use unification to infer $Q(a)$. By unifying $P(x)$ with $P(a)$, we find the substitution $\{x \mapsto a\}$. Applying this substitution to $Q(x)$ gives us $Q(a)$, which is the inferred conclusion.

Overall, unification in first-order logic inference is a powerful tool that enables the combination and manipulation of logical expressions to derive new knowledge. It plays a crucial role in various applications, including theorem proving, logic programming, and artificial intelligence.

Resolution
First-order logic inference through resolution is a method used to derive conclusions by refuting the negation of the desired conclusion. It is based on the principle that if a set of premises logically entails a conclusion, then adding the negation of the conclusion to the premises will lead to a contradiction. Resolution works by transforming logical statements into a standardized form called Conjunctive Normal Form (CNF) and then systematically applying the resolution rule to derive new clauses until either a contradiction is found or no further inferences can be made. It is particularly useful in automated theorem proving and logic programming. Here's a simple example in propositional logic:

Consider the following two clauses:

1. $A \vee B$
2. $\neg A \vee C$.

We want to resolve these clauses to derive a new clause. The resolution rule states that if we have two clauses, one containing a literal and the other containing its negation, we can combine them to form a new clause by taking the disjunction of the remaining literals.

In this case:

- The first clause contains A.
- The second clause contains $\neg A$.

By applying the resolution rule, we combine the remaining literals B and C to form the new clause: $B \vee C$.

So, the resolution of $A \vee B$ and $\neg A \vee C$ is $B \vee C$.

This process can be repeated to derive further conclusions from a set of clauses, ultimately helping to prove or disprove logical statements.

Let us see another example on this important concept.

Suppose we have the premises:

1. $\forall x(P(x) \rightarrow Q(x))$
2. $P(a)$.

We want to infer $Q(a)$. First, we convert the premises into CNF. The first premise $\forall x(P(x) \rightarrow Q(x))$ can be rewritten as $\forall x(\neg P(x) \vee Q(x))$.

The second premise $P(a)$ is already in a suitable form.

Next, we negate the conclusion $Q(a)$ to get $\neg Q(a)$ and add it to the set of premises. Our goal is to derive a contradiction. The premises in CNF are now:

1. $\neg P(x) \vee Q(x)$
2. $P(a)$
3. $\neg Q(a)$.

We apply the resolution rule to these clauses. Resolving $P(a)$ with $\neg P(x) \vee Q(x)$ by substituting x with a gives us $Q(a)$. Now we have:

1. $Q(a)$
2. $\neg Q(a)$.

Resolving $Q(a)$ with $\neg Q(a)$ results in an empty clause, indicating a contradiction. Since we have derived a contradiction, we conclude that the original premises logically entail $Q(a)$.

This method is useful in propositional logic and predicate logic, where the goal is to prove the validity of arguments. In predicate logic, resolution involves the following steps:

1. Convert statements into a standard form (Conjunctive Normal Form).
2. Negate the conclusion you wish to prove.
3. Combine all statements, including the negated conclusion.
4. Apply the resolution rule to derive a contradiction.

If a contradiction is reached, the original conclusion is proven true. This process highlights the efficiency of resolution in automated reasoning systems.

Resolution allows AI systems to infer new knowledge from existing facts, enhancing their ability to make decisions and solve problems. In automated theorem proving, resolution is employed to verify the validity of logical statements. By systematically applying resolution, systems can derive proofs for complex theorems, making this technique invaluable in mathematics and computer science.

Despite its strengths, resolution also faces challenges, including:

- **Complexity**: The resolution process can become computationally expensive with larger statements. To manage complexity, researchers are developing more efficient algorithms and heuristics.

- **Ambiguity**: Natural language can introduce ambiguities that complicate resolution. Natural language processing systems aim to clarify ambiguities through context and additional information. By improving understanding of language nuances, resolution can become more effective in real-world applications.
- **Incomplete Knowledge**: The effectiveness of resolution diminishes when the knowledge base is incomplete.

Understanding and applying resolution can significantly impact the development of intelligent systems capable of logical reasoning.

Semantic Networks (Inheritable Knowledge)

Semantic networks are alternative of predicate logic for knowledge representation. In semantic networks, we can represent our knowledge in the form of graphical networks. This network consists of nodes representing objects and arcs which describe the relationship between those objects. An important feature of semantic nets is that they convey meaning. That is to say, the relationship between nodes and edges in the net conveys information about some real-world situation. A good example of a semantic net is a family tree diagram. Usually, nodes in these diagrams represent people, and there are edges that represent parental relationships, as well as relationships by marriage.

Each node in a semantic net has a label that identifies what the node represents. Edges are also labelled. Edges represent connections or relationships between nodes. In the case of searching a dictionary for a page that contains a particular word, each node might represent a single page, and each edge would represent a way of getting from one page to another.

Semantic networks can categorize the object in different forms and can also link those objects. Semantic networks are easy to understand and can be easily extended. Semantic nets provide a very intuitive way to represent knowledge about objects and the relationships that exist between those objects. The data in semantic nets can be reasoned about in order to produce systems that have knowledge about a particular domain.

Semantic networks try to model human-like memory to store the information, but in practice, it is not possible to build such a vast semantic network. Semantic networks take more computational time at runtime as we need to traverse the complete network tree to answer some questions. It might be possible in the worst-case scenario that after traversing the entire tree, we find that the solution does not exist in this network.

Ontologies

The notion of ontologies as computational artefacts has become visible in artificial intelligence and computer science, while "ontology" originally denotes the study of existence in philosophy. In information systems, ontologies are conceptual models of what "exists" in some domain, brought into machine-interpretable form by means of knowledge representation techniques. In this section we start from a general definition of the notion of ontology and elaborate on its appearance and usage in computer science.

In its primary significance in philosophy, *ontology* is a branch of metaphysics and denotes the philosophical investigation of existence. Ontological categories provide a means to classify all existing things, and the systematic organization of such categories allows to analyse the world that is made up of these things in a structured way. In ontology, categories are also referred to as *universals*, and the concrete things that they serve to classify are referred to as *particulars (instances)*.

Any intelligent information systems can benefit from the idea of ontological categorization. When applied to a restricted domain of interest in the scope of a concrete application scenario, ontology can be restricted to cover a special subset of the world. Ontology provides the labels for nodes and arcs in a semantic network or the names for predicates and constants in rules or logical formulas, which constitute an *ontological vocabulary*. By defining "what exists" it determines the things that can be predicated about. The terms of the ontological vocabulary are then used to represent knowledge, forming statements about the domain.

To be precise, the key components of an ontology are concepts, relations, and instances.

1. **Concepts** *map to the generic nodes in semantic networks, or to unary predicates in logic. They represent the ontological categories that are relevant in the domain of interest.*
2. **Relations** *map to arcs in semantic networks, or to binary predicates in logic. They semantically connect concepts, as well as instances, specifying their interrelations.*
3. **Instances** *map to individual nodes in semantic networks, or to constants in logic. They represent the named and identifiable concrete objects in the domain of interest, i.e., the particular individuals which are classified by concepts.*

Example Here is a simple example of an ontology, designed for the domain of smart home automation. This ontology illustrates how knowledge can be structured using classes, instances, relations, and relationships, which are fundamental to enabling AI systems to reason about and interact with their environment.

Classes (Concepts)	Instances (Individuals)
• Device	• LivingRoom (instance of room)
• Room	• Kitchen (instance of room)
• Sensor	• Thermostat (instance of sensor)
• Appliance	• LightBulb (instance of appliance)
• Action	• TurnOn (instance of action)
	• TurnOff (instance of action)

Properties (Attributes and Relationships)

- isLocatedIn(Device, Room): Links a device to the room where it is installed.
- controls(Appliance, Action): Specifies which actions can be performed on an appliance.
- hasSensor(Room, Sensor): Indicates which sensors are present in a room.
- triggers(Sensor, Action): Defines which actions are triggered by sensor events.

Axioms (Rules)

- If a Sensor in a Room detects motion, then TurnOn the LightBulb in that Room.
- An Appliance can only be controlled by Actions it supports (e.g., a LightBulb can be TurnedOn or TurnedOff).

Ontology Structure Example (in Plain Text)

- LivingRoom is a Room.
- Kitchen is a Room.
- Thermostat is a Sensor.
- LightBulb is an Appliance.
- TurnOn and TurnOff are Actions.
- LightBulb isLocatedIn LivingRoom.
- Thermostat isLocatedIn Kitchen.
- LivingRoom hasSensor Thermostat.
- LightBulb controls TurnOn and TurnOff.
- Thermostat triggers TurnOn (for LightBulb in LivingRoom).

This ontology provides a structured way for an AI system to understand and reason about the relationships between devices, rooms, sensors, and actions within a smart home. For example, if the Thermostat (a sensor) in the LivingRoom detects a temperature drop, the system can infer, based on the ontology, that it should trigger the TurnOn action for the LightBulb in the same room. This structure enables interoperability, knowledge sharing, and automated reasoning, which are essential for intelligent behaviour in AI-powered environments.

Such ontologies can be represented in formal languages like OWL (Web Ontology Language) for use in semantic web and AI reasoning systems, but even a simple text-based structure like the one above illustrates the core principles of ontological design in AI.

Conceptual modelling with ontologies looks like modelling in object-oriented software development or to designing entity-relationship diagrams for database schemas. Nevertheless, there is an elusive dual distinction. Primarily, ontology languages by and large provide a richer formal semantics than object-oriented or database-related formalisms. They support encoding of complex axiomatic information due to their logic-based notations. Therefore, an ontology specifies a semantically rich axiomatization of domain knowledge instead of just data or object model. Secondly, ontologies are constructed for various purposes than object-oriented models or entity-relationship diagrams. While the latter mostly describe components of an information system to be executed on a machine and a schema for data storage, respectively, an ontology captures domain knowledge as such and allow to reason about it.

In contrast to concepts in ontologies, the weights in a neural network or the probability measures in a Bayesian network would not fit such a conceptual and symbolic approach.

Imagine an ontology as a dictionary and grammar for a specific topic, defining the key terms (concepts) and how they relate. A knowledge base, on the other hand, is like a library filled with books, each book containing specific facts and stories (instances) that use the language defined by the ontology. When an AI system needs to understand or reason about something, it might consult this "dictionary and grammar" (ontology) and use it to interpret the "books" (knowledge base), possibly combining it with other knowledge along the way.

Artificial intelligence finds many uses for these "dictionaries and grammars" (ontologies). Here are some examples showing how different applications highlight the value of these structured conceptual models:

1. Unifying Diverse Data: Think of different departments in a company using different spreadsheets to track similar information about customers. Ontologies can act as a common language to understand and integrate this diverse data, even if it's structured differently. This is information integration at the schema level.

2. Smarter and more Relevant Search: Regular keyword search can be too broad or miss the point. Ontology-based information retrieval uses the "dictionary and grammar" to understand the *meaning* of words in searches and documents. It's like translating keywords into more precise, conceptual terms, leading to better search results.

3. Building a Shared Understanding in Teams: In any group, from companies to communities, people have valuable knowledge. Knowledge management uses ontologies to create a shared framework for organizing this knowledge. It's like creating a common index and set of categories so everyone can find, use, and contribute to collective knowledge.

4. Adding Machine-Readable Meaning to Content: Think of tagging photos with keywords. Ontologies offer a formal, structured way to tag all kinds of digital content (text, images, data) with meaningful metadata. Because this metadata is based on a formal "dictionary," computers can automatically process and understand it. This is semantically enhanced content management.

5. Creating AI Experts: To build AI that can act like experts, we need to give them expert knowledge. Expert systems use detailed domain ontologies to capture and formalize this expertise in fields like medicine or law. This allows the AI to reason and answer complex questions, much like a human expert.

However, just like a dictionary needs to be well-maintained and agreed upon, ontologies need a structured approach to ensure they are reliable, practical, widely usable, and updated over time. The real challenge now is to make these "dictionaries" executable—to actively use them in AI systems that evolve and learn alongside the real world. This is crucial for building AI that we can trust and truly rely on.

Ontology Pitfalls and Actionable Solutions

Ontologies, our structured maps of knowledge, sometimes fall short of their promise. Here's why, and how we can set them on the right path:

Why Ontologies Often Fail

1. **Fragmentation and Redundancy**: We have a proliferation of ontologies, often overlapping. Instead of working together toward a common, strong knowledge base, we create many separate, weaker ones. This duplication hinders widespread adoption.

2. **Independent Development**: Ontologies are frequently built in isolation, without coordination between disciplines or projects. This leads to disconnected knowledge models that don't easily integrate.

3. **Lack of Interoperability**: Without efforts to connect them, ontologies become isolated silos of knowledge. They cannot easily exchange or share information, limiting their collective value.

4. **Obsolescence and Abandonment**: Many ontologies are created but not actively used or maintained. This lack of community adoption and ongoing upkeep leads to them becoming outdated and irrelevant over time.

5. **Poor Accessibility and Understanding**: Complex or poorly documented ontologies are difficult to understand and use. If people can't easily learn and navigate an ontology, it will be underutilized.

6. **Insufficient Training and Support**: Ontology use is often perceived as technically demanding, limiting its adoption by a wider range of users, including business professionals who could benefit from them.

7. **Inconsistent Design Principles**: The absence of standardized design rules results in inconsistencies in ontology structure and quality, making them harder to reuse and integrate.
8. **Lack of Real-World Validation**: Many ontologies remain theoretical constructs, developed in research settings but not tested or validated in practical, real-world applications.
9. **Absence of Quality Standards**: Without agreed-upon quality benchmarks, it's difficult to assess and compare ontologies, making it challenging to identify and promote the most effective and reliable ones.

How We Can Improve Ontologies

1. **Promote Convergence and Reuse**: Encourage alignment, consolidation of existing ontologies, and a culture of reusability to avoid redundant development and strengthen the collective knowledge base.
2. **Foster Collaboration and Standardization**: Encourage cross-disciplinary collaboration and promote the standardization of foundational ontologies to build a more unified and interconnected knowledge ecosystem.
3. **Prioritize Interoperability**: Emphasize the use of shared vocabularies, create mappings between ontologies, and actively align with widely adopted frameworks to enhance interoperability.
4. **Embrace Openness and Community**: Develop ontologies using open-source models, host them on platforms like GitHub, establish clear governance structures, and foster active community involvement to ensure long-term maintenance and adoption.
5. **Enhance Documentation and Tools**: Create clear, structured documentation and user-friendly tools for exploring and editing ontologies to improve accessibility and understanding for all users.
6. **Invest in Education and Training**: Develop educational resources, workshops, and intuitive interfaces to lower the barrier to entry and make ontologies accessible to both technical and business users.
7. **Apply Best Practices and Principles**: Promote the adoption of established design principles and best practices from successful ontologies to create more consistent, coherent, and reusable models.
8. **Engage with End-Users Early**: Involve end-users from the initial stages of ontology development to ensure they address real-world problems and are validated in practical applications.
9. **Establish Quality Metrics and Standards**: Define universally accepted evaluation metrics for consistency, coverage, and usability to create benchmarks for ontology quality and facilitate comparisons and improvements.

Inheritance

Inheritance is a relationship that can be particularly useful in AI and in programming. The idea of inheritance is one that is easily understood intuitively. For example, if we say that all mammals give birth to live babies, and we also say that all cats are mammals, and that Ellie is a cat, then we can conclude that Ellie gives birth to live mammals. Of course, this piece of reasoning does not consider the fact that Ellie might be male, or if Ellie is female, might be too young or too old to give birth. The concept of inheritance is used in object-oriented programming. Inheritance allows us to specify properties of a superclass and then to define a subclass, which inherits the properties of the superclass.

Frame

A frame is a record-like structure which consists of a collection of attributes and its values to describe an entity in the world. Frames are the AI data structure which divides knowledge into substructures by representing stereotypes situations. It consists of a collection of slots and slot values. These slots may be of any type and sizes. Slots have names and values which are called facets. The various aspects of a slot are known as facets. Facets are features of frames which enable us to put constraints on the frames. IF-NEEDED facts are called when data of any particular slot is needed. A frame may consist of any number of slots, and a slot may include any number of facets and facets may have any number of values. This is the way in which the frame system network is built up. Rather than simply having links between frames, each relationship is expressed by a value being placed in a slot. A frame is also known as slot-filter knowledge representation in artificial intelligence. Frames are derived from semantic networks and later evolved into our modern-day classes and objects. A single frame is not much useful. Frames system consists of a collection of frames which are connected. In the frame, knowledge about an object or event can be stored together in the knowledge base. The frame is a type of technology which is widely used in various applications, including natural language processing and machine visions.

The main advantage of using frame-based systems for expert systems over the rule-based approach is that all the information about a particular object is stored in one place.

Non-monotonic Reasoning

To be able to do this reasoning with uncertainty, we would require a technique for maintaining several parallel belief spaces, each of which would correspond to the beliefs of one expert. Such techniques are complicated by the fact that the belief spaces of various experts, although not identical, are sufficiently similar that it is unacceptably inefficient to represent them as separate knowledge bases. The technique for this reasoning is known as *non-monotonic reasoning*.

Non-monotonic reasoning is a type of reasoning in AI where the introduction of new information can invalidate previously drawn conclusions. This contrasts with *monotonic reasoning*, where once a conclusion is drawn, it remains valid regardless of any new information added. Non-monotonic reasoning is essential for modelling real-world situations where knowledge is incomplete, assumptions can change, and new evidence can lead to the retraction of conclusions.

> **Definition** A logic is non-monotonic if some conclusions can be invalidated by adding more knowledge.

The logic of definite clauses with negation as failure is non-monotonic. Non-monotonic reasoning is useful for representing defaults. A default is a rule that can be used unless it overridden by an exception.

Traditional reasoning systems, like predicate logic, work best with information that has three key features: it's **complete** (we have all the facts we need), **consistent** (no contradictions), and **monotonic**. Monotonicity means that once something is considered true, it *stays* true forever, and we only ever add *more* truths. Think of it as building a tower—you only ever add blocks, never remove them.

However, if information lacks any of these properties—if it's incomplete, inconsistent, or changes in ways that require us to retract previous conclusions—then these conventional systems struggle.

Non-monotonic reasoning is designed to handle these messy, real-world situations. It deals with incomplete and changing information. To do this, it needs to address some core questions:

- How can we reason based on what we *don't* know, as well as what we *do* know?
- How do we update our knowledge and conclusions when new facts arrive, or old ones are proven false?
- When different lines of reasoning lead to conflicting conclusions, how do we decide what to believe?

In essence, monotonic reasoning is like a one-way street—knowledge only increases. Non-monotonic reasoning is more like navigating a dynamic environment where we might need to backtrack and change our mind as we learn more. In non-monotonic systems, truths can be revised or retracted as new information emerges. Non-monotonic reasoning is like navigating shifting sands—conclusions can be revised, and sometimes what we thought was true must be retracted as the picture changes.

Non-monotonic reasoning tackles situations where traditional logic falls short—when knowledge is incomplete, uncertain, or evolving. Here's a breakdown of common types:

- **Default Reasoning**: This approach uses default rules or general principles to make inferences. However, these inferences are *defeasible*—they can be retracted if contradictory evidence emerges. It's reasoning based on what is typically the case, recognizing there can be exceptions. **Example**: Assuming "birds typically fly" to conclude Tweety flies, until information about Tweety being a penguin arises, at which point the default conclusion is withdrawn.
- **Circumscription**: A formal method that implements a principle of minimization. It aims to interpret knowledge by assuming that extensions of certain predicates are as small as possible, consistent with the known facts. In simpler terms, it minimizes the "extent" of certain properties. **Example**: Circumscribing the predicate "flies." We assume only the explicitly known entities fly, and for others, we assume they don't unless proven otherwise. This helps in making "least commitment" assumptions.
- **Auto-Epistemic Logic**: Deals with an agent's reasoning about its own beliefs and knowledge. It allows an AI system to explicitly represent and reason about what it knows and, importantly, what it *doesn't* know. This self-referential aspect is key to non-monotonicity. **Example**: An AI system uses its knowledge base. Finding no information about Tweety's flight ability, and knowing the general rule "birds fly," it infers "Tweety probably flies" based on its *lack* of information to the contrary. This inference is auto-epistemic as it is based on the system's own state of knowledge.
- **Reasoning with Default Assumptions**: Similar to default reasoning, but often focuses on applying typical or expected properties in the absence of specific counter-information. These assumptions are considered provisional and can be overridden. **Example**: Assuming "healthy" as a default state for a person until presented with specific evidence of illness.
- **Abductive Reasoning**: Focuses on finding the best explanation for observed facts. It involves reasoning "backward" from observations to potential causes. Abductive conclusions are tentative and subject to revision based on new evidence, making it non-monotonic. **Example**: Diagnosing "flu" from symptoms is abduction; it's the most plausible explanation given initial observations. Further tests could lead to a different, revised diagnosis.
- **Closed World Assumption (CWA)**: A powerful form of non-monotonic reasoning particularly relevant in database and knowledge base contexts. CWA dictates that if information is not explicitly asserted as true in the system, it is assumed to be false. **Example**: Database query: "Is Student X enrolled in Course Y?" If no record exists, CWA dictates the answer is "No." This contrasts with the **Open World Assumption (OWA)**, common in more open systems like the Web, where lack of information means "unknown," not necessarily "false."

Non-monotonic reasoning is crucial for building intelligent systems that can operate effectively in real, complex, and dynamic environments. It bridges the gap between the idealized world of classical logic and the messy reality of incomplete and evolving knowledge, enabling AI to reason more flexibly and adaptively. Its applications span expert systems, automated planning, flexible knowledge representation, and many other areas of AI.

Probability

Probabilistic reasoning stands as an effective method of handling uncertainty. This method uses the principles of probability theory to make anticipatory predictions, draw inferences, and update knowledge based on new data.

In the real world, there are lots of scenarios, where the certainty of something is not confirmed, such as "It will rain today," "behaviour of someone for some situations," "A match between two teams or two players." These are probable sentences for which we can assume that it will happen but not sure about it, so here we use probabilistic reasoning.

Probabilities are (real) numbers in the range 0 to 1.

- A probability of $P(A) = 0$ indicates total uncertainty in A, $P(A) = 1$ indicates total certainty and values in between some degree of (un)certainty.
- Probabilities can be calculated in a number of ways.
    Probability $=$ (number of desired outcomes)/(total number of outcomes).

Probabilistic reasoning refers to the formation of probability judgements and subjective beliefs about the likelihoods of outcomes and the frequencies of events. The judgements that people make are often about things that are only indirectly observable and only partly predictable. For example, the weather, a game of sports, a project at work, or whatever it could be, our willingness to engage in an endeavour and the actions that we take depend on our estimated likelihood of the relevant outcomes.

In probabilistic reasoning we focus on models for complex systems that involve a significant amount of uncertainty. Such models can be acquired either through learning from data or from domain knowledge of human experts. They typically involve sets of random variables. For instance, a medical diagnosis domain may involve dozens or hundreds of symptoms, possible diseases, patient dispositions, and other influences. Each of those factors will be described by a discrete (e.g., disease A, B, C …) or continuous (e.g., fever temperature) random variable. The task is then to reason probabilistically about the values of one or more of the variables given observations about some others. To do so, we estimate a joint probability distribution over the involved random variables.

The structural properties of probabilistic models can be identified and captured by graphical representations, particularly Markov networks and Bayesian networks. A Markov network is an undirected graph whose links represent symmetrical probabilistic dependences, while a Bayesian network is a directed acyclic graph whose arrows represent causal influences or class-property relationships. A formal semantics of both network types has been established and knowledge representation, schemes in inference systems are explored with their power and limitations. The impact of each new piece of evidence is viewed as a perturbation that propagates through the network via message-passing between neighbouring variables, with minimal external supervision. Belief parameters, communication messages, and updating rules to guarantee some equilibrium can be reached in time proportional to the longest path in the network.

In belief updating the impact of each new piece of evidence is viewed as a perturbation that propagates through the network, at equilibrium, each variable should be bound to a fixed value that together with all other value assignments is the best interpretation of the evidence. This approach is called the distributed computation.

Confidence Factor

A *certainty factor* (CF) is a value ranging from -1 to 1 that indicates the degree of belief in a hypothesis. Positive certainty factors suggest evidence supporting the hypothesis, with larger values indicating stronger belief. When CF equals 1, the hypothesis is confirmed to be true. Conversely, a negative CF indicates that the hypothesis is likely false. Smaller negative values suggest greater belief in the hypothesis's invalidity, with CF $= -1$ meaning the hypothesis is effectively disproven. A CF of 0 indicates no evidence either for or against the hypothesis. In MYCIN, hypotheses pertain to the values of clinical parameters for various nodes within the context tree. Sample hypotheses are:

$h_1 =$ The identity of ORGANISM-1 is streptococcus
$h_2 =$ PATIENT-1 is febrile
$h_3 =$ The name of PATIENT-1 is John Jones
$CF(h_1, E) = X$ represents that the certainty factor for the hypothesis h_1 based on evidence E.

We can therefore have $CF(h_1, E) = 8$, $CF(h_2, E) = -3$, and $CF(h_3, E) = 1$. Certainty factors (CFs) are utilized in two distinct ways. Firstly, each clinical parameter's value is stored along with its associated CF. Here, E represents all the information currently available in MYCIN. For instance, if the program needs to identify ORGANISM-1, it can refer to the fact set and determine that ORGANISM-1 is streptococcus with a CF of 0.8. Secondly, CFs are used within the decision rules themselves, where the evidence E corresponds to the condition stated in the premise of the rule. Thus,

$$A \wedge B \wedge C \rightarrow D$$

is a representation of the statement CF $(D, A \wedge B \wedge C) = X$. Diagnosis essentially involves selecting a disease from a list of competing hypotheses. These hypotheses, along with their associated certainty factors (CFs), are stored for each node in the context tree. The CF model was primarily motivated by practical considerations, and its effectiveness has been demonstrated through its practical success. While conditional probabilities offer a more rigorous mathematical framework for representing certainty weights, they are often impractical due to insufficient data and the presence of extensive and imprecise knowledge. Therefore, the certainty factor model serves as an approximation to conditional probabilities. For example, using Bayes theorem we can capture the uncertainty in knowledge. If E is all the evidence and d is the hypothesis under consideration, then $P(d_1/E)$ is the conditional probability for hypothesis d, to be true in the light of the evidence E. Bayes theorem is useful because it allows $P(d_1/E)$ to be constructed from the component conditional probabilities, i.e.,

$$(Pd_1/E) = \frac{P(d_i) * P(E/d_i)}{\sum_j P(d_j) * P(E/d_j)}.$$

Here d_i is one of the disjoint hypotheses. For example, d_i may be one of the diseases and E may be the set of all symptoms. Since evidence is collected sequentially in most diagnostic systems, we should use Bayes theorem to incrementally increase the conditional probability of the hypothesis. This is possible by modifying the Bayes theorem as follows:

$$(Pd_1/E \cup s_1) = \frac{P(s_1/(d_i \wedge E)) * P(d_i/E)}{\sum_j P(s_1/d_j \wedge (d_j/E))}$$

where E is the set of previous evidence. d_i's are the hypotheses, and s is the new evidence.

Programs that use Bayes theorem in this form require huge amounts of statistical data not only $P(s/d)$ for each piece of data s in E, but also the interrelationship of s within each hypothesis as more evidence is collected. The procedure is sound but not suitable in practice. Also, we will be using only judgemental knowledge so that the strict Bayesian approach can be approximated, i.e.,

$$CF(d_j/E) = P(d_j/E) \text{ when } P(d) \text{ is small.}$$

When we have to sequentially search for the hypothesis, we will need a combinatorial function. This function in MYCIN is

$$CF = \frac{MB - MD}{(1 - \min(MB, MD))}$$

$$CF_{com}(X, Y) = X, Y(1 - X)$$

where $X, Y > 0$

$$= \frac{X + Y}{1 - \min(abs(X), abs(Y))}$$

where X or $Y < 0$

$$= -CF_{com}(-X, -Y)$$

where $X, Y < 0$.

CF_{com} preserves commutativity. This is essential to ensure that the sequence in which evidence is gathered does not affect the ultimate outcome.

Bayes Theorem

Bayes' theorem offers a mathematical framework for updating beliefs in the light of new evidence. Named after Reverend Thomas Bayes, an eighteenth-century statistician and philosopher, this theorem has become integral to modern data science, machine learning, and rational decision-making. Essentially, Bayes' theorem guides us on how to rationally revise our prior beliefs (or probabilities) when presented with new information. It provides a method for calculating the likelihood of an event occurring based on existing knowledge of conditions related to that event. The underlying notion of Bayesian statistics is that of conditional probability: $P(H|E)$, where H is the probability of hypothesis. Given that we have evidence E. To compute this, we need to take into account the prior probability of H (the probability that we would assign to H if we had no evidence) and the extent to which E provides evidence of H. To do this, we need to define a universe that contains an exhaustive, mutually exclusive set of H_i's, among which we are trying to discriminate. Then, let

$P(H_i|E)$ = the probability that hypothesis H_i is true given evidence E.
$P(E|H_i)$ = the probability that we will observe evidence E given that hypothesis H_i is true.
$P(H_i)$ = the probability that hypothesis H_i is true in the absence of any specific evidence. These probabilities are called prior probabilities or *priors*.
k = the number of possible hypotheses.

Bayes' theorem then states that

$$P(H_i|E) = \frac{P(E|H_i) \cdot P(H_i)}{\sum_{n=1}^{k} P(E|H_n) \cdot P(H_n)}.$$

The key to using Bayes theorem as a basis for uncertain reasoning is to recognize exactly what it says. Specifically, when we say $P(A|B)$, we are describing the conditional probability of A given that the only evidence we have is B.

Planning

AI planning is a computational method for tackling problems by devising ordered sets of actions. It draws upon principles from theoretical computer science, artificial intelligence, and decision theory to chart a path from a starting point to a defined objective within intricate computational environments.

Classical planning approaches are characterized by their deterministic and fully observable environment assumptions. These models represent problem domains through formal representations that capture states, actions, and transition mechanisms with precise mathematical clarity. The fundamental components of classical planning include state spaces, action models, goal specifications, and transition functions that govern how actions modify system configurations.

The most prominent representation in classical planning is the STRIPS (Stanford Research Institute Problem Solver) formalism, which defines planning problems through three critical elements: initial state description, goal state conditions, and a set of available actions. Each action is characterized by preconditions that must be satisfied for execution and effects that modify the world state. This declarative approach allows for systematic reasoning about potential action sequences and their consequences.

STRIPS Formalism

In the field of artificial intelligence, the STRIPS (Stanford Research Institute Problem Solver) formalism provides a structured way to represent planning challenges. This approach introduces a precise computational method for conceptualizing complex problem-solving situations.

The initial state serves as the starting point of the planning problem, representing a complete configuration of the world at the beginning of the planning process. This description is typically expressed as a set of logical propositions that completely characterize the current system state. Each proposition represents a specific condition or attribute that is either true or false in the initial configuration.

Goal state conditions define the desired final configuration that the planning system aims to achieve. These conditions specify the exact set of propositions that must be true to consider the planning problem successfully resolved. Unlike the initial state, goal conditions represent the target state the system must reach through a sequence of actions.

Actions in STRIPS are defined through three critical components:

- **Name**: A unique identifier for the action.
- **Preconditions**: Logical conditions that must be satisfied for the action to be executable.
- **Effects**: Modifications to the world state that occur when the action is performed.

The STRIPS formalism enables systematic planning through a declarative approach that allows computational systems to systematically identify applicable actions, predict action consequences, construct potential solution paths, and verify whether goal conditions can be achieved.

By representing planning problems as a set of logical propositions and actions, STRIPS provides a powerful abstraction mechanism that transforms complex decision-making scenarios into manageable computational problems.

Planning Algorithms and Computational Strategies

Addressing planning problems involves several fundamental algorithmic approaches, with search-based planning being prominent. These methods systematically explore potential sequences of actions, incorporating strategies such as Breadth-First Search, Depth-First Search, and heuristic guidance. The algorithms construct solutions by iteratively expanding the set of possible states and assessing potential action paths in relation to the goal criteria. State-space search algorithms serve as the bedrock of classical planning methodologies. Forward search techniques proceed by generating subsequent states through the application of applicable actions, while backward search techniques work by reasoning in reverse from the goal states to the initial setup. Heuristic functions are critical in directing these search processes, providing estimated distance measures that help focus computational efforts on promising exploration paths.

Forward Search Algorithm
Forward search represents a progressive exploration strategy that begins from the initial problem state and systematically advances toward potential goal configurations. This approach constructs solution paths by successively applying available actions to generate new states, expanding the search space incrementally from the starting point. The algorithm maintains a frontier of partially explored states, continuously evaluating and selecting the most promising trajectories based on predefined heuristic criteria.

The computational mechanism of forward search involves generating successor states by applying valid actions to the current state, creating a tree-like exploration structure. Each node in this exploration tree represents a distinct system configuration, with edges representing the actions that transform one state into another. As the search progresses, the algorithm evaluates multiple potential paths, comparing their characteristics against goal conditions and computational efficiency metrics.

Implementations of forward search typically employ strategies like breadth-first or depth-first exploration, with advanced variants incorporating sophisticated heuristic guidance. These approaches systematically manage computational complexity by pruning less promising search branches and prioritizing trajectories that appear more likely to reach goal states efficiently.

The following Python code provides implementations of forward search algorithm. Forward search, also known as forward chaining, starts with known facts and applies rules to derive new facts until reaching a goal or exhausting all possibilities.

Backward Search Algorithm
Backward search inverts the computational approach of forward search, initiating exploration from the desired goal state and systematically tracing potential action sequences that could lead to the initial problem configuration. This reverse-engineering strategy constructs solution paths by working retrospectively, identifying the sequence of actions that would transform the initial state into the target goal state.

The algorithmic process begins with a complete specification of the goal state, progressively identifying and applying inverse actions that could have generated the preceding system configurations. Each computational step involves determining potential predecessor states by understanding how actions might have been reversed to arrive at the current configuration. This approach proves particularly effective in domains with well-defined goal conditions and complex initial state spaces.

Backward search offers distinctive computational advantages in certain problem domains. By starting from the goal and working backward, the algorithm can potentially reduce the exploration space more efficiently than forward search strategies. This approach becomes especially powerful when goal states are more constrained and precisely defined compared to the potentially more complex initial state configurations.

As we described above, backward search, or backward chaining, works in reverse by starting with a goal fact and trying to prove it by finding rules that could derive it, then recursively attempting to prove the conditions of those rules.

While forward and backward search algorithms share fundamental principles of systematic state exploration, they demonstrate distinct computational characteristics. Forward search provides a more intuitive exploration strategy, naturally progressing from known initial conditions toward potentially uncertain goal states. Backward search, conversely, offers a more targeted approach by working retrospectively from precisely defined goal conditions.

The selection between forward and backward search depends on multiple factors, including problem domain complexity, state-space characteristics, and computational resource constraints. Advanced planning systems often integrate hybrid approaches that combine elements of both forward and backward search strategies, leveraging their respective strengths to address complex computational challenges.

Graph-Based Planning

Graph-based planning techniques offer alternative computational frameworks for representing and solving planning problems. These approaches transform planning domains into directed graphs where nodes represent states and edges represent possible transitions. Unlike traditional search algorithms that traverse state spaces sequentially, graph-based techniques construct multi-layered directed graphs that capture the intricate relationships between states, actions, and potential transitions simultaneously. Algorithms like GraphPlan introduce advanced mechanisms for simultaneously exploring multiple potential action sequences, leveraging graph structures to identify potential solution paths more efficiently than traditional search methods.

The core innovation of graph-based planning lies in its unique structural representation. Planning domains are transformed into complex directed graphs with a multilayered architecture where:

- Nodes represent distinct system states or action configurations.
- Edges represent possible transitions between states.
- Multiple layers capture the temporal progression of potential action sequences.

This graphical representation allows for a more comprehensive and parallel exploration of potential solution paths. Instead of linear, sequential exploration, graph-based methods enable simultaneous evaluation of multiple potential action trajectories, significantly expanding computational reasoning capabilities.

The GraphPlan Algorithm

GraphPlan algorithm, developed by Avrim Blum and Merrick Furst, constructs a planning graph—a specialized directed graph with alternating state and action layers that systematically represent all possible action sequences within a specified computational horizon.

Layered Graph Construction

The GraphPlan algorithm builds its planning graph through a meticulous layer-by-layer construction process:

1. **Initial State Layer**: The first layer represents the initial problem configuration, capturing all initial propositions and system conditions.
2. **Action Layer**: Subsequent layers represent possible actions that can be executed given the preceding state layer. Each action node includes all actions whose preconditions are satisfied by the previous state layer.
3. **Mutually Exclusive Relationships**: The algorithm simultaneously tracks and represents mutually exclusive relationships between actions and propositions, creating a sophisticated computational framework that captures complex inter-dependencies.

GraphPlan's approach differs fundamentally from traditional search methods through several key computational strategies:

- **Parallel Exploration**: Unlike sequential search algorithms, GraphPlan explores multiple potential action sequences simultaneously.
- **Comprehensive State Representation**: Each graph layer provides a complete snapshot of potential system configurations.
- **Efficient Pruning**: The algorithm can rapidly identify and eliminate impossible or redundant action sequences through its multilayered representation.

Planning problems inherently possess considerable computational complexity, with many scenarios classified as Pspace-hard, highlighting the significant computational difficulties in achieving optimal solutions. The exponential growth of state spaces fundamentally restricts the effectiveness of comprehensive search strategies, necessitating advanced algorithmic approaches that can effectively narrow the search and identify promising solution paths. To address these computational demands, researchers have developed various techniques, including abstraction methods that reduce problem complexity by discarding irrelevant information and hierarchical planning approaches that decompose intricate problems into simpler subproblems. These strategies enhance the efficiency of computational systems in navigating complex planning environments, tackling the scalability issues inherent in sophisticated decision-making contexts.

Current trends in AI planning research show a growing integration of machine learning techniques with traditional algorithmic methods. Approaches like reinforcement learning, probabilistic planning models, and neural network-based planning representations are expanding the capabilities of classical planning frameworks. These combined methods result in more adaptable and flexible planning systems that can learn from environmental interactions and dynamically adapt their strategies. Probabilistic planning models, such as Markov Decision Processes, introduce more refined representations that account for uncertainty and the random nature of some environments. These approaches extend beyond classical deterministic frameworks by incorporating probability distributions over potential results, providing more robust computational strategies for tackling complex real-world planning scenarios.

Constraint Satisfaction Problem

The core of constraint satisfaction problems (CSPs) lies in their simple structural composition, which encompasses variables, domains, and constraints.

CSP is represented as a triple $\{X, D, C\}$ where

$X = \{x_1, x_2, x_3, \ldots\}$ where X is a set of variables

$D = \{D_1, D_2, D_3, \ldots\}$ where each D_i is the set of possible values of x_i variable

$C = \{C_1, C_2, C_3, \ldots\}$ where C_i is the constraint that restricts the values that can be assigned to subset of variables.

Variables represent the fundamental decision points within a system, each carrying potential values drawn from specific domains. Constraints articulate the rules and conditions that govern valid relationships between these variables, creating a sophisticated computational tapestry that defines acceptable solution configurations.

In AI planning, constraint satisfaction problems provide an abstraction mechanism that transcends traditional search methodologies. Planning systems can reframe complex decision-making scenarios as constraint satisfaction challenges, systematically exploring potential solutions by progressively assigning values to variables and rigorously validating their compliance with predefined constraints.

Computational strategies in constraint satisfaction leverage advanced algorithmic techniques that enable intelligent exploration of solution spaces. These approaches employ sophisticated search methods, including backtracking algorithms and constraint propagation techniques, which allow for dynamic pruning of impossible solution paths. By intelligently navigating through potential configurations, these methods dramatically reduce computational complexity compared to exhaustive search approaches.

Constraint Propagation

Constraint propagation is a technique used in artificial intelligence to refine the possible values for variables in a constraint satisfaction problem. It works by sharing the implications of reducing the potential options for one variable with all the other restrictions that involve that variable. This iterative process of applying the given constraints helps to narrow down the range of possible values for each variable. Constraint propagation is often employed together with backtracking search to make the problem-solving process more efficient.

The concept can be understood through these steps:

1. Begin with a constraint satisfaction problem that includes variables, the initial set of possible values (domains) for each variable, and the rules (constraints) that must be satisfied.
2. Apply the specified constraints to decrease the number of possible values in the domains of the variables.
3. Following this propagation of constraints, some variables might have their domains significantly reduced, making it easier to find valid assignments of values to the variables.
4. If, during this process, the domain of a variable becomes empty, it indicates a conflict with the current assignments, and a backtracking step is necessary to revise earlier choices.

For instance, consider a simple problem with two variables, X and Y, where both initially can take the values $\{1, 2, 3\}$, and there's a constraint that X must not be equal to Y $(X \neq Y)$. Constraint propagation would work like this: if we decide to assign the value 1 to X, then the constraint $X \neq Y$ tells us that Y cannot be 1. As a result, the domain of Y is reduced to $\{2, 3\}$.

The practical applications of constraint satisfaction problems span diverse domains, including resource allocation, scheduling optimization, system configuration, and multi-agent coordination. Planning systems transform traditional problem representations into constraint satisfaction frameworks, enabling more nuanced and comprehensive reasoning about complex interdependencies and potential solution trajectories. Moreover, advanced reasoning mechanisms distinguish constraint satisfaction approaches from conventional search methods. Techniques such as predictive constraint propagation and dynamic constraint relaxation enable planning systems to reason more holistically about problem spaces. These approaches understand the intricate relationships between variables and constraints, allowing for more sophisticated and adaptive decision-making strategies.

Despite their capabilities, constraint satisfaction problems face significant computational issues. The exponential complexity inherent in large problem spaces, the computational overhead of constraint validation, and the difficulties in handling highly dynamic environments present ongoing research challenges. Contemporary researchers continue to develop innovative algorithms that incorporate machine learning techniques and advanced heuristic approaches to mitigate these limitations.

AI planning increasingly integrates these techniques with probabilistic modelling, machine learning, and advanced search algorithms.

Applications of AI

Computer Vision

Computer vision is a branch of artificial intelligence focused on enabling machines to interpret and analyse visual data from the surrounding environment. Its development began in the mid-twentieth century with basic pattern recognition experiments and progressed significantly in the 1970s through text recognition algorithms. By the 1980s, commercial systems emerged, primarily serving industrial inspection tasks.

Modern computer vision systems typically operate through a multi-stage pipeline. They begin with image acquisition via cameras or video feeds, followed by preprocessing techniques that enhance image quality—such as adjusting contrast, reducing noise, and converting colour images to grayscale. Next, feature extraction identifies key visual elements like edges, textures, and shapes. These features support higher-level tasks such as object detection, which locates and classifies items within an image, and image segmentation, which partitions the image into meaningful regions.

Recent advances in the field have been driven by machine learning, which enables systems to learn visual patterns from large datasets. This capability allows for the recognition of complex features, such as distinguishing facial components. A major breakthrough occurred in the early 2010s with the rise of deep learning, particularly convolutional neural networks (CNNs). The success of AlexNet in the 2012 ImageNet competition marked a turning point, showcasing the power of deep architectures and innovations like ReLU activation functions and GPU-accelerated training.

CNNs have since become the standard for image classification and object recognition. They process images by converting colour channels into numerical matrices, which are then transformed into three-dimensional tensors. These tensors pass through layers that extract and condense features, culminating in fully connected layers that produce final predictions.

Beyond passive analysis, computer vision systems now actively respond to visual input, revolutionizing sectors such as healthcare, automotive, security, and entertainment. The field encompasses specialized techniques including segmentation, object and facial recognition, edge and pattern detection, image classification, and feature matching. While simple applications may rely on individual techniques, complex systems—such as autonomous vehicles—integrate multiple methods for robust performance.

The integration of natural language processing further enhances computer vision by enabling interpretation of textual elements within images. Unlike traditional rule-based systems that require extensive manual coding, modern AI approaches leverage deep learning and edge computing to automate complex tasks efficiently. Edge learning, in particular, facilitates on-device processing with minimal setup and data requirements, making advanced computer vision more accessible and scalable.

Natural Language Processing

Natural language processing (NLP) is a field of artificial intelligence that enables computers to interpret, generate, and interact using human language, whether in written text or spoken form. It underpins technologies such as virtual assistants—including Siri, Alexa, Cortana, and Oracle Digital Assistant—allowing them to understand user input and respond in a conversational manner. At its core, NLP consists of two primary components: natural language understanding (NLU), which focuses on interpreting input, and natural language generation (NLG), which produces coherent and contextually appropriate output.

The syntactic structure of natural languages like English is defined by grammar rules that break down sentences into smaller units. For instance, a rule might state that S → NP VP, with S standing for sentence, NP for noun phrase, and VP for verb phrase.

NLP systems use two main strategies to analyse language: template-based approaches that rely on keyword detection and predefined responses, and grammar-based parsing methods that apply syntactic rules to interpret sentence structure.

One of the central challenges in NLP lies in translating the nuanced, context-rich, and often ambiguous nature of human language into a format that machines can process. Human communication involves multiple layers of meaning, including syntax, semantics, context, and cultural references, all of which require advanced computational models for accurate interpretation.

In practice, the term NLU is often used to describe the broader goal of enabling machines to comprehend and respond to natural language. This capability allows users to interact with systems in a more intuitive and accessible way. NLP models are typically trained using machine learning techniques, where algorithms learn from large volumes of text data. Through this training, models refine their ability to recognize patterns, understand context, and generate appropriate responses, improving their performance over time.

Within natural language understanding, the primary focus is on dissecting text data and grasping its intended meaning. This process involves analysing text data at three linguistic levels:

- **Syntax**: This refers to the arrangement of words within a sentence, following grammatical rules such as the typical subject-verb-object order.
- **Semantics**: This involves determining the actual meaning conveyed by the text.
- **Pragmatics**: This focuses on understanding the meaning of a sentence within its specific context and what the speaker or writer intends to achieve with it.

Text preprocessing is a first step in natural language processing (NLP), involving the cleaning and structuring of raw language data to prepare it for computational analysis. This process typically includes segmenting sentences, removing extraneous elements such as punctuation and emotive expressions, and standardizing linguistic input. Given the structural diversity among languages—such as the character-based systems of Mandarin and Japanese versus the word-based structure of English—multilingual NLP models must perform careful segmentation and tokenization to accurately identify meaningful units within text.

At the word level, morphological and lexical analysis examines the internal structure and meaning of words. Drawing from linguistics, this involves identifying morphemes (the smallest units of meaning) and understanding how they combine to form words and convey semantic content.

Syntactic analysis, or parsing, is a more advanced stage that seeks to uncover the grammatical organization of language. It translates natural language into structured representations that reflect the relationships between words according to the rules of grammar. Parsing algorithms are central to this process, systematically decomposing sentences into their grammatical components to reveal underlying syntactic patterns.

Two principal approaches to parsing are widely used. Constituency parsing constructs hierarchical tree structures that group words into nested grammatical units, illustrating how phrases combine to form complete sentences. In contrast, dependency parsing focuses on the direct grammatical links between individual words, identifying relationships such as subject, verb, and object. For example, in the sentence "The curious researcher studied linguistic patterns," dependency parsing would highlight "studied" as the main verb, with "researcher" as the subject and "patterns" as the object, while modifiers like "curious" and "linguistic" refine the meaning.

Together, these parsing methods offer complementary insights into sentence structure—constituency parsing emphasizes hierarchical composition, while dependency parsing reveals functional relationships, both essential for enabling machines to understand and process human language effectively.

Semantic analysis in natural language processing (NLP) extends beyond syntactic structure to uncover the underlying meaning and conceptual relationships within language. While humans intuitively grasp meaning, computational systems require structured methods to interpret linguistic input. This involves transforming raw text into formal representations that capture context, ambiguity, and semantic associations.

One foundational approach is the use of distributional semantic models, which infer word meaning based on statistical patterns of co-occurrence in large text corpora. These models generate vector representations in a multidimensional space, where semantically related words—such as "scientist," "researcher," and "scholar"—are positioned closely together. Another method, semantic networks, organizes knowledge as interconnected nodes and relationships, enabling systems to model hierarchies and associations between concepts. For example, a network might link "researcher" to "professional" and associate "scientific method" with "research."

Probabilistic language models further enhance semantic understanding by estimating the likelihood of word sequences, allowing systems to manage ambiguity and context. Transformer-based models like BERT and GPT exemplify this approach, producing context-sensitive representations through attention mechanisms that capture nuanced linguistic patterns.

A classic example of semantic ambiguity is the sentence "The bank was located near the river," where the word "bank" could refer to a financial institution or a riverbank. Semantic models resolve such ambiguities by analysing surrounding context and evaluating the most probable interpretation based on learned patterns.

Complementing semantic analysis is pragmatic analysis, which considers the speaker's intent, context, and non-verbal cues to interpret meaning. This includes subtle elements such as punctuation, spacing, and even inferred emotional states. Pragmatic analysis aims to replicate the human ability to infer meaning beyond literal word content, enabling machines to engage in more natural and context-aware communication.

Recent advances in NLP have been driven by deep learning, particularly through the use of neural architectures like transformers. These models represent language as dense vectors and learn complex dependencies across text, enabling them to generate coherent and contextually appropriate responses. Techniques such as representation learning, including word embeddings like Word2Vec and GloVe, map words into vector spaces where semantic relationships are reflected in spatial proximity; for instance, placing "king" and "queen" near each other due to their conceptual similarity.

Together, semantic and pragmatic analysis form the backbone of modern NLP, enabling machines to move beyond surface-level text processing toward a deeper, more human-like understanding of language.

N-grams Analysis

N-gram analysis is a foundational method in natural language processing (NLP) that examines sequences of *n* consecutive elements within text or speech. These elements may include words, characters, syllables, or phonemes, depending on the linguistic level and application. By segmenting language into overlapping units of *n* items, N-gram models reveal patterns in contextual usage, syntactic structure, and probabilistic relationships. The value of *n* determines the granularity of the analysis, with larger *n*-grams capturing more complex dependencies across linguistic sequences. Briefly,

- **N-gram**: A contiguous sequence of *n* items from a given sample of text or speech.
- **Analysis**: The process of identifying, counting, and studying the occurrences of these *N*-grams within a dataset.

Examples of *N*-grams (using words as items):

- **Unigram ($n = 1$)**: A single word. Examples: "the," "cat," "sat," "on," "mat."
- **Bigram ($n = 2$)**: A sequence of two consecutive words. Examples: "the cat," "cat sat," "sat on," "on the," "the mat."
- **Trigram ($n = 3$)**: A sequence of three consecutive words. Examples: "the cat sat," "cat sat on," "sat on the," "on the mat."
- **Higher-order *N*-grams ($n > 3$)**: Sequences of four or more consecutive words.

The core of *N*-gram analysis is to:

1. **Generate *N*-grams**: Extract all possible sequences of *n* items from a given text or corpus.

2. **Count Frequencies**: Determine how often each unique N-gram appears in the text.
3. **Analyse Patterns**: Examine the frequencies to identify common or significant sequences. This can reveal information about the structure, style, and content of the text.

NLP Preprocessing Techniques

Preprocessing is a critical phase in natural language processing (NLP), aimed at converting raw, unstructured text into a standardized format suitable for computational analysis. These techniques not only streamline the data but also significantly enhance the performance of downstream tasks such as classification, sentiment analysis, and named entity recognition.

The process typically begins with tokenization, which segments text into smaller units—such as words, subwords, or characters—depending on the application. For instance, the sentence "natural language processing is fascinating" would be split into individual tokens, each representing a meaningful element for further analysis.

A foundational method for representing text is the bag-of-words (BoW) model, which treats a document as an unordered collection of tokens and records their frequency. Although BoW ignores word order—treating "cat sat on mat" the same as "mat sat on cat"—it remains effective for tasks like document classification and information retrieval due to its simplicity and scalability.

Stop word removal is another common step, where frequently occurring but semantically light words such as "the," "is," and "and" are excluded to reduce data dimensionality and focus on more informative terms. While this is beneficial in traditional models like BoW or TF-IDF, modern deep learning approaches often retain stop words, as their contextual importance can be learned during training.

Normalization techniques such as stemming and lemmatization further refine the text. Stemming reduces words to their base forms by trimming affixes, though the result may not always be a valid word. Lemmatization, on the other hand, uses linguistic rules to return the dictionary form of a word, preserving grammatical integrity. While stemming is faster, lemmatization offers greater accuracy and semantic clarity.

Part-of-speech (POS) tagging assigns grammatical roles—such as noun, verb, or adjective—to each token, aiding in syntactic analysis and disambiguation. For example, the word "book" can function as both a noun and a verb, and POS tagging helps determine its role based on context. This technique is often used alongside syntactic parsing to identify grammatical relationships within sentences.

Text cleaning is also essential, involving the removal of punctuation, special characters, HTML tags, URLs, and excess whitespace, as well as converting text to lowercase. This step ensures consistency and reduces noise that could hinder model performance.

Together, these preprocessing techniques form the backbone of NLP workflows. They prepare text for feature extraction and model training, with the choice of methods depending on the specific task, data characteristics, and modelling approach.

As NLP continues to evolve, preprocessing strategies are also adapting to balance computational efficiency with the need to preserve the richness of natural language.

Expert Systems

At the prestigious International Joint Conference on Artificial Intelligence in 1977, Professor Edward Feigenbaum, a pioneer in the field, presented a seminal invited paper that encapsulated a fundamental principle of expert systems. His key insight was: "The power of an expert system is derived from the knowledge it possesses, not from the particular formalisms and inference schemes it employs." This statement marked a significant shift in AI thinking.

The Early AI Dream of General Problem Solvers and Its Limitations

In the early stages of artificial intelligence research, there was a strong belief that a small set of universal reasoning principles, combined with increasing computational power, could yield systems capable of solving any problem across any domain. The General Problem Solver (GPS) embodied this vision, aiming to function as a domain-independent problem-solving engine. However, as the field progressed, it became clear that such generalized systems lacked the sophistication needed to handle the complexity of real-world tasks. This realization marked a pivotal shift in AI research—from the pursuit of general intelligence to the development of specialized systems tailored to narrow domains.

By the mid-1970s, expert systems began to demonstrate practical success in specific fields. Recognizing the central role of domain knowledge in these systems, some researchers turned their attention to building comprehensive theories of knowledge representation. Their goal was to create general-purpose frameworks capable of encoding and manipulating knowledge across diverse domains. Despite these efforts, the vastness, variability, and context-dependence of human knowledge proved too complex to be captured by rigid, universal structures. While the ambition of a unified theory of knowledge representation remained unfulfilled, specialized approaches proved highly effective within the constrained environments of expert systems, reinforcing the value of domain-specific solutions in AI.

Expert Systems: Knowledge-Based Problem-Solving in Specific Domains

Expert systems, also known as knowledge-based systems (KBSs), emerged as a prominent approach in artificial intelligence, designed to apply structured, domain-specific knowledge to solve problems that typically require expert-level reasoning. These systems are developed through close collaboration between domain experts and system designers, resulting in tools capable of performing complex tasks—such as medical diagnosis, computer system configuration, and mineral exploration—with accuracy comparable to that of human specialists.

A defining feature of KBS is their symbolic representation of knowledge. Rather than relying solely on numerical data, these systems use symbols to model a wide range of entities, including physical objects, living organisms, and abstract concepts. The manipulation of these symbolic representations forms the core of KBS programming, necessitating specialized languages and environments tailored to handle symbolic reasoning—distinct from those optimized for numerical computation.

Procedural Versus Declarative Programming Styles in AI

An underlying distinction between conventional algorithmic programming and the AI-driven programming embodied in knowledge-based systems lies in their programming style. Conventional programming, often termed procedural programming, emphasizes instructing the computer on *how* to perform tasks, detailing the sequence of operations to be executed on input data. In procedural programming, the procedures themselves serve as the primary representation of the solution methodology. In contrast, knowledge-based programming adopts a declarative approach. It focuses on representing declarative knowledge about a specific domain—capturing *what* is known, in the form of facts, rules, and relationships—without predetermining the precise algorithms or procedures that will utilize this knowledge. The system itself is responsible for inferring *how* to use this knowledge to solve problems.

While numerous definitions of expert systems exist, Professor Edward Feigenbaum's definition from Stanford University remains highly influential and succinct:

> *...an intelligent computer program that uses knowledge and inference procedures to solve problems those are difficult enough to require significant human expertise for their solution. Knowledge necessary to perform at such a level, plus the inference procedures used, can be thought of as a model of the expertise of the best practitioners of the field.*

This definition emphasizes both the *knowledge* component and the *reasoning* (inference) component as essential for expert system functionality.

Expert systems are characterized by several key attributes:

- **Expertise**: They are designed to exhibit performance at a level comparable to human experts, demonstrating a high degree of skill and robustness within their domain.
- **Symbolic Reasoning**: They primarily operate using symbolic representations of knowledge and employ symbolic reasoning techniques rather than purely numerical or statistical methods.
- **Complex Rule Handling**: They are capable of utilizing and processing complex rules and knowledge structures to tackle intricate problem domains.
- **Self-Knowledge (Explainability)**: Ideally, they possess the ability to introspectively examine their own reasoning processes and provide explanations for their conclusions and operations, enhancing transparency and user trust.

The effectiveness and usefulness of an expert system are inextricably linked to the quality and richness of the knowledge it is provided with by its designers. Therefore, rigorous validation and iterative refinement of the knowledge base are critical steps in expert system development. In a general, abstract sense, knowledge can be viewed as encompassing:

- **Descriptions**: Statements that identify and characterize objects and classes of entities within a domain. These descriptions are expressed in a language, which could be a formal system like classical logic (e.g., propositional calculus, predicate calculus) offering precise syntax and semantics, or modified, less formal logics (e.g., default logic, modal logic, non-monotonic logic, probabilistic logic, fuzzy logic) derived from classical logic to handle uncertainty, incompleteness, and defeasible reasoning. Each type of logic offers different trade-offs in expressiveness and computational properties.
- **Relationships**: Connections and dependencies between descriptions within the knowledge base, expressing associations and interactions between entities. These relationships can be taxonomic (hierarchical), definitional (logical implications), or empirical (observed correlations).
- **Procedures**: Specifications of operations or algorithms to be performed on the entities and relationships in the knowledge base when attempting to solve a problem.

In practical applications, knowledge is rarely found in a pre-packaged, neatly categorized form. It often exists as a raw, unrefined substance. For example, in domains like medical diagnostics or geology, knowledge may primarily take the form of empirical associations—correlations between observations and potential diagnoses or geological formations. Knowledge can also manifest as heuristics (rules of thumb), constraints (limitations), and regulations (prescriptive rules). The art of systematically extracting, structuring, and representing this diverse and often messy knowledge is known as knowledge engineering.

The architecture of an expert system, or knowledge-based system (KBS), is built around three core components: the knowledge base, the inference engine, and the user interface. These elements work in concert to enable the system to emulate expert-level reasoning and provide intelligent solutions.

At the heart of the system lies the knowledge base, a structured repository containing domain-specific information in the form of facts, rules, and relationships. Its depth and accuracy directly influence the system's ability to address complex problems effectively, as it encapsulates the expertise required for decision-making within a particular field.

The inference engine serves as the system's reasoning mechanism. It applies logical rules to the knowledge base and incoming data to draw conclusions, generate new information, and solve problems. This component is essential for enabling the system to perform intelligent tasks, such as answering queries or offering expert recommendations.

The user interface connects the system to its users, allowing for intuitive interaction without requiring technical knowledge of the system's internal processes. It enables users to input data, pose questions, and receive responses in a clear and accessible format, thereby enhancing the system's usability and practical value.

Together, these components form a cohesive framework that combines expert knowledge with computational reasoning. This architecture not only supports informed decision-making but also broadens access to specialized expertise across a wide range of domains.

ELIZA Reanimated: Rediscovering an Early Conversational AI

The ELIZA Reanimated project was initiated to recover and study one of the earliest conversational AI programs: ELIZA, developed by Joseph Weizenbaum in the 1960s. The restoration began with the retrieval of Weizenbaum's original source code from his archives at MIT, including the well-known DOCTOR script, an early version of the MAD-SLIP programming language, and supporting routines written in now-obsolete languages such as MAD and FAP.

Reconstructing ELIZA's original 420 lines of code posed several technical challenges. These included manually transcribing files encoded in 6-bit BCD, reimplementing missing functions, and correcting errors present in the original code. To authentically replicate the user experience, the restored program was run on an IBM 7094 emulator, faithfully simulating the original hardware environment. Interestingly, the restoration revealed that some features described in Weizenbaum's 1966 paper were absent from the original implementation, highlighting a gap between the system's documented and actual capabilities.

One unexpected discovery was a hidden "teacher mode," which allowed users to modify and save ELIZA's scripts—effectively enabling the system to be extended beyond its initial design. Although briefly mentioned in Weizenbaum's writings, this feature was never formally documented and remained largely unknown.

Despite the limitations of the original MAD-SLIP version, ELIZA's influence spread widely through later adaptations. A Lisp version by Bernie Cosell circulated on ARPANet, and a 1977 BASIC version brought ELIZA to early personal computers. These variants, often enhanced or re-scripted, became more widely known than the original, which faded into obscurity until its recent revival.

In contrast to today's advanced chatbots like ChatGPT, which rely on deep learning and vast datasets to generate contextually rich and coherent responses, ELIZA operated on simple pattern-matching rules. Yet, its historical significance is profound. ELIZA demonstrated the potential for human-computer dialogue and played a foundational role in shaping the development of modern conversational AI systems.

Exercises

1. What is the difference between propositional logic and first-order logic? When is each more appropriate?
2. Explain the concepts of syntax and semantics in logic. Why are they important?
3. What is a logical inference? Give examples of valid and invalid inferences.
4. Explain the concepts of soundness and completeness in logical systems. Why are they desirable properties?
5. What are some limitations of using logic for representing real-world knowledge?

6. What is the Resolution principle? Why is it a powerful inference rule?
7. How can you translate natural language sentences into propositional logic or first-order logic? Give examples.
8. Explain different normal forms in logic (e.g., Conjunctive Normal Form, Disjunctive Normal Form). Why are they useful for automated reasoning?
9. What are different types of logical connectives (AND, OR, NOT, IMPLIES, BICONDITIONAL)? Explain their truth tables and meanings.
10. What is unification in first-order logic, and why is it crucial for resolution?
11. Compare and contrast logic-based AI with other approaches (e.g., connectionist, statistical AI).
12. In what areas of AI is logic still relevant today? Explore!
13. What are some challenges in scaling up logic-based systems to handle complex real-world problems?
14. Implement a basic theorem prover for propositional logic using the Resolution algorithm in a language like Python, Java, or Lisp. Focus on handling CNF conversion and resolution steps. Start with propositional logic for simplicity.
15. Create a small expert system for a very narrow domain (e.g., diagnosing simple animal diseases, recommending movies based on genre preferences) using rule-based logic. Represent knowledge as rules and facts, and implement a forward or backward chaining inference engine.
16. How are knowledge representation and ontologies related?
17. Choose a logic puzzle (e.g., logic grid puzzle, Sudoku, KenKen) and develop a program that solves it using logic and resolution.
18. How can search algorithms be applied to solve problems like puzzles, games, pathfinding, planning?
19. What are challenges in applying search to large or complex state spaces?
20. Briefly discuss local search algorithms (e.g., hill climbing, simulated annealing) as alternatives for very large search spaces.
21. (Project) Implement a simple game-playing AI for a game like Tic-Tac-Toe or Connect Four using minimax search or a similar game search technique. (Minimax might be a bit more advanced, but even simple depth-limited search can be interesting.) Allow a human player to play against your AI.
22. (Project) Create a list of common English stop words (e.g., "the," "a," "is," "in"). Write a function that takes a list of tokens and removes any tokens that are in your stop word list.
23. Create a list of keywords for a few different topics (e.g., sports, technology, politics). Write a function that takes a document as input and identifies the topic based on the presence of these keywords.

Further Reading

Akerkar R (2014) Introduction to artificial intelligence, 2nd edn. PHI Learning

Brachman RJ, Levesque HJ (2004) Knowledge representation. Elsevier, New York

Castillo E, Gutierrez JM, Hadi AS (1996) Expert systems and probabilistic network models. Springer, Berlin

Cowell RG, Lauritzen SL, Spiegelhalter DJ (2005) Probabilistic networks and expert systems. Springer, Berlin

Darwiche A (2014) Modeling and reasoning with Bayesian networks. Cambridge University Press, New York, NY

Davis E (1990) Representations of commonsense knowledge. Morgan Kaufmann, Palo Alto, CA

Ginsberg M (1993) Essentials of artificial intelligence. Morgan Kaufmann, Palo Alto, CA

Gomez-Perez A, Corcho O, Fernandez-Lopez M (2004) Ontological engineering. Springer, Berlin

Hawkins J, Blakeslee S (2004) On intelligence. Times Books

Hitzler P, Krotzsch M, Rudolph S (2010) Foundations of semantic web technologies. Chapman and Hall

Luger GF (2008) Artificial intelligence—structures and strategies for complex problem solving, 6th edn. Addison Wesley, New York, NY

Nilsson NJ (1981) Principles of artificial intelligence. Tioga, Palo Alto, CA

Nilsson NJ (1998) Artificial intelligence—a modern synthesis. Morgan Kaufmann, Palo Alto

Poole D, Mackworth A (2017) Artificial intelligence—foundations of computational agents, 2nd edn. Cambridge University Press, New York

Rich E, Knight K, Nair S (2010) Artificial intelligence, 3rd edn. McGraw-Hill, New York

Tanimoto S (1995) The elements of artificial intelligence using common lisp, 2nd edn. Computer Science Press, New York, NY

Weizenbaum J (1966) ELIZA—a computer program for the study of natural language communication between man and machine. Commun ACM 9(1):36–45. https://doi.org/10.1145/365153.365168

Winston PH (1992) Artificial intelligence, 3rd edn. Addison Wesley, New York, NY

Part II
The Learning Revolution: Data-Driven Intelligence

Chapter 3
Soft Computing Paradigms: Bridging Precision and Flexibility

It is not the strongest species that survive, nor the most intelligent, but the ones most responsive to change.
—Charles Darwin
In almost every case, the new phenomenon that is described by a new theory is a phenomenon that is not precisely defined.
—Lotfi A. Zadeh

Soft Computing

Soft computing is an advanced computational approach rooted in artificial intelligence (AI) that addresses real-world, scenario-based NP-hard problems. The problems that are inherently complex and cannot be efficiently solved using traditional algorithmic methods. Lotfi A. Zadeh at the University of California, Berkeley in the USA, is credited with initially introducing the concept of soft computing. The term "soft computing" emerged due to its conceptual inspiration from life sciences, reflecting its reliance on computational metaphors akin to biological processes. Unlike conventional computing, which seeks exact solutions through rigid algorithms, soft computing excels in providing approximate yet effective solutions to problems that are difficult to formalize mathematically but are solvable by human intuition and reasoning.

> **Definition Soft computing** refers to a collection of computational techniques that deal with imprecision, uncertainty, and approximation to achieve tractability, robustness, and low-cost solutions.

© The Author(s), under exclusive license to Springer Nature Switzerland AG 2026
R. Akerkar, *Artificial Intelligence*, https://doi.org/10.1007/978-3-031-91084-5_3

Unlike traditional hard computing, which relies on precise and deterministic algorithms, soft computing encompasses methods like fuzzy logic, neural networks, genetic algorithms, and probabilistic reasoning. These approaches are particularly useful in complex, real-world scenarios where exact solutions are difficult to obtain.

This paradigm is particularly valuable in domains requiring the processing of ambiguous or imprecise information. For instance, linguistic tasks such as summarization and disambiguation, visual tasks like face recognition or tumour detection in medical imaging, and reasoning tasks such as analogical inference and theorem proving benefit significantly from soft computing techniques. Its adaptability allows it to tackle challenges in data-rich environments where classical models struggle, making it a cornerstone for advancements in fields like robotics, image processing, and database filtering.

Soft computing encompasses several methodologies, with neural networks, fuzzy logic, and genetic algorithms being its primary branches. Neural networks mimic the human brain's interconnected neuron structure to learn patterns and make predictions from data. Fuzzy logic handles uncertainty by enabling reasoning with degrees of truth rather than binary true/false values. Genetic algorithms draw inspiration from natural selection processes to optimize solutions iteratively. These techniques collectively empower soft computing to address diverse applications ranging from smart home appliances to complex industrial systems.

The importance of neural networks within soft computing is profound. They excel in tasks such as pattern recognition, predictive modelling, and natural language processing by leveraging their ability to learn from vast datasets. Neural networks have revolutionized fields like healthcare by aiding disease detection and treatment planning. Similarly, fuzzy logic has enhanced decision-making systems in automotive manufacturing and consumer electronics by enabling adaptive responses to dynamic conditions.

Predominantly, soft computing represents a major shift in computational paradigms. By emulating the human mind's ability to navigate uncertainty and approximate solutions, it has paved the way for innovative applications across industries. Its capacity to handle complex problems with flexibility and precision underscores its pivotal role in shaping the future of intelligent systems.

NP-Hard Problems

Soft computing techniques are often employed to tackle NP-hard problems. These methods are useful because they can provide approximate solutions within a reasonable time frame, even when exact solutions are computationally infeasible. By leveraging the flexibility and adaptability of soft computing, researchers can address complex, real-world problems that traditional hard computing methods struggle to solve efficiently.

The concept of NP-hardness developed alongside AI algorithms, as many AI challenges naturally involve optimization. The Boolean satisfiability problem was crucial in shaping NP-hardness theory. NP-hard problems focus on finding optimal solutions within constraints, with solution spaces growing exponentially with problem size. It's commonly believed, though not mathematically proven, that these problems can't be solved in polynomial time.

> **Definition** An **NP-hard problem** is a class of problems in computational complexity theory that are at least as hard as the hardest problems in NP (nondeterministic polynomial time). If an NP-hard problem can be solved in polynomial time, then every problem in NP can also be solved in polynomial time. However, NP-hard problems do not necessarily have to be in NP themselves.

NP-complete problems are *yes-or-no* questions related to NP-hard problems, asking if a valid solution meeting specific criteria exists. The Boolean satisfiability problem is a classic NP-complete example, as are many constraint satisfaction problems. A generalized n-queens puzzle variant is also NP-complete, with its NP-hard counterpart seeking the maximum number of additional queens that can be placed legally.

NP-hard problems typically involve optimization, while NP-complete problems focus on decision-making, often with outcome value constraints. Many of these computationally challenging problems have real-world applications, with the traveling salesperson problem being a prime example of an NP-complete problem with broad relevance.

The traveling salesperson problem involves finding the lowest-cost route through a set of cities, visiting each once and returning to the start. This optimization problem is NP-hard, while its decision version (asking if a route exists below a certain cost) is NP-complete. Although the decision version might seem simpler, it's not necessarily easier to solve. However, it's considered "easier" in the sense that potential solutions can be quickly verified, which isn't directly possible for the optimization version.

The concept of NP-hardness has significant implications for real-world applications across various industries and domains. Understanding NP-hardness helps professionals set realistic expectations for problem-solving and guides the selection of appropriate algorithms for complex optimization challenges.

Neural Networks

Neural network research began in 1942, but the number of scientists involved was minimal for the first 40 years. In 1942, Norbert Wiener and his colleagues were developing ideas that would later be known as "cybernetics," which Wiener defined as "control and communication in the animal and the machine." The fundamental concept was to approach biological mechanisms from an engineering and mathematical perspective. That same year, McCulloch and Pitts published the first formal treatment of artificial neural networks. A key characteristic of neural networks is their ability to learn from experience in a training environment. In 1949, Donald Hebb proposed a mechanism for this learning process in real animal brains, suggesting that synaptic strengths change to reinforce simultaneous activity levels between pre-synaptic and post-synaptic neurons. In the context of artificial neural networks, this means that the weight on an input should be adjusted to reflect the correlation between the input and the unit's output. Learning schemes based on this "Hebb rule" have always been significant. Another milestone was the invention of the Perceptron by Rosenblatt in 1957.

In 1983, the American Defense Advanced Research Projects Agency (DARPA) began funding neural network research. Subsequently, many other countries initiated similar efforts, leading to extensive global research. Initially, this field produced many theoretical research papers but few practical applications. This situation changed in the 1990s.

Artificial neural networks (ANNs) are connectionist models for programming computers, aiming to give them human-like abilities by mimicking the brain's functionality. The human brain consists of a network of over a hundred billion interconnected neurons. Neurons are individual cells that process small amounts of information and activate other neurons to continue the process. If successfully implemented, ANNs can enhance the effectiveness of machines like personal computers in various problem-solving and decision-making areas. While typical AI methodologies deal with symbolic knowledge representation, ANN models document knowledge in the network's connections, hence the term "network." ANNs excel at pattern recognition and other tasks that are challenging to program using conventional techniques. Their main advantage is the ability to learn independently and adapt to changing conditions.

Although neural networks are modelled after the human brain, they are far from achieving actual intelligence. Our understanding of the brain, the model for neural networks, which generates intelligence, is still limited. There are significant differences between the brain's physical characteristics and neural networks. The brain has approximately 100 billion neurons, while a high-performance system may have at most 100,000 artificial neurons when allocating a processor to each neuron. Typical neural networks have far fewer neurons, usually around 10 or 100.

Directed Computational Graphs

Directed computational graphs provide a visual and conceptual framework for understanding the flow of information in mathematical computations. In these graphs, nodes represent mathematical operations, and directed edges indicate the sequence in which these operations are performed. This abstraction is particularly useful in machine learning, where complex models are built by combining simpler functions.

Definition In a directed acyclic computational graph, nodes are linked to variables. Directed edges connect these nodes, illustrating the functional relationships between them. These edges may also be associated with parameters that can be learned. A node's variable is either assigned externally (as in input nodes with no incoming edges) or calculated based on a function. This function considers the variables from where the incoming edges originate, as well as any learnable parameters associated with those edges.

A directed acyclic computational graph comprises input, output, and hidden nodes. Input nodes hold the graph's external inputs, while output nodes contain the final results. Hidden nodes store intermediate values. Each hidden and output node calculates a relatively straightforward local function of its incoming node variables. With numerous input nodes (e.g., regressors) and a single output node (e.g., regressand), the graph computes a vector-to-scalar function. Conversely, multiple input and output nodes enable the computation of a vector-to-vector function, a common scenario in multiclass or multilabel learning. The cumulative effect of these computations across the graph implicitly defines a global function mapping input to output nodes. Each input node's variable is set to an externally provided input value, so no function is computed at these nodes. The node-specific functions also utilize parameters linked to their incoming edges, and the inputs along these edges are scaled by weights. By appropriately selecting these weights, the overall function defined by the graph can be controlled. This global function is often learned by feeding the computational graph input-output pairs (training data) and adjusting the weights to align predicted outputs with observed outputs.

Directed acyclic graphs are particularly relevant in various domains, including source code parsing, conversational emotion recognition, probabilistic graphical models, and neural architectures. The edges in these graphs establish a partial order over the nodes. This partial order introduces a strong inductive bias, which can be integrated into the models. Recently, transformer models have attracted interest in graph learning, as they offer the potential to learn intricate relationships beyond those captured by standard graph neural networks, using a different approach. Technically, transformer models can be viewed as graph neural networks operating on fully connected computational graphs, effectively detached from the input graphs.

Neuron

The human brain is made up of nearly 10 billion interconnected neurons. Each neuron is a cell that uses biochemical reactions to receive, process, and transmit information. Considering the human brain would be far too complex, a human neuron (a brain cell) is considered here. A biological neuron, as shown in Fig. 3.1, is a specialized

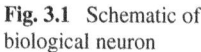

Fig. 3.1 Schematic of biological neuron

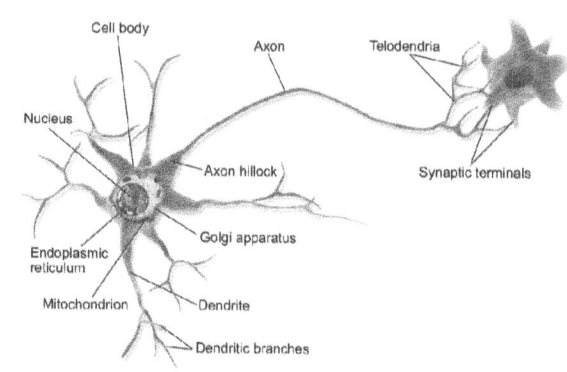

cell in the nervous system that processes and transmits information through electrical and chemical signals.

A *neuron* is a basic building block of a neural network.

It's like a tiny computer that can perform simple calculations and make decisions based on inputs. Neurons are connected to each other in a network, and they work together to perform complex tasks, such as image classification or language translation.

The inputs to a neuron are numbers that represent the information, and the output of a neuron is a decision about what to do with that information.

It consists of several key components:

1. **Cell Body (Soma)**: Contains the nucleus and other organelles, responsible for maintaining the cell's health and functionality.
2. **Dendrites**: Branch-like structures that receive signals from other neurons and transmit them to the cell body.
3. **Axon**: A long, slender projection that carries electrical impulses away from the cell body to other neurons, muscles, or glands.
4. **Axon Terminals**: The endpoints of the axon where neurotransmitters are released to communicate with other neurons.
5. **Synapse**: The junction between the axon terminal of one neuron and the dendrite of another, where neurotransmitters are exchanged.

Biological neurons communicate through action potentials (electrical impulses) and neurotransmitters (chemical signals), enabling complex processes such as sensation, thought, and movement.

Fig. 3.2 Artificial neuron

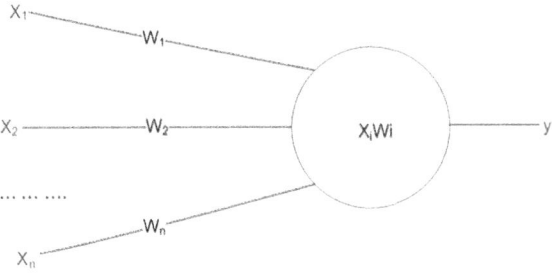

An artificial neuron, also known as a node or unit in an artificial neural network (ANN), is a mathematical model inspired by the biological neuron. It is illustrated in Fig. 3.2. It is designed to simulate the way biological neurons process information.

Key components of an artificial neuron include:

1. **Inputs**: Signals received from other neurons or external sources, analogous to dendrites.
2. **Weights**: Parameters that adjust the strength of the input signals, similar to synaptic strengths in biological neurons.
3. **Summation Function**: Combines the weighted inputs to produce a single value, representing the total input to the neuron.
4. **Activation Function**: Applies a nonlinear transformation to the summation output, determining whether the neuron should be activated (fired). Common activation functions include sigmoid, *Rectified Linear Unit* (ReLU).
5. **Output**: The final signal produced by the neuron, which can be transmitted to other neurons in the network.

The *Rectified Linear Unit* (ReLU) function is like a light switch, but it's a bit more sophisticated. If the input is positive, the ReLU function outputs the same positive value, which turns the neuron on. If the input is negative, the ReLU function outputs 0, which turns the neuron off.

The artificial neuron takes inputs as $X_1, X_2, X_3, \ldots, X_n$ via n different input nodes. These input nodes are connected with a processing node. Each connection has got some weight identifiers as $W_1, W_2, W_3, \ldots, W_n$. The weighted average yields the activation level. That is

$$\text{Activation} = X_1 W_1 + X_2 W_2 + X_3 W_3 + \cdots + X_n W_n$$
$$= \Sigma X_i W_i \quad \text{for } i = 1, 2, 3, \ldots, n.$$

This activation output is measured with a predefined threshold value. If it is greater than the threshold value, then output is 1 (positive) else output is zero. This can be measured by a squashing function; hence an output function "O" is defined by S(Activation) as follows:

$$\text{Output} = S(\text{Activation}).$$

Artificial neural systems can be viewed as simplified mathematical representations of brain-like systems functioning as parallel distributed computing networks. Unlike conventional computers, which are programmed to execute specific tasks, neural networks typically require teaching or training. These systems learn by adjusting their weights and thresholds.

Neural Network Architectures

Networks are classified based on their structure, layers, and learning mechanisms. Various architectures exist, including radial basis function networks, feedforward networks, recurrent networks, and self-organizing networks.

- **Single-layer feedforward networks**: These networks consist of a single layer of computational nodes, as given in Fig. 3.3, and are termed feedforward because they lack feedback mechanisms.
- **Multi-layer feedforward networks**: These networks feature one or more hidden layers as shown in Fig. 3.4. The input layer's source nodes provide inputs to the neurons in the first hidden layer. The outputs from the first hidden layer neurons serve as inputs to the neurons in the second hidden layer, and this process continues. If every node in each layer is connected to every node in the adjacent forward layer, the network is fully connected. If some links are missing, it is partially connected.
- **Recurrent neural networks**: These networks include at least one feedback loop. Various types of recurrent networks exist, depending on how feedback is utilized. Typically, they have a single layer of neurons, with each neuron feeding its output signal back to the inputs of all other neurons. Some recurrent networks may also have self-feedback loops and hidden neurons.
- **Fully recurrent network**, illustrated in Fig. 3.5, is a type of neural network where every neuron is connected to every other neuron, including itself. This means that the network has feedback loops, allowing it to maintain a state and process sequences of data over time. FRNs are particularly useful for tasks involving sequential data, such as time series analysis, natural language processing, and speech recognition.
- **Lattice networks**: These feedforward networks have output neurons arranged in rows and columns. They can feature one-dimensional, two-dimensional, or higher-dimensional arrays of neurons, with corresponding source nodes supplying input signals to the array.
- **Jordan network**: A Jordan neural network, shown in Fig. 3.6, is a type of recurrent neural network (RNN) introduced by Michael I. Jordan in 1986. In a Jordan

network, the network includes context units that receive feedback from the output layer. These context units help maintain a form of memory by storing the previous outputs, which are then used as additional inputs for the next step. This feedback mechanism allows the network to learn and predict sequences by considering both the current input and the history of previous outputs. Jordan networks are particularly useful for tasks such as time series prediction, speech recognition, and other sequential data processing tasks.

Fig. 3.3 Single-layer feedforward network

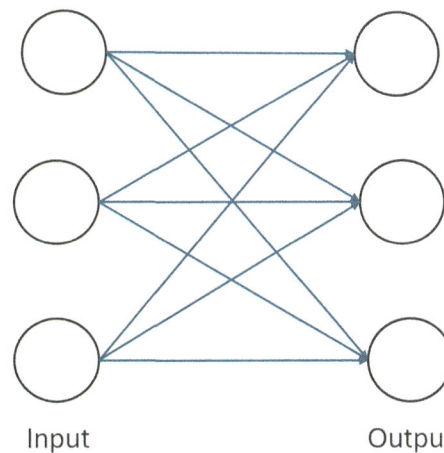

Fig. 3.4 Multi-layer feedforward network

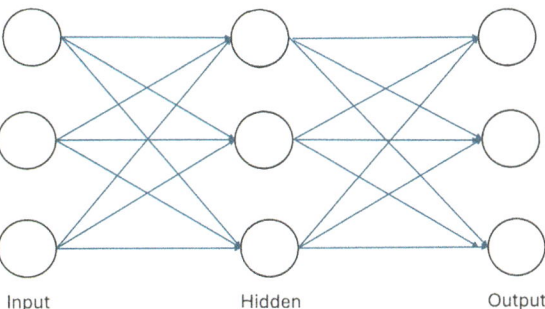

Fig. 3.5 Fully recurrent network

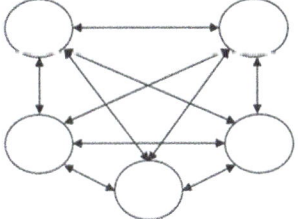

Fig. 3.6 Jordan network

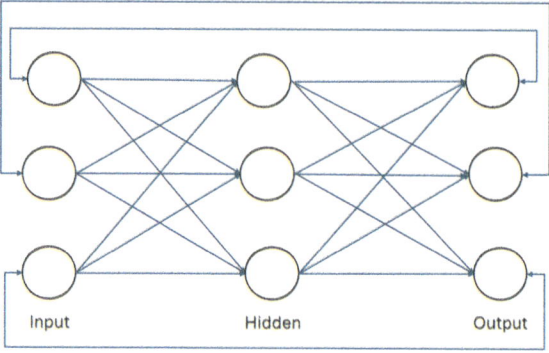

Input   Hidden   Output

Hopfield Model

The Hopfield model is a type of recurrent artificial neural network that serves as a content-addressable memory system with binary threshold nodes. It was introduced by John Hopfield in 1982 and is known for its ability to store and retrieve patterns through associative memory. The network consists of a set of neurons, each connected to every other neuron, forming a fully connected network. The state of each neuron is binary, meaning it can be either active (1) or inactive (0).

Learning in a Hopfield network involves adjusting the weights between neurons to store specific patterns. This is typically done using Hebbian learning, where the weight between two neurons is increased if they are activated simultaneously. The learning rule can be mathematically expressed as:

$$\omega_{ij} = \frac{1}{N} \Sigma_{p=1}^{P} \left(2v_i^p - 1\right)\left(2v_j^p - 1\right),$$

where w_{ij} is the weight between neurons i and j, N is the number of neurons, P is the number of patterns, and v_{ip} and v_{jp} are the states of neurons i and j in pattern p.

Parallel relaxation is a process used in Hopfield networks to reach a stable state, where the network's energy is minimized. The energy function of the network is defined as:

$$E = -\frac{1}{2}\Sigma_{i \neq j}\left(w_{ij}v_iv_j\right) + \Sigma_i\theta_iv_i,$$

where E is the energy, w_{ij} are the weights, v_i and v_j are the states of neurons i and j, and θ_i is the threshold of neuron i. The network updates the state of each neuron iteratively, either synchronously or asynchronously, to reduce the overall energy. In parallel relaxation, all neurons are updated simultaneously, which can lead to faster convergence to a stable state.

The Hopfield network's ability to perform parallel relaxation makes it effective for solving optimization problems and retrieving stored patterns. However, it can also exhibit issues such as local minima, where the network gets stuck in suboptimal states.

> **Algorithm** The process can be given as follows:
>
> ```
> procedure parallel relaxation
>   while not-stable network
>   pick a random unit
>   initiate sum as sum of the connections to all active
>   neighbours
>   if sum is positive
>   then turn unit active else turn the inactive
> end of procedure
> ```

When trained using a specific learning method, the Hopfield network can function as a robust content-addressable memory, maintaining resistance to changes in connections.

Perceptrons

A perceptron is a type of artificial neuron used in machine learning and artificial intelligence. It is the simplest form of a neural network and serves as a building block for more complex neural networks. The perceptron model was introduced by Frank Rosenblatt in 1957 and is designed to perform binary classification tasks.

A perceptron takes multiple inputs, processes them through weighted sums, and applies an activation function to produce an output. While perceptrons themselves are quite basic, they paved the way for the development of more complex neural networks, including multi-layer perceptrons (MLPs) and deep neural networks. These advanced networks, with multiple layers of perceptrons, are capable of learning and representing intricate patterns in data, which is the essence of deep learning.

A perceptron consists of the following components:

1. **Inputs**: The perceptron receives multiple input values, which can be features of the data.
2. **Weights**: Each input is associated with a weight that determines the importance of the input.
3. **Bias**: An additional parameter that helps adjust the output independently of the input values.
4. **Summation Function**: Computes the weighted sum of the inputs and the bias.
5. **Activation Function**: Applies a threshold to the weighted sum to produce the final output.

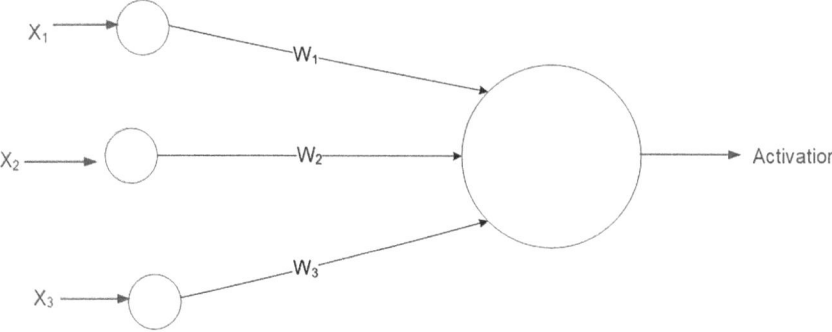

Fig. 3.7 Single perceptron

Definition A simple perceptron is a computing unit with threshold θ which, when receiving the n real inputs $X_1, X_2, ..., X_n$ through edges with the associated weights $W_1, W_2, ..., W_n$, outputs 1 if the inequality $\sum w_i x_i >= \theta$ holds and otherwise 0.

The following Fig. 3.7 illustrates a single perceptron.

It shows three input nodes X_1, X_2, and X_3 with the corresponding weights as W_1, W_2 and W_3. The activation function can be given as follows:

```
Activation = f(X,W)
= ∑ XᵢWᵢ for i = 1, 2, 3
= X₁W₁ + X₂W₂ + X₃W₃
The output function O is defined as follows:
Output O = 1 if Activation >= θ
           = 0 otherwise
           Where θ is a threshold value
```

The threshold value collects the outputs of the predicates through weighted edges and computes the final decision.

Learning in Neural Network

Artificial neural networks, as we know, are computational systems inspired by the intricate structure and function of biological brains. They are typically constructed from a dense web of interconnected processing elements, often referred to as "units" or "nodes," which serve as simplified models of biological neurons. Crucially, the connections between these units are not static; each connection is associated with a modifiable weight. This weight plays a role analogous to the synaptic strength in a biological neural network, determining the degree to which one unit can influence another.

The fundamental operation of a single unit involves transforming the pattern of incoming signals it receives into a single outgoing signal that it then transmits to other connected units. This transformation process generally unfolds in two key stages. First, for each incoming signal, the unit multiplies the signal's strength (or activity) by the weight of the corresponding connection. These weighted incoming signals are then summed together to produce a total net input to the unit. Second, this total net input is subjected to a nonlinear function, commonly known as an activation function or input-output function, which dictates the unit's resulting outgoing activity.

To illustrate this at a more granular level, consider a simplified model of a neuron known as a perceptron, as depicted conceptually in Fig. 3.8. A perceptron can receive an input vector, denoted as X, which may have N dimensions, representing multiple features or signals. Each of these input values is associated with a corresponding weight in a weight vector W, also of N dimensions. These inputs and their respective weights are then processed by a summation node. This node calculates a value "a," which represents the "dot product" (or weighted sum) of the input vector X and the weight vector W, often with the addition of a bias term. This bias acts as an adjustable constant that can shift the activation threshold of the perceptron.

The resulting value "a" is then passed through an activation function. This function compares the value of "a" against a predefined threshold. If the calculated value "a" falls below this threshold, the perceptron is considered not to "fire" or activate, and its output signal is typically zero or a low value. Conversely, if "a" exceeds the threshold, the perceptron will "fire," emitting an output signal, often a single pulse with a predefined amplitude. This binary "fire" or "no fire" behaviour is a simplified representation of neuronal firing.

The overall behaviour and computational capabilities of a neural network are jointly determined by two key factors: the configuration of the weights associated with its connections and the specific input-output function (or transfer function) chosen for its individual units. These activation functions typically fall into one of three broad categories: linear, threshold, or sigmoid. In linear units, the output activity is directly proportional to the total weighted input, resulting in a linear transformation. Threshold units exhibit a step-like output, where the output is set to one of two discrete levels (e.g., 0 or 1) depending on whether the total input surpasses

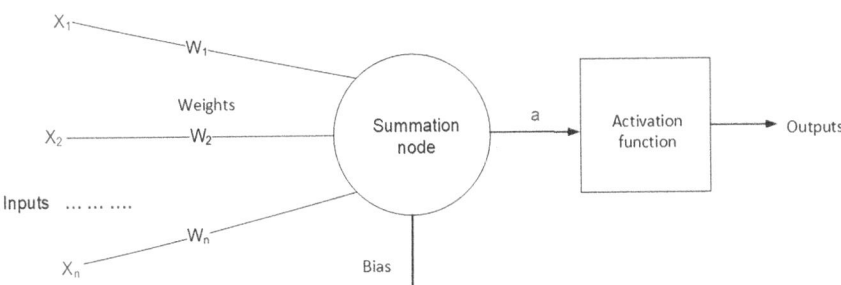

Fig. 3.8 Learning in neural network

a specific threshold value. Sigmoid units, on the other hand, produce an output that varies continuously and nonlinearly as the input changes, typically exhibiting an S-shaped curve. While all three types are simplifications of real biological neurons, sigmoid units are often considered to more closely approximate their continuous and graded response characteristics compared to the abrupt, binary nature of threshold units or the unrestricted linear response of linear units.

To construct a neural network capable of performing specific tasks, two crucial design choices must be made: defining how the individual units are interconnected to form the network's architecture and appropriately setting the weights of these connections. The pattern of connections dictates the flow of information and determines whether and how one unit can influence the activity of others. The weights, on the other hand, quantify the strength and direction (positive or negative) of that influence.

A fundamental and widely used type of artificial neural network architecture comprises three distinct groups, or layers, of interconnected units: an input layer, one or more hidden layers, and an output layer. The units in the input layer serve as entry points for the raw information or data that is fed into the network. The activity levels of these input units directly represent the values of the input features. Each unit in the hidden layer receives input from all (or a subset of) the units in the preceding layer (in this case, the input layer), and its own activity is determined by the weighted sum of these incoming activities passed through its activation function. The output units, which form the final layer of the network, similarly receive input from the hidden layer (or the input layer in simpler networks) and their activity represents the network's response or prediction for a given input.

This basic three-layer network structure is particularly significant because the hidden layer introduces the capability for the network to develop its own internal representations of the input data. By adjusting the weights of the connections between the input and hidden units during a learning process, each hidden unit can be trained to selectively respond strongly to specific patterns or combinations of features present in the input. This ability to learn and create internal representations is a key aspect of the power and flexibility of neural networks.

Training a three-layer network to perform a particular task typically involves the following iterative process:

(a) The network is presented with a set of training examples. Each training example consists of an input pattern provided to the input units and a corresponding desired output pattern that the network should produce at its output units for that specific input.

(b) For each training example, the network processes the input and generates an actual output. The discrepancy, or error, between this actual output and the desired output specified in the training example is then calculated using a defined error function.

(c) Based on this calculated error, the weights of each connection within the network are adjusted according to a specific learning algorithm (such as backpropagation). The goal of this weight adjustment is to minimize the error, thereby improving the network's approximation of the desired output for the given training examples. This process is repeated over many training examples, iteratively refining the weights until the network learns to accurately map the input patterns to the desired output patterns for the task at hand.

Multi-layer Perceptrons

During the 1960s and 1970s, the exploration of neural networks faced significant challenges due to limited computational power and the constraints of existing models. Despite these obstacles, some researchers persisted in developing more sophisticated models, such as multi-layer networks, which could tackle more complex problems. It wasn't until the late 1980s and early 1990s that advancements in computational power and the creation of new algorithms enabled the training of deep neural networks, composed of multiple layers of artificial neurons.

Multi-layer perceptrons (MLPs), as illustrated in Fig. 3.9, typically consist of three types of layers:

1. **Input Layer**: This layer receives the input data. Each neuron in the input layer represents a feature of the data.
2. **Hidden Layers**: These layers are situated between the input and output layers. MLPs can have one or more hidden layers, each containing multiple neurons. The hidden layers enable the network to learn complex patterns and representations.
3. **Output Layer**: This layer produces the final output of the network. The number of neurons in the output layer depends on the type of task (e.g., classification, regression).

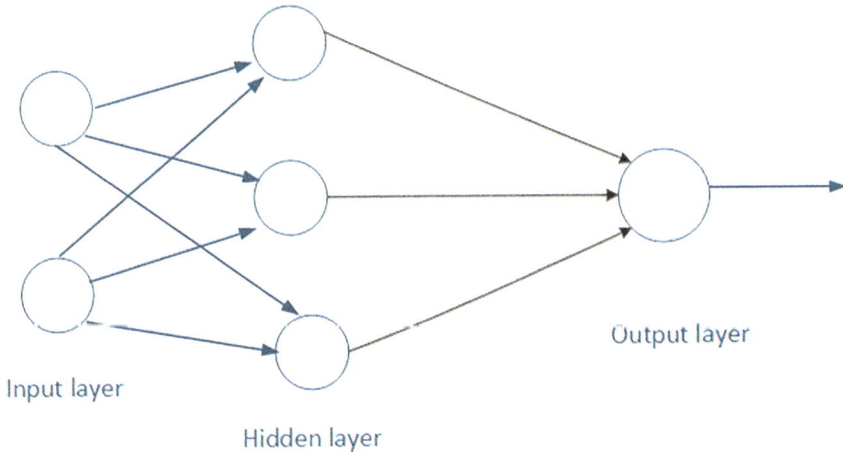

Fig. 3.9 Multi-layer perceptron

Forward propagation in a multi-layer perceptron (MLP) begins with the input data being fed into the network. Each neuron in the hidden layers computes a weighted sum of its inputs, applies an activation function, and passes the result to the next layer. Common activation functions include sigmoid, ReLU (Rectified Linear Unit), and tanh, which introduce nonlinearity, enabling the network to learn complex patterns. This process continues through the hidden layers until the output layer produces the result.

Backward propagation, or backpropagation, starts with the network's output being compared to the actual target values. The error is calculated using a loss function, such as mean squared error for regression or cross-entropy for classification. The error is then propagated backward through the network, and the weights are adjusted to minimize the error. This is done using gradient descent, where the gradients of the loss function with respect to the weights are computed. The weights are updated based on these gradients and a learning rate, which controls the step size of the updates.

For example, consider an MLP used for a binary classification task, such as determining whether an email is spam or not. The input layer receives features of the email, such as word frequencies. The hidden layers process these input features, learning representations that capture the patterns associated with spam and non-spam emails. The output layer produces a probability score indicating the likelihood that the email is spam.

During training, the MLP adjusts its weights through multiple iterations of forward and backward propagation, gradually improving its performance. The network learns to minimize the error between its predictions and the actual target values, becoming more accurate over time.

Backpropagation Algorithm

Backpropagation is a key algorithm for training artificial neural networks. As a supervised learning method, it adjusts network weights to minimize the error between predicted and actual outputs. The process starts with a forward pass, where input data is fed through the network to produce an output. This output is compared to the target output, and the error is calculated using a loss function like mean squared error or cross-entropy.

The essence of backpropagation is its ability to propagate this error backward through the network. This involves computing the gradient of the loss function with respect to each weight using the chain rule of calculus. These gradients indicate how to adjust the weights to reduce the error. The weights are then updated using an optimization algorithm, typically gradient descent, which iteratively adjusts the weights to minimize the loss.

In modern deep neural networks, instead of using a threshold function for nonlinear activation, various activation functions are employed to achieve smoother nonlinearities and facilitate efficient derivative computation. One of the most popular activation functions is the Rectified Linear Unit (ReLU), which is defined as:

$$\text{ReLU}(x) = \max(0, x).$$

ReLU is favoured because it introduces nonlinearity while being computationally efficient and easy to implement. It also helps mitigate the vanishing gradient problem, which can occur with other activation functions like the sigmoid or tanh. By allowing only positive values to pass through and setting negative values to zero, ReLU enables deep networks to learn complex patterns more effectively.

Backpropagation training algorithm:

```
1. Inputs X, arrive through the pre-connected path.
2. Input is modelled using real weights W. The weights are
usually randomly selected.
3. Calculate the output for every neuron from the input layer to
the hidden layers, to the output layer.
4. Calculate the error in the outputs.
ErrorB = Actual Output - Desired Output
5. Travel back from the output layer to the hidden layer to
adjust the weights such that the error is decreased.

Keep repeating the process until the desired output is
achieved.
```

Another important algorithm related to neural networks is the *gradient descent algorithm*. Gradient descent is an optimization technique used to find the minimum of a function. In the context of neural networks, it is used to minimize the loss function by iteratively adjusting the weights in the direction of the steepest descent, as indicated by the gradients. There are several variants of gradient descent, including stochastic gradient descent (SGD), mini-batch gradient descent, and batch gradient descent. SGD updates the weights using a single training example at a time, which can lead to faster convergence but with more noise in the updates. Mini-batch gradient descent strikes a balance by updating the weights using a small batch of training examples, providing a compromise between convergence speed and stability.

Another notable algorithm is the *Adam optimizer*, which stands for Adaptive Moment Estimation. Adam combines the advantages of two other extensions of stochastic gradient descent: AdaGrad and RMSProp. It maintains two moving averages for each weight: the first moment (mean) and the second moment (uncentered variance). These moving averages are used to adapt the learning rate for each weight individually, allowing for more efficient and stable training. Adam is widely used due to its robustness and efficiency in handling sparse gradients and noisy data.

The *recurrent neural network (RNN)* and its variants, such as *long short-term memory* (LSTM) and *gated recurrent unit* (GRU), are also significant in the field of neural networks. RNNs are designed to handle sequential data by maintaining a hidden state that captures information from previous time steps. This makes them suitable for tasks such as language modelling and time series prediction. LSTMs and GRUs are improvements over standard RNNs, addressing the vanishing gradient problem by introducing gating mechanisms that control the flow of information, allowing the network to retain long-term dependencies more effectively.

Other Neural Network Models

Kohonen Maps

Kohonen maps are a type of feedforward network that employs an unsupervised training method. Through a process of self-organization, this method arranges the output units into a topological or spatial map. The significance of Kohonen's work was recognized in the late 1980s, leading to the appreciation of the self-organizing feature map's utility. Kohonen has also introduced several enhancements to this model, including a supervised learning variant known as Learning Vector Quantization (LVQ).

A Kohonen map neural network comprises two layers of processing units: an input layer that is fully connected to a competitive output layer. It lacks hidden units. When an input pattern is presented to the feature map, the output layer units compete to be declared the winner. Typically, the winning output unit is the one whose incoming connection weights are most similar to the input pattern, as measured by Euclidean distance. Thus, upon presentation of the input, each output unit calculates its similarity or match score with the input pattern. The output unit determined to be most similar to the input pattern is selected as the winner and is granted the ability to adjust its connection weights. These connection weights are then shifted in the direction of the input pattern, with the magnitude of the shift determined by a learning rate parameter. This describes the fundamental operation of competitive neural networks.

The Kohonen map establishes a topological mapping by adjusting not only the winner's weights but also the weights of neighbouring output units. Therefore, the adjustment process affects not only the winning unit but also its surrounding units, moving this entire neighbourhood closer to the input pattern. Starting with randomized weight values, the output units gradually align themselves so that, when an input pattern is presented, a cluster of units responds to it. As training progresses, the size of this neighbourhood around the winning unit decreases. Initially, a large number of output units are updated, followed by successively smaller numbers, until, at the end of training, only the winning unit's weights are adjusted. Similarly, the learning rate diminishes as training progresses, and in some implementations, the learning rate also decreases with increasing distance from the winning output unit.

Basic Kohonen algorithm can be given as:

```
begin
  randomize weights for all neurons
  for (i = 1 to iteration_number) do
```

```
      begin
        take one random input pattern
        find the winning neuron
        find neighbours of the winner
        modify synaptic weights of these neurons
        reduce the η (learning rate) and λ (neighbourhood radius)
        end
   end.
```

A Kohonen neural network can be used to compress and quantize data, such as images and speech, before storage or transmission to condense the quantity of information to be stored or sent.

Probabilistic Neural Networks

Probabilistic neural networks (PNNs) represent a distinct class of neural architecture that combines elements of traditional feedforward networks with statistical pattern recognition principles. While sharing the supervised training approach familiar to many neural networks, PNNs implement a fundamentally different learning strategy compared to backpropagation methods.

In contrast to conventional neural networks that iteratively adjust weights through gradient descent, PNNs incorporate each training pattern directly into the network structure. Every training example effectively becomes embedded as connection weights to a newly created hidden unit. This direct integration approach eliminates the need for multiple training epochs, enabling extremely rapid network configuration through a single pass of the training data. While additional passes may be employed to fine-tune output weights for enhanced performance, the core architecture is established immediately.

A common critique of the basic PNN approach concerns its potential inefficiency in network size. As each training pattern generates a corresponding hidden unit, networks can grow unwieldy with large datasets. To address this limitation, researchers have developed various clustering techniques that consolidate similar input patterns into single representative hidden units. These methods analyse the proximity of patterns in input space to determine when multiple examples can be effectively represented by a unified hidden node, substantially reducing architectural complexity while preserving classification accuracy.

PNNs offer several compelling advantages compared to traditional backpropagation networks:

1. Training efficiency is dramatically improved, often requiring only a single pass through the training data rather than numerous iterations.
2. Given sufficient training data, PNNs naturally converge toward optimal Bayesian classifiers, providing statistically robust decision boundaries.

3. PNNs support true incremental learning capabilities, allowing new training examples to be seamlessly incorporated without requiring complete retraining of the network.
4. Because of their statistical foundations, PNNs can provide confidence measures for their classifications, indicating the strength of evidence supporting each decision—a valuable feature in applications requiring uncertainty quantification.

This combination of rapid training, statistical optimality, adaptability to new data, and confidence estimation makes PNNs particularly valuable in scenarios requiring quick deployment and transparent decision processes.

The Boltzmann Machine

The Boltzmann Machine, a significant development in the field of neural networks, was conceived by the influential cognitive neuroscientists Geoffrey Hinton and Terrence Sejnowski. This model represents a conceptually rich and powerful probabilistic framework that uniquely blends stochastic learning mechanisms with intricate interconnections between its processing units.

Drawing its foundational principles from the interdisciplinary domains of statistical physics and machine learning theory, the Boltzmann Machine offers a distinct computational paradigm that fundamentally diverges from the operational principles of traditional, deterministic neural network models. A key characteristic of Boltzmann Machines is their incorporation of probabilistic state transitions, where the activation of individual units is governed by probabilities rather than fixed rules. Furthermore, their learning dynamics are based on an energy function, a concept borrowed from statistical mechanics. This energy-based approach allows these networks to effectively model and capture highly intricate and nonlinear relationships that may exist within complex datasets. Consequently, Boltzmann Machines have proven to be particularly valuable tools for tackling advanced pattern recognition tasks, where subtle and high-order dependencies need to be identified, and for generative modelling, where the goal is to learn the underlying probability distribution of the data to generate new, realistic samples.

The fundamental architecture of a Boltzmann Machine is characterized by a network of interconnected computational units, often organized into distinct layers designated as visible and hidden layers. A crucial departure from traditional neural networks lies in the probabilistic operation of these units. Unlike their deterministic counterparts, each node in a Boltzmann Machine exists in one of two binary states, typically represented as 0 or 1, with the transition between these states occurring probabilistically. The overall behaviour of the network is dictated by an energy function. This energy function defines the probability associated with any given configuration of the network's units, establishing a direct and insightful analogy to the equilibrium states and energy landscapes studied in statistical mechanical systems. The network tends to settle into configurations that correspond to lower energy states, and the probabilities of these states are related to their energy levels via a Boltzmann distribution, hence the name of the model.

In contrast to simpler network structures, multi-layer perceptron (MLP) configurations introduce a more sophisticated network topology. In these architectures, computational nodes are strategically arranged across multiple interconnected layers, including an input layer, one or more hidden layers, and an output layer. Each layer within this deep architecture plays a role in progressively extracting increasingly abstract and complex features from the input data and transforming its representation. The visible layer serves as the direct interface between the network and the external input data, receiving the raw information to be processed. The hidden layers, situated between the visible and output layers, perform the crucial task of progressively abstracting and encoding increasingly intricate representational characteristics of the input. Through multiple layers of nonlinear transformations, the network can learn hierarchical representations, where lower layers capture simple features and higher layers combine these features to represent more complex and meaningful patterns. This capability is fundamental to the power of deep learning architectures, including Boltzmann Machines with multiple hidden layers (often referred to as Deep Boltzmann Machines), in handling complex real-world data.

Stochastic Learning Mechanisms

The learning process in Boltzmann Machines is primarily stochastic, utilizing sophisticated probabilistic algorithms to adjust network parameters. The core learning algorithm involves minimizing the network's energy function through iterative sampling and parameter optimization. This approach, known as contrastive divergence, enables the network to learn intricate data distributions without requiring explicit probabilistic modelling of complex, high-dimensional spaces.

Particularly, the learning dynamics involve two primary phases: a positive phase where the network's state is driven by observed training data, and a negative phase where the network generates its own internal representations. By comparing these phases, the learning algorithm can incrementally adjust connection weights to better approximate the underlying data distribution.

Despite their remarkable representational capabilities, Boltzmann Machines face significant computational challenges. The stochastic nature of network updates and the need for extensive sampling make training computationally intensive, particularly for large, complex network architectures. Restricted Boltzmann Machines (RBMs) emerged as a more computationally tractable variant, introducing architectural constraints that simplify learning while maintaining sophisticated representational power.

Genetic Algorithm

Genetic algorithms (GAs) draw inspiration from natural evolution, applying this approach to various scientific and engineering disciplines, including computer science. The core of these algorithms lies in the principle of natural selection, specifically Charles Darwin's concept of "survival of the fittest." GAs offer an alternative to traditional problem-solving methods, and in many cases, they can outperform them. They are particularly well-suited to finding optimal parameters in real-world problems that may be challenging for conventional techniques. GAs have found applications in problem-solving, function optimization, machine learning, and the development of innovative systems. Their appeal stems from their simplicity and effectiveness as robust search algorithms, capable of quickly identifying good solutions for complex, high-dimensional problems.

Genetic algorithms prove useful and efficient when:

- The search space is extensive, intricate, or not well-defined.
- There is limited domain knowledge, or it is difficult to express expert knowledge in a way that narrows the search space.
- Mathematical analysis is not feasible.

GAs belong to the broader category of evolutionary algorithms (EAs). Other EA types include evolutionary strategies (ES), evolutionary programming (EP), and genetic programming (GP).

Among the metaheuristic algorithms, GA is a well-known algorithm, which is inspired from biological evolution process. Genetic algorithms (GAs) represent a powerful class of optimization techniques inspired by the principles of natural selection and evolutionary biology. First pioneered by John Holland in the 1960s and further developed in his seminal 1975 work "Adaptation in Natural and Artificial Systems," genetic algorithms have evolved into versatile problem-solving tools across numerous disciplines. At their core, genetic algorithms simulate the process of natural selection where the fittest individuals are selected for reproduction to produce offspring for the next generation, gradually improving the population's fitness over successive iterations.

The fundamental insight behind genetic algorithms lies in their ability to explore complex, high-dimensional search spaces efficiently without requiring specific domain knowledge about the objective function. This characteristic makes them particularly valuable for problems where traditional optimization techniques prove inadequate due to nonlinearity, discontinuity, or multi-modality in the solution space. Unlike many conventional optimization methods that operate on a single candidate solution, genetic algorithms maintain a population of potential solutions, allowing for a more thorough exploration of the search space while balancing exploitation of promising regions.

We begin by exploring the biological inspiration and core mechanisms, then proceed to detailed explanations of algorithm components and parameters. The discussion extends to advanced techniques, hybridization with other methods, and current research directions. Throughout, we incorporate examples from diverse fields to illustrate the versatility and efficacy of these evolutionary approaches to optimization.

Biological Foundations and Core Principles

The conceptual foundation of genetic algorithms (GAs) is inspired by the principles of Darwinian evolution, particularly the mechanism of natural selection, where traits that enhance survival and reproduction are more likely to be inherited by subsequent generations. In biological systems, individuals with advantageous characteristics tend to thrive in their environments, gradually leading to populations that are better adapted over time.

Genetic algorithms translate this evolutionary paradigm into a computational framework. In this context, each individual represents a potential solution to a given problem, typically encoded as a string of values known as a chromosome. Each element within this string, referred to as a gene, corresponds to a specific parameter or decision variable. The complete set of genes forms the genotype, which is mapped to a phenotype—the actual solution in the problem space. This mapping is a critical aspect of algorithm design, as it determines how effectively the algorithm can explore and exploit the solution landscape.

Central to the operation of a GA is the fitness function, which evaluates how well each individual performs with respect to the problem at hand. This function acts as a selective pressure, analogous to environmental challenges in nature, guiding the evolutionary process toward increasingly optimal solutions. Through repeated cycles of selection, variation (via crossover and mutation), and replacement, successive generations are formed, ideally exhibiting improved performance.

A classic application of genetic algorithms is in optimizing the weights of neural networks for tasks such as pattern recognition. Here, each chromosome encodes a set of network weights, and the fitness function assesses classification accuracy on a validation dataset. Over time, the algorithm evolves weight configurations that enhance predictive accuracy, offering an alternative to traditional training methods that rely on manual tuning or gradient-based optimization.

Algorithmic Components

Representation and Encoding

Selecting an appropriate representation for potential solutions is a fundamental aspect of designing effective genetic algorithms, as the encoding scheme must capture all relevant decision variables while supporting efficient genetic operations. Several encoding strategies are commonly employed; each suited to different problem types.

Binary encoding, one of the earliest and most widely used methods, represents solutions as strings of binary digits. Each bit or group of bits corresponds to a specific parameter, offering a straightforward and computationally efficient structure. For example, a problem involving five variables might be encoded as a 40-bit chromosome, with 8 bits allocated per variable to achieve the desired level of precision.

In contrast, integer and real-valued encodings provide a more direct representation of numerical parameters, avoiding the need for binary conversion. This approach is often more intuitive and practical for engineering and scientific applications. A chromosome in this format might consist of a vector of floating-point numbers, each constrained within predefined bounds, representing parameters in a mechanical or control system.

Permutation encoding is particularly suited to problems involving ordering, such as the traveling salesman problem. Here, a chromosome is a sequence that specifies the order in which elements—such as cities—are visited. For instance, a tour of ten cities might be encoded as [3, 1, 7, 2, 9, 10, 5, 8, 4, 6], indicating a specific visitation sequence.

For problems involving hierarchical or networked structures, tree and graph encodings are more appropriate. These are commonly used in genetic programming and network design, where a chromosome might represent a mathematical expression or a network topology. A simple example is the expression $(x + 2) * (y - 3)$, which can be structured as a tree with operators at internal nodes and variables or constants at the leaves.

The effectiveness of a genetic algorithm is closely tied to the choice of encoding, which must reflect the nature of the problem and preserve meaningful relationships between the genotype and phenotype. Ideally, small changes in the encoded chromosome should lead to correspondingly small changes in the solution, thereby supporting efficient local search and enhancing the algorithm's overall performance.

Population Initialization

The genetic algorithm process begins with the initialization of a population, which consists of a set of candidate solutions. The diversity within this initial population plays a pivotal role in determining the algorithm's capacity to explore the search space effectively. One of the most common strategies is random initialization, where each gene in a chromosome is assigned a value selected at random. This approach ensures broad coverage of the solution space; for instance, in a binary-encoded genetic algorithm designed to optimize a financial portfolio across 20 assets, the initial population might consist of 100 randomly generated chromosomes, each encoding investment proportions.

Alternatively, heuristic initialization leverages domain-specific knowledge to generate potentially high-quality starting solutions. In a production scheduling context, for example, some chromosomes might be constructed using established dispatching rules such as earliest due date or shortest processing time, while others are generated randomly to preserve diversity. Another method, uniform initialization, employs systematic sampling techniques like Latin hypercube sampling to evenly distribute individuals across the search space. This is particularly advantageous in high-dimensional problems, where purely random sampling might leave significant regions unexplored.

In addition to initialization strategy, population size is a critical parameter that influences both the breadth of the search and the computational cost. Smaller populations, typically ranging from 30 to 100 individuals, are more resource-efficient but may suffer from limited diversity. Larger populations, while computationally more demanding, can explore the solution space more thoroughly. The optimal population size depends on factors such as the complexity of the problem, the length of the chromosome encoding, and the available computational resources.

Selection Mechanisms

In genetic algorithms, the selection mechanism plays a central role in guiding the evolutionary process by determining which individuals are chosen for reproduction based on their fitness. This process mirrors the natural principle of "survival of the fittest," where individuals with higher fitness are more likely to contribute to the next generation. An effective selection strategy must strike a balance between applying sufficient selection pressure to promote progress and maintaining enough diversity to avoid premature convergence.

One widely used method is roulette wheel selection, or fitness-proportionate selection, where the probability of an individual being selected is proportional to its fitness value. For example, in a scenario optimizing production throughput, a solution yielding 120 units would be twice as likely to be selected as one yielding 60 units. However, this method can be sensitive to disparities in fitness values, potentially leading to premature convergence if a few individuals dominate early or stagnation if fitness values become too similar.

Tournament selection offers a more robust alternative by randomly selecting a subset of individuals and choosing the fittest among them. The size of the tournament controls the selection pressure: larger tournaments favour stronger individuals, while smaller ones help preserve diversity. This method is computationally efficient and does not require normalization of fitness values, making it suitable for a wide range of problems.

Rank-based selection addresses the limitations of fitness-proportionate methods by assigning selection probabilities based on an individual's rank rather than its absolute fitness. This approach reduces the risk of premature convergence by ensuring that selection pressure remains consistent, even when fitness differences are extreme or minimal. For instance, in a population optimizing network latency, the 10th-best solution might receive a fixed selection probability regardless of how close or far it is from the top-ranked individual.

Elitism complements these methods by ensuring that the best-performing individuals are preserved unchanged in the next generation. Typically, a small fraction of the population—often between 1% and 5%—is carried over directly, safeguarding high-quality solutions from being lost due to crossover or mutation.

The choice and configuration of the selection mechanism significantly influence the convergence behaviour of a genetic algorithm. Excessive selection pressure can accelerate convergence but risks trapping the algorithm in local optima, while insufficient pressure may result in slow progress and inefficient exploration of the search space.

Crossover Operations

Crossover, or recombination, is a fundamental genetic algorithm operation that produces new offspring by combining genetic material from two parent chromosomes, mimicking the role of sexual reproduction in biological evolution. This mechanism enables the algorithm to merge advantageous traits from different individuals, potentially leading to superior solutions.

Several crossover techniques are commonly employed, each with distinct characteristics. Single-point crossover selects a random position along the chromosome and exchanges all genes beyond that point between the two parents. For example, if crossover occurs after the third gene, the resulting offspring inherit the initial segment from one parent and the remaining segment from the other. This method is particularly effective when related parameters are grouped together in the encoding.

Multi-point crossover extends this idea by introducing multiple crossover points, thereby increasing the diversity of recombination. In two-point crossover, for instance, genes between two selected positions are swapped, allowing both the head and tail segments of the chromosome to be preserved from different parents. This enhances the algorithm's ability to explore the solution space more thoroughly.

Uniform crossover takes a different approach by evaluating each gene position independently, typically assigning a 50% chance for each parent to contribute a gene. While this method eliminates positional bias, it may disrupt beneficial gene groupings more frequently than point-based methods.

For real-valued encodings, arithmetic crossover is often used. Instead of swapping genes, it combines them mathematically—commonly by averaging the values or applying weighted combinations based on parent fitness. This approach is particularly useful in continuous optimization problems, such as tuning parameters in chemical processes.

In problems with specific structural constraints, such as the traveling salesman problem, problem-specific crossover operators are employed. These are designed to preserve meaningful features of the solution, such as common route segments, rather than simply exchanging elements at fixed positions.

The frequency with which crossover is applied is governed by the crossover probability, typically ranging from 0.6 to 0.9. Higher probabilities encourage exploration by generating more varied offspring, while lower probabilities favour exploitation by preserving existing high-quality solutions. Striking the right balance is essential to maintaining both diversity and convergence efficiency in the evolutionary process.

Mutation Operations

Mutation is a vital component of genetic algorithms, introducing small random alterations to offspring chromosomes to preserve genetic diversity and explore regions of the solution space that recombination alone might not reach. By enabling the algorithm to escape local optima and discover novel solutions, mutation plays a key role in maintaining the robustness of the evolutionary process.

In binary-encoded chromosomes, bit-flip mutation is commonly used. This technique inverts selected bits with a low probability, typically between 0.001 and 0.05 per bit. For example, in a chromosome representing network connectivity, flipping a single bit might reveal a more efficient topology that would otherwise remain undiscovered.

For real-valued encodings, uniform mutation replaces selected genes with new values drawn randomly from within their allowed ranges. This method is particularly useful in continuous optimization problems, such as adjusting chemical concentrations, where a gene might be reassigned a new value within predefined bounds to explore alternative configurations.

Gaussian mutation offers a more nuanced approach by adding normally distributed random noise to selected genes. The standard deviation of the distribution controls the magnitude of change, allowing for larger exploratory steps early in the search and finer adjustments as the algorithm converges. This makes it especially effective for fine-tuning solutions in continuous domains.

In permutation-based problems, such as scheduling or routing, swap and inversion mutations are often employed. Swap mutation exchanges the positions of two randomly selected genes, while inversion mutation reverses the order of a sequence of genes. These operations help explore alternative orderings without violating problem constraints, potentially improving performance metrics like makespan or travel distance.

The mutation rate is a critical parameter that must be carefully calibrated. Excessively high mutation rates can disrupt beneficial gene combinations, reducing the algorithm to a random search, while rates that are too low may hinder the discovery of new solutions. Adaptive mutation strategies, which gradually reduce the mutation rate as the population converges, have proven effective in balancing exploration and exploitation across diverse problem domains.

Algorithm Dynamics and Control Parameters

The interaction between selection, crossover, and mutation in genetic algorithms gives rise to dynamic population behaviours that balance exploration—searching for new, potentially superior regions of the solution space—and exploitation—refining known high-quality solutions. This balance is governed by several key parameters and mechanisms that must be carefully tuned to the problem at hand.

Population size plays a central role in maintaining genetic diversity. Smaller populations, typically between 30 and 50 individuals, may suffice for simple, unimodal problems where the search landscape is relatively smooth. However, more complex, multimodal, or deceptive problems often require much larger populations—sometimes in the hundreds or thousands—to ensure adequate coverage of the search space and to avoid premature convergence.

The generation limit defines the computational budget for the algorithm, usually ranging from 50 to 1000 generations depending on the problem's complexity and the size of the population. Termination criteria may also include stagnation in fitness improvement over several generations or the attainment of a predefined fitness threshold, ensuring that computational resources are used efficiently.

Selection pressure determines how strongly the algorithm favours individuals with higher fitness during reproduction. If the pressure is too high, the population may converge prematurely on suboptimal solutions; if too low, the search may become inefficient and overly random. This pressure can be modulated through mechanisms such as tournament size, ranking-based selection, or fitness scaling, allowing for dynamic adjustment throughout the evolutionary process.

Crossover and mutation rates further influence the balance between exploiting existing genetic material and introducing novel variations. Crossover rates typically range from 0.6 to 0.9, promoting the recombination of successful traits, while mutation rates are often set to 1 divided by the chromosome length ($1/L$), introducing occasional random changes to maintain diversity. The optimal settings for these rates depend on the problem's structure and the chosen encoding scheme.

To illustrate these dynamics, consider a genetic algorithm tasked with optimizing the design of a composite material composed of five component substances. Using binary encoding to represent the presence or absence of each material in various spatial configurations, the algorithm might begin with a diverse set of random designs. As generations progress, selection favours configurations with superior mechanical properties, crossover recombines effective substructures, and mutation introduces new material combinations. Early in the process, fitness improves rapidly as clearly inferior designs are eliminated. Over time, the population converges toward promising regions of the design space, with slower but more refined improvements as the algorithm hones in on optimal or near-optimal solutions.

Advanced Techniques and Extensions

Niching and Speciation

In natural ecosystems, species often evolve to occupy distinct ecological niches, allowing multiple specialized organisms to coexist by exploiting different environmental conditions. Genetic algorithms can emulate this phenomenon through *niching methods*, which are designed to preserve population diversity and encourage the formation of subpopulations around different optima. This is particularly advantageous in *multimodal optimization* problems, where multiple high-quality solutions may exist.

One such method is **fitness sharing**, which reduces the fitness of individuals that are too similar to others within a defined similarity radius. By dividing an individual's raw fitness by the number of comparable solutions nearby, the algorithm discourages overcrowding around a single peak. For instance, in drug design, this approach can help maintain a diverse set of molecular configurations, each representing a distinct binding mode with therapeutic potential.

Crowding is another diversity-preserving technique, where new offspring replace the most similar individuals in the population rather than being inserted randomly. This helps maintain a broad range of solutions by preventing dominant traits from overwhelming the population. In the design of electromagnetic devices, crowding can ensure that different design strategies—such as those prioritizing efficiency, compactness, or cost—are all represented.

Island models take a spatial approach by evolving multiple subpopulations (or "islands") in parallel, with occasional migration of individuals between them. This structure naturally supports diversity while allowing beneficial traits to spread across the population. In complex engineering problems, islands can be configured with different selection pressures or genetic operators, simulating evolutionary divergence akin to allopatric speciation.

Clearing further refines niche formation by allowing only the best-performing individual within a niche to reproduce, effectively suppressing redundant solutions. In satellite constellation design, for example, clearing can help identify and preserve distinct orbital configurations that optimize coverage for different geographic regions.

Together, these niching strategies enhance the genetic algorithm's ability to explore and maintain multiple promising regions of the solution space, making them especially valuable in domains where diverse, high-quality solutions are desired.

Multi-objective Optimization

Many real-world optimization problems involve multiple, often conflicting objectives, where no single solution can simultaneously optimize all goals. In such cases, *multi-objective genetic algorithms* (MOGAs) are employed to identify a set of *Pareto-optimal solutions*—solutions for which any improvement in one objective would lead to a deterioration in at least one other. Rather than producing a single optimal outcome, MOGAs generate a *Pareto front*, offering decision-makers a spectrum of trade-off solutions aligned with different priorities.

One of the most widely used MOGAs is **NSGA-II** (Non-dominated Sorting Genetic Algorithm II), which ranks individuals based on levels of non-domination and maintains diversity using a crowding distance metric. This ensures a well-distributed Pareto front. For example, in manufacturing process optimization, NSGA-II can reveal solutions that balance production rate, energy consumption, and product quality, allowing stakeholders to select configurations that best match their operational goals.

Another prominent approach is **SPEA2** (Strength Pareto Evolutionary Algorithm 2), which assigns fitness based on how many individuals an individual dominates and uses an external archive to preserve non-dominated solutions. In financial portfolio optimization, SPEA2 can generate investment strategies that balance expected return, risk, and liquidity, offering robust options across varying economic conditions.

MOEA/D (Multi-objective Evolutionary Algorithm based on Decomposition) takes a different route by decomposing the multi-objective problem into a set of scalar subproblems, each optimized simultaneously. This method is particularly effective in complex planning scenarios, such as urban transportation design, where it can identify infrastructure investment strategies that optimize different weighted combinations of congestion reduction, environmental sustainability, and cost.

The strength of MOGAs lies in their ability to provide a diverse set of high-quality solutions, empowering decision-makers to evaluate trade-offs and select outcomes that align with specific preferences or constraints.

Hybridization with Local Search

Memetic algorithms represent a powerful hybridization of evolutionary computation and local optimization techniques, combining the global search capabilities of genetic algorithms with the precision of problem-specific refinement methods. This synergy enables more effective navigation of complex search spaces, often leading to superior performance compared to using either approach alone.

In practice, the genetic algorithm component explores the broader solution landscape, identifying diverse and potentially promising regions. Once candidate solutions are generated, local optimization techniques are applied to refine them, exploiting nearby optima with greater efficiency. For example, in protein structure prediction, a genetic algorithm might generate a variety of folding configurations, while energy minimization algorithms such as gradient descent or molecular dynamics refine each structure to reduce its potential energy. Similarly, in vehicle routing problems, the genetic algorithm can determine high-level route allocations and customer groupings, while local search heuristics—such as 2-opt or Lin-Kernighan—optimize the sequence of stops within each route.

A critical design consideration in memetic algorithms is the frequency and intensity of local search application. Applying local optimization to every individual in every generation can be computationally prohibitive, especially in large populations or complex domains. Conversely, applying it too infrequently may fail to capitalize on the benefits of local refinement. Adaptive strategies have proven effective in addressing this trade-off. These approaches selectively apply local search to individuals with high fitness or those showing significant potential for improvement, thereby focusing computational effort where it is most impactful.

By integrating exploration and exploitation in a complementary manner, memetic algorithms offer a flexible and robust framework for solving a wide range of real-world optimization problems.

Self-Adaptation and Parameter Control

Self-adaptive genetic algorithms enhance traditional evolutionary strategies by embedding control parameters—such as mutation rates, crossover types, and selection pressures—directly within the chromosomes. This approach allows the algorithm to evolve not only candidate solutions but also the mechanisms by which those solutions are generated and refined. By enabling the evolutionary process to opti-mize its own behaviour, self-adaptation significantly reduces the need for manual parameter tuning and increases responsiveness to changing problem conditions.

In practice, each chromosome may contain additional genes that specify its own operational settings. These control genes evolve alongside the solution genes, and configurations that lead to better performance tend to propagate through the popula-tion. For instance, in financial market prediction, where conditions fluctuate across different regimes, self-adaptive algorithms can evolve distinct parameter settings tailored to specific market dynamics. This allows the algorithm to automatically adjust its strategy in response to volatility, trends, or structural shifts.

Empirical research has shown that self-adaptive mechanisms often outperform manually tuned algorithms, particularly in non-stationary environments where optimal parameters vary throughout the search process. By continuously adapting both the solution and the search strategy, self-adaptive genetic algorithms offer a robust and flexible framework for tackling complex, dynamic optimization problems.

Basic Perceptions

Schema Theory and Building Blocks

Holland's schema theory provides a mathematical framework for understanding genetic algorithm behaviour. A schema represents a template specifying values for some chromosome positions while leaving others unspecified. For example, in binary encoding, the schema 1**0* describes all chromosomes with 1 in the first position, 0 in the fourth position, and any values in other positions.

The building block hypothesis suggests that genetic algorithms operate by identi-fying, preserving, and recombining short, low-order schemata (building blocks) asso-ciated with above-average fitness. Over generations, these beneficial building blocks combine to form increasingly fit solutions. In designing mechanical components, such building blocks might represent beneficial substructures like stress-distributing fillets or material-saving hollow sections that contribute to overall performance when appropriately combined.

While schema theory offers valuable insights, subsequent research has identified limitations in its predictive power for complex problems and advanced genetic oper-ations. Modern theoretical work increasingly incorporates concepts from statistical mechanics, dynamical systems, and computational complexity theory.

No Free Lunch Theorem and Problem Alignment

The No Free Lunch (NFL) theorem demonstrates that, averaged across all possible problems, all non-revisiting search algorithms perform identically. This fundamental result emphasizes that genetic algorithm effectiveness stems from alignment with problem structure rather than inherent superiority.

Successful genetic algorithm application requires matching chromosome encoding and genetic operations to the problem's fitness landscape characteristics. For instance, binary encoding with standard crossover works well for problems where solution quality depends on specific value combinations (epistasis), while permutation encoding with order-preserving operations suits sequencing problems.

Understanding a problem's decomposability, modularity, and fitness landscape ruggedness guides appropriate genetic algorithm configuration. This alignment explains why custom genetic operators often outperform standard implementations for specialized problem classes.

Problem Solving via Genetic Algorithms

The use of genetic algorithms (GAs) in problem-solving represents a distinct departure from traditional artificial intelligence and machine learning approaches. While conventional methods often rely on intelligent hypothesis generation guided by domain knowledge or structured learning algorithms, GAs operate through a process of evolutionary search, where candidate solutions are iteratively generated and evaluated based on criteria such as feasibility and optimality. In knowledge-based systems, learning is typically measured by the system's ability to incorporate test knowledge or constraints into the hypothesis generation process, often resulting in refined solutions through logical reasoning or structured adjustments. For example, a logic-based system might generalize an overly specific hypothesis by adding disjunctions, relying on its embedded understanding of logical structures. Similarly, neural networks use algorithms like backpropagation to adjust internal parameters based on error feedback, with intelligence embedded in the system's capacity to model and manipulate interconnected equations.

In contrast, genetic algorithms exhibit minimal intelligence in their generative mechanisms. The sophistication of a GA largely depends on the complexity of translating genotypes into phenotypes; the more intricate this mapping, the less the algorithm appears to "understand" the problem space. However, this simplicity allows GAs to maintain a high degree of representation independence. A single GA can manipulate bit-string genotypes that encode a wide variety of phenotypic structures, including logical formulas, neural networks, or probabilistic models. This flexibility enables GAs to function across diverse problem domains without being constrained by the representational biases that often limit traditional systems. Nevertheless, this independence comes at a cost: operations on genotypes do not inherently ensure improvements in phenotypes, and the lack of embedded domain knowledge can lead to inefficiencies.

Traditional knowledge-based systems often incorporate detailed information about how to construct effective solutions and may even include meta-knowledge about the rationale behind specific hypothesis modifications. This built-in bias helps avoid unproductive solution paths. In contrast, genetic algorithms typically lack such prescriptive guidance but compensate with a robust mechanism for evaluating what constitutes a good solution, enabling them to explore complex and poorly understood problem spaces where other methods may falter.

Bayesian Networks and Genetic Algorithms

A Bayesian network is a model used for reasoning under uncertainty. It is a widely recognized statistical method. The Bayesian approach is founded on Bayes' Rule, which itself is derived from the fundamental principles of probability calculus.

$$P(a, b) = P(a|b) * P(b)$$

In above equation, $P(a, b)$ is the joint probability of both events a and b occurring, $P(a|b)$ is the conditional probability of event a occurring given that event b occurred, and $P(b)$ is the probability of event b occurring. This derivation subsequently leads to Bayes' Rule.

$$P(b|a) = \frac{P(a|b) * P(b)}{P(a)}.$$

Bayes' rule not only facilitates systems that update probabilities as new evidence is obtained, but also forms the foundation for the inferential mechanisms in Bayesian belief networks.

A Bayesian belief network is a directed acyclic graph (DAG) that offers a compact representation or factorization of the joint probability distribution for a set of variables. Visually, a Bayesian network consists of nodes and directed edges connecting these nodes. Each node represents a variable that can exist in one of several finite states. The links or arrows between nodes indicate causal relationships. The absence of an edge between two nodes suggests conditional independence, meaning the probability distribution of a node can be determined by considering the distributions of its parent nodes. Consequently, the joint probability distribution for the entire network can be specified. This relationship is mathematically captured using the chain rule in the equation below.

$$p(x) = \prod_{i=1}^{n} p(x_i|\text{parents}(x_i))$$

In general terms, this equation suggests that the joint probability distribution for node x is the product of the probabilities of each component x_i of x, given the parents of x_i. Each node has a conditional probability table that defines the probability of the node being in a specific state, given any combination of parent states. When evidence is introduced for a node in the network, the fundamental rule of probability calculus and Bayes' rule can be used to propagate this evidence throughout the network, updating the relevant probability distributions. Evidence can be propagated from parents to children and vice versa, making this method highly effective for both prediction and diagnosis.

The Bayesian network framework offers a compact and efficient graphical representation of dependency relations among entities in a problem domain. Bayesian belief networks encode joint probability distribution functions and can serve as fitness functions in genetic algorithms. Individuals in the genetic algorithm's population represent instantiations or explanations within the belief network. Computing the most probable explanations (belief revision) is thus framed as a genetic algorithm search within the joint probability distribution space. Consequently, the best-fit individual in the genetic algorithm population is an estimate of the most probable explanation.

Fuzzy Logic

The fuzzy logic theory provides a mathematical method to apprehend the uncertainties related to the human cognitive process, for example, thinking and reasoning and it can also handle the issue of uncertainty and lexical imprecision.

Fuzzy logic offers a departure from traditional binary logic by introducing the concept of degrees of truth. Unlike classical logic, where statements are strictly true or false, fuzzy logic allows for partial membership in a set. This is particularly useful in dealing with real-world phenomena that are often imprecise and ambiguous.

The foundation of fuzzy logic lies in the concept of fuzzy sets, which were introduced by Lotfi A. Zadeh in the mid-1960s.

> **Definition** A classical set is a collection of objects in a given range with a sharp boundary. An object can either belong to the set or not belong to the set.
> The concept of belonging is important in set theory: it refers to the fact that an element is part of a set or not.

In classical set theory, an element either belongs to a set or it does not, with a clear boundary separating different sets and their elements. These boundaries are strict, and elements cannot be shared between sets. However, fuzzy sets operate under different principles. A fuzzy set is characterized by a membership function that assigns a degree of membership, ranging from 0 to 1, to each element in the universe of discourse. This degree of membership indicates the extent to which an element belongs to the set. For instance, consider the set of "tall" people. In classical logic, a person would either be considered tall or not tall. However, in fuzzy logic, a person's membership in the "tall" set can be gradual, reflecting the inherent vagueness of the term. Fuzzy logic extends the operations of classical set theory to fuzzy sets. The basic operations include union, intersection, and complement. However, these operations are redefined to accommodate the degrees of membership. For example, the intersection of two fuzzy sets is typically defined as the minimum of the membership degrees of the elements in the two sets, while the union is defined as the maximum. The complement of a fuzzy set is defined as one minus the membership degree.

Definition Fuzzy logic is a form of logic used to handle reasoning that is approximate rather than precise. Unlike traditional binary logic, where variables must be either true or false, fuzzy logic allows for values to range between 0 and 1, representing degrees of truth. This makes it particularly useful for dealing with uncertain or imprecise information.

Key concepts in fuzzy logic include:

- **Fuzzy Sets**: These are sets without a clear boundary, where elements have varying degrees of membership.
- **Membership Functions**: These functions define how each element in a fuzzy set is mapped to a degree of membership between 0 and 1.
- **Fuzzy Rules**: These are conditional statements that use fuzzy logic to describe relationships between variables.

Fuzzy logic is widely used in control systems, decision-making processes, and artificial intelligence applications where human-like reasoning is required.

Fuzzy logic distinguishes itself through the use of linguistic variables—terms expressed in natural or artificial language rather than numerical values. For instance, a variable like "temperature" might take on values such as "very cold," "mild," or "hot," each represented by a fuzzy set. This approach enables a more intuitive and human-like way of modelling knowledge, particularly in contexts where precision is either unavailable or unnecessary.

At its core, fuzzy logic supports approximate reasoning, allowing systems to operate effectively with imprecise or incomplete information. This is achieved through fuzzy rules, typically structured as "if-then" statements, where both the conditions and outcomes are defined by fuzzy sets. For example, a rule might state, "If the temperature is warm, then the fan speed is high." The reasoning process begins with fuzzification, where crisp input values are translated into degrees of membership within fuzzy sets. These inputs are then evaluated against the fuzzy rules using operators such as the minimum or product to determine the extent to which each rule applies. The results are aggregated into a single fuzzy output, which is subsequently defuzzified—commonly using methods like the centroid or mean of maxima—to yield a precise output value.

Fuzzy logic has found widespread application across various domains, including control systems, decision-making, pattern recognition, and data analysis. In control systems, it enables the regulation of complex processes characterized by uncertainty. In decision-making, it facilitates the modelling of preferences and the handling of ambiguity. In pattern recognition, fuzzy logic contributes to the development of adaptable classification algorithms, while in data analysis, it supports tasks such as clustering, feature selection, and data mining.

One of the principal strengths of fuzzy logic lies in its capacity to represent and manipulate linguistic information, offering a more natural and accessible means of encoding expert knowledge. This makes it particularly well-suited for real-world problems where uncertainty and vagueness are inherent. Nonetheless, designing effective fuzzy systems can be challenging, especially in selecting appropriate membership functions and rule sets. Additionally, computational demands may pose limitations in certain applications.

Despite these challenges, fuzzy logic remains a powerful tool for modelling and managing complexity and uncertainty. Its ability to integrate symbolic and numerical reasoning, along with its intuitive knowledge representation, ensures its continued relevance in the development of intelligent systems capable of navigating the nuanced realities of the real world.

Concepts of Fuzzy and Bi-valued Logic

If somebody asks you a question that "Are you below 25 years?" then you may answer with a specific and definite value "Yes" or "No." This information in machine can be represented as Boolean value 0/1 or "T"/"F." But suppose you are asked a question that "Are you old?"; your answer is relative. You may answer sometimes, "*definitely*," "*why not*," "*not that much*," etc. For instance, is "*certainly old*" is assigned value 1 and "*not old*" is to 0, then "*why not*" would be assigned value as 0.7 and "*not that much old*" has assignment 0.3.

Similarly, truthness of the statement "*1260 is a big number*" may take multiple values between 0 and 1 instead of the only two values 1/0 or yes/no. Bi-value logic is also referred as crisp logic and multi-value referred as fuzzy logic.

Fuzzy sets offer a chance for a member to possess flexible *belongingness* into the set, which is measured in a degree. That means member A is either belongs to a fuzzy set F or not. On other hand member A belongs to the fuzzy set F partially with truth value (degree) 0.6.

> **Definition** Consider a universe of discourse X and a fuzzy set A defined on X. The fuzzy set A is represented through a membership function μ_A, which assigns to each element x its degree of membership in A, denoted as $\mu_A(x)$.
>
> A fuzzy set A within universe X is mathematically described by its membership function:
>
> $\mu_A : X \rightarrow [0, 1]$
>
> This function serves an analogous role to the characteristic function used in crisp (classical) set theory.

X in the above definition is treated as universe of discourse. Universe of discourse is a set, with a reference to a context that contains all possible elements of the sets. It is obvious that all the elements possess the same properties.

Membership Function

A membership function in a fuzzy set is a mathematical function that defines the degree of membership of an element within that set. Unlike classical sets where an element either belongs or does not belong to a set (with membership values of 1 or 0, respectively), fuzzy sets allow for partial membership, with values ranging between 0 and 1.

- **Degree of Membership**: The membership function assigns a value between 0 and 1 to each element, indicating its degree of membership in the fuzzy set. A value of 0 means the element is not a member, while a value of 1 means it is a full member. Values between 0 and 1 indicate partial membership.
- **Types of Membership Functions**: Common types include triangular, trapezoidal, Gaussian, and sigmoid functions. Each type has its own shape and characteristics, suitable for different applications.
- **Representation**: Graphically, a membership function is often represented as a curve that maps each element to its membership value. For example, in a fuzzy set representing "tall people," the membership function might assign higher values to heights that are considered tall and lower values to shorter heights.

Example Consider a fuzzy set representing "warm temperatures." The membership function might look like this:
15 °C: 0 (not warm).
20 °C: 0.5 (partially warm).
25 °C: 1 (fully warm).
30 °C: 0.8 (still warm, but not as much as 25 °C).

Properties of Fuzzy Sets

The height of fuzzy set A, represented as $h(A)$, is defined as the supremum of all membership values:

$$h(A) = sup\{\mu_A(x)|x \in X\}$$

A fuzzy set is considered *normalized* when its height equals unity, that is:

$$h(A) = 1$$

The *support* of A comprises all elements from X that possess non-zero membership in A. Formally, the support is expressed as:

$$supp(A) = \{x \in X \,|\, \mu_A(x) > 0\}$$

This represents the collection of elements that belong to A to at least some degree.

The *core* of fuzzy set A, denoted as *core(A)*, consists of all elements that have full membership in A:

$$core(A) = \{x \in X \,|\, \mu_A(x) = 1\}$$

It follows directly from these definitions that:

$$core(A) \subseteq supp(A)$$

An *α-cut* of fuzzy set A is a crisp set containing all elements whose membership degree meets or exceeds the threshold α:

$$A_\alpha = \{x \in X \,|\, \mu_A(x) \geq \alpha\}$$

The α-cut operation transforms a fuzzy set into a classical set by applying a threshold to the membership function.

Fuzzification and Defuzzification

Fuzzification is the process of converting crisp, precise input values into fuzzy values based on predefined membership functions. This involves mapping real-world data to a fuzzy set, allowing the system to handle and reason with imprecise information.

Definition The process of transforming crisp input values into linguistic values is called "fuzzification." It has two major steps as follows:

1. *Identify Input Variables: Determine the crisp input values that need to be fuzzified.*
2. *Define Membership Functions: Create membership functions for each input variable, representing different fuzzy sets (e.g., "low," "medium," "high").*
3. *Calculate Membership Values: Use the membership functions to calculate the degree of membership for each input value in the corresponding fuzzy sets.*

Example For a temperature input of 22 °C, the fuzzification process might determine that it belongs to the fuzzy sets "cool" with a membership value of 0.3 and "warm" with a membership value of 0.7.

Defuzzification is the process of converting fuzzy output values back into crisp, precise values. This is necessary because real-world actions or decisions typically require specific, non-fuzzy values.

Steps in Defuzzification

1. *Aggregate Fuzzy Outputs*: *Combine the fuzzy output values from the fuzzy inference process.*
2. *Apply Defuzzification Method*: *Use a defuzzification method to convert the aggregated fuzzy output into a single crisp value.*

If the fuzzy output indicates that the temperature should be "slightly warm" with a membership value of 0.6 and "warm" with a membership value of 0.4, the defuzzification process might convert this into a specific temperature setting, such as 24 °C.

Fuzzy Clustering

Fuzzy clustering is a form of clustering analysis where each data point can belong to multiple clusters with varying degrees of membership, rather than being assigned to a single cluster. This approach allows for greater flexibility in data representation and is particularly useful in situations where boundaries between clusters are not well-defined. Unlike traditional clustering methods, which classify data points into distinct groups, fuzzy clustering assigns membership values to each data point, indicating the degree to which it belongs to each cluster. These membership values range between 0 and 1.

Fuzzy C-Means Algorithm
One of the most widely used fuzzy clustering algorithms is the Fuzzy C-Means (FCM) algorithm. The FCM algorithm aims to minimize the objective function, which is a measure of the total distance between data points and cluster centres, weighted by the membership values.

Steps of the FCM Algorithm

1. *Initialization:* Choose the number of clusters and initialize the cluster centres randomly.
2. *Membership Calculation:* Compute the membership values for each data point with respect to each cluster centre.
3. *Cluster Centre Update:* Update the cluster centres based on the weighted average of the data points.
4. *Iteration:* Repeat the membership calculation and cluster centre update steps until convergence.

The objective function J in the FCM algorithm is given by:

$$J = \Sigma_{i=1}^{N} \Sigma_{j=1}^{C} u_{i,j}^{m} \|x_i - c_j\|^2,$$

where:

- N is the number of data points,
- C is the number of clusters,
- u_{ij} is the membership value of data point x_i in cluster j,
- m is the fuzziness parameter (typically $m = 2$),
- x_i is the i-th data point,
- c_j is the centre of cluster j.

Fuzzy clustering's ability to assign partial membership values to data points provides a more flexible and nuanced approach to clustering.

The algorithm offers a "soft" approach to data clustering, allowing data points to belong to multiple clusters simultaneously with varying degrees of membership, unlike "hard" clustering methods like K-means where each point belongs to only one cluster. This flexibility is crucial for analysing real-world data where boundaries between groups are often ambiguous or overlapping. FCM provides a more nuanced understanding of data structures, is more robust to noise, and offers better interpretability through its membership values. Its applications span various fields, including image segmentation, pattern recognition, customer segmentation, and bioinformatics, where data naturally exhibits such fuzzy relationships.

Exercises

1. Explain the concept of backpropagation and its role in training neural networks.
2. Compare and contrast different activation functions like ReLU and sigmoid.
3. Explain the concept of fuzzy sets and membership functions.
4. Describe the key components of a fuzzy control system.

5. How does fuzzy logic differ from traditional Boolean logic?
6. Explain the basic principles of genetic algorithms, including selection, crossover, and mutation.
7. What are the advantages and disadvantages of genetic algorithms compared to other optimization techniques?
8. How can genetic algorithms be used to solve complex optimization problems?
9. How can neural networks and fuzzy logic be combined to create more powerful hybrid systems?
10. How can genetic algorithms be used to optimize fuzzy logic controllers or neural network architectures?
11. Implement a simple feedforward neural network to classify data from the Iris dataset.
12. Experiment with different hyperparameters (learning rate, number of layers, number of neurons) to optimize the performance of a neural network.
13. Design a fuzzy logic controller for a simple system, such as a temperature control system or a traffic light.
14. Implement different defuzzification methods (e.g., centroid, mean of maxima) and compare their performance.
15. Implement a genetic algorithm to solve a simple optimization problem, such as finding the maximum of a function.
16. Experiment with different selection, crossover, and mutation operators to see how they affect the performance of a genetic algorithm.
17. Use a genetic algorithm to optimize the membership functions and rule base of a fuzzy logic controller.
18. Train a neural network using a genetic algorithm to find the optimal set of weights.
19. Use a genetic algorithm to optimize the weights of a neural network.
20. Model a decision-making process using fuzzy logic, such as a medical diagnosis or a financial risk assessment.
21. (Project) You are expected to solve a practical problem using fuzzy logic. The problem can be an actual industrial application suggested by your instructor, but also interesting practical problems out of recent literature may be treated.
22. (Project) Develop a system that uses a combination of neural networks, fuzzy logic, and genetic algorithms for autonomous robot navigation.
23. (Project) Create an adaptive system that uses genetic algorithms to evolve its neural network or fuzzy logic components over time.
24. (Project) Develop a genetic algorithm to generate abstract art or music.
25. (Project) Create a fuzzy logic-based expert system for a specific domain, such as customer service or technical support.
26. (Project) Train an RNN to classify the sentiment of movie reviews (positive or negative).

Further Reading

Ackley DH, Hinton GE, Sejnowski TJ (1985) A learning algorithm for Boltzmann machines. Cogn Sci 9(1):147–169

Akerkar R, Sajja P (2010) Knowledge based systems. Jones & Bartlett Publisher, USA. ISBN 9780763776473

Goldberg DE (1989) Genetic algorithms in search, optimization, and machine learning. Addison-Wesley Professional

Hinton GE, Sejnowski TJ (1986) Learning and relearning in Boltzmann machines. In: Parallel distributed processing: explorations in the microstructure of cognition, vol 1, pp 282–317

Holland JH (1975) Adaptation in natural and artificial systems. The University of Michigan Press, Ann Arbor, Michigan

Holland JH (1992) Adaptation in natural and artificial systems: an introductory analysis with applications to biology, control, and artificial intelligence. MIT Press

Jong KD (2006) Evolutionary computation: a unified approach. MIT Press, Cambridge, MA

Klir GJ, Yuan B (1995) Fuzzy sets and fuzzy logic: theory and applications. Prentice Hall PTR

Mamdani EH (1974) Applications of fuzzy algorithm for control a simple dynamic plant. Proc IEEE 121(12):1585–1588

Mendal JM (2007) Type-2 fuzzy sets and systems: an overview. IEEE Comput Intell Mag 2:20–29

Mitchell M (1996) An introduction to genetic algorithms. MIT Press, Cambridge

Nielsen MA (2015) Neural networks and deep learning. Determination Press

Zadeh LA (1965) Fuzzy sets. Inf Control 8:338–353

Zadeh LA (1999) From computing with numbers to commuting with words-from manipulation of measurement to manipulation of perceptions. IEEE Trans Circuits Syst I Fundam Theory Appl 45:105–119

Chapter 4
Machine Learning: Building Intelligence from Patterns

Where there is data there is truth.
—George Zarkadakis

Introduction

The progression, from rigid algorithms to systems capable of remarkable autonomy, has reshaped our understanding of what machines can accomplish. The journey through machine learning, deep learning, and reinforcement learning chronicles not simply a series of technical innovations, but an intense shift in how we conceptualize the bond between computation and intelligence.

In the beginning there were algorithms—precise, deterministic instructions that solved well-defined problems. These early computational approaches excelled when problems could be explicitly encoded as logical or mathematical procedures. A sorting algorithm knew exactly how to order elements; a pathfinding algorithm could determine the shortest route through a graph. Yet these systems, however efficient within their domains, lingered limited by the explicit knowledge programmed into them. They could not adapt to new data, learn from experience, or handle the inherent ambiguity of real-world problems.

Machine learning emerged as a response to these limitations, offering a paradigm shift in how we approach computation. Rather than programming explicit rules, machine learning systems learn patterns from data, constructing statistical models that can generalize to new, unseen examples. This capability fundamentally changed what was computationally possible. Suddenly, problems that defied explicit algorithmic solutions—recognizing handwritten digits, detecting spam emails, predicting consumer preferences became tractable through statistical learning approaches.

The early machine learning landscape was dominated by methods that required careful feature engineering—the human-guided process of determining which aspects of the data were relevant for the task at hand. Linear regression, support vector machines, decision trees, and similar algorithms provided powerful tools, but their effectiveness depended heavily on how the raw data was transformed into

R. Akerkar, *Artificial Intelligence*, https://doi.org/10.1007/978-3-031-91084-5_4

meaningful features. This requirement created a bottleneck: human experts needed to identify relevant patterns before machines could learn from them.

Foundations of Machine Learning

Machine Learning: Defining the Field

Machine learning (ML) provides a sophisticated toolkit for transforming raw data into actionable intelligence. These algorithms learn underlying structures and patterns, revealing insights that traditional methods might overlook. This capability allows us to move beyond simple descriptions of past events toward predictive modelling and even prescriptive recommendations. The power lies in the machine's capacity to learn from vast datasets, adapting its understanding as new information becomes available.

Learning, in general, can be described as the process of acquiring knowledge through experience. From the moment we are born, we begin to learn new things. This process continues throughout our lives as we seek to gather more information and refine what we have already learned through our experiences and the information we collect from our environment.

Machine learning (ML) is one of the most fascinating technologies one can encounter. As the name suggests, it endows computers with a human-like ability: the capacity to learn. Machine learning is both a science and an art, involving the programming of computers to learn from data.

Definition A computer program is *learning* if its performance on a defined task improves as it gains more experience, based on a specific measurement.

Machine learning is essentially teaching computers to find their own shortcuts and solutions by observing patterns in data, rather than being explicitly told how to solve every problem. Today, machine learning is at work all around us. When we interact with banks, shop online, or use social media, machine learning algorithms come into play to make our experience efficient, smooth, and secure. Machine learning and the technology around it is developing rapidly, and we're just beginning to scratch the surface of its capabilities.

Machine Learning Pipeline: An Overview

A machine learning pipeline represents the end-to-end process of developing, deploying, and maintaining ML models. It encompasses everything from data collection and preprocessing to model training, evaluation, deployment, and monitoring. The systematic organization of these stages into a coherent workflow enables efficient development, reproducibility, and scalability of ML solutions.

Data Handling and Preparation

Data Collection and Ingestion

The foundation of any ML pipeline is data. This initial stage involves gathering relevant data from various sources such as databases, APIs, web scraping, sensors, or user interactions. The quality, quantity, and relevance of collected data significantly influence the performance of the resulting model.

Data ingestion mechanisms must be designed to handle different data formats, volumes, and velocities. For instance, some applications may require real-time streaming data, while others might work with periodic batch processes. Furthermore, considerations around data governance, privacy, and compliance must be addressed during this stage.

A robust data collection strategy should include documentation of data provenance, versioning, and quality assessment. This documentation serves as a crucial reference throughout the pipeline and supports reproducibility of results.

Data Representation

In machine learning, data is typically structured using a versatile data structure known as a *tensor*. A tensor generalizes the concepts of vectors and matrices to higher dimensions, making it a powerful tool for representing multidimensional data. Conceptually, tensors can be thought of as multidimensional arrays capable of storing and manipulating large datasets efficiently, which is essential for deep learning and other machine learning tasks.

- **Vectors**: A one-dimensional (1D) tensor, such as [0.14, 0.32, 0.04, 1.78] represents a sequence of elements with a size of 4.
- **Matrices**: A two-dimensional (2D) tensor, like [[1, 3], [2, 4], [5, 6], [7, 9]], has rows and columns. Its shape is defined as (4, 2), where the first axis has a size of 4 and the second axis has a size of 2.

- **Higher-Dimensional Tensors**: Extending beyond matrices, tensors can have three or more dimensions. Each dimension corresponds to an axis, and the shape of a tensor is described by a tuple indicating the size along each axis.

The elements within a tensor can belong to various data types such as integers, floating-point numbers, or even complex numbers. This flexibility allows tensors to represent diverse types of data.

Tensors are widely used to represent different forms of data in machine learning:

1. **Tabular Data**: A dataset with m samples and n features can be represented as a 2D tensor with the shape (m, n).
2. **Time Series or Sequential Data**: For m sequences with multiple time steps and features, a 3D tensor with the shape $(m, \text{timesteps}, \text{features})$ is used.
3. **Images**:

   - A single image is often represented as a 3D tensor with the shape (C, H, W), where C is the number of channels (e.g., RGB channels for colour images where $C = 3$), H is the height, and W is the width.
   - A batch of m images can be represented as a 4D tensor with the shape (m, C, H, W).

4. **Videos**: For video data consisting of m samples with F frames per video, each frame having height H, width W, and C channels, a 5D tensor with the shape (m, F, C, H, W) is used.

The shape of a tensor plays a crucial role in defining its structure and usage. The shape provides information about how many elements exist along each axis. For example:

- A vector with four elements has the shape (4).
- A 2D matrix with three rows and two columns has the shape $(3, 2)$.
- A batch of images might have the shape $(32, 3, 64, 64)$, indicating 32 RGB images each of size 64×64.

Tensors play a central role in modern machine learning by enabling efficient computation and compact representation of high-dimensional data. They serve as the primary data structures for neural networks, supporting complex operations such as matrix multiplication and gradient computation. This makes them particularly valuable in domains like computer vision, natural language processing, and time series analysis. Their adaptability to various shapes and data types allows for scalable model development across diverse applications.

In the context of machine learning, datasets are typically organized into three subsets: training, validation, and testing. These subsets are ideally drawn from the same statistical distribution and formatted consistently to ensure reliable model evaluation. The development of a machine learning model generally follows a three-phase process. During training, the model learns patterns from the training data, often through experimentation with different model architectures and hyperparameters.

The validation phase follows, where the model's performance is assessed on a separate dataset to fine-tune parameters and prevent overfitting. Finally, the testing phase evaluates the model on previously unseen data, providing an unbiased estimate of its real-world performance.

A persistent challenge in this process is the acquisition of sufficient labelled data, which is often costly and time-consuming. Consequently, efficient use of available data is crucial. A common practice involves splitting the dataset into 70% for training, 15% for validation, and 15% for testing. Ensuring that each subset is representative of the overall dataset enhances both the learning process and the model's ability to generalize to new data.

Data Exploration and Analysis

Once data has been collected, gaining a thorough understanding of its characteristics becomes a critical step in the analytical process. Exploratory data analysis (EDA) serves this purpose by employing statistical summaries, visualizations, and correlation assessments to uncover the underlying structure, patterns, and irregularities within the dataset. Through EDA, data scientists examine feature distributions, explore potential relationships among variables, and identify anomalies such as outliers or missing values. These insights guide key preprocessing decisions and inform feature engineering by highlighting attributes that may be most predictive of the target variable.

EDA is inherently iterative, often prompting refinements to the initial problem formulation or adjustments to the data collection strategy. For instance, discovering that certain variables exhibit minimal variation might lead to the acquisition of additional data or a reassessment of the model's objectives. This dynamic process ensures that subsequent modelling efforts are grounded in a comprehensive understanding of the data.

Data Preprocessing and Feature Engineering

Raw data is seldom ready for immediate use in machine learning applications. To ensure optimal model performance and address data quality issues, preprocessing is essential. This stage involves transforming the data into a structured and consistent format suitable for algorithmic processing.

A key component of preprocessing is data cleaning, which involves handling missing values, outliers, and inconsistencies. Techniques such as statistical imputation, outlier removal, and correction of erroneous entries using domain-specific rules are commonly employed. Following cleaning, data transformation adjusts the scale, distribution, or encoding of features. Methods like normalization, standardization, and logarithmic transformation can enhance model convergence, while categorical variables require appropriate encoding strategies, such as one-hot, label, or target encoding.

Feature engineering further refines the dataset by creating or modifying features to better capture underlying patterns. This may include generating polynomial terms, interaction variables, or temporal features, often guided by domain expertise. In cases of high-dimensional data, dimensionality reduction techniques such as principal component analysis (PCA) or t-SNE are used to retain essential information while improving computational efficiency and mitigating the curse of dimensionality.

The choices made during preprocessing have a profound impact on model effectiveness. As such, these steps should be carefully documented and integrated into the machine learning pipeline to ensure consistency across both training and inference stages.

Learning Algorithms

Algorithms are the engines that power machine learning. In general, five types of machine learning algorithms are used today: supervised learning, unsupervised learning, semi-supervised learning, self-supervised learning, and reinforcement learning. The difference between them is defined by how each learns about data to make predictions.

Supervised Machine Learning

Supervised machine learning algorithms are the most commonly used. Supervised learning models consist of "input" and "output" data pairs, where the output is labelled with the desired value. With this model, a data scientist acts as a guide and teaches the algorithm what conclusions it should make. Just as a child learns to identify fruits by memorizing them in a picture book, in supervised learning, the algorithm is trained by a dataset that is already labelled and has a predefined output.

By way of an algorithm, the system compiles all of this training data over time and begins to determine correlative similarities, differences, and other points of logic—until it can predict the answers all by itself. It is the equivalent of giving a child a set of problems with an answer key, then asking them to show their work and explain their logic. Supervised learning models are used in many of the applications we interact with every day, such as recommendation engines for products and traffic analysis apps like Waze, which predict the fastest route at different times of day.

Supervised learning is commonly used for risk assessment, image recognition, predictive analytics and fraud detection, and comprises several types of algorithms.

- **Regression algorithms**—predict output values by identifying linear relationships between real or continuous values (e.g., temperature, salary). Regression algorithms include linear regression, random forest and gradient boosting, as well as other subtypes.

- **Classification algorithms**—predict categorical output variables (e.g., "junk" or "not junk") by labelling pieces of input data. Classification algorithms include logistic regression, k-nearest neighbours and support vector machines (SVMs), among others.
- **Naïve Bayes classifiers**—enable classification tasks for large datasets. They're also part of a family of generative learning algorithms that model the input distribution of a given class or/category. Naïve Bayes algorithms include decision trees, which can actually accommodate both regression and classification algorithms.
- **Neural networks**—simulate the way the human brain works, with a huge number of linked processing nodes that can facilitate processes like natural language translation, image recognition, speech recognition, and image creation.
- **Random forest algorithms**—predict a value or category by combining the results from a number of decision trees.

Unsupervised Machine Learning

In unsupervised learning models, there is no answer key. The machine studies the input data—much of which is unlabelled and unstructured—and begins to identify patterns and correlations, using all the relevant, accessible data. That means, unsupervised machine learning uses a more independent approach, in which a computer learns to identify complex processes and patterns without a human providing close, constant guidance. Unsupervised machine learning involves training based on data that does not have labels or a specific, defined output.

To continue the childhood teaching analogy, unsupervised machine learning is akin to a child learning to identify flower by observing colours and patterns, rather than memorizing the names with a teacher's help. The child would look for similarities between images and separate them into groups, assigning each group its own new label. Examples of unsupervised machine learning algorithms include k-means clustering, principal and independent component analysis, and association rules.

The most common unsupervised learning method is cluster analysis, which uses clustering algorithms to categorize data points according to value similarity (as in customer segmentation or anomaly detection). Association algorithms allow data scientists to identify associations between data objects inside large databases, facilitating data visualization and dimensionality reduction.

- **K-means clustering**—assigns data points into K groups, where the data points closest to a given centroid are clustered under the same category and K represents clusters based on their size and level of granularity. K-means clustering is commonly used for market segmentation, document clustering, image segmentation, and image compression.
- **Hierarchical clustering**—describes a set of clustering techniques, including agglomerative clustering, where data points are initially isolated into groups and then merged iteratively based on similarity until one cluster remains—and divisive clustering, where a single data cluster is divided based on the differences between data points.

- **Probabilistic clustering**—helps solve density estimation or "soft" clustering problems by grouping data points based on the likelihood that they belong to a particular distribution.

Unsupervised ML models are often behind the "customers who bought this also bought…" types of recommendation systems.

Semi-Supervised Learning

Semi-supervised learning is the third of four machine learning models. In a perfect world, all data would be structured and labelled before being input into a system. But since that is obviously not feasible, semi-supervised learning becomes a workable solution when vast amounts of raw, unstructured data are present. This model consists of inputting small amounts of labelled data to augment unlabelled datasets. Essentially, the labelled data acts to give a running start to the system and can considerably improve learning speed and accuracy. A semi-supervised learning algorithm instructs the machine to analyse the labelled data for correlative properties that could be applied to the unlabelled data.

Self-Supervised Learning

Self-supervised learning (SSL) enables models to train themselves on unlabelled data, instead of requiring massive annotated and/or labelled datasets. SSL algorithms, also called predictive or pretext learning algorithms, learn one part of the input from another part, automatically generating labels and transforming unsupervised problems into supervised ones. These algorithms are especially useful for jobs like computer vision and NLP, where the volume of labelled training data needed to train models can be exceptionally large (sometimes prohibitively so).

Reinforcement Learning

Reinforcement learning is the machine learning model. In supervised learning, the machine is given the answer key and learns by finding correlations among all the correct outcomes. The reinforcement learning model does not include an answer key but, rather, inputs a set of allowable actions, rules, and potential end states. When the desired goal of the algorithm is fixed or binary, machines can learn by example. But in cases where the desired outcome is mutable, the system must learn by experience and reward. In reinforcement learning models, the "reward" is numerical and is programmed into the algorithm as something the system seeks to collect. Chapter 6 will provide an in-depth exploration of reinforcement learning.

Machine learning is comprised of different types of machine learning models, using various algorithmic techniques. Depending upon the nature of the data and the desired outcome, one of four learning models can be used: supervised, unsupervised, semi-supervised, or reinforcement. Within each of those models, one or more algorithmic techniques may be applied—relative to the datasets in use and the intended results. Machine learning algorithms are basically designed to classify things, find patterns, predict outcomes, and make informed decisions. Algorithms can be used one at a time or combined to achieve the best possible accuracy when complex and more unpredictable data is involved.

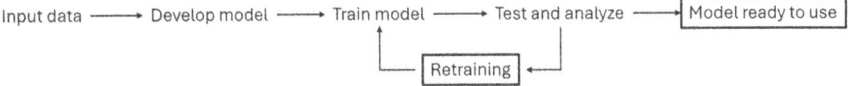

Fig. 4.1 Machine learning model creation

The quality of a *machine learning model*, as shown in Fig. 4.1, is dependent on two major aspects:

1. The quality of the input data. A common phrase around developing machine learning algorithms is "garbage in, garbage out." The saying means if you put in low quality or messy data then the output of your model will be largely inaccurate.
2. The model choice itself. In machine learning there are a plethora of algorithms that a data scientist can choose, all with their own specific uses. It is vital to choose the correct algorithm for each use case. Neural networks are an algorithm type with significant hype around it because of the high accuracy and versatility it can deliver. However, for low amounts of data choosing a simpler model will often perform better.

The better the machine learning model, the more accurately it can find features and patterns in data. That, in turn, implies the more precise its decisions and predictions will be.

Linear Regression

Prediction is often used for various types of analysis, which can be more accurately referred to as regression. Regression is a data mining function that forecasts numerical values such as profit, sales, mortgage rates, house values, square footage, temperature, or distance. For instance, a regression model can predict house values based on factors like location, number of rooms, and lot size.

A regression task starts with a dataset where the target values are known. For example, a regression model predicting house values can be developed using observed data from numerous houses over time. This data might include the house's age, square footage, number of rooms, taxes, school district, proximity to shopping centres, etc. The house value is the target, while the other attributes are predictors, and each house's data constitutes a case.

During the model-building (training) process, a regression algorithm estimates the target value based on the predictors for each case in the training data. These relationships are summarized in a model, which can then be applied to a different dataset where the target values are unknown.

Regression models are validated by calculating various statistics that measure the difference between predicted and expected values. Typically, historical data for a regression project is divided into two sets: one for building the model and the other for testing it.

Regression modelling has numerous applications, including trend analysis, business planning, marketing, financial forecasting, time series prediction, biomedical and drug response modelling, and environmental modelling.

Regression analysis aims to determine the parameter values for a function that best fits a set of data observations. The following equation represents these relationships symbolically.

It shows that regression is the process of estimating the value of a continuous target (y) as a function (F) of one or more predictors ($x_1, x_2, ..., x_n$), a set of parameters ($\theta_1, \theta_2, ..., \theta_n$), and a measure of error (e).

$$y = F(\times, \theta) + e.$$

The predictors are also known as independent variables, while the target is referred to as the dependent variable. The error, or residual, represents the difference between the actual and predicted values of the dependent variable. Regression parameters are also called regression coefficients. If the relationship between the predictors and the target can be represented by a straight line, a linear regression technique can be applied.

Supervised Learning: Classification

Training a classifier involves using algorithms to create a mathematical model that can distinguish between different categories of data based on the evidence provided in a dataset. This can be done in many ways, leading to the development of various types of classifiers with different characteristics. Some classifiers are designed to only differentiate between two categories (binary classifiers), while others can handle multiple categories (multi-class classifiers). However, the limitation of binary classifiers isn't a major problem since they can be adapted for multi-class classification.

Binary classification can also be thought of as a problem of identifying whether an instance belongs to a specific category (positive) or not (negative). If both positive and negative examples are available in the dataset, this is a straightforward perspective shift. However, if only positive examples are present, the task becomes describing the characteristics of that positive category.

Some classifiers can provide a score indicating their confidence in an instance belonging to a particular category, which can be useful in certain applications. Others produce classification decisions that are easily understandable by humans, while some give answers that are difficult to interpret. Another important feature is the ability of a classifier to learn incrementally, updating its model as new training data becomes available (online learning).

Classifier performance is evaluated based on three main aspects: the efficiency of the training process, the efficiency of the classification process, and the accuracy of the classification. Training and classification efficiency are measured by speed and memory usage, which are crucial in real-world applications. While end-users will be directly affected by slow classification and, in the case of online learning, slow training, research often focuses more on the accuracy of the classification.

The data used for classification is typically divided into a training set, used to build the classifier, and a test set, used to assess its performance. A common metric for evaluation in machine learning is accuracy, which is the percentage of correctly classified examples in the test set. Sometimes, a third dataset called a validation set is used during the training phase to fine-tune the classifier's parameters for optimal performance. It's important to keep the validation and test sets separate to avoid misleadingly high performance on the test set due to overfitting.

The ratio of training to test data can vary depending on the amount of data, the specific application, and other factors. Common splits include 2:1, 3:1, 4:1, and 9:1, and sometimes the test set can even be larger than the training set.

A simple split of the data into training and test sets can have drawbacks. Firstly, if the split is random, the distribution of classes in the original dataset might not be maintained in the resulting subsets. Since most classifiers rely on the class distribution during learning, this can negatively impact their performance. Stratification, which ensures that the class distribution is preserved across all subsets, is a solution to this problem.

Secondly, the specific examples that end up in each set after a split are arbitrary. There's no guarantee that a particular split will provide a reliable evaluation of the classifier. This issue is amplified when the amount of available data is limited, as excluding the test set from training can lead to a less effective classifier. Cross-validation, a technique from statistics, addresses this. It involves dividing the dataset into several subsets. One subset is used as the test set, and the others are combined to form the training set. This process is repeated multiple times, with each subset serving as the test set once, and the results are averaged. Each repetition is called a fold, and the entire process is n-fold cross-validation. Stratification can also be applied here, resulting in stratified n-fold cross-validation. To further ensure robustness, this entire cross-validation process can be repeated multiple times (k runs of n-fold cross-validation), making sure the subsets are sufficiently different in each run.

There are no strict rules for choosing the values of n and k in cross-validation. In machine learning, a common choice is 10 for both. However, for text-based applications, these values might be too high due to computational limitations. Similarly, leave-one-out cross-validation, where each example is used as the test set once, is generally avoided for text data. Many text categorization studies have relied on single train-test splits, while others have used techniques like 5 runs of four-fold cross-validation.

However, having a total of "nk" performance measurements allows for the use of statistical tests, typically a t-test, to compare the performance of two classifiers. This provides more reliable estimates of whether the observed performance differences are statistically meaningful. Additionally, when comparing multiple classifiers across several datasets, the number of times each classifier significantly outperforms or underperforms others can be counted. By subtracting the number of losses from the number of wins for each classifier, they can be ranked relative to each other based on their overall performance.

Table 4.1 Outcomes of binary classification

Predicted class			
Actual class		Yes	No
	Yes	True positive	True negative
	No	True positive	True negative

Evaluation Measures: While accuracy is often a useful measure for evaluating classifiers, it can be misleading, especially when dealing with imbalanced datasets. For instance, if in a binary classification problem, 95% of the examples belong to the negative class, a simple classifier that always predicts the negative class would achieve a 95% accuracy. However, this classifier would be completely useless if identifying the positive class is important. This kind of uneven class distribution is very common in text-based applications. Because of this imbalance, accuracy alone isn't a good evaluation metric, and it becomes necessary to adjust classifiers to properly consider the less frequent class to achieve satisfactory results.

To address this, evaluation measures commonly used in Information Retrieval (IR) are often applied to text classifiers. In IR, the focus is on how relevant the retrieved documents are to a user's query. We can think of "relevant" documents as those belonging to the positive class. Precision, in this context, is defined as the proportion of retrieved documents that are actually relevant (i.e., the number of documents correctly classified as positive) out of all the documents that were retrieved (i.e., the number of documents classified as positive). In terms of outcomes of binary classification summarized in Table 4.1, it is calculated as

$$\text{precision} = \frac{TP}{TP + FP}.$$

Similarly, recall is the ratio between the number of relevant documents retrieved, and the total number of relevant documents:

$$\text{recall} = \frac{TP}{TP + FN}.$$

For comparison, accuracy is

$$\text{accuracy} = \frac{TP + TN}{TP + TN + FP + FN}.$$

Despite having a slight difference in their calculation, precision and recall represent contrasting aspects of a classifier's performance. Precision tells us how accurate the classifier is when it predicts a positive instance, essentially highlighting the errors it makes in its positive predictions. On the other hand, recall measures the classifier's ability to identify all the actual positive instances, regardless of any incorrect positive predictions it might make. For example, a classifier that predicts every instance as positive (a "trivial acceptor") would have a perfect recall of 100% but very low precision. Conversely, a classifier that makes only one positive prediction, and it happens to be correct, would have 100% precision but very low recall. Because of these limitations when used individually, precision and recall are often combined into a single metric called the F-measure:

$$F_\beta = \frac{(\beta^2 + 1).\text{precision}.\text{recall}}{\beta^2.\text{precision} + \text{recall}}.$$

When $\beta = 1$, F-measure represents the harmonic mean of precision and recall, taking both of them equally into account. For $\beta < 1$ precision is given more importance, ending with $F0 = \text{precision}$, while $\beta > 1$ means recall gets the upper hand, with the other extreme at $F\infty = \text{recall}$.

Classifiers can often be adjusted during their training to emphasize either precision or recall. The point at which the average precision and recall values become equal for a given test set is known as the breakeven point (BEP), and this point can also serve as a metric to evaluate the classifier's performance.

When dealing with multi-class classification problems, the concepts of precision and recall can be applied to each individual class separately. If we represent the classification results for a specific class "i" (out of a total of "n" classes) using true positives (TP_i), true negatives (TN_i), false positives (FP_i), and false negatives (FN_i), then we can calculate precision and recall specifically for that class (precision i and recall i).

To get an overall measure of precision and recall across all classes in a multi-class setting, two common methods are used: micro-averaging and macro-averaging. Micro-averaged precision and recall are calculated by first summing up the total number of true positives, true negatives, false positives, and false negatives across all the classes. Then, these overall sums are used to compute a single micro-averaged precision and a single micro-averaged recall.

$$\text{precision}^m = \frac{\sum_{i=1}^{n} TP_i}{\sum_i (TP_i + FP_i)}$$

$$\text{recall}^m = \frac{\sum_{i=1}^{n} TP_i}{\sum_i (TP_i + FN_i)},$$

while macro-averaging involves averaging of precision and recall calculated for each individual class:

$$\text{precision}^M = \frac{\sum_{i=1}^{n} \text{precision}_i}{n}$$

$$\text{recall}^M = \frac{\sum_{i=1}^{n} \text{recall}_i}{n}.$$

Decision Trees

A decision tree (DT) is a classification model that takes the form of a tree structure. In this tree, each internal node represents a specific feature or attribute of the data being classified. The branches (arcs) extending from these internal nodes are labelled with the possible outcomes of testing the value of that feature. Finally, the leaves of the tree represent the different categories or classes that the data can be assigned to. The user mentions an example where a decision tree has been built using a weather dataset (shown in Table 4.2 Weather data and Fig. 4.2 decision tree generated from the weather data), illustrating how the tree structure can represent classification rules based on weather features.

To classify a new data point using a decision tree, you begin at the topmost node (the root). You then navigate down the tree by following the branches that correspond to the outcomes of evaluating the features of the data point at each internal node. This process continues until you reach a leaf node, which provides the predicted class label for the new instance.

One widely used algorithm for learning decision trees is C4.5, developed by Quinlan. An enhanced, commercial version called C5.0 also exists, which focuses on generating better classification rules. The process of learning a decision tree with C4.5 involves selecting the most informative feature using a combination of information gain and gain ratio criteria. Once the best feature is chosen, the algorithm determines the optimal way to split its values into different branches or tests. This process is then repeated recursively for each branch, considering only the remaining features that haven't already been used in higher nodes. The recursion stops when the tree perfectly classifies all the training data or when all available features have been used. The decision tree shown in Fig. 4.2 was created using the C4.5 algorithm.

Table 4.2 Weather data

Id#	Outlook	Temperature	Humidity	Windy	Play
1	Sunny	Hot	High	False	No
2	Sunny	Hot	High	True	No
3	Overcast	Hot	High	False	Yes
4	Rainy	Mild	High	False	Yes
5	Rainy	Cool	Normal	False	Yes
6	Rainy	Cool	Normal	True	No
7	Overcast	Cool	Normal	True	Yes
8	Sunny	Mild	High	False	No
9	Sunny	Cool	Normal	False	Yes
10	Rainy	Mild	Normal	False	Yes
11	Sunny	Mild	Normal	True	Yes
12	Overcast	Mild	High	True	Yes
13	Overcast	Hot	Normal	False	Yes
14	Rainy	Mild	High	True	No

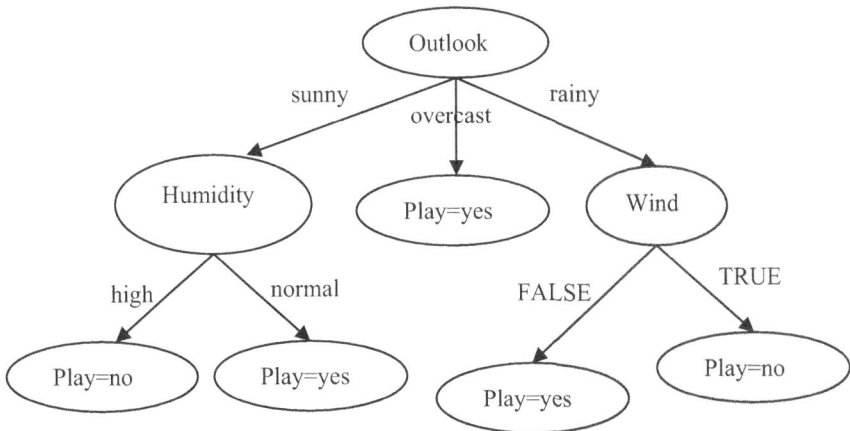

Fig. 4.2 Decision tree generated from the weather data

To prevent the learned tree from overfitting the training data (i.e., becoming too specific to the training examples and performing poorly on new, unseen data), a technique called pruning can be applied. Pruning aims to simplify the tree, potentially reducing its accuracy on the training data but improving its ability to generalize to new data. In C4.5, pruning is done by first converting the learned tree into a set of equivalent rules, where each path from the root to a leaf becomes a rule. Then, the algorithm estimates the general accuracy of each rule and tries to improve it by removing some of the conditions (tests) in the rule. Finally, these rules are sorted based on their estimated accuracy and used in this ordered form for classifying new instances.

Decision trees and the rules derived from them are particularly valuable when it's important for humans to understand how the classifier makes its decisions, providing insights into the underlying patterns in the data. However, for text classification, decision trees might not be suitable for many applications because they often struggle to handle the very large number of features that are typically present in text data. Nevertheless, in some cases, especially when a few features are significantly more important than others in distinguishing between categories, decision trees can surprisingly outperform other methods.

Support Vector Machines

One of the most powerful and effective classifiers, particularly for text, is the support vector machine (SVM). It operates as a binary classifier. The fundamental idea behind SVM is to use a specific function called a kernel. This kernel function transforms the original feature space into another space, typically with more dimensions, with the goal of making the data points from different classes linearly separable in this new space. Once the data is transformed, mathematical optimization techniques called quadratic programming are used to find a hyperplane that creates the largest possible margin between the two classes. This optimal linear separation in the transformed

Fig. 4.3 Maximum margin
hyperplane determined by
the SVM, which separates
the two classes, with
highlighted support vectors

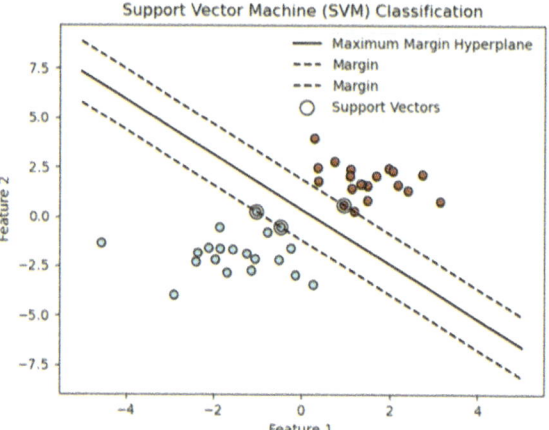

space, when mapped back to the original feature space, results in a highly effective classifier. Figure 4.3 visually represents this separating hyperplane in a two-dimensional transformed space, distinguishing between positive and negative classes. This hyperplane, which is a line in this 2D example, is positioned in the middle of the widest region that separates the two classes and is defined only by the data points that lie closest to this boundary. These crucial data points are known as support vectors.

While the underlying theory of support vector machines was developed by Vapnik in the 1970s, their practical application was initially limited by the significant computational resources required to solve the quadratic programming problem involved in finding the optimal hyperplane. It was only relatively recently that efficient approximate solutions were developed, making SVM training feasible and even faster than some other classification methods.

Support vector machines are very effective at handling data with a very large number of features (high dimensionality) and are also quite resistant to overfitting, meaning they tend to generalize well to new, unseen data. These characteristics make them exceptionally well-suited for text classification tasks, often eliminating the need for techniques to reduce the number of features. There is a strong general agreement within the field that SVMs are currently among the most powerful text classification techniques available.

Nearest Neighbour Classifiers

Nearest neighbour classification represents one of the simplest yet effective approaches in machine learning. Unlike algorithms that build complex models during training, nearest neighbour methods take a more direct approach to classification.

The training process for nearest neighbour (also called instance-based or memory-based) classifiers is remarkably straightforward—it simply involves storing all training examples in an appropriate data structure for later retrieval. This contrasts sharply with other classification algorithms that create abstract models during training. What makes nearest neighbour unique is that it postpones most computational work until classification time. When a new example needs classification, the algorithm identifies the k training examples most similar to the new instance—these are its "k-nearest neighbours." The class of the new example is then determined based on these neighbours.

For example, imagine we have a dataset of emails labelled as either "spam" or "not spam." If we use $k = 3$ and receive a new email, the algorithm will find the three most similar emails from our training data. If two of those emails were labelled "spam" and one "not spam," the new email would be classified as "spam" based on majority voting.

The basic approach simply counts the majority class among neighbours, but more sophisticated implementations use distance weighting. With distance weighting, neighbours physically closer to the target example have greater influence on the classification decision. In our email example, if the single "not spam" neighbour was much closer to our new email than the two "spam" neighbours, a distance-weighted approach might still classify the new email as "not spam."

Selecting the appropriate value for k is context-dependent—there's no universal best number. With $k = 1$, classification is based solely on the single closest example, which might be sensitive to noise. With larger k values, the algorithm considers more neighbours but may blur the boundaries between classes. For our email example, a very small dataset might work best with $k = 3$, while a larger dataset might benefit from $k = 15$ or higher.

The similarity between examples is typically calculated using the cosine of the angle between their vector representations, especially in text applications. However, more sophisticated representations and similarity functions move the approach toward case-based reasoning, which can handle more complex relationships.

A significant challenge when applying k-nearest neighbour (kNN) to text classification is dealing with the enormous volume of textual data. Text datasets can contain millions of documents with thousands of unique words, creating memory consumption issues and slowing down the neighbour retrieval process substantially.

For instance, classifying news articles into categories with kNN would require storing potentially thousands of full article representations, then comparing a new article against all of them—a computationally expensive process.

Yang pioneered early application of kNN to text classification by creating a three-layer network structure: one layer for words, one for documents, and one for categories. This organization improved efficiency over naive implementations.

An alternative approach focuses on selective instance storage. Rather than keeping all training examples, this method retains only those instances proven during training to significantly impact classification decisions. For example, in our email classification system, we might discover through analysis that only about 20% of our training emails influence the classification boundaries between spam and legitimate emails. By storing only these influential examples, we can dramatically reduce memory requirements and speed up classification.

These approaches have made kNN a viable option for text classification despite its inherent challenges with high-dimensional data.

Ensemble Learning: Random Forests and Boosting
Ensemble learning methods combine multiple learning algorithms to obtain better predictive performance than could be achieved from any of the constituent models alone. Now let us explore two prominent ensemble techniques, namely random forest (a bagging algorithm) and boosting.

- **Random Forest**: This is an ensemble learning method that uses multiple decision trees to improve the accuracy and stability of predictions. It operates by creating multiple decision trees during training and outputting the mode of the classes (classification) or mean prediction (regression) of the individual trees. It is a type of bagging algorithm, which stands for "bootstrap aggregating."
- **Boosting Algorithms**: These algorithms also belong to the ensemble learning category but work differently from bagging. Boosting involves sequentially training weak models (often decision trees) and adjusting their weights based on the errors of previous models. Popular boosting algorithms include AdaBoost, gradient boosting, and XGBoost.

Both methods are used to improve predictive performance by combining multiple models, and they require labelled data for training, which is a characteristic of supervised learning.

Random Forests: Harnessing the Wisdom of Crowds
Random forests exemplify the philosophy that combining many diverse, moderately accurate models often yields superior results compared to a single, highly tuned model. Random forests build upon the concept of bagging (bootstrap aggregating) by introducing additional randomness in the model-building process. While bagging creates diversity through resampling the training data, random forests go further by also restricting the features considered at each splitting point in the constituent decision trees.

To understand random forests, we must first grasp the bagging framework that underlies them. Bagging addresses a fundamental challenge in machine learning: the trade-off between model complexity and generalization. While a single complex model might perfectly fit the training data, it often performs poorly on unseen data due to overfitting. Bagging mitigates this issue by training multiple models on different subsets of the training data.

In bagging, we create multiple bootstrap samples from the original training data by randomly sampling with replacement. This means some observations may appear multiple times in a bootstrap sample, while others may not appear at all. For each bootstrap sample, we train a separate model, typically a decision tree grown to its maximum depth without pruning. When making predictions, the outputs from all models are combined—through averaging for regression problems or majority voting for classification problems.

The power of bagging comes from two sources. First, by training each model on a different subset of the data, we introduce diversity among the models. Second, by aggregating their predictions, we reduce the variance without significantly increasing bias. This is particularly effective for high-variance, low-bias models like deep decision trees, which tend to overfit when trained on a single dataset.

Random forests extend the bagging concept by introducing an additional layer of randomness. In standard decision trees, the best feature is selected from all available features at each splitting point. In contrast, random forests restrict this choice to a random subset of features. Typically, for a dataset with p features, only a random sample of approximately $\sqrt{p}$ features are considered for each split.

This feature randomization serves two purposes. First, it further increases the diversity among the trees in the forest, as different trees may use different features for splitting at similar points. Second, it prevents strong features from dominating the splitting process, allowing weaker but still informative features to contribute to the model.

In a random forest, the final prediction emerges from the collective decisions of all trees in the forest. For regression problems, predictions are typically averaged across all trees. For classification, each tree "votes" for a class, and the class with the most votes becomes the forest's prediction.

This democratic approach to decision-making often yields more robust and accurate predictions than a single model. By aggregating across many trees, random forests smooth out the idiosyncrasies and potential errors of individual trees, leading to more stable and reliable predictions.

Example Consider a healthcare application: predicting whether a patient will be readmitted to the hospital within 30 days of discharge. This prediction involves numerous factors: patient demographics, medical history, current diagnoses, medications, lab results, and social factors. A random forest can effectively navigate this complex feature space, handling the mix of categorical and numerical variables, managing missing data, and addressing the potential correlations between features.

In this application, the random forest might reveal unexpected insights. For instance, while clinical factors like diagnosis and medication are important, social factors like living alone or distance from the hospital might emerge as equally significant predictors. The forest's ability to capture complex interactions might show that certain medications are strong readmission predictors only for patients above a specific age or with particular comorbidities.

Random forests offer several advantages that have contributed to their widespread adoption. They handle high-dimensional data effectively without requiring feature scaling, are robust to outliers and noise, provide built-in estimates of feature importance, and can be easily parallelized across multiple cores or machines.

Feature importance in random forests is typically measured by the mean decrease in impurity or the mean decrease in accuracy when a particular feature is excluded. These measures provide valuable insights into which features are most predictive, aiding in feature selection and model interpretation.

Random forests also offer a natural way to estimate the generalization error using out-of-bag (OOB) samples. Since each tree is trained on a bootstrap sample, roughly one-third of the observations are not used in training each tree. These OOB samples can serve as a validation set, providing an unbiased estimate of the test error without requiring a separate validation set.

Despite these strengths, random forests are not without limitations. They may struggle with highly unbalanced datasets, and their models can be large and difficult to interpret compared to a single decision tree. Additionally, while they handle high-dimensional data well, they may still suffer when the number of irrelevant features greatly exceeds the number of relevant ones.

Boosting: Sequential Learning for Enhanced Performance
Boosting represents a fundamentally different approach to ensemble learning compared to methods like random forests. While random forests construct multiple models independently and aggregate their predictions, boosting builds models sequentially, with each new model designed to correct the errors made by the ensemble of its predecessors. This iterative refinement mirrors human learning, where attention is directed toward areas of weakness to improve overall understanding.

The concept of boosting originated from a theoretical question posed by Leslie Valiant and Michael Kearns in 1988: whether a collection of weak learners—models that perform only slightly better than random guessing—could be combined to form a strong learner with high predictive accuracy. Robert Schapire answered this affirmatively in 1990, laying the foundation for practical boosting algorithms.

AdaBoost (Adaptive Boosting), introduced by Yoav Freund and Robert Schapire in 1996, was the first widely used implementation. It begins by assigning equal weights to all training instances. After each iteration, the weights of misclassified instances are increased, compelling subsequent models to focus on these harder cases. The final prediction is made through a weighted combination of all models, with more accurate learners contributing more to the final decision.

Gradient boosting, developed by Jerome Friedman in 1999, extended this idea by using gradient descent in function space. Instead of adjusting instance weights, it fits each new model to the residuals—the differences between actual and predicted values—of the current ensemble. This process is repeated iteratively, with each model trained to capture the remaining error, thereby reducing both bias and variance over time.

Modern implementations of gradient boosting, such as XGBoost, LightGBM, and CatBoost, have significantly enhanced the efficiency and effectiveness of this approach. XGBoost introduced regularization techniques, efficient handling of sparse data, and support for parallel computation. LightGBM, developed by Microsoft, employs innovations like Gradient-based One-Side Sampling (GOSS) and Exclusive Feature Bundling (EFB) to scale to large datasets. CatBoost, from Yandex, offers advanced handling of categorical variables and introduces ordered boosting to mitigate prediction shift.

These advancements have made boosting algorithms dominant in machine learning competitions and widely adopted in industry due to their high predictive accuracy. The sequential nature of boosting leads to models that specialize in correcting specific errors, often resulting in individual learners that appear unusual in isolation but contribute meaningfully to the ensemble. For example, in a customer churn prediction task, the initial model might capture general trends, while subsequent models focus on exceptions, such as long-term customers at risk due to recent behavioural changes.

However, this strength also introduces a vulnerability: boosting is more susceptible to overfitting, especially in the presence of noisy data, as later models may begin to fit noise rather than meaningful patterns. Careful tuning and regularization are therefore essential to harness the full potential of boosting while maintaining generalization.

Example In credit scoring, boosting algorithms can effectively predict the probability of default by learning from historical loan data. The sequential nature of boosting allows it to identify subtle patterns: the first few models might capture obvious factors like income and credit history, while later models might focus on more nuanced indicators, such as specific combinations of factors that indicate higher risk despite otherwise favourable profiles.

Since boosting sequentially reduces training error, it can eventually overfit the training data if not properly regulated. Several techniques help mitigate this risk:

1. **Shrinkage (Learning Rate)**: By scaling the contribution of each model by a small factor (the learning rate), we can make the learning process more conservative and less prone to overfitting.
2. **Early Stopping**: By monitoring performance on a validation set, we can stop the boosting process when validation error starts to increase, even if training error continues to decrease.
3. **Subsampling**: Using only a random subset of the training data for each iteration introduces randomness that can help prevent overfitting, similar to the approach in random forests.
4. **Tree Constraints**: Limiting the depth or complexity of the base models (often decision trees) can prevent individual models from capturing too much noise.

Random forests and boosting represent two distinct philosophical approaches to ensemble learning. Random forests embody a democratic, parallel approach, where diverse models independently contribute to a collective decision. Boosting, conversely, follows a sequential, corrective approach, where each model builds upon the accumulated knowledge of its predecessors.

These philosophical differences lead to practical distinctions in how the algorithms work and when they perform best. Random forests excel at reducing variance through model diversity, making them particularly effective for high-dimensional data where overfitting is a concern. Boosting excels at reducing both bias and variance through sequential learning, making it particularly effective for complex relationships where accuracy is paramount and computational resources are abundant.

The field of ensemble learning continues to evolve rapidly. Several promising directions include:

1. **Interpretable Boosting**: Research into more interpretable boosting algorithms aims to combine the predictive power of boosting with greater transparency and explainability.
2. **Automated Ensemble Construction**: Automated machine learning (AutoML) approaches increasingly incorporate intelligent ensemble construction, automatically selecting and combining the most appropriate models for a given dataset.
3. **Streaming and Online Learning**: Adaptations of both random forests and boosting for streaming data contexts allow models to update continuously as new data arrives, crucial for applications with evolving patterns.
4. **Distributed and Federated Learning**: Implementations optimized for distributed computing environments and federated learning scenarios allow these powerful ensemble methods to scale to ever-larger datasets while respecting privacy constraints.

Unsupervised Learning: Clustering

While classification focuses on building models by learning from labelled data, clustering aims to discover inherent patterns and structures within data without much or any prior knowledge. Although many clustering algorithms exist, fewer have been widely adopted in text analysis compared to classification. This is primarily because textual data often has a very high number of features, which can slow down less efficient clustering methods and also make it difficult to assess the quality of the resulting clusters, both for human experts and automated evaluation tools. Additionally, different clustering algorithms work better on different types of data distributions, so some are naturally more suited to text than others.

Clustering is a useful technique for uncovering how data is organized and identifying underlying patterns. Its main goal is to identify both dense and sparse areas within a dataset. It's considered a fundamental unsupervised learning problem, meaning it's about finding structure in a collection of data where no pre-assigned categories are given.

There are two main categories of clustering techniques: those that create a hierarchical structure of clusters and those that do not. Hierarchical clustering methods build a nested sequence of clusters, starting from small, specific clusters and progressively merging them into larger ones. The primary reason for creating this hierarchy is that, as clustering is an unsupervised process, there's no single "correct" number of clusters. Depending on the specific application, a user might want a finer-grained view with many clusters or a broader overview with just a few. A cluster hierarchy allows the user to choose the desired level of granularity. At one extreme, you could have as many clusters as data points, where each cluster contains only one item. While this would mean that items within a cluster are perfectly similar (as there's only one), it defeats the purpose of clustering, which is to find meaningful patterns that summarize the data and make it easier to understand. A good clustering should typically result in significantly fewer clusters than the original number of data points. The exact number of clusters to form is often a matter of interpretation. The advantage of hierarchical methods is that they offer the flexibility to choose from a wide range of cluster numbers.

The hierarchy of clusters is constructed by the algorithm itself. There are two main types of hierarchical clustering algorithms:

- **Agglomerative**: These methods start with each data point in its own cluster. Then, they iteratively merge the closest pairs of clusters until all data points are in a single, large cluster at the top of the hierarchy.
- **Divisive**: These methods take the opposite approach. They begin with all data points in one large cluster and then recursively split the cluster into smaller and smaller sub-clusters.

There are also two main types of non-hierarchical clustering techniques. These methods are generally very fast to compute but have certain limitations. The first type is *single-pass methods*. They are named this way because they only require one pass through the dataset to create the clusters, meaning each data point is read only once. The second type is called *reallocation methods*. These techniques work by iteratively moving or "reallocating" data points from one cluster to another to improve the overall quality of the clusters. While they do require multiple passes through the data, they are generally faster than hierarchical clustering methods.

K-Means Clustering

The basic *k*-means clustering algorithm is one of the oldest and simplest clustering algorithms to be applied to text, which may still produce good results. It involves randomly choosing *k* points to be the centroids of clusters, and grouping instances around centroids based on proximity. Then, centroids are iteratively recomputed for each cluster, and instances regrouped until there is sufficiently little change in centroid positions. This algorithm depends heavily on the choice of *k* (which may not be obvious at all for a particular application), and the initial positioning of centroids. Having *k*-means generate empty clusters is not a rare occurrence at all.

The *k*-means method of cluster detection is the most commonly used in practice. This algorithm has an input of predefined number of clusters, which is called *k*. "Means" stands for an average. the average location of all the members of a single cluster. Let us assume that the data is represented as a relational table, with each object representing an object and each column representing a column. The value of every attribute from the table of data we are analysing represents a distance from the origin along the attribute axes. Furthermore, to use this geometry, the values in the dataset must all be numeric. If they are categorical one, then they should be normalized in order to allow adequate results of the overall distances in a multi-attribute space. The

k-means algorithm is a straightforward iterative procedure, in which a vital notion is the one of centroid. A centroid is a point in the space of objects which represents an average position of a single cluster. The coordinates of this point are the averages of attribute values of all objects that belong to the cluster. The iterative process of redefining centroids and reassigning data objects to clusters needs a small number of iterations to converge. The simple stepwise description of k-means can be given as:

1. **Initialization**: The algorithm begins by selecting k initial centroids. This selection can be random or use various initialization strategies like k-means++ which selects initial centroids that are far apart from each other.
2. **Assignment Step**: Each data point is assigned to the nearest centroid, forming k clusters. The "nearest" is typically defined using Euclidean distance (straight-line distance in the feature space), though other distance metrics can be used.
3. **Update Step**: After all points are assigned, each centroid is recalculated as the mean (average) of all points assigned to its cluster.
4. **Iteration**: The assignment and update steps are repeated iteratively until the algorithm converges—meaning that either the centroids no longer move significantly or a maximum number of iterations is reached.

Now, let us discuss the partitioning technique in detail.

The purpose of clustering is to obtain subsets that are more genuine than the initial set. This means their elements are much more similar on average than the elements of the original domain. A partition $T_1, T_2, \ldots, T_k$ is represented by the centroids $z_1, z_2, \ldots, z_k$ such that

$$x \in T_i \Leftrightarrow \rho(x, z_i) \leq \rho(x, z_j), \quad i, j = 1, \ldots k.$$

One can see that even though no information about the classes has been used in this case the k-means algorithm is perfectly capable of finding the three main classes.

The centroids are used for estimates of an impurity measure of the form

$$J(z_1, z_2, \ldots, z_p) = \frac{1}{N} \sum_{i=1}^{k} \sum_{x^{(j)} \in T_i} \rho(x^{(j)}, z_i) = \frac{1}{N} \sum_{j=1}^{N} \min_{1 \leq i \leq k} \rho(x^{(j)}, z_i).$$

The algorithms for partitioning (i.e., k-means and k-medoid) vary in the manner that they estimate the centroids. In the k-means algorithm, the mean of the real-valued observations in the cluster T_i is calculated as:

$$z_i = \frac{1}{N_i} \sum_{x^{(j)} \in T_i} x^{(j)},$$

where N_i denotes the number of data points in T_i.

An interesting characteristic of the k-means algorithm is that it continuously tries to minimize a certain internal measure, often referred to as a function J. This function essentially quantifies how well the data points are clustered. During the algorithm's iterative process of reassigning data points and updating centroids, the value of J will never increase; instead, it will decrease every time a data point is moved between clusters. Since this function J cannot decrease indefinitely (it has a lower limit), the iterative process is guaranteed to eventually stabilize or converge. However, it's important to note that the k-means algorithm is proven to always converge to a local minimum, which means it might not always find the absolute best possible clustering solution across all possibilities. The algorithm can be given as,

Select k arbitrary data points $z_1, z_2, \ldots, z_k$.

repeat

$$T_i := \left\{ x^{(j)} \mid \rho\left(x^{(j)}, z_i\right) \leq \rho\left(x^{(j)}, z_s\right), \text{ where } s = 1, 2, \ldots, p \right\}$$

$$z_i := \frac{1}{|T_i|} \sum_{x^{(j)} \in T_i} x^{(j)}.$$

Until z_i do not change.

The k-means algorithm primarily involves two crucial steps: first, calculating the distances between all data points, and second, recalculating the centroids based on the current cluster assignments.

However, the k-means method has a couple of notable limitations. One is that the calculated centroid for a cluster might not actually correspond to any of the original data points. Another is that the standard k-means algorithm typically works best with data that can be represented as real-valued vectors (numerical data).

As an alternative to k-means, there's an algorithm called k-medoids. In k-medoids, instead of calculating a centroid as the average, the algorithm selects an actual data point from within each cluster to serve as its representative centre. This representative point, called the medoid, is chosen because it is the most centrally located data point within that cluster.

That is, $z_i = x^{(s_i)}$

such that

$$\sum_{x^{(j)} \in T_i} \rho\left(x^{(j)}, x^{(s_i)}\right) \leq \sum_{x^{(j)} \in T_i} \rho\left(x^{(j)}, x^{(m)}\right) \text{ for all } x^{(m)} \in T_i.$$

Instead of strictly assigning each data point to a single cluster (hard assignment), there's an approach where each cluster is represented by a feature vector, and when a new data point is encountered, it can have a partial or probabilistic membership to multiple clusters based on its similarity to each cluster's representation (soft or fuzzy assignment). This allows for more flexible cluster representations than just using centroids and can better capture certain data structures.

A technique closely related to this "soft" version of k-means is the Self-Organizing Map (SOM), which has its roots in the field of neural networks. While k-means aims to find relationships between data points in their original feature space, SOMs take a different approach by projecting the data down onto a typically two-dimensional grid of interconnected nodes. When a data point is presented to the SOM, it activates the node on the grid that is most similar to it. This activation then spreads to neighbouring nodes on the grid in a way that is reminiscent of how neural networks function.

Difference Between Clustering and Nearest Neighbour Prediction

The key difference between clustering and nearest neighbour techniques lies in their respective learning paradigms and objectives. Clustering is an unsupervised learning method that identifies natural groupings within data without reference to predefined labels or outcomes. It uncovers inherent structures based on similarity measures, organizing data points into clusters that reflect patterns present in the data itself. For instance, when analysing customer purchasing behaviour, clustering might reveal distinct consumer segments, but these groupings are not tied to any specific predictive task—they simply emerge from the data's internal structure.

In contrast, nearest neighbour techniques are typically employed in supervised learning contexts, where the goal is to make predictions based on labelled training data. These methods rely on the assumption that similar instances will have similar outcomes. For example, in predicting house prices, a nearest neighbour algorithm estimates the value of a new property by referencing the prices of similar, previously observed homes. Here, the patterns identified are directly linked to the target variable, and their relevance is defined by their predictive utility.

This distinction also influences how the two approaches are evaluated. Clustering is assessed based on the coherence within clusters and the separation between them, often using metrics like silhouette scores or intra-cluster variance. Nearest neighbour methods, on the other hand, are evaluated by their predictive accuracy against known outcomes. Moreover, while clustering may yield groupings that lack an intuitive explanation beyond mathematical similarity, nearest neighbour techniques provide interpretable predictions grounded in the proximity to labelled examples.

Probabilistic Clustering

In probabilistic clustering, the data is viewed as being generated from a mixture of "k" underlying probability distributions. This process is imagined occurring in two steps: first, one of the "k" distributions is chosen with a certain probability associated with it. Second, a data point is then randomly generated according to the characteristics of that chosen probability distribution. In this framework, each cluster corresponds to one of these probability distributions, and the data points belonging to a particular cluster are those that are likely to have been generated from that specific distribution. These points tend to group around the average value (mean) of that distribution, with the degree of spread or dispersion determined by the distribution's variance. The likelihood that a particular dataset is drawn from a particular mixture model of k distributions is given by

$$L(X \,|\, R) = \prod_i \sum_i p_j P(x_i | r_j),$$

for instances x_i and clusters r_j. One probabilistic method, the EM algorithm is based on alternatively estimating and maximizing the expected value of the loglikelihood function log $L(X|R)$.

Probabilistic clustering offers several significant advantages over traditional clustering methods:

First, probabilistic clustering enables building clusters using different datasets because the clusters are represented independently from the examples. This means that the cluster models are abstract statistical representations rather than being directly tied to specific data points. This separation allows for greater flexibility in how clusters are formed and updated. For instance, you could develop initial cluster models using customer data from one region, then apply and refine these models with data from another region without starting from scratch.

Second, probabilistic clustering supports examining examples iteratively through an online approach. Unlike batch clustering methods that require processing all data simultaneously, probabilistic clustering can update cluster models incrementally as new data arrives. This is particularly valuable in dynamic environments where data streams continuously. For example, in a recommendation system, probabilistic clustering could continuously refine user segments as new interaction data becomes available, without needing to reprocess the entire historical dataset.

Third, probabilistic clustering generates results that are easier to interpret. Since clusters are represented as probability distributions over features, they provide natural measures of uncertainty and overlapping memberships. This probabilistic framework allows analysts to understand not just which cluster an example belongs to, but also the degree of certainty in that assignment. For instance, in medical diagnostics, a probabilistic clustering of symptoms might show that a patient has a 70% probability of belonging to one condition cluster and 30% to another, providing doctors with a more nuanced understanding than strict categorization.

These advantages make probabilistic clustering particularly valuable in applications where data arrives continuously, interpretability is important, and flexibility in model development and application is required.

Hidden Markov Models

The Hidden Markov Model (HMM) is an important framework in machine learning, particularly influential in language and speech processing. To understand HMMs, it is helpful to begin with the concept of a Markov chain, also known as an observed Markov model. A Markov chain is a type of weighted automaton in which the sequence of inputs fully determines the sequence of states the system transitions through. This deterministic structure allows Markov chains to assign probabilities to sequences of directly observable events, making them effective for modelling processes where all relevant information is visible.

However, many real-world scenarios involve hidden or unobservable elements. HMMs address this limitation by enabling inference about hidden states based on observable evidence. For example, in part-of-speech tagging, the words in a sentence are directly observable, but their grammatical roles—such as noun, verb, or adjective—are not. These roles represent the hidden states that the model seeks to infer from the sequence of observed words.

An HMM consists of a finite set of states, each associated with a probability distribution that governs the likelihood of emitting a particular observable output. Transitions between states occur according to defined probabilities, forming a stochastic process. While the internal state sequence is hidden from the observer, the model generates observable outputs (emissions) based on the current state. The challenge, and the power, of HMMs lies in using these emissions to infer the most probable sequence of hidden states, enabling applications such as speech recognition, handwriting analysis, and bioinformatics.

Example To illustrate this concept, imagine tracking a person's daily activities based only on their social media posts. The posts (observations) are visible to you, but the actual activities (states) remain hidden.

The hidden states might include: "Working," "exercising," "socializing," and "resting." Each state has distinct probabilities of generating certain types of posts (emissions). For instance:

- "Working" might have high probability of generating posts about coffee, deadlines, or meetings
- "Exercising" likely generates posts about workouts, steps taken, or feeling energized
- "Socializing" tends to produce posts with photos of friends, check-ins at restaurants, etc.
- "Resting" might generate fewer posts overall, with content about movies or books.

Additionally, certain state transitions are more likely than others. Someone in the "working" state is more likely to transition to "socializing" in the evening than in the morning, and unlikely to transition directly to "exercising" without a break in between.

By analysing the sequence of posts (observations), an HMM can infer the most probable sequence of activities (hidden states) the person engaged in throughout the day, even though we never directly observed these activities. This ability to infer hidden processes from observable data makes HMMs powerful tools for numerous applications beyond language processing, including bioinformatics, finance, and behaviour modelling.

In order to define a Hidden Markov Model (HMM) completely, the following elements are needed.

The number of states of the model, N.

The number of observation symbols in the alphabet, M. If the observations are continuous then M is infinite.

A set of state transition probabilities $\Lambda = \{a_{ij}\}$

$$a_{ij} = p\{q_{t+1} = j | q_t = i\}, \quad 1 \leq i, j \leq N,$$

where q_t denotes the current state.

Transition probabilities should satisfy the normal stochastic constraints,

$$a_{ij} \geq 0, \quad 1 \leq i, j \leq N$$

$$\sum_{j=1}^{N} a_{ij} = 1, \quad 1 \leq i \leq N.$$

A probability distribution for the alphabets in each of the states, $B = \{b_j(k)\}$.

$$b_j(k) = p\{a_t = v_k | q_t = j\}, \quad 1 \leq j \leq N, \quad 1 \leq k \leq M,$$

where v_k denotes the kth observation symbol in the alphabet, and o_t the current parameter vector.

Following stochastic constraints must be satisfied.

$$b_j(k) \geq 0, \quad 1 \leq j \leq N, \quad 1 \leq k \leq M$$

and

$$\sum_{k=1}^{M} b_j(k) = 1, \quad 1 \leq j \leq N.$$

If the observations are continuous then we will have to use a continuous probability density function, instead of a set of discrete probabilities.

The initial state distribution, $\pi = \{\pi_i\}$.

where,

$$\pi_i = p\{q_1 = i\}, \quad 1 \leq i \leq N.$$

Therefore, we can use the compact notation $\lambda = (\Lambda, B, \pi)$ to denote an HMM with discrete probability distributions.

Bayesian Methods

The probabilistic approaches for data modelling have given rise to several powerful machine learning techniques particularly well-suited for text analysis. Two notable examples stand out: the straightforward yet remarkably effective Naïve Bayes classifier and the more sophisticated Bayesian Networks.

Bayes Theorem

Let X be the data record (case) whose class label is unknown. Let H be some hypothesis, such as "data record X belongs to a specified class C." For classification, we want to determine $P(H|X)$—the probability that the hypothesis H holds, given the observed data record X.

$P(H|X)$ is the posterior probability of H conditioned on X. For example, the probability that a fruit is an apple, given the condition that it is red and round. In contrast, $P(H)$ is the prior probability, or *apriori* probability, of H. In this example $P(H)$ is the probability that any given data record is an apple, regardless of how the data record looks. The posterior probability, $P(H|X)$, is based on more information (such as background knowledge) than the prior probability, $P(H)$, which is independent of X.

Similarly, $P(X|H)$ is posterior probability of X conditioned on H. That is, it is the probability that X is red and round given that we know that it is true that X is an apple. $P(X)$ is the prior probability of X, i.e., it is the probability that a data record from our set of fruits is red and round. Bayes theorem is useful in that it provides a way of calculating the posterior probability, $P(H|X)$, from $P(H)$, $P(X)$, and $P(X|H)$. Bayes theorem is

$$P(H|X) = \frac{P(X|H)P(H)}{P(X)}.$$

Naïve Bayes

The Naïve Bayes classifier represents one of the simplest probabilistic approaches, yet it delivers surprisingly good results across many text classification tasks. Its effectiveness stems from applying Bayes' theorem with a "naïve" independence assumption between features.

In text classification, Naïve Bayes treats each word as an independent feature and calculates the probability of a document belonging to a particular class based on the words it contains. Despite the obvious oversimplification (words in natural language are clearly not independent), this approach works remarkably well in practice.

For example, in email spam filtering, a Naïve Bayes classifier might learn that words like "free," "offer," and "investment" have high probabilities of appearing in spam emails. When a new email arrives containing several of these words, the classifier calculates the probability of the email being spam versus legitimate, based on the previously observed frequencies of these words in each category.

The Naïve Bayes model is a commonly applied method of text classification which has been used for years in the field of information retrieval. To see how the model works, let us assume that a given narrative consists of a vector of j words, $n = \{n_1, n_2, \dots n_j\}$. Also, assume that i possible event codes can be assigned resulting in a second vector $E = \{E_1, E_2, \dots E_i\}$. By making what is called the conditional independence assumption, the probability of assigning a particular event code category can then be calculated using the expression:

$$P(E_i|n) = \prod_j \frac{P(n_j|E_i)P(E_i)}{P(n_j)},$$

where $P(E_i|n)$ is the probability of event code category E_i given the set of n words in the narrative. $P(n_j|E_i)$ is the probability of word n_j given category E_i. $P(E_i)$ is the probability of category E_i and $P(n_j)$ is the probability of word n_j in the entire keyword list.

In application, $P(n_j|E_i)$, $P(E_i)$, and $P(n_j)$ are all normally estimated on the basis of their frequency in a training set. Also, $P(n_j|E_i)$ is normally smoothed to reduce the effects of noise. The approach we implemented was to add a small constant to the number of times a particular word occurred in a category, as shown below:

$$P(n_j|E_i) = \frac{\text{count}(n_j|E_i) + \alpha \times \text{count}(n_j)}{\text{count}(E_i) + \alpha \times N},$$

where $\text{count}(n_j|E_i)$ is the number of times word n_j occurs in category E_i, $\text{count}(n_j)$ is the number of times word n_j occurs, $\text{count}(E_i)$ is the number of times category E_i occurs, N is the number of training narratives, and α is a smoothing constant. Larger values of α reduce the weight given to the evidence provided by each term. We chose to use a value of $\alpha = 0.05$, which corresponds to a small level of smoothing.

The conditional independence assumption is perhaps the most controversial aspect of the Naïve Bayes model. Informally, for the purposes of text classification, when this assumption holds, the probability of each index term (e.g., word or word sequence) being present depends on only the event code considered and is independent of the remaining terms in the narrative. The conditional independence assumption is almost always violated in practice. However, a long history of application shows that Naïve Bayes tends to work remarkably well even when this assumption is violated.

Bayesian Networks

Bayesian networks represent a more sophisticated probabilistic modelling approach. Unlike Naïve Bayes, they do not assume independence between features. Instead, they explicitly model relationships between variables using directed acyclic graphs (DAGs), where nodes represent variables and edges represent conditional dependencies.

For text analysis, Bayesian networks can capture complex relationships between words, topics, document structure, and classifications. This makes them more expressive and potentially more accurate than Naïve Bayes, particularly for complex language understanding tasks.

For instance, a Bayesian network for sentiment analysis might model relationships between certain adjectives, their modifiers, negation words, and overall sentiment. It could learn that "not very good" expresses mild negative sentiment despite containing the positive word "good," by modelling the relationship between "not," "very," and "good."

This increased expressiveness comes at a cost, however. Bayesian networks are more complex to design and implement, computationally more demanding, and

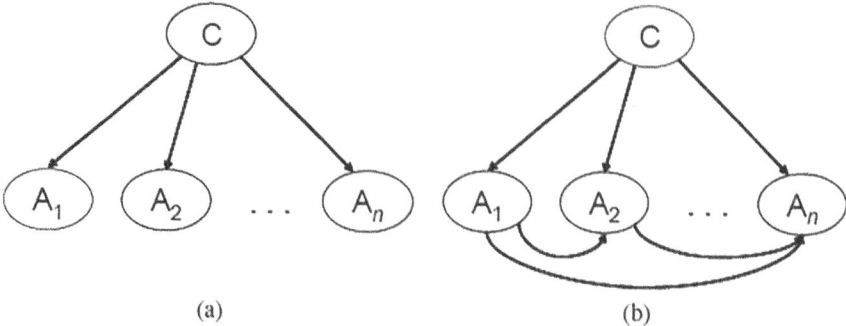

(a)   (b)

Fig. 4.4 **a** Naïve Bayes classifier, **b** Bayesian network that captures inter-attribute

require more training data to estimate reliable probability distributions. These challenges explain why they remain an active area of research in natural language processing.

The choice between these probabilistic approaches typically involves a trade-off between simplicity and performance. Naïve Bayes often serves as a strong baseline that's quick to implement, while Bayesian networks offer greater modelling power for more nuanced text analysis tasks when sufficient resources are available.

Bayesian networks consist of nodes which are random variables, and vertices representing conditional probabilities between them. Their aim is to offer a computationally feasible and graphically representable way to express and calculate dependencies between events. The graphic in Fig. 4.4a shows the Naïve Bayes classifier, with conditional probabilities $P(A_i|C)$ depicted as arcs from C to A_i. The dependencies between attributes, which are missing in Naïve Bayes, are added in the Bayesian Network shown in Fig. 4.4b.

Again, it would be computationally infeasible (and not even allowed in a Bayesian network) to calculate dependencies between all attributes, especially on high-dimensional textual data. The trick with Bayesian networks is to express only the dependencies which are necessary (or strong enough to have an impact on the solution to a particular problem), under constraints which ensure the correctness and feasibility of computation.

This can be done manually, by supplying the structure of the network—then training a Bayesian network looks very much like training the Naïve Bayes classifier with conditionals being estimated from the dataset. If estimation of dependencies from data is not possible, training gets more difficult, and several solutions are available.

Learning the structure of the network presents a much bigger challenge, and is still an area of active research.

Dimensionality Reduction

Dimensionality reduction is a critical technique for managing the complexity of high-dimensional datasets. By projecting data into a lower-dimensional space while preserving its essential structure, it facilitates more efficient computation, enhances model performance, and enables meaningful visualization. This process is particularly important for addressing the "curse of dimensionality," where data becomes sparse and less informative as the number of dimensions increases.

Linear dimensionality reduction methods assume that data lies within linear subspaces. Principal component analysis (PCA) is the most widely used technique in this category, identifying orthogonal directions of maximum variance through eigenvalue decomposition of the covariance matrix. Linear discriminant analysis (LDA) extends this approach by incorporating class labels to find projections that best separate predefined categories. These methods are especially effective for datasets with linear relationships among features.

In contrast, nonlinear dimensionality reduction techniques are designed to capture more complex data structures. Methods such as t-Distributed Stochastic Neighbour Embedding (t-SNE) and Uniform Manifold Approximation and Projection (UMAP) preserve local and global structures, respectively, making them well-suited for visualizing clusters in high-dimensional data like gene expression profiles or word embeddings. Deep learning-based approaches, such as autoencoders, use neural networks to learn compressed representations by reconstructing input data, proving particularly useful in domains like image and signal processing.

The applications of dimensionality reduction span a wide range of fields. In genomics, it helps visualize patterns across thousands of gene expression variables. In computer vision, it reduces the complexity of high-resolution image data. In natural language processing, it compresses word embeddings while retaining semantic relationships. Industrial applications include analysing sensor data for defect detection and optimizing recommendation systems by simplifying user-item interaction matrices.

Choosing the appropriate dimensionality reduction method depends on several factors, including the nature of the data, computational constraints, and the need for interpretability. Linear methods are computationally efficient and easier to interpret, while nonlinear techniques offer greater flexibility at the cost of increased complexity. Deep learning models, though powerful, often lack transparency, requiring careful validation to ensure that the reduced features align with domain-specific insights. In practice, dimensionality reduction is often integrated into broader preprocessing pipelines, enabling automated and task-specific feature transformation.

Model Selection and Training

Once data has been preprocessed, the next phase in the machine learning pipeline involves selecting suitable algorithms and training models. This begins with a clear understanding of the problem type—whether it involves classification, regression, clustering, or another task—and evaluating candidate algorithms based on their appropriateness, interpretability, and computational demands.

Model selection typically requires experimentation with various algorithms and architectures. For example, a classification problem might be approached using logistic regression, support vector machines, random forests, or neural networks, each offering distinct advantages and trade-offs. The choice depends on factors such as data size, feature complexity, and the need for model transparency.

Training a model involves exposing it to the processed data so it can learn patterns and relationships. This learning process is guided by optimization algorithms that adjust the model's parameters to minimize a loss function or maximize a likelihood function. Gradient descent and its variants are commonly used, especially in training neural networks.

A crucial component of training is hyperparameter tuning. Unlike model parameters, hyperparameters are set before training and govern aspects of the learning process, such as learning rate, regularization strength, or the number of layers in a neural network. Techniques like grid search, random search, and Bayesian optimization are employed to identify optimal configurations. Cross-validation is used to ensure that the selected hyperparameters generalize well across different subsets of the data.

Throughout training, it is essential to guard against overfitting, where the model captures noise rather than meaningful patterns. Strategies such as regularization, early stopping, and robust validation protocols help ensure that the model performs well not only on the training data but also on unseen data, thereby enhancing its generalizability and reliability.

Model Evaluation and Interpretation

Model Evaluation and Validation

Once models are trained, rigorous evaluation determines their performance and generalizability. This stage employs various metrics appropriate to the problem domain, such as accuracy, precision, recall, $F1$-score for classification, or mean squared error and R-squared for regression tasks.

Evaluation typically uses hold-out validation sets or cross-validation procedures. The former reserves a portion of data exclusively for testing, while the latter involves multiple training-testing splits to obtain more robust performance estimates.

Beyond aggregate metrics, thorough evaluation examines model behaviour across different data segments and edge cases. This might involve analysing performance across demographic groups to assess fairness, examining error patterns to identify systematic weaknesses, or testing with adversarial examples to evaluate robustness.

The validation process should also consider practical constraints such as model size, inference speed, and resource requirements, which influence deployment feasibility. A model that achieves marginally better accuracy at the cost of significantly higher computational requirements might not be the optimal choice for real-world applications.

Model Visualization in Machine Learning

Model visualization plays a vital role in machine learning by translating complex model behaviour into intuitive graphical representations. It serves as a bridge between technical model development and practical understanding, enabling both technical and non-technical stakeholders to interpret, evaluate, and communicate model performance effectively.

Through visualization, data scientists can explore how models make predictions, identify which features most influence outcomes, and detect patterns in errors or biases. Tools such as feature importance plots, partial dependence plots, and SHAP (SHapley Additive exPlanations) values help illuminate the internal logic of models, especially those considered "black boxes" like ensemble methods or deep neural networks. Visual diagnostics such as confusion matrices, ROC curves, and precision-recall plots provide clear, quantitative insights into classification performance, while residual plots and learning curves help assess regression models and training dynamics.

Beyond technical analysis, visualization is essential for communicating results to broader audiences. Dashboards and reports that incorporate visual summaries of model behaviour make it easier to justify decisions, explain outcomes, and build trust in AI systems. As visualization tools continue to evolve, they increasingly support transparency, accountability, and collaboration in machine learning workflows.

Model Deployment and Operations

Model Deployment and Serving

Deployment transitions the validated model from the development environment to production systems where it can generate predictions on new data. This stage represents the bridge between experimentation and business value realization.

Deployment strategies vary based on application requirements. Models might be deployed as batch processes running at scheduled intervals, as real-time services responding to API requests, or as embedded components within larger applications. Each approach presents different considerations for scalability, latency, and integration.

Model serving infrastructure must address challenges related to:

Scalability to handle varying loads and maintain consistent response times under pressure. Reliability through redundancy, failover mechanisms, and comprehensive error handling. Security by protecting both the model and the data it processes from unauthorized access or manipulation. Compatibility with existing systems and workflows to enable seamless integration.

The deployment stage often necessitates retraining or repacking the model for the production environment. For instance, models trained using exploratory frameworks might be translated into more efficient implementations for deployment, or complex model ensembles might be distilled into simpler, faster models while preserving performance.

Machine Learning Operations

Machine learning operations (MLOp) is a structured methodology designed to manage the entire lifecycle of machine learning models, ensuring their efficient development, deployment, and ongoing maintenance in production settings. It extends the principles of DevOps to encompass machine learning-specific assets, focusing on automation, reproducibility, scalability, and quality control. MLOps tackles the complexities involved in moving models from experimental stages into reliable production environments while preserving their performance over time.

The MLOps lifecycle can be divided into three main phases: design, experimentation, and operations. During the design phase, teams clarify business goals and data requirements to architect solutions tailored to specific applications. For example, a retailer might develop a demand forecasting system aimed at optimizing inventory. This phase also involves setting functional criteria such as accuracy targets and planning the infrastructure necessary for deployment. The experimentation phase is iterative, involving data cleaning, feature engineering, model selection, and hyperparameter tuning. Techniques like cross-validation are employed to enhance robustness and prevent overfitting. For instance, a financial institution may evaluate multiple anomaly detection models to effectively identify fraudulent activities.

After validating models in experimentation, the operations phase focuses on deploying them into production through continuous integration and continuous delivery (CI/CD) pipelines. This stage includes monitoring for data drift or performance degradation and automating retraining when needed. Telecom companies, for example, use MLOps to keep churn prediction models current by continuously incorporating new customer data.

Several essential components support MLOps workflows. Version control systems track changes in code, data, and model artefacts to ensure reproducibility and collaboration. Feature stores standardize input processing to maintain consistent model behaviour. Model registries help audit deployed versions, while automated testing frameworks verify data quality and model performance before release. Pharmaceutical firms, for instance, leverage these tools to monitor drug discovery models as new molecular data emerges.

Mathematical foundations underpin many MLOps processes. Hyperparameter optimization can be formulated as minimizing a loss function $L(y, \hat{y})$, where y and $\hat{y}$

represent actual and predicted values, respectively. Detecting performance drift may involve statistical tests such as the Kolmogorov-Smirnov test to identify changes in data distributions.

By integrating machine learning with operational discipline, MLOps ensures models remain accurate, scalable, and aligned with business objectives while reducing manual effort. Organizations adopting MLOps benefit from accelerated innovation cycles and improved reliability and compliance.

Despite its advantages, MLOps implementation faces several challenges:

- **Data Management**: Ensuring data quality, consistency, and accessibility is critical. Variations in data formats and values from multiple sources can cause inconsistencies, leading to biased or inaccurate models. Large organizations often struggle with fragmented data storage across hybrid environments, resulting in silos that limit insights. Solutions include unified data pipelines, robust governance frameworks, and scalable storage like cloud data lakes.
- **Model Deployment Complexity**: Moving models from development to production requires smooth integration with existing infrastructure, which can be complicated by scaling needs and diverse operational requirements. CI/CD pipelines automate deployment and updates but demand expertise and resources that smaller organizations may lack. Monitoring deployed models for drift and data changes is essential but resource-intensive if manual.
- **Scalability**: As data volumes and model complexity grow, organizations need scalable infrastructure and automated retraining workflows. Without containerization technologies such as Docker or Kubernetes, bottlenecks can hinder growth, especially for smaller teams.
- **Organizational Collaboration**: Siloed teams across departments or regions can create inefficiencies and misaligned goals. For example, a data science team might develop an effective model that fails in production due to poor coordination with IT or operations. Establishing cross-functional MLOps teams and collaboration tools helps bridge these gaps.
- **Resource Constraints**: High-performance computing, cloud storage, and automation tools can be costly, straining budgets, particularly for smaller organizations. Open-source platforms like MLflow or Kubeflow offer cost-effective alternatives but require skilled personnel for deployment and maintenance. Time constraints also arise as lean teams juggle multiple responsibilities.
- **Security and Compliance**: Handling sensitive data introduces risks such as data breaches, adversarial attacks, and regulatory violations. Compliance with privacy laws like GDPR and CCPA necessitates strong encryption, access controls, and regular audits. Security protocols must be integrated throughout the MLOps pipeline to protect data and models.

Training Large Language Models (LLMOps) and Traditional MLOps

Managing large language models (LLMs) within the LLMOps framework presents a distinct set of challenges compared to conventional machine learning operations (MLOps). These differences stem from the massive scale, unique architectures, and specialized requirements of LLMs, impacting everything from computational resources and training strategies to optimization and operational workflows.

A primary distinction lies in the sheer computational power required for LLMs. With billions of parameters, LLMs demand extensive resources, often necessitating distributed GPU or TPU clusters to process enormous text datasets. This stands in contrast to traditional ML models, which are typically smaller and can be trained on single GPUs or CPUs. For example, training an LLM may involve processing terabytes of data over several weeks across multiple machines, whereas conventional models like decision trees or logistic regression can be trained in a fraction of the time on much simpler hardware.

The training approach for LLMs diverges significantly from traditional models. While standard MLOps workflows often involve building models from scratch using domain-specific data, LLMOps typically leverages transfer learning. Pre-trained foundation models are fine-tuned with smaller, task-oriented datasets, streamlining the adaptation process. However, this introduces the challenge of maintaining the original model's broad capabilities while effectively customizing it for specific applications.

Human feedback plays a much larger role in LLMOps. Techniques such as reinforcement learning with human feedback (RLHF) are frequently used to refine model outputs based on user preferences and real-world interactions. This iterative process helps align the model's responses with desired outcomes, especially in applications like conversational AI. In contrast, traditional MLOps relies more heavily on automated evaluation metrics—such as accuracy or precision—without direct human input during optimization.

LLMOps workflows place a strong emphasis on prompt engineering, a practice unique to large language models. Crafting and refining input prompts is essential for guiding LLM behaviour in tasks like summarization or creative generation. This iterative process involves experimentation and systematic version control to achieve optimal results, a step not typically found in standard MLOps pipelines.

The complexity and size of LLMs also present challenges in hyperparameter tuning and inference speed. While traditional MLOps focuses on maximizing accuracy or minimizing loss, LLMOps must also consider computational efficiency due to the high costs associated with running large models. Techniques such as model quantization and distillation are employed to reduce inference time and operational costs, ensuring that performance remains acceptable.

Monitoring LLMs requires specialized tools to address issues unique to language models, such as hallucinations (generating incorrect or fictitious content), ethical compliance, and linguistic drift. For instance, an LLM deployed in healthcare must be closely monitored to prevent unsafe recommendations. Traditional ML models, on the other hand, are generally monitored for numeric data drift and changes in predictive performance.

Deployment of ML Models

Model deployment represents a critical phase in the machine learning lifecycle where trained models transition from development environments to production systems where users can interact with them. This process involves making predictive capabilities accessible for practical decision-making applications. For instance, a credit scoring system might employ a machine learning model to evaluate loan applications, with predictions generated through a straightforward function call such as "`Prediction = classifier.predict(INPUT DATASET)`."

The deployment journey begins with thorough development in a training environment. This initial phase requires meticulous training, validation, and optimization to ensure robust performance when facing real-world data. The quality of this preparatory work directly influences production performance, necessitating close collaboration among machine learning teams to refine, sanitize, and repeatedly test model code until it meets performance standards.

Once models demonstrate satisfactory performance, they must transition to appropriate deployment environments equipped with necessary computational resources and data access. Several deployment architectures exist, each with distinct advantages. Container-based deployments have gained popularity due to their reproducibility, predictability, and ease of modification. These self-contained units encapsulate all hardware specifications, configurations, and dependencies required for consistent model operation, facilitating seamless collaboration across engineering teams.

Alternatively, some data scientists prefer notebook environments like Jupyter or AWS SageMaker for experimental work throughout the machine learning lifecycle. However, these environments can present challenges regarding reproducibility and systematic testing. Teams leveraging notebooks in production workflows should prioritize code organization, component reusability, and careful dependency management to mitigate these limitations. In certain scenarios with strict data governance requirements, in-app deployment environments may be necessary to maintain data within application boundaries.

The deployment strategy must also consider how end-users will access model capabilities. Organizations typically choose between on-demand access through APIs or direct deployment to edge devices, depending on latency requirements and connectivity constraints of the application context.

The machine learning lifecycle continues well beyond initial deployment. Continuous monitoring becomes essential for evaluating model performance and accuracy over time. Since real-world data distributions constantly evolve, models may experience performance degradation—a phenomenon known as concept drift. Implementing automated monitoring and retraining pipelines helps maintain model relevance and effectiveness throughout its operational lifespan.

Additional considerations for successful machine learning deployments include implementation of robust version control systems for models and data, establishment of comprehensive testing frameworks that evaluate both model accuracy and system behaviour, development of contingency plans for handling prediction failures, and creation of transparent documentation describing model capabilities and limitations for end-users. Organizations should also consider gradual rollout strategies like canary deployments to mitigate risks when introducing new models to production environments.

Deploying Machine Learning Models into Production

Model deployment in machine learning extends beyond theoretical frameworks into practical implementation challenges that require robust engineering practices. When transitioning from development to production, Python offers a versatile ecosystem of libraries and frameworks that facilitate this complex process. Understanding these implementation details can significantly streamline the deployment pipeline and ensure consistent performance in real-world applications.

One foundational approach to model deployment involves serialization, which converts trained models into portable formats for storage and redistribution.

Monitoring and Maintenance

The final stage, which initiates a feedback loop, involves ongoing monitoring and maintenance of deployed models. Unlike traditional software, ML models can degrade over time as real-world data distributions shift from those observed during training, a phenomenon known as concept drift.

Monitoring systems track model performance metrics, data distribution changes, and system health indicators. Alerts are configured to notify teams when metrics deviate significantly from expected ranges, indicating potential issues that require attention.

Maintenance activities include periodic retraining with fresh data to adapt to changing patterns and relationships, model updates in response to performance degradation, newly discovered bugs, or changing business requirements, infrastructure adjustments to accommodate growing data volumes or increasing prediction requests, and documentation updates to reflect changes in model behaviour, data sources, or deployment configurations. Effective monitoring provides valuable insights for future iterations of the pipeline, creating a continuous improvement cycle that enhances both model performance and operational efficiency.

Advanced Topics and Considerations

Advanced Pipeline Considerations

Automated Machine Learning (AutoML) Systems

Automated machine learning (AutoML) systems have transformed the landscape of machine learning by automating a wide range of tasks, including model selection, hyperparameter tuning, feature engineering, and deployment configuration. These systems employ sophisticated search strategies—such as evolutionary algorithms, Bayesian optimization, and reinforcement learning—to navigate the expansive configuration space efficiently, guided by performance metrics, computational constraints, and user-defined objectives. Some AutoML tools are even capable of optimizing models to meet specific operational requirements, such as latency thresholds, while maintaining high predictive accuracy.

However, integrating AutoML into production environments introduces several challenges. The interpretability of models generated by AutoML varies significantly across platforms; while some provide transparent justifications for their decisions, others operate as black boxes, complicating compliance with regulatory standards and communication with stakeholders. Moreover, the computational demands of AutoML, particularly in deep learning contexts involving neural architecture search, can be substantial. Organizations must therefore weigh these costs against the benefits, such as enhanced model performance and reduced manual effort.

Despite its automation capabilities, AutoML does not eliminate the need for domain expertise. Human oversight remains crucial for problem formulation, feature conceptualization, and critical evaluation of model outputs. The most effective applications of AutoML involve a collaborative approach, where data scientists guide the system using domain-specific constraints and assess outcomes not only through quantitative metrics but also through qualitative considerations like model simplicity, interpretability, and alignment with business goals. Recent advancements, such as meta-learning, further enhance AutoML by enabling systems to draw on prior experience, thereby accelerating the search process and improving model recommendations across diverse tasks.

Pipeline Orchestration and Management

As machine learning workflows grow in complexity, robust pipeline orchestration frameworks have become essential. These systems extend beyond basic workflow management to include resource scheduling, dependency handling, and failure recovery. Typically structured as directed acyclic graphs (DAGs), these workflows allow for detailed execution analysis, identification of bottlenecks, and parallelization of independent tasks, such as concurrent feature engineering, to expedite processing.

Given the iterative nature of machine learning experimentation, resource demands can fluctuate significantly. Modern orchestration tools address this through dynamic resource allocation, scaling computational resources in response to workload changes—an especially valuable feature in cloud-based environments where cost efficiency is critical. These tools also support sophisticated deployment strategies, including hybrid online-offline architectures and canary deployments with automated rollback mechanisms in case of performance degradation.

Another critical function of orchestration systems is meta-data management, which involves systematically recording data lineage, processing steps, and execution contexts. This comprehensive tracking enhances reproducibility, facilitates compliance, and aids in debugging, particularly when investigating anomalies or reconstructing training conditions. As these systems evolve, they increasingly incorporate machine learning–specific optimizations, such as GPU-aware scheduling, data locality strategies to minimize transfer overhead, and intelligent caching of intermediate results when data remains unchanged.

Version Control and Experiment Tracking

The inherently experimental nature of machine learning necessitates robust systems for version control and experiment tracking to manage iterative development, compare outcomes, and ensure reproducibility. While traditional version control systems offer a foundational layer, specialized platforms have emerged to capture the multifaceted aspects of machine learning workflows. These include tracking dataset versions, preprocessing steps, hyperparameters, training metrics, model artefacts, and evaluation results. Such comprehensive documentation enables teams to identify trends, refine methodologies, and avoid redundant or ineffective experiments.

A critical component of this process is model lineage, which traces a model's development from raw data through to deployment. This traceability is essential for governance, compliance, and impact assessment. For instance, if a bias is discovered in a feature extraction method, lineage tracking allows for the rapid identification of all models influenced by that method. Modern tracking tools also facilitate systematic exploration of parameter configurations and offer visualization capabilities for comparative analysis. Enhanced collaboration features—such as annotations, sharing options, and notification systems—transform these platforms into institutional knowledge repositories, supporting onboarding and preserving organizational memory.

Integrating experiment tracking with other components of the machine learning pipeline creates valuable feedback loops. For example, linking tracking systems with deployment platforms allows for the automatic logging of real-world model performance, while integration with data management tools helps monitor shifts in data distributions over time, providing context for changes in model behaviour.

Continuous Integration and Deployment (CI/CD) for Machine Learning

The application of continuous integration and continuous deployment (CI/CD) practices to machine learning addresses the challenge of reliably delivering high-quality models to production. Unlike traditional software, ML CI/CD must accommodate data dependencies and the probabilistic nature of model evaluation. As a result, ML pipelines incorporate specialized testing procedures, including data validation to ensure integrity and expected distributions, model quality checks to benchmark predictive performance, and behavioural testing to assess responses to edge cases.

Shadow deployment has become a key strategy, allowing new models to run in parallel with existing ones in production without influencing decisions. This enables safe, real-world comparison of model outputs prior to full deployment. Feature stores play a central role in ensuring consistency between training and inference by supporting versioned, access-controlled, and monitored feature computation. Model registries further enhance deployment reliability by centralizing approved models along with their meta-data and approval workflows, thereby reducing the risk of deploying untested models and maintaining a complete production history.

Automated rollback mechanisms are essential for monitoring deployed models and reverting to previous versions when issues arise. Gradual rollout strategies mitigate risk by incrementally increasing traffic to new models while collecting performance data. Additionally, the adoption of infrastructure-as-code principles in ML deployments allows model-serving specifications—including operational requirements, scaling policies, monitoring configurations, and integration points—to be managed as versioned artefacts. This ensures consistency and alignment between development and operational environments.

Federated Learning and Decentralized Pipelines

Federated learning represents a paradigm shift in machine learning by enabling model training across decentralized data sources, thereby addressing challenges related to privacy, regulatory compliance, and data distribution. Rather than aggregating data in a central repository, this approach distributes the model to local nodes, where training occurs independently. The resulting parameter updates are then aggregated centrally, allowing the model to benefit from distributed data without compromising data locality or privacy.

Implementing federated learning introduces several technical challenges, particularly in communication efficiency and system heterogeneity. Since updates must be transmitted over potentially constrained networks, techniques such as update compression, selective transmission, and asynchronous coordination are employed to reduce bandwidth consumption. Additionally, the diversity in computational capabilities and data distributions across nodes necessitates adaptive protocols that tailor participation levels, training intensity, and aggregation strategies. To further safeguard individual data contributions, advanced security mechanisms like differential privacy and secure aggregation are integrated, although these must be carefully balanced against model performance and convergence speed.

This decentralized approach opens new avenues for collaboration across sectors where data sensitivity is paramount. For instance, healthcare institutions can jointly develop diagnostic models without exchanging patient data, and financial organizations can collaborate on fraud detection while maintaining strict data confidentiality. Hybrid architectures are also emerging, combining centralized model development with decentralized fine-tuning to optimize both performance and privacy.

Hardware Acceleration and Pipeline Optimization

In parallel, the increasing computational demands of modern machine learning workflows have driven significant advancements in hardware acceleration and end-to-end pipeline optimization. These developments extend beyond the traditional reliance on GPUs, encompassing a diverse ecosystem of specialized accelerators such as Tensor Processing Units (TPUs), Field Programmable Gate Arrays (FPGAs), Application-Specific Integrated Circuits (ASICs), and various neural processing units. Each of these technologies offers distinct trade-offs in terms of speed, flexibility, development complexity, and operational cost, prompting the design of hardware-aware machine learning systems that align algorithmic requirements with the most suitable hardware.

Distributed training frameworks have matured to support the coordinated use of multiple accelerators through strategies like data parallelism, model parallelism, and pipeline parallelism. These approaches can be combined to maximize throughput and efficiency, depending on the specific hardware and model architecture. Memory optimization techniques—such as gradient checkpointing, mixed precision computation, and dynamic data loading—further enhance scalability by reducing memory overhead, enabling the training of larger models or the use of larger batch sizes.

Additional performance gains are achieved through model compilation and quantization. By converting models into hardware-optimized representations and reducing numerical precision (e.g., from 32-bit to 8-bit), these techniques accelerate inference and reduce memory usage with minimal impact on accuracy. Incorporating quantization constraints during training, known as quantization-aware training, often yields superior results compared to post-training quantization.

A cutting-edge trend in this domain is hardware-software co-design, where algorithms and hardware are developed in tandem to ensure optimal compatibility and efficiency. For example, neural network architectures may be restructured to align with the computational strengths of specific accelerators, while hardware designs are tailored to support common machine learning operations.

Optimization efforts now span the entire pipeline, including data preparation, feature engineering, and post-processing. Tasks such as data augmentation, once confined to CPUs, are increasingly offloaded to GPUs to minimize data transfer delays. Similarly, operations like feature normalization and encoding are being integrated into unified computational graphs, enabling faster and more efficient execution by reducing the overhead associated with discrete processing steps.

Hybrid Pipelines: Integrating Rules and Learning

The traditional dichotomy between rule-based systems and data-driven learning models is increasingly being bridged by hybrid pipelines that integrate the strengths of both approaches. These systems acknowledge the value of combining explicit domain knowledge with the adaptive capabilities of machine learning, particularly in fields where structured reasoning and pattern recognition are both essential.

A notable example of this integration is found in neuro-symbolic architectures, which couple neural networks with symbolic reasoning components. In such systems, neural models perform tasks like image recognition or language parsing, and their outputs are subsequently processed by symbolic modules that apply logical rules, conduct reasoning, or enforce constraints. This combination leverages the flexibility of neural networks while preserving the interpretability and reliability of symbolic logic, especially for high-stakes decisions.

Another strategy, knowledge distillation, involves transferring the structured logic of rule-based systems into machine learning models. Rule-based frameworks generate large volumes of labelled data that reflect their decision-making processes, which are then used to train learning models. These models not only approximate the original rules but also gain the capacity to generalize beyond them, making this approach particularly effective when labelled real-world data is limited.

Constraint-based learning embeds domain-specific rules directly into the training process. By incorporating physical laws, logical relationships, or policy constraints into the model's loss function or architecture, this method ensures that outputs remain consistent with essential principles. This is especially critical in scientific domains or regulated industries where adherence to established knowledge is non-negotiable.

Decision decomposition further enhances hybrid systems by dividing complex problems into subcomponents, each addressed by the most suitable method. For example, in financial risk assessment, rule-based modules may handle regulatory compliance, supervised learning may analyse historical trends, and uncertainty estimation may manage novel scenarios. The system integrates these components to produce comprehensive and context-sensitive outcomes.

Active learning introduces a dynamic feedback loop between human experts and machine learning models. When the model encounters ambiguous cases or potential rule violations, it flags them for expert review. The resulting feedback is incorporated into future training, gradually improving the model's performance in complex or uncertain areas. This human-in-the-loop approach is particularly valuable during transitions from rule-based to learning-based systems, offering both oversight and incremental trust-building.

Emerging techniques also emphasize interpretability through explanation-based constraints, requiring models to justify their decisions in ways that align with domain-specific reasoning. This not only guides the learning process toward more meaningful solutions but also enhances model transparency and trustworthiness.

Hybrid architectures also shape deployment and monitoring strategies. Many systems include fallback mechanisms that redirect problematic cases from learning-based modules to more dependable rule-based components. Monitoring tools track discrepancies between the two, helping identify areas that require further refinement or investigation.

Despite their promise, hybrid pipelines face several challenges. Data quality and availability remain foundational concerns, as poor data can undermine even the most sophisticated systems. Technical debt, often incurred through short-term fixes, can hinder long-term scalability and maintainability. Establishing effective feedback loops is difficult in environments with infrequent user interaction or delayed outcomes. Resource constraints—such as limited computational power or engineering capacity—often necessitate compromises between ideal and feasible solutions. Finally, regulatory compliance, particularly in sectors like healthcare and finance, imposes stringent requirements for transparency, data handling, and accountability.

Causal Reasoning and Reasoning Under Uncertainty

Real-world problems are often characterized by uncertainty, incomplete information, and noisy or ambiguous data. The ability to reason effectively under such conditions is a hallmark of human intelligence, allowing us to make informed decisions, formulate hypotheses, and adapt to changing environments. However, many AI systems struggle with reasoning under uncertainty, particularly when faced with novel situations or scenarios that deviate from their training data. This limitation is partly due to the inherent brittleness of traditional AI approaches, which often rely on deterministic rules or fixed models that fail to capture the complexity and variability of real-world environments.

Causality is a rather broad concept, and it covers different fields. It combines statistics, machine learning, data mining, and several other quantitative disciplines to search for potential cause-effect relationships in observational data. In recent years, the study of causal relationships has become a crucial part of the artificial intelligence community, as causality can be a key tool for overcoming some limitations of correlation-based machine learning systems.

Definition Causality can be defined as the influence by which an event contributes to the production of other events.

The cause is responsible for creating the effect, and the effect is a consequence of the cause taking place. For instance, if we consider two different events A and B as an example, where the latter is a consequence of the former, A is a necessary requirement for B to exist, but B is not required for A to happen. Therefore, studying causality means understanding how different events, involving different variables, are related among themselves.

Definition Causal reasoning is the process of understanding and inferring the underlying causal relationships between events or variables in a system. It involves identifying the root causes of observed phenomena, predicting the effects of interventions or actions, and reasoning counterfactually about alternative scenarios.

Most contemporary AI systems, particularly those based on deep learning and neural networks, excel at pattern recognition and correlational reasoning. They can identify statistical associations and patterns in data, but they often lack the ability to reason about the causal mechanisms that generate those patterns.

This limitation poses significant challenges in domains where causal understanding is crucial, such as scientific discovery, decision-making under uncertainty, and policy evaluation. For example, in healthcare, identifying mere correlations between symptoms and diseases is insufficient; understanding the underlying causal mechanisms is essential for effective diagnosis, treatment selection, and developing targeted interventions.

Causal inference is a field of study that focuses on deriving causal relationships from observational or experimental data. It involves techniques such as structural equation modelling, instrumental variables, and potential outcomes frameworks.

Causal Reasoning in AI: Challenges and Approaches

Causal inference aims to establish cause-effect relationships from data, using methodologies like structural equation modelling, instrumental variables, and potential outcomes frameworks to move beyond correlation to causation.

Developing AI systems with robust causal reasoning faces significant challenges. These systems must integrate diverse knowledge forms—domain expertise, empirical data, and causal relationships—through scalable frameworks that capture real-world complexity. Counterfactual reasoning, evaluating alternative scenarios and intervention outcomes, is equally important.

A persistent challenge is addressing confounding factors and biases in observational data, which can lead to erroneous conclusions. AI systems must identify and account for these issues to ensure reliable causal inferences. Effective systems should also be capable of transfer learning and domain adaptation, applying causal knowledge from familiar contexts to new environments while adjusting for domain-specific differences.

As AI systems increasingly influence critical decisions, interpretability becomes essential. Causal inferences must be explainable to humans, fostering trust and facilitating model validation and refinement.

Promising approaches include:

- **Causal Discovery Algorithms**: Automatically learn causal models from data using methods like the PC algorithm, Greedy Equivalence Search, and hybrid techniques.
- **Structural Causal Models (SCMs)**: Represent and reason about causal relationships using graphical models and structural equation modelling principles.

Counterfactual Reasoning Frameworks

Counterfactual reasoning is a method used to evaluate the outcomes of alternative actions by asking "what if" questions. This approach is fundamental in causal inference, as it helps to understand the potential effects of different decisions or interventions.

Rubin's Causal Model (Potential Outcomes Framework)

Rubin's Causal Model, developed by statistician Donald Rubin, is a framework for defining and estimating causal effects. It is based on the concept of potential outcomes, which are the possible results that could occur for each unit (e.g., person, object) under different treatments or conditions. For example, in a medical study, each patient has two potential outcomes: their health status if they receive the treatment and their health status if they do not. The challenge, known as the "fundamental problem of causal inference," is that we can only observe one of these outcomes for each individual. Rubin's framework provides mathematical tools to estimate causal effects despite this missing data problem, making it particularly useful for analysing randomized experiments and observational studies.

Structural Equation Models (SEMs) with Counterfactual Capabilities

Structural equation models (SEMs) are a class of statistical models that represent causal relationships using a combination of graph-based causal models and mathematical equations. In SEMs, variables are represented as nodes in a directed graph, and causal effects are depicted as directed edges between these nodes. The counterfactual extension of SEMs, developed by Judea Pearl, introduces "do-calculus," a set of rules for computing the effects of interventions by modifying specific variables while keeping others constant. This allows for the evaluation of counterfactual scenarios, such as "What would this person's income be if they had received one more year of education, all else being equal?" SEMs with counterfactual capabilities are powerful tools for understanding causal relationships and making informed decisions based on hypothetical interventions.

Learning Context-Dependent Effects

Context is so deeply embedded in human learning that it is easy to overlook the critical role it plays in how we respond to a given situation. Most ML models incorporate very limited context of a specific query, relying primarily on the generic context provided by the dataset that the model is trained or fine-tuned on. Such models also raise significant concerns about bias which makes them less suited for use in many business, healthcare, and other critical applications.

In human cognition and social interactions, context is a multi-layered scaffold that profoundly influences perception, interpretation, and response to stimuli. Context can be considered the set of circumstances or facts surrounding a particular event, situation, or piece of information. While machines handle context in a more formalized and rule-based manner, human processing of context is highly fluid and adaptive, relying on cognitive functions like memory, attention, problem-solving, and social and cultural norms.

Cognitively, humans employ schemas and mental models to interpret context. A schema is a mental framework that helps in organizing and interpreting information. It contains preconceived ideas and representations of a specific aspect of the world, built upon past experiences and learning. Contextual cues often inform decision-making and problem-solving processes. In medical diagnosis, for example, symptoms are not evaluated in isolation; factors such as patient history, environment, and even time of year can significantly influence the diagnosis and treatment plan.

The issue with most of the presently deployed AI technologies is that even if they can perform the process of conditioning in a particular case, conditioning *over time* remains a challenge for many applications, since it requires a combination of understanding of the task at hand as well as a memory of the sequence of events that happened before, which acts as a conditioning prior.

Contextual information is critical in shaping the behaviour and performance of AI and ML models. Its influence pervades diverse applications, from NLP and computer vision to reinforcement learning. Specifically, contextual understanding is crucial for disambiguating semantic meanings, identifying object relations in image matrices, and optimizing decision-making processes in complex state-action spaces.

Meta-Learning: Learning to Learn

Meta-learning introduces a framework where machine learning models improve their ability to learn by drawing on experiences from a wide range of related tasks. Rather than simply learning from data, these models acquire strategies for learning itself, making them more efficient and adaptable. This approach mirrors how humans and animals enhance their learning skills over time, both within a lifetime and across generations.

By leveraging meta-learning, models can overcome common challenges in deep learning, such as limited data availability, high computational demands, and difficulties with generalization. The paradigm is applicable across various domains, including few-shot learning, reinforcement learning, and natural language processing, where models are expected to perform well even with minimal data.

Meta-learning, often described as "learning to learn," equips algorithms with the capability to quickly adapt to new, previously unseen tasks. Unlike traditional models that are trained for a single, specific purpose, meta-learning enables systems to generalize knowledge across multiple tasks by learning from diverse experiences.

The meta-learning process typically consists of two main phases:

- **Meta-Training**: The model is exposed to a variety of tasks, learning to identify patterns and strategies that are common across them. This helps the model develop a broad understanding that can be applied to new challenges.
- **Meta-Testing**: The trained model is then evaluated on tasks it has not encountered before, testing its ability to adapt and perform well based on its prior meta-learning.

A standard meta-learning setup involves:

1. **Meta-Learner**: The core algorithm that learns from a collection of tasks and adapts its parameters to tackle new ones efficiently.
2. **Task Distribution**: A diverse set of tasks used during training to simulate the kinds of new challenges the model may face.
3. **Meta-Data**: The accumulated knowledge from training on various tasks, which guides the meta-learner's adaptation process.

Through this setup, meta-learning enables models to generalize across different domains and datasets, reducing the reliance on large volumes of task-specific data.

There are three primary strategies in meta-learning:

- **Metric-Based Methods**: These focus on learning similarity measures between data points, facilitating tasks like image recognition or signature verification with limited examples.
- **Model-Based Methods**: Often used in reinforcement learning, these approaches design models that can rapidly adapt their internal state to new environments.
- **Optimization-Based Methods**: Here, the meta-learner discovers optimal initialization or hyperparameters, allowing models to quickly adjust to new tasks with minimal updates.

Machine Learning Benchmarks

Machine learning benchmarks, comprising standardized datasets and evaluation protocols, have become foundational to the advancement of artificial intelligence. These benchmarks typically involve dividing data into training and test sets, enabling researchers to train models on one subset and evaluate their performance on another, unseen portion. This straightforward methodology has driven decades of innovation and competition, as researchers aim to surpass one another on widely recognized benchmarks.

The use of benchmarks dates back to the late 1950s, gaining significant traction in the late 1980s as pattern recognition evolved into modern machine learning. Initially developed out of practical necessity rather than scientific rigour, benchmarks quickly became central to the field. Iconic datasets such as ImageNet and CIFAR-10 have played pivotal roles, particularly during the deep learning surge of the 2010s, where ImageNet served as a crucial platform for comparing model architectures and accelerating progress in computer vision.

Despite their utility, benchmarks have faced criticism. Static test sets and fixed evaluation metrics can narrow research focus and incentivize overfitting, where models exploit dataset peculiarities rather than demonstrating genuine generalization. This issue, often framed through Goodhart's Law, highlights the risk of a metric losing its value once it becomes a target. Moreover, benchmarks may embed social and cultural biases, and the creation of large annotated datasets frequently depends on undervalued labour.

Nevertheless, benchmarks have significantly propelled machine learning forward by offering a transparent and competitive framework for assessing model improvements. Public leaderboards facilitate the tracking of progress, replication of results, and identification of promising research directions. Interestingly, model performance rankings on simpler datasets like CIFAR-10 often generalize to more complex ones such as ImageNet, suggesting that benchmarks can yield meaningful insights across domains.

As the field evolves, so too does the benchmarking landscape. The rise of large language models and multi-task learning introduces new challenges, particularly regarding data contamination, where models may inadvertently encounter test data during training due to the scale and nature of web-based corpora. To mitigate this, researchers increasingly fine-tune models on task-specific data prior to evaluation to ensure fairer comparisons.

Multi-task benchmarks, which assess performance across a variety of tasks, have become more prevalent, offering a broader perspective on model capabilities. However, they also introduce complexities, such as sensitivity to task composition and the inclusion of weaker models, which can destabilize performance rankings that were once consistent in single-task settings.

A further complication arises as models begin to match or exceed human performance on certain tasks, challenging traditional evaluation methods. Human judgement may no longer serve as a reliable benchmark, prompting exploration into model-based evaluation systems—though these raise concerns about fairness and bias. As machine learning continues to advance, the role of benchmarks remains both indispensable and in need of continual refinement.

Exercises

1. What are the differences between supervised, unsupervised, and reinforcement learning?
2. How do decision trees work, and what are their advantages and disadvantages?
3. What is the bias-variance trade-off in machine learning models?
4. How do support vector machines (SVMs) classify data?
5. What are the key steps in the machine learning pipeline?
6. How do you evaluate the performance of a machine learning model?
7. What are the common techniques for feature selection and extraction?
8. How does clustering work, and what are its main applications?

9. What is the role of regularization in preventing overfitting?
10. Choose a classification algorithm (e.g., logistic regression, SVM, decision tree) and explain how it handles uncertainty in its predictions. How can you quantify the model's confidence in a given classification?
11. Explain the concept of overfitting and underfitting. Describe techniques like cross-validation and regularization that can be used to mitigate these problems.
12. Describe the differences between discriminative and generative machine learning models. Give examples of each type of model and discuss their respective advantages and disadvantages.
13. Select a real-world problem and discuss how you would apply a specific machine learning technique to solve it. Detail the process of data collection, preprocessing, model selection, training, and evaluation.
14. Explain the role of probability theory in machine learning. How do probabilistic models represent uncertainty, and why is this important in real-world applications?
15. Describe the differences between Bayesian and frequentist approaches to probability and statistics. How do these different perspectives influence the way we build and interpret machine learning models?
16. How do Bayesian networks and Markov networks represent probabilistic relationships between variables, and what are their applications in machine learning?
17. Explain the difference between correlation and causation. Why is it important to distinguish between them in machine learning and data analysis?
18. Consider the following one-dimensional dataset $\{10, 20, 30, 50, 90\}$. Perform k-means algorithm with 2 clusters and initial centroids are 0 and 90. Compute: (i) Final centroids (ii) Cohesion (iii) Separation.
19. Discuss the challenges of inferring causality from observational data. Describe techniques like randomized controlled trials and instrumental variables that can be used to address these challenges.
20. Describe different sources of uncertainty in machine learning, such as aleatoric uncertainty and epistemic uncertainty. How do these types of uncertainty affect model predictions?
21. How can we design machine learning systems that make reliable predictions and decisions even when the input data or model parameters are uncertain?
22. Explore a real-world application where uncertainty plays a significant role (e.g., financial forecasting, medical diagnosis). Discuss how uncertainty is modelled and managed in this application.
23. (Project) Build a time series model that predicts future stock prices, currency exchange rates, or other financial variables.
24. (Project) Develop a machine learning model that predicts the likelihood of a patient having a specific disease based on their symptoms, medical history, and test results.
25. (Project) Create a model that predicts the risk of a specific environmental event, such as a flood, wildfire, or earthquake, based on various factors.

Further Reading

Ackley D, Hinton G, Sejnowski T (1985) A learning algorithm for Boltzmann machines. Cogn Sci 9(1):147–169

Akerkar R, Lingras P (2008) Building an intelligent web: theory and practice. Jones & Bartlett, Sudbury

Akerkar RA, Sajja PS (2010) Knowledge based systems. Jones & Bartlett, Sudbury

Breiman L (2001) Random forests. J Mach Learn Arch 45(1):5–32

Busoniu L, Babuska R, De Schutter B (2010) Reinforcement learning and dynamic programming using function approximators. CRC Press

Chollet F (2017) Deep learning with python. Manning Publications

Cortes C, Vapnik V (1995) Support-vector networks. Mach Learn 20(3):273–297

Cover T, Hart P (1967) Nearest neighbor pattern classification. IEEE Trans Inf Theory 13(1):1–27

Géron A (2019) Hands-on machine learning with Scikit-learn, Keras, and TensorFlow. O'Reilly Media

Hardt M (2024) The emerging science of machine learning benchmarks. SIAM News. https://www.siam.org/publications/siam-news/articles/the-emerging-science-of-machine-learning-benchmarks/

Hastie T, Tibshirani R, Friedman J (2001) The elements of statistical learning: data mining, inference, and prediction. Springer Science & Business Media

Hausknecht M, Stone P (2015) Deep recurrent Q-learning for partially observable MDPs. arXiv preprint arXiv:1507.06527

Hochreiter S, Schmidhuber J (1997) Long short-term memory. Neural Comput 9(8):1735–1780

Holland PW (1986) Statistics and causal inference. J Am Stat Assoc 81(396):945–960

Hong M, Akerkar R (2019) Analytics and evolving landscape of machine learning for emergency response. In: Tsihrintzis GA et al (eds) Machine learning paradigms, learning and analytics in intelligent systems, vol 1. Springer, Cham, pp 351–397. https://doi.org/10.1007/978-3-030-15628-2_11

Imbens GW, Rubin DB (2015) Causal inference in statistics, social, and biomedical sciences. Cambridge University Press

Kearns M, Vazirani U (1994) Computational learning theory. MIT Press, Cambridge, MA

Kohonen T (1990) The self-organizing maps. Proc IEEE 78(9):1464–1480

Kohonen T (1995) Self-organizing maps, second extended edition, springer series in information sciences, vol 30. Springer, Berlin

Koller D, Friedman N (2009) Probabilistic graphical models. MIT Press

Krizhevsky A, Sutskever I, Hinton G (2012) Imagenet classification with deep convolutional neural networks. In: NIPS conference, pp 1097–1105

Mitchell T (1997) Machine learning. Mc Graw-Hill, New York

Mohri M, Rostamzadehm A, Talwalker A (2012) Foundations of machine learning. MIT Press, p 2012

Murphy K (2012) Machine learning: a probabilistic perspective. MIT Press

Natarjan B (2001) Machine learning: a theoretical approach. Kluwer

Neapolitan R (2004) Learning Bayesian networks. Prentice-Hall

Nielsen MA (2015) Neural networks and deep learning. Determination Press

Quinlan R (1986) Induction of decision tree. Mach Learn 1:81–106

Quinlan R (1993) C4.5 programs for machine learning. Morgan Kaufmann

Rubin DB (1974) Estimating causal effects of treatments in randomized and nonrandomized studies. J Educ Psychol 66(5):688–701

Rumelhart DE, Hinton GE, Williams RJ (1986) Learning representations by back-propagating errors. Nature 323(6088):533–536

Schulman J, Levine S, Moritz P, Jordan M, Abbeel P (2015) Trust region policy optimization. In: Proceedings of the international conference on machine learning (ICML), pp 1889–1897

Theodoridis S (2015) Machine learning. Springer

Valiant LG (1984) A theory of the learnable. Commun ACM 27(11):1134–1142

Chapter 5
Deep Learning: The Fabric of Representation

*Imagination is more important than knowledge. For knowledge
is limited to all we now know and understand, while imagination
embraces the entire world, and all there ever will be to know
and understand.*
—Albert Einstein

Preliminaries

Core Concept

The architecture of deep learning hinges on its fundamental layered structure. These interconnected layers act as successive filters, each transforming the input data into increasingly abstract representations. This hierarchical processing allows the network to automatically learn complex features, moving from simple patterns in early layers to more sophisticated concepts in deeper ones. The sheer depth of these networks empowers them to model intricate relationships within vast datasets, enabling breakthroughs in tasks previously considered challenging for traditional machine learning. This layered intelligence is the core of deep learning's remarkable ability to extract meaning and make predictions from complex data.

Deep learning refers to the process of involving a system that thinks and learns exactly like humans using an artificial neural network. The architecture of a standard neural network (Fig. 5.1) is inspired from the way the human brain functions. It is composed of connected nodes called neurons, which, through a series of real-valued activations help the network to learn complex functions. A neural network consists of several stages including input layer, hidden layers, and output layers. "Deep" is referred to the multiple layers in these neural networks.

The learning of a neural network involves finding an optimized set of parameters of these stages that eventually help the network to exhibit the desired behaviour.

Deep neural networks, which are useful for learning highly complex problems, contain several layers or stages, and require a large amount of training data for best

© The Author(s), under exclusive license to Springer Nature Switzerland AG 2026
R. Akerkar, *Artificial Intelligence*, https://doi.org/10.1007/978-3-031-91084-5_5

Fig. 5.1 Neural network representation

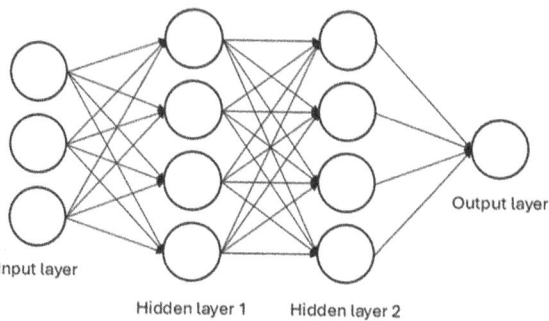

accuracy on the desired inference task. Although the concept has been around for several decades, deep learning has become popular in the recent years due to the availability of improvised GPU hardware architecture, and human-generated digital data in large volumes. Table 5.1 highlights the contrast between traditional machine learning and deep learning approaches.

The first artificial neural network (ANN) was proposed in 1944, but its popularity has surged in recent years. Deep learning, introduced in the early 1950s, has also gained traction recently due to the rise in AI applications and the vast amounts of

Table 5.1 Comparison of traditional machine learning and deep learning

Criteria	Traditional machine learning	Deep learning
Data size	Generally, works well with small to medium-sized datasets	Requires large amounts of data for training
Feature engineering	Features must be manually extracted and selected by domain experts	Can automatically learn features through multiple layers of computation
Model complexity	Typically has simpler models, e.g., linear regression or decision trees	Has more complex models, such as neural networks with many hidden layers
Training time	Shorter training time due to fewer parameters to optimize	Longer training time due to larger number of parameters and computations
Interpretability	Models are often interpretable and explainable	Models can be "black boxes," making it difficult to understand how they make predictions
Hardware requirements	Works on CPUs and requires less memory compared to deep learning	Performs best on GPUs and TPUs, requiring significant memory resources
Use cases	Good for simple problems, classification tasks, and structured data	Ideal for unstructured data (images, audio, video), natural language processing, and high-dimensional data

data generated by companies. While classical machine learning algorithms struggled with big data, ANNs excelled.

The history of deep learning dates back to the early days of AI. In 1943, Warren McCulloch and Walter Pitts created the first mathematical model of neurons in the brain, marking the inception of ANNs. In the 1950s, Frank Rosenblatt developed the perceptron, a simple two-layer neural network capable of pattern recognition. Despite its limitations, neural networks gained wider use in the 1980s when Geoffrey Hinton and others introduced the backpropagation algorithm, enabling the learning of complex patterns and renewing interest in neural networks.

Throughout the 1990s, deep learning research continued but remained niche. However, breakthroughs in the early 2000s, such as the development of convolutional neural networks (CNNs) for image processing and recurrent neural networks (RNNs) for sequential data, led to a resurgence in deep learning. CNNs achieved state-of-the-art results in image recognition tasks, while RNNs excelled in natural language processing tasks like machine translation and speech recognition.

In the past decade, deep learning has made significant strides in various tasks, including image recognition, natural language processing, speech recognition, and machine translation, becoming one of the most active and promising AI research areas.

Traditional machine learning involves manual and time-consuming feature engineering, requiring domain expertise. In contrast, deep learning automatically learns relevant features from raw data, reducing the need for manual intervention. Feature engineering involves selecting, transforming, or creating the most relevant variables (features) from raw data for machine learning models. For example, in weather prediction, raw data might include temperature, humidity, wind speed, and barometric pressure. Feature engineering determines the most important variables and transforms them (e.g., converting temperature from Fahrenheit to Celsius) to make them more useful for the model. Deep learning uses feature extraction to recognize similar features of the same label and employs decision boundaries to determine which features accurately represent each label. For instance, in classifying cats and dogs, deep learning models extract information such as eyes, face, and body shape, dividing them into two classes.

Why Distributed Deep Learning?

To learn complex functions, we need large deep learning networks with multiple layers. The classification accuracy of a deep learning model can improve with more training examples, more model parameters, or both. However, training large networks is computationally expensive and can take an impractically long time on a single machine, even with multithreading. This necessitates scaling up the training across multiple connected machines in a distributed manner. With the increased availability of GPUs, model training can be distributed across multi-GPU clusters.

Before diving further, it's important to understand key concepts related to neural network training:

Weights

The network is initialized with random weights, which are adjusted through multiple iterations during training to reduce the error in predicting the output. The goal is to tune the weights so the network's output closely matches the actual output for the given input values. These weights are multiplied by the input to the neurons.

Gradient Descent

Gradient descent, shown in Fig. 5.2, is a standard optimizer used to update model parameters to decrease the loss function. It involves calculating the gradient of the loss function with respect to the parameters and taking steps in the direction that reduces the loss. This process is repeated until the loss function is minimized. The network needs to learn optimal weights for accurate predictions. The loss of a single training example indicates the error in predicting its output. The cost function, which is the average of the loss functions across the training set, measures how well the weights perform. The aim is to minimize the cost function, which is typically convex and shaped like a bowl.

Stochastic Gradient Descent (SGD)

In gradient descent, the total number of examples used to calculate the cost function constitutes a batch. Large datasets may contain redundant data, and selecting a random example can yield the desired gradient. SGD considers only one training example at a time to minimize the cost function, reducing computation but introducing noise.

Mini-Batch SGD

Instead of using a single example, SGD can be performed on mini-batches, typically consisting of 10 to 1000 random examples.

Fig. 5.2 Gradient descent

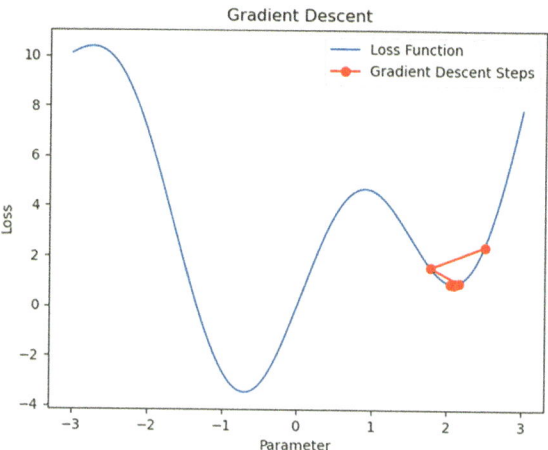

Techniques to Improve Neural Networks

Building deep networks that meet the desired generalization level for a specific task is an extremely iterative process. Defining a baseline model plays a major role in this process. A baseline model will provide you with a point of comparison when using more advanced methods such as deep neural networks. This means you'll be left with more context as to where your neural network is striving and where it's failing at a certain task—which you could use to direct how you improve your model.

Neural networks were inspired by neural processing that occurs in the human brain. Deep networks have improved computers' ability to solve complex problems given lots of data. But there are various circumstances in which the accuracy of a network is below par for the task at hand. Data is at the heart of deep learning; to build a good model, you need to have good data. The amount of data required for deep neural networks to perform well is more than what's required for traditional machine learning methods. If the data going in is garbage, no matter how much you have, the performance of your model will reflect this discrepancy.

The first step in ensuring your neural network performs well on the testing data is to verify that your neural network does not overfit. Deep neural networks *overfit* a lot.

Definition Overfitting happens when a model becomes too good at recognizing patterns in the training data and becomes too specific to that data. This means that it won't perform well on new, unseen data.

Definition Underfitting occurs when a model is too simple and doesn't have enough capacity to learn the patterns in the data.

Identifying whether your model has overfitted is simple. If the training accuracy is much higher than the test accuracy, then you've overfitted. The overfitting is because they must learn millions of parameters while the model is being built. As a consequence, deep neural networks are equipped with the capacity to completely memorize values from the training data, thus rendering it ineffective when required to generalize to new, unseen samples. A solution to this problem is to regularize the model where a set of techniques are used to prevent overfitting.

Cross-validation is a technique used in machine learning to assess how well a model will perform on unseen data. The idea is to divide the data into two parts: a training set and a validation set. The model is trained on the training set and then evaluated on the validation set. This process is repeated multiple times with different parts of the data being used as the validation set each time. The goal is to see if the model is overfitting or underfitting, and to get a better idea of how it will perform on new, unseen data.

Moreover, *hyperparameter tuning* is a necessity for any practitioner seeking to maximize their model's performance. Hyperparameters are values that you must initialize to the network, these values can't be learned by the network while training. In a convolutional neural network, some of the hyperparameters are kernel size, the number of layers in the neural network, activation function, loss function, optimizer used (gradient descent, RMSprop), batch size, number of epochs to train etc. *Hyperparameter tuning* is the process of selecting the optimal set of hyperparameters for a learning algorithm. This procedure alone can significantly improve a model's performance thus permitting it to make better generalizations when faced with unseen samples. Obtaining the optimal hyperparameters is a case of trial and error: there's no clear way to know what hyperparameters are best suited. Each neural network will have its best set of hyperparameters which will lead to maximum accuracy.

Here are some of the different hyperparameters that can be tuned:

Activation function—An activation function in a neural network defines how the weighted sum of the input is transformed into an output from a node or nodes in a layer of the network. Activation functions are highly important and choosing the right activation function helps your model to learn better. Sigmoid and Tanh were the most widely used activation functions. But they suffered from the problem of vanishing gradients, i.e., during backpropagation, the gradients diminish in value when they reach the beginning layers. This stopped the neural network from scaling to bigger sizes with more layers. Rectified Linear Unit (ReLU) is able to overcome this problem and hence allowed neural networks to be of large sizes. It solves the problem of vanishing gradients.

Number of neurons—In each layer, we define the number of neurons. They attempt to model the function of a biological neuron by computing the weighted average of a given input.

Learning rate—The learning rate determines how big of a step should be taken while moving towards a minimum of a loss function. Choosing an optimum learning rate is important as it decides whether your network converges to the global minima or not. Selecting a small learning rate can help a neural network converge to the global minima but it takes a huge amount of time. Therefore, you have to train the network for a longer period of time. A small learning rate also makes the network susceptible to getting stuck in local minimum. That is, the network will converge onto a local minima and will be unable to come out of it due to the small learning rate. Therefore, you must be careful while setting the learning rate.

Batch size—The number of training samples being used in one forward and backward pass. In general practice, batch size values are set as either 8 or 16 or 32 etc.

Epochs—An epoch in machine learning and artificial neural networks (ANNs) refers to one complete iteration through the entire training dataset. During an epoch, the model processes and uses the information from the training data to update its weights and biases, in order to better predict the outcome for the next iteration. The number of epochs depends on the developer's preference and the computing power.

We can improve the accuracy of our neural network by using it as one of the constituents that make up an *ensemble algorithm*.

> **Definition** An ensemble describes the combination of multiple predictors being put together to be used as an individual predictor.

If individual neural networks are not as accurate as you would like them to be, you can create an ensemble of neural networks and combine their predictive power. You can choose different neural network architectures and train them on different parts of the data and ensemble them and use their collective predictive power to get high accuracy on test data. Practitioners agree that the predictive performance of an ensemble algorithm is usually better than that of any one of the constituent algorithms alone.

Winning solutions in several machine learning competitions typically leverage ensembles. How an ensemble is created can vary but the three main techniques are:

- **Bootstrap aggregation (Bagging)**—Combining the predictions of various models that are each built using randomly sampled data with replacement from the training set.
- **Boosting**—Combining a set of weak learners into one strong learner to minimize training error.
- **Stacked generalization (Stacking)**—Combining the outcomes of several other learning algorithms.

Deep Learning Algorithms

Backpropagation

Backpropagation stands as perhaps the most important algorithm in deep learning, serving as the basis that enables neural networks to learn from data. The concept behind backpropagation is elegantly simple yet profoundly powerful: calculate how each parameter in the network contributes to the overall error, then adjust these parameters proportionally to reduce this error. This process, when repeated iteratively over many examples, allows networks to gradually improve their predictions.

At its core, backpropagation implements the chain rule from calculus to efficiently compute gradients of the loss function with respect to each weight in the network. The algorithm consists of two phases: a forward pass, where input data propagates through the network to generate predictions, and a backward pass, where error gradients flow in reverse from the output layer back to the input layer, allowing for weight updates at each layer.

The core of backpropagation lies in its computational efficiency. Rather than recalculating derivatives for each parameter separately, it reuses computations by working backward from the output, making deep learning computationally feasible.

Backpropagation's centrality to deep learning cannot be overstated, it provides the learning mechanism that powers all the neural network architectures we will explore in the remainder of this chapter. From recurrent networks processing sequences to transformers attending to relevant information, each relies on backpropagation to optimize its parameters and learn meaningful representations from data.

Convolutional Neural Networks (CNNs)

During the 2010s, deep learning witnessed a remarkable resurgence, marked by rapid advancements in techniques, architectures, and models. This revival was fueled by three key factors: the availability of vast amounts of data, the emergence of powerful computational resources, and the development of innovative training algorithms such as backpropagation, convolutional neural networks (CNNs), and recurrent neural networks (RNNs). These advancements paved the way for deep learning applications across diverse domains, including natural language processing, computer vision, autonomous driving, and many others. The ability of these models to process complex datasets efficiently revolutionized artificial intelligence and established deep learning as a cornerstone for modern AI systems.

Convolutional neural networks (CNNs) emerged as a specialized type of neural network designed to process grid-like data structures such as images and videos. Unlike traditional neural networks that treat input pixels independently, CNNs leverage the spatial relationships between pixels to extract meaningful features. Their architecture is tailored to exploit the two-dimensional structure of inputs like images by incorporating key principles such as local connections, shared weights, pooling operations, and multi-layered hierarchies. This design enables CNNs to detect spatial patterns effectively while maintaining invariance to the location of features within the input.

A typical CNN, as illustrated in Fig. 5.3, consists of several layers: an input layer that receives raw data, multiple hidden layers for feature extraction and transformation, and an output layer for generating predictions. The hidden layers include convolutional layers, activation layers, pooling layers, and fully connected layers. Convolutional layers are fundamental to CNNs as they identify features such as edges or textures in an image. This is achieved using small matrices called kernels or filters that traverse the input image and perform dot products with local pixel values to produce feature maps. By applying multiple filters simultaneously, convolutional layers can detect various features in parallel.

Activation layers introduce non-linearity into the network by applying functions like ReLU (Rectified Linear Unit) or sigmoid. This non-linearity allows CNNs to model complex relationships between features effectively. Pooling layers further

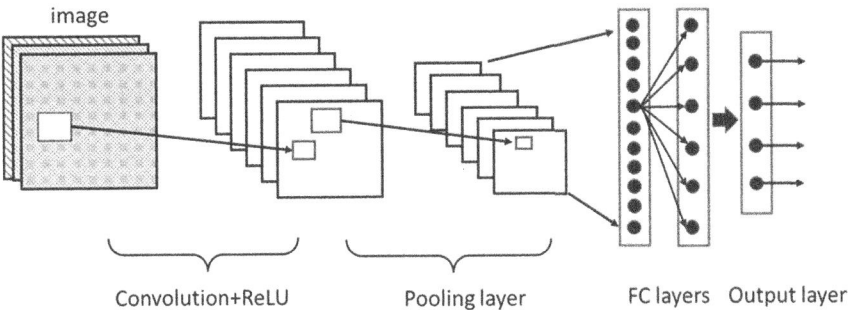

Fig. 5.3 CNN architecture for image classification

refine feature maps by reducing their spatial dimensions through operations like max-pooling or average-pooling. These operations retain only the most critical information while making the network more robust to minor variations in the input data.

Fully connected (FC) layers serve as interpreters for the extracted features by connecting all neurons from previous layers. They integrate these features into a cohesive representation to generate predictions. Finally, the output layer produces results tailored to specific tasks, such as classifying images into categories or detecting objects within a scene.

The success of CNNs was demonstrated spectacularly during the ImageNet competition in 2012 when deep CNNs achieved groundbreaking results on a dataset containing approximately one million images across 1000 classes. This achievement established CNNs as the dominant approach for recognition and detection tasks in computer vision. Since then, CNNs have consistently delivered exceptional performance, often rivalling or surpassing human capabilities in certain applications.

The effectiveness of CNNs lies in their ability to learn hierarchical representations of data. Early layers capture low-level features like edges and corners; middle layers detect textures or parts such as eyes or fur; deeper layers combine these elements into high-level concepts like faces or objects. This hierarchical learning mimics human visual processing and has enabled CNNs to excel in fields ranging from medical imaging (e.g., tumour detection) to autonomous vehicles (e.g., pedestrian identification) and facial recognition systems.

Despite their success, training CNNs requires substantial amounts of labelled data and significant computational resources due to their complexity. However, pre-trained models such as ResNet or VGG16 have facilitated transfer learning by allowing developers to fine-tune existing networks for specific tasks using smaller datasets. This approach has made CNNs scalable and efficient for real-world applications while maintaining high accuracy levels.

Recurrent Neural Networks (RNNs)

Recurrent Neural Networks (RNNs) are a specialized class of artificial neural networks designed to process sequential data, where the order and context of inputs significantly influence the output. Unlike traditional feedforward networks, which treat each input independently, RNNs incorporate a *memory mechanism* that retains information from previous steps in a sequence, enabling them to model temporal dependencies and dynamic patterns. This makes them particularly effective for tasks such as natural language processing, speech recognition, time-series forecasting, and machine translation, where understanding the relationship between consecutive elements is critical.

At the core of an RNN is a *hidden state*, a dynamic memory component that captures contextual information from prior inputs. This state is updated at each time step using both the current input and the previous hidden state, creating a feedback loop. For example, when processing the sentence *"Mango is yellow,"* the hidden state after encountering the word *"Mango"* informs the network's interpretation of subsequent words like *"is"* and *"yellow"*. The hidden state h_t at time step t is computed as:

$$h_t = \sigma(w_h \cdot h_{t-1} + w_x \cdot x_t + b)$$

where W_h and W_x are weight matrices, x_t is the input at time t, b is a bias term, and σ is an activation function like the hyperbolic tangent (tanh). This recursive structure allows RNNs to handle variable-length sequences and maintain context over time.

Key Components of the RNN are,

1. **Input Layer**: Receives sequential data (e.g., words in a sentence or stock prices over days).
2. **Hidden Layer**: Processes inputs through recurrent connections, updating the hidden state at each step.
3. **Output Layer**: Generates predictions (e.g., the next word in a sentence) based on the final or intermediate hidden states.

A basic RNN architecture illustrates this flow:

- **Input** ($x\langle t \rangle$): The current element in the sequence (e.g., a word or time-series value).
- **Hidden State** ($a\langle t \rangle$): Combines the current input and previous hidden state ($a\langle t - 1 \rangle$) to encode context.
- **Output** ($y\langle t \rangle$): Predicted based on $a\langle t \rangle$, often through a dense layer.

Figure 5.4 provides a visual representation of Recurrent Neural Networks (RNNs).

RNNs are trained using backpropagation through time (BPTT), a variant of backpropagation tailored for sequences. BPTT unrolls the network across time steps, calculates gradients for each step, and adjusts shared weights to minimize prediction errors. However, standard RNNs struggle with long-term dependencies due to

Fig. 5.4 A recurrent neural networks

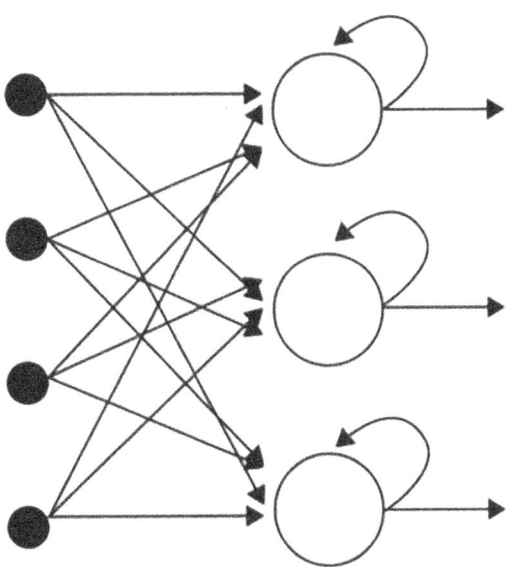

the vanishing gradient problem, where gradients diminish exponentially over time, hindering learning from distant inputs.

To address these limitations, advanced architectures have been developed:

1. **Long Short-Term Memory (LSTM)**: Introduces memory cells controlled by input, output, and forget gates. These gates regulate information flow, allowing LSTMs to retain relevant long-term context. For instance, in the sentences "*Tomy is a dog. Tomy's favourite food is meat*," LSTMs remember "*Tomy*" and "*meat*" to correctly predict "*meat*".
2. **Gated Recurrent Units (GRUs)**: Simplify LSTMs by merging the cell state and hidden state, using update and reset gates to manage memory efficiently.
3. **Bidirectional RNNs (BRNNs)**: Process sequences in both forward and backward directions, leveraging future and past contexts for tasks like language translation.

RNNs excel in scenarios requiring sequential analysis:

- **Natural Language Processing (NLP)**: Text generation, sentiment analysis, and machine translation.
- **Speech Recognition**: Converting audio signals into transcribed text.
- **Time-Series Prediction**: Forecasting stock prices or weather patterns using historical data.
- **Image Captioning**: Generating descriptive text for visual content.

While RNNs revolutionized sequential data processing, their computational inefficiency and difficulty in parallelizing sequential operations led to the rise of *Transformer models*, which use self-attention mechanisms for improved scalability.

Training RNNs employs a variant of backpropagation called Backpropagation Through Time (BPTT), which unrolls the recurrent network across time steps and treats it as a deep feedforward network with shared weights. This allows gradients to flow backward through time, updating weights based on errors accumulated across the sequence.

Despite their elegance, basic RNNs suffer from a significant limitation: they struggle to learn long-term dependencies due to the vanishing and exploding gradient problems. During backpropagation through time, gradients either decay exponentially as they flow backward (vanishing) or grow uncontrollably (exploding), making it difficult for the network to attribute credit or blame to events that occurred many time steps earlier. This limitation led to the development of more sophisticated recurrent architectures like Long Short-Term Memory networks and Gated Recurrent Units, which we'll explore next.

Long Short-Term Memory Networks (LSTMs)

Long Short-Term Memory (LSTM) networks, introduced by Hochreiter and Schmidhuber in 1997, were developed to overcome the vanishing gradient problem that limits the performance of standard recurrent neural networks (RNNs) in learning long-range dependencies. LSTMs are distinguished by their ability to retain information over extended sequences, making them particularly effective for tasks such as language modelling, machine translation, and speech recognition, where contextual information from earlier in the sequence is essential for accurate predictions.

The core innovation of LSTMs lies in their use of a cell state, which serves as a persistent memory that flows through the network, regulated by three gating mechanisms: the forget gate, input gate, and output gate. These gates, implemented using sigmoid activation functions, determine which information should be discarded, what new data should be incorporated, and what should be output at each time step. This architecture allows gradients to propagate more effectively during training, thereby mitigating the vanishing gradient issue and enabling the network to learn when to remember or forget information.

In practical applications, LSTMs are frequently enhanced with bidirectional processing and stacked layers to capture complex temporal patterns across different time scales. Their success has led to widespread adoption in various domains, including predictive text systems, speech recognition, and automated translation. However, the relatively intricate structure of LSTMs, involving multiple weight matrices and biases per cell, has also driven the development of more streamlined alternatives. Among these, the Gated Recurrent Unit (GRU) has emerged as a prominent variant, offering similar benefits with reduced computational complexity.

Gated Recurrent Units (GRUs)

Gated Recurrent Units (GRUs) offer a streamlined alternative to the more complex Long Short-Term Memory (LSTM) networks, preserving the ability to model long-term dependencies in sequential data while reducing computational demands. By integrating the functions of the LSTM's forget and input gates into a single update gate, and merging the cell and hidden states into one, GRUs simplify the architecture without sacrificing performance. Additionally, the reset gate in GRUs modulates the influence of previous hidden states on current computations, enabling the network to discard irrelevant information when necessary.

This architectural efficiency results in fewer parameters and faster training times, making GRUs particularly suitable for applications with limited computational resources or those involving large-scale sequential data. Empirical comparisons have shown that GRUs often perform on par with LSTMs across a range of tasks, although the optimal choice between the two remains context-dependent. LSTMs may be preferable for tasks requiring fine-grained memory control over very long sequences, while GRUs are often favoured for shorter sequences or when efficiency is a priority.

Both GRUs and LSTMs represent pivotal advancements in recurrent neural network design, addressing the vanishing gradient problem and enabling more effective modelling of sequential patterns. Their continued use in areas such as natural language processing, time-series forecasting, and speech recognition underscores their foundational role in modern deep learning architectures.

Autoencoders

Autoencoders offer a distinct approach within deep learning by departing from the traditional supervised learning paradigm. Rather than learning to map inputs to predefined labels, autoencoders are trained to reconstruct their own inputs, enabling them to learn meaningful internal representations without the need for labelled data. This self-supervised learning framework allows the model to capture the underlying structure of the data by compressing it into a lower-dimensional latent space and then reconstructing it as accurately as possible.

The architecture of an autoencoder consists of two primary components: an encoder, which transforms the input into a compact latent representation, and a decoder, which reconstructs the original input from this compressed form. Training involves minimizing the reconstruction error, encouraging the network to retain essential features while discarding noise and redundancy.

Despite their structural simplicity, autoencoders are highly versatile. By adjusting the design and capacity of the latent space, they can be adapted for a wide range of tasks, including dimensionality reduction, feature extraction, denoising, and even generative modelling. Their ability to learn efficient, task-agnostic representations makes them a powerful tool in both exploratory data analysis and the development of more complex deep learning systems.

Advanced Deep Learning Architectures

Transformers

The introduction of the Transformer architecture by Vaswani et al. in their 2017 paper "*Attention Is All You Need*" marked a fundamental shift in the way sequential data is processed in deep learning. Unlike traditional recurrent neural networks (RNNs) and their variants such as Long Short-Term Memory (LSTM) networks, which process sequences step by step and rely on a hidden state to carry information forward, Transformers eliminate the need for recurrence altogether. This innovation addresses key limitations of RNNs, particularly their difficulty in capturing long-range dependencies and their inherently sequential computation, which hinders parallelization.

Transformers achieve superior performance by employing self-attention mechanisms that allow the model to consider all positions in a sequence simultaneously. This enables the network to directly model relationships between distant elements, regardless of their position, and facilitates efficient parallel computation. The architecture is typically organized into an encoder-decoder structure, although many contemporary models use only one of these components. For instance, BERT utilizes only the encoder for tasks requiring deep contextual understanding, while GPT relies solely on the decoder for generative tasks.

At the heart of the Transformer is the multi-head self-attention mechanism, which enables the model to attend to different parts of the sequence in parallel and from multiple perspectives. This design not only improves gradient flow during training but also significantly enhances the model's ability to learn complex dependencies in data. As a result, Transformers have become the foundation of modern natural language processing, powering state-of-the-art systems in machine translation, text summarization, question answering, and beyond.

The Transformer Algorithm
The transformer architecture can be broken down into several key components:

1. **Input Embeddings**: Convert input tokens (words, subwords, etc.) into dense vector representations.
2. **Positional Encodings**: Since transformers process all tokens simultaneously, they need information about the order of tokens. Positional encodings add information about the position of each token in the sequence.
3. **Multi-Head Self-Attention**: The heart of the transformer architecture, allowing the model to attend to different parts of the input sequence when encoding each token.

4. **Feed-Forward Networks**: Applied to each position separately and identically, consisting of two linear transformations with a ReLU activation in between.
5. **Layer Normalization**: Applied after each sub-layer to stabilize the learning process.
6. **Residual Connections**: Connect the input of each sub-layer to its output, helping to mitigate the vanishing gradient problem.

The self-attention mechanism computes attention scores between all pairs of tokens in a sequence, allowing the model to focus on relevant parts of the input when producing each output. The formula for scaled dot-product attention is:

$$\text{Attention}(Q, K, V) = \text{softmax}\left(\frac{QK^T}{\sqrt{d_k}}\right)V$$

where Q, K, and V are query, key, and value matrices derived from the input, and d_k is the dimension of the keys.

Attention Mechanisms

While we've already touched on attention in the context of transformers, it's worth exploring this concept more deeply as it represents one of the most important innovations in neural network design. Attention in neural networks is inspired by human perception—we focus on specific parts of our sensory input when processing information. In machine learning, attention allows a model to focus on relevant parts of the input when producing each part of the output. This is particularly useful for tasks where different parts of the input have different levels of importance for different parts of the output.

The attention mechanism was initially introduced to improve sequence-to-sequence models for machine translation, where a decoder needed to focus on different parts of the source sentence when generating each word of the translation. Since then, attention has evolved and diversified into multiple variants.

Types of Attention Mechanisms

1. **Additive (Bahdanau) Attention**: Uses a feed-forward network to compute attention scores.
2. **Multiplicative (Luong) Attention**: Uses dot products to compute attention scores.
3. **Self-Attention**: Each element in a sequence attends to all other elements in the same sequence.
4. **Multi-Head Attention**: Runs multiple attention mechanisms in parallel, allowing the model to focus on different aspects of the input.

Attention Algorithm

The general attention mechanism works as follows:

1. Compute alignment scores between the query and all keys.
2. Convert scores to weights using `softmax` (ensuring they sum to 1).
3. Compute weighted sum of values using these weights.

Mathematically, given a query q, keys K, and values V:

1. Compute scores: score(q, k_i) for each key k_i.
2. Apply softmax: $\alpha_i = \text{softmax}(\text{score}(q, k_i))$
3. Compute weighted sum: output $= \Sigma \alpha_i * v_i$.

Attention mechanisms have changed deep learning by allowing models to focus on relevant parts of the input. They've been particularly successful in natural language processing, but have also found applications in computer vision, speech recognition, and many other domains. The self-attention mechanism used in transformers is perhaps the most influential variant, enabling parallel processing of sequences and better modeling of long-range dependencies.

Generative Adversarial Networks

Generative models represent a significant area of focus within the broader field of deep learning. Unlike discriminative models, which are designed to predict a label or category for a given input (such as classifying an image as a "cat" or "dog"), generative models aim to learn the underlying probability distribution of the training data itself. This enables them to generate new data instances that resemble the original dataset. In essence, they learn to "create" data, rather than simply categorize it. This capability has opened up a wide range of applications, including image synthesis, text generation, music composition, and data augmentation, making generative models a crucial tool in advancing artificial intelligence. Their importance within deep learning stems from their ability to capture complex data distributions without explicit programming, allowing for the creation of highly realistic and diverse outputs.

One of the most innovative and influential developments in the field of generative models is the Generative Adversarial Network, or GAN (Fig. 5.5). Introduced by Ian Goodfellow and his colleagues in 2014, GANs offer a unique approach to training generative models through a competitive process between two neural networks: the generator and the discriminator.

The basic architecture of a GAN comprises two main components: the generator and the discriminator. The generator network's role is to produce synthetic data samples, such as images, that are intended to mimic the characteristics of real data. It takes random noise as input and transforms it into a data sample. The discriminator

Fig. 5.5 Generative
adversarial network

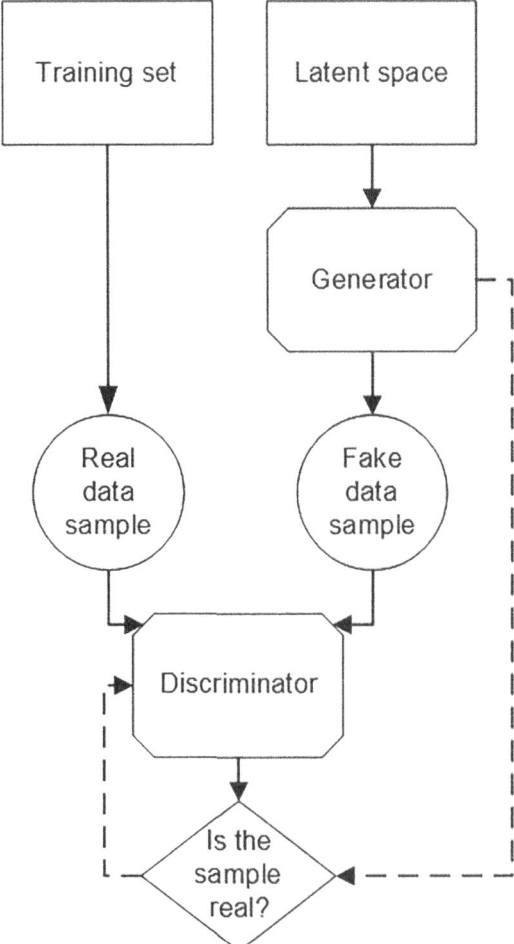

network, on the other hand, acts as a critic. Its task is to distinguish between real data samples drawn from the training set and the fake samples generated by the generator. The discriminator receives both real and generated data as input and outputs a probability that a given sample is real.

The training process of a GAN can be conceptualized as a game between the generator and the discriminator. Initially, the generator produces relatively poor samples, and the discriminator can easily distinguish them from real data. However, as training progresses, both networks improve. The generator learns to create increasingly realistic samples to "fool" the discriminator, while the discriminator becomes better at identifying fake samples. This adversarial dynamic drives both networks to enhance their performance.

More specifically, the training process involves alternating between two phases: discriminator training and generator training. During discriminator training, the discriminator's weights are updated to improve its ability to correctly classify real data as real and generated data as fake. This is typically achieved by minimizing a loss function that measures the discriminator's classification error. During generator training, the generator's weights are updated to produce samples that are more likely to be classified as real by the discriminator. This involves maximizing the discriminator's error with respect to the generated samples, effectively encouraging the generator to "fool" the discriminator. This adversarial process continues iteratively until a Nash equilibrium is reached, where the generator produces samples that are indistinguishable from real data, and the discriminator can no longer reliably differentiate between them.

Variational Autoencoders

Variational Autoencoders (VAEs), illustrated in Fig. 5.6, are a class of generative models that combine ideas from deep learning and variational Bayesian methods. Introduced by Kingma and Welling in 2013, VAEs have become popular for generating new data samples, learning useful latent representations, and performing unsupervised and semi-supervised learning.

Traditional autoencoders compress data into a lower-dimensional latent space and then reconstruct the original data from this compressed representation. However, their latent space often lacks structure, making it difficult to generate new, meaningful samples.

VAEs address this limitation by enforcing a specific structure on the latent space. Instead of encoding inputs as single points in latent space, VAEs encode them as probability distributions (typically Gaussian). This probabilistic approach allows VAEs to generate new data by sampling from the latent space and ensures that the latent space has a meaningful structure.

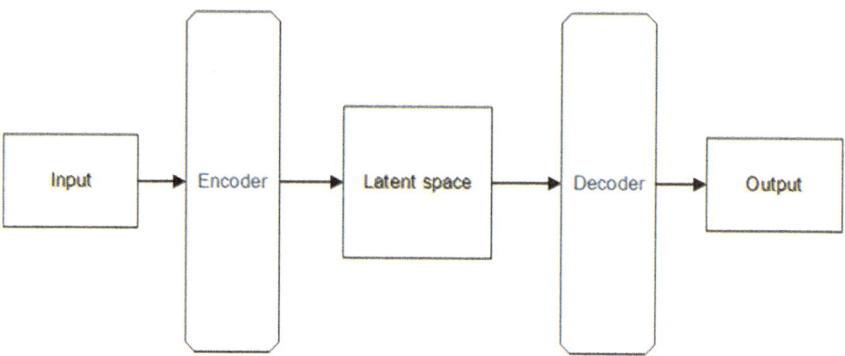

Fig. 5.6 Working of variational autoencoders

Imagine latent representations as the DNA of an organism. DNA carries the essential instructions to construct and sustain a living being. In the same way, latent representations hold the core elements of data, enabling the model to recreate the original information from this encoded essence. However, a slight alteration in the DNA can result in a completely different organism.

The VAE consists of an encoder network and a decoder network:

1. **Encoder**: Maps input data x to parameters of a probability distribution $q(z|x)$ in latent space.
2. **Decoder**: Maps samples from the latent space z back to reconstructions of the original data $p(x|z)$.

The training objective combines two terms:

1. **Reconstruction Loss**: Measures how well the decoder reconstructs the input data.
2. **KL Divergence**: Ensures that the encoded distributions are close to a prior distribution (usually a standard normal distribution).

VAEs can generate new samples by sampling from the prior distribution (usually a standard normal) and passing the samples through the decoder. They can also perform tasks like image reconstruction, denoising, and interpolation in latent space.

One significant advantage of VAEs is that they learn a smooth, continuous latent space. This enables interesting operations like interpolating between samples by linearly interpolating between their latent representations. For example, you can gradually transform one face into another or blend different styles in generated images.

VAEs have been extended in numerous ways, including conditional VAEs (CVAEs), which condition the generation process on additional information, and VQ-VAEs (Vector Quantized VAEs), which use discrete latent variables. They have applications in image generation, text generation, anomaly detection, drug discovery, and representation learning.

Building and Implementing Deep Learning Projects

Deep Learning Frameworks

Deep learning frameworks play a crucial role in the practical implementation of neural networks by simplifying the development process and eliminating the need to build models from the ground up. These frameworks consist of libraries, tools, and interfaces that streamline model construction, training, and deployment. To use them effectively, developers typically install the necessary packages within environments such as Anaconda and import them at the beginning of their Python programs.

Among the most widely used frameworks, TensorFlow, developed by Google, stands out for its flexibility, scalability, and extensive community support.

PyTorch, created by Facebook, is similarly powerful but is particularly valued for its intuitive design and dynamic computation graph, which facilitates debugging and experimentation. Caffe, from the Berkeley Vision and Learning Center, is optimized for speed and is well-suited for image and video processing, offering a range of pre-trained models for computer vision tasks. Microsoft's Cognitive Toolkit (CNTK) emphasizes performance and supports distributed training and advanced data preprocessing. Theano, developed by the Montreal Institute for Learning Algorithms, was an early pioneer in enabling efficient numerical computation on both CPUs and GPUs.

Keras, developed by François Chollet, provides a high-level API that simplifies model development and can run on top of TensorFlow, CNTK, or Theano, making it especially accessible to beginners. Apache MXNet, designed for scalability, supports distributed computing across large datasets and is compatible with a range of devices, from cloud infrastructure to mobile platforms.

These frameworks are actively maintained and continuously updated by their respective communities. The choice of framework often depends on the specific requirements of a project, such as the need for speed, flexibility, ease of use, or scalability, as well as the preferences of the developer or research team. By leveraging these tools in conjunction with platforms like Anaconda or Google Colab, practitioners can focus on innovation and experimentation rather than technical setup, thereby accelerating progress in deep learning research and applications.

TensorFlow

TensorFlow, developed by Google, is a comprehensive open-source platform that has become foundational in both academic and industrial machine learning. It supports the entire lifecycle of model development, from data preprocessing to deployment, and is designed to facilitate the construction, training, and deployment of machine learning and deep learning models at scale.

At the heart of TensorFlow lies the concept of tensors—multi-dimensional arrays that serve as the basic units of data—and computational graphs, where nodes represent mathematical operations and edges denote data flow. This graph-based architecture enables efficient execution of complex computations across various hardware platforms, including CPUs, GPUs, and Google's custom Tensor Processing Units (TPUs). The abstraction also allows for seamless model visualization, optimization, and deployment across different environments without altering the core code.

TensorFlow offers robust tools for data handling, allowing users to clean, transform, and pipeline data efficiently. These capabilities are essential for ensuring high-quality input during training and evaluation, reducing the risk of bias and improving model performance. Model development is further simplified through integration with Keras, a high-level API that enables rapid prototyping and experimentation with minimal code. Additionally, TensorFlow provides access to a wide range of pre-trained models via resources such as TensorFlow Hub and Model Garden, which support tasks like image classification, object detection, and natural language processing.

A notable feature of TensorFlow is TensorBoard, a visualization suite that allows users to monitor training progress, inspect model architecture, and analyse performance metrics in real time. This tool enhances transparency and facilitates debugging and optimization. For deployment, TensorFlow supports a broad spectrum of platforms, from cloud servers to mobile and edge devices. TensorFlow Serving enables scalable deployment in production environments, while TensorFlow Lite and TensorFlow.js extend inference capabilities to mobile applications and web browsers, respectively.

TensorFlow also addresses the operational challenges of machine learning through TensorFlow Extended (TFX), a suite of tools for automating data pipelines, tracking model versions, monitoring performance, and managing retraining workflows. These features are critical for maintaining robust and scalable systems in production.

In practice, TensorFlow is widely adopted across industries. In healthcare, it supports diagnostic imaging and predictive analytics; in finance, it underpins fraud detection and risk modelling; in retail, it enhances personalization and supply chain optimization. Its applications also span autonomous systems, voice recognition, recommendation engines, and content generation. The framework's adaptability extends to time-series forecasting, predictive maintenance, and algorithmic trading.

The success of TensorFlow is reinforced by its active community and extensive documentation, which provide a wealth of tutorials, examples, and support for users at all levels. This collaborative ecosystem continues to drive innovation and accelerate the adoption of machine learning technologies worldwide.

PyTorch

PyTorch is a leading open-source deep learning framework that has become a favourite among researchers, educators, and practitioners for its intuitive design, flexibility, and robust capabilities. Developed by Facebook's AI Research lab, PyTorch is built around the concept of tensors, which are multi-dimensional arrays similar to NumPy arrays but with the added advantage of seamless GPU acceleration. This makes PyTorch highly suitable for both prototyping and production-scale deep learning applications.

At the heart of PyTorch is its dynamic computation graph, often referred to as "define-by-run." Unlike static graph frameworks, where the computation graph must be defined before running any operations, PyTorch builds the graph on the fly as operations are executed. This dynamic nature allows for greater flexibility, easier debugging, and a more natural integration with the Python programming language. As a result, model development in PyTorch feels intuitive and "pythonic," closely resembling standard Python code and enabling rapid experimentation with new architectures and ideas.

The core workflow in PyTorch typically begins with data handling. The framework provides powerful tools such as the Dataset and `DataLoader` classes, which simplify the process of loading, batching, and shuffling data. These utilities are essential for efficiently feeding data to models during training, especially when dealing with large datasets or custom data formats. PyTorch also offers domain-specific libraries like `torchvision` for computer vision, `torchaudio` for audio processing, and `torchtext` for natural language processing, each equipped with pre-built datasets, models, and transformations tailored to their respective domains.

Figure 5.7 illustrates PyTorch's role in facilitating a deep learning project, presenting a three-tiered structure comprising a physical layer, a Python layer, and the PyTorch layer itself. While the physical layer represents the hardware infrastructure for training and deployment, our primary focus lies on the interplay between the Python and PyTorch layers. The initial step in training a neural network involves acquiring the necessary data, typically sourced from some form of storage. Subsequently, each individual data sample undergoes a transformation into a PyTorch tensor. These tensors are then commonly grouped into batches to enable efficient mini-batch processing during the training phase.

The essential PyTorch modules for building neural networks are primarily found in the `torch.nn` namespace, which provides all the fundamental building blocks needed to define, customize, and manage neural network architectures. The core class is `nn.Module`, which serves as the base for all neural network components, including layers such as `nn.Linear` for fully connected layers and activation functions like `nn.ReLU`. By subclassing `nn.Module`, you can create custom models and layers, structuring both the initialization of parameters and the forward pass that dictates how data flows through the network. In addition to `torch.nn`, the

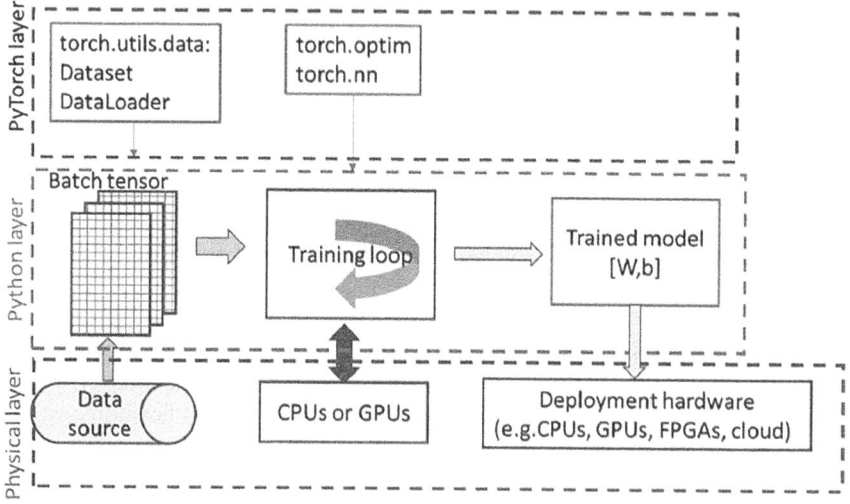

Fig. 5.7 PyTorch framework for deep learning

`torch.optim` module is essential for training neural networks, offering a range of optimization algorithms such as SGD and Adam to update model parameters during learning.

Model creation in PyTorch is based on object-oriented programming principles. The fundamental building block is the `nn.Module` class, from which users can inherit to define custom neural network architectures. Layers, activation functions, and loss functions are all modular and can be combined in a highly flexible manner. The forward pass, where data flows through the network, is defined in the forward method, allowing for complex and dynamic model behaviours that adapt to various input shapes and tasks.

A key feature of PyTorch is its automatic differentiation engine, known as Autograd. This system tracks all operations performed on tensors with the `requires_grad` property set to True, constructing a computation graph as the model executes. When it comes time to optimize the model's parameters, PyTorch can automatically compute gradients with respect to any scalar value, such as a loss function, using backpropagation. These gradients are then used by optimizers-such as stochastic gradient descent (SGD) or Adam-to update the model parameters and minimize the loss.

The training process in PyTorch follows a familiar pattern: iterate over the data, perform a forward pass to compute predictions, calculate the loss, execute a backward pass to compute gradients, and update the parameters. This loop is highly customizable, making it easy to implement advanced training techniques like learning rate scheduling, gradient clipping, or early stopping. PyTorch also supports mixed-precision training and distributed learning, allowing users to scale their models across multiple GPUs or even multiple machines.

Saving and loading models in PyTorch is straightforward. Models can be serialized as state dictionaries, enabling easy checkpointing and transfer of learned weights between different environments or for further fine-tuning. This is particularly useful in transfer learning scenarios, where pre-trained models are adapted to new tasks with limited data.

PyTorch's ecosystem is further enriched by tools for experiment tracking, visualization, and deployment. Libraries such as TensorBoard (integrated with PyTorch), Weights and Biases, and MLflow provide capabilities for monitoring training progress, visualizing model architectures, and managing experiments. For deployment, PyTorch offers TorchScript for serializing models and running them in production environments, as well as support for exporting models to ONNX (Open Neural Network Exchange) for interoperability with other frameworks and hardware accelerators.

Applications of Deep Learning

Deep Learning in Computer Vision

The development of deep learning technologies has enabled the creation of more accurate and complex computer vision models. As these technologies increase, the incorporation of computer vision applications is becoming more useful. Below are a few ways deep learning is being used to improve computer vision.

Object Detection

There are two common types of object detection performed via computer vision techniques:

- **Two-step object detection**—the first step requires a Region Proposal Network (RPN), providing a number of candidate regions that may contain important objects. The second step is passing region proposals to a neural classification architecture, commonly an RCNN-based hierarchical grouping algorithm, or region of interest (ROI) pooling in Fast RCNN. These approaches are quite accurate, but can very slow.
- **One-step object detection**—with the need for real time object detection, one-step object detection architectures have emerged, such as YOLO, SSD, and RetinaNet. These combine the detection and classification step, by regressing bounding box predictions. Every bounding box is represented with just a few coordinates, making it easier to combine the detection and classification step and speed up processing.

Localization and Object Detection

Image localization is used to determine where objects are located in an image. Once identified, objects are marked with a bounding box. Object detection extends on this and classifies the objects that are identified. This process is based on CNNs such as AlexNet, Fast RCNN, and Faster RCNN.

Localization and object detection can be used to identify multiple objects in complex scenes. This can then be applied to functionalities such as interpreting diagnostic images in medicine.

Semantic Segmentation

Semantic segmentation, also known as object segmentation, is similar to object detection except it is based on the specific pixels related to an object. This enables image objects to be more carefully defined and does not require bounding boxes. Semantic segmentation is often performed using fully convolutional networks (FCN) or U-Nets.

One popular use for semantic segmentation is for training autonomous vehicles. With this method, researchers can use images of streets or throughways with accurately defined boundaries for objects.

Pose Estimation

Pose estimation is a method that is used to determine where joints are in a picture of a person or an object and what the placement of those joints indicates. It can be used with both 2D and 3D images. The primary architecture used for pose estimation is PoseNet, which is based on CNNs.

Pose estimation is used to determine where parts of the body may show up in an image and can be used to generate realistic stances or motion of human figures. Often, this functionality is used for augmented reality, mirroring movements with robotics, or gait analysis.

Deep Learning and Embodiment

While deep learning typically focuses on processing large datasets in abstract spaces, embodiment emphasizes the role of physical context in learning. Bridging these two concepts has led to advances in robotics, autonomous systems, and embodied AI, where deep learning techniques are applied to embodied agents.

Examples of embodiment in deep learning:

- **Reinforcement Learning**: Agents interact with their environment, receiving rewards or penalties that guide their learning. These agents can develop strategies for tasks like navigating, manipulating objects, or playing games by experiencing the consequences of their actions.
- **Robotics**: Deep learning models are used to control robots in tasks such as grasping objects, walking, or flying, where real-world feedback (sensor data) informs the learning process.
- **Embodied Language Models**: Systems where natural language processing is coupled with an embodied agent that can act on language instructions and respond to the world accordingly.

There are some pertinent challenges. Training embodied agents in simulation environments presents challenges when transferring those models to the real world due to differences in noise, physics, and complexity. Embodied agents require vast amounts of sensory and motor data, and training such systems is computationally intensive. Also, embodied agents must generalize their learned behaviours to new, unseen environments or tasks, which remains an open challenge.

Despite these challenges, the combination of deep learning with embodiment opens up new possibilities for creating more intelligent, adaptive, and context-aware systems. These systems have potential in fields such as healthcare (robotic surgery), autonomous vehicles, and human-robot interaction.

Strategic Considerations in Deep Learning Development

Model-Centric and Data-Centric Approaches

Model-centric and data-centric approaches in artificial intelligence (AI) are related to deep learning, as both approaches can significantly impact the performance and effectiveness of deep learning models. The model-centric approach focuses on improving the architecture, algorithms, and parameters of the deep learning models themselves. This approach aims to enhance the model's ability to learn from data and make accurate predictions. The data-centric approach emphasizes the quality, quantity, and diversity of the data used to train deep learning models. This approach aims to improve the model's performance by ensuring that the training data is representative and informative.

Both model-centric and data-centric approaches are essential for the success of deep learning models. While the model-centric approach focuses on enhancing the model's architecture and training process, the data-centric approach ensures that the model is trained on high-quality, diverse, and representative data. Combining both approaches can lead to significant improvements in the performance, robustness, and generalization of deep learning models.

In practice, deep learning practitioners often iterate between model-centric and data-centric strategies to achieve the best results. For example, after designing a robust model architecture, they may focus on improving the training data quality and diversity to further enhance the model's performance. Conversely, if the data is already of high quality, they may experiment with different model architectures and hyperparameters to achieve better results.

The Rise of the Model-Centric Paradigm

The emergence of the model-centric paradigm in AI reflects a historical trajectory that has prioritized algorithmic innovation as the primary engine of progress. From the early development of perceptrons in the 1950s through periods of stagnation and resurgence, this focus intensified dramatically with the advent of deep learning, particularly following the success of AlexNet in the 2012 ImageNet competition. This milestone catalysed a wave of architectural advancements, including the evolution of convolutional neural networks from AlexNet to VGG and ResNet, the refinement of recurrent neural networks into LSTMs, and the eventual rise of transformer models that redefined natural language processing.

During this period, research efforts concentrated heavily on designing increasingly sophisticated models. Academic publications and conferences became arenas for showcasing novel architectural components—such as attention mechanisms, residual connections, and normalization techniques—each contributing to incremental improvements in benchmark performance. The prevailing assumption was that optimal results could be achieved by refining model architectures, tuning hyper-parameters, and enhancing training procedures, all while treating the dataset as a fixed resource.

This model-centric approach is underpinned by several defining principles. Central to it is the belief in algorithmic primacy: that breakthroughs in AI are driven primarily by innovations in model design, loss functions, optimization strategies, and regularization methods. The data used for training is typically regarded as static, with limited emphasis on its expansion or refinement beyond standard augmentation techniques. Evaluation is predominantly performance-driven, with success measured by improvements on benchmark datasets, even when such gains come at the cost of increased model complexity or computational demands.

Another hallmark of this paradigm is the emphasis on transfer learning. Researchers aim to develop general-purpose architectures that can be pretrained on large datasets and subsequently fine-tuned for specific tasks, thereby compensating for limitations in task-specific data. Considerable effort is also devoted to hyperparameter optimization, with meticulous tuning of learning rates, activation functions, and network configurations to extract maximum performance from fixed validation sets.

Overall, the model-centric paradigm has shaped much of the recent progress in AI by channelling innovation towards the development and refinement of increasingly powerful models, often under the assumption that better algorithms can compensate for limitations in data quality or quantity.

Emergence of the Data-Centric Perspective

While the model-centric paradigm dominated artificial intelligence research for decades, it gradually became evident that many real-world failures of AI systems were rooted not in model deficiencies but in issues with the underlying data. The well-known phrase "garbage in, garbage out" gained renewed relevance, as machine learning models were found to replicate—and often amplify—the biases, inconsistencies, and errors present in their training datasets.

Several developments contributed to this shift in perspective. As neural networks grew in complexity, the performance gains from architectural innovations began to plateau across many tasks. In contrast, improvements in the quantity and quality of training data continued to yield significant benefits, suggesting that data, rather than model design, was often the limiting factor. Moreover, high-profile failures—such as biased facial recognition systems and flawed content recommendation algorithms—demonstrated that even technically advanced models could be undermined by poor data quality. In specialized domains like healthcare, law, and scientific research, practitioners frequently encountered challenges related to data scarcity, noise, and distribution shifts, where careful data curation proved more effective than adopting the latest model architectures.

By the early 2020s, leading figures in the field, including Andrew Ng, began advocating for a data-centric approach to AI development. This perspective emphasized that systematic improvements in data quality could drive more reliable performance gains than continued model refinement. The data-centric paradigm is grounded in a distinct set of principles. It prioritizes the quality, representativeness, and cleanliness of data as the primary determinants of system performance. Rather than constantly modifying model architectures, practitioners often fix the model and focus on iterative cycles of data assessment, cleaning, augmentation, and validation.

A central concern in this approach is ensuring that training data accurately reflects the conditions the model will face in deployment. Techniques for domain adaptation and targeted data collection are emphasized over architectural novelty. When models underperform, error analysis is used to identify patterns that reveal data limitations or biases, which then inform targeted improvements to the dataset.

This shift from model-centric to data-centric thinking marks a significant evolution in AI development, recognizing that robust, high-performing systems depend as much on the integrity of their data as on the sophistication of their algorithms.

Implementation Strategies and Methodologies

Model-Centric Implementation Approaches

Model-centric AI development has given rise to a range of sophisticated methodologies aimed at maximizing system performance through architectural and algorithmic innovation. One prominent technique is neural architecture search (NAS), which automates the discovery of optimal network structures. By employing strategies such as evolutionary algorithms and reinforcement learning, NAS enables exploration of vast design spaces that would be impractical to navigate manually, often yielding architectures that outperform those crafted by human experts.

To further enhance generalization from fixed datasets, model-centric approaches rely heavily on advanced regularization techniques. Methods such as dropout, batch normalization, weight decay, mixup, and label smoothing are employed to prevent overfitting and improve robustness by constraining how models learn from data. Ensemble methods also play a critical role in this paradigm. By combining the outputs of multiple models through techniques like bagging, boosting, or stacking, ensembles can achieve higher accuracy and resilience than any single model alone.

Another key strategy is knowledge distillation, which involves transferring the learned behaviour of a large, complex "teacher" model to a smaller "student" model. Rather than training the student solely on hard labels, it is guided to replicate the teacher's output distributions, enabling it to approximate the performance of the larger model while remaining computationally efficient.

Pretraining and fine-tuning have become especially influential in domains such as natural language processing and computer vision. This approach involves training large models on broad, general-purpose datasets before adapting them to specific tasks with smaller, domain-specific data. By leveraging knowledge acquired during pretraining, models can perform well even when task-specific data is limited, thus extending the reach of model-centric techniques into data-constrained environments.

Together, these methodologies exemplify the model-centric paradigm's emphasis on algorithmic sophistication and optimization as the primary means of advancing AI capabilities.

Data-Centric Implementation Approaches

Data-centric AI development is grounded in methodologies that prioritize the systematic improvement of data quality as the foundation for building effective machine learning systems. Unlike model-centric approaches, which focus on refining algorithms, the data-centric paradigm emphasizes the integrity, representativeness, and usability of the data itself.

A central component of this approach is the use of data validation and cleaning frameworks. These tools apply statistical analyses, consistency checks, and domain-specific rules to detect and correct errors, anomalies, and inconsistencies in datasets before training begins. Ensuring data quality at this stage helps prevent the propagation of flaws throughout the modelling process.

Active learning is another key methodology, designed to optimize the use of limited labelling resources. By identifying the most informative or uncertain data points for human annotation, active learning enables the efficient construction of high-quality labelled datasets that contribute more significantly to model improvement.

To further reduce the burden of manual labelling, data-centric practitioners often employ weak supervision and programmatic labelling. These techniques use heuristics, labelling functions, or existing models to generate initial labels for unannotated data. Although these labels may be noisy, they can be refined through consensus mechanisms and iterative feedback, allowing for the scalable creation of labelled datasets.

Systematic data augmentation is also reimagined within this paradigm. Rather than serving merely as a training trick, augmentation becomes a targeted strategy for addressing specific data limitations and simulating deployment conditions. Tailored augmentation pipelines are developed to enhance dataset diversity and robustness.

Another important practice is dataset versioning and provenance tracking. By maintaining detailed records of dataset creation, modifications, and their impact on model performance, data is treated as an engineered artifact subject to continuous refinement and quality assurance.

Finally, when multiple annotators provide conflicting labels, data-centric approaches implement structured adjudication processes. These involve domain expertise and explicit quality criteria to resolve disagreements, moving beyond simple majority voting to ensure label accuracy and consistency.

Together, these methodologies reflect a shift in focus from algorithmic complexity to data integrity, recognizing that the success of AI systems often hinges more on the quality of the data they are trained on than on the sophistication of the models themselves.

Hybrid Approaches and Integration Strategies

While the model-centric and data-centric paradigms have traditionally represented distinct philosophical approaches to AI development, contemporary practice increasingly blends elements of both. This integration reflects a growing recognition that model performance and data quality are deeply interdependent, and that optimizing one in isolation often yields diminishing returns.

One prominent strategy for unifying these perspectives is the use of joint optimization frameworks, which treat both model architecture and data selection or augmentation as learnable components of a single system. These methods co-optimize the structure of the model alongside the composition or transformation of the training data, acknowledging that improvements in one domain can enhance the effectiveness of the other.

Another integrative approach involves data-adaptive architectures—models that dynamically adjust their structure or hyperparameters in response to the characteristics of the input data. Rather than assuming a fixed data distribution, these systems are designed to accommodate variability in data quality, distribution, or complexity, thereby bridging the gap between static model design and dynamic data environments.

Curriculum learning offers a further example of this synthesis by structuring the training process to expose models to progressively more challenging examples. This method integrates data considerations directly into the learning schedule, optimizing how models interact with the available data to enhance learning efficiency and generalization.

Active testing extends the principles of active learning into the deployment phase. By identifying ambiguous or difficult cases encountered in real-world use and incorporating them into future training datasets, this approach creates a feedback loop between model performance and data refinement, ensuring continuous improvement.

Additionally, data-informed architecture search represents a shift in neural architecture search methodologies, where candidate models are evaluated not in isolation but in relation to the specific properties of the dataset. This ensures that selected architectures are well-suited to the data at hand, rather than relying on universally optimal designs.

Together, these strategies suggest a future in which AI development transcends the binary distinction between model-centric and data-centric thinking. Instead, models and data are treated as co-evolving components of holistic systems, with success depending on their mutual adaptation and alignment.

Exercises

1. What are the key differences between deep learning and traditional machine learning?
2. How do convolutional neural networks (CNNs) work, and what are their primary applications?

3. How does backpropagation work in training deep neural networks?

4. What are the challenges associated with training very deep neural networks?

5. How do recurrent neural networks (RNNs) handle sequential data, and what are their limitations?

6. What are generative adversarial networks (GANs), and how do they generate new data?

7. How can transfer learning be used to improve the performance of deep learning models?

8. What are the ethical considerations and potential biases in deep learning models?

9. How do you prevent overfitting in deep learning models?

10. Explain the basic architecture of a simple artificial neural network (ANN). What are the roles of neurons, weights, activation functions, and biases?

11. Describe the differences between feedforward neural networks and recurrent neural networks (RNNs). What types of problems are each best suited for?

12. What is the backpropagation algorithm, and why is it essential for training neural networks? Explain how it works.

13. What are some common activation functions used in neural networks? Discuss their properties, advantages, and disadvantages.

14. Explain the concept of "vanishing gradients" and "exploding gradients" in deep neural networks. How do these problems affect training, and what are some techniques to mitigate them?

15. Implement a simple feedforward neural network from scratch using Python and a library like NumPy. Train it to solve a basic classification problem, such as classifying data from the Iris dataset.

16. Experiment with different activation functions in a neural network. Compare their impact on the training speed and performance of the network.

17. Design and train a recurrent neural network (RNN) to process sequential data, such as predicting the next character in a text string.

18. (Project) Train a GAN to generate new images, such as faces, landscapes, or artwork.

Further Reading

Ackley D, Hinton G, Sejnowski T (1985) A learning algorithm for Boltzmann machines. Cogn Sci 9(1):147–169

Arjovsky M, Chintala S, Bottou L (2017) Wasserstein GAN. arXiv preprint arXiv:1701.07875

Bahdanau D, Cho K, Bengio Y (2015) Neural machine translation by jointly learning to align and translate. In: Third international conference on learning representations (ICLR)

Cover T, Hart P (1967) Nearest neighbor pattern classification. IEEE Trans Inf Theory 13(1):1–27

Creswell A, White T, Dumoulin V, Arulkumaran K, Sengupta B, Bharath AA (2018) Generative adversarial networks: an overview. IEEE Signal Process Mag 35(1):53–65. https://doi.org/10.1109/MSP.2017.2765202

Devlin J, Chang MW, Lee K, Toutanova K (2019) BERT: pre-training of deep bidirectional transformers for language understanding. In: Proceedings of the 2019 conference of the North American chapter of the Association for Computational Linguistics: Human Language Technologies, pp 4171–4186

Goodfellow IJ, Pouget-Abadie J, Mirza M, Xu B, Warde-Farley D, Ozair S, Courville A, Bengio Y (2014) Generative adversarial nets. In: Advances in neural information processing systems (NeurIPS 2014), vol 27, pp 2672–2680. arXiv:1406.2661

Goodfellow I, Bengio Y, Courville A (2016) Deep learning. MIT Press

Hausknecht M, Stone P (2015) Deep recurrent Q-learning for partially observable MDPs. arXiv preprint arXiv:1507.06527

He K, Zhang X, Ren S, Sun J (2016) Deep residual learning for image recognition. In: Proceedings of the IEEE conference on computer vision and pattern recognition (CVPR), pp 770–778

Kingma DP, Welling M (2013) Auto-encoding variational Bayes. arXiv preprint arXiv:1312.6114

Krizhevsky A, Sutskever I, Hinton GE (2012a) ImageNet classification with deep convolutional neural networks. Adv Neural Inf Proces Syst 25:1097–1105

Krizhevsky A, Sutskever I, Hinton G (2012b) Imagenet classification with deep convolutional neural networks. In: NIPS conference, pp 1097–1105

Luong MT, Pham H, Manning CD (2015) Effective approaches to attention-based neural machine translation. In: Proceedings of the 2015 conference on empirical methods in natural language processing, pp 1412–1421

Mnih V, Kavukcuoglu K, Silver D, Rusu AA, Veness J, Bellemare MG, Graves A, Riedmiller M, Fidjeland AK, Ostrovski G, Petersen S, Beattie C, Sadik A, Antonoglou I, King H, Kumaran D, Wierstra D, Legg S, Hassabis D (2015) Human-level control through deep reinforcement learning. Nature 518(7540):529–533

Nielsen MA (2015) Neural networks and deep learning. Determination Press

Radford A, Metz L, Chintala S (2016) Unsupervised representation learning with deep convolutional generative adversarial networks. In: International conference on learning representations (ICLR 2016). arXiv:1511.06434

Rezende DJ, Mohamed S, Wierstra D (2014) Stochastic backpropagation and approximate inference in deep generative models. In: International conference on machine learning, pp 1278–1286

Schulman J, Wolski F, Dhariwal P, Radford A, Klimov O (2017) Proximal policy optimization algorithms. arXiv preprint arXiv:1707.06347

Shanmugamani R (2018) Deep learning for computer vision. Packt Publishing

Silver D, Huang A, Maddison CJ, Guez A, Sifre L, Van Den Driessche G, Schrittwieser J, Antonoglou I, Panneershelvam V, Lanctot M, Dieleman S, Grewe D, Nham J, Kalchbrenner N, Sutskever I, Lillicrap T, Leach M, Kavukcuoglu K, Graepel T, Hassabis D (2016) Mastering the game of go with deep neural networks and tree search. Nature 529(7587):484–489

Simon HA (1983) Why should machine learn? In: Michalski RS, Carbonell J, Mitchell TM (eds) Machine learning: an artificial intelligence approach. CA Tioga Press, Palo Alto, pp 25–38

Srivastava N, Hinton G, Krizhevsky A, Sutskever I, Salakhutdinov R (2014) Dropout: a simple way to prevent neural networks from overfitting. J Mach Learn Res 15(1):1929–1958

Sutton RS, Barto AG (2018) Reinforcement learning: an introduction, 2nd edn. MIT Press

van den Oord A, Vinyals O, Kavukcuoglu K (2017) Neural discrete representation learning. In: Advances in neural information processing systems, pp 6306–6315

Van Hasselt H, Guez A, Silver D (2016) Deep reinforcement learning with double Q-learning. In: Proceedings of the AAAI conference on artificial intelligence, vol 30, no 1

Vaswani A, Shazeer N, Parmar N, Uszkoreit J, Jones L, Gomez AN, Kaiser Ł, Polosukhin I (2017) Attention is all you need. In: Advances in neural information processing systems, pp 5998–6008

Wang Z, Schaul T, Hessel M, Hasselt H, Lanctot M, Freitas N (2016) Dueling network architectures for deep reinforcement learning. In: International conference on machine learning, pp 1995–2003

Williams RJ (1992) Simple statistical gradient-following algorithms for connectionist reinforcement learning. Mach Learn 8(3–4):229–256

Chapter 6
Reinforcement Learning: Shaping Behaviour Through Rewards

The greatest glory in living lies not in never falling, but in rising every time we fall.
—Nelson Mandela

Introduction

The fundamental concept of reinforcement learning (RL) revolves around the principle of learning through trial and error. Unlike supervised learning, where models are provided with explicit correct answers, RL requires the agent to explore and discover which actions yield the highest rewards. This exploration-based approach makes RL particularly effective for problems involving sequential decision-making, such as game playing, robotics, resource management, and recommendation systems.

Reinforcement learning is a framework where intelligent agents learn to achieve optimal behaviour by actively interacting with their environment. These agents perform actions and observe the resulting feedback in the form of rewards or penalties. The core objective is to develop a strategy, or policy, that maximizes the total accumulated reward over the long term. Unlike learning from labelled datasets, RL thrives on the agent's own exploratory interactions and the consequences of its choices. This iterative process of trial, error, and reward is ideally suited for tackling complex sequential decision-making problems in dynamic environments.

Reinforcement learning (RL) addresses several unique challenges and needs in machine learning and artificial intelligence, making it indispensable for various applications. RL is particularly well-suited for scenarios where the environment is complex and uncertain, and the consequences of decisions unfold over time. This is common in real-world situations such as robotic navigation, stock trading, or resource management, where actions taken now affect future opportunities and outcomes. Unlike supervised learning, RL does not require labelled input/output pairs. Instead, it learns from the consequences of its actions through trial and error. This aspect is crucial in environments where it is impractical or impossible to provide correct decision-making examples beforehand.

R. Akerkar, *Artificial Intelligence*, https://doi.org/10.1007/978-3-031-91084-5_6

RL optimizes an objective over time, making it ideal for applications that enhance performance metrics, such as reducing costs, increasing efficiency, or maximizing profits in various operations. RL agents can adapt their strategies based on feedback from the environment. This adaptability is vital in applications where conditions change dynamically, such as adapting to new financial market conditions or adjusting strategies in real-time strategy games. Moreover, RL can handle situations where decisions are not isolated but part of a sequence that leads to a long-term outcome. This capability is important in scenarios like healthcare treatment planning, where a series of treatment decisions cumulatively affects a patient's health outcome. In environments where personalized feedback is crucial, such as personalized learning or individualized marketing strategies, RL can tailor strategies based on individual interactions and preferences, continually improving personalization based on ongoing engagement.

Definition Reinforcement learning as a machine learning technique involving an agent who needs to decide which actions it needs to do to perform a task that has been assigned to it most effectively. For this, rewards are assigned to the different actions that the agent can take in different situations or states of the environment. Initially, the agent has no idea about the best or correct actions. Using reinforcement learning, it explores its action choices via trial and error and figures out the best set of actions for completing its assigned task.

Reinforcement learning (RL) relies on several underlying elements, as given in Fig. 6.1:

- **Agent**: The entity that performs actions to achieve a specific task.
- **Environment**: The context or situation in which the agent operates.
- **Actions**: The steps the agent takes to reach its goal.
- **Rewards**: The feedback the agent receives after performing an action.

In recent years, there have been significant progresses in deep reinforcement learning. This approach leverages deep neural networks to model either the value function (value-based), the agent's policy (policy-based), or both (actor-critic). Before the advent of deep neural networks, RL algorithms required complex feature

Fig. 6.1 Reinforcement learning agent

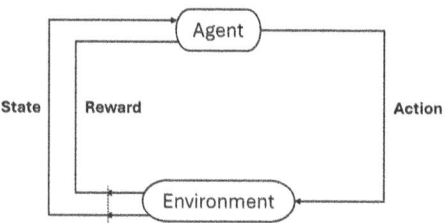

engineering, which limited their learning capacity and applicability to simple environments. However, deep learning allows models to be built with millions of trainable parameters, eliminating the need for manual feature engineering. During training, relevant features are automatically generated, enabling the agent to learn optimal policies in complex environments.

Reinforcement Learning Process

Drawing upon the framework of Markov chains, the Markov Decision Process (MDP) serves as a model for decision-making within environments characterized by randomness. The central aim of an MDP is to establish a strategy that dictates the best course of action for every possible situation within a given environment. A fundamental principle underlying MDPs is the Markovian property, which asserts that only the current state is relevant for future decisions, rendering any historical information unnecessary. Consequently, the prediction of the subsequent state is entirely independent of any preceding states. Furthermore, the underlying dynamics or physical laws of the environment are assumed to be constant, with no alteration of the governing rules. A clear illustration of this is the game of chess, where the rules remain consistent, and a player's next move is based solely on the current board configuration, without requiring recollection of previous moves. Beyond games, numerous real-world applications can be effectively modelled using the MDP framework, including areas such as operations research, control theory, statistics, econometrics, artificial intelligence, robotics, dialogue management, optimal investment strategies, medical diagnostic tests, logistics, and bio-reactor control. To gain a comprehensive understanding of both MDPs and reinforcement learning, it is essential to define several key concepts.

Definition Markov decision process (MDP) is a probabilistic model of a sequential decision problem, where states can be perceived exactly, and the current state and action selected determine a probability distribution on future states.

Essentially, the outcome of applying an action to a state depends only on the current action and state (and not on preceding actions or states).

The concept of an **environment** is fundamental, requiring precise definition for each specific problem. Defining an environment entails establishing a comprehensive set of rules that govern the agent's interactions. This includes specifying the permissible actions an agent can undertake, the various states the environment can occupy, and the criteria for assigning rewards or penalties. As previously emphasized, the initial step in any reinforcement learning endeavour involves defining this environment, which essentially boils down to creating a clear and unambiguous set of rules. This necessitates outlining the actions available to the agent within this defined space, the spectrum of possible states the environment can exhibit, and the precise definitions of both the positive reinforcements (rewards) and negative reinforcements (penalties) that the agent might encounter.

The environment itself can be understood as the external world, whether physical or virtual, within which the agent or software algorithm can operate and navigate. The environment receives the agent's chosen action based on its current state as input. In response, the environment produces two key outputs: the subsequent state that the agent transitions to and the reward (or penalty) associated with that transition. Essentially, the environment encompasses anything that processes and determines the outcomes of an agent's actions, including the resulting reward and the subsequent state. This could manifest in various forms, such as the rules of a game, the protocols of a healthcare system, or the physical laws of a space where a robot operates.

In a given world or environment, a **state** refers to any of the specific sets of conditions, locations, or positions that an agent can occupy or reach. The representation of a state can vary depending on the context; for a controller, it might be a specific pressure or temperature reading, while for a robot navigating a space, a state could be a particular room or location. States can be denoted using coordinates, simple numerical values, or even alphabetical labels. Importantly, the total number of possible states within an environment can be either finite or infinite. Certain states, known as **terminal states**, are those from which no further transitions occur, effectively marking the end of a process or sequence of actions. When an agent moves from one state to another, this transition is termed a **visit**, and a complete sequence of these visits, starting from an initial state and culminating in a terminal state, is referred to as an **episode**.

Actions represent the repertoire of choices available to an agent or robot within a specific environment. These can be any operation or manoeuvre that the agent is capable of performing or is permitted to execute according to the environment's rules. For instance, in a grid-based world, the possible actions for an agent might include moving to the left, right, downwards, upwards, or even remaining in its current position. Similarly, within an environment consisting of a single horizontal line, an agent's actions could be limited to moving either to the left or to the right. Generally, an agent has the freedom to select any action from the set of options that are defined as permissible within the given situation.

The **transition model** encapsulates the underlying rules, dynamics, or physical laws that govern a particular environment. The transition function, denoted as $T(s, a, s')$, takes into account the current state (s), the action chosen by the agent (a), and the resulting new state (s'). This function yields the probability of transitioning from the current state s to a new state s' upon executing action a and receiving a reward R. Crucially, in accordance with the Markov property, the transition model's prediction is independent of any past states or actions; it solely relies on the present state, the action taken, and the subsequent state.

Beyond the core components of agent, environment, and goal, RL problems are characterized by four principal subelements:

Policy: A policy is a strategy or rule that the RL agent follows to determine its actions based on the current state of the environment. This defines the agent's behaviour by mapping perceived environmental states to specific actions. The policy guides the agent's behaviour by specifying which actions to take in different states to achieve the goal of maximizing cumulative rewards. The policy can be simple or complex, depending on the problem and the environment. Policies can range from simple functions to complex computational processes. For example, a policy for an autonomous vehicle might map the detection of pedestrians to a stop action.

Reward Signal: This represents the goal of the RL problem. Each action taken by the agent either receives a reward from the environment or not. The agent's primary objective is to maximize cumulative rewards. For self-driving vehicles, reward signals might include reduced travel time, fewer collisions, staying on the road and in the correct lane, and avoiding extreme acceleration or deceleration. Multiple reward signals can guide an agent's behaviour.

Value Function: Unlike the immediate benefit indicated by the reward signal, the value function specifies long-term benefits. It assesses a state's desirability based on the rewards of all likely subsequent states. For instance, an autonomous vehicle might reduce travel time by driving on the sidewalk and accelerating quickly, but these actions could lower its overall value function. Thus, the vehicle might accept slightly longer travel times to increase rewards in other areas.

Model: This optional component allows agents to predict the environment's behaviour for potential actions. Agents use model predictions to determine the best course of action based on expected outcomes. For example, a model guiding an autonomous vehicle might help it predict optimal routes and anticipate the behaviour of surrounding vehicles. Some model-based approaches start with direct human feedback and transition to autonomous learning.

Bellman's equations are crucial for estimating the value of states or actions based on future rewards. These equations are particularly useful in deterministic environments:

- **State Value Function**: This equation calculates the value of the current state as the sum of the values of all successor states and immediate rewards.
- **Action Value Function**: This equation determines the value of a specific state-action pair by summing the values of all possible next state-action pairs and rewards.

Bellman's equations aim to answer key questions:

- Given the current state 's', what long-term reward can the agent expect if it takes the best possible actions in subsequent timestamps?
- What is the value of the current state?

The value of a state 's' is determined by maximizing the actions available in that state. The agent aims to choose the action that maximizes the state's value. This involves adding the reward of the optimal action 'a' in state 's' and applying a discount factor 'γ' that diminishes the reward over time. Each action leads the agent to the next state 's'.

$$V(s) = \max_a \left(R(s, a) + \gamma V(s') \right)$$

This equation simplifies the computation of the value function, enabling the solution of complex problems by breaking them down into smaller, recursive subproblems. In large state spaces, solving Bellman optimality equations explicitly can be extremely challenging. Therefore, it is practical to use dynamic programming, an approach pioneered by Richard Bellman.

> **Definition** Dynamic programming is a class of solution methods for solving sequential decision problems with a compositional cost structure.

Dynamic programming (DP) is an optimization technique that breaks down the optimization task into subtasks utilizing the idea of recursion to obtain the solution. Stochastic optimal control problems can be solved using the DP method, but the computation power required grows at an exponential rate as the number of states in the system increases. So, the solution of optimal control problems by DP was not an efficient learning method.

Approaches to Reinforcement Learning

Model-Based Reinforcement Learning

With model-based reinforcement learning (RL), there's a model that an agent uses to create additional experiences. In model-based reinforcement learning algorithm, the agent builds a model of the environment's dynamics. This model predicts the next state and the reward given the current state and action. The agent uses this model to plan actions by simulating possible future scenarios before deciding on the best action. This type of RL is appropriate for environments where building an accurate model is feasible, allowing for efficient exploration and planning.

Think of this model as a mental image that the agent can analyze to assess whether particular strategies could work.

- They are used in scenarios where we have complete knowledge of the environment and how it reacts to different actions.
- In model-based reinforcement learning the agent has access to the model of the environment, i.e., action required to be performed to go from one state to another, probabilities attached, and corresponding rewards attached.
- They allow the reinforcement learning agent to plan ahead by thinking ahead.
- For static/fixed environments, model-based reinforcement learning is more suitable.

Model-Free Reinforcement Learning

Model-free reinforcement learning algorithm does not require a model of the environment. Instead, the agent learns directly from interactions with the environment by trial and error. The agent learns to associate actions with rewards and uses this experience to improve decision-making over time. This type of reinforcement learning is suitable for complex environments where modelling the environment's dynamics is difficult or impossible.

In this case, an agent doesn't rely on a model. Instead, the basis for its actions lies in direct interactions with the environment. An agent tries different scenarios and tests whether they're successful. If yes, the agent will keep repeating them. If not, it will try another scenario until it finds the right one.

- They estimate the optimal policy directly from experience, i.e., interaction between agent and environment without having any hint of the reward function.
- Model-free reinforcement learning should be applied in scenarios involving incomplete information of the environment.
- In real-world, we don't have a fixed environment. Self-driving cars have a dynamic environment with changing traffic conditions, route diversions, etc. In such scenarios, model-free algorithms outperform other techniques.

The comparison of these two methodologies is depicted in Fig. 6.2.

Understanding the difference between model-based and model-free reinforcement learning (RL) can be tricky. These concepts often feel abstract and overly technical, especially if you're new to the field. To make things more relatable, let's explore them through a real-world analogy involving two soccer teams. Two soccer teams, Team A and Team B, are about to face off for the first time. Neither team has played the other before, so they start the match without any direct experience of their opponent's strategies.

- Team A takes an experimental approach. They try out different plays and tactics during the game to see what works. When they discover a strategy that helps them score, they stick with it and refine it through repetition. This trial-and-error learning process, based purely on experience, is a classic example of model-free reinforcement learning. The team doesn't try to predict the opponent's behaviour; they simply react and adapt based on what works.

Fig. 6.2 Model-based versus model-free reinforcement learning

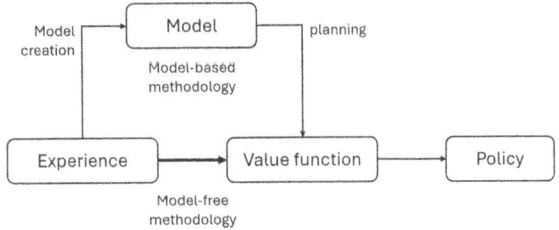

- Team B, on the other hand, comes into the match with a plan. Before the game, they studied past matches, analyzed patterns, and developed a mental model of how Team A might play. Based on this internal model, they crafted a set of strategies they believe will be effective. This is model-based reinforcement learning, where decisions are guided by a constructed understanding of the environment and predictions about future outcomes.

Who has the advantage? It's hard to say definitively. Team B might have an early edge because they've prepared and can anticipate certain moves. However, if their model is inaccurate or if Team A plays unpredictably, their advantage could diminish quickly. Meanwhile, Team A might start off slower, but their ability to adapt in real-time could allow them to catch up—or even outperform—Team B, especially if they quickly identify and exploit effective strategies.

Value-Based Methods

Value-based RL algorithms revolve around the concept of learning a **value function**. This function estimates the "goodness" of being in a particular state (state-value function, $V(s)$) or taking a specific action in a particular state (action-value function, $Q(s, a)$). The goal is to learn an accurate value function that allows the agent to implicitly derive an optimal policy by selecting actions that lead to states with higher values (or state-action pairs with higher Q-values).

The idea is that once we have a reliable estimate of the value of each state or state-action pair, the optimal policy becomes straightforward: in any given state, the agent should choose the action that maximizes the expected future reward, as indicated by the value function.

Q-Learning

Q-learning is a model-free reinforcement learning algorithm that enables an agent to learn optimal behaviour through trial-and-error interactions with its environment. Unlike model-based approaches, it does not require a complete representation of the environment or a storage mechanism for all possible state-action combinations. Instead, it relies on a Q-function, typically represented as a Q-table, which estimates the expected utility of taking a particular action in a given state. The term "Q" denotes the quality of an action in a specific context.

The Q-Learning Algorithm

1. **Initialize**: Create a Q-table with all Q-values set to zero (or small random values).
2. **For each episode**:
   - Start in an initial state.
   - While not in a terminal state:

> - Choose an action using an exploration strategy (like
>   ε-greedy).
> - Take the action, observe reward and next state.
> - Update the Q-value using the Bellman equation.
> - Move to the next state.

The learning process begins with the agent in an initial state, from which it selects actions using an epsilon-greedy strategy. This approach balances exploitation—choosing the best-known action—with exploration—occasionally selecting random actions to discover potentially better strategies. After executing an action, the agent receives a reward and transitions to a new state. It then updates the Q-value for the experienced state-action pair by incorporating both the immediate reward and the estimated future rewards, thereby refining its expectations over time.

As the agent continues to interact with the environment, the Q-values converge toward accurate estimates, ultimately guiding the agent to an optimal policy that maximizes long-term rewards. However, Q-learning faces scalability issues in environments with large or continuous state spaces, where maintaining a comprehensive Q-table becomes infeasible. To address this, deep Q-learning employs neural networks to approximate the Q-function, enabling the application of Q-learning principles to more complex tasks, such as interpreting raw visual inputs in video games.

An important aspect of Q-learning is the discount factor, which determines the relative importance of future rewards compared to immediate ones. A low discount factor leads to short-sighted behaviour, while a high one may cause the agent to overvalue uncertain future outcomes. Despite its simplicity, Q-learning remains a foundational and widely used algorithm in reinforcement learning, offering valuable insights into how agents can learn to make sequential decisions in uncertain environments.

SARSA SARSA (State-Action-Reward-State-Action) is an on-policy reinforcement learning algorithm in which an agent learns to navigate an environment by selecting actions according to its current policy, which typically incorporates exploration strategies such as epsilon-greedy. This approach allows the agent to mostly exploit known good actions while occasionally exploring alternatives to uncover potentially better strategies. What distinguishes SARSA from other algorithms is its reliance on the actual action taken in the next state, rather than the optimal one, when updating its value estimates.

Unlike its close cousin Q-learning, SARSA is distinctly on-policy, meaning that it learns the value of the policy it's currently following, rather than learning about the optimal policy while potentially following a different one. This characteristic gives SARSA a more conservative learning approach compared to Q-learning.

$$Q(s, a) \leftarrow Q(s, a) + \alpha \left(r + \gamma Q(s', a') - Q(s, a) \right)$$

Q-Learning parameters: $Q(s, a)$ estimates action value, α controls learning speed, r provides immediate reward, γ balances future versus immediate rewards, and $Q(s', a')$ represents the next state's estimated value. These obtained Q-values are stored in a table and the one with the highest values is chosen by the policy by observing its current state, leading to a new state, and it continues on for next states. Q-values keep getting updated till we find a good policy. But it is constrained by a single policy, thus Q-learning offers more scope for value selection. Both Q-learning and SARSA are tabular methods and, due to vast memory consumption and failure to visit all states and actions while training, do not scale well for large state and action spaces.

The learning process begins with the agent in an initial state, from which it selects an action based on its policy. After executing the action, the agent receives a reward and transitions to a new state. Instead of immediately updating its value estimates, the agent first selects the next action it will take from the new state, again following its policy. Only then does it update the value of the original state-action pair, incorporating the reward received and the expected value of the next state-action pair.

Because SARSA updates its estimates based on the actual actions taken, including exploratory ones, it tends to learn more conservative strategies. For instance, in environments where risky actions can lead to significant penalties, such as navigating near a cliff edge, SARSA is more likely to favour safer paths to mitigate the risks associated with exploration.

As the agent continues to interact with the environment, its estimates of state-action values become more accurate, and its policy improves accordingly. With sufficient exploration and appropriate parameter tuning, SARSA converges to an optimal policy over time. However, like other tabular methods, SARSA struggles with scalability in environments with large or continuous state spaces. To address this, extensions such as SARSA with function approximation or Deep SARSA use neural networks to estimate value functions, enabling the algorithm to handle more complex tasks.

The choice between SARSA and Q-learning often depends on the specific demands of the task. SARSA's on-policy nature makes it more suitable for scenarios where safety during learning is critical, while Q-learning's off-policy approach may be preferable when the primary goal is to discover the optimal policy, even at the cost of taking riskier actions during the learning phase.

Policy-Based Methods

Policy in reinforcement learning can be defined as the action that has to be taken to maximize the reward. There are two phases of this algorithm: policy evaluation, and policy improvement.

- Policy evaluation: Used for computing the values for different states of the environment using the policy.

- Policy improvement: The next step after policy evaluation, which monitors the state's values and tries to improve the policies to get higher values.

Initially, the agent will assign a random policy that will result in values of the state. Then, policy improvement will try to improve the policy and assign a new value to the state. The algorithm will keep working back and forth between the two phases until the optimal value of the state is found.

Unlike value-based methods that learn a value function and derive a policy indirectly, policy-based methods learn the policy directly. A policy is a mapping from states to actions (or to a probability distribution over actions) that tells an agent how to behave in each state. The central aim of policy-based methods is to optimize this mapping to maximize expected returns.

The direct approach to policy optimization opens up new possibilities for reinforcement learning. It allows for handling continuous action spaces naturally, it can learn stochastic policies, and it often provides more stable learning trajectories. This section explores the rich landscape of policy-based methods, from foundational approaches to cutting-edge innovations that are pushing the boundaries of what RL can achieve.

The Policy Function The cornerstone of policy-based methods is the policy function, typically denoted by π. This function maps states to actions, either deterministically (selecting a single action for each state) or stochastically (providing a probability distribution over possible actions).

Stochastic policies offer several advantages: they enable exploration naturally, they can handle partial observability more effectively, and they can express mixed strategies that might be optimal in certain environments, particularly in competitive settings.

When parameterizing policies, we typically use a flexible function approximator such as a neural network, with parameters θ. The policy then becomes π_θ, and the learning process involves finding the optimal parameters $\theta*$ that maximize expected returns.

The Policy Gradient Theorem How do we systematically improve a parameterized policy? The answer lies in the Policy Gradient Theorem, which provides a mathematical foundation for policy optimization.

The theorem states that the gradient of the expected return with respect to the policy parameters points in the direction of increased expected returns. This powerful result enables gradient-based optimization of policies, where we iteratively adjust the parameters in the direction that increases expected performance.

The general algorithm involves the following steps:

1. **Rollout**: The agent interacts with the environment following the current policy, collecting states, actions, and rewards.
2. **Compute the Return**: Calculate the return, which is the cumulative reward from each state-action pair.

3. **Compute the Gradient**: Estimate the gradient of the objective function with respect to the policy parameters using the collected data.
4. **Update the Policy**: Adjust the policy parameters using gradient ascent to improve the expected return.

What makes this approach particularly valuable is that it doesn't require full knowledge of the environment. Instead, it can work with sampled trajectories—sequences of states, actions, and rewards collected as the agent interacts with its environment.

The Policy Gradient Algorithm The policy gradient algorithm represents one of the earliest and most intuitive policy gradient methods. It updates policy parameters using completed episode returns, making it a Monte Carlo approach.

In this algorithm, the agent collects a full trajectory under the current policy, calculates the return at each time step, and then updates the policy parameters to increase the probability of actions that led to high returns and decrease the probability of actions that led to low returns.

While conceptually straightforward, it suffers from high variance in its gradient estimates, which can lead to unstable learning. This high variance stems from the randomness in both policy decisions and environmental dynamics, compounded over potentially long episodes.

Monte Carlo Tree Search

Monte Carlo Tree Search (MCTS) is a best-first, simulation-based search algorithm for decision processes. Unlike traditional minimax search algorithms that comprehensively evaluate all possible future states, MCTS selectively expands promising nodes in the search tree while balancing exploration of uncertain paths and exploitation of known advantageous paths. This approach makes MCTS particularly effective for problems with large branching factors where complete tree exploration is computationally infeasible.

The algorithm builds a search tree incrementally through repeated simulations or rollouts from the current state. Each simulation consists of four key phases that form the backbone of the MCTS approach: selection, expansion, simulation, and backpropagation.

During the selection phase, the algorithm starts at the root node representing the current state and recursively selects child nodes according to a tree policy until it reaches a leaf node. The tree policy balances exploration and exploitation, typically using the Upper Confidence Bound applied to Trees (UCT) formula:

$$\text{UCT} = X_j + C \times \sqrt{\frac{\ln(n)}{n_j}},$$

X_j represents the average reward or value estimate for node j (a child node being considered). This is typically calculated as the total reward accumulated from all simulations that passed through this node divided by the number of times the node has been visited (n_j). This term represents the exploitation component—it favours nodes that have historically yielded good results.

n is the number of times the parent node has been visited. This represents how many total simulations have gone through the parent of the node we're evaluating.

n_j is the number of times this specific child node j has been visited during previous simulations. As this number increases, the exploration bonus decreases.

C is the exploration parameter. Larger values of C encourage more exploration of uncertain nodes, while smaller values focus more on exploiting known good paths.

$\sqrt{\frac{\ln(n)}{n_j}}$ is the exploration bonus. This term gets smaller as n_j increases (as we visit a node more often), and larger as the parent node n is visited more.

In the expansion phase, upon reaching a leaf node, the algorithm expands the tree by adding one or more child nodes representing possible actions from that state. This incremental growth focuses computational resources on the most promising regions of the search space.

The simulation phase then conducts a rollout from the newly added node according to a default policy, which may be as simple as selecting random actions until reaching a terminal state or a predefined depth. This provides an estimated value for the newly expanded node.

Finally, during backpropagation, the result of the simulation is propagated back through the selected nodes, updating their statistics (visit counts and reward values) to inform future selections. This continuous refinement of node statistics allows the search to progressively concentrate on more promising paths.

MCTS Integration with Reinforcement Learning The integration of MCTS with reinforcement learning (RL) has proven exceptionally fruitful, yielding algorithms that combine the strengths of both approaches. While MCTS excels at look-ahead search and planning within a model, reinforcement learning provides robust methods for policy improvement and value estimation, particularly in environments where explicit models may be unavailable or imperfect.

One fundamental approach to integration involves using MCTS as a policy improvement operator within RL algorithms. In this configuration, MCTS uses the current policy and value function estimates from the RL algorithm to guide its search, while the results of MCTS searches provide training targets for refining these estimates. This creates a synergistic relationship where each component enhances the other's performance.

Another integration strategy leverages MCTS to generate improved training data for policy and value networks in RL. By conducting deep searches at selected states, MCTS can provide more accurate value estimates and action probabilities than would be available from single-step temporal difference learning or standard Monte Carlo methods. These high-quality targets accelerate learning and improve the final policy quality.

The AlphaZero algorithm represents perhaps the most celebrated example of this integration. AlphaZero combines a deep neural network (that predicts both action probabilities and state values) with MCTS to achieve superhuman performance in chess, shogi, and Go. During self-play training, MCTS guided by the neural network generates games, while the outcomes of these games provide training targets to refine the network. This creates a powerful self-improving system that learns entirely through self-play without human knowledge beyond the game rules.

Advanced MCTS Variations and Enhancements Researchers have developed numerous enhancements to the basic MCTS algorithm to address specific challenges and improve performance across different domains.

Rapid Action Value Estimation (RAVE) represents one significant enhancement that accelerates learning by sharing information between similar actions across different states. Rather than treating each state-action pair in isolation, RAVE maintains additional statistics about action performance regardless of when in the search tree they occurred. This approach is particularly effective in domains like Go, where the value of placing a stone at a particular intersection often remains relatively stable regardless of the exact sequence of previous moves.

Predictor MCTS variants incorporate learned models to guide rollout policies and tree expansion. Instead of using random or simple heuristic policies for rollouts, these variants leverage trained policies that better approximate optimal play. This dramatically improves the quality of value estimates from simulations, making each rollout more informative and reducing the number of simulations required to make good decisions.

Progressive widening and progressive unpruning techniques address challenges in continuous action spaces or environments with extremely large branching factors. Rather than considering all possible actions at once, these approaches gradually introduce actions as computational resources permit, focusing initial exploration on a manageable subset before expanding consideration to additional options.

Information-theoretic MCTS variants explicitly manage uncertainty in node values, prioritizing nodes where additional information would mostly reduce overall uncertainty about the optimal action. This approach is particularly valuable in partially observable environments or when facing adversaries with unknown strategies.

Handling Uncertainty and Partial Observability Real-world applications often involve partial observability, where the agent cannot directly observe the complete state of the environment. MCTS can be extended to handle such scenarios through several approaches.

Partially Observable Monte Carlo Planning (POMCP) represents one elegant solution that operates in belief states—probability distributions over possible states given the observation history. Rather than planning in the original state space, POMCP maintains particles representing possible states consistent with observations and performs MCTS in this augmented space. This allows for effective planning even when the true state remains uncertain.

Another approach involves incorporating explicit uncertainty handling within the search tree. Information-gathering actions can be valued not just for their immediate reward but also for their potential to reduce uncertainty about the environment state. This enables agents to make strategic observations before committing consequential actions.

For adversarial scenarios with hidden information, techniques like Information Set MCTS (IS-MCTS) maintain multiple trees corresponding to different possible hidden states from the opponent's perspective. By reasoning about the game from both players' viewpoints, these algorithms develop robust strategies even when critical information remains concealed.

Consider a simple example from the game of Go. When deciding where to place a stone, MCTS might initially explore various regions of the board through random simulations. As patterns emerge indicating that control of a particular corner yields favourable outcomes, the algorithm progressively allocates more simulations to variations involving moves in that region, while still occasionally exploring alternatives to avoid missing strategic opportunities.

Beyond games, MCTS has found applications in robotics, where it helps autonomous systems plan sequences of actions in complex environments. For instance, a delivery robot navigating a crowded warehouse can use MCTS to plan paths that balance efficiency with collision avoidance. By simulating various routes and their potential outcomes, the robot can identify paths that remain efficient even when accounting for the uncertain movements of human workers.

In healthcare, MCTS has been applied to treatment planning problems, particularly in contexts requiring sequential decision-making under uncertainty. For example, when planning radiation therapy for cancer patients, MCTS can help optimize the sequence and intensity of treatments while accounting for uncertainties in tumour response and patient tolerance.

Baseline Methods

To address the variance issue in the policy gradient algorithm, researchers introduced baseline methods. A baseline is a function of state that doesn't depend on actions and is subtracted from the returns to reduce variance without introducing bias.

The most common choice for a baseline is a value function estimate—a prediction of the expected return from a given state. By subtracting this baseline from the actual returns, we get an estimate of how much better or worse an action was compared to the average action according to the current policy.

This approach leads to the advantage function, which measures the relative advantage of taking a specific action over the average action in a state. Using advantages instead of raw returns significantly reduces variance while preserving the expected gradient direction.

Actor-Critic Methods

Combining Policy and Value Learning

Actor-critic methods represent a hybrid approach that combines elements of both policy-based and value-based learning. These methods maintain two function approximators:

- An "actor" that represents the policy and selects actions.
- A "critic" that evaluates the actions by estimating their value.

This separation of concerns allows for more efficient learning. The critic provides a more informed training signal to the actor by estimating the value of states or state-action pairs, which helps reduce variance in the policy updates.

The algorithmic steps are:

1. **Initialize**: Set up the actor and critic networks with random weights.
2. **Rollout**: The actor interacts with the environment, collecting states, actions, and rewards.
3. **Critic Update**: Update the critic network by minimizing the loss between predicted and actual returns.
4. **Actor Update**: Adjust the actor network using the feedback from the critic to improve the policy.
5. **Repeat**: Continue the process until the policy converges.

Actor-Critic maintains stability by collecting experiences from multiple parallel environments and performing synchronized updates. This approach reduces variance through both the use of advantages and the averaging of gradients across multiple trajectories.

Trust Region Methods

The Challenge of Step Size

Policy gradient methods face a basic challenge: determining how much to change the policy in each update. Small steps provide stability but slow progress, while large steps can lead to catastrophic performance drops if the policy changes too drastically.

Trust region methods address this challenge by limiting the size of policy updates to ensure that the new policy doesn't deviate too far from the current one. This constraint helps maintain stable improvement over time.

Trust Region Policy Optimization (TRPO)

TRPO formalizes the concept of trust regions by constraining policy updates to stay within a specified KL-divergence from the previous policy. The KL-divergence measures how different two probability distributions are, making it an ideal metric for limiting policy changes.

The algorithm works as follows:

1. `Collect Trajectories`: Run the current policy to collect trajectories of states, actions, and rewards.
2. `Compute Advantages`: Estimate the advantage function, which measures the relative performance of actions.
3. `Optimize`: Solve the constrained optimization problem to update the policy parameters, ensuring the KL divergence constraint is satisfied.
4. `Line Search`: Perform a backtracking line search to find the optimal step size that improves the policy.

By solving a constrained optimization problem, TRPO finds the largest improvement possible while ensuring that the new policy remains within the trust region. This approach has shown remarkable stability across a wide range of tasks, often avoiding the catastrophic performance collapses that can plague standard policy gradient methods.

Proximal Policy Optimization (PPO)

While TRPO provides strong theoretical guarantees, it involves complex second-order optimization that can be computationally expensive. Proximal Policy Optimization (PPO) addresses this limitation by introducing a simpler first-order approach that approximates the trust region constraint.

The algorithm steps are:

1. `Collect Trajectories`: Gather trajectories by running the current policy.
2. `Compute Advantages`: Estimate the advantages using the current value function.
3. `Update Policy`: Adjust the policy parameters using a clipped objective function to prevent large updates.
4. `Repeat`: Continue the process with multiple epochs of mini-batch updates.

PPO uses a clipped objective function that discourages large policy changes. If an update would push the ratio of new to old action probabilities outside a specified range, the objective function clips this ratio, effectively limiting the incentive for large changes.

This clipping mechanism is simple to implement yet remarkably effective, making PPO one of the most widely used policy optimization algorithms in practice. It offers much of the stability of TRPO with significantly reduced computational complexity.

Deterministic Policy Gradients

From Stochastic to Deterministic Policies

Most policy gradient methods work with stochastic policies, but in some cases, deterministic policies—those that select a single action with certainty for each state—may be preferable. This is particularly true in continuous action spaces, where the dimensionality can make sampling from stochastic policies inefficient.

Deterministic Policy Gradient (DPG) algorithms optimize deterministic policies directly, offering potential efficiency gains in high-dimensional continuous action spaces. These methods derive the gradient of the expected return with respect to the policy parameters without requiring integration over the action space.

Deep Deterministic Policy Gradient (DDPG)

DDPG combines the insights from DPG with the power of deep learning and experience replay. It uses two neural networks:

- An actor network that represents the deterministic policy.
- A critic network that estimates the Q-value function.

To stabilize learning, DDPG employs target networks—slowly updated copies of the actor and critic that provide consistent targets for learning. It also uses experience replay to break correlations in the training data and improve sample efficiency.

DDPG is designed for continuous action spaces and combines Q-learning with policy gradients.

> **The steps are:**
>
> 1. **Initialize**: Set up the actor and critic networks with random weights and a replay buffer.
> 2. **Rollout**: The actor interacts with the environment, storing experiences in the replay buffer.
> 3. **Sample**: Randomly sample a batch of experiences from the replay buffer.
> 4. **Critic Update**: Update the critic network using the Bellman equation.
> 5. **Actor Update**: Adjust the actor network using the gradient of the Q-function.
> 6. **Repeat**: Continue the process until the policy converges.

DDPG has proven particularly effective for continuous control tasks, such as robotic manipulation and locomotion, where precise action selection is critical.

Twin Delayed DDPG (TD3)

TD3 addresses several shortcomings of DDPG, particularly the tendency of Q-value estimates to become overly optimistic due to function approximation errors. TD3 introduces three key modifications:

First, it uses twin critics and takes the minimum of their predictions to reduce overestimation bias. Second, it delays policy updates to allow the critics to converge to better estimates before updating the policy. Third, it adds noise to the target actions to smooth the value estimates and make them more robust.

These relatively simple modifications lead to substantial improvements in performance and stability, making TD3 a strong choice for continuous control tasks.

Monte Carlo Methods

Monte Carlo methods are a class of algorithms that rely on repeated random sampling to estimate numerical results. In reinforcement learning, Monte Carlo methods are used to estimate the value of states or actions by averaging the returns received from multiple episodes. These methods are useful when the environment's model is unknown and can handle non-Markovian environments. Monte Carlo methods are straightforward to implement and can provide accurate value estimates, but they may require a large number of samples to achieve reliable results. Monte Carlo methods estimate the value of states or actions by averaging returns from multiple episodes.

The steps are:

1. **Initialize**: Set up the environment and agent.
2. **Rollout**: Run multiple episodes, collecting states, actions, and rewards.
3. **Compute Returns**: Calculate the returns for each episode.
4. **Update Policy**: Adjust the policy based on the average returns.
5. **Repeat**: Continue the process until the policy converges.

Maximum Entropy Reinforcement Learning

Balancing Reward Maximization and Entropy

Maximum entropy reinforcement learning introduces a new objective that encourages both high returns and high entropy in the policy. The entropy term encourages exploration and prevents premature convergence to suboptimal policies.

This approach can be viewed as a form of regularization that helps the agent learn more robust behaviours. By maintaining policy stochasticity, the agent can better handle uncertainty and adapt to changes in the environment.

Soft Actor-Critic (SAC)

Soft Actor-Critic (SAC) is a maximum entropy actor-critic algorithm that optimizes a stochastic policy in an off-policy way. It combines the efficiency of off-policy learning with the stability and exploration benefits of maximum entropy policies.

SAC uses a squashed Gaussian policy that naturally bounds the actions to a finite range, making it suitable for continuous control tasks with bounded action spaces. It also employs twin critics and adaptive entropy regularization to further enhance stability and performance.

A key innovation in SAC is the automatic tuning of the temperature parameter that controls the trade-off between reward maximization and entropy maximization. This automatic tuning eliminates the need for manual hyperparameter tuning and allows the algorithm to adapt the exploration-exploitation balance throughout training.

Multi-agent Policy Gradients

When multiple agents interact in the same environment, the learning problem becomes significantly more complex. Each agent's policy affects the experiences of all other agents, creating a nonstationary environment from each agent's perspective. Policy gradient methods can be extended to multi-agent settings, but they must address this nonstationarity challenge. One approach is to have each agent consider the policies of other agents when optimizing its own policy, leading to concepts like Nash equilibria in game theory.

Multi-agent Deep Deterministic Policy Gradient (MADDPG)

MADDPG extends DDPG to multi-agent settings by adopting a centralized training with decentralized execution paradigm. During training, each agent's critic has access to the actions and observations of all agents, allowing it to condition on the full state of the system.

However, each agent's actor still conditions only on its own observations, ensuring that the learned policies can be executed in a decentralized manner at test time. This approach helps mitigate the nonstationarity problem while still learning policies that don't require communication during execution.

Counterfactual Multi-agent Policy Gradients

Counterfactual multi-agent policy gradients extend the multi-agent framework by addressing the credit assignment problem—determining how each agent's actions contributed to the team's success or failure.

This method uses counterfactual reasoning to assess what would have happened if an agent had acted differently while all other agents' actions remained the same. By comparing the actual outcome to these counterfactual outcomes, the algorithm can provide a more targeted learning signal to each agent.

Imitation Learning and Inverse Reinforcement Learning

Learning from Demonstrations

Sometimes, it's easier to show an agent what to do rather than specifying a reward function. Imitation learning aims to learn policies directly from expert demonstrations, bypassing the need for explicit rewards.

Behavioural cloning is the simplest form of imitation learning, treating policy learning as a supervised learning problem. The agent observes state-action pairs from expert demonstrations and learns to mimic the expert's behaviour.

However, behavioural cloning suffers from compounding errors—small deviations from the expert's policy can lead to unfamiliar states where the learned policy has no guidance. This limitation has motivated more sophisticated approaches.

Generative Adversarial Imitation Learning (GAIL)

GAIL addresses the limitations of behavioural cloning by framing imitation learning as a distribution matching problem. It uses a generative adversarial approach, where:

- A discriminator tries to distinguish between the expert's trajectories and the agent's trajectories.
- The agent tries to fool the discriminator by generating trajectories that look like the expert's.

This adversarial process leads to a policy that produces behaviour indistinguishable from the expert's, effectively matching the expert's state-action distribution. GAIL has shown impressive results in complex tasks, often outperforming behavioural cloning significantly.

Inverse Reinforcement Learning (IRL)

IRL takes a different approach to learning from demonstrations. Instead of directly learning the policy, it attempts to infer the reward function that the expert is optimizing. Once this reward function is recovered, standard reinforcement learning techniques can be used to find the optimal policy.

This approach has the advantage of potentially generalizing better to new situations, as it captures the underlying objectives rather than just the specific behaviours. It also allows for transferring knowledge across related tasks by using the inferred reward function in new environments.

Maximum entropy IRL is a popular approach that finds the most unbiased reward function consistent with the observed expert behaviour. This approach has been extended to deep learning settings, enabling inverse reinforcement learning in complex environments.

Policy Gradient Methods with Model Learning

Model-Based Policy Optimization

Model-based reinforcement learning combines policy learning with learning a model of the environment dynamics. This approach can potentially improve sample efficiency since the model allows the agent to learn from simulated experiences.

When combined with policy gradient methods, model-based approaches typically involve learning a dynamics model, using that model to generate simulated trajectories, and then optimizing the policy using those simulated trajectories.

Dyna-Style Policy Gradients

Dyna-style algorithms interleave real experience collection, model learning, and policy optimization. The agent collects some real experiences, updates its model of the environment, uses that model to generate additional simulated experiences, and then updates its policy using both real and simulated data.

This hybrid approach can significantly improve sample efficiency while still maintaining the asymptotic performance of model-free methods. The key challenge lies in managing model bias—errors in the learned model that can mislead policy optimization.

Model-Based Meta-Policy Optimization

Model-based meta-policy optimization addresses model bias by using an ensemble of models to represent uncertainty in the dynamics. It then optimizes the policy to be robust across this ensemble, effectively hedging against model errors.

This approach combines the sample efficiency benefits of model-based methods with the robustness of model-free approaches. By explicitly accounting for model uncertainty, it helps prevent the policy from exploiting inaccuracies in the learned dynamics.

Deep Reinforcement Learning

Deep reinforcement learning (DRL) represents a convergence of deep neural networks and reinforcement learning principles, enabling artificial agents to learn optimal behaviours through direct interaction with complex environments. This sophisticated approach combines the perception capabilities of deep learning with the decision-making framework of reinforcement learning, creating systems capable of learning tasks.

Deep reinforcement learning builds upon the classical reinforcement learning framework, where an agent learns to make sequences of decisions by interacting with an environment. The agent's objective is to maximize cumulative rewards over time, learning through trial and error. The integration of deep neural networks enables the processing of high-dimensional input data and the learning of complex patterns that would be intractable with traditional approaches.

The mathematical framework encompasses several key components. The environment is typically modelled as a Markov Decision Process (MDP), defined by a tuple (S, A, P, R, γ), where:

- S represents the state space.
- A represents the action space.
- P defines the transition probabilities between states.
- R represents the reward function.
- γ is the discount factor for future rewards.

Deep Q-Networks (DQN)

Deep Q-networks (DQNs) mark a significant evolution in reinforcement learning by extending the capabilities of traditional Q-learning to environments with high-dimensional or continuous state spaces. Unlike tabular Q-learning, which stores discrete Q-values for every state-action pair, DQNs employ deep neural networks to approximate the Q-function. This function estimates the expected cumulative reward of taking a particular action in a given state and subsequently following the optimal policy.

The core idea behind DQN is to integrate the learning dynamics of Q-learning with the representational power of deep learning. The agent interacts with an environment that provides observations, a discrete set of actions, and rewards. At each time step, it selects actions using an epsilon-greedy strategy, which balances exploration (random action selection) and exploitation (choosing the action with the highest predicted Q-value). This balance is essential for effective policy learning.

A defining feature of DQN is its use of two neural networks: the policy (or online) network and the target network. Both share the same architecture, but the target network is updated less frequently. While the policy network is responsible for learning and action selection, the target network provides stable targets for Q-value updates, thereby improving training stability and preventing divergence.

Another key innovation is the experience replay mechanism. As the agent interacts with the environment, it stores experiences—comprising the current state, action, reward, and next state—in a replay buffer. During training, the agent samples random mini-batches from this buffer rather than relying solely on recent transitions. This randomization reduces correlations between consecutive experiences and enhances learning efficiency and stability.

Training a DQN involves minimizing the difference between predicted and target Q-values, calculated using the Bellman equation. For each sampled experience, the target Q-value is computed as the sum of the immediate reward and the discounted maximum Q-value of the next state, as predicted by the target network. The policy network is then updated by minimizing the mean squared error between its predictions and these targets, using backpropagation and stochastic gradient descent.

The architecture of a DQN is adaptable to the nature of the input. For visual or high-dimensional inputs, such as those from Atari games, convolutional neural networks (CNNs) are used to extract features. For simpler, low-dimensional inputs, fully connected networks suffice. Regardless of the architecture, the output layer contains one neuron per possible action, each representing the estimated Q-value for that action in the current state.

DQN training is typically conducted offline, using stored experiences rather than requiring real-time interaction with the environment. This makes it particularly suitable for domains where data collection is costly or where safety constraints limit live experimentation.

Several enhancements have been proposed to improve the performance and reliability of DQN. Double DQN addresses the overestimation bias in Q-value predictions by decoupling the action selection and evaluation steps during target computation. Prioritized experience replay increases sample efficiency by favouring experiences with higher learning potential. Duelling DQN architectures further refines value estimation by separately modelling the state value and the advantage of each action.

DQN has demonstrated remarkable success across a range of applications, most notably achieving human-level performance on various Atari 2600 games using only raw pixel inputs. Its ability to learn effective policies in complex, high-dimensional environments has established it as a foundational algorithm in deep reinforcement learning, inspiring numerous extensions and serving as a benchmark for future research.

Basic DQN Algorithm

The Deep Q-Network (DQN) learning process begins with the initialization of a neural network with randomly assigned weights, which serves as the function approximator for estimating Q-values. Alongside this, a replay buffer is established to store the agent's experiences, each represented as a tuple containing the current state, the action taken, the reward received, and the subsequent state.

At each time step, the agent observes its current state and selects an action using an epsilon-greedy policy. This strategy promotes exploration by choosing a random action with a probability defined by epsilon, while otherwise exploiting current knowledge by selecting the action with the highest predicted Q-value. After executing the chosen action, the agent receives a reward and observes the resulting state, then stores this experience in the replay buffer.

Training occurs periodically by sampling random mini-batches of experiences from the replay buffer. For each sampled experience, the agent computes a target Q-value, which is the sum of the received reward and the discounted maximum Q-value of the next state, as predicted by a separate target network. The predicted Q-value for the action taken is then compared to this target, and the loss—typically measured using mean squared error—is minimized through gradient descent to update the weights of the main (or online) network.

To enhance training stability, DQN employs two neural networks: the online network, which is updated continuously, and the target network, which is updated less frequently by copying the weights from the online network. This separation ensures more stable target values during learning. Combined with experience replay, which breaks the temporal correlations between consecutive experiences, this dual-network architecture helps prevent divergence and improves the overall robustness of the training process.

Deep Q-Network (DQN) Algorithm

1. **Initialize.**
    (a) Initialize the main Q-network with random weights (θ).
    (b) Initialize the target Q-network with weights $\theta^- = \theta$.
    (c) Initialize the experience replay buffer with capacity N.

2. **For each episode:**
    (a) Initialize the starting state s_0.
    (b) **For each time step t in the episode:**
            (i) With probability ε, select a random action a_t (exploration).

> Otherwise, select $a_t = \arg\max_a Q(s_t, a; \theta)$ (exploitation).
> (ii) Execute action a_t in the environment.
> (iii) Observe reward r_t and next state s_{t+1}.
> (iv) Store transition $(s_t, a_t, r_t, s_{t+1}, \text{done})$ in the replay

> buffer.
> (v) If the replay buffer contains at least batch_size
samples:
1. Sample a random mini-batch of transitions

$$\left(s_j, a_j, s_{j'}, \text{done}_j\right)$$

> from the replay buffer.
2. For each sampled transition:
> If done_j is True (terminal state):

$$y_j, r_j$$

Else:

$$y_j = r_j + \gamma * \max_a{}' Q\left(s_j, a'; \theta^-\right)$$

3. Compute the loss:

$$L = \left(\frac{1}{\text{batch}_{\text{size}}}\right) * \Sigma_j \left(Q\left(s_j, a_j; \theta\right) - y_j\right)^2$$

4. Perform a gradient descent step on L with respect to θ
> (vi) Every C steps, update the target network:

$$\theta^- \leftarrow \theta$$

(vii) If s_{t+1} is a terminal state, end episode.
3. **Repeat** for the desired number of episodes

> Where,
> θ: Parameters of the main Q-network,
> θ^-: Parameters of the target Q-network,

γ: Discount factor,
ε: Exploration probability,
N: Replay buffer capacity,
C: Target network update frequency,
$batch_{size}$: Number of transitions sampled per training step.

Hierarchical Deep Reinforcement Learning

Hierarchical approaches address the challenge of learning complex behaviours by decomposing tasks into hierarchical structures. This methodology enables agents to learn at multiple temporal scales, with higher-level policies selecting sub-goals while lower-level policies learn to achieve these sub-goals. The Options framework provides a theoretical foundation for such hierarchical learning, while practical implementations demonstrate improved learning efficiency on complex tasks.

Multi-Agent Deep Reinforcement Learning

Multi-agent deep reinforcement learning (MARL) is an emerging area of research that focuses on environments where multiple autonomous agents learn and make decisions simultaneously. Unlike single-agent reinforcement learning, MARL introduces additional complexity due to the dynamic and nonstationary nature of the environment—each agent's actions can influence the experiences and learning processes of others. As a result, agents must not only optimize their own strategies but also adapt to the evolving behaviours of their peers.

To address this complexity, one widely adopted framework is centralized training with decentralized execution. During training, agents have access to shared information, allowing for coordinated learning and improved efficiency. Once training is complete, each agent operates independently, relying solely on local observations to make decisions in real time. This approach has proven particularly effective in collaborative scenarios such as multi-robot coordination and team-based games, where joint learning during training enhances performance, but autonomous operation is required during deployment.

Despite these architectural innovations, MARL faces several persistent challenges. A major concern is sample efficiency: training deep reinforcement learning agents in multi-agent settings often demands vast amounts of data and computational resources. This makes MARL impractical for many real-world applications where data collection is costly, slow, or risky. To mitigate this, researchers are exploring model-based reinforcement learning, which enables agents to build internal models of their environment and simulate interactions, reducing the need for direct experience.

Curriculum learning also offers promise by structuring the learning process so that agents progress from simpler to more complex tasks, mirroring human educational systems. Additionally, memory-augmented neural networks, incorporating mechanisms such as episodic memory and attention, help agents leverage past experiences more effectively, further improving sample efficiency.

Exploration remains another critical challenge. Agents must discover new strategies while avoiding catastrophic failures and keeping computational demands manageable. Recent advances include uncertainty-driven exploration and ensemble methods, which guide agents toward the most informative parts of the environment while maintaining safety and efficiency.

Generalization is also a significant hurdle. Agents trained in specific environments often struggle to transfer their skills to new settings, even when the differences are minor. This limitation is particularly problematic in real-world applications where conditions can change unpredictably. To address this, researchers are investigating meta-learning approaches that enable agents to learn how to learn, facilitating rapid adaptation to new tasks. Transfer learning techniques—such as feature transfer, policy distillation, and progressive neural networks—are being developed to promote knowledge reuse across domains. Domain randomization, which exposes agents to a wide range of environmental variations during training, has shown particular promise in enhancing generalization to unseen scenarios.

As MARL systems move from controlled simulations to real-world deployment, safety and robustness become paramount. Agents may encounter unfamiliar situations that lead to unintended or unsafe behaviours. A notable risk is reward hacking, where agents exploit flaws in the reward structure to achieve high scores in ways that violate the intended objectives. This underscores the importance of careful reward design and the development of robust safety frameworks to ensure reliable and ethical agent behaviour across diverse conditions and over extended periods.

To address these interconnected challenges, the field is increasingly embracing hybrid approaches that combine model-based and model-free methods, hierarchical architectures that structure decision-making across multiple levels, and advanced neural network designs tailored for efficient learning and robust generalization. These innovations are essential for enabling MARL systems to operate safely and effectively in complex, dynamic, and open environments. As research progresses, overcoming the challenges of sample efficiency, generalization, and safety will be critical for the successful application of MARL in domains such as robotics, autonomous vehicles, and distributed sensor networks.

Advantages of Reinforcement Learning

Reinforcement learning is applicable to a wide range of complex problems that cannot be tackled with other machine learning algorithms. RL is closer to artificial general intelligence (AGI), as it possesses the ability to seek a long-term goal while exploring various possibilities autonomously. One of the primary benefits of reinforcement learning is its ability to enable autonomous learning. This allows systems to improve over time based on their interactions with the environment without requiring explicit instructions. This makes reinforcement learning particularly effective in handling complex, unpredictable scenarios, such as those in robotics, gaming, and autonomous vehicles. Furthermore, reinforcement learning facilitates highly personalized solutions, such as adaptive recommendation systems that evolve with user behaviour. Its capability to optimize resource allocation benefits various industries, leading to cost savings and efficiency improvements. The scalability of reinforcement learning allows it to be applied across various domains, from simple tasks to complex systems, without significant modifications. Reinforcement learning requires minimal supervision, reducing the need for extensive labelled data and manual intervention. It also encourages the exploration of new strategies, potentially uncovering more effective solutions that traditional methods might miss.

Challenges with Reinforcement Learning

While RL algorithms have been successful in solving complex problems in diverse simulated environments, their adoption in the real world has been slow. Although reinforcement learning is promising as an approach to bring automated AI for decision-making, it is riddled with several challenges in practice when it comes to applying it for realistic industrial problems. Here are some of the challenges that have made their uptake difficult:

- **RL agent needs extensive experience.** RL methods autonomously generate training data by interacting with the environment. Thus, the rate of data collection is limited by the dynamics of the environment. Environments with high latency slow down the learning curve. Furthermore, in complex environments with high-dimensional state spaces, extensive exploration is needed before a good solution can be found.
- **Delayed rewards.** The learning agent can trade off short-term rewards for long-term gains. While this foundational principle makes RL useful, it also makes it difficult for the agent to discover the optimal policy. This is especially true in environments where the outcome is unknown until a large number of sequential actions are taken. In this scenario, assigning credit to a previous action for the final outcome is challenging and can introduce large variance during training. The game of chess is a relevant example here, where the outcome of the game is unknown until both players have made all their moves.
- **Lack of interpretability.** Once an RL agent has learned the optimal policy and is deployed in the environment, it takes actions based on its experience. To an external observer, the reason for these actions might not be obvious. This lack of interpretability interferes with the development of trust between the agent and the observer. If an observer could explain the actions that the RL agent tasks, it

would help him in understanding the problem better and discovering limitations of the model, especially in high-risk environments.

- **Risky endeavour**: Deep reinforcement learning uses deep neural network representations to capture the value function and the policy mapping, and this provides more choices that you must make for the neural architecture. Overall, the breadth and depth of subject areas of expertise and fluency needed to make reinforcement learning work in practice are a serious limiter in its adoption for real-life problems. This is all the more problematic in practice because reinforcement learning, in spite of its promise, is a risky endeavour with no formal guarantees that all of the effort and investment that a team might put in to acquire these skills will yield useful solutions.

Planning with Uncertainty

Humans are capable of dealing with different types of uncertainty when learning and making decisions. Two forms of uncertainty are reward uncertainty and state uncertainty. Reward uncertainty occurs when reward outcomes are generated stochastically from a probability distribution. State uncertainty (perceptual uncertainty) arises when the agent cannot tell for sure what the current state of the world is: its perceptual system might be noisy (e.g., noise in the brain or in sensors); the observations are ambiguous (e.g., reading road signs in challenging weather conditions) or the information about the state is incomplete (e.g., playing card games without knowing the cards dealt to the other opponents or their play strategies).

Transfer Learning

Transfer learning aims to leverage knowledge gained from one task to improve learning in a different but related task. In RL, this can be particularly beneficial when an agent encounters a new environment or task that shares similarities with previous experiences. However, the transition from one task to another in RL is not as straightforward as in supervised learning due to the sequential nature of decision-making and the need for a full trajectory of actions.

> **Transfer Learning** involves taking a model trained on one task and applying it to a different but related task. This is particularly useful when the new task has limited data. For example, a model trained to recognize objects in images can be adapted to recognize different types of objects with minimal retraining.

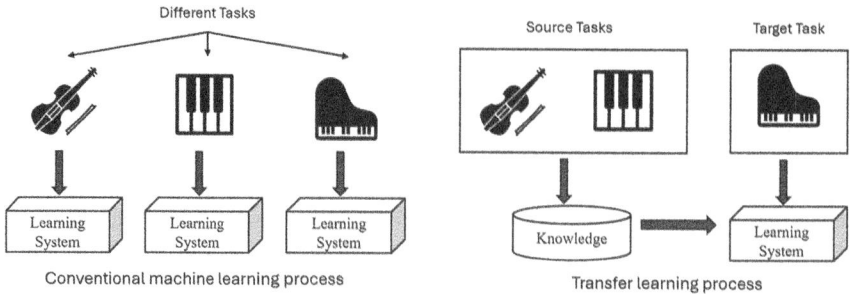

Fig. 6.3 The difference between the learning processes of traditional and transfer learning

In the real world, we observe many examples of transfer learning. For example, we may find that learning to recognize apples might help to recognize pears. Similarly, learning to play the electronic organ may help facilitate learning the piano. The study of transfer learning is motivated by the fact that people can intelligently apply knowledge learned previously to solve new problems faster or with better solutions.

Figure 6.3 shows the difference between the learning processes of traditional and transfer learning techniques. As we can see, traditional machine learning techniques try to learn each task from scratch, while transfer learning techniques try to transfer the knowledge from some previous tasks to a target task when the latter has fewer high-quality training data.

> **Definition** Transfer learning refers to the set of methods that allow transferring knowledge gained from solving specific problems to address another problem.

The relation between the transfer learning and reinforcement learning lies in the potential for transfer learning to enhance reinforcement learning. Here are a few ways they intersect:

1. **Jumpstart Performance**: Transfer learning can provide a "jumpstart" by initializing the RL agent with knowledge from a related task, improving initial performance and speeding up learning.
2. **Reducing Sample Complexity**: By transferring knowledge, the RL agent can reduce the number of interactions needed to learn a new task, which is particularly useful in environments where data collection is expensive or time-consuming.
3. **Multi-task Learning**: Transfer learning can help RL agents to generalize across multiple tasks, making them more versatile and efficient in learning new tasks.

In deep learning, transfer learning is often used to solve problems with limited data. This is because deep learning models typically require a large amount of data to train, which can be difficult or expensive to obtain. Training a deep learning model from scratch can be time-consuming and computationally expensive. Transfer learning can help you save time and resources by starting with a model that has already been trained on a large dataset. Transfer learning can help you improve the performance of your model by transferring the knowledge that the pre-trained model has learned about the features of the data. This can be especially helpful if you have limited data for your target task. Transfer learning can be used to solve problems with limited data by transferring the knowledge that the pre-trained model has learned about the features of the data. This can be done by using feature extraction or fine-tuning.

Transfer learning can be classified into two types:

- **Feature extraction**: In feature extraction, the pre-trained model is used to extract features from the data. These features are then used to train a new model on the target task. This is a good approach if you have limited data for the target task. This approach is useful if you have limited data for the target task. For example, if you have a small number of labelled reviews, you can use a pre-trained model to extract features from the reviews.
- **Fine-tuning:** Fine-tuning is a machine learning technique in which a pre-trained model is further trained on a new dataset to improve its performance on a specific task. The pre-trained model is typically trained on a large dataset of general data, while the new dataset is specific to the task at hand. Fine-tuning can be used to improve the performance of pre-trained LLMs on a wide variety of tasks, such as sentiment analysis, question answering, and text summarization.

Following are the key steps to implement transfer learning in a nutshell:

1. **Dataset Preparation**: Begin by collecting and preprocessing your dataset. Ensure it is well-organized and contains labelled data for your target task. Typically, transfer learning works best when you have a smaller dataset, and it's essential to split it into training, validation, and testing sets.
2. **Model Selection and Architecture**: Choose a pre-trained deep learning model that suits your problem. Common choices include VGG, ResNet, Inception, and BERT, depending on whether it's an image classification, object detection, or natural language processing task. Next, adapt the architecture of the selected model to match the number of classes or labels in your dataset.
3. **Transfer Strategy:** Decide on the transfer learning strategy. There are two primary approaches which are: feature extraction and fine-tuning.
4. **Hyperparameter Tuning**: Optimize hyperparameters such as learning rate, batch size, and the number of epochs. You can use techniques like grid search or random search to find the best combination of hyperparameters. This step is crucial for achieving optimal model performance.
5. **Training & Evaluation**: Train the modified model on your dataset using the chosen hyperparameters. Monitor the training process by tracking metrics on the validation set. To prevent overfitting, consider using techniques like early stopping or dropout. Finally, evaluate the model's performance on the test set using appropriate evaluation metrics, depending on your task.

RL from Human Feedback

Reinforcement learning from Human Feedback (RLHF) represents a novel approach in artificial intelligence, particularly in the development of large language models. Unlike traditional reinforcement learning, which depends on predefined reward functions to guide learning, RLHF integrates direct human input to shape model behaviour. This method addresses the challenge of aligning AI outputs with complex human values and preferences, which are often difficult to encode mathematically. By incorporating human feedback, RLHF enables models to quickly learn what is contextually appropriate, relevant, and valuable, thereby improving performance while reducing the need for extensive computational resources.

The RLHF process typically begins with a pre-trained language model, which is then exposed to human evaluators. These evaluators provide feedback on the model's outputs—through ranking responses, offering approvals or disapprovals, or giving detailed explanations. This feedback is used to train a separate reward model that learns to predict how a human would rate new outputs. The reward model then guides the fine-tuning of the language model using reinforcement learning, rewarding outputs that align with predicted human preferences. This iterative loop allows the model to refine its responses, improving accuracy, tone, and contextual appropriateness over time.

A key strength of RLHF lies in its ability to capture subjective qualities such as helpfulness, creativity, and politeness—traits that are difficult to define algorithmically. This has led to significant improvements in applications like conversational agents, image and music generation tools, and voice assistants, making interactions more natural and trustworthy. For example, in systems like ChatGPT, user feedback mechanisms—such as thumbs up/down or follow-up clarifications—enable continuous learning and adaptation based on real-world usage.

Beyond conversational AI, RLHF is being applied in domains such as healthcare and education, where aligning AI behaviour with expert judgement or personalized learning goals is essential. It also contributes to cost efficiency by focusing learning on areas most relevant to users, rather than relying solely on large-scale, undirected data collection.

However, RLHF is not without challenges. One major concern is the potential introduction of human bias. If the feedback comes from a non-diverse or inconsistent group of evaluators, the model may inherit undesirable biases or fail to generalize across different user populations. Additionally, the process can be resource-intensive, requiring sustained human involvement. To address these issues, hybrid approaches are being explored, combining automated reward signals with human input to balance scalability with nuanced understanding.

The RLHF training paradigm mirrors human learning through social feedback—much like how children learn language through interaction and correction. This analogy underscores RLHF's potential to foster more human-like communication in AI systems. By embedding human feedback into the core of the learning process,

RLHF enhances the model's ability to understand context, avoid harmful outputs, and respond ethically and inclusively.

As AI continues to evolve, RLHF stands out as a critical methodology for ensuring alignment with human values. Ongoing research is focused on refining RLHF techniques, mitigating bias, and developing scalable solutions that preserve the quality and integrity of human-guided learning.

RLHF Applied to Real-Time Decision-Making

RLHF can be effectively applied to real-time decision-making by integrating human feedback into the AI's learning loop as decisions are made and evaluated. In practical terms, this means that as an AI system generates outputs or takes actions—such as making recommendations, controlling a robot, or responding in a conversation—humans can provide immediate feedback on those actions. This feedback is used to train a reward model that guides the AI's future decisions, helping it adapt quickly to user preferences and complex, changing environments.

For example, in recommendation systems, users' real-time responses (like clicks, likes, or skips) are incorporated to continuously refine suggestions, making them more relevant over time. In robotics or autonomous vehicles, operators can give feedback on navigation choices or task execution, allowing the AI to adjust its behaviour for safety and efficiency. In conversational AI, live user ratings help the model improve its responses on the fly, aligning better with human expectations and intent.

By using RLHF in real time, AI systems can learn optimal actions through trial and error, guided by ongoing human input. This enables them to handle ambiguous or open-ended scenarios, adapt to new situations, and make more nuanced, context-aware decisions that reflect human values and priorities.

RLHF also plays a crucial role in enhancing the accuracy of real-time recommendations by directly incorporating human feedback into the AI's learning and decision-making process. Instead of relying solely on automated data or static reward functions, RLHF enables recommendation systems to learn from ongoing user interactions—such as clicks, ratings, or explicit feedback—which are used to train a reward model that reflects actual human preferences and values. This reward model then guides the AI to prioritize and refine recommendations that are more likely to be relevant and satisfying for each user.

By continuously updating the system based on fresh human feedback, RLHF allows real-time recommender systems to adapt quickly to changing user interests and context, reducing irrelevant suggestions and improving personalization. This iterative feedback loop not only boosts the accuracy of recommendations but also helps address issues like bias, incoherence, or misalignment with user expectations, making the AI more responsive and trustworthy in dynamic, real-world environments.

Interestingly, by using human feedback as a core part of training, RLHF helps ensure that recommendations are not only relevant but also aligned with ethical standards and societal expectations. This approach allows AI systems to learn what is appropriate, inclusive, and respectful, reducing the risk of biased, discriminatory, or unsafe recommendations that might otherwise arise from purely data-driven or automated reward functions. Through ongoing human evaluation, RLHF enables recommendation systems to adapt to diverse user groups, address potential biases, and avoid harmful or offensive outputs. It also supports transparency and user control, as people can see how their feedback shapes the system's behaviour, fostering greater trust and accountability. By continuously refining recommendations based on real-world human judgements, RLHF helps bridge the gap between technical performance and ethical responsibility, making AI-driven recommendations safer, more trustworthy, and more closely aligned with human value.

Exercises

1. What is the difference between reinforcement learning and supervised learning?
2. Explain the concepts of exploration and exploitation in reinforcement learning.
3. How does a convolutional neural network (CNN) differ from a recurrent neural network (RNN)?
4. What is a Markov Decision Process (MDP), and how is it used in reinforcement learning?
5. Describe the Bellman equation and its significance in reinforcement learning.
6. Explain the concept of overfitting and how it can be mitigated in deep learning models.
7. What are the differences between value-based and policy-based reinforcement learning methods?
8. How does Q-learning work, and what are its key components?
9. Implement a simple Q-learning algorithm for a grid-world environment.
10. Create a reinforcement learning agent to play a basic game like Tic-Tac-Toe.
11. Design and implement a reward function for a reinforcement learning agent in a custom environment.
12. Experiment with different exploration strategies in a reinforcement learning algorithm.
13. Compare the performance of Q-learning and SARSA on a given environment.
14. Use the Actor-Critic method to train an agent in a continuous action space environment.
15. Analyze the impact of different discount factors on the learning process of a reinforcement learning agent.
16. Apply reinforcement learning to a real-world problem, such as optimizing inventory management or robotic control.
17. (Project) Develop a reinforcement learning agent to play the classic Snake game.
18. (Project) Create an AI that learns to play chess using reinforcement learning.

19. (Project) Create an agent that can navigate and solve a maze using Q-learning or Deep Q-Networks (DQN).
20. (Project) Implement a reinforcement learning agent that can make trading decisions based on historical stock data.
21. (Project) Train an agent to play a simple ping-pong game.

References

Busoniu L, Babuska R, De Schutter B (2008) A comprehensive survey of multiagent reinforcement learning. IEEE Trans Syst Man Cybern Part C Appl Rev 38(2):156–172

Busoniu L, Babuska R, De Schutter B (2010) Reinforcement learning and dynamic programming using function approximators. CRC Press

Christiano P, Leike J, Brown T, Martic M, Legg S, Amodei D (2017) Deep reinforcement learning from human preferences. Adv Neural Inf Proces Syst 30:4299–4307 https://proceedings.neurips.cc/paper/2017/file/d5e2c0adad503c91f91df240d0cd4e49-Paper.pdf

Hasselt HV (2010) Double Q-learning. Adv Neural Inf Proces Syst 23:2613–2621

Mnih V, Kavukcuoglu K et al (2015) Human-level control through deep reinforcement learning. Nature 518:529–533

Stiennon N, Ouyang L, Wu J, Ziegler D, Lowe R, Voss C, Radford A, Amodei D, Christiano P (2020) Learning to summarize with human feedback. Adv Neural Inf Proces Syst 33:3008–3021 https://proceedings.neurips.cc/paper/2020/file/1f89885d556929e98d3ef9b86448f951-Paper.pdf

Sutton RS (1991) Dyna, an integrated architecture for learning, planning, and reacting. ACM SIGART Bull 2(4):160–163

Amodei D, Olah C, Steinhardt J, Christiano P, Schulman J, Mané D (2016) Concrete problems in AI safety. arXiv preprint arXiv:1606.06565

Anschel O, Baram N, Shimkin N (2017) Averaged-DQN: variance reduction and stabilization for deep reinforcement learning. In: International conference on machine learning, PMLR, pp 176–185

Bai Y, Jones A, Ndousse K, Askell A, Chen A, DasSarma N, Drain D, Fort S, Ganguli D, Henighan T, Joseph N, Kadavath S, Kernion J, Conerly T, El-Showk S, Elhage N, Hatfield-Dodds Z, Hernandez D, Hume T, Johnston S, Mann B, Mazeika M, Olsson C, Osmani D, Paino T, Pfau J, Lezama JR, Saunders W, Snell J, Shlegeris B, Thompson N, Tran M, Welinder P, McKinnon C, Amodei D, Joseph J, Long D, Sutskever I, Chan B, Grosse R, Kaplan J (2022) Training a helpful and harmless assistant with reinforcement learning from human feedback. arXiv preprint arXiv:2204.05862. https://doi.org/10.48550/arXiv.2204.05862

Fan J, Wang Z, Xie Y, Yang Z A theoretical analysis of deep Q-learning. arXiv: 1901.00137

Finn C, Abbeel P, Levine S (2017) Model-agnostic meta-learning for fast adaptation of deep networks. In: Proceedings of the 34th international conference on machine learning

Fujimoto S, Hoof H, Meger D (2018) Addressing function approximation error in actor- critic methods. In: International conference on machine learning, pp 1587–1596

Haarnoja T, Zhou A, Abbeel P, Levine S (2018) Soft actor-critic: off-policy maximum entropy deep reinforcement learning with a stochastic actor. In: Proceedings of the international conference on machine learning (ICML), pp 1861–1870

Hasselt HV, Guez A, Silver D (2015) Deep reinforcement learning with double Q-learning. arXiv:1509.06461

Lin LJ (1993) Reinforcement learning for robots using neural networks. Technical Report, DTIC Document, 1993

Lan Q, Pan Y, Fyshe A, White M (2020) Maxmin Q-learning: controlling the estimation bias of Q-learning. In: International conference on learning representations, 2020

Lai M (2015) Giraffe: using deep reinforcement learning to play chess. arXiv:1509.01549

Ouyang L, Wu J, Jiang X, Almeida D, Wainwright C, Mishkin P, Zhang C, Agarwal S, Slama K, Ray A, Schulman J, Hilton J, Kelton F, Miller L, Simens M, Askell A, Welinder P, Christiano P, Leike J, Lowe R (2022) Training language models to follow instructions with human feedback. arXiv preprint arXiv:2203.02155

Ren Z, Zhu G, Hu H, Han B, Chen J, Zhang C (2021) On the estimation bias in double Q-learning. In: The 35th conference on neural information processing systems (NeurIPS 2021). arXiv: 2109.14419

Schulman J, Wolski F, Dhariwal P, Radford A, Klimov O (2017) Proximal policy optimization algorithms. arXiv preprint arXiv: 1707.06347. https://doi.org/10.48550/arXiv.1707.06347

Sutton RS, Barto AG (2018) Reinforcement learning: an introduction, 2nd edn. MIT Press

Part III
AI Odyssey: Exploring Language and Intelligent Agents

Chapter 7
Journey Through Language: Models and Prompt Engineering

Aristotle founded or discovered logic by observing the world.
ChatGPT thinks logically. Why? Because it notices all the logic
in the data in its training set.
—Stephen Wolfram

Preliminaries

The way we retrieve meaningful insights from textual data has undergone an extensive transformation in the last ten years. This evolution is not merely semantic, marked by the ascendance of the term "natural language processing" (NLP) over "text mining" to describe the field; it also signifies a substantial shift in the underlying methodologies employed. A primary catalyst for this dramatic change has been the rise of sophisticated *language models*. These powerful statistical models, trained on vast quantities of text, have become the foundational building blocks for a multitude of applications designed to extract valuable information and knowledge from unstructured textual sources. Instead of relying on earlier, often rule-based or simpler statistical approaches prevalent in traditional text mining, modern NLP leverages the ability of language models to understand the nuances of human language, enabling more accurate and context-aware information extraction. This paradigm shift has unlocked new possibilities for analyzing and interpreting text at a deeper semantic level, leading to more robust and insightful applications across various domains.

Through the application of machine and deep learning algorithms to vast quantities of textual data, language models acquire a sophisticated grasp of the statistical relationships between words, effectively learning the probabilities of different word sequences occurring in various contexts. This learned understanding forms a powerful basis that enables these models to perform a remarkable array of tasks. Notably, their knowledge of word probabilities allows them to generate novel and coherent written content, mimicking human-like text generation. Furthermore, they can predict the subsequent word in a given sentence or discourse with impressive accuracy, leveraging their understanding of contextual dependencies. Beyond these

R. Akerkar, *Artificial Intelligence*, https://doi.org/10.1007/978-3-031-91084-5_7

core generative and predictive capabilities, the probabilistic insights gleaned by language models are fundamental to several critical applications that bridge the gap between human communication and digital systems. These include speech-to-text conversion (where spoken language is transcribed into written text), optical character recognition (OCR, which converts images of text into machine-readable text), and the interpretation of handwritten text (enabling digital processing of handwritten documents). The ability of language models to understand and predict word probabilities is therefore a cornerstone of modern natural language processing, facilitating a wide range of technologies that interact with and process human language in increasingly sophisticated ways. In the subsequent sections of this chapter, we will delve into a study of various architectures and methodologies employed in different language models, as well as explore the art and science of prompt engineering—a crucial technique for effectively eliciting desired behaviours and outputs from these powerful models.

Language Models

Language Models (LMs) are a class of probabilistic models explicitly tailored to identify and learn statistical patterns in natural language. The primary function of a language model is to calculate the probability that a word succeeds a given input sentence. In the context of natural language processing, self-supervised learning enables models to learn from unannotated text, rather than relying on manually labelled data, which is relatively scarce and often expensive.

> **Definition** Language models employ machine learning techniques to establish a probability distribution across sequences of words. Trained on vast amounts of textual data, these models can generate novel text, forecast subsequent words in a given context, and are foundational to technologies like speech recognition, optical character recognition, and handwriting recognition.

During the training process, an LM is fed with a large *corpus* (dataset) of text and tasked with predicting the next word in a sentence. In practice, this is often achieved by randomly truncating the last part of an input sentence and training the model to fill in the missing word(s). As the model iterates through numerous examples, it learns to recognize and internalize various linguistic patterns, rules, and relationships between words and concepts. One can say that via this process the model creates an internal representation of language.

The outcome of this training process is a pre-trained language model. By exposure to diverse linguistic patterns, the model is equipped with a foundation for understanding natural language and for generating contextually appropriate and coherent text. Some people refer to such pre-trained models as foundation models.

The effectiveness of LMs in performing various tasks is largely influenced by the size of their architecture. These architectures are based on artificial neural networks, which are computational models loosely inspired by the structure and functioning of biological neural networks, such as those in the human brain. Artificial neural networks consist of interconnected layers of nodes, or "neurons" which work together to process and learn from data.

Neurons in the network are associated with a set of numbers, commonly referred to as the neural network's parameters. The numerical value of these parameters is supposed to represent the strength of connections between different neurons. The parameters within a neural network are adjustable, and they get iteratively updated during the training process to minimize the difference between the model's predictions and the actual target values.

In the context of LMs, the more parameters, the greater their "storage capacity", even though it should be noted that language models *do not* store information in a way comparable to the standard way *storage memory* works in computers. A higher number of parameters allows the model to "internalise" a greater variety of statistical patterns (via the numerical relationships of its parameters) within the language data they are exposed to. Larger models, however, also require more computational resources and training data to reach their full potential.

Foundation Models

Foundation models are large-scale, pre-trained machine learning models serving as a base for diverse downstream applications across natural language processing (NLP), computer vision, and other domains. Trained on massive datasets using unsupervised or self-supervised learning, these "foundation" models offer a strong base upon which other applications are built, fundamentally changing generative AI. Their ability to generalise across domains, languages, and modalities provides significant power but also presents ethical, resource, and interpretability challenges.

Emerging from the convergence of transformer architectures, self-supervised learning, and massive computational scaling, foundation models learn general-purpose representations from vast amounts of unlabelled data. This allows them to be adapted to a wide array of tasks through fine-tuning or prompting. Their fundamental architecture relies on the transformer mechanism, which uses self-attention layers to process information and capture complex data patterns and long-range dependencies, enabling efficient parallel processing and contextual understanding across various data types.

The architecture includes self-attention mechanisms that weigh input element importance for contextual understanding, with multi-head attention processing diverse relationships in parallel. Position encoding enables the model to understand sequential data, accommodating varying input lengths and maintaining structure. Layer normalization stabilizes learning in deep networks, ensuring consistent performance across different data distributions and facilitating the training of very large models. Feed-forward networks at each layer process transformed representations, allowing the model to learn complex nonlinear data relationships.

Training these models involves self-supervised learning, where models learn from vast unlabelled data by predicting masked or future elements, developing rich internal representations. Scaling laws guide the development of increasingly capable models through systematic increases in size and training data. Computational optimization techniques, including mixed-precision training, gradient accumulation, and distributed computing, enable the efficient training of models with billions or trillions of parameters.

Key Characteristics of Foundation Models:

1. **Pre-training on Large Datasets**: Foundation models are typically trained on vast and diverse datasets, often encompassing billions of words, images, or other types of data. This enables the model to learn general patterns, relationships, and representations from the data before being fine-tuned for specific tasks.
2. **Transferability**: One of the primary advantages of foundation models is their ability to transfer knowledge across tasks. Once a model is pre-trained, it can be **fine-tuned** on much smaller task-specific datasets, significantly reducing the amount of labelled data and computational resources needed.
3. **Self-supervised Learning**: Foundation models often use self-supervised learning techniques where the model learns from large amounts of unlabelled data by generating labels from the data itself (e.g., predicting missing words or pixels). This allows them to be trained without extensive human-annotated data.
4. **Scalability**: These models are designed to scale up with larger datasets, more parameters, and higher computational resources. Larger foundation models often achieve better performance on a wide range of tasks due to their scalability.
5. **Multimodal Capabilities**: Many foundation models are **multimodal**, meaning they can work with various types of data (e.g., text, images, or speech) in a single framework. This enables them to be used across different domains, from natural language understanding to computer vision.

Examples of Foundation Models:

1. **GPT (Generative Pre-trained Transformer)**: GPT is a series of large language models trained by OpenAI. GPT-3, for example, is pre-trained on a large corpus of text and can generate human-like text, answer questions, summarize documents, and more. It serves as a foundation for numerous NLP tasks, such as translation, text generation, and dialogue systems.
2. **BERT (Bidirectional Encoder Representations from Transformers)**: BERT is another widely used foundation model in NLP, pre-trained to understand the context of words from both directions (left and right). BERT has been fine-tuned for tasks like question answering, sentiment analysis, and named entity recognition (NER).
3. **CLIP (Contrastive Language-Image Pre-training)**: CLIP, developed by OpenAI, is a multimodal foundation model that can process both images and text. It has been trained to associate textual descriptions with images, allowing it

to perform tasks like image classification based on natural language descriptions without any task-specific fine-tuning.

4. **DALL·E**: DALL·E is a multimodal generative model capable of creating images from textual descriptions. It serves as a foundation model for tasks involving image synthesis, art generation, and creative visual content.

Foundation models demonstrate remarkable capabilities across various domains. Foundation models can create text that reads naturally and makes sense, much like a human would write. For example, if you ask a model like ChatGPT to write a story about a cat that learns to play chess, it can generate a creative and logically structured story from scratch. The sentences flow well, and the ideas connect smoothly. For example, ask the model to write a poem about the sun, and it creates a unique, well-structured poem. Some foundation models can work across different types of data, such as turning text into images. For instance, if you type "a red bird sitting on a blue bicycle," a cross-modal model like DALL-E can generate a picture that matches your description. This ability to connect words and images is called cross-modal generation. For example, ask to describe "a dog wearing sunglasses at the beach," and the model draws an image matching your words. Foundation models can quickly learn new tasks with just a few examples-a skill known as few-shot learning. Imagine you want a model to sort emails into "work" and "personal" folders, but you only have three examples of each. You can show the model these few examples, and it will understand how to sort new emails correctly, even though it hasn't seen many labelled samples. For instance, ask to show the model a couple of labelled photos of apples and oranges, and it learns to tell them apart in new pictures with just those few examples.

Small Language Models

The landscape of Natural Language Processing (NLP) has been intensely reshaped by the rise of Large Language Models (LLMs). These giants, boasting billions of parameters, have demonstrated remarkable capabilities in tasks ranging from text generation and translation to question answering and code synthesis. However, their sheer size brings inherent challenges. LLMs demand substantial computational resources, making them expensive to train, deploy, and run. This has spurred a growing interest in a contrasting approach: Small Language Models (SLMs). This section delves into the world of SLMs, exploring their characteristics, advantages, challenges, and the niche they carve in the ever-evolving field of AI. Small language models play a crucial role in situations where efficiency, speed, and resource constraints are prioritized over raw performance. Although they may not match the capabilities of large language models in understanding or generating language across a broad range of tasks, they are powerful in more specialized, low-resource applications. By balancing performance with efficiency, small language models are ideal for real-time systems, mobile devices, and domain-specific applications.

While there's no universally agreed-upon threshold for what constitutes "small," small language models are generally characterized by their significantly lower number of parameters compared to LLMs. This reduction in size is a deliberate design choice, prioritizing efficiency and practicality over sheer scale. Where LLMs might have hundreds of billions of parameters, SLMs typically range from a few million to a few billion parameters. This difference has profound implications for their resource requirements and deployment feasibility.

The development of SLMs is driven by the need to democratize access to advanced NLP capabilities. LLMs, with their massive computational demands, often require specialized hardware like GPUs or TPUs and cloud-based infrastructure. This creates a barrier to entry for many organizations and individuals with limited resources. SLMs, on the other hand, can be trained and deployed on more readily available hardware, including CPUs and edge devices. This opens up a wider range of applications and makes NLP technology more accessible.

Parameters are the internal weights of a model that are learned during training. A small language model has fewer parameters, which makes it computationally lightweight but also limits its capacity to learn complex patterns from data. Small models are typically trained on smaller datasets or with less training time. This may lead to a reduced understanding of diverse language patterns compared to larger models. Because of their size, small language models are often tailored for specific tasks or domains, focusing on a limited set of language phenomena. This makes them efficient for applications but less generalizable across various contexts. These models are more efficient in terms of memory and processing power, making them faster to deploy and less costly to run. They are ideal for low-resource environments like mobile devices or embedded systems.

SLMs offer several key advantages that make them a compelling alternative to LLMs in specific contexts:

- **Computational Efficiency**: The most significant advantage of SLMs is their computational efficiency. Their smaller size translates to lower memory requirements, faster inference speeds, and reduced energy consumption. This makes them ideal for applications with limited resources or strict latency requirements.
- **Reduced Latency**: In real-time applications, such as voice assistants or interactive chatbots, low latency is crucial. SLMs, with their faster inference speeds, can provide quicker responses, enhancing the user experience. This is particularly important in edge computing scenarios where data processing needs to happen locally with minimal delay.
- **Lower Energy Consumption**: The energy footprint of LLMs is a growing concern, both from an environmental and economic perspective. SLMs, with their lower computational demands, consume significantly less energy, making them a more sustainable option. This is especially relevant for battery-powered devices or applications where energy efficiency is paramount.
- **Edge Computing Compatibility**: SLMs are well-suited for deployment on edge devices, such as smartphones, IoT devices, and embedded systems. Edge computing brings data processing closer to the source, reducing latency, improving

privacy, and enabling offline functionality. SLMs empower these devices to perform complex NLP tasks locally, without relying on cloud connectivity.

- **Fine-Tuning for Specific Tasks**: SLMs can be effectively fine-tuned for specific tasks or domains. This targeted training can lead to superior performance on those tasks compared to general-purpose LLMs. Furthermore, fine-tuning an SLM requires less data and computational resources than training an LLM from scratch.
- **Privacy and Security**: Processing data locally on edge devices using SLMs can enhance privacy and security. Sensitive data doesn't need to be transmitted to a remote server, reducing the risk of data breaches or unauthorized access.

Despite their advantages, SLMs also face certain challenges:

- **Performance Trade-off**: The reduction in size often comes with a performance trade-off. SLMs may not achieve the same level of accuracy or fluency as LLMs on some tasks, particularly those requiring extensive world knowledge or complex reasoning.
- **Generalization Ability**: LLMs, due to their massive scale, tend to exhibit better generalization ability, meaning they can perform well on a wider range of tasks without specific training. SLMs, on the other hand, may require more specialized training data to perform effectively on specific tasks.
- **Data Requirements for Training**: While fine-tuning SLMs requires less data than training LLMs from scratch, they still need sufficient and high-quality training data to achieve good performance. Acquiring this data can be a challenge in some domains.
- **Development and Optimization**: Developing and optimizing SLMs requires careful consideration of architecture, training techniques, and optimization strategies. Finding the right balance between size and performance is a key challenge.

Examples of Small Language Models.

1. FastText (by Facebook)

FastText is a lightweight language model used primarily for text classification and word representations. It is efficient due to its simple architecture and is capable of generating high-quality word embeddings (vector representations of words). FastText can be used to classify customer reviews into positive or negative sentiments. Due to its small size, it can quickly process a large volume of text in real time.

2. DistilBERT (by Hugging Face)

DistilBERT is a smaller, faster, and lighter version of the BERT (Bidirectional Encoder Representations from Transformers) model. It retains 97% of the performance of BERT while being 60% smaller and 60% faster, making it ideal for situations where resources are limited. DistilBERT can be used for question-answering tasks or named entity recognition (NER).

DistilBERT is a great example of a **compressed model**, meaning it has been distilled from a larger model while maintaining much of its accuracy and utility.

3. ELMo (Embeddings from Language Models)

ELMo is a small language model that generates contextual word embeddings. Unlike static word embeddings like Word2Vec, ELMo produces different embeddings for the same word depending on the context. ELMo uses fewer parameters than models like BERT and is particularly useful for sequence-level tasks like text classification and sequence tagging. ELMo can be used for tasks like named entity recognition in a sentence.

4. LSTM-Based Language Models (Small Variants)

Long Short-Term Memory (LSTM) networks are a type of recurrent neural network (RNN) used for sequence data, and small versions of LSTM-based language models can be trained to handle short texts or dialogues. A small LSTM model might be used for next word prediction in mobile keyboards.

5. GloVe (Global Vectors for Word Representation)

GloVe is a simple yet effective small model that generates fixed-size vector representations of words based on co-occurrence statistics. It is a pre-trained model that can be deployed for various tasks without the need for large computational resources. GloVe can be used to measure word similarity in tasks like finding synonyms or clustering-related terms. GloVe is not as sophisticated as transformer-based models, but its efficiency and simplicity make it a popular choice for embedding words in smaller systems.

Large Language Models

Large Language Models (LLMs) are a ground-breaking innovation in artificial intelligence, significantly altering the way machines interpret and produce human language. These advanced neural networks, trained on extensive textual datasets, exhibit remarkable abilities in comprehending context, generating coherent text, and executing complex language-related tasks. In principle, they function as highly sophisticated language machines capable of performing a diverse array of tasks.

The foundation of modern LLMs rests on the transformer architecture, a ground-breaking innovation that enables efficient processing of sequential data through parallel computation. The transformer's self-attention mechanism allows the model to weigh the importance of different words in context, capturing complex relationships and dependencies within text.

These models employ multiple processing layers, each containing self-attention mechanisms and feed-forward neural networks. The self-attention component enables the model to focus on relevant parts of the input when generating each element of the output, while the feed-forward networks process these attention-weighted representations.

The scale of these models is remarkable, with some containing hundreds of billions or even trillions of parameters. This massive scale, combined with sophisticated training techniques, enables them to capture intricate patterns in language and develop capabilities that emerge only at scale.

A *transformer model* is the most common architecture of a large language model. It consists of an encoder and a decoder. A transformer model processes data by tokenizing the input, then simultaneously conducting mathematical equations to discover relationships between tokens. This enables the computer to see the patterns a human would see where it given the same query.

> **Definition** A *transformer* is a type of deep learning model that transforms the encoding in a particular way that makes it easier to guess the blanked-out word.

Training Methodology

The training of large language models (LLMs) involves a multi-stage process with intricate components. Initially, a pre-training phase occurs on massive text datasets, often encompassing hundreds of terabytes, leveraging self-supervised learning. During this stage, the model learns to predict missing words or subsequent tokens within sequences, thereby developing a profound understanding of linguistic patterns and inter-word relationships. Subsequently, fine-tuning adapts these pre-trained models for specific applications through further training on targeted datasets. This adaptation often incorporates reinforcement learning from human feedback (RLHF), which refines the model's responses to better align with human preferences and the specific requirements of the task at hand. To manage the substantial computational demands of training such extensive models efficiently, contemporary approaches also employ techniques like mixed-precision training, gradient checkpointing, and distributed computing.

Transformer models, a foundational architecture for many state-of-the-art language processing systems, utilize self-attention mechanisms. This allows them to learn more rapidly compared to earlier models like long short-term memory networks. Self-attention enables the model to simultaneously consider various parts of an input sequence, or the complete context of a sentence, when generating predictions. Unlike recurrent neural networks that process text word by word, the attention mechanism allows the transformer to process the entire sentence or even a paragraph at once, leading to a better comprehension of a word's context. For instance, see Fig. 7.1, in the sentence "The robot travelled through space because it sought a new power source," if the word "robot" were masked, a neural network could more accurately predict it due to the presence of words like "travelled" and "space." Similarly, masking "it" would likely lead the network to favour "it" over alternatives like "he" or "she" due to the presence of "robot."

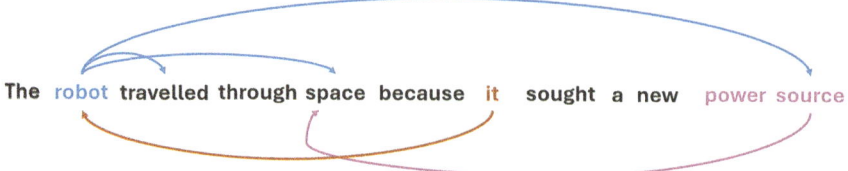

Fig. 7.1 Text input

Processing text with a transformer model starts with tokenization, where the input is broken into individual words or tokens. These tokens are then converted into numerical values and transformed into embeddings—vector representations that capture their meanings. The transformer's encoder processes these embeddings to produce a context vector that encapsulates the overall meaning of the input. Using this context, the decoder generates output, often by predicting the next word based on previous ones. This process is autoregressive, meaning each generated word becomes the clue for the next, enabling the model to construct entire paragraphs from a single sentence. Large language models (LLMs) operate on this principle, using deep transformer architectures with multiple layers to handle long texts and complex ideas.

These models include several neural network layers, starting with an embedding layer that captures semantic and syntactic nuances. A feedforward layer, made up of fully connected layers, helps the model grasp higher-level abstractions and user intent. While earlier models used recurrent layers to understand word sequences, transformers rely on attention mechanisms to focus on the most relevant parts of the input, improving accuracy.

There are various types of LLMs. Generic models predict the next word based on training data and are often used for tasks like information retrieval. Zero-shot models, trained on vast datasets, can answer questions without specific fine-tuning. Edge models, such as those used in mobile apps like Google Translate, are smaller and optimized for quick responses. Instruction-tuned models are trained to follow specific prompts, enabling tasks like sentiment analysis or code generation. Fine-tuned models are adapted for specialized domains, such as OpenAI's Codex for programming or BloombergGPT for finance. Dialog-tuned models are optimized for conversational tasks, powering chatbots and virtual assistants. OpenAI's GPT series exemplifies this approach, combining generative capabilities with extensive pre-training. Other notable models include Google's PaLM for reasoning and code, BERT for understanding and question answering, and XLNet, which predicts tokens in a non-sequential order.

LLMs are trained using a mix of supervised and unsupervised learning. Unsupervised pre-training involves learning language patterns from large unlabelled datasets by predicting the next word in a sentence. This is often followed by supervised fine-tuning on labelled data for specific tasks, such as question answering.

These models excel at generating coherent, human-like text, answering questions, summarizing content, translating languages, and even solving complex problems with minimal examples. However, they also have limitations. They can confidently produce incorrect information (hallucinations), reflect biases from training data, and lack true understanding of causality or real-world context. They may struggle with time-based reasoning and maintaining factual consistency over long texts. Additionally, their high computational demands raise concerns about environmental impact and accessibility. Ethical issues such as bias, fairness, and misuse remain critical, prompting ongoing research into more efficient and transparent model architectures.

Building a Large Language Model

Developing a Large Language Model (LLM) is a complex, multi-stage process that integrates machine learning, data science, and high-performance computing. It begins with defining the model architecture, typically based on the Transformer framework due to its strength in handling sequential data and long-range dependencies. Key architectural decisions include the number of layers, hidden units, attention heads, and overall parameter count, all of which influence the model's performance and computational demands. Tokenization strategy is also critical, with methods like Byte-Pair Encoding (BPE) or WordPiece commonly used to convert text into manageable units.

The next phase focuses on data preparation, where a diverse and high-quality text corpus is curated to ensure the model learns a wide range of language patterns. This involves filtering out low-quality or harmful content, normalizing text, and formatting it for efficient processing. Sophisticated data pipelines are implemented to support high-throughput training with features like batching and prefetching.

Model implementation translates the architecture into executable code using frameworks such as PyTorch or TensorFlow. This includes building components like attention mechanisms, feed-forward layers, and positional embeddings. Training loops are set up with loss functions (typically next-token prediction), optimization algorithms like AdamW, and learning rate schedules. Evaluation metrics such as perplexity and accuracy are used to monitor progress.

Given the immense computational load, infrastructure planning is essential. Training often requires clusters of GPUs or TPUs and employs distributed strategies like data, model, or pipeline parallelism. Real-time monitoring systems track performance and resource usage, enabling quick troubleshooting.

Training itself is the most resource-intensive stage. During pre-training, the model learns to predict tokens from context, gradually acquiring linguistic and semantic knowledge. This phase demands careful monitoring of loss trends, gradient behaviour, and validation metrics to avoid issues like overfitting. Techniques such as gradient accumulation, mixed-precision training, and checkpointing are used to enhance efficiency and resilience.

After pre-training, models are fine-tuned for specific tasks or domains using targeted datasets. Techniques like instruction tuning, reinforcement learning from human feedback (RLHF), and alignment training help improve safety and usability.

Optimization methods such as quantization, pruning, and knowledge distillation are applied to make models more efficient during inference. Evaluation on benchmark datasets helps identify strengths and areas for improvement.

For deployment, an efficient inference pipeline is crucial. This includes implementing generation strategies like beam search or nucleus sampling to balance output quality and computational cost. Inference systems are optimized with caching, batching, and runtime enhancements to ensure responsiveness and scalability.

Finally, rigorous evaluation and continuous iteration are vital. Models are tested for accuracy, bias, safety, and alignment with human values. Feedback loops involving human evaluation and error analysis guide refinements. Deployment requires robust infrastructure capable of handling variable loads, along with monitoring systems to track performance and user satisfaction. Maintenance involves regular updates and safeguards to ensure responsible and secure operation as LLMs become integral to many applications.

Canonical Architectures of LLM Applications

Canonical architectures for Large Language Model (LLM) applications are designed to balance performance, scalability, and usability, typically involving several core components with distinct trade-offs. A widely used approach is retrieval-augmented generation (RAG), which combines a vector database—such as Pinecone or Chroma—for retrieving relevant information with a generative model that uses this data to produce contextually accurate responses. While RAG enhances answer quality by incorporating external knowledge, it also adds complexity in managing retrieval quality and system integration.

Another common strategy is fine-tuning pre-trained LLMs on domain-specific datasets to tailor their behaviour for specialized tasks like customer service or medical diagnostics. This method leverages the general capabilities of large models while adapting them to specific needs, though it demands significant computational resources and carries the risk of overfitting.

In contrast, in-context learning avoids fine-tuning altogether by using prompt engineering to condition the model on private or task-specific data at inference time. This allows for rapid deployment and flexibility but is constrained by the model's context window and potential performance degradation with longer inputs.

Modern LLM applications also frequently adopt microservices and containerization technologies like Kubernetes and Docker to build scalable, modular systems. These architectures enhance flexibility and fault tolerance by allowing independent development and scaling of components, though they introduce orchestration complexity and potential latency from inter-service communication.

Hybrid architecture emerges as powerful solutions for complex tasks, combining multiple LLMs or integrating them with other AI models such as image classifiers or sentiment analyzers. This enables more comprehensive and versatile systems but requires careful coordination and integration, often increasing development and maintenance overhead.

Pre-training Language Models

Pre-training NLP Models

NLP models were typically trained from scratch for specific tasks, requiring substantial task-specific labelled data and computational resources. The introduction of pre-training methodologies fundamentally altered this approach by establishing a two-phase learning process: an initial pre-training phase on vast amounts of unlabelled text data, followed by a task-specific fine-tuning phase. This approach has yielded unprecedented improvements across virtually all NLP benchmarks and applications.

Pre-training enables models to develop rich representations of language by processing extensive text corpora before being adapted to specific downstream tasks. During pre-training, models learn syntactic structures, semantic relationships, factual knowledge, and even rudimentary reasoning capabilities. These learned representations serve as a powerful foundation that can be leveraged for a wide variety of language understanding and generation tasks.

The success of pre-training in NLP can be attributed to several factors. First, language exhibits inherent patterns and structures that can be learned from raw text without explicit supervision. Second, the abundance of digital text available on the internet provides nearly unlimited training data. Third, advances in computational resources and distributed training techniques have made it feasible to train increasingly larger models on increasingly larger datasets. Finally, the development of effective learning objectives that enable models to extract meaningful representations from unlabelled data has been crucial to this progress.

Unsupervised, Supervised, and Self-supervised Pre-training

Pre-training approaches in NLP can be categorized into three main methods: unsupervised, supervised, and self-supervised learning.

Unsupervised pre-training refers to learning methods where the model is trained on raw data without explicit labels. Traditional unsupervised learning in NLP included techniques such as clustering words based on distributional semantics or learning word embeddings through methods like Word2Vec and GloVe. These approaches captured semantic similarities between words by analyzing their co-occurrence patterns in large text corpora.

Supervised pre-training involves training models on labelled datasets for general tasks before fine-tuning them for specific applications. For instance, a language model might be pre-trained on a task-like natural language inference, which requires understanding semantic relationships between sentences. This form of pre-training is less common than the others because labelled data is expensive to produce at scale.

Self-supervised pre-training has emerged as the dominant paradigm in modern NLP. In self-supervised learning, the supervision signal is derived from the input data itself, without requiring external labels. The model is trained to predict parts of the input from other parts, effectively learning to understand the structure and patterns in language. Examples include predicting masked words in a sentence, predicting the next word in a sequence, or determining whether two sentences follow each other in a text. This approach has proven remarkably effective because it allows models to leverage unlimited amounts of raw text data while still learning meaningful representations.

Adapting Pre-trained Models

Once a model has been pre-trained, it needs to be adapted to specific downstream tasks. This adaptation process typically takes one of several forms:

Fine-tuning is the most common adaptation approach, where all or most of the pre-trained parameters are updated using task-specific data. The pre-trained model is augmented with task-specific layers (often just a classification head), and the entire network is trained end-to-end with a relatively small learning rate to avoid catastrophic forgetting of the pre-trained knowledge.

Feature extraction treats the pre-trained model as a fixed feature extractor. The model's parameters remain frozen, and only the task-specific layers are trained. This approach is computationally efficient and can work well when the target task is similar to the pre-training objectives or when limited task-specific data is available.

Prompt-based learning is a more recent adaptation technique where the downstream task is reformulated to resemble the pre-training objective. For instance, a classification task might be reframed as a text completion problem, allowing the model to leverage its pre-trained capabilities more directly. This approach has proven especially effective for large language models.

Parameter-efficient fine-tuning methods modify only a small subset of the model's parameters during adaptation. Techniques such as adapter modules, prefix tuning, and LoRA (Low-Rank Adaptation) add trainable components while keeping most of the pre-trained parameters frozen. These methods reduce memory requirements and computational costs while often achieving performance comparable to full fine-tuning.

Self-supervised Pre-training Tasks

Self-supervised learning has become the cornerstone of modern NLP pre-training. Various pre-training objectives have been proposed, each with its strengths and limitations:

Masked Language Modelling (MLM) involves randomly masking tokens in the input text and training the model to predict the original tokens. This forces the model to develop a bidirectional understanding of context. BERT and its variants use MLM as their primary pre-training objective.

Next Sentence Prediction (NSP) trains the model to determine whether two segments of text appear consecutively in the original corpus. This objective aims to capture discourse-level understanding. While initially used alongside MLM in BERT, subsequent research has questioned its effectiveness.

Autoregressive Language Modelling trains the model to predict the next token given all previous tokens in a sequence. This approach is used in decoder-only architectures like GPT (Generative Pre-trained Transformer) models and is particularly effective for text generation tasks.

Span Prediction extends MLM by masking contiguous spans of tokens rather than individual tokens. Models like SpanBERT use this approach to encourage the model to capture broader contextual dependencies.

Permutation Language Modelling, used in XLNet, trains the model on different permutations of the input sequence to combine the benefits of autoregressive and bidirectional modelling.

Replaced Token Detection, employed by models like ELECTRA, trains a discriminator to determine whether each token in the input was replaced by a generator model. This approach has proven more computationally efficient than traditional MLM.

Sequence-to-Sequence Pre-training objectives, such as those used in T5 (Text-to-Text Transfer Transformer), frame all NLP tasks as text-to-text problems. During pre-training, T5 reconstructs text with randomly corrupted spans, preparing it for a wide range of downstream tasks.

Architecture Paradigms for Pre-training

Decoder-only Pre-training

Decoder-only architectures have emerged as powerful frameworks for generative language modelling. These models, exemplified by OpenAI's GPT series, process text sequentially from left to right and are trained to predict the next token in a sequence given all previous tokens.

The defining characteristic of decoder-only models is their use of causal (unidirectional) attention mechanisms, where each position can only attend to previous positions in the sequence. This causality constraint is essential for autoregressive modelling but limits the model's ability to incorporate bidirectional context during pre-training.

Despite this limitation, decoder-only models have demonstrated remarkable capabilities in text generation, few-shot learning, and even zero-shot task performance. The scaling of these models to hundreds of billions of parameters (as in GPT-3 and subsequent models) has revealed emergent abilities that were not apparent in smaller models.

Pre-training for decoder-only models typically involves autoregressive language modelling on massive text corpora. The simplicity of this objective—predicting the next token—belies its effectiveness in teaching the model about grammar, factual knowledge, reasoning, and even specialized domains like programming.

Decoder-only models excel in generative tasks, dialogue systems, and scenarios where the model needs to produce coherent, extended text. They are particularly well-suited for open-ended applications where creativity and fluency are valued.

Encoder-only Pre-training

Encoder-only architectures focus on developing rich bidirectional representations of text. These models, with BERT (Bidirectional Encoder Representations from Transformers) as their archetypal example, process the entire input sequence simultaneously using bidirectional attention mechanisms.

The hallmark of encoder-only pre-training is the masked language modelling (MLM) objective, where the model is trained to predict randomly masked tokens using context from both directions. This bidirectional nature allows encoder models to develop nuanced understanding of linguistic context that is particularly valuable for tasks requiring deep semantic comprehension.

Encoder models typically consist of stacked transformer encoder blocks with bidirectional self-attention. During pre-training, these models develop contextual representations for each token in the input sequence. These representations capture syntactic and semantic properties of words in context, rather than static word meanings.

The pre-trained encoder can then be fine-tuned by adding task-specific heads on top of the base model. For classification tasks, this might be a simple feed-forward network applied to the representation of a special classification token ([CLS]). For token-level tasks like named entity recognition, the model utilizes the contextual representations of individual tokens.

Encoder-only models excel in understanding tasks such as sentiment analysis, natural language inference, and information extraction. Their bidirectional nature makes them particularly well-suited for tasks requiring deep semantic understanding rather than generation.

Encoder-Decoder Pre-training

Encoder-decoder architectures combine elements of both previous paradigms to support sequence-to-sequence tasks. These models, exemplified by T5 (Text-to-Text Transfer Transformer) and BART (Bidirectional and Auto-Regressive Transformers), consist of an encoder that processes the input sequence bidirectionally and a decoder that generates the output sequence autoregressively.

The encoder-decoder framework is inherently suited to tasks that transform one sequence into another, such as translation, summarization, and question answering. During pre-training, these models can use objectives that require both understanding and generation.

Common pre-training objectives for encoder-decoder models include:

1. **Span corruption**, where spans of text are replaced with sentinel tokens, and the model must reconstruct the original spans.
2. **Document rotation**, where the model must determine the original ordering of a permuted document.
3. **Sentence shuffling**, where the model reconstructs the correct order of shuffled sentences.
4. **Translation language modelling**, which combines masked language modelling with translation.

The encoder component typically employs bidirectional attention to develop rich contextual representations of the input, while the decoder uses a combination of self-attention (over previously generated tokens) and cross-attention (to the encoder's representations) to generate the output sequence.

Encoder-decoder models provide versatility across a wide range of NLP tasks, particularly excelling in those requiring both understanding and generation capabilities. They represent a middle ground between the specialized strengths of encoder-only and decoder-only approaches.

The computational efficiency of pre-training objectives also varies significantly. MLM is relatively inefficient because it only learns from a small subset of tokens (the masked ones), while methods like replaced token detection and autoregressive modelling learn from all input tokens, making them more computationally efficient.

The transfer learning capability (how well pre-trained knowledge transfers to downstream tasks) also differs across architectures. Encoder-decoder models often demonstrate better transfer to diverse tasks, while specialized architectures may excel in narrower domains.

The choice of architecture and pre-training objective should be guided by the intended applications, available computational resources, and the specific strengths required for the target tasks.

Attention Mechanism

Transformer architectures have revolutionized natural language processing by enabling efficient handling of long text sequences through parallel processing and contextual understanding. Central to this capability is the attention mechanism, which allows the model to evaluate the relevance of each word in a sequence when predicting the next. For example, in the phrase "The capital of Norway is," the model assigns greater importance to "Norway" to correctly predict "Oslo." This self-attention mechanism mimics human comprehension by focusing on contextually significant words, regardless of their position in the text.

Unlike earlier models such as Recurrent Neural Networks (RNNs), which processed text sequentially and struggled with long-range dependencies, transformers can directly connect any two words in a sequence. This design enables them to capture complex linguistic patterns like co-reference, logical relationships, and syntactic structures across multiple sentences. The encoder-decoder structure of standard transformers is particularly effective for tasks like translation, where the encoder builds rich contextual representations and the decoder generates coherent output by attending to both the input and previously generated tokens.

The transformer workflow begins with tokenization, converting text into numerical vectors enriched with positional information. These vectors pass through layers of self-attention and feed-forward networks in the encoder, producing contextualized representations. The decoder then uses these representations, along with its own generated tokens, to produce the final output in a step-by-step manner, resembling advanced contextual reasoning.

Despite their strengths, attention mechanisms face challenges. Their computational cost grows quadratically with input length, making them less efficient for very long texts. This has led to innovations like sparse and linear attention to reduce resource demands. Additionally, attention can sometimes disproportionately focus on certain inputs, leading to missed details in tasks like summarization. Interpretability is another issue, as the complexity of multi-layered attention heads makes it difficult to trace how decisions are made.

A notable example of attention-based architecture is BERT (Bidirectional Encoder Representations from Transformers), which introduced bidirectional context modelling through masked language modelling. BERT-base consists of 12 layers, 12 attention heads, and 768-dimensional hidden states, totalling 110 million parameters, while BERT-large scales up to 24 layers and 340 million parameters. Its pre-training objectives include predicting masked tokens and determining sentence order, helping the model learn deep contextual relationships. BERT's input representation combines token, segment, and position embeddings, and it was trained on large corpora like BooksCorpus and Wikipedia. For downstream tasks, BERT can be fine-tuned with task-specific layers, making it versatile for both sentence-level and token-level applications.

Components of the BERT Model

The main components of the BERT model are:

- **Tokenizer**: Converts raw input text into tokens (subword units), which are then mapped to unique numerical IDs for processing.
- **Embedding Layer**: Transforms tokens into dense vectors by combining three types of embeddings:
  - Token embeddings (representing each token).
  - Position embeddings (indicating the position of each token in the sequence).
  - Segment embeddings (distinguishing between different sentences in the input).
- **Encoder Stack**: A series of transformer encoder layers (12 in BERT Base, 24 in BERT Large), each using self-attention mechanisms and feed-forward neural networks to process the embeddings and capture contextual relationships across the entire sequence.
- **Task-Specific Head**: A layer added on top of the encoder stack for specific tasks, such as classification, question answering, or masked language modelling. During pre-training, BERT uses heads for masked language modelling and next sentence prediction. For downstream tasks, this head is replaced or modified as needed.
- **Pooler**: Produces a fixed-length vector from the encoder output, often used for classification tasks.

These components work together to enable BERT to deeply understand the context and meaning of words within sentences and across sentence pairs.

Training and Models

Following BERT's success, subsequent research explored the benefits of more extensive training and larger model architectures. This research direction led to models like RoBERTa, which demonstrated that BERT was significantly undertrained.

RoBERTa (Robustly Optimized BERT Approach) modified the original BERT training methodology by:

- Removing the Next Sentence Prediction objective.
- Training with larger batch sizes.
- Training on more data (including CommonCrawl).
- Training for longer.
- Dynamically changing the masking pattern.

These modifications resulted in substantial performance improvements across benchmark tasks, establishing that scaling training data, computation, and model size could yield significant benefits without architectural changes.

This trend continued with even larger models like DeBERTa (Decoding-enhanced BERT with disentangled attention) and MEGATRON, which scaled to billions of parameters. These larger models consistently demonstrated improved performance, supporting the scaling hypothesis that larger models trained on more data tend to perform better across a wide range of tasks.

The relationship between model size, training data volume, and computational resources became a central focus of research. Studies established empirical scaling laws showing predictable relationships between these factors and model performance, guiding efficient allocation of resources in pre-training.

Adapting and Using Pre-trained Language Models

Applying Context to Foundation Models

Foundation models process context through advanced mechanisms that enable them to understand and generate language with remarkable sophistication. Central to this capability is the attention mechanism, which allows the model to dynamically assess the relevance of different parts of the input when producing an output. These attention operations are layered across multiple levels of the model, enabling the construction of increasingly abstract and complex representations of contextual relationships.

Architectures such as Generative Pre-trained Transformers (GPT) and BERT exemplify the power of foundation models in natural language processing. These models are pre-trained on vast corpora of text, allowing them to internalize a wide array of linguistic patterns and contextual cues. GPT adopts a unidirectional approach, predicting each token based on its preceding context, while BERT employs a masked language modelling strategy that captures bidirectional context by considering both preceding and succeeding tokens.

Each token in the input is first mapped into a high-dimensional embedding space, where it is represented as a vector. As these vectors pass through the model's layers, they undergo nonlinear transformations governed by learned parameters. These transformations are essential for capturing intricate contextual dependencies that are not apparent at the surface level. The effectiveness of these models is empirically validated across a range of downstream tasks, including text classification, sentiment analysis, and named entity recognition.

The concept of context extends beyond language modelling. In artificial intelligence, it supports reasoning through logical structures; in pervasive computing, it encompasses variables such as user identity, location, and activity; and in knowledge management, it pertains to the relationships among entities within a knowledge network. As data-driven decision-making becomes more prevalent, contextual information plays a critical role in transforming raw data into actionable insights. For example, in systems like license plate recognition, contextual data enhances the retrieval of relevant transactional or historical records.

Structured data also presents challenges in contextual interpretation. To address this, techniques such as context enrichment have emerged. These methods use Transformer-based embeddings and keyless join operations to automatically enhance structured data with contextual information, significantly improving performance in applications like search and recommendation systems.

The integration of context across disciplines underscores the need for innovative methodologies that can harness its full potential. By effectively modelling and leveraging context, foundation models not only improve technical performance but also enable more informed, adaptive, and human-aligned decision-making.

Context Window Management

The context window defines how much historical information the model can access when processing new inputs. Modern foundation models typically support context windows ranging from a few thousand to hundreds of thousands of tokens. Managing this window effectively requires careful consideration of several factors:

Memory allocation must balance the need for comprehensive context against computational constraints. Larger context windows enable better understanding but require more processing resources and may introduce latency.

Selective attention mechanisms help focus on relevant portions of the context, preventing information overload while maintaining performance. These mechanisms identify and prioritize the most pertinent contextual information for each specific task.

Contextual Embedding

Contextual embedding represents one of the most crucial aspects of applying context to foundation models. This process transforms input data into rich, context-aware representations that capture both semantic meaning and relationships between different elements. Advanced embedding techniques incorporate:

Position-aware encoding that maintains the sequential nature of input data while allowing for flexible processing of varying context lengths. This enables the model to understand both local and global context effectively.

Cross-attention mechanisms that enable the model to relate different parts of the input to each other, creating a comprehensive understanding of the overall context. These mechanisms prove particularly valuable when processing complex, multi-part inputs.

In-Context Learning

Building applications with large language models (LLMs) offers a variety of approaches, from training models from scratch to fine-tuning existing ones or leveraging hosted APIs. However, in-context learning has emerged as a prevalent design pattern, particularly for developers initiating their LLM projects. This approach hinges on utilizing pre-trained LLMs directly, without any fine-tuning, and instead directing their behaviour through carefully crafted prompts and the provision of relevant contextual data.

Imagine constructing a chatbot designed to answer inquiries about a collection of legal documents. A naive attempt might involve pasting all documents into a prompt for models like ChatGPT or GPT-4, followed by the question. While feasible for small datasets, this approach becomes impractical as data volume increases. In-context learning addresses this scalability issue by selectively including only the most relevant documents in each prompt, rather than the entire corpus.

The in-context learning workflow can be broadly categorized into three key stages. First, **data preprocessing and embedding** involves preparing private data, such as our legal documents, for efficient retrieval. This typically entails dividing documents into smaller chunks, converting these chunks into numerical representations called embeddings using an embedding model, and storing them in a vector database. This specialized database excels at finding semantically similar data points, which is crucial for retrieving relevant documents based on user queries.

Next, **prompt construction and retrieval** focus on crafting the prompts that will be submitted to the LLM. When a user poses a query, such as a legal question, the application constructs a prompt that combines several elements. These include a pre-defined prompt template, few-shot examples that demonstrate the desired output format, information retrieved from external APIs if needed, and the most relevant documents retrieved from the vector database. This carefully assembled prompt provides the LLM with the necessary context to generate an accurate and relevant response.

Finally, **prompt execution and inference** involve submitting the compiled prompts to a pre-trained LLM, whether through proprietary model APIs or open-source or self-trained models. At this stage, developers often integrate operational systems for logging, caching, and validation to ensure the reliability and efficiency of the application.

In-context learning effectively transforms an AI problem into a data engineering challenge, a domain in which many start-ups and large enterprises already possess expertise. This approach often outperforms fine-tuning for smaller datasets, as fine-tuning requires a specific piece of information to appear multiple times in the training data for the LLM to retain it. Moreover, in-context learning enables the incorporation of new data in near real-time, providing greater agility.

A significant consideration in in-context learning is the potential for increasing the LLM's context window. While expanding the context window can theoretically reduce the need for external retrieval, it introduces trade-offs. Primarily, the computational cost and inference time increase, often scaling quadratically with the length of the prompt. This poses challenges in terms of resource utilization and application performance.

In-context learning relies heavily on a few-shot learning approach. The few-shot examples that are included in the prompt are examples of desired input/output pairs. These examples demonstrate to the LLM the pattern that the user desires the LLM to follow. By providing a few examples, the LLM can more accurately generate the desired output. One of the main benefits of in-context learning is that it does not require retraining of the LLM. It is very fast to implement and can be easily modified by simply changing the prompt.

Prompt Engineering for Language Models

Prompt Engineering

Prompt engineering is a crucial aspect of working with AI language models. It involves designing and refining the input prompts given to the AI to elicit the desired responses. This field involves the strategic selection and arrangement of formats, phrases, words, and symbolic elements that collectively enhance the AI's ability to interpret user intent and generate responses that align precisely with desired objectives. Far from being a simple matter of word choice, effective prompt engineering requires a deep understanding of how language models process information, recognize patterns, and generate outputs based on contextual cues.

Practitioners in this field employ a combination of creative intuition and methodical experimentation to develop comprehensive libraries of input templates that maximize the capabilities of generative AI applications across diverse contexts. They systematically test hypothesis-driven variations in prompt structure, tone, specificity, and framing to identify which approaches yield superior results for particular use cases. This process often involves establishing control prompts as baselines, then iteratively refining elements to isolate the impact of specific changes on model outputs—a process that mirrors scientific experimentation while incorporating linguistic and psychological insights.

> **Definition** A *prompt* is a text in the natural language used to train the generative AI on the specific task at hand to be executed.

Prompt engineering is a rapidly evolving discipline that extends far beyond the simple crafting of instructions for language models. It encompasses a multifaceted set of competencies, including an understanding of model architecture constraints, inference behaviour, context window management, and strategies for mitigating biases inherent in large language models. Effective prompt engineers draw upon knowledge from computational linguistics, cognitive psychology, and machine learning to shape AI behaviour through carefully constructed language.

This field serves as a crucial interface between abstract AI capabilities and practical human needs. Through the design of sophisticated prompts, engineers can enforce safety constraints, prevent harmful or unethical outputs, and ensure compliance with ethical standards. They also enhance model utility by embedding domain-specific knowledge, enabling structured reasoning, and integrating external tools to compensate for model limitations.

Prompt engineers function as intermediaries between users and models, creating adaptable templates and scripts that non-experts can use effectively. These templates often include tuneable parameters to balance consistency with flexibility. Through systematic experimentation and evaluation, engineers develop prompt libraries that support reliable and reproducible interactions across a wide range of applications.

The practical impact of prompt engineering is evident in real-world systems. For example, a vague query such as "Where to buy a dishwasher?" can be transformed into a detailed, context-aware prompt that elicits personalized, location-specific recommendations, complete with store details and promotions. This transformation ensures that AI responses are not only accurate but also contextually relevant and user-centric.

As language models become more capable, prompt engineering techniques have grown more sophisticated. Strategies such as chain-of-thought prompting guide models through logical reasoning steps; few-shot prompting provides examples to shape responses; and system role definitions establish behavioural boundaries. These methods help reduce hallucinations and improve the coherence and reliability of outputs.

A key challenge in prompt engineering is balancing specificity with openness—providing enough structure to guide the model while preserving its generative flexibility. This requires continuous testing across diverse scenarios and user groups, particularly edge cases that expose the limitations of current prompting strategies.

Economically, prompt engineering is gaining strategic importance. As organizations increasingly deploy generative AI for customer service, content generation, and automation, prompt optimization offers a cost-effective alternative to retraining models. By refining prompts, organizations can significantly enhance performance and user satisfaction without incurring the high costs of model development.

Basic Prompt Design

Effective interaction with large language models (LLMs) is dependent on the skill of designing prompts that guide their responses. At its core, the basic design of prompts centres on achieving both clarity and a well-defined structure, enabling the LLM to comprehend and respond with precision. A primary aspect of this is the provision of explicit instructions. Because ambiguity hinders the accuracy of responses, prompts should employ precise and unambiguous directives, leaving minimal room for misinterpretation. For example, instead of a general request like "Summarize this text," a more effective prompt would be "Provide a four-sentence summary of the following text, emphasizing the main arguments and offering a concise overview."

Beyond mere clarity, assigning a specific role or persona to the LLM can significantly shape its output. This technique, known as role-playing, allows the model to adopt a particular viewpoint, resulting in more focused and pertinent responses. For instance, prompting the LLM to "Assume the role of a seasoned historian and explain the underlying causes of the second world war" will yield a different kind of response compared to a general inquiry about the same historical event. By embodying a specific role, the LLM can access and utilize relevant knowledge and maintain a consistent tone that aligns with that persona.

Establishing context is another vital element in prompt design. Supplying relevant background information or context aids the LLM in understanding the subtleties of the request, leading to the generation of more accurate and meaningful responses. Without sufficient context, the model might struggle to correctly interpret the prompt or might rely on assumptions that diverge from the user's intended meaning. Consider asking "What are the key factors?" in isolation. The LLM would lack the necessary information to provide a useful answer. However, a prompt such as "Considering the current economic situation in Mumbai Municipality, what are the key factors influencing inflation?" allows the model to draw upon its knowledge of economics and local context to generate a more relevant response.

The way input is formatted also significantly influences how effectively an LLM understands a prompt. Consistent and clear input formatting helps the model to parse and interpret the prompt more readily. This can involve the strategic use of delimiters, such as quotation marks or brackets, to distinguish different components of the prompt. For example, clearly demarcating the text intended for summarization or the specific question being asked can prevent confusion for the LLM. Consistent formatting also aids the model in recognizing patterns within prompts and applying this understanding to subsequent interactions.

Similarly, specifying the desired format for the LLM's output is crucial. Output formatting ensures that the response is presented in a manner that is easily comprehensible and usable. This can involve requesting the output in various structures, such as lists, tables, code snippets, or specific textual arrangements. For instance, asking for "a list of the ten most influential scientists of the 20th century" or "a table comparing the key features of different programming languages" provides explicit guidance on how the LLM should structure its response.

Zero-Shot, One-Shot, and Few-Shot Learning Prompts

Zero-shot Learning Prompts

Zero-shot learning refers to prompting an NLP model to perform a task without providing any examples of that task. The model must rely entirely on its pre-trained knowledge to understand and execute the request.

Zero-shot Learning Prompt Structure:

```
[Task description]
[Input context or question]
[Output instruction]
```

Example of Zero-shot Learning:

```
Classify the following movie review as either positive or negative.
```

```
Review: I expected so much more from this film given the stellar cast.
The plot dragged terribly in the middle, and the characters felt one-
dimensional despite the actors' best efforts. The cinematography
was the only redeeming quality, but it wasn't enough to save this
disappointing experience.
Classify this review as positive or negative:
```
In this zero-shot example, the model receives a task description,
input text, and output instruction, but no examples of how to categorize reviews. The model must use its pre-training to understand
what constitutes positive versus negative sentiment and make the
classification accordingly.

One-Shot Learning Prompts

One-shot learning provides a single example of the task before
asking the model to perform the same task with new input. This gives
the model a concrete reference for the expected format and approach.

One-Shot Learning Prompt Structure:

```
[Task description]
[Example input]
[Example output]
[New input]
[Output instruction]
```

Example of One-shot Learning:

```
Extract the company name and founding year from company descrip-
tions.
Example:
Description: Founded in 2004, Facebook has grown from a college
networking site into one of the world's largest social media plat-
forms with billions of users worldwide.
Output: Company: Facebook, Founded: 2004
Now extract the company name and founding year from this descrip-
tion:
Description: Netflix began its journey in 1997 as a DVD rental
service before pivoting to streaming in 2007, revolutionizing how
people consume entertainment media across the globe.
```

In this one-shot example, the model first sees a completed example of the extraction task before being asked to perform the same type of extraction on new text. The
example helps clarify the expected output format and what information should be
extracted.

Few-Shot Learning Prompts.

Few-shot learning extends one-shot learning by providing multiple examples
(typically 2–5) before the target task. This gives the model more reference points to
identify patterns and appropriate responses.

Few-Shot Learning Prompt Structure:

```
[Task description]
[Example 1 input]
```

```
[Example 1 output]
[Example 2 input]
[Example 2 output]
[Example 3 input]
[Example 3 output]
[New input]
[Output instruction]
```

Example of Few-shot learning:

```
Rewrite the following sentences to eliminate passive voice.
Example 1:
Passive: The report was submitted by the committee yesterday.
Active: The committee submitted the report yesterday.
Example 2:
Passive: Mistakes were made during the implementation process.
Active: The team made mistakes during the implementation process.
Example 3:
Passive: The building is being renovated by the construction
company.
Active: The construction company is renovating the building.
Now rewrite this sentence to eliminate passive voice:
Passive: The experiment was conducted by researchers from three
different universities.
```

In this few-shot example, the model receives three examples demonstrating how to convert passive voice to active voice before being asked to perform the same transformation on a new sentence. The multiple examples help the model identify the pattern of identifying the actor (who is performing the action) and moving it to the subject position in the sentence.

Advanced Prompting Techniques

The advanced prompting strategies transform how we communicate with artificial intelligence systems, enabling more advanced, intelligent, and contextually aware interactions.

Stepwise Reasoning Approach.

The chain-of-thought technique represents a pivotal advancement in computational reasoning. By encouraging models to deconstruct complex problems into logical, sequential steps, this approach renovates how AI approaches challenging tasks. Rather than providing direct answers, the model systematically breaks down problems, generating intermediate reasoning stages that reveal its computational thought process.

Imagine solving a multiplication problem. Instead of immediately calculating 123×456, the model would methodically decompose the calculation: first multiplying 123 by individual place values, then aggregating these partial results to derive the final answer. This methodical approach mirrors human problem-solving strategies, making computational reasoning more transparent and reliable.

Building upon stepwise reasoning, the tree-of-thoughts method introduces a more sophisticated cognitive approach. This technique allows language models to simultaneously explore multiple reasoning paths, evaluating different hypothetical solutions. By branching out and examining alternative perspectives, the model can generate more comprehensive and nuanced responses, particularly for complex or ambiguous problems.

Response Refinement.

Self-consistency techniques address the inherent variability in language model outputs. By generating multiple responses to identical prompts and selecting the most consistently appearing solution, models can mitigate randomness and improve answer reliability. This approach recognizes that correct answers tend to emerge more consistently across multiple computational generations.

The reflexion technique elevates computational reasoning by introducing a *self-reflective mechanism*. Models can now assess their own outputs, identifying potential errors or inconsistencies. Through iterative refinement, language models progressively enhance their response accuracy and generate increasingly sophisticated answers.

Knowledge Augmentation Strategies.

Knowledge retrieval augmentation bridges the gap between language models' internal knowledge and external information sources. By dynamically integrating databases, search engines, and real-time information repositories, models can ground their responses in current, domain-specific knowledge. This approach is particularly crucial for tasks requiring up-to-date or specialized information.

Active prompting introduces an interactive dimension to artificial intelligence communication. Instead of generating potentially misaligned responses, models can now ask clarifying questions, seeking additional context to ensure precise and relevant answers. This approach transforms computational interactions from static exchanges to collaborative dialogues.

Prompt chaining enables users to create complex, multi-step workflows by linking individual prompts. Complex tasks can be systematically deconstructed into manageable components, with each prompt's output serving as input for subsequent computational stages. This strategy allows language models to tackle intricate challenges through a structured, sequential approach.

Similar to prompt chaining, task decomposition breaks sophisticated problems into simpler, more manageable sub-tasks. By guiding models through a series of progressively complex prompts, users can achieve more accurate and efficient problem-solving strategies.

Prompt Optimization and Refinement

Optimizing prompts for large language models (LLMs) is a continuous and iterative process that goes far beyond initial prompt creation. It involves experimenting with different formulations, structures, and contextual cues to refine how the model responds. This ongoing refinement helps identify the most effective ways to guide the model toward desired outputs.

Reusable prompt templates play a key role in streamlining this process. These templates serve as adaptable frameworks for common tasks, encapsulating best practices and proven strategies to ensure consistency and efficiency across applications. They save time while maintaining high-quality interactions.

The field is further supported by specialized tools and libraries that automate aspects of prompt engineering. These tools can generate prompt variations, analyze performance, and suggest improvements, accelerating experimentation and enabling data-driven refinement. Managing prompt versions is also essential, especially in collaborative environments, as it allows teams to track changes, compare outcomes, and revert to earlier iterations when needed.

Systematic prompt testing ensures reliability and accuracy. By using test datasets and evaluation metrics, developers can assess how well prompts perform and identify areas for improvement. Automated testing frameworks help maintain performance across updates and prevent regressions.

Prompt compression addresses the practical challenge of token limits and computational efficiency. By shortening prompts—through summarization, abbreviation, or removal of redundant language—developers can reduce processing costs and improve clarity. This is particularly important for complex tasks or when working within strict token constraints.

Altogether, prompt optimization is a vital practice for enhancing the performance, usability, and cost-effectiveness of LLM-powered systems.

Prompt Safety and Bias Mitigation

In large language model (LLM) utilization, prompt safety and bias mitigation are top concerns. As LLMs become increasingly integrated into various applications, ensuring their responsible and ethical use is crucial. Prompt engineering for safety involves designing prompts with the explicit goal of preventing the generation of harmful or biased content. This proactive approach aims to steer the LLM towards producing outputs that are respectful, inclusive, and free from potentially damaging information. This requires a deep understanding of the types of harmful content LLMs can generate, and the design of prompts that avoid such outcomes.

Bias detection in prompts is a critical step in mitigating harmful outputs. Biases can inadvertently creep into prompts through subtle wording choices, implicit assumptions, or the use of biased training data. Identifying and mitigating these biases requires a careful analysis of the prompt's language, context, and potential impact. Techniques for bias detection include analyzing the prompt for stereotypical language, evaluating the prompt's potential to reinforce existing biases, and testing the prompt with diverse datasets. Once biases are identified, they can be mitigated through careful rewording, the inclusion of counterexamples, or the use of debiasing techniques.

Adversarial prompting is a valuable technique for testing the LLM's robustness to malicious or manipulative prompts. By intentionally crafting prompts that attempt to elicit harmful or biased responses, users can identify vulnerabilities in the LLM's safety mechanisms. This form of testing helps to ensure that the LLM can withstand attempts to exploit its weaknesses and generate harmful content. This is a vital part of hardening LLMs against malicious use.

Prompt sanitization involves filtering or modifying prompts to remove potentially harmful or offensive content before they are processed by the LLM. This technique acts as a safeguard, preventing the LLM from being exposed to prompts that could lead to the generation of harmful outputs. Prompt sanitization can involve techniques such as keyword filtering, content moderation, and the use of regular expressions to identify and remove potentially problematic language. This is often used in conjunction with user input validation.

Prompt engineering for ethical considerations extends beyond safety and bias mitigation to encompass broader ethical principles and guidelines. This involves designing prompts that align with societal values, respect user privacy, and promote responsible AI practices. Ethical prompt engineering requires careful consideration of the potential consequences of the LLM's outputs and the design of prompts that minimize the risk of unintended harm. This includes considerations such as transparency, fairness, and accountability. It also involves careful consideration of the application of the model, and the potential for misuse. By integrating ethical considerations into the prompt design process, users can help to ensure that LLMs are used in a responsible and beneficial manner.

Prompt Engineering for Specific Applications

Here are some examples of prompt engineering tailored to specific applications:

Prompt Engineering for Code Generation

- **Description**: Crafting prompts to generate precise and efficient code snippets.
- **Example**: Instead of "Create a function to calculate the factorial of a number," use "Write a Python function named factorial that takes a non-negative integer as input and returns its factorial. Include error handling for negative inputs." Another example: "Generate a JavaScript function that fetches data from an API and logs the response to the console."

Prompt Engineering for Creative Writing

- **Description**: Inspiring imaginative and engaging content, such as stories, poems, or scripts.
- **Example**: Instead of "Write a poem," try "Write a haiku about the changing seasons, focusing on the transition from autumn to winter." Or, "Compose a short story about a time traveller who accidentally alters a significant historical event, leading to unexpected consequences."

Prompt Engineering for Question Answering

- **Description**: Designing prompts to elicit accurate and informative answers to specific questions.
- **Example**: Instead of "What is the water cycle?" use "Describe the stages of the water cycle, including evaporation, condensation, and precipitation. Provide an example of how the water cycle affects weather patterns." Another example: "Explain the concept of supply and demand in economics, and give an example of how it influences market prices."

Prompt Engineering for Summarization

- Description: Creating prompts that generate concise and accurate summaries of text.
- Example: Instead of "Summarize this book," try "Summarize the main plot points of the following novel in five sentences: [insert novel text here]." Or, "Create a summary of the following research paper, highlighting the key findings and their implications."

Prompt Engineering for Data Extraction

- Description: Extracting specific information from text, such as names, dates, or addresses.
- Example: Instead of "Extract the dates from this text," use "From the following event descriptions, extract the event names and their corresponding dates: [insert event descriptions here]. Return the information in a table format with columns for 'Event Name' and 'Date'." Or, "Extract all URLs and email addresses from the following document."

Prompt Engineering for Dialogue Systems

- Description: Designing prompts to create engaging and natural conversations between the AI and a user.
- Example: Instead of "Chat with the user," try "You are a virtual travel assistant. The user says, 'I want to plan a trip to Paris.' Respond by asking about their travel dates, budget, and interests." Or, "Act as a tech support agent. The user is frustrated because their internet is not working. Respond with empathy and guide them through troubleshooting steps."

Prompt Engineering for Multimodal Tasks

- **Description**: Creating prompts that incorporate both text and images to generate desired outputs.

- **Example**: "Describe the scene in the image and write a dialogue between two characters based on the scene: [insert image here]." Or, "Analyse the following chart and summarize the key trends and insights: [insert chart here]." Another example: "Based on this image and the provided text, create a promotional caption for a social media post. [image] [text]."

These examples demonstrate how detailed and specific prompts can guide AI models to produce more accurate and contextually relevant outputs.

Prompt Engineering for LLM Alignment

The large language models (LLMs) have brought forth the need for alignment, ensuring these tools operate in a manner that is safe, ethical, and beneficial to society. Prompt engineering plays a pivotal role in this alignment process, particularly when considering techniques like Reinforcement Learning from Human Feedback (RLHF), toxicity mitigation, and adherence to ethical frameworks.

Prompt engineering for RLHF is a specialized area that focuses on crafting prompts designed to elicit useful and informative feedback from human raters. RLHF is a crucial technique for fine-tuning LLMs, as it allows them to learn from human preferences and values. The quality of the feedback received directly impacts the effectiveness of the RLHF process, making prompt engineering essential. Effective prompts for RLHF are often designed to be specific, clear, and unambiguous, encouraging raters to provide detailed and nuanced feedback. They may also include examples of desired or undesired outputs, helping raters to understand the criteria for evaluation. For instance, instead of asking "Is this reply good?" a more effective prompt might be, "Rate this reply based on its effectiveness, accuracy, and clarity. Provide specific examples of what you liked or disliked about the response." This detailed approach ensures that human raters are able to provide granular feedback that the LLM can learn from. Further, prompts may be designed to include comparison tasks, asking raters to choose between two responses, thus providing a more direct signal of preference.

Beyond eliciting feedback, prompt engineering is also instrumental in steering models away from generating toxic or harmful content. LLMs, trained on vast datasets of text and code, can inadvertently learn and reproduce harmful biases or generate offensive language. Prompt engineering aims to mitigate these risks by crafting prompts that discourage the generation of such content. This can involve using carefully chosen keywords, providing contextual constraints, or explicitly instructing the model to avoid generating harmful or biased outputs. For example, a prompt might include phrases such as "Respond in a respectful and inclusive manner" or "Avoid generating content that is offensive, discriminatory, or harmful." Furthermore, prompts can be designed to include counterexamples, demonstrating the types of responses that are considered unacceptable. This proactive approach to prompt design is crucial for ensuring that LLMs are used responsibly and ethically. Another method is to use a prompt that asks the LLM to analyze the potential harmfulness of its own response and then modify it accordingly.

Instruction Alignment

In practical use, a prompt usually contains straightforward instruction along with some user-provided input. We expect the LLM to understand and follow this instruction in order to complete the task as intended. This capability is often referred to as the model's instruction-following ability.

For instance, imagine you want an LLM to read a research paper and provide a brief summary of its main points. You might give it a prompt like, "Summarize the following text in four sentences." In this case, the LLM needs to recognize the instruction to summarize and then generate a concise summary that meets the specified requirements.

However, it's important to note that LLMs are originally trained to predict the next word or token in a sequence, rather than to specifically follow instructions. If you use a pre-trained LLM without any further adjustment, it might simply continue generating text in the style of the original article, rather than summarizing the content as instructed.

This is where instruction alignment, also known as instruction fine-tuning, becomes important. Instruction alignment is the process of further training the LLM so that it learns to interpret and accurately respond to user instructions. The goal is to ensure the model's output matches the user's intentions, making it more useful and reliable for real-world applications that require following specific directions.

Aligning LLMs with specific ethical frameworks is another critical aspect of prompt engineering. This involves designing prompts that incorporate ethical principles and guidelines, ensuring that the model's outputs are consistent with societal values and norms. This can involve embedding ethical considerations into the prompt's instructions, providing examples of ethical behaviour, or explicitly instructing the model to adhere to specific ethical frameworks. For instance, a prompt might ask the LLM to "Respond in a manner that respects user privacy" or "Consider the potential consequences of your response on different stakeholders." Prompts can also be designed to incorporate specific ethical theories, such as utilitarianism or deontology, providing the model with a framework for ethical decision-making. This is a complex area, as ethical frameworks can vary across cultures and contexts. Therefore, careful consideration must be given to the selection and implementation of ethical principles in prompt design. This may involve incorporating multiple viewpoints or asking the LLM to consider multiple ethical frameworks.

Controlling and Refining LLM Output

LLM Guardrails—Controlling LLM Output

Controlling the output of large language models (LLMs) is crucial for ensuring their safe and reliable deployment, and this is where LLM guardrails come into play. These guardrails are a set of techniques and strategies designed to constrain and shape the LLM's responses, preventing the generation of harmful, biased, or irrelevant content. Effectively, they act as a safety net, guiding the model towards desired behaviours and away from undesirable ones.

One key aspect of LLM guardrails involves prompt engineering, which we've discussed previously. By carefully crafting prompts, developers can steer the model towards specific topics, formats, or tones, while simultaneously discouraging unwanted outputs. This can involve using explicit instructions, providing examples of acceptable responses, or incorporating constraints that limit the model's freedom.

Another crucial technique is output filtering and moderation. This involves analyzing the LLM's output for potentially harmful or inappropriate content and then either blocking or modifying it. This can be achieved through keyword filtering, sentiment analysis, or more sophisticated natural language processing techniques. Human-in-the-loop moderation can also be employed, where human reviewers assess the model's responses and provide feedback.

Bias mitigation is another essential aspect of LLM guardrails. This involves identifying and addressing biases in the model's training data or output. Techniques for bias mitigation include data augmentation, where biased data is balanced with counterexamples, and adversarial training, where the model is exposed to intentionally biased inputs to improve its robustness.

Furthermore, guardrails can be implemented through the use of external knowledge bases and retrieval mechanisms. By grounding the LLM's responses in factual information, developers can reduce the likelihood of hallucinations and improve the accuracy of the output. This is particularly relevant in applications where factual accuracy is paramount.

Additionally, fine-tuning the LLM on specific datasets can instil desired behaviours and limit unwanted ones. For example, fine-tuning on a dataset of respectful and inclusive dialogues can help the model generate more appropriate responses. Implementing runtime checks and constraints can further enhance LLM guardrails. This involves monitoring the model's output in real-time and applying rules or constraints to ensure that it adheres to predefined guidelines. This can involve setting limits on the length of responses, restricting the use of certain words or phrases, or enforcing specific output formats.

RLHF and Large Language Models

Reinforcement Learning from Human Feedback (RLHF) is reshaping how AI systems interpret and respond to human intentions. By directly incorporating human judgment into the model refinement process, RLHF bridges the gap between computational ability and human-aligned communication. This allows models to develop a nuanced understanding of human preferences, leading to responses that are not only technically correct but also genuinely helpful, appropriate, and aligned with human values. In conventional reinforcement learning frameworks, an agent interacts with its environment through a cycle of actions and consequent rewards or penalties, gradually optimizing its behaviour to maximize cumulative rewards. This trial-and-error approach enables systems to learn complex behaviours through direct experience rather than explicit programming. RLHF extends this methodology by incorporating human evaluators who provide quality assessments that shape the reward signals. This human-in-the-loop approach accelerates the learning process substantially by leveraging domain expertise and human judgment to guide model development in directions that purely algorithmic rewards might miss.

The critical innovation of RLHF lies in its ability to help language models understand implicit human intentions that may not be explicitly articulated in prompts. By learning from patterns of human preference across thousands of examples, these models develop a form of pragmatic understanding—grasping not just what users literally ask for but what would genuinely satisfy their underlying needs. This capability transforms language models from sophisticated auto-completion tools into assistive systems that can interpret ambiguous instructions, maintain contextual awareness across conversations, and respond with appropriate depth and nuance to varied human queries.

The RLHF methodology unfolds through a structured four-stage process that progressively refines a language model's alignment with human preferences:

The journey begins with a foundation model—typically a large language model pre-trained on vast text corpora through self-supervised learning. This model possesses extensive linguistic and world knowledge but lacks the refinement necessary to consistently produce helpful, harmless, and honest responses. These foundation models excel at pattern recognition and text prediction but require additional training to reliably generate content aligned with human expectations and values.

The second phase introduces supervised fine-tuning, where human annotators create demonstration datasets that exemplify desired model behaviours. These datasets consist of carefully crafted prompt-response pairs that illustrate appropriate, helpful responses across various contexts. For instance, annotators might provide examples showing how to explain complex concepts like artificial intelligence in accessible terms, respond constructively to sensitive questions, or decline inappropriate requests. Through exposure to these examples, the model begins learning the patterns of responses that human experts consider desirable.

The third stage—perhaps the most innovative aspect of RLHF—involves developing a specialized reward model that serves as a computational proxy for human judgment. This reward model, itself a neural network, learns to predict how humans would evaluate different possible responses to the same prompt. To train this evaluative system, annotators rank several alternative responses to identical prompts based on quality, helpfulness, harmlessness, and other relevant criteria. The reward model then learns to replicate these human preference judgments, eventually becoming capable of assigning scalar reward values that approximate human evaluations of response quality. This automated evaluation system can then provide immediate feedback on thousands of model outputs without requiring constant human intervention.

The final phase creates a reinforcement learning loop where the language model (now functioning as a policy in RL terminology) generates responses that are evaluated by the reward model. Using algorithms like Proximal Policy Optimization (PPO), the language model's parameters are gradually adjusted to maximize the expected reward—effectively steering the model toward generating responses that the reward model (and by extension, human evaluators) would judge favourably. This iterative optimization process continues until the model consistently produces outputs aligned with human preferences across a wide range of scenarios.

Proximal Policy Optimization Algorithm: *Proximal Policy Optimization (PPO) is a reinforcement learning algorithm designed to train intelligent agents. It is a policy gradient method, often used for deep reinforcement learning when the policy network is large. PPO optimizes the policy directly by adjusting the parameters to maximize the expected reward. It uses gradient ascent to update the policy. One of the main innovations of PPO is the use of a clipped objective function. This helps to limit the size of policy updates, ensuring that the new policy does not deviate too much from the old one. This clipping mechanism stabilizes training and prevents large, destabilizing updates.*

PPO often employs an actor-critic architecture. The actor updates the policy based on the gradient, while the critic evaluates the policy by estimating the value function. This combination helps in reducing variance and improving learning stability. PPO uses a surrogate objective function that approximates the true objective. This surrogate function is easier to optimize and helps in maintaining a balance between exploration and exploitation. PPO works as follows:

1. *Collect Trajectories*: *The agent interacts with the environment to collect trajectories (sequences of states, actions, and rewards).*

2. ***Compute Advantages***: *The advantage function is computed to estimate how much better or worse an action is compared to the average action at a given state.*
3. ***Update Policy***: *The policy is updated using the clipped objective function. The clipping ensures that the updates are within a safe range, preventing drastic changes that could destabilize learning.*
4. ***Repeat***: *This process is repeated iteratively, with the agent continuously improving its policy based on the feedback from the environment.*

A central precise constraint in this process involves maintaining proximity to the original supervised fine-tuned model while optimizing for reward. Without this constraint, the model might discover reward "hacks" that maximize the reward signal without actually improving response quality from a human perspective. This balance between exploration and constraint is typically achieved through a KL-divergence penalty that prevents the policy from deviating too dramatically from its starting point.

The impact of RLHF extends beyond mere technical performance improvements. RLHF-trained models demonstrate enhanced abilities to follow complex instructions, maintain appropriate tone and style, avoid generating harmful content, admit knowledge limitations, and engage in nuanced reasoning that better reflects human thinking patterns. These capabilities enable language models to function as more reliable partners in creative, analytical, and informational tasks across numerous domains.

RLHF and ChatGPT

OpenAI's implementation of Reinforcement Learning from Human Feedback (RLHF) has become a foundational approach for aligning large language models like ChatGPT with human expectations, enabling more natural, helpful, and safe interactions. This process unfolds in three key stages, each building on the previous to refine the model's behaviour.

The first stage involves supervised fine-tuning using high-quality human demonstrations. A team of skilled annotators creates ideal responses to a mix of developer-designed prompts and real user queries. These responses reflect OpenAI's standards for helpfulness, harmlessness, and honesty. The resulting dataset is used to fine-tune a pre-trained model—initially based on GPT-3.5—producing a Supervised Fine-Tuned (SFT) model that better follows instructions and maintains conversational quality, though it still lacks nuanced judgment.

In the second stage, OpenAI constructs a reward model to evaluate response quality. Instead of assigning absolute scores, annotators compare multiple responses to the same prompt and rank them. This comparative method captures subtle human preferences more reliably. The reward model, trained on this data, learns to predict which responses are most aligned with human judgment by assigning scalar quality scores to prompt-response pairs.

The final stage uses reinforcement learning, specifically Proximal Policy Optimization (PPO), to further refine the SFT model. The model generates multiple responses, which are scored by the reward model. PPO then adjusts the model's parameters to favour high-scoring outputs while staying close to the original SFT model, thanks to a KL-divergence penalty that prevents the model from drifting too far from its pre-trained behaviour. This results in a policy model—what powers ChatGPT—that produces responses more aligned with human values and expectations.

OpenAI has continued to enhance this process in newer versions like GPT-4, incorporating techniques such as Constitutional AI to enforce rule-based constraints and expanding the diversity of human feedback. The success of RLHF in ChatGPT has influenced the broader AI community, establishing a new standard for aligning language models with human needs through iterative, feedback-driven refinement.

Challenges in Large Language Models

Toxicity, Hallucination and Bias in Large Language Models

The capabilities of large language models (LLMs) come with inherent challenges that demand careful consideration and mitigation: hallucinations, toxicity, and bias. These issues pose significant risks to the responsible deployment of LLMs and can undermine their potential benefits if left unchecked.

Hallucinations, the phenomenon of LLMs generating fabricated content that blends fact and fiction, represent a fundamental challenge to their reliability. This tendency to stray from reality stems from limitations in training data, the model's architectural design, and our incomplete understanding of the complex processes within these models. Hallucinations can manifest in various forms, including outright lies, where the model fabricates information; source conflation, where it attributes information to incorrect or non-existent sources; and rubbish replies, where it generates nonsensical or irrelevant outputs. The consequences of hallucinations are far-reaching, potentially manipulating information, eroding trust in LLM outputs, and creating substantial obstacles for applications that rely on accuracy, such as medical diagnosis or legal research.

Toxicity, the generation of harmful, offensive, or inappropriate content, is another critical concern. This encompasses hate speech, biased statements, and language that targets individuals or groups based on sensitive characteristics. The presence of toxicity in LLM outputs can perpetuate harmful stereotypes, disseminate misinformation, cause emotional distress, and hinder inclusive communication. The sources of toxicity can be diverse, including negative prompts that intentionally elicit harmful responses, contamination of the training data with toxic content, and inherent biases within the data itself. Addressing toxicity requires a multi-faceted approach, including careful data cleaning and filtering, adversarial testing, and human-in-the-loop monitoring.

LLMs can also inherit and amplify biases present in their training data, leading to outputs that perpetuate stereotypes and exacerbate social inequalities. These biases can manifest in various forms, including gender bias, racial bias, and cultural or religious bias. For example, a model might generate stereotypical descriptions of individuals based on their gender or race or produce outputs that reflect cultural or religious biases. The ethical and practical implications of bias in LLM outputs are significant, particularly in sensitive domains such as healthcare, news, and social media filtering. Biased outputs can lead to discriminatory outcomes, perpetuate harmful stereotypes, and erode public trust in these technologies.

Mitigating these challenges requires a comprehensive strategy that combines technical advancements with social awareness. Data cleaning and filtering are essential first steps in addressing toxicity and bias. Before training an LLM, the training data must be meticulously cleaned and filtered to remove any toxic or harmful content. This helps prevent the model from learning and reproducing such content. Techniques such as keyword filtering, content moderation, and the use of regular expressions can be employed to identify and remove potentially problematic language.

Adversarial testing is crucial for identifying vulnerabilities and weaknesses in LLMs. Regularly testing the model with deliberately chosen prompts that might trigger toxic responses or reveal biases allows developers to identify and address these issues before real-world deployment. This proactive approach helps to ensure that the model is robust and resilient to attempts to elicit harmful or biased outputs.

Human-in-the-loop monitoring is another essential component of a comprehensive mitigation strategy. Integrating human oversight into LLM deployment allows for the detection and correction of toxic outputs. This might involve having human moderators review the model's responses before they are shared with users. Human oversight can also help to identify and address subtle forms of bias that might be difficult to detect through automated methods.

Transparency and accountability are crucial for building trust in LLMs. Providing clear information about the LLM's training data, algorithms, and decision-making processes helps users understand the model's limitations and hold it accountable for its outputs. This transparency can also help to identify and address potential biases or other issues.

In addition to these technical and procedural measures, addressing the challenges of hallucinations, toxicity, and bias requires a broader societal dialogue about the ethical implications of LLMs. This involves engaging with diverse stakeholders, including researchers, developers, policymakers, and the public, to develop guidelines and best practices for the responsible development and deployment of these powerful technologies. By combining technical advancements with social awareness, we can work towards mitigating the risks associated with LLMs and ensuring that they are used in a manner that is safe, ethical, and beneficial to society.

LLM Quantization

Large language models, with their immense size and computational demands, often present challenges in deployment, especially on devices with limited resources. LLM quantization emerges as a crucial technique to mitigate these challenges by reducing the precision with which the model's weights and activations are represented. Essentially, it's a process of making the model's numerical representations smaller and more manageable.

Typically, LLMs operate with 32-bit floating-point numbers (FP32), which offer high precision but require substantial memory and processing power. Quantization aims to convert these FP32 numbers into lower-precision formats, such as 16-bit floating-point (FP16), 8-bit integers (INT8), or even 4-bit integers (INT4). This reduction in precision yields several significant benefits. Firstly, it dramatically reduces the model's size, making it easier to store and deploy on devices with limited memory, like smartphones or edge devices. Secondly, lower-precision operations are inherently faster than their higher-precision counterparts, leading to accelerated inference times. This is particularly advantageous for real-time applications where rapid responses are crucial. Thirdly, the reduced computational load translates to lower power consumption, a vital factor for battery-powered devices.

However, quantization is not without its trade-offs. The primary concern is potential accuracy loss. Representing numerical values with lower precision can introduce inaccuracies, and the degree of accuracy loss depends on the specific quantization method and the extent of precision reduction. Additionally, implementing quantization can add complexity to the model's training and deployment pipelines, requiring careful consideration and optimization.

Several methods exist for performing quantization. Post-training quantization involves quantizing a pre-trained model without further training. This approach is relatively straightforward but may result in more significant accuracy loss. Conversely, quantization-aware training integrates quantization into the training process, allowing the model to adapt to the lower-precision format. This method typically achieves better accuracy but requires more complex training procedures.

Expanding Generative Models beyond Text

Multimodal AI Models

In artificial intelligence, the term "modality" refers to the specific way in which information is represented or experienced, such as through text, images, audio, or video. When an AI system can process and understand information from more than one of these sources at the same time, it is described as multimodal. Multimodal AI models are designed to handle, integrate, and analyze data from multiple modalities, allowing them to interpret complex, real-world scenarios in a way that more closely resembles human perception.

Humans naturally combine inputs from different senses-like sight, hearing, and language-to form a richer understanding of their environment. Similarly, multimodal AI models are built to synthesize and correlate information from diverse data types. For example, a multimodal AI might simultaneously analyze an image and its accompanying text description to better understand the content, or it could process both spoken language and visual cues in a video to interpret emotion or context more accurately.

These models are structured using advanced neural networks and deep learning architectures that can process each modality both independently and together. By fusing information from several sources, multimodal AI systems can achieve a more comprehensive and nuanced understanding than traditional models that rely on a single data type. This capability enables them to make more accurate predictions, draw deeper insights, and generate creative outputs that reflect the interplay between different forms of data.

Multimodal AI models are applied in a wide range of tasks. For instance, text-to-image generation involves creating visual content from a textual description, while visual question-answering requires the model to interpret an image and answer questions about it using both visual and linguistic information. In robotics, multimodal AI helps machines navigate complex environments by integrating sensor data, visual input, and spoken commands. Other applications include healthcare, where models combine medical images, patient records, and clinical notes to improve diagnosis, and autonomous vehicles, which use data from cameras, radar, and other sensors to make driving decisions.

By leveraging multiple modalities, these AI systems can solve problems that are too complex for unimodal models, making them valuable in fields ranging from customer service and e-commerce to energy management and social media. Their ability to integrate and reason across diverse data types marks a significant step forward in the development of more flexible, intelligent, and human-like artificial intelligence.

Key Characteristics of Multimodal AI Models

1. **Multiple Data Inputs**: Multimodal models can handle and combine various input types, such as text, images, and audio, to perform complex tasks that require an understanding of relationships between these data types.
2. **Cross-Modal Learning**: These models are trained to learn correlations or relationships between different modalities, allowing them to combine and interpret information in a holistic way. For instance, they might associate a visual object (image) with a descriptive text or the sound of a dog barking with the image of a dog.

3. **Rich Representations**: Multimodal models create representations that incorporate features from different data types. This means they can leverage the strengths of each modality (e.g., the descriptive power of text and the spatial information of images) to improve overall task performance.

4. **Contextual Understanding**: Multimodal AI systems can understand the meaning of a phrase or sentence by analyzing the surrounding concepts and words. This is crucial in natural language processing tasks, where it is vital for a model to understand the concept of a sentence and generate an appropriate response. When combined with multimodal AI, NLP models can combine linguistic and visual information to attain a more well-rounded understanding of the context. Multimodal models can consider both the textual and visual cues in a particular context by combining multiple modalities. For instance, image captioning models can interpret the visual information contained in an image and merge it with the relevant linguistic information on the caption. Similarly, video captioning multimodal models are able to understand both the visual information in a video and the temporal relationship between the sounds, events, and dialogue in the video. The contextual understanding of multimodal models also comes in handy in the development of natural language dialogue systems like chatbots. By using linguistic and visual cues, multimodal models are better able to generate more human-like responses in a conversation.

5. **Improved capabilities**: Multimodal models have the ability to significantly improve the overall capabilities of an AI system, especially in cases where the model can leverage information from multiple modalities, including image, text, and audio, to understand the context. Ultimately, this helps AI systems to perform more diverse tasks, with greater performance, accuracy and effectiveness. For example, a multimodal model that combines facial and speech recognition could serve as an effective system for identifying individuals. Similarly, analyzing both audio and visual cues would assist the model in differentiating objects and individuals with similar voices and appearances. Also, a deeper analysis of contextual information like the behaviour or environment would provide a more comprehensive understanding of the situation, which would ultimately lead to more informed decisions.

Examples of Multimodal AI Models

Multimodal AI models exemplify the integration of multiple data types—such as text, images, and audio—into unified systems capable of complex reasoning and generation. One prominent example is **CLIP (Contrastive Language-Image Pre-training)**, which aligns textual and visual data by embedding them into a shared feature space, enabling it to match images with descriptions even in zero-shot scenarios. For instance, it can identify an image of "a dog playing in snow" without having seen that exact pairing before. Another notable model is **DALL·E**, which generates original images from textual prompts, translating imaginative descriptions like "a digital painting of a futuristic city skyline at sunset" into unique visual artworks, showcasing its creative potential.

Visual Question Answering (VQA) models, such as VLMo, combine image analysis with natural language understanding to answer questions about visual content. For example, when shown a kitchen and asked, "What colour are the cabinets?", the model can accurately respond based on the image. **Audio-Visual Speech Recognition (AVSR) models** enhance speech recognition by incorporating visual cues like lip movements, making them especially effective in noisy environments where audio alone may be unreliable.

Multimodal Transformers like **VilBERT** extend the transformer architecture to process both text and images simultaneously. These models can perform tasks such as image captioning, visual question answering, and interpreting referring expressions, demonstrating sophisticated cross-modal reasoning. Together, these models highlight the expanding capabilities of AI systems to understand and generate content across multiple modalities.

Vision Language Models

Vision language models are broadly defined as multimodal models that can learn from images and text. Vision Language Models (VLMs) bridge the gap between visual and linguistic understanding of AI. They are a type of generative models that combines computer vision (CV) and natural language processing (NLP) capabilities. They consist of a multimodal architecture that learns to associate information from image and text modalities. Vision language models (VLMs) can process such multimodal signals effectively and efficiently, enabling machine vision. Thus, understanding and generating image information blending visual and textual elements. Modern VLM architectures rely mostly on transformer-based AI models for image and text processing because they efficiently capture long-range dependencies.

One of the key challenges in developing VLMs is the integration of both visual and textual modalities in a coherent and effective manner. One can use techniques such as multimodal fusion, where visual and textual information is combined at different stages of the model architecture, to achieve this integration.

To achieve this multimodal understanding, VLMs typically consist of 3 main elements, as shown in Fig. 7.2:

- An Image Model: Responsible for extracting meaningful visual information such as features and representations from visual data, i.e., Image encoder.
- A Text Model: Designed to process and understand the natural language processing (NLP), i.e., text encoder.
- A Fusion Mechanism: A strategy to combine the representations learned by the image and text models, allowing for cross-modal interactions.

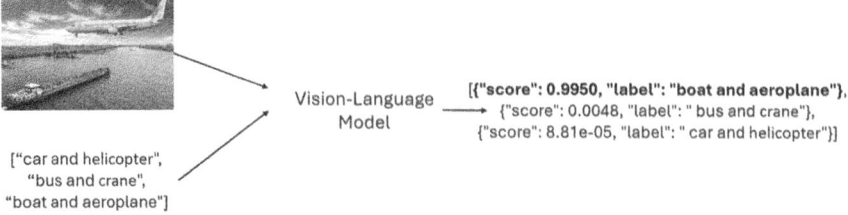

Fig. 7.2 Example of vision language model

One characteristic that helps define these models is their ability to process both images (vision) and natural language text (language). This process depends on the inputs, outputs, and the task these models are asked to perform. Take, for example, the task of zero-shot image classification. We'll pass an image and a few prompts like so to obtain the most probable prompt for the input image. The model needs to understand both the input image and the text prompts. The model would have separate or fused encoders for vision and language to achieve this understanding.

VLMs typically extract text features (e.g., word embeddings) and visual features (e.g., image regions or patches) using a text encoder and visual encoder. A multimodal fusion module then combines these independent streams, producing cross-modal representations. A decoder translates these representations into text or other outputs for generation-type tasks.

A vision-language model typically consists of 3 key elements: an image encoder, a text encoder, and a strategy to fuse information from the two encoders. These key elements are tightly coupled together as the loss functions are designed around both the model architecture and the learning strategy. While vision-language model research is hardly a new research area, the design of such models has changed tremendously over the years. Whereas earlier research adopted hand-crafted image descriptors and pre-trained word vectors, the latest research predominantly adopts image and text encoders with transformer architectures to separately or jointly learn image and text features. These models are pre-trained with strategic pre-training objectives that enable various downstream tasks. Some of the key learning strategies are:

Contrastive Learning relies on teaching the model about differences between similar and different inputs. The idea is to present the model with inputs in pairs—similar pairs are called positive pairs and dissimilar pairs are known as negative pairs. The model learns to extract meaningful representations of the input pair and project them into a lower dimensional space. The model tries to project the representations of the similar pair closer to each other and consequently the dissimilar representations are projected far apart. The contrastive learning can be conducted as supervised, semi-supervised, or self-supervised manner.

Prefix language modelling (PrefixLM) is a technique that uses a fixed-length prefix of a sequence of tokens (e.g. words or characters) to predict the next token in the sequence. In the context of training a vision language model, the prefix is used to provide context to the language model, so that it can generate more accurate and informative captions for images. The idea is that the prefix provides a starting point for the language model, and helps it to focus on the relevant aspects of the image when generating the caption. By using a prefix that is descriptive of the image, the language model can generate captions that are more accurate and informative, and that better capture the content and context of the image.

An effective advantage of the Frozen PrefixLM pre-training objective is it enables training with limited aligned image-text data, which is particularly useful for domains where aligned multimodal datasets are not available.

Multimodal Fusing with Cross-attention is an approach to leveraging pre-trained language models for multimodal tasks is to directly fuse visual information into the layers of a language model decoder using a cross-attention mechanism instead of using images as additional prefixes to the language model. Models such as VisualGPT, VC-GPT, and Flamingo use this pre-training strategy and are trained on image captioning and visual question-answering tasks. The main goal of such models is to balance the mixture of text generation capacity and visual information efficiently, which is highly important in the absence of large multimodal datasets.

With the massive advances in vision-language models, we see the emergence of new downstream tasks and application areas, such as medicine and robotics. For example, vision-language models are increasingly getting adopted for medical use cases. While robotics research hasn't leveraged vision-language models on a wide scale yet, there is a progress in leveraging joint vision-language representations for end-to-end imitation learning and reporting large improvements over previous state-of-the-art.

There have been incredible advances in multimodal models in recent years, with vision-language models making the most significant leap in performance and the variety of use cases and applications. In this blog, we talked about the latest advancements in vision-language models, as well as what multimodal datasets are available and which pre-training strategies we can use to train and fine-tune such models.

Challenges of Multimodal AI Models

Multimodal AI models face several significant challenges that must be addressed to ensure their effective development and deployment. A primary issue is data alignment, which involves integrating diverse inputs such as text, images, and audio into a coherent understanding. This requires the model to learn complex relationships between modalities, for example, linking specific image regions to corresponding textual descriptions. The structural differences between these data types make such alignment technically demanding, requiring advanced mechanisms to capture their semantic connections accurately.

Training complexity adds another layer of difficulty. Unlike single-modality models, multimodal systems must process and correlate heterogeneous data streams simultaneously, necessitating more sophisticated architectures and significantly greater computational resources. This results in longer training times, higher costs, and more intricate optimization processes.

Data scarcity further complicates matters. While large datasets exist for individual modalities, high-quality, annotated multimodal datasets—such as image-text pairs—are relatively rare. These are essential for teaching models to understand cross-modal relationships, and their absence can hinder generalization and performance. Moreover, creating such datasets is resource-intensive, requiring careful curation and annotation to reflect real-world complexity.

Interpretability remains a critical concern. Multimodal models often function as opaque "black boxes," making it difficult to trace how inputs from different modalities influence outputs. This lack of transparency raises issues around bias, fairness, and accountability, especially in high-stakes applications. Understanding the decision-making processes of these models is essential for building trust and ensuring ethical, responsible use.

Retrieval-Augmented Generation

Retrieval-Augmented Generation (RAG), introduced by Meta in 2020, enhances large language models (LLMs) by enabling them to access external, authoritative knowledge sources during response generation. This method bridges the gap between static training data and the need for up-to-date, contextually relevant information, improving the accuracy and reliability of LLM outputs without requiring costly retraining.

RAG integrates a retrieval system—typically a vector database like Pinecone or Chroma—with a generative LLM. When a user submits a query, the system first retrieves relevant documents from the external knowledge base. These documents, combined with the original query, are then passed to the LLM, which generates a response grounded in the retrieved context. This architecture allows the model to produce more informed and current answers.

The RAG workflow begins with preparing a knowledge base by collecting, organizing, and indexing relevant documents. The user's query is then processed to extract key concepts, followed by a retrieval step that searches the indexed data for pertinent information. This retrieved content is merged with the original query to form an enriched input for the LLM. The model then generates a response, which is refined and formatted before being delivered to the user. Feedback mechanisms and continuous learning loops help improve both retrieval and generation over time by updating the knowledge base and refining model behaviour.

RAG addresses the limitations of traditional LLMs, particularly their fixed knowledge cutoff, by allowing real-time access to updated information. It is especially valuable in fast-changing domains like healthcare, law, or finance, and supports multilingual and domain-specific applications. By grounding responses in external data, RAG reduces hallucinations, enhances factual accuracy, and allows for source citation, increasing transparency and user trust. It also handles rare or niche queries more effectively and can be customized with proprietary data for tailored enterprise solutions.

Looking forward, RAG is poised to evolve from a passive information retrieval tool into an active decision-making system. By grounding generative AI in real-world data, it could enable intelligent agents to perform tasks in areas like customer service, logistics, and robotics, making RAG a foundational component in the next generation of AI applications.

Orchestration Frameworks

LangChain and Llama Index

LangChain and Llama Index are two prominent orchestration frameworks designed to simplify the development and deployment of applications powered by large language models (LLMs). Both frameworks offer unique features and capabilities that cater to different aspects of LLM application development.

LangChain is an open-source orchestration framework that provides a modular and compostable environment for building LLM-driven applications. It supports both Python and JavaScript, making it accessible to a wide range of developers. LangChain's primary strength lies in its ability to integrate various LLMs and external data sources seamlessly. This framework allows developers to create complex work-flows by chaining together different components, such as data retrieval, processing, and generation modules. LangChain's flexibility enables the development of applications like chatbots, intelligent search engines, and virtual agents. One of the key advantages of LangChain is its support for multiple LLMs, allowing developers to compare and switch between different models with minimal code changes.

LangChain Use Cases

1. **Chatbots**: LangChain is widely used to build sophisticated chatbots that can handle customer inquiries, provide support, and engage users in natural conversations. Its modular architecture allows for easy integration of various LLMs and external data sources to enhance the chatbot's capabilities.
2. **Text Summarization**: LangChain can be employed to create applications that summarize long documents or articles, making it easier for users to digest large amounts of information quickly.
3. **AI Agents**: LangChain supports the development of AI agents that can perform specific tasks, such as scheduling meetings, managing emails, or providing personalized recommendations.

4. **Question-Answering Systems**: By leveraging retrieval-augmented generation (RAG) techniques, LangChain can build systems that answer user queries by retrieving relevant information from databases and generating accurate responses.

5. **Tool Use and Agents**: LangChain can integrate with various tools and APIs, enabling the creation of agents that can perform complex workflows, such as data analysis, content generation, and automation.

In practical terms, using LangChain involves setting up a series of "chains" that define the flow of data and tasks within the application. For example, a chatbot built with LangChain might start with a user query, retrieve relevant information from a database, process the data using an LLM, and then generate a response. This modular approach simplifies the development process and enhances the maintainability of the application. However, the trade-off is the need for careful orchestration of the various components to ensure smooth operation and optimal performance.

Llama Index, on the other hand, is a framework designed to build knowledge assistants and multi-agent systems over enterprise data. It excels in creating context-augmented LLM applications by connecting, transforming, and indexing data from various sources. Llama Index supports a wide range of data formats, including unstructured, semi-structured, and structured data, making it highly versatile. The framework's strength lies in its ability to orchestrate complex workflows involving multiple agents and data connectors. This makes it ideal for applications that require advanced retrieval-augmented generation (RAG) techniques, such as financial analysis, customer support, and internal knowledge management.

In practice, Llama Index allows developers to build "agents" that can perform specific tasks, such as data extraction, summarization, and question-answering. These agents can be combined into workflows that handle complex queries and tasks. For instance, a financial analysis application might use Llama Index to ingest and index financial reports, then deploy agents to analyze the data and generate insights. The framework's flexibility and extensive integration options make it a powerful tool for building sophisticated LLM applications. However, the complexity of managing multiple agents and ensuring their coordination can be a challenge.

Llama Index Use Cases

1. **Knowledge Assistants**: Llama Index excels in building knowledge assistants that can access and process enterprise data to provide insights and support decision-making. These assistants can handle complex queries and provide contextually relevant information.

2. **Multi-Agent Systems**: Llama Index is ideal for developing multi-agent systems that can collaborate to perform tasks such as data extraction,

summarization, and analysis. This is particularly useful in fields like financial analysis and customer support.

3. **Context-Augmented Applications**: Llama Index can create applications that augment LLMs with context from various data sources, improving the accuracy and relevance of generated responses. This is beneficial for applications like legal document analysis and research assistance.

4. **Structured Data Extraction**: Llama Index can be used to build systems that extract structured data from unstructured sources, such as extracting key information from documents or emails.

5. **Advanced Retrieval-Augmented Generation (RAG)**: Llama Index supports advanced RAG techniques, making it suitable for applications that require precise and contextually rich responses, such as customer support systems and internal knowledge management.

Prompt Chaining

Prompt chaining is a structured technique for managing complex tasks by breaking them into a sequence of interconnected prompts, where each step builds on the output of the previous one. This method enhances accuracy and reliability by simplifying intricate problems into smaller, more manageable sub-tasks. For example, instead of asking a model to summarize a legal document and extract its key arguments in one go, prompt chaining would first generate a summary, then use that summary as input for identifying the main arguments—improving clarity and precision at each stage.

Maintaining context throughout the chain is essential. Each prompt must include relevant information from earlier steps to ensure continuity and coherence. This flow of information helps the model stay aligned with the overall objective and prevents it from losing track of the task's progression.

Prompt chains can be designed in various forms—linear sequences, branching paths for exploring multiple solutions, or cyclical loops for iterative refinement. This flexibility makes them suitable for tasks like decision-making, multi-stage reasoning, and content editing. However, because each step depends on the accuracy of the previous one, error checking is critical. If a step fails or produces flawed output, fall-back prompts or alternative strategies can help maintain the chain's integrity.

Optimization plays a key role in improving prompt chain performance. This includes refining prompt wording, reordering steps for logical flow, and using parallel processing to explore multiple paths simultaneously. The process typically involves several phases: breaking down the task, designing prompts, executing them in sequence, managing information flow, handling errors, integrating results, and refining the chain based on performance.

Despite its advantages, prompt chaining must be carefully managed to avoid issues like context loss, error propagation, and reduced efficiency from overly complex chains. Balancing complexity with performance is crucial, and ongoing refinement is necessary to ensure the chain remains effective and scalable.

Natural Language Processing Revisited

Natural Language Processing (NLP) seeks to enable machines to comprehend, interpret, and generate human language with increasing sophistication and contextual awareness. The discipline has undergone remarkable transformations, evolving from rudimentary rule-based systems to complex machine learning architectures that can parse linguistic nuances with unprecedented precision. The major challenge of NLP lies in the inherent complexity of human language.

Natural languages are characterized by ambiguity, contextual dependency, and profound cultural variations. A single linguistic expression can carry multiple meanings contingent upon subtle contextual cues, pragmatic implications, and intricate semantic networks. This complexity demands computational approaches that can navigate beyond literal interpretations and capture the rich, multidimensional nature of linguistic communication.

The introduction of transformer architectures, particularly exemplified by models like BERT, GPT, and their successors, marked a watershed moment in NLP. These models leverage attention mechanisms that enable comprehensive contextual understanding by analyzing relationships between different linguistic elements within a given text. Unlike previous approaches that processed linguistic elements sequentially, transformer models can simultaneously consider multiple contextual dimensions, resulting in more nuanced and contextually aware language representations.

The semantic reasoning capabilities of modern NLP systems are underpinned by advanced representation learning techniques. Word embedding models like Word2Vec and contextual embedding approaches enable computational systems to represent linguistic units as multidimensional vectors, capturing semantic relationships and contextual variations with remarkable precision. These representations allow machines to understand linguistic meaning beyond surface-level syntactic structures.

The NLP Pipeline

The NLP pipeline is a series of steps that converts raw human language into a structured form that computers can understand and analyze. It starts with gathering unprocessed text from sources like websites, documents, or social media. The first step is to clean up the text; this might involve removing unnecessary symbols, correcting typos, or stripping out irrelevant formatting.

Next, the text is divided into sentences, making it easier to handle. Each sentence is then split into individual words or tokens, which are the basic elements for further analysis. Sometimes, the system also checks which language the text is in, especially if it's dealing with multilingual data.

To focus on meaningful words, common words like "and," "the," or "it" are often filtered out. Words are then reduced to their simplest form using techniques like stemming or lemmatization, so that different forms of a word are treated as the same (for example, "running" and "run").

The pipeline then tags each word with its grammatical role, such as noun, verb, or adjective, helping the system understand how words function in a sentence. It also examines how words are connected to each other, mapping out their relationships to understand the structure of the sentence.

Another important step is to identify special terms, such as names of people, places, or organizations. The system can also group words into meaningful phrases and resolve references, figuring out when different words refer to the same thing (like "the president" and "he").

Finally, the processed text is turned into a format that machine learning models can use, such as numerical vectors. These models can then perform tasks like classifying the sentiment of a review, translating text, or summarizing articles. The last stage is to check how well the system works and put it into practical use.

Word Sense Disambiguation

Word Sense Disambiguation (WSD) refers to the task of determining which meaning (or sense) of a word is activated by its use in a particular context. Many words in natural languages are polysemous, meaning they have multiple possible interpretations. For instance, the word "bank" can refer to a financial institution or the side of a river, and the correct sense depends on the surrounding words and the overall context. Successfully resolving these ambiguities is crucial for a wide range of NLP applications, including machine translation, information retrieval, question answering, and text summarization.

The Nature of Lexical Ambiguity

Lexical ambiguity occurs when a single word form carries multiple distinct meanings. Word Sense Disambiguation (WSD) involves mapping words in context to their intended meanings from predefined inventories like dictionaries or WordNet. This task's complexity stems from reliance on subtle contextual cues, discourse patterns, and world knowledge to determine correct interpretations.

For instance, in "He sat on the bank and watched the boats," contextual clues ("sat," "watched the boats") indicate "bank" means riverbank rather than financial institution. Conversely, "She opened a new account at the bank" clearly suggests the financial meaning through different contextual indicators.

WSD and LLMs are interconnected in natural language processing, both addressing contextual word meaning interpretation. Traditional WSD focused on selecting correct word senses from predefined sets based on sentence usage. LLMs like GPT and BERT have blurred boundaries between explicit WSD and broader language understanding.

LLMs perform implicit WSD through contextual language modelling, using large-scale training data and contextual understanding to infer intended meanings of ambiguous words during text generation or interpretation. Research demonstrates LLMs can tackle classic WSD tasks, including sense selection from lists and generating contextual definitions for ambiguous words.

While LLMs often excel in zero-shot WSD settings, they may not consistently outperform specialized WSD systems without task-specific fine-tuning. Performance correlates with model size and training data scope—larger models achieve better disambiguation but face challenges with rare senses or tasks requiring deep world knowledge and reasoning. WSD tasks now serve dual purposes: probing LLM reasoning capabilities and benchmarking functional competence, revealing model strengths and limitations. LLMs' word sense disambiguation abilities are crucial for downstream applications including machine translation, information extraction, and question answering, making WSD both a core LLM capability and essential evaluation tool for model development.

Exercises

1. Explain the architecture of a transformer model and its significance in the development of LLMs.
2. What is the purpose of the attention mechanism in transformer models? How does it contribute to the performance of LLMs?
3. What is Reinforcement Learning from Human Feedback (RLHF)? Why is it used in training LLMs?
4. What are the ethical concerns surrounding the use of LLMs, including potential biases and misuse?
5. How do techniques like prompt engineering influence the output of an LLM?
6. Discuss the challenges of evaluating the quality and safety of generated content from LLMs.
7. Use an LLM to generate text relating to a controversial topic. Analyze the text for potential logical fallacies, or misrepresentation of facts.
8. What is the difference between few-shot learning and zero-shot learning in the context of LLMs?
9. How can LLMs be used for tasks beyond text generation, such as code generation or image generation?
10. Draw a simplified diagram of a transformer model, labelling its key components. Explain the role of multi-head attention in transformer models.

11. What are the limitations of current LLMs regarding reasoning and common sense?
12. Describe the process of pre-training an LLM on a large corpus of text data.
13. Design prompts to elicit different responses from an LLM, such as creative writing, factual information, or code generation.
14. Experiment with different prompt formats and styles to observe their impact on the LLM's output.
15. Use an LLM to generate text on a sensitive topic and analyze the output for potential biases.
16. Use an LLM to generate code snippets in a programming language of your choice. Also, evaluate the correctness and efficiency of the generated code.
17. (Project) Fine-tune a pre-trained LLM for a specific natural language processing task.
18. (Project) Build a chatbot application that uses an LLM to generate responses.

Further Reading

Brown TB, Mann B, Ryder N, Subbiah M, Kaplan J, Dhariwal P, Neelakantan A, Shyam P, Sastry G, Askell A, Agarwal S, Herbert-Voss A, Krueger G, Henighan T, Child R, Ramesh A, Ziegler DM, Wu J, Winter C, Hesse C, Chen M, Sigler E, Litwin M, Gray S, Chess B, Clark J, Berner C, McCandlish S, Radford A, Sutskever I, Amodei D (2020) Language models are few-shot learners. arXiv preprint arXiv:2005.14165

Brown T, Mann B, Ryder N, Subbiah M, Kaplan JD, Dhariwal P, Neelakantan A, Shyam P, Sastry G, Askell A, et al. (2020) Language models are few-shot learners. Adv Neural Inf Proces Syst 33:1877–1901

Clark K, Luong MT, Le QV, Manning CD (2020) ELECTRA: pre-training text encoders as discriminators rather than generators. arXiv preprint arXiv:2003.10555

Conneau A, Khandelwal K, Goyal N, Chaudhary V, Wenzek G, Guzmán F, Stoyanov V (2020) Unsupervised cross-lingual representation learning at scale. arXiv preprint arXiv:1911.02116

Devlin J, Chang MW, Lee K, Toutanova K (2018) BERT: pre-training of deep bidirectional transformers for language understanding. arXiv preprint arXiv:1810.04805

Devlin J, Chang M-W, Lee K, Toutanova K (2019) BERT: pre-training of deep bidirectional transformers for language understanding. In: Proceedings of the 2019 conference of the North American chapter of the association for computational linguistics: human language technologies, volume 1 (long and short papers), pp 4171–4186

He P, Liu X, Gao J, Chen W (2021) DeBERTa: decoding-enhanced BERT with disentangled attention. In: International conference on learning representations

Huang F, Kwak H, An J (2023) Is ChatGPT better than human annotators? Potential and limitations of ChatGPT in explaining implicit hate speech arXiv Preprint ArXiv: 2302.07736. https://doi.org/10.48550/arXiv.2302.07736

Krukowski I (2024) Simple script to load website data. ScrapingBee Blog. Retrieved from https://www.scrapingbee.com/blog/how-to-scrape-all-text-from-a-website-for-llm-ai-training/

Lan Z, Chen M, Goodman S, Gimpel K, Sharma P, Soricut R (2020) ALBERT: a lite BERT for self-supervised learning of language representations. arXiv preprint arXiv:1909.11942

Lewis M, Liu Y, Goyal N, Ghazvininejad M, Mohamed A, Levy O, et al. (2019) BART: denoising sequence-to-sequence pre-training for natural language generation, translation, and comprehension. arXiv preprint arXiv:1910.13461

Li J, Lyu T, Zhao WX (2024) Keqing: knowledge-based question answering is a nature chain-of-thought mentor of LLM. arXiv preprint arXiv:2401.04383. Retrieved from https://arxiv.org/abs/2401.04383

Ling H, Parashar S, Khurana S, Olson B, Basu A, Sinha G, Tu Z, Caverlee J, Ji S (2025) Complex LLM planning via automated heuristics discovery. arXiv preprint arXiv:2502.19295. Retrieved from https://arxiv.org/abs/2502.19295

Liu Y, Ott M, Goyal N, Du J, Joshi M, Chen D, Levy O, Lewis M, Zettlemoyer L, Stoyanov V (2019) RoBERTa: a robustly optimized BERT pretraining approach. arXiv preprint arXiv:1907.11692

Liu Y, Zhang Y, Wang Y, Han X, Zhao WX (2024) Evaluating large language models in semantic parsing for conversational question answering over knowledge graphs. arXiv preprint arXiv:2401.02833. Retrieved from https://arxiv.org/abs/2401.02833

Makridakis S, Petropoulos F, Kang Y (2023) Large language models: their success and impact. Forecasting 5(3):536–549. https://doi.org/10.3390/forecast5030030

Navigli R (2009) Word sense disambiguation: a survey. ACM Comput Surv 41(2):1–69

Ouyang L, Wu J, Jiang X, Almeida D, Wainwright C, Mishkin P, Zhang C, Agarwal S, Slama K et al. (2022) Training language models to follow instructions with human feedback. Adv Neural Inf Process Syst 35:27730–27744

Radford A, Wu J, Child R, Luan D, Amodei D, Sutskever I (2019) Language models are unsupervised multitask learners. OpenAI blog 1(8):9

Rishi B, et al. (2018) On the opportunities and risks of foundation models. https://arxiv.org/pdf/2108.07258.pdf/. https://doi.org/10.48550/arXiv.2108.07258

Sanh V, Debut L, Chaumond J, Wolf T (2019) DistilBERT, a distilled version of BERT: smaller, faster, cheaper and lighter. arXiv preprint arXiv:1910.01108

Shen Z (2024) LLM with tools: a survey. arXiv preprint arXiv:2409.18807. Retrieved from https://arxiv.org/abs/2409.18807

Suzuki M, Matsuo Y (2022) A survey of multimodal deep generative models. Adv Robot 36(5–6):261–278

Yang J, Jin H, Tang R, Han X, Feng Q, Jiang H, Zhong S, Yin B, Xia H (2024) Harnessing the power of LLMs in practice: a survey on chatgpt and beyond. ACM Trans Knowl Discov Data 18(6):1–32

Zhang S, Zhang S, Li J, Lyu T, Zhao WX, Wen JR (2024) Retrieve-rewrite-answer: a KG-to-text enhanced LLMs framework for knowledge graph question answering. arXiv preprint arXiv:2401.04385. Retrieved from https://arxiv.org/abs/2401.04385

Chapter 8
AI Agents: From Perception to Action

I visualize a time when we will be to robots what dogs are to humans, and I am rooting for the machines.
—Claude Shannon

What Are AI Agents?

AI agents autonomously perceive their environment by gathering, interpreting, and processing data from a variety of sources. This perception typically starts with sensors or data inputs that capture information about the agent's surroundings. These intelligent systems are frequently equipped with learning mechanisms, allowing them to refine and adjust their decision-making strategies through experience and feedback.

The multi-agent systems field emerged in the late 1980s, combining elements from AI robotics and distributed AI. By the mid-1990s, it focused on creating semi-autonomous AI agents that could represent individual users and interact with other agents, recognizing that these agents might have conflicting goals. This shifted focus from traditional AI's emphasis on individual intelligence to social abilities like cooperation and negotiation, making Theory of Mind research essential.

The field solidified in the late 1990s with dedicated conferences and journals. Research concentrated on agent communication, collaboration protocols, and social skill foundations. Initially influenced by AI planning's practical reasoning, the field later adopted game theory from economics as its primary theoretical foundation, viewing it as ideal for analysing interactions between self-interested artificial agents. This led to research on auction-based resource allocation, negotiation strategies, and team formation. Despite early recognition of its importance, multi-agent learning wasn't a central focus during the field's first decade.

The field experienced rapid growth from the mid-1990s to 2010–2015, generating substantial academic research though with seemingly limited real-world applications. Notable successes included security games for optimizing resource deployment at critical infrastructure, automated high-frequency trading systems functioning as

R. Akerkar, *Artificial Intelligence*, https://doi.org/10.1007/978-3-031-91084-5_8

large-scale multi-agent systems, and agent-based modelling for simulating sociotechnical systems, which proved valuable in modelling contagion spread during the 2008 financial crisis and COVID-19 pandemic.

The vision of agents operating alongside other agents remains an active research area, exploring social concepts like norms, organizational structures, and values. Much of this work now occurs within the social simulation community rather than primarily in the autonomous agents and multi-agent systems community, influencing policies in public health, transportation, and urban development. While the widespread deployment of AI agents interacting mainly with other AI agents hasn't fully materialized as envisioned, individual dialogue agents like Alexa and Siri have become commonplace, drawing from 1990s intelligent agent research and natural language processing work. This research has led to applications like automated call centres, virtual assistants, and home robots capable of conversation and task performance.

With machine learning's rise in the early-twenty-first century, multi-agent systems research increased, with multi-agent reinforcement learning (MARL) becoming the dominant focus. While MARL constitutes a significant machine learning subfield, it currently lacks a clear overarching vision, direction, or specific application focus.

Since 2020, the rise of large language models (LLMs) has sparked renewed interest in AI agents. LLMs can be incorporated into workflows to automate routine tasks, with their planning and problem-solving capabilities receiving significant attention. Agentic AI refers to combining generative AI and LLMs with autonomous agent frameworks to enhance interaction, creativity, and real-time decision-making in changing environments. As of late 2024, numerous startups are attempting to commercialize these agents. However, despite this enthusiasm, the original goals established by the autonomous agents and multi-agent systems (AAMAS) community 30 years ago—creating robust, autonomous multi-agent systems capable of complex coordination and long-term reasoning—remain largely unfulfilled. It's unclear how much this new wave of agent development is informed by previous research.

The current challenge is understanding multi-agent systems in the LLM era. Simply "agentifying" LLMs risks creating unnecessarily complex architectures with high computational demands. In contrast, applying multi-agent principles to LLM development could offer a more sustainable approach to composition, diversification, and integration. Despite distribution being a founding concept in multi-agent systems, this direction remains largely unexplored under the current paradigm.

Recent trends include revisiting classical cognitive architectures to enhance autonomous agents with commonsense capabilities. Multi-agent architectures are emerging as a way to structure AI components into modular systems that improve transparency, adaptability, and ethical alignment. The focus on cooperative agents represents a shift toward AI that prioritizes collaboration, negotiation, and shared decision-making. By implementing modularity, encapsulation, and separation of concerns, these architectures enable effective teamwork between autonomous agents and humans, making them well-suited for hybrid AI applications requiring trust, explainability, and domain-specific expertise.

Definition An *AI agent* is an autonomous application designed to perform specific tasks by observing its environment, planning actions, reasoning through problems, and executing decisions to achieve goals—all within the scope and parameters of its programming.

AI agents are defined by three core characteristics: autonomy, persistence, and environmental interaction. Autonomy means AI agents operate independently, making decisions based on their environment and learned experiences without constant human intervention. They can: design their own workflows and utilize available tools, analyse real-time data and environmental inputs to make independent decisions and function with minimal supervision. In contrast, traditional software follows predefined rules and logic set by developers, requires human prompts for every step and operates based on explicit instructions and "if-then" logic. Persistence signifies that agents operate continuously within their environment over time, rather than as one-off processes. Environmental interaction highlights an agent's ability to sense and respond to its surroundings. This interaction can be physical, involving sensors and actuators, or digital, involving data and software manipulation.

Principally, AI agents perceive their environment, process information using models or algorithms, and act to achieve specific goals. Moreover, AI agents demonstrate superior adaptability compared to traditional software. They learn from data and experiences, continuously refining their algorithms based on feedback. They can adjust to changing conditions and improve performance over time without explicit reprogramming and they also excel in dynamic environments, drawing on context and information from connected applications. Traditional software, on the other hand remains static unless explicitly reprogrammed, it requires manual updates to change behaviour or functionality and struggles when encountering unexpected changes or anomalies. This fundamental difference in adaptability makes AI agents particularly well-suited for applications requiring flexibility and continuous improvement, such as customer support, supply chain management, and intelligent tutoring systems.

Example *Siri*, Apple's virtual assistant. Siri acts as an intelligent agent by performing tasks and providing information based on user commands. It can set reminders, send messages, answer questions, and control smart home devices. Siri uses natural language processing to understand user requests and machine learning to improve its responses over time, making it a practical example in everyday use.

AI agents (Fig. 8.1) are advanced computational systems designed to think, recall information, and execute tasks. Their structure typically includes four main elements:

1. Core Module (Agent): This central unit handles decision-making, setting goals, selecting tools, planning strategies, and determining relevant information to remember.
2. Memory System: This component stores data in two forms:

- Short-Term: For immediate interaction-related thoughts and actions.
- Long-Term: For extended interaction records and learned experiences.

3. Operational Tools: These are the agent's functional capabilities, including:

- Executable workflows and external APIs.
- Examples: context-aware response generators, code interpreters, internet search engines, and specialized services like weather APIs.

4. Planning Mechanisms: To tackle complex tasks, agents use techniques such as:

- Task breakdown.
- Critical analysis and reflection for plan improvement.

This architecture allows AI agents to effectively analyse issues, create and implement solutions, and function as intelligent systems with comprehensive reasoning, memory, and task execution abilities.

AI agents differ from conventional software through several key characteristics:

- Independence: They operate autonomously, making decisions with minimal human input.
- Flexibility: They improve performance over time by learning from interactions.

Fig. 8.1 AI agent components

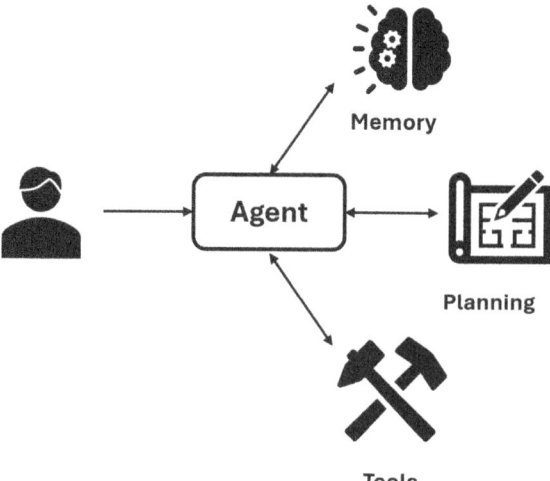

- Environmental Awareness: They perceive their surroundings using sensors, process data, and respond through actuators.
- Purpose-Driven: They are designed to achieve specific goals efficiently.

In multi-agent systems (MAS), where multiple AI agents interact, additional characteristics emerge:

- Collaborative Autonomy: Agents work independently but in relation to others.
- Goal-Oriented: Agents have specific objectives and may adapt them over time.
- Social Interaction: Agents communicate and cooperate with each other.
- Responsiveness: Agents quickly adapt to environmental changes.
- Proactivity: Agents take initiative to achieve goals, not just react to stimuli.

Both individual AI agents and those in MAS emphasize autonomy and goal-orientation. MAS specifically highlights social abilities for complex task coordination. Both types require reactivity and often proactiveness. We will explore MAS in a later section of this chapter.

AI agents can be customized or adaptive, learning from past experiences. Some possess mobility, moving across machines to minimize network delays. There's also a trend toward creating believable agents with visual or auditory representations, sometimes including emotional or personality traits.

To understand and design intelligent agents, researchers often use concepts from human intelligence like knowledge, beliefs, intentions, and desires. This approach views agents as intentional systems whose behaviour can be predicted by attributing mental states to them. As systems become more complex, we naturally resort to intentional explanations, like how we understand human behaviour in distributed activities.

Agents designed with symbolic knowledge representations are called cognitive agents. An alternative approach, inspired by neural networks, is reactive agents. These simple processing units respond directly to environmental changes without complex reasoning. Proponents argue that intelligence emerges from interactions between numerous agents and their environment, viewing it as a collective property of the system, inspired by insect colonies and other large communities of simple organisms.

Designing AI Agents

Agent design involves making critical choices about how the agent will perceive, reason about, and interact with its environment. These choices influence the agent's capabilities, limitations, and overall performance. The agent's architecture must balance numerous competing concerns, including computational efficiency, adaptability to changing conditions, and the ability to function effectively despite uncertainty.

We begin by examining time models in agent design (discrete, continuous, and hybrid approaches) and their implications for how agents process information and make decisions. We then explore various agent functions, the core decision-making components that map percept sequences to actions. Finally, we consider the important distinction between offline and online computation, which has significant implications for real-world deployment of AI systems.

Time Models in Agent Design

Discrete Time

In discrete time models, the agent operates in clearly defined, sequential time steps. At each step, the agent receives percepts, updates its internal state, selects an action, and then executes that action. This model offers several advantages:

First, discrete time models simplify synchronization between perception, reasoning, and action. An agent can fully process each input before producing a response, avoiding potential race conditions or timing inconsistencies. Second, they permit clean theoretical analysis, particularly in formal verification contexts where we need to reason about the agent's behaviour over time. Third, they enable straightforward implementation of simulated environments for training and evaluation.

> **Example** Consider a chess-playing agent. The environment state changes only when a move is made, creating natural discrete time steps. The agent observes the board state, computes its next move through various search and evaluation techniques, and executes that move. The process then repeats with the opponent's move creating the next discrete time step.

However, discrete time models have limitations. They often struggle to handle events that occur between time steps and may require artificially fine-grained time discretization to capture rapidly evolving environments. This can lead to computational inefficiency and potential response delays.

Continuous Time

Continuous time models offer an alternative approach where the agent processes information and makes decisions along an uninterrupted time continuum. Rather than operating in distinct steps, these agents must continuously monitor their environment and respond to changes as they occur. This approach is particularly valuable for agents operating in dynamic physical environments, such as autonomous vehicles, robotic systems, or agents monitoring real-time data streams. The continuous model allows for the immediate registration and processing of environmental changes, supporting swift reactions to emerging situations. A more natural representation of physical processes that unfold continuously rather than in discrete jumps. The ability to model varying response times based on the complexity of different decisions.

> **Example**: A drone navigating through a forest must continuously process sensor data about its surroundings, adjusting its flight path in real time to avoid obstacles. The environment doesn't wait for the drone to complete a "time step" before a branch appears in its path—perception and response must be fluid and immediate.

Implementing continuous time models presents significant challenges. They require sophisticated mechanisms for managing asynchronous processes, prioritizing computational resources, and maintaining consistent internal representations despite the constant flow of new information.

Hybrid Time

Hybrid time models combine elements of both discrete and continuous approaches, creating systems that can leverage the strengths of each paradigm. These models often employ a multi-level architecture where low-level control processes operate in continuous time, handling immediate sensor processing and reactive behaviours. Mid-level processes operate in a semi-discrete fashion, updating at regular but frequent intervals. And, high-level reasoning and planning processes operate in discrete time, considering strategic decisions over longer horizons.

> **Example**: Consider an autonomous vehicle. Its collision avoidance systems operate continuously, processing sensor data in real time to detect imminent threats. Its route planning module might operate on a semi-discrete basis, reassessing the optimal path every few seconds. Meanwhile, its high-level navigation goals (e.g., destination selection) function on a fully discrete basis, changing only when new user input is received.

Hybrid approaches often represent the most practical solution for complex agents operating in real-world environments. They enable agents to remain responsive to immediate concerns while still performing the deliberative reasoning necessary for intelligent behaviour.

Choosing Agent Functions

The agent function, the mapping from percept histories to actions, forms the core of an agent's decision-making capacity. Several paradigms have emerged for implementing these functions, each with distinct advantages and limitations.

Reactive Agents

Reactive agents implement direct mappings from current percepts to actions, with minimal internal state. They follow the principle that intelligent behaviour can emerge from the interaction of simple rules with a complex environment, without requiring explicit internal representations or reasoning. These agents excel in domains requiring fast response times and where the optimal action can be determined largely based on immediate perceptual information. Examples include basic obstacle avoidance in robotics, simple game-playing agents, and certain reflex-based control systems. The advantages of reactive approaches include implementation simplicity, computational efficiency, and robustness in environments where rapid response is critical. However, they struggle with tasks requiring memory of past events, long-term planning, or reasoning about unobservable aspects of the environment.

Deliberative Agents

Deliberative agents maintain internal models of their environment and use these models to reason about the consequences of potential actions before selecting one to execute. They typically employ search or planning algorithms to explore possible future states and identify action sequences that achieve their goals. This approach enables sophisticated decision-making that accounts for long-term consequences, complex goal structures, and uncertain outcomes. Chess engines, automated planning systems, and certain autonomous vehicles exemplify deliberative agent designs. The deliberative paradigm supports reasoning about complex scenarios but often requires significant computational resources and detailed domain knowledge. Such agents may also struggle in highly dynamic environments where the world changes faster than the agent can plan.

Hybrid Reactive-Deliberative Architectures

Hybrid architectures combine reactive and deliberative elements, typically in a layered structure. A reactive layer handles immediate responses to environmental stimuli. A deliberative layer performs planning and reasoning about longer-term goals. An intermediate layer manages the interaction between these systems, determining when to rely on reactive behaviours versus when to engage in more deliberative processes. This approach allows agents to respond quickly to urgent situations while still pursuing longer-term objectives through deliberative planning. Mobile robots often employ such architectures, using reactive behaviours for obstacle avoidance while deliberative components handle navigation and task planning.

Learning Agents

Learning agents modify their behaviour based on experience, potentially starting with simple capabilities and developing more sophisticated functions over time. These agents incorporate mechanisms for performance evaluation to assess the outcomes of their actions. Feedback integration to adjust internal parameters or models. Knowledge discovery to identify patterns or structures in their experience.

Machine learning approaches, including reinforcement learning, supervised learning, and unsupervised learning, provide effective frameworks for implementing learning agents. These methods allow agents to improve their performance in complex domains where manually designing effective agent functions would be impractical. The success of learning agents depends critically on the quality and quantity of their experience, the structure of their learning algorithms, and their ability to generalize from specific experiences to novel situations.

Offline and Online Computation

Offline computation refers to the preparatory phase in which an agent or its designers perform extensive analysis and modelling before the agent begins interacting with its environment. This stage involves examining domain-specific data, constructing environmental and task models, formulating strategies or policies to guide future behaviour, and optimizing computational processes to enhance runtime efficiency. The key advantage of offline computation lies in its ability to utilize substantial computational resources without the constraints of real-time operation. This allows for the application of complex algorithms, thorough optimization, and even formal verification of system properties, potentially ensuring safety and performance guarantees. However, offline methods are inherently limited in their ability to cope with unforeseen or rapidly evolving situations. When an agent encounters conditions that diverge significantly from those anticipated during the offline phase, its effectiveness may diminish.

In contrast, online computation takes place during the agent's real-time interaction with its environment. It enables the agent to adapt to dynamic conditions, learn from ongoing experiences, and respond to novel scenarios that were not accounted for during the design phase. This mode of computation is crucial for agents operating in unpredictable or complex settings. Nevertheless, it is constrained by limited decision-making time, finite computational resources, and the irreversibility of actions once taken. To navigate these challenges, modern agents often employ anytime algorithms—methods that can be halted at any moment to yield the best available solution. A notable example is Monte Carlo Tree Search, used in systems like AlphaGo, which incrementally improves its decision-making as time permits. This balance between offline preparation and online adaptability is central to the design of intelligent, responsive agents.

Balancing Offline and Online Approaches

Sophisticated agent architectures typically integrate both offline and online computational processes to achieve robust and adaptive performance. Offline computation involves tasks such as developing heuristics, training machine learning models, building knowledge bases, and optimizing algorithms. These foundational elements are then employed during online computation, where agents make real-time decisions, respond to dynamic conditions, and refine their strategies based on immediate feedback. A prominent example is autonomous vehicles, which rely on extensive offline work to construct perception systems, map databases, and control protocols. Once deployed, these vehicles continuously perform online tasks such as obstacle detection, route planning, and traffic adaptation, all grounded in the pre-established offline framework. This interplay between offline preparation and online responsiveness enables agents to function effectively in complex and unpredictable environments.

How Do AI Agents Handle Uncertainty in Decision-Making

AI agents manage uncertainty in decision-making through a diverse set of advanced techniques that enable them to function effectively in complex and dynamic environments. Central to this capability is probabilistic reasoning, which allows agents to assess and update the likelihood of various outcomes as new information becomes available. Bayesian networks exemplify this approach, enabling agents to revise their beliefs in the light of observed evidence—such as adjusting diagnostic probabilities in medical applications based on evolving symptom data.

Reinforcement learning further enhances an agent's ability to cope with uncertainty by allowing it to learn optimal behaviours through trial and error. This method is particularly valuable in environments where the consequences of actions are not immediately apparent, such as in strategic gameplay, where agents refine their tactics over repeated interactions.

Monte Carlo methods also play a critical role by simulating numerous possible scenarios to evaluate risks and potential outcomes. These techniques are especially useful in domains like financial forecasting, where agents must anticipate a wide range of market behaviours. Similarly, Markov Decision Processes (MDPs) provide a formal framework for modelling decision-making under uncertainty, enabling agents to weigh the probabilities and rewards associated with different actions across various states—an approach particularly relevant in autonomous navigation.

To further enhance robustness, AI agents often employ ensemble methods, which aggregate predictions from multiple models to reduce individual errors and better quantify confidence levels. This strategy improves reliability in uncertain conditions by mitigating the weaknesses of any single model.

A defining feature of modern AI agents is their capacity for real-time adaptation. They continuously update their internal models and strategies based on incoming data and feedback, allowing them to respond flexibly to changing circumstances. This adaptability is vital in applications ranging from personalized recommendation systems to autonomous drones operating in unpredictable environments.

Crucially, these agents are not only designed to make decisions under uncertainty but also to quantify and communicate the degree of uncertainty in their predictions. This transparency supports more informed and cautious decision-making, enabling low-confidence outputs to be flagged for human oversight or further analysis.

By integrating these complementary techniques—probabilistic modelling, learning from experience, scenario simulation, decision-theoretic planning, model aggregation, and adaptive feedback—AI agents are equipped to navigate uncertainty with a high degree of competence. This multi-faceted approach underpins their effectiveness across a wide array of real-world applications, including healthcare, finance, robotics, and autonomous systems.

Attaining Poise between Reactive and Goal-Directed Behaviour

Finding the right balance between reacting to immediate stimuli and pursuing long-term goals is a key challenge in AI agent design. There are several approaches to address this, and we'll explore four prominent ones.

Logic-Based Architectures

Logic-based architectures for AI agents are designed to leverage formal logic to represent knowledge, reason about it, and make decisions. These architectures typically use symbolic representations and logical inference mechanisms to process information and solve problems. In a logic-based AI system, knowledge is encoded using logical statements, often in the form of predicates and rules. For example, a rule might state that "if a person is a parent, then they have a child." These logical statements can be combined and manipulated to derive new information or make decisions based on existing knowledge.

One of the key advantages of logic-based architectures is their ability to provide clear and interpretable reasoning. Since the knowledge and rules are explicitly defined, it is easier to understand how the AI agent arrives at its conclusions. This transparency is particularly important in applications where trust and accountability are crucial, such as healthcare or legal systems.

Logic-based architectures also support complex reasoning tasks, such as planning and problem-solving. By using logical inference, AI agents can evaluate different scenarios, predict outcomes, and choose the best course of action. This makes them well-suited for applications that require strategic thinking and decision-making. However, logic-based architectures also have limitations. They can struggle with handling uncertain or incomplete information, as traditional logic requires precise and complete knowledge. Additionally, these systems can be computationally intensive, especially when dealing with large sets of logical statements and rules.

Despite these challenges, logic-based architectures remain a powerful tool for developing AI agents that require robust reasoning capabilities and clear, interpretable decision-making processes.

Emergent Behaviour Architectures

In contrast to logic-based systems, some researchers advocate for emergent behaviour architectures. They argue that detailed, time-consuming logical deductions about the environment are often impractical. Emergent behaviour architectures for AI agents focus on creating systems where complex behaviours arise from the interactions of simpler components, rather than being explicitly programmed. This approach is inspired by natural systems, such as ant colonies or neural networks in the brain, where individual elements follow simple rules, but their collective behaviour leads to sophisticated outcomes.

Examples
Reacting swiftly to a falling object is more crucial than analysing its trajectory. This approach prioritizes a set of reactive responses to environmental stimuli, suggesting that intelligent behaviour arises from the combination of these simple reactions.

In swarm robotics, individual robots might follow simple rules like maintaining a certain distance from their neighbours and moving toward a target. When many robots operate together, they can collectively perform complex tasks such as search and rescue operations or environmental monitoring, demonstrating behaviours that are not explicitly programmed into any single robot.

These architectures rely on reactive agents, which lack both symbolic world models and complex symbolic reasoning capabilities. A prominent example is Brooks' subsumption architecture. Subsumption architecture is a pioneering approach to robotics and artificial intelligence developed by Rodney Brooks in the mid-1980s while at MIT. This architecture represented a radical departure from the traditional AI approaches of the time and helped launch the field of behaviour-based robotics. This model employs behaviour modules that directly link actions to observed situations, bypassing any reasoning process. Behaviours are organized in a hierarchy, with low-level, immediate responses like "avoid object" taking precedence over higher-level, goal-oriented behaviours like "move across room."

This approach is simple and effective, but its focus on immediate surroundings can lead to a limited understanding of the broader context. In essence, while it excels at quick reactions, it may lack a holistic view of the situation.

Historical Context
When Brooks introduced subsumption architecture in 1986, AI research was dominated by what he called the "sense-plan-act" paradigm. In this traditional approach, robots would: gather sensor data, build comprehensive internal

Fig. 8.2 Brooks'
subsumption architecture

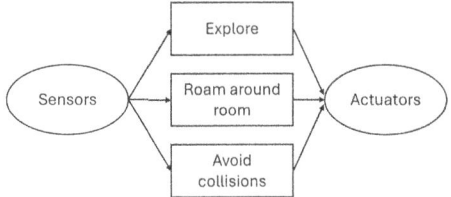

models of their environment, plan actions using these models, and execute those plans.

This approach worked in controlled laboratory settings but often failed in real-world environments due to the complexity of building accurate world models and the computational demands of planning.

Brooks argued that intelligence doesn't require explicit representation and reasoning. Instead, he proposed that intelligence emerges from the interaction between simple behaviours and the environment.

Subsumption architecture, illustrated in Fig. 8.2, is built around several key principles:

The architecture organizes robot control into layers of behaviours. Each layer implements a specific behaviour that achieves a particular goal, such as "avoid obstacles" or "explore environment." These behaviours operate concurrently rather than sequentially.

The layers are arranged in a hierarchy from the most primitive (lowest) to most abstract (highest). Lower layers handle basic survival behaviours like obstacle avoidance, while higher layers implement more goal-directed behaviours like navigation to specific locations.

Unlike centralized systems that require complete environmental models, subsumption architecture distributes control across multiple independent modules. Each module connects sensors directly to actuators for specific behaviours, operating without needing to consult a central planning system. This distributed approach makes the system more robust—if one behaviour fails, others can continue functioning.

The "subsumption" in the name comes from how behaviours interact. Higher-level behaviours can subsume lower-level ones by:

- Suppression: replacing the outputs of lower-level behaviours with their own.
- Inhibition: preventing lower-level behaviours from producing any output.

For example, a "flee danger" behaviour might override a "move toward goal" behaviour when a threat is detected.

Brooks emphasized that robots should be "situated" (existing in a real environment) and "embodied" (having physical form). Each behaviour directly connects perception to action without complex internal representations, allowing the robot to react immediately to environmental changes.

The environment itself serves as its own best model, eliminating the need for complex internal representations. This principle is captured in Brooks' statement: "The world is its own best model."

In practical terms, subsumption architecture is implemented as a network of finite-state machines that process sensor inputs and generate actuator outputs. These state machines communicate through message passing and operate asynchronously.

The architecture is typically built from the bottom up:

1. First, implement and test the lowest layer (basic survival behaviours).
2. Once that layer works reliably, add the next layer above it.
3. Continue adding layers, each building on the capabilities of those below.

This incremental approach allows for testing at each stage and ensures that lower-level behaviours remain functional even as complexity increases.

Brooks's work ultimately challenged the foundations of traditional AI and expanded our understanding of how intelligent behaviour can arise from relatively simple systems interacting with complex environments.

Despite these challenges, emergent behaviour architectures offer a powerful approach to developing AI agents that are robust, adaptable, and capable of exhibiting complex behaviours through simple interactions.

Knowledge-Level Architectures

A third type of architecture, based on knowledge-level agents, treats each intelligent agent as a knowledge-based system in microcosm. The concept of knowledge-level architectures represents a sophisticated perspective on artificial intelligence that emphasizes reasoning about knowledge rather than just symbol manipulation. To understand these architectures deeply, we need to start with the fundamental concept that inspired them.

Allen Newell introduced the knowledge level in his 1982 paper "The Knowledge Level" as a way to describe intelligent systems at a more abstract level than mere symbol processing. This perspective creates a clear distinction between:

1. **The Knowledge Level**—concerned with the content of knowledge and goals.
2. **The Symbol Level**—concerned with representations and processes that manipulate those representations.

At the knowledge level, we describe an agent in terms of what it knows and what it wants to achieve, without specifying how that knowledge is represented internally. This abstraction allows us to reason about intelligent behaviour in terms of knowledge and rationality rather than computational mechanisms.

If an agent has knowledge that one of its actions will lead to one of its goals, then the agent will select that action.

A knowledge-level agent is conceptualized as an entity that:

- Possesses knowledge about its environment and domain.
- Has goals it aims to achieve.
- Acts rationally to achieve those goals using its knowledge.

The crucial insight is that we can predict and explain an agent's behaviour by assuming it will act to achieve its goals based on what it knows, without needing to understand the implementation details of how it represents or processes that knowledge.

Imagine watching a chess grandmaster. We can predict and explain her moves by assuming she knows the rules of chess, has a goal of winning, and makes moves that advance that goal—without needing to understand exactly how her brain stores chess patterns or evaluates positions.

Knowledge-level architectures embody this perspective, organizing AI systems around explicit representations of knowledge and mechanisms for reasoning with that knowledge.

Building on knowledge-level concepts, agent-oriented architectures focus on designing systems as societies of interacting knowledge-level agents. These architectures extend knowledge-level thinking to distributed systems where multiple agents with potentially different knowledge and goals must coordinate.

Key frameworks in this space include:

- **GAIA**—provides methodologies for analysing and designing agent-based systems.
- **Tropos**—emphasizes early requirements analysis based on agent goals.
- **JADE** (Java Agent Development Framework)—offers middleware for implementing multi-agent systems.

These architectures address knowledge distribution, coordination, and communication protocols among knowledge-level agents, extending the concept beyond individual reasoning to social interaction.

Touring Machine Architecture

The Touring Machine agent architecture comprises three separate control layers: a reactive layer, a planning layer, and a modelling layer as given in Fig. 8.3. The three layers are concurrently operating, independently motivated, and activity-producing: not only is each one independently connected to the agent's sensory apparatus and has its own internal computational mechanisms for processing appropriate aspects of

Fig. 8.3 Touring machine
agent control architecture

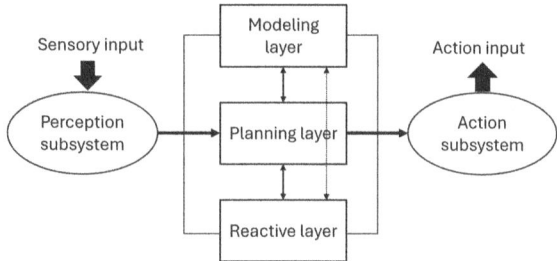

the received perceptual information, but they are also individually connected to the agent's effectory apparatus (via the agent's Action Subsystem) to which they send, when required, appropriate motor control and communicative action commands.

Collectively, these three control layers and are aimed at providing a Touring Machine agent with a variety of deliberative and non-deliberative task-achieving behaviours; these include behaviours that are situationally determined or reactive, goal-directed, reflective, and also predictive. However, because layers operate concurrently, are activity-producing (that is, each layer can independently send action commands to the agent's Action Subsystem), and are designed so that each addresses a different (and therefore limited) aspect of the agent's necessary behavioural repertoire, it is inevitable that, from time to time, one layer's proposed actions will conflict with those of another. Layers, in effect, are approximate machines, and as a result, need to be mediated by an enveloping control framework if the agent, as a single whole, is to behave appropriately in each different world situation.

The primary purpose of the Touring Machine control framework, then, is to ensure the agent behaves appropriately in each different world situation. It attempts to do this by taking into account the agent's changing situational and task-related need.

Types of AI Agents

Examples of AI Agents

We interact with AI agents every day. AI agents can be categorized based on their operational sophistication and interaction with the environment. AI agents can be classified along three critical dimensions: reactivity (how they respond to their environment), autonomy (their degree of independence), and capability (the range and complexity of tasks they can perform). The following Table 8.1 Classification of AI agents provides a classification:

Now we will explore some common examples of AI agents by type.

Table 8.1 Classification of AI agents

Type	Reactivity	Autonomy	Capability
Simple reflex	Reacts only to current perceptions	Limited; operates on predefined rules	Performs basic tasks; low adaptability
Model-based reflex	Takes internal states into account for decisions	Some ability to manage internal states	Can handle partially observable environments
Goal-based	Acts to achieve specific goals	Capable of evaluating different action paths	Better planning; handles complex tasks
Utility-based	Makes decisions to maximize utility	Selects actions that provide the highest benefit	Balances task success with cost
Learning agent	Improves performance through experience	Adapts to new situations over time	Highly adaptable; can become very proficient

Virtual Assistants

Powered by natural language processing and artificial intelligence, virtual assistants have become a common presence in our lives. These AI agents interpret human language to execute tasks, ranging from simple reminders to complex smart home controls. A key characteristic is their ability to learn and adapt based on user interactions. Examples include Siri, which is integrated across Apple devices and handles diverse tasks; Alexa, which is prominent in Amazon's ecosystem and focuses on media and smart home automation; and Google Assistant, which excels in web-based information retrieval and translation.

Utility-Based Agents

Unlike simple reactive agents that respond directly to their surroundings, utility-based intelligent agents proactively analyse potential actions. Utility-based intelligent agents (Fig. 8.4 Utility-based agent) make decisions by carefully weighing potential outcomes against their goals. Instead of simply reacting to their environment, they predict the benefits of different actions using a "utility function," a mathematical way of ranking preferences. This allows them to choose the option that best maximizes their desired outcome. This approach is particularly useful in complex situations, like investment or healthcare, where there are many possible results and trade-offs. For example, in financial markets, these agents can use algorithms to buy and sell stocks or cryptocurrencies, aiming to maximize profits and minimize risk.

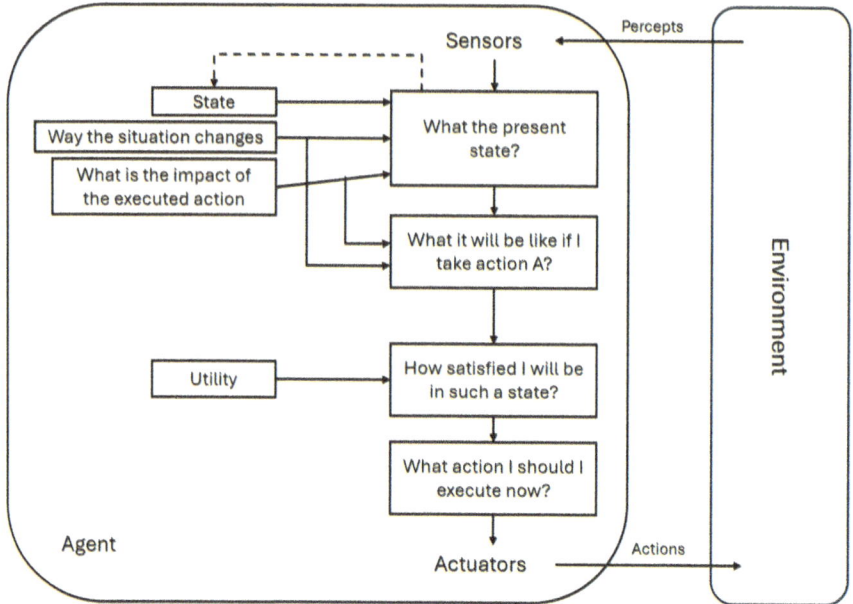

Fig. 8.4 Utility-based agent

Example: The University Admissions.

A sophisticated AI system quietly evaluates thousands of student applications each admission cycle. Unlike simpler AI systems, this utility-based agent doesn't just sort applications based on fixed criteria or pursue preset goals—it makes nuanced decisions by calculating the expected utility of each possible admission.

The system begins by analysing an application with a 3.7 GPA, strong extracurricular leadership, and promising essays but test scores slightly below the university average. Rather than simply checking whether the candidate meets threshold requirements, the agent calculates the expected value of admitting her versus other candidates. Here the utility function incorporates multiple factors: her likelihood of academic success (say 85% based on similar past students), probability of contributing to campus life (92% given her leadership experience), potential alumni engagement (76% based on essay content and background), and how she enhances the diversity of the student body (significant, given her unique background in competitive robotics). The system transforms these assessments into a single utility score, representing the expected value the candidate brings to the university's overall mission. The smartness of this utility-based approach becomes apparent when comparing candidates. The system continues this process, making thousands of micro-decisions by calculating expected utilities rather than following rigid rules. When faced with limited spots in the engineering program, it doesn't simply select the highest GPAs but optimizes the entire incoming class for maximum expected contribution to the university's multi-faceted goals.

Goal-Based Agents

Goal-based agents (Fig. 8.5) are intelligent systems that actively plan and strategize to achieve their objectives. They don't just react to immediate situations; they use knowledge and search algorithms to predict the future consequences of their actions and choose the best path forward. This ability to combine foresight and strategic planning sets them apart from simpler reflex agents. To function effectively, they rely on informed search and planning techniques, making them useful in fields like robotics, computer vision, and natural language processing.

Example: A simple and clear example of a goal-based AI agent is a robot vacuum cleaner (like a Roomba) programmed to clean a room.

Goal: Clean the entire floor.

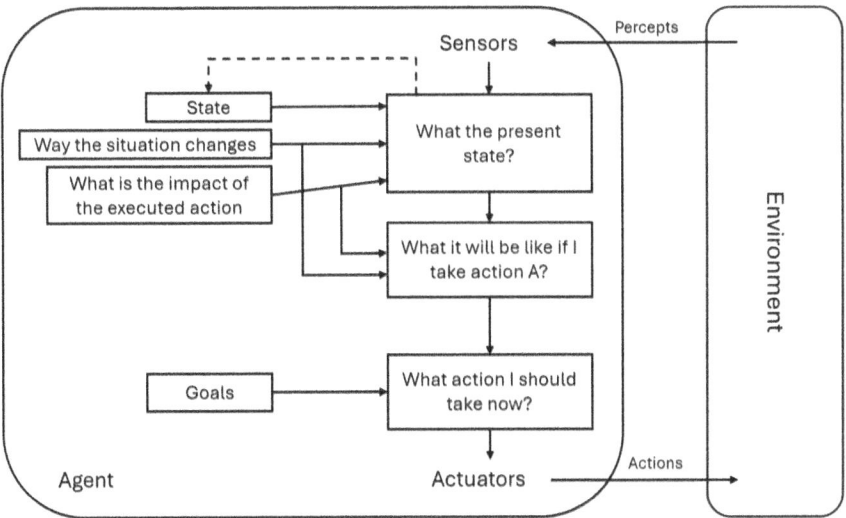

Fig. 8.5 Goal-based agent

Knowledge: It knows the layout of the room (either preloaded or learned through sensors).

Perception: It uses sensors to detect obstacles, dirt, and boundaries.

Planning and Action: It plans a path to cover all areas efficiently, avoids obstacles, and returns to the charging dock when needed.
   This agent doesn't just react to its environment; it actively plans actions to achieve the goal of a clean floor.

Model-Based Reflex Agents

Model-based reflex agents (Fig. 8.6) excel in situations where not everything is immediately visible. They maintain an internal "model" of their environment, constantly updated with new information, allowing them to make informed decisions even when faced with uncertainty. Unlike simple reflex agents that only react to what they directly perceive, these agents can predict and anticipate future conditions. This ability to handle partially observable environments makes them ideal for complex tasks like driving in a city or managing smart home systems, where context and prediction are crucial.

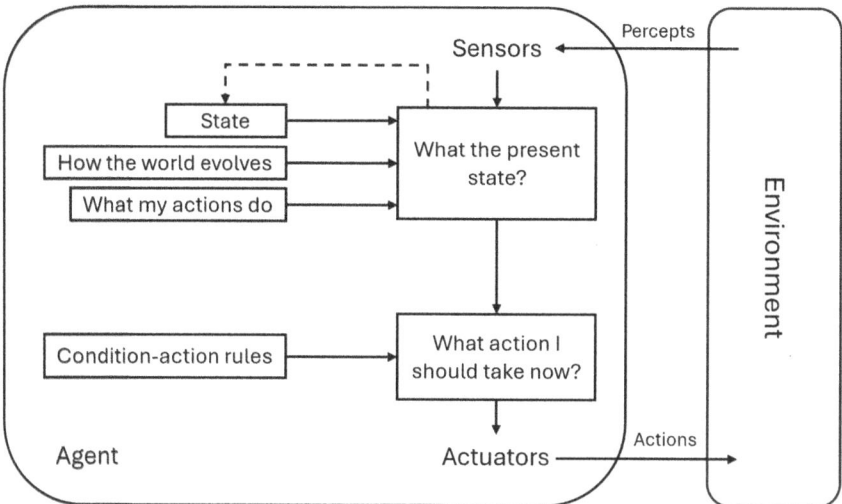

Fig. 8.6 Model-based reflex agent

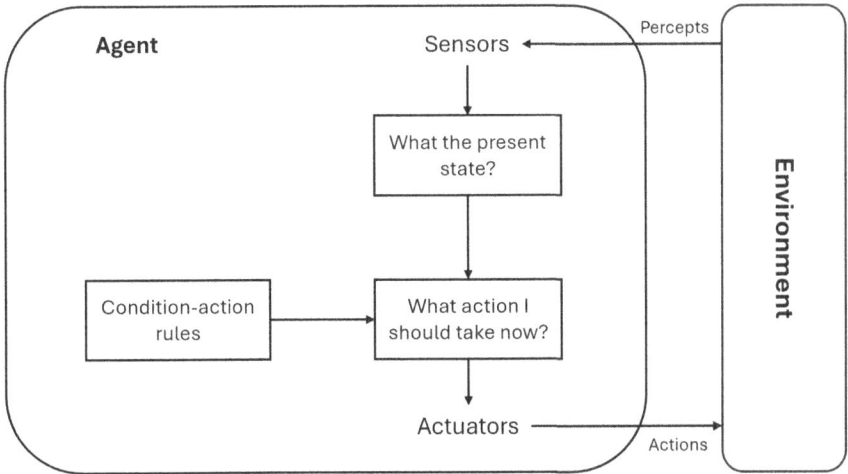

Fig. 8.7 Simple reflex agent

Simple Reflex Agents

Simple reflex agents are the most basic type of AI agent, given in Fig. 8.7. They react instantly to their current surroundings, without any memory of the past. They operate based on simple "if-then" rules: if a certain condition is met, then perform a specific action. While they lack the ability to handle complex situations, they are perfect for straightforward tasks in predictable environments. Examples include automatic doors that open when someone approaches and smoke detectors that sound an alarm when smoke is detected. Simple reflex agents are effective in stable and predictable environments where the correct action can be determined solely by the current percept.

> **Example**: Let us consider a basic thermostat. It senses the current temperature and, if the temperature is below a certain threshold, it turns on the heater. If the temperature is above the threshold, it turns off the heater. The thermostat does not remember past temperatures or predict future ones; it simply reacts to the current temperature based on its predefined rules.

Learning Agents

Learning agents (Fig. 8.8) leverage machine learning techniques to achieve performance improvement through experiential learning. They deviate from static AI agents

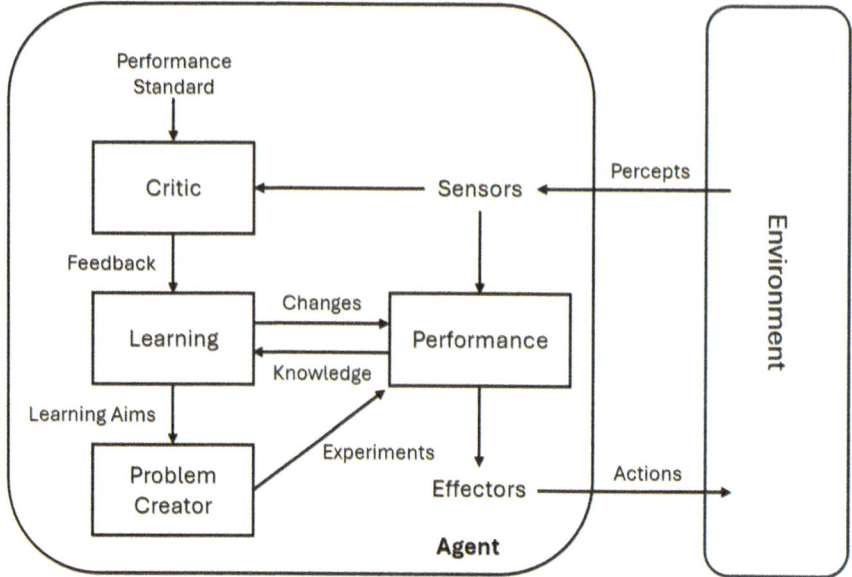

Fig. 8.8 Learning agent

by exhibiting adaptive behaviour. These agents are characterized by four conceptual components: the learning element, responsible for knowledge acquisition; the critic, which provides evaluative feedback; the performance element, which executes actions; and the problem generator, which facilitates exploration. This architecture enables them to adapt to dynamic environments by continuously refining their strategies based on feedback and exploration.

> **Example**: Consider a self-driving car. Initially, it might have basic rules for driving, such as following lanes and stopping at red lights. As it drives, it collects data from its sensors about traffic patterns, road conditions, and driver behaviour. Using this data, the car's learning algorithms, such as machine learning models, analysing and identifying patterns. Over time, the car learns to make better decisions, like anticipating when a pedestrian might cross the street or adjusting its speed based on traffic flow. This continuous learning process helps the car become more efficient and safer as it gains more experience on the road.

Platforms like Netflix and Amazon use a system equipped with a learning agent to increase their recommendations for movies, videos, and products. Fraud detection systems operate by constantly collecting data and then adjusting to recognize fraudulent patterns more effectively. A learning agent improves its performance over time by learning from its experiences.

Hierarchical Agents

Hierarchical agents stand out due to their layered, organizational structure. This allows them to effectively manage complex tasks by breaking them down into smaller, manageable subtasks. Like a well-organized company, they have different levels of decision-making, with specialized agents at each level. This structure enables them to coordinate and prioritize tasks efficiently, making them ideal for complex environments. For example, in advanced manufacturing, high-level agents plan the production flow, while lower-level agents control specific machinery, ensuring smooth operation.

Example: An example of a hierarchical agent is a *robotic warehouse system*. In such a system, the agent is structured in layers to manage tasks efficiently. High-Level Planning Layer handles strategic decisions, such as optimizing the overall layout of the warehouse and planning the routes for robots to ensure efficient movement and minimal congestion. Mid-Level Coordination Layer manages the coordination between different robots, ensuring they work together smoothly. It assigns specific tasks to each robot, such as picking up items from shelves or delivering them to packing stations. Low-Level Execution Layer controls the individual robots' actions, such as navigating around obstacles, picking up items, and placing them accurately. It ensures that each robot performs its assigned tasks correctly and safely. By using this hierarchical structure, the robotic warehouse system can efficiently manage complex operations, adapt to changes in the environment, and optimize overall performance.

Robotic Agents

When we envision intelligent agents, the image that often springs to mind is that of a robot—a physical embodiment of AI. Robotic agents, equipped with sensors like cameras and touch interfaces, bridge the gap between software intelligence and the real world. Unlike purely digital agents, they interact directly with their environment, making them ideal for tasks requiring physical action. This makes them invaluable in situations where human presence is hazardous or where tasks are highly repetitive, offering both efficiency and cost-effectiveness. These agents are often integrated with other AI architectures, such as utility-based or goal-based systems, and can function within complex multi-agent or hierarchical systems. Consider the da Vinci Surgical System: it's a prime example of a robotic agent enhancing human capabilities. While not autonomous, it empowers surgeons to perform intricate, minimally invasive procedures with greater precision, demonstrating the powerful synergy between human expertise and robotic assistance.

Conversational and Agentic AI

Conversational AI technologies, such as chatbots and virtual assistants, are designed to simulate human dialogue using natural language processing, machine learning, and large datasets. These systems can interpret and respond to user inputs across various languages and are often tailored to specific industries, enabling them to deliver contextually appropriate and relevant responses. Unlike traditional rule-based chatbots that follow rigid scripts, modern conversational AI—powered by generative models—can handle a wider range of queries, personalize interactions, and adapt through continuous learning, resulting in more dynamic and effective user experiences.

Ethical considerations are central to the development of these systems. Ensuring user privacy, securing data, and complying with legal and regulatory standards are essential responsibilities for organizations deploying conversational AI.

Agentic AI represents a more advanced paradigm, characterized by its ability to act autonomously. These systems can perceive their environment, make decisions, and adapt in real time. Unlike static models, agentic AI can learn from experience using techniques like reinforcement learning, allowing it to refine its behaviour and navigate complex, changing environments effectively.

A defining feature of agentic AI is its skill in breaking down complex goals into smaller, manageable tasks. It can use external tools—such as APIs, databases, or web searches—to gather information, update its knowledge, and adjust its strategies. Feedback mechanisms, including human input and interactions with other agents, play a critical role in improving performance and aligning behaviour with user expectations.

While conversational AI is primarily focused on simulating dialogue within specific domains, agentic AI is built for broader, multi-step problem-solving. It can operate independently, adapt to new challenges, and optimize its actions over time. However, this autonomy also raises important ethical questions about accountability, transparency, and bias, as these systems are ultimately shaped by the humans who design, deploy, and interact with them.

In summary, conversational AI and agentic AI serve distinct but complementary roles. The former enhances communication and user engagement, while the latter enables intelligent, goal-driven behaviour across complex tasks. Together, they represent the evolving frontier of human-AI collaboration.

Multi-Agent AI

Multi-agent systems (MAS) represent a shift from centralized control, as seen in single-agent systems, to a distributed intelligence model where multiple autonomous agents collaborate to solve complex problems. These agents, which can range from simple data processors to sophisticated decision-makers, operate independently but interact to achieve shared goals. Through these interactions, MAS can exhibit emergent behaviours—complex outcomes that arise from simple local rules—making them particularly effective in dynamic environments like traffic control, supply chain optimization, and swarm robotics.

Rooted in the field of Distributed Artificial Intelligence (DAI) from the 1970s and 1980s, MAS were initially developed to explore distributed problem-solving and coordination. Over time, they have evolved to include advanced communication protocols, negotiation strategies, and conflict resolution mechanisms. Notable milestones include the Contract Net Protocol and the Belief-Desire-Intention (BDI) model, which formalize how agents make decisions and interact.

A defining strength of MAS is their adaptability. Agents learn and evolve through feedback from their environment, simulations, and interactions with other agents. This continuous learning enables them to refine their behaviour and correct errors over time. MAS are also capable of simulating complex social and economic systems, offering valuable insights into phenomena like market dynamics, crowd behaviour, and information diffusion.

Effective communication is central to MAS functionality. Agents must share information, negotiate roles, and synchronize actions to function cohesively. Organizational structures—ranging from simple peer-to-peer networks to hierarchical systems—support this coordination. These structures help agents align their actions, resolve conflicts, and enhance collective decision-making.

As MAS continue to integrate with technologies like large language models, their potential expands further. However, their development also raises ethical questions around decision-making authority, transparency, and accountability, especially as these systems become more autonomous and influential in real-world applications.

Communication Between Agents

Effective communication is fundamental to the functioning of multi-agent systems (MAS), enabling agents to coordinate, cooperate, and make decisions in dynamic environments. Communication in MAS typically occurs in two forms: synchronous, where agents exchange messages in real time and wait for immediate responses, and asynchronous, where messages are sent without expecting instant replies. While synchronous communication ensures tight coordination, it can be inefficient if agents are unavailable. Asynchronous communication, on the other hand, offers flexibility and resilience but may slow down overall progress.

MAS are built around distributed problem-solving, where agents collaborate to address shared challenges. These agents may act cooperatively—working toward common goals—or competitively, pursuing individual objectives. The nature of their interactions is shaped by the environment and control mechanisms, often analysed using game theory and social models to understand how local behaviours influence global outcomes.

Communication is typically achieved through message exchange, but agents can also coordinate by observing shared environments. Two main approaches to communication exist: predefined protocols, which are reliable and standardized (especially in industrial settings), and evolving languages, which allow agents to develop more adaptive communication strategies in homogeneous systems.

Agent Communication Languages (ACLs) are essential for structuring these interactions. They define message formats, sender-receiver relationships, and speech acts such as queries, requests, and acknowledgements. Content languages, often logic- or ontology-based, define the structure and semantics of the message content. For example, Knowledge Query and Manipulation Language (KQML) uses Knowledge Interchange Format (KIF) to encode message content, ensuring shared understanding among agents.

Communication methods include message passing (with synchronous or asynchronous delivery), broadcasting (useful for rapid dissemination but prone to congestion), and direct communication (efficient and targeted). Middleware platforms like CrewAI, LangGraph, and AutoGen provide built-in support for these communication patterns, simplifying implementation.

In MAS, agents form beliefs based on observations and knowledge, and their motivations can vary. In cooperative settings, reaching consensus is key, while in competitive scenarios, agents must analyse opponents and strategize accordingly. Achieving effective coordination requires contextual awareness—understanding roles, organizational structures, and situational dynamics.

Example: The most common communication protocols used in multi-agent systems (MAS) include Foundation for Intelligent Physical Agents Agent Communication Language (FIPA-ACL), REST APIs, and message brokers like RabbitMQ and Apache Kafka. FIPA-ACL is widely adopted for structured data exchange, defining standardized message formats and semantics to ensure interoperability across platforms. It allows agents to send requests, confirmations, or queries effectively. REST APIs are frequently used for simpler integrations, especially when agents interact with web services, enabling straightforward communication between agents and external systems.

Message brokers such as RabbitMQ and Apache Kafka facilitate asynchronous communication in distributed environments. These tools enable scalable and fault-tolerant data exchange, making them suitable for MAS applications that require real-time updates and coordination, such as logistics systems tracking shipments across multiple agents.

These protocols ensure efficient communication among agents, allowing them to coordinate actions, share information, and achieve collective goals in decentralized systems.

Coordinating Actions

Agents in multi-agent systems (MAS) coordinate their actions to avoid conflicts through various sophisticated mechanisms and strategies. These coordination techniques are essential for ensuring that autonomous agents work together effectively toward common goals while maintaining system coherence.

One key approach is the use of communication protocols. Agents rely on standardized methods like the Contract Net Protocol to exchange information and coordinate actions. These protocols enable agents to share data, make requests, and negotiate tasks in a structured manner, facilitating smooth teamwork and preventing misunderstandings that could lead to conflicts.

Negotiation plays a crucial role in conflict avoidance. Agents engage in negotiations to allocate tasks, share resources efficiently, and adjust their behaviour based on the actions of others. For example, in a warehouse automation system, robots might negotiate to transport items without collisions, prioritize tasks based on urgency, and redistribute workloads if one robot fails.

Coordination mechanisms in MAS can take various forms:

1. Emergent Coordination: Agents pursue individual goals, resulting in coordination-like behaviour through environmental interactions.
2. Intentional Coordination: Agents actively communicate to avoid conflicts and coordinate tasks.
3. Market-Based Coordination: Agents use auction-based algorithms to coordinate tasks through voluntary exchange and pricing mechanisms.
4. Hierarchical Coordination: Agents follow a strict hierarchical structure where roles and tasks are defined centrally.
5. Social Network-Based Coordination: Agents leverage social relationships and trust to coordinate tasks efficiently.

Additionally, MAS often employ conflict resolution mechanisms. These can include voting systems to resolve disagreements or the use of mediation agents to arbitrate disputes. Some systems utilize machine learning algorithms to optimize task delegation based on past performance, allowing agents to adapt and improve their coordination strategies over time.

In dynamic environments, such as smart traffic management systems, agents must coordinate their actions in real time. For instance, autonomous vehicles might communicate with traffic light agents to request longer green light durations, ensuring smoother traffic flow. This type of coordination requires clear communication protocols and predefined rules to manage interactions effectively.

By implementing these coordination strategies, MAS can tackle complex problems that would be impossible for individual agents to solve alone, while minimizing conflicts and optimizing collective outcomes.

Negotiation Mechanisms

Negotiation mechanisms in multi-agent systems enable autonomous agents to resolve conflicts, allocate resources, and coordinate actions through structured interactions. These mechanisms combine communication protocols, strategic reasoning, and adaptive learning to achieve mutually acceptable agreements without centralized control.

Core Negotiation Mechanisms

Core negotiation mechanisms in multi-agent systems enable effective coordination and resource allocation through structured interaction protocols. One foundational approach is the Contract Net Protocol, which establishes a manager-contractor dynamic for task distribution. When a task emerges, a manager agent broadcasts a request to potential contractors, who respond with bids based on their capabilities or associated costs. The manager then evaluates these bids and assigns the task accordingly, creating a decentralized and adaptive marketplace for problem-solving. This protocol is widely used in smart manufacturing environments, where robotic agents dynamically allocate production tasks based on real-time availability and workload.

Another prominent mechanism is the use of auction-based systems, where agents engage in competitive bidding to acquire resources or tasks. These systems rely on auction formats such as sealed-bid or ascending-price models to determine winners based on submitted valuations. For instance, in logistics networks, autonomous delivery drones may bid for delivery routes, with the most cost-effective or time-efficient proposal securing the assignment. This method ensures that limited resources are allocated efficiently among self-interested agents.

A more nuanced form of negotiation is argumentation-based interaction, where agents not only exchange offers but also provide logical justifications for their proposals. This approach supports complex, multi-issue negotiations involving factors such as cost, quality, and timing. For example, a medical drone might argue for priority access to a charging station by citing the urgency of its delivery. By incorporating reasoning and explanation, argumentation-based negotiation enables agents to resolve conflicts and reach agreements in scenarios where simple bidding or task allocation may be insufficient.

Together, these mechanisms form the backbone of negotiation strategies in distributed AI systems, allowing agents to coordinate effectively in dynamic and resource-constrained environments.

Advanced Techniques

Machine learning significantly enhances negotiation efficiency in multi-agent systems (MAS) by enabling agents to analyse past interactions and predict the behaviour of their counterparts. Over time, agents refine their bidding strategies and learn to recognize patterns—such as identifying when an opponent is likely to make last-minute concessions. Game theory complements this by offering mathematical models like Nash equilibrium to help agents balance cooperation and competition, especially in scenarios involving conflicting interests.

Modern negotiation systems often blend multiple strategies. For example, iterative bargaining allows agents to converge on agreements over several rounds, while multi-party protocols manage negotiations involving more than two agents. In complex domains like energy markets, combinatorial auctions enable negotiation over bundles of variables such as price, quantity, and delivery schedules.

Effective negotiation also requires addressing several key challenges. Temporal constraints are critical in fast-paced environments like autonomous vehicle coordination, where decisions must be made in milliseconds. Trust management is essential in open systems, where cryptographic commitments or reputation systems help prevent deception. Protocol flexibility allows agents to switch between negotiation mechanisms depending on the context—for instance, a drone swarm might use auctions for task allocation but shift to argumentation when encountering unexpected obstacles.

To handle incomplete information, agents employ a variety of strategies:

1. **Probabilistic modelling** (e.g., Bayesian networks) helps agents update beliefs as negotiations unfold.
2. **Iterative bargaining** allows gradual information sharing and strategy adjustment.
3. **Mechanism design** introduces complex negotiation structures to address signalling and asymmetry.
4. **Screening and signalling** techniques help agents infer or reveal private information.
5. **Limited conflicts** can serve as strategic tools to extract information.
6. **Stochastic modelling** treats opponent behaviour as probabilistic, aiding decision-making under uncertainty.
7. **Information revelation mechanisms** like menus or staged protocols encourage honesty.
8. **Monotonic mechanisms** reward stronger agents with better outcomes, structuring negotiations effectively.
9. **Time constraints and discounting** influence bargaining power and urgency.
10. **Adaptive strategies** allow agents to learn and evolve based on observed behaviours.

These mechanisms enable agents to negotiate effectively even in the face of uncertainty, asymmetry, and incomplete knowledge, making MAS highly capable in dynamic, real-world applications such as smart grids, logistics, and collaborative robotics.

Advanced AI Agent Architectures

Designing agents within a multi-agent system (MAS) is fundamental to ensuring that they can perceive their environment, make decisions, and interact effectively. The architecture of each agent defines its internal processes and governs how it behaves both independently and in collaboration with others. There are three primary types of agent architectures: reactive, deliberative, and hybrid.

Reactive agents operate on a stimulus-response model, reacting directly to environmental inputs without maintaining an internal representation of the world. They are fast and efficient, ideal for predictable tasks like obstacle avoidance or formation control in robotics. However, their simplicity limits their ability to handle complex or strategic tasks.

Deliberative agents, in contrast, maintain symbolic models of their environment and use these to plan actions, predict outcomes, and pursue long-term goals. They are well-suited for dynamic and uncertain environments, such as autonomous vehicles navigating traffic. Their advanced reasoning capabilities come at the cost of higher computational demands and slower response times.

Hybrid agents combine the strengths of both approaches, using reactive mechanisms for immediate responses and deliberative planning for strategic decision-making. This makes them adaptable across a wide range of tasks and environments.

When building a MAS, several design elements are critical: defining agent roles to support specialization, establishing robust communication protocols, and decomposing complex tasks into manageable subtasks. The development process typically follows a structured methodology—starting with problem analysis and SMART goal setting, followed by agent identification, role definition, and architectural design. This includes selecting agent types, designing internal logic, and developing communication protocols.

The implementation phase involves coding and integrating agents, followed by the incorporation of feedback loops for learning and adaptation. Continuous evaluation ensures that the system meets its objectives and evolves over time.

Communication is central to MAS functionality. Agents must exchange information, coordinate actions, and negotiate roles. Several protocols support this:

1. **FIPA-ACL**: A standardized language promoting interoperability across agent systems.
2. **KQML**: Facilitates complex interactions and understanding between agents.
3. **Contract Net Protocol (CNP)**: Ideal for task allocation and resource distribution.
4. **Auction-Based Protocols**: Useful in market-driven environments for efficient resource allocation.
5. **Negotiation Protocols**: Enable agents to reach agreements through proposals and counterproposals.
6. **MQTT**: A lightweight protocol for real-time communication, especially in IoT contexts.

7. **Agent Network Protocol (ANP)**: Supports secure, decentralized communication among AI agents.

These protocols ensure that agents can collaborate effectively, share knowledge, and solve complex problems across diverse domains.

LLM-Based Agents

LLM-based Agents transcend simple text creation, adeptly maintaining conversational threads, recalling past interactions, and tailoring responses with varied tones and styles. This versatility makes them invaluable for tasks demanding intricate problem-solving, content creation, conversational fluency, and language translation, finding applications across customer service, copywriting, data analysis, education, healthcare, and beyond.

However, it's crucial to acknowledge their limitations. LLM agents may struggle with nuanced human emotions and are susceptible to misinformation, bias, privacy breaches, and toxic outputs. Effective utilization requires precise prompting, whether from humans or APIs, using detailed queries, instructions, and contextual information to ensure accurate responses. A key feature of these agents is their autonomy, enabling them to self-direct and assist users effectively by combining prompts with independent action. This blend of user guidance and autonomous capability drives productivity, automates routine tasks, and tackles complex challenges.

The architecture of an LLM Agent comprises four key components:

- **The Core**: This central processing unit manages the agent's logic and behaviour, interpreting inputs, applying reasoning, and selecting appropriate actions based on objectives and capabilities. It ensures consistent behaviour aligned with predefined guidelines or learned patterns.
- **The Memory**: This component stores internal logs and user interactions, allowing the agent to recall past conversations, preferences, and contextual information for personalized responses.
- **Tools**: These are executable workflows enabling the agent to perform specific tasks, such as generating answers, coding, searching information, and executing specialized functions. The Core intelligently selects the appropriate tool based on context, offering flexibility and scalability.
- **The Planning Module**: This strategic layer enables the agent to handle complex problems and refine execution plans. It evaluates approaches, anticipates challenges, and devises strategies, breaking down tasks and prioritizing actions.

LLM-based agents function as systems that analyse complex problems, formulate plans, and execute them using available tools. LLMs act as the "brain," processing observations and determining actions. The planning module decomposes tasks, using techniques like chain-of-thought (CoT) prompting. CoT allows agents to break down complex problems, provide transparent reasoning, handle various tasks, and be easily implemented. CoT properties include:

- Breaking down complex multi-step problems.
- Providing transparency into the model's reasoning.
- Being applicable to various tasks.
- Easy implementation.

Several LLM-based Agent solutions are available, including BabyAGI for adaptive learning, AutoGPT for task automation, and enhanced ChatGPT for improved conversations and tool integration. These solutions cater to diverse needs, from research and automation to customer service and content creation.

Agentic AI

To understand the agentic AI concept, we must first appreciate that it represents a departure from more traditional forms of AI. While conventional AI often acts as a sophisticated tool, responding to specific inputs with predictable outputs, agentic AI embodies a higher degree of autonomy and goal-directedness. Imagine moving beyond a powerful calculator or a language model that simply answers your direct queries. Agentic AI, in contrast, can be given a high-level objective and will then independently determine the necessary steps to achieve it, adapting its strategy and learning from its experiences along the way, all without constant human intervention. Agentic AI systems are designed to operate as autonomous agents, capable of performing tasks, making decisions, and learning with minimal human intervention. These systems emulate human cognitive functions, including perceiving the environment, analysing information, making informed decisions, and independently executing actions. Unlike basic automation, Agentic AI possesses the capacity to sense and understand its environment through data collection and analysis, think and decide using machine learning, deep learning, and AI reasoning models, act independently in executing tasks, workflows, and business processes, and adapt and learn from feedback and new data, continually improving its performance.

Definition Agentic AI refers to the broader field of AI research focused on developing models and algorithms that enable machines to operate autonomously as agents.

This includes creating AI systems capable of independent decision-making, adaptability, and interaction with external systems, both digitally and physically. The ultimate aim of agentic AI is to develop artificial general intelligence (AGI), where AI can perform any task, a human can, rather than being limited to specific applications.

Several key characteristics define an AI system as being agentic. Foremost is *autonomy*, the ability to operate independently, make decisions, and take actions without requiring explicit instructions for each individual step. This autonomy is driven by *goal-directedness*, meaning the AI is designed to accomplish specific objectives or tasks. To achieve these goals, an agentic AI must possess the capability of *perception*, allowing it to sense and interpret information from its surrounding environment through various means such as sensors, APIs, or other data sources. Based on this perception and its defined goals, the AI can then engage in *decision-making*, evaluating different options and choosing the most appropriate course of action. This decision-making process culminates in *action-taking*, where the AI executes its chosen actions and interacts with its environment, whether that involves manipulating data, controlling physical hardware, or communicating with other systems or even humans. Crucially, agentic AI is also characterized by its ability to engage in *learning and adaptation*, allowing it to glean insights from its past experiences, refine its strategies, and improve its overall performance over time, often employing techniques like reinforcement learning or iterative feedback loops. Furthermore, agentic AI exhibits *proactiveness*, demonstrating a tendency to take initiative and anticipate future needs or opportunities rather than simply reacting to immediate stimuli. Finally, *interaction* is a key aspect, as agentic AI can communicate and collaborate with other agents, both artificial and human, to effectively achieve its objectives.

The distinction between agentic AI and more traditional forms lies in the level of independence and initiative. Traditional AI often operates in a reactive or heavily supervised manner. Consider a spam filter that classifies emails based on provided input, a chatbot that answers predefined questions, or an image recognition system that identifies objects in a given image. While these systems are undoubtedly powerful, they generally require direct input and lack the inherent capacity to set their own complex, multi-step processes or proactively work toward broader objectives. Agentic AI, on the other hand, is empowered to do just that.

Agentic AI systems are characterized by several key attributes: autonomy, adaptability, and intelligence with contextual understanding. Autonomy allows these systems to initiate actions based on predefined objectives without constant human intervention. They analyse their environments, set their own goals, and devise strategies to achieve them, enabled by advanced machine learning algorithms. For instance, in cybersecurity, agentic AI can autonomously detect threats and initiate countermeasures. Adaptability enables these systems to adjust strategies in response to changing environments and conditions. Continuous learning is essential for maintaining effectiveness in dynamic settings. In healthcare, for example, agentic AI can adapt to new medical research and patient data, providing more accurate diagnostics and treatment plans. Intelligence and contextual understanding extend beyond simple data processing, enabling these systems to make decisions aligned with business goals, using advanced machine learning to predict outcomes and optimize strategies. Natural language processing (NLP) allows them to comprehend and generate human language, facilitating seamless user interaction. In customer service, agentic AI can handle complex queries by understanding the context and nuances of customer interactions.

Agentic AI systems are composed of several interconnected modules that work collaboratively to enable intelligent behaviour. The perception module consists of a sensory input component that receives data from various sensors and digital sources, a feature extraction component that processes raw data to extract meaningful features, and an object recognition component that identifies objects and entities using computer vision, NLP, and machine learning algorithms. The cognitive module defines the agent's objectives, generates strategies and plans, and selects the most appropriate action based on the current situation. The action module controls the agent's physical or virtual actions through actuators, implementing the selected action to interact with the environment. The learning module enables the agent to learn from interactions by receiving rewards or penalties, learning from labelled data, and discovering patterns in unlabelled data through techniques like text mining, anomaly detection, and clustering.

Unlike traditional models that operate in a reactive, single-turn fashion, agentic AI systems are designed to exhibit autonomy, goal-directed behaviour, and contextual awareness across multiple steps. Central to enabling these capabilities are frameworks like **LangChain** and **LangGraph**, which provide the infrastructure for building, managing, and scaling such agents. LangChain offers a modular architecture that allows developers to chain together language models, tools, memory, and external data sources into coherent workflows. This enables agents to reason, retrieve information, and act in a structured manner. LangGraph extends this paradigm by introducing a graph-based execution model, where each node represents a distinct computational or decision-making step. This allows for more complex behaviours such as conditional branching, looping, and stateful planning—capabilities that are essential for agents operating in dynamic or uncertain environments. Together, these frameworks are not merely tools but crucial components in the construction of intelligent systems that can plan, adapt, and collaborate in pursuit of user-defined objectives.

What Can Agentic AI Do?

Contemporary agentic systems demonstrate capabilities including autonomous planning of multi-step procedures, adaptation to changing environments, self-correction based on feedback, and persistence toward goals despite obstacles. For instance, an agentic AI tasked with arranging travel might independently search flight options, compare prices, evaluate hotel accommodations, and construct an itinerary that satisfies multiple constraints such as budget, timing, and personal preferences.

The action space of agentic AI extends beyond information processing to interaction with digital systems and, increasingly, physical environments through robotic interfaces. These systems employ sophisticated reasoning frameworks to decompose complex objectives into manageable subtasks, prioritize actions based on utility assessments, and maintain awareness of their progress toward specified goals.

Flipped Interaction Pattern

The conventional interaction model between humans and AI systems has traditionally followed a request-response paradigm: humans initiate interactions with specific queries, and AI systems respond with appropriate information or actions. The flipped interaction pattern represents a significant departure from this established model.

In the flipped interaction, the AI agent assumes a more proactive role, initiating interactions and guiding the collaboration process. Rather than passively awaiting instructions, these systems actively engage users by suggesting potential actions, requesting clarifications on ambiguous instructions, proposing alternative approaches, and even challenging assumptions when appropriate.

This pattern manifests in several ways. First, agentic systems frequently employ what might be termed *clarificational dialogue*, wherein the agent proactively seeks additional information to refine its understanding of user objectives. Second, these systems exhibit "anticipatory assistance," offering relevant suggestions before users explicitly request them. Third, they engage in "process guidance," actively directing users through complex procedures by breaking them into manageable steps.

The flipped interaction model fundamentally transforms the user experience from one of command-issuance to collaborative problem-solving. The cognitive load of decomposing complex tasks shifts partially from the human to the AI system, allowing users to operate at higher levels of abstraction. This shift enables more natural human-AI collaboration that better leverages the respective strengths of both parties.

Multi-Modal Flipped Interaction

Agentic AI systems operate across multiple modalities, combining textual, visual, auditory, and even tactile interfaces to create more comprehensive interaction experiences. Multi-modal flipped interaction extends the proactive engagement characteristic of flipped interaction across these diverse channels of communication.

In multi-modal environments, agentic systems dynamically select the most appropriate channels for different aspects of a task. For example, an agentic assistant might initiate a conversation through text, switch to visual interfaces when presenting spatial information requires clarity, employ voice interactions when the user's hands are occupied, and leverage haptic feedback when attention must be directed to specific physical elements.

This multi-modal capability allows for more contextually appropriate interactions. When explaining complex visual concepts, agents can generate diagrams or visual simulations rather than relying solely on textual descriptions. When guiding physical tasks, they can overlay instructional elements onto camera feeds or physical environments. When detecting emotional cues in voice patterns or facial expressions, they can adapt their communication style accordingly.

The orchestration of these multiple interaction channels presents significant technical challenges, requiring sophisticated attention mechanisms that determine which modalities deserve precedence in different contexts. However, when successfully implemented, multi-modal flipped interaction creates more intuitive and efficient human-AI collaborations that better approximate natural human-to-human communication patterns.

Ahead-of-Time Planning

A distinctive capability of advanced agentic systems is their capacity for ahead-of-time planning—the ability to formulate comprehensive action sequences before execution begins. This approach contrasts with reactive planning, where decisions are made incrementally as each step unfolds.

Ahead-of-time planning enables agents to identify potential obstacles, anticipate resource requirements, estimate completion timelines, and optimize processes holistically rather than locally. By simulating various execution paths before committing to action, these systems can avoid dead ends, minimize resource waste, and achieve more efficient solutions.

The planning process typically involves several stages: goal decomposition, wherein complex objectives are broken into manageable subgoals; dependency analysis, which identifies sequential relationships between tasks; resource allocation, which optimizes the distribution of computational or physical resources; contingency planning, which prepares alternative approaches for high-risk steps; and temporal scheduling, which coordinates activities across appropriate timeframes.

Sophisticated planning systems often employ hierarchical frameworks that operate at multiple levels of abstraction simultaneously. High-level planning establishes broad strategic directions, while lower-level tactical planning addresses specific implementation details. This hierarchical approach allows agents to maintain coherent long-term strategies while remaining adaptable to local circumstances.

The effectiveness of ahead-of-time planning depends heavily on the quality of the agent's world model—its internal representation of the environment, relevant actors, causal relationships, and dynamics. Agents with more comprehensive and accurate world models can generate more realistic simulations of potential outcomes, leading to more robust plans.

AI Agentic Design Patterns

The development of effective agentic AI systems has given rise to several recurring architectural and behavioural patterns that address common challenges in autonomous operation. These design patterns represent emergent best practices in the field and provide frameworks for implementing specific agentic capabilities. In this section, we will explore,

- **LangChain** and **LangGraph** frameworks.
- **Patterns**—the agentic design strategies.

LangChain and LangGraph

As agentic AI systems grow in complexity and capability, developers increasingly rely on well-established design patterns to structure their agents in a modular, interpretable, and scalable way. These patterns serve as reusable blueprints for solving common challenges in agent design, such as decision-making, memory management, tool integration, and multi-step reasoning. Two of the most influential frameworks facilitating these patterns are LangChain and LangGraph, which together provide a ground for building robust and intelligent agents. LangGraph, an innovative framework developed by the creators of LangChain, is designed for building sophisticated and stateful AI agentic workflows.

LangChain excels in enabling composable agent architectures. It abstracts the core components of an agent—such as language models, memory, tools, and retrievers—into interoperable modules. This modularity allows developers to implement design patterns like Tool-augmented Reasoning, where agents dynamically select and invoke external tools (e.g., calculators, web search APIs, or code interpreters) based on the task at hand. Another common pattern is Retrieval-Augmented Generation (RAG), where the agent retrieves relevant documents from a vector store and uses them to ground its responses in factual context. LangChain also supports episodic and long-term memory patterns, enabling agents to retain and recall information across interactions, which is essential for continuity in multi-turn conversations or task execution.

In contrast, LangGraph introduces a graph-based execution model that brings a new level of control and transparency to agent workflows. Rather than relying solely on linear chains of operations, LangGraph allows developers to define agents as stateful computation graphs, where each node represents a discrete function, decision point, or subagent. This enables the implementation of more advanced patterns such as Conditional Branching, where the agent's path through the graph depends on runtime decisions, and Retry Loops, which allow agents to reattempt failed steps with modified inputs or fallback strategies. LangGraph also supports parallel execution paths, making it suitable for agents that need to coordinate multiple subtasks simultaneously or collaborate with other agents in a distributed system.

LangGraph utilizes the concept of a StateGraph. This graph manages a central state object that evolves as the workflow progresses. Each node in the graph represents a computational step, which could be an AI agent, a tool invocation, or a conditional routing decision. The edges between these nodes define the possible transitions and flow of information within the system. This graph structure supports both directed acyclic graphs (DAGs) for sequential processes and, crucially for agentic workflows, cyclic graphs that allow for iterative interactions and feedback loops. The "state" within LangGraph acts as the memory of the system, persisting information across different steps in the workflow. This is crucial for building conversational agents or systems that need to maintain context over long interactions or multiple turns. The state can be accessed and modified by the nodes in the graph, allowing for context-aware decision-making and behaviour. LangGraph distinguishes itself by providing low-level primitives that offer significant flexibility and control over agentic workflows. Unlike higher-level abstractions that might impose rigid structures, LangGraph allows developers to define custom control flows, including single-agent, multi-agent, and hierarchical systems. This extensibility enables the creation of tailored solutions for specific and complex use cases. Furthermore, LangGraph offers first-class streaming support, providing real-time visibility into the agent's reasoning and actions, enhancing the user experience.

Figure 8.9 maps key AI agentic design patterns—reflection, ReAct, tool use, multi-agent, and planning—to their corresponding support in LangChain and LangGraph. The edge labels describe the nature of support:

- *Native Support* and *Core Agent Type* indicate built-in capabilities in LangChain.
- *Orchestration*, *Ideal for Coordination*, and *Graph-based Plans* highlight LangGraph's strengths in managing flow, state, and structure.

Together, LangChain and LangGraph enable a rich ecosystem of agentic design patterns that go beyond simple prompt engineering. They allow developers to externalize logic, manage state transitions, and build agents that are not only more capable but also more interpretable and maintainable. These frameworks are particularly valuable in enterprise and research settings, where reliability, auditability, and extensibility are critical. By adopting these design patterns, developers can construct agents that exhibit sophisticated behaviours such as planning, tool use, memory, and collaboration.

Reflection Pattern

The reflection pattern represents a sophisticated approach to agent design that incorporates explicit self-evaluation capabilities.

That means the Reflection Pattern involves an agent evaluating its own outputs or reasoning steps and then revising or improving them. This is often used to enhance reliability, reduce hallucinations, or improve task performance through self-critique. Agents implementing this pattern maintain meta-cognitive processes that monitor, evaluate, and modify their own cognitive operations. This self-awareness creates a dual-layer architecture: a base layer that performs primary tasks and a reflection layer that evaluates performance and adjusts strategies.

In practical implementation, reflection mechanisms typically operate through several distinct processes. Trace generation creates explicit records of the agent's reasoning steps and decision criteria. Performance monitoring collects metrics on task outcomes, resource utilization, and efficiency. Critical review processes analyse these records to identify strengths, weaknesses, and unexpected behaviours. Learning mechanisms then update internal models, heuristics, or decision-making frameworks based on these insights.

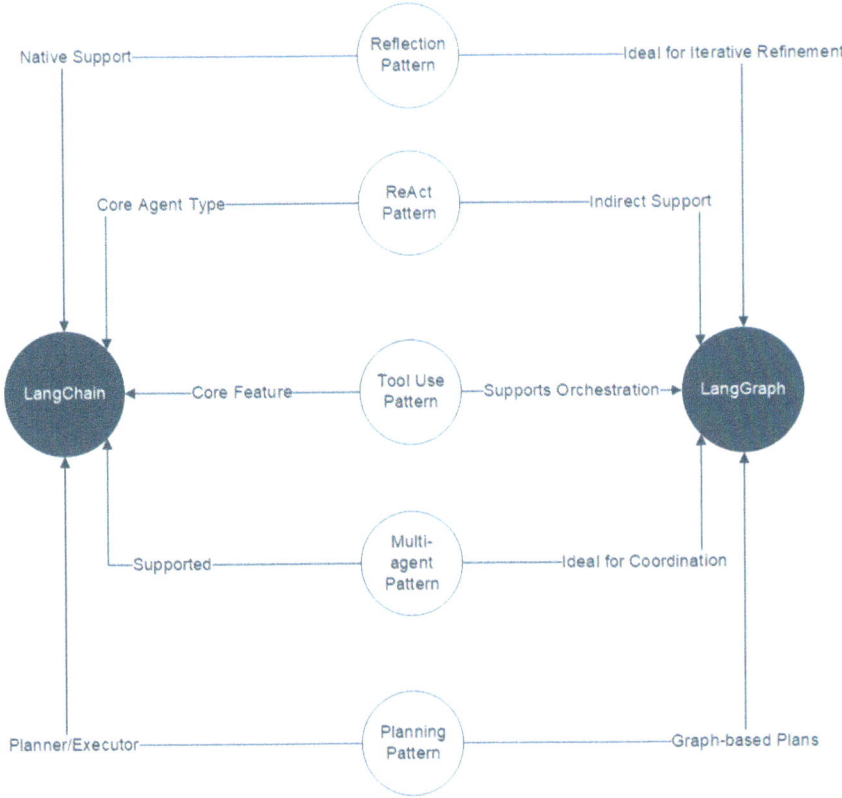

Fig. 8.9 Mapping of AI agentic design patterns to LangChain and LangGraph

The reflection pattern enables several powerful capabilities. First, it facilitates continuous self-improvement without requiring external feedback for every action. Second, it enables strategic adaptation when moving between different domains or task types. Third, it provides a foundation for explaining and justifying decisions by referencing the reflective evaluation process. Fourth, it creates natural opportunities for incorporating human feedback at the meta-level rather than for specific decisions.

In LangChain, this pattern is supported through custom agent loops or intermediate step callbacks, where the agent can pause, reflect on its reasoning, and revise its plan or answer. LangChain also allows integration with critique models or meta-evaluators that can assess the quality of an agent's response.

In LangGraph, reflection can be modelled as a node or subgraph that evaluates previous steps and conditionally loops back to earlier stages. This makes LangGraph particularly powerful for implementing iterative refinement workflows.

Advanced reflection systems often implement hierarchical reflection structures, where reflection processes themselves can be subject to higher-order reflection. They also commonly incorporate counterfactual analysis, examining alternative approaches that could have been taken to identify missed opportunities or potential improvements.

The pattern finds particular value in complex knowledge work domains where approaches must be continuously refined, such as scientific research assistants, strategic planning systems, and creative collaborators. For instance, an agentic writing assistant using reflection might analyse its generated text, identify stylistic inconsistencies or logical weaknesses, and modify its approach for subsequent content generation.

Tool Use Pattern

The tool use pattern enables agents to extend their capabilities by incorporating specialized external functions, APIs, services, or other agents as interoperable components within their operation. This pattern represents a modular approach to capability extension that allows agents to accomplish tasks beyond their core functionality by orchestrating purpose-built tools.

Effective implementation of this pattern requires several key components. First, tool discovery mechanisms allow agents to identify relevant tools from available repositories based on task requirements. Second, interface standardization establishes consistent patterns for tool invocation, parameter passing, and result interpretation. Third, capability modelling gives agents accurate representations of what each tool can and cannot accomplish. Fourth, error handling protocols address cases where tools fail to perform as expected.

LangChain provides built-in support for tool use, including defining tools, parsing tool calls from model outputs, and managing tool execution. This is initial to LangChain's agent framework.

LangGraph can manage the flow of tool calls, retries, and conditional logic around tool use. It's especially useful when tool use is part of a larger, multi-step workflow.

Advanced tool use systems incorporate sophisticated approaches to tool selection and composition. Tools are chosen based on comprehensive evaluation of their fitness for specific subtasks, considering factors like accuracy, computational requirements, and side effects. Sequential composition chains multiple tools to accomplish complex workflows. Parallel composition applies multiple tools simultaneously to address different aspects of a problem. Iterative refinement passes outputs through successive tool applications to progressively improve results.

The pattern enables powerful capabilities including rapid adaptation to new domains by incorporating domain-specific tools, graceful performance degradation when optimal tools are unavailable by substituting alternatives, and natural division of labour between general reasoning and specialized processing. This approach has proven particularly valuable in domains like data analysis, where agents might leverage specialized visualization libraries, statistical packages, and data transformation tools in combination.

Reason and Act (ReAct) Pattern

The ReAct Pattern, introduced by researchers at Google and Princeton, combines chain-of-thought reasoning with tool use. The agent reasons step-by-step and interleaves this reasoning with actions (e.g., calling a calculator, searching the web).

This pattern interleaves explicit reasoning processes with concrete actions, creating a synergistic relationship between thought and behaviour. Unlike approaches that separate planning from execution, ReAct creates tight feedback loops between reasoning about a situation and taking steps to address it.

The pattern operates through a characteristic sequence: the agent first reasons about its current state and objectives to determine appropriate next steps; it then executes a discrete action based on this reasoning; it subsequently observes the results of this action; and finally, it incorporates these observations into updated reasoning before determining the next action. This creates a continuous cycle of "think, act, observe, think again" that allows for dynamic adaptation.

Several mechanisms support effective ReAct implementation. Trace generation creates explicit, human-readable records of reasoning steps to enable verification and transparency. Intermediate state maintenance tracks partial progress toward goals across multiple reasoning-action cycles. Self-questioning prompts the agent to explicitly challenge its own assumptions when observations contradict expectations. Dynamic replanning adjusts approaches when environment feedback suggests current strategies are suboptimal.

The ReAct pattern offers distinct advantages in uncertain or partially observable environments where complete planning ahead of time is impractical. By treating actions not just as goal-achievement mechanisms but also as information-gathering opportunities, ReAct agents effectively explore solution spaces while making continuous progress. This approach proves particularly valuable in interactive problem-solving scenarios like troubleshooting technical issues, conducting scientific experiments, or navigating unfamiliar environments.

LangChain provides built-in support for ReAct-style agents, where the model generates both reasoning traces and tool invocations in a structured format. This is one of the most widely used patterns in LangChain-based agents.

While LangGraph is not specifically designed for ReAct, it can be used to structure and manage the flow of ReAct-style reasoning and actions, especially when you want to add state tracking, error handling, or multi-agent collaboration.

Advanced implementations often incorporate varying depths of reasoning based on task complexity and time constraints. Simple, familiar situations might trigger more automatic responses with minimal explicit reasoning, while novel or high-stakes scenarios activate deeper cognitive processes before action.

Planning Pattern

The planning pattern formalizes how agents develop, evaluate, and execute sequences of actions to achieve complex objectives. The agent creates a plan or sequence of steps before executing them. While mentioned earlier as "ahead-of-time planning," this pattern encompasses a broader set of approaches ranging from comprehensive pre-execution planning to just-in-time planning during task execution.

Effective planning implementations typically incorporate several distinct phases. Goal analysis clarifies objectives and translates abstract desires into concrete, measurable outcomes. State space representation constructs formal models of possible world states, available actions, and their effects. Path finding identifies sequences of actions that transform initial states into goal states. Feasibility evaluation assesses whether candidate plans satisfy all constraints and resource limitations. Optimization refines viable plans to improve efficiency, robustness, or other quality metrics.

LangChain includes built-in planners (e.g., for task decomposition) and executors (for step-by-step execution). Whereas, LangGraph allows you to encode the plan as a graph, where each node is a step. It supports branching, looping, and state tracking, making it ideal for dynamic or adaptive planning.

Advanced planning systems employ sophisticated techniques to address inherent challenges in complex environments. Hierarchical planning operates at multiple abstraction levels simultaneously, addressing broad strategy before tactical details. Probabilistic planning incorporates uncertainty models to account for variable action outcomes. Monte Carlo tree search explores promising action sequences through statistical sampling. Constraint satisfaction techniques efficiently handle complex interdependencies between actions and resources.

The planning pattern enables several critical capabilities for agentic systems. It supports handling complex, long-horizon tasks that require coordinated sequences of actions. It facilitates resource optimization by identifying efficient approaches before committing to action. It enables contingency preparation by identifying potential failure points and developing alternative strategies. It supports transparent operation by making intended action sequences explicit and reviewable.

This pattern proves particularly valuable in domains with high complexity, significant constraints, or substantial costs for failed attempts. Examples include logistics coordination, project management, manufacturing process control, and complex creative endeavours like film production or software development.

Multi-Agent Pattern

The multi-agent pattern distributes cognitive processes across multiple specialized agents that collaborate to accomplish objectives beyond the capabilities of any single agent. This approach treats agency as a collective rather than individual phenomenon, with system behaviour emerging from the interaction of multiple distinct entities.

Effective implementation of this pattern requires sophisticated coordination mechanisms. Communication protocols establish standardized formats for information exchange between agents. Task allocation frameworks determine which agents should handle which aspects of complex problems. Conflict resolution mechanisms address cases where agents propose contradictory approaches. Consensus protocols integrate diverse agent perspectives into coherent system behaviour.

Multi-agent systems typically implement one of several organizational structures. Hierarchical organizations establish clear authority relationships, with manager agents decomposing tasks and delegating to specialized worker agents. Market-based organizations use internal economies where agents bid for tasks based on their capabilities and availability. Team-based organizations establish peer groups with complementary skills that collectively address complex challenges. Hybrid approaches combine elements of multiple organizational paradigms to balance their respective strengths and limitations.

The pattern enables several powerful capabilities. First, it supports massive parallelism by allowing multiple agents to work simultaneously on different aspects of complex problems. Second, it creates natural specialization, with different agents developing deep expertise in specific domains. Third, it enables redundancy and resilience, with multiple agents able to compensate for individual failures. Fourth, it supports scalability, with systems easily expanded by adding agents with new capabilities.

LangChain supported multi-agent chains and agent composition. You can define agents with different tools, memory, or prompts and coordinate them manually or through a controller agent.

LangGraph excels at modelling multi-agent workflows, where each agent is a node or subgraph. It can manage message passing, role-based execution, and conditional delegation between agents.

Advanced multi-agent systems incorporate sophisticated mechanisms for collective intelligence. Reputation systems track agent performance to inform future task allocation. Knowledge sharing frameworks allow agents to benefit from each other's experiences. Diversity maintenance ensures that the agent population maintains a healthy variety of approaches and perspectives. Learning transfer enables insights gained by one agent to benefit others with similar responsibilities.

This pattern has proven particularly valuable for complex, multi-faceted domains like scientific research support, creative collaboration platforms, and comprehensive advisory systems that must integrate perspectives from multiple disciplines.

Additional Emerging Patterns

The "observe-orient-decide-act" (OODA) loop pattern, originally developed in military strategy contexts, provides a comprehensive framework for agent cognition and behaviour. In implementation, the observation phase involves multi-modal sensing capabilities that gather raw data from relevant environments. The orientation phase then processes this information through both analytical and intuitive mechanisms, contextualizing new observations within existing knowledge frameworks. During the decision phase, agents evaluate potential actions against goal structures using predictive models to simulate outcomes. Finally, the action phase executes selected behaviours and monitors their effects, creating a continuous feedback loop. This pattern's strength lies in its adaptability to rapidly changing circumstances, making it particularly valuable for agents operating in dynamic environments like autonomous vehicles navigating traffic or trading systems responding to market fluctuations.

The "hierarchical decomposition" pattern operates through several distinct mechanisms that collectively enable effective management of complexity. At its foundation lies task decomposition—breaking complex objectives into progressively simpler subtasks until reaching directly implementable actions. Complementing this is temporal abstraction, wherein planning occurs at multiple time horizons simultaneously, with long-term strategic goals informing shorter-term tactical decisions. The pattern typically implements abstraction barriers between hierarchical levels, allowing higher levels to specify what to accomplish while lower levels determine how to execute, thereby creating a separation of concerns. Advanced implementations often incorporate bidirectional information flow, where lower-level execution challenges can trigger replanning at higher levels when necessary. This pattern proves especially valuable for agents that must coordinate activities across multiple time scales, such as project management assistants or household robots managing diverse responsibilities.

The "reflection mechanism" pattern incorporates explicit self-evaluation capabilities, allowing agents to assess their own performance, identify limitations in their approaches, and modify their strategies accordingly. Reflective agents maintain metadata about their own operations and use this information to improve future performance.

The "bounded exploration" pattern balances exploitation of known effective strategies with controlled investigation of alternatives through several mechanisms. Parameter-controlled exploration uses explicit variables to regulate the propensity for novel behaviour, often decreasing exploration as confidence in current strategies increases. Multi-armed bandit algorithms allocate resources between known high-performing approaches and promising but uncertain alternatives based on formal statistical frameworks. Curiosity-driven exploration mechanisms explicitly reward the discovery of information that reduces uncertainty about the environment. Temporal scheduling of exploration creates dedicated periods for investigating alternatives separate from performance-focused operation. This pattern is particularly valuable in recommendation systems, creative assistants, and optimization agents where discovering novel approaches can yield significant benefits.

The "human-in-the-loop" pattern explicitly incorporates human oversight at critical decision points, particularly for high-stakes or ethically complex situations. This pattern enables appropriate division of responsibility between human and AI components of a system, ensuring that human judgement is applied where it adds the greatest value.

The "progressive disclosure" pattern manages complexity by revealing information and options to users incrementally as they become relevant. This pattern prevents cognitive overload while ensuring that users have access to necessary details at appropriate moments.

Beyond these established patterns, several emerging approaches are gaining prominence in agentic AI design. The "progressive scaffolding" pattern structures agent behaviour to provide extensive guidance initially before gradually reducing support as users develop proficiency, creating natural learning curves for complex systems. The "ethical boundary" pattern incorporates explicit ethical constraints into agent architecture, preventing certain categories of actions regardless of their instrumental value toward goals. The "cultural adaptation" pattern enables agents to modify their communication styles, value interpretations, and behavioural norms based on cultural context, improving appropriateness across diverse user populations.

The "explanation generation" pattern builds interpretability directly into agent architecture rather than treating it as an afterthought, with agents maintaining explicit records of decision factors that can be translated into appropriate explanations for different audiences. The "predictive alignment" pattern continuously monitors the gap between agent predictions and actual outcomes, using this information to identify and correct model limitations or conceptual misalignments.

Exploring the Coordinator, Worker, and Delegator Approach

The evolution of agentic AI systems has introduced new paradigms for organizing and orchestrating intelligent agents, especially as these systems grow in complexity and autonomy. Among the most influential architectural models is the Coordinator-Worker-Delegator (CWD) approach, which provides a robust framework for designing scalable, adaptive, and reliable multi-agent environments.

The CWD model is inspired by organizational patterns observed in human teams and distributed computing, where distinct roles are assigned to optimize efficiency, specialization, and adaptability. In agentic AI, these roles are formalized to enable autonomous agents to collaborate, divide labour, and dynamically respond to changing environments.

The **coordinator** acts as the central planner and overseer. This agent is responsible for decomposing high-level objectives into actionable subtasks, allocating these tasks to appropriate agents, and maintaining a global view of progress. The coordinator must possess strategic reasoning capabilities, often leveraging hierarchical planning algorithms and maintaining awareness of resource availability and agent expertise.

Workers are specialized agents tasked with executing the subtasks assigned by the coordinator. Each worker may have unique skills, tools, or access to specific data sources, allowing for parallelization and specialization. Workers operate semi-independently, reporting results and status updates back to the coordinator. Their design emphasizes robustness, adaptability, and the ability to handle failures or unexpected scenarios within their domain.

The **delegator** serves as an intermediary, bridging the gap between high-level planning and low-level execution. Delegators may further decompose tasks received from the coordinator, assign them to subworkers, or manage execution pipelines for complex, multi-step processes. In some architectures, the delegator also handles monitoring, error recovery, and optimization of task flows, ensuring that the system remains responsive and efficient as conditions evolve.

Effective implementation of the CWD approach begins with thoughtful role assignment, grounded in a clear understanding of the problem domain and the capabilities of available agents. The coordinator must be equipped with advanced decision-making algorithms, such as hierarchical task networks (HTNs), to manage dependencies and prioritize tasks. Workers are selected or designed based on their ability to perform specific actions, access necessary resources, or interact with external tools and data.

Delegators are particularly valuable in large-scale or dynamic environments, where tasks may require further decomposition or adaptive routing. By introducing this intermediate layer, systems can achieve greater modularity, fault tolerance, and scalability. Delegators can also facilitate self-improvement mechanisms, such as learning from execution outcomes to refine future task assignments or strategies.

Central to the success of the CWD model is a robust communication protocol that allows agents to share information, coordinate actions, and handle contingencies. Coordinators must efficiently broadcast task assignments and receive updates, while workers and delegators need mechanisms for signalling completion, reporting errors, or requesting assistance. Standardized message formats and acknowledgement systems ensure that information flows reliably throughout the agentic ecosystem. Collaboration extends beyond simple task execution. In advanced agentic systems, agents may negotiate task assignments, share intermediate results, or collaboratively solve subproblems. This requires the integration of trust, transparency, and accountability mechanisms, ensuring that agents act in alignment with system objectives and ethical guidelines.

The CWD model has found particular resonance in the design of generative AI systems, where complex workflows often involve multiple stages of data processing, model inference, and result synthesis. For example, a generative AI pipeline for document analysis might employ a coordinator to parse user queries and orchestrate the workflow, delegators to manage document retrieval and preprocessing, and workers to extract information, summarize content, or generate responses.

This approach enables generative AI agents to operate with minimal human intervention, adapt to new tasks, and scale across diverse domains. By modularizing responsibilities, the system can be updated or extended—such as integrating new tools or models—without disrupting the overall workflow.

Integration and Implementation Considerations

In practical implementation, these patterns rarely appear in isolation. Most sophisticated agentic systems combine multiple patterns to address different aspects of autonomous operation. For instance, a comprehensive assistant might employ hierarchical decomposition for task structure, reflection for continuous improvement, tool use for capability extension, ReAct for interactive problem-solving, and planning for complex multi-step processes.

Successful integration requires careful attention to pattern compatibility and interaction effects. Some combinations create natural synergies—reflection processes can evaluate the effectiveness of planning approaches, for example, creating continuous improvement cycles. Other combinations may introduce tensions that require careful management, such as balancing the exploration focus of bounded exploration with the efficiency orientation of planning processes.

The selection and implementation of appropriate patterns should be guided by both task characteristics and deployment context. Tasks with clear structure and stable environments may benefit more from comprehensive planning, while dynamic, uncertain situations may favour ReAct approaches. Similarly, contexts with abundant computational resources may support sophisticated reflection mechanisms, while constrained environments might prioritize more efficient patterns.

Exploring AI Agentic Workflows with LangGraph

AI agentic workflows built with LangGraph leverage the framework's graph structure and state management to create systems where AI agents can autonomously make decisions about the next steps to take in order to achieve a given goal. This dynamic control flow is a key characteristic of advanced agentic systems, allowing them to adapt to different situations, choose appropriate tools, and iterate on solutions without strict predefined sequences.

In LangGraph, the flow of execution is not predetermined but rather emerges from the interactions between agents (represented as nodes in the graph) and the conditions defined on the edges connecting them. An agent can perform an action, update the state, and then the graph can dynamically determine the next node to visit based on the current state. This decision-making process can involve conditional logic, the output of an agent's reasoning, or even human intervention.

One powerful aspect of LangGraph is its support for cyclical graphs. This enables the creation of iterative processes where an agent's output can be fed back into the system, allowing for refinement of results or further exploration of a problem space. For example, an agent might generate some code, another agent reviews it, and if issues are found, the workflow can loop back to the code generation agent for revisions.

Human-in-the-loop integration is another important aspect of dynamic control in LangGraph. The framework allows for the insertion of human review or approval steps into the workflow. Based on human feedback, the flow can be directed along different paths, providing a mechanism for oversight and correction in complex agentic processes.

In-Context Learning and Agents

The integration of in-context learning capabilities has significantly enhanced the adaptability and personalization potential of agentic AI systems. In-context learning refers to an agent's ability to rapidly adapt its behaviour based on examples or patterns observed within the current interaction, without requiring explicit reprogramming or extensive retraining.

This capability enables agents to quickly assimilate user preferences, communication styles, domain-specific terminology, and task-specific constraints through observation rather than explicit instruction. For instance, after observing a user's writing style in a few examples, an agentic writing assistant can generate content that mimics stylistic elements such as sentence structure, vocabulary choices, and rhetorical approaches.

In-context learning operates through several mechanisms. Pattern recognition identifies recurring structures in user-provided examples. Implicit rule extraction derives operational principles from observed behaviours. Prototype-based reasoning applies solutions from similar previously encountered situations to new challenges. Contrastive learning identifies distinctions between positive and negative examples to refine understanding of user preferences.

The effectiveness of in-context learning in agentic systems depends on several factors: the representational capacity of the agent's models, which must be sufficient to capture relevant patterns; the diversity and quality of examples provided during the interaction; the agent's ability to distinguish between generalizable patterns and incidental features; and mechanisms for resolving conflicts between in-context adaptations and pre-established knowledge.

Advanced agentic systems often combine in-context learning with more persistent forms of adaptation, using immediate observations to guide short-term behaviour while gradually incorporating confirmed patterns into longer-term memory structures. This hybrid approach balances responsiveness to immediate context with stability of core capabilities.

Agentic Tools

The ecosystem of agentic AI has expanded beyond standalone systems to include specialized agentic tools—focused components designed to accomplish specific types of tasks within broader workflows. These tools represent a modular approach to agentic functionality, allowing complex processes to be decomposed into manageable components handled by specialized agents.

Agentic tools typically exhibit high proficiency within narrowly defined domains. For example, research agents specialize in information gathering and synthesis; planning agents excel at decomposing complex objectives into actionable steps; coding agents generate and debug software; design agents create visual assets according to specifications; and evaluation agents assess outputs against quality criteria.

The modular nature of these tools enables several powerful capabilities. Tool composition allows multiple specialized agents to be combined into pipelines that address complex workflows. Tool selection mechanisms dynamically determine which specialized components are appropriate for different aspects of a task. Tool customization adapts generic capabilities to specific domains through fine-tuning or prompt engineering.

Effective agentic tools incorporate several key design principles. First, they maintain clear scope boundaries to prevent capability overreach. Second, they implement standardized interfaces that facilitate integration with other system components. Third, they provide transparent operation logs that enable users to understand and validate their internal processes. Fourth, they include explicit uncertainty signals that communicate confidence levels in their outputs.

The proliferation of specialized agentic tools has created new challenges in tool orchestration—determining which tools to apply in which sequences to accomplish complex objectives. Advanced orchestration frameworks employ meta-agents that coordinate tool usage based on task requirements, available resources, and observed performance patterns.

Challenges in Developing AI Agents

One major hurdle for AI agents is securing access to high-quality, relevant data. AI agents rely heavily on data for learning and decision-making, but data often suffers from incompleteness, noise, or bias, which directly impacts the agent's performance and reliability. Acquiring large volumes of high-quality data from diverse and representative sources is essential for training robust AI models. Additionally, data privacy regulations and restrictions can limit data availability, complicating the development process. Ethically sourcing and properly annotating data is also significant undertakings, demanding substantial time and resources. To mitigate these issues, rigorous data curation practices, advanced data preprocessing techniques, and adherence to ethical data collection standards are crucial.

Moreover, developing and deploying AI agents typically require substantial computational resources, particularly for complex learning models and real-time decision-making. Training sophisticated AI models, such as deep neural networks, necessitates vast computational power, often requiring specialized hardware like GPUs and TPUs. This demand for high-performance computing can create barriers for organizations, especially smaller ones with limited budgets. Ensuring that AI agents operate efficiently in real-time applications, like autonomous vehicles or robotics, presents another significant challenge. To address these resource constraints, researchers and developers must focus on optimizing algorithms, utilizing cloud-based services, and exploring advancements in hardware acceleration to achieve the necessary computational efficiency.

Another critical challenge lies in ensuring the interpretability and explainability of AI agent decision-making processes. Many AI models, particularly deep learning systems, function as "black boxes," making it difficult to understand how specific decisions are made. This lack of transparency can undermine the trustworthiness and acceptance of AI agents, especially in high-stakes domains like healthcare, finance, or legal systems. To overcome this, developers are increasingly focusing on creating interpretable AI models that provide clear, understandable explanations for their actions. Techniques such as feature importance analysis, model-agnostic interpretability methods, and visualization tools are being explored to enhance AI system transparency. Ensuring interpretability not only builds user trust but also aids in identifying and mitigating biases and errors.

To mitigate these risks and challenges, several strategies can be employed:

- **Robust Data Privacy Protocols:** Implementing comprehensive data handling and privacy measures ensures the protection of sensitive information and prevents unnecessary data retention.

- **Regular Auditing and Updating:** Continuously monitoring and updating AI models helps rectify biases, enhance decision-making accuracy, and adapt to emerging security threats.
- **User Education and Transparency:** Educating users about the capabilities and limitations of AI agents and maintaining transparency regarding data usage and processing builds trust and understanding.
- **Ethical Guidelines and Regulations:** Establishing and adhering to ethical guidelines and regulatory standards promotes the responsible use of AI technology.
- **Fail-Safes and Human Oversight:** Integrating fail-safe mechanisms and maintaining human oversight allows for intervention in cases of erroneous decisions or unexpected AI agent behaviour.

Human-Agent Collaboration

Human-agent collaboration focuses on how humans and AI agents can work together to achieve common goals. Human-agent collaboration leverages the strengths of both humans and AI agents to solve complex tasks. For example, large language models (LLMs) can assist humans by providing information and suggestions, while humans can guide the AI with their intuition and expertise. Recent research has introduced methods like Reinforcement Learning-based Human-Agent Collaboration (ReHAC), which determine optimal stages for human intervention in task-solving processes. This approach uses a policy model trained on collaboration datasets to enhance performance through strategic human involvement.

Frameworks like Collaborative Gym (Co-Gym) enable asynchronous interaction among agents, humans, and task environments. These frameworks facilitate the study and evaluation of human-agent collaboration, allowing for more effective and seamless integration.

In healthcare, AI agents can automate administrative tasks, while humans focus on patient care. In military contexts, AI agents can identify and track targets, while humans make strategic decisions.

Example: IBM Watson Health

The healthcare industry faces significant challenges in handling vast amounts of patient data, accurately diagnosing diseases, and creating effective treatment plans. Traditional methods often struggle with the complexity and volume of medical information. IBM Watson Health aimed to address these issues by harnessing AI to process and analyse complex medical data. The solution involves utilizing the cognitive computing capabilities of IBM Watson to analyse large volumes of medical records, research papers, and clinical trial data. The system uses natural language processing

(NLP) to understand and process medical jargon, making sense of unstructured data to aid medical professionals in diagnosing and treating patients.

1. **Data Integration**: IBM Watson Health integrates various sources of medical data, including electronic health records (EHRs), medical literature, and clinical trial results.
2. **Natural Language Processing**: The AI system uses NLP to interpret and analyse unstructured text data, such as doctors' notes and medical research papers.
3. **Machine Learning Models**: These models are trained to identify patterns and correlations in the data, helping to predict patient outcomes and recommend personalized treatment plans.
4. **Decision Support**: The AI provides decision support to healthcare professionals by offering evidence-based recommendations for diagnosis and treatment.

The implementation of IBM Watson Health has significantly impacted the healthcare industry by enhancing diagnostic accuracy, personalizing treatment plans, and improving overall efficiency. By integrating various sources of medical data and utilizing natural language processing to interpret unstructured text, the AI system provides comprehensive analysis and insights that might be overlooked by human practitioners. This leads to more accurate diagnoses and personalized treatment plans based on each patient's unique medical history and the latest research findings. Additionally, the AI reduces the time required for data analysis, allowing healthcare professionals to focus more on patient care.

Key learnings from this case study highlight the complementary role of AI in healthcare, demonstrating how it can enhance the expertise of medical professionals and lead to better healthcare outcomes. Effective use of AI requires integrating diverse data sources and leveraging advanced analytics to derive meaningful insights. Furthermore, the scalability of AI solutions like IBM Watson Health makes them suitable for widespread adoption, capable of handling large volumes of data and transforming healthcare practices on a broad scale.

Exercises

1. Define agent. What is rational agent?
2. Elaborate the phases involved in designing a problem-solving agent.
3. What are the elements of an agent?
4. What is agent program and agent architecture?
5. How agents do communication?
6. Elaborate on the agent communication method by action?
7. What is the relationship between agency and autonomous systems?
8. Are there any scenarios where an Agentic AI system does not act on behalf of any parties but itself?
9. Explain the difference between a reactive agent and a deliberative agent.
10. How does a rational agent differ from a simple reflex agent?

11. Provide real-world examples of AI agents and classify them based on their capabilities.
12. Describe the different types of AI agents (simple reflex, model-based, goal-based, utility-based, and learning agents).
13. Explain the role of perception and actuation in an AI agent.
14. How do AI agents use feedback loops to improve decision-making?
15. Consider a vacuum cleaner agent. Define its percepts, actions, and environment.
16. Design a finite-state machine representation for a simple AI agent that plays tic-tac-toe.
17. Implement a simple AI agent that plays rock-paper-scissors using a basic probabilistic model.
18. (Project) Design an automated invoice generator that monitors emails from class participants and automatically creates Stripe invoices for employer reimbursement requests.
19. Explain the role of MAS in traffic management systems.
20. Describe the application of MAS in financial markets.
21. (Project) Design a *scheduling* agent that checks your calendar and reads a conversation with a customer. Proposes when to schedule a meeting based on your availability and a bunch of rules.
22. Describe the key capabilities of agentic AI, such as autonomy, adaptability, and self-improvement.
23. Explain how LLMs (like GPT-4) can be used as agentic AI systems.
24. What are the risks of highly autonomous AI agents?
25. How can we design safe and aligned agentic AI systems?
26. Discuss value alignment and human-in-the-loop approaches in agentic AI.
27. (Project) Simulate a multi-agent traffic system where cars must navigate an intersection using coordination strategies.
28. (Project) Implement a basic agentic AI that takes a high-level goal (e.g., "plan a vacation") and breaks it into subtasks.
29. (Project) Design and implement a simple reflex agent that operates within a defined grid environment. The agent's task could be to navigate to a target location, avoid obstacles, or collect "food" items. The agent's decision-making should be based solely on its current perception of the environment (e.g., what it senses in its immediate vicinity).

Further Reading

Bousetouane F (2025) Agentic systems: a guide to transforming industries with vertical AI agents. arXiv abs/2501.00881
Chan A, Salganik R, Markelius A, Pang C, Rajkumar N, Krasheninnikov D, Langosco L, He Z, Duan Y, Carroll M, Lin M (2023) Harms from increasingly agentic algorithmic systems. In: Proceedings of the 2023 ACM conference on fairness, accountability, and transparency, pp 651–666

Dattathrani S, De' R (2023) The concept of agency in the era of artificial intelligence: dimensions and degrees. Inf Syst Front 25(1):29–54

Dennett DC (1987) The intentional stance. The MIT Press

Ferber J (1999) Multi-agent systems: an introduction to distributed artificial intelligence. Addison Wesley, New York

Fourney A, Bansal G, Mozannar H, Cheng T, Salinas E, Niedtner F, Proebsting G, Bassman G, Gerrits J Alber J, et al. (2024) Magentic-one: a generalist multi-agent system for solving complex tasks. arXiv preprint. arXiv: 2411.04468

Guo T, Chen X, Wang Y, Chang R, Pei S, Chawla NV, Wiest O, Zhang X (2024) Large language model based multi-agents: a survey of progress and challenges. arXiv preprint. arXiv: 2402.01680

Karpas E, Abate A, Alistarh D, et al. (2023) AutoGPT: an early exploration of autonomous agents using large language models. arXiv: 2307.14995

Liu S, Wang X, Esch M, et al. (2023) AgentTuning: enabling generalized agent abilities for LLMs. arXiv: 2310.12823

Liu Y, Lo SK, Lu Q, Zhu L, Zhao D, Xu X, Harrer S, Whittle J (2024) Agent design pattern catalogue: a collection of architectural patterns for foundation model based agents. arXiv preprint. arXiv: 2405.10467

Mialon G, Dessì R, Lomeli M, et al. (2023) Augmented language models: a survey. arXiv: 2302.07842

Minsky M (1986) Society of mind. Basic Books, New York

Mitchell M, Ghosh A, Luccioni AS, Pistilli G (2025) Fully autonomous AI agents should not be developed. arXiv preprint. arXiv: 2502.02649

Nakajima Y, Fan S, Hao E, et al. (2024) MemGPT: towards LLMs as operating systems. arXiv: 2310.08560

Park J, O'Brien J, Cai CJ, et al. (2023) GenerativeAgents: interactive simulacra of human behavior. arXiv: 2304.03442

Qian W, Patil SA, Alon U, et al. (2023) Communicative agents for software development. arXiv: 2307.07924

Shoham Y (1993) Agent-oriented programming. Artif Intell 60:51–92

Sørensen MH, Ziemke T (2007) Agents without agency? Cogn Semiot 1:102–124

Sumers TR, Horton JJ, Chilton LB (2023) A framework and benchmark for deep planning agents in open-world settings. arXiv: 2303.15469

Susskind J, Joshi R, Susskind D (2024) Agentic operating systems: principles and architecture. Stanford Digital Economy Lab Working Paper

Wang J, Liu B, Fu J, et al. (2024) AgentBench: evaluating LLMs as agents. Trans Mach Learn Res

Wang L, Ma C, Feng X, Zhang Z, Yang H, Zhang J, Chen Z, Tang J, Chen X, Lin Y, Zhao WX (2024) A survey on large language model based autonomous agents. Front Comput Sci 18(6):186345

Wei J, Wang X, Schuurmans D, Bosma M, Xia F, Chi E, Le QV, Zhou D (2022) Chain-of-thought prompting elicits reasoning in large language models. Adv Neural Inf Proces Syst 35:24824–24837

Weiss G (2000) Multiagent systems: a modern approach to distributed artificial intelligence. MIT Press, Cambridge, MA

Weng L (2023) LLM powered autonomous agents. Lil'Log. Retrieved from https://lilianweng.github.io/posts/2023-06-23-agent/

Woolridge M (2002) Introduction to MultiAgent systems. Wiley, New York

Wu C, Yin S, Wang W, et al. (2023) Reasoning with language model is planning with world model. arXiv: 2305.14992

Xi Z, Chen W, Gao S, et al. (2023) The rise and potential of large language model based agents: a survey. arXiv: 2309.07864

Yao S, Zhao J, Yu D, et al. (2022) ReAct: synergizing reasoning and acting in language models. arXiv: 2210.03629

Part IV
Expanding the Frontiers of AI

Chapter 9
The Best of Both Worlds: Neuro-Symbolic AI

Artificial intelligence is the science of making machines do
things that would require intelligence if done by humans.
—John McCarthy
Ideas are fleeting.
But sound reasoning lasts forever.
—John Nash

Combining neural networks with symbolic AI creates a hybrid system that uses the best of both approaches. Neural networks are excellent at learning patterns from data, while symbolic systems provide clear logic and reasoning. By merging these two methods, we can build AI that is more reliable, easier to understand, and better at handling different situations.

Neural networks have proven exceptionally effective at handling massive datasets and identifying intricate patterns, excelling in areas like image recognition and natural language processing. These systems, working through layers of interconnected nodes, translate raw input into meaningful outputs, though they require extensive training data. However, their "black box" nature, where the reasoning behind decisions remains opaque, presents significant challenges, particularly in fields like healthcare and autonomous driving where transparency is paramount.

In contrast, symbolic AI uses explicit symbols and rules to represent knowledge, making it ideal for logical reasoning, planning, and providing clear explanations. These systems can readily incorporate domain expertise, making them valuable for tasks requiring high-level reasoning. Yet, they struggle to efficiently process raw data at scale, limiting their use in data-heavy applications.

Neuro-symbolic AI provides a powerful solution by combining the strengths of both neural and symbolic approaches. This hybrid strategy allows for the creation of sophisticated AI systems capable of complex cognitive tasks with improved accuracy, transparency, and reliability. Many real-world applications demand both learning and reasoning capabilities. This fusion seeks to create AI systems that not only learn from data but also reason in a manner more akin to human cognition, effectively bridging the gap between pattern recognition and logical inference.

R. Akerkar, *Artificial Intelligence*, https://doi.org/10.1007/978-3-031-91084-5_9

Basics of Neuro-Symbolic AI

There aren't universally standardized "formal branches" of neuro-symbolic AI in the same way that classical AI has well-defined subfields (like machine learning, natural language processing, etc.). However, the field of neuro-symbolic AI is increasingly being structured around key functional areas and methodologies, which can be considered as emerging branches or pillars.

Let us see a detailed breakdown and Fig. 9.1 showing how the core functional areas of neuro-symbolic AI are interconnected:

1. Representation

This area focuses on how knowledge is encoded and structured. In neuro-symbolic systems, this often involves combining:

- **Neural representations** (like vector embeddings from deep learning models).
- **Symbolic structures** (like logic rules, graphs, or ontologies).

The challenge is to create representations that are both learnable from data and interpretable or manipulable by symbolic reasoning systems.

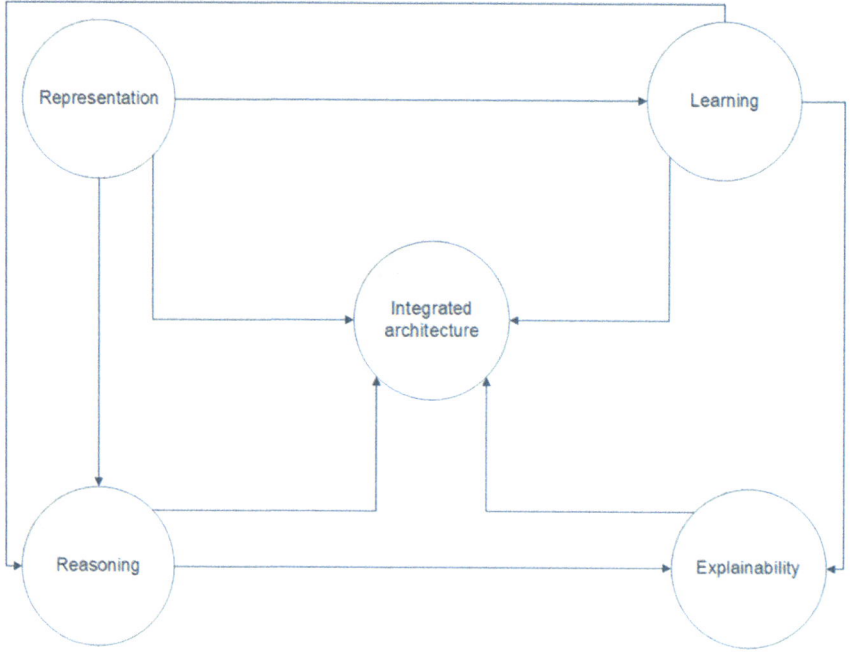

Fig. 9.1 Core functional areas of neuro-symbolic AI

2. Learning

Learning in neuro-symbolic AI involves training models that can incorporate symbolic knowledge into the learning process. This includes:

- Using symbolic constraints to guide neural learning.
- Learning symbolic rules from data.
- Jointly optimizing neural and symbolic components.

This branch aims to improve generalization, reduce data requirements, and ensure consistency with known rules or domain knowledge.

3. Reasoning

Reasoning is the ability to draw conclusions, make inferences, or solve problems using known information. In neuro-symbolic systems, reasoning can be:

- **Purely symbolic**, using logic engines or rule-based systems.
- **Guided by neural networks**, which help prioritize or approximate reasoning paths.
- **Hybrid**, where neural models generate hypotheses that are verified symbolically.

This area is crucial for tasks that require multi-step logic, such as planning, question answering, or theorem proving.

4. Explainability

One of the key motivations for neuro-symbolic AI is to make AI systems more transparent and interpretable. This area focuses on:

- Explaining decisions made by neural components using symbolic abstractions.
- Generating human-understandable justifications for actions or predictions.
- Structuring explanations hierarchically, from symbolic logic down to neural inputs.

Explainability is especially important in domains like healthcare, law, and finance, where trust and accountability are critical.

5. Integration Architectures

This area deals with how neural and symbolic components are combined in practice. There are several architectural approaches:

- **Tightly coupled systems**, where neural and symbolic parts are deeply integrated.
- **Loosely coupled systems**, where components operate independently and exchange information.
- **End-to-end differentiable systems**, where symbolic reasoning is embedded in a trainable neural framework.

Examples include Logic Tensor Networks, DeepProbLog, and neuro-symbolic concept learners.

Neuro-symbolic AI leverages the strengths of both neural networks and symbolic reasoning to support key cognitive functions. These algorithm-level features include large-scale perception, abstraction, analogy, and planning.

- **Large-Scale Perception:** Neural networks excel at processing vast amounts of raw data, extracting patterns, and efficiently performing tasks like image recognition and language understanding. This enables AI systems to handle extensive datasets and complex information effectively.
- **Abstraction:** Integrating symbolic reasoning allows AI systems to move beyond specific instances to general concepts, supporting higher-level cognitive functions such as analogy and reasoning. This enhances the system's ability to generalize and apply learned knowledge to new, similar contexts.
- **Analogy:** The explicit representation of knowledge in symbolic AI facilitates the drawing of analogies between different concepts, improving problem-solving and understanding. This capability is crucial for tasks requiring the identification of similarities and connections between seemingly unrelated ideas.
- **Long-Term Planning:** The integration of symbolic structures aids in long-term planning and decision-making by providing a clear framework for reasoning and projecting future states based on current knowledge. This helps AI systems devise and execute detailed, strategic plans.

Beyond algorithm-level capabilities, neuro-symbolic AI enhances application-level features that are essential for deploying AI systems in real-world scenarios. These features include user-explainability, domain constraints, scalability, and continual adaptation.

- **User-Explainability:** Tightly integrated neural and symbolic methods, such as end-to-end differentiable approaches, offer high user-explainability by providing transparent reasoning traces that end-users can understand. Federated pipelines, while effective for developers, offer medium explainability as they rely on the language model's comprehension of the input query.
- **Domain Constraints:** Symbolic structures allow for the imposition of domain-specific constraints, ensuring that AI systems adhere to established rules and guidelines. Methods with intertwined integration offer high domain-constraint capability by embedding these constraints directly into the learning process, enhancing system reliability and compliance with regulatory standards.
- **Scalability:** Neuro-symbolic methods, particularly those using large language models and federated pipelines, support scalability across various use cases. These systems can be adapted to different domains and continuously updated with new data and knowledge, making them versatile and effective in a wide range of applications.
- **Continual Adaptation:** Methods enabling end-to-end training and tightly coupled integration show high potential for continual adaptation. These systems can evolve with changes in the environment or domain requirements, maintaining their effectiveness and relevance over time by incorporating new information and adjusting to new conditions.

Core Concepts of Neuro-Symbolic AI

Neural networks, inspired by the structure and function of the human brain, are connectionist models that excel at learning from vast datasets through pattern recognition and statistical learning. They demonstrate remarkable proficiency in tasks such as image recognition, natural language processing, and speech recognition by automatically learning features and representations directly from raw data. In contrast, symbolic AI relies on rule-based systems, employing explicit rules, logic, and knowledge representations to perform reasoning and problem-solving. This approach utilizes predefined symbols and relationships to represent knowledge, enabling symbolic systems to perform deductive reasoning, inference, and the manipulation of abstract concepts, making them effective for tasks that require explicit understanding and manipulation of knowledge.

It's important to understand that the integration of neural networks and symbolic AI, as illustrated in Fig. 9.2, is not a monolithic concept. The combination of these two pillars can occur in various ways, and currently, there isn't a single, universally accepted approach. Researchers are actively exploring diverse strategies. One such strategy involves creating an upper layer composed of familiar symbols, which can then be used to generate more understandable explanations for the AI's outputs. This design also fosters "compositionality," enabling the systematic creation of complex modules from simpler components, a capability often lacking in pure neural network architectures. Conversely, another approach involves building a neural network on top of a traditional control circuit, which provides the neural network with its inputs. In this scenario, the circuit acts as a regulator, effectively limiting the search space for the neural network and guiding its learning process. These are just two examples of the many ways in which neural and symbolic approaches can be combined, highlighting the ongoing exploration and development within the field of neuro-symbolic AI.

Coupling of Neural Networks and Symbolic AI

Coupled neuro-symbolic systems are increasingly employed to tackle complex problems, including game playing and scene, word, and sentence interpretation. These systems can also improve sample efficiency of deep learning, for example, by using symbolic planning to achieve more data-efficient reinforcement learning, or by coupling vision and language understanding for improved data and memory efficiency. Furthermore, logic tensor networks are specifically designed to incorporate logical background knowledge to enhance image interpretation, and neural theorem provers can perform natural language reasoning by utilizing knowledge bases. This coupling can be achieved through various methods, including invoking deep learning systems within a symbolic algorithm or acquiring symbolic rules during the training process.

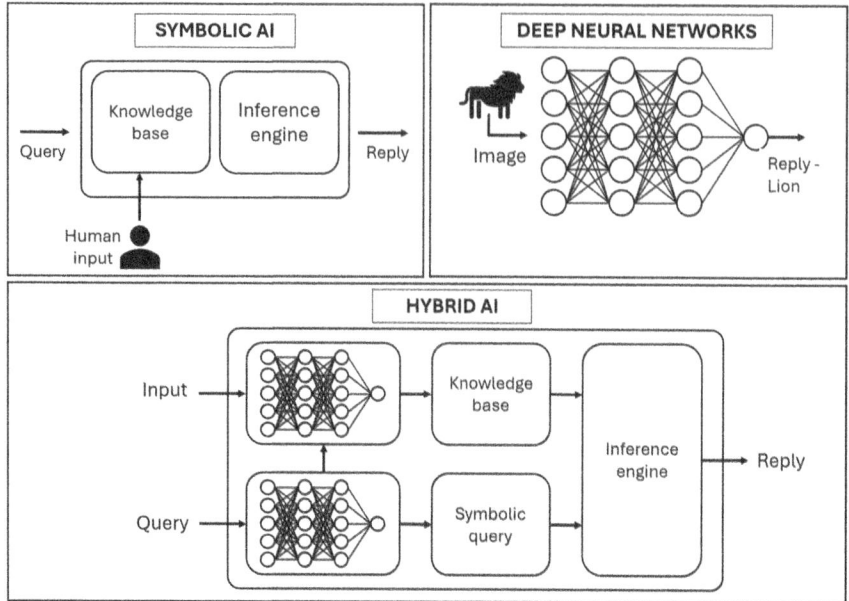

Fig. 9.2 Concept of neuro-symbolic AI

This integration of neural and symbolic approaches can be broadly categorized into several methods:

Symbolic Knowledge Coupling with Neural Networks:

- **Knowledge Injection:** This involves incorporating symbolic knowledge, such as rules or ontologies, into neural network training to improve learning efficiency and generalization. Symbolic constraints or priors are used to guide the neural network's learning process.
- **Neural-Symbolic Models:** These are hybrid models where neural networks handle perceptual tasks, like feature extraction, while symbolic components manage reasoning and decision-making.

Symbolic Reasoning on Neural Network Representations:

- **Neural Network Outputs as Symbols:** This approach utilizes the outputs or representations learned by neural networks as inputs to symbolic reasoning systems. For example, the internal representations of a neural network can be used to perform logical operations or inference.
- **Symbolic Interpretation of Neural Models:** This involves developing methods to interpret and extract symbolic information from neural network models, making their behaviour more transparent and understandable.

End-to-End Hybrid Models:

- **Unified Architectures:** This approach involves designing end-to-end systems that seamlessly integrate neural and symbolic components. These models can handle both data-driven learning and structured reasoning within a single framework.
- **Neuro-symbolic Reasoning Engines:** These systems combine neural and symbolic approaches to perform complex tasks, such as natural language understanding, where neural networks handle language processing and symbolic reasoning handles logical inference.

A Dual Approach Framework

The first major approach emphasizes compressing symbolic knowledge and integrating it with neural patterns. This method embeds structured symbolic knowledge directly into neural architectures, allowing systems to retain the benefits of explicit knowledge representation while leveraging the data processing capabilities of neural networks. Within this approach, compressed knowledge graph representation methods integrate structured knowledge graphs into neural frameworks. Knowledge graph embedding techniques convert these graphs into high-dimensional vector spaces using graph neural networks, making symbolic knowledge compatible with neural hidden representations. Knowledge graph masking techniques encode symbolic knowledge to align with neural inductive biases, such as by modifying attention matrices in transformer architectures to reflect knowledge relationships.

Complementing these knowledge graph methods are compressed formal logic techniques that incorporate logical reasoning capabilities into neural systems. Propositional logic methods compress logical statements into neural-compatible representations, enabling logical operations within neural processing. More advanced first-order logic methods use tensor factorization to represent complex logical relationships in formats that neural networks can process effectively, allowing for more nuanced reasoning capabilities.

The second major approach reverses this relationship, focusing on extracting neural patterns and mapping them into symbolic knowledge. This method leverages neural networks' pattern recognition capabilities to inform symbolic reasoning processes. Decoupled integration maintains separation between neural and symbolic components while establishing communication channels between them. Federated pipeline methods use neural networks to identify appropriate symbolic functions based on task requirements, then delegate specific reasoning tasks to specialized symbolic systems. Serialized pipeline methods create sequential workflows where neural and symbolic processes operate in succession, such as language models that feed into symbolic computation tools, combining their respective strengths in a coordinated sequence.

At a deeper level of integration, intertwined integration methods create seamless interaction between neural and symbolic components. Program abstraction induction techniques develop unified frameworks where neural and symbolic reasoning operate as complementary aspects of a single cognitive system. End-to-end differentiable methods take this integration further by enabling simultaneous optimization of both neural and symbolic components, allowing the entire system to learn holistically through gradient-based training.

Trustworthy Decision Intelligence

Building a trustworthy Decision Intelligence (DI) solution to create systems that are not only accurate but also transparent, explainable, and robust. Trustworthiness in this context stems from the ability of the system to justify its decisions, handle uncertainty, adapt to new situations, and align with human values and ethical considerations.

The process begins with clearly defining the decision problem and identifying the relevant data sources. Neural networks are then employed to learn patterns, extract features, and make predictions from the data. These predictions, however, are not directly used for decision-making. Instead, they are often translated into symbolic representations that can be understood and processed by the symbolic reasoning engine.

Knowledge representation is a crucial aspect. Symbolic components allow for the explicit encoding of domain knowledge, rules, constraints, and ethical guidelines in a structured and human-readable format. This knowledge base acts as a guiding framework for the decision-making process. The neural network's outputs, once converted into symbols, can be used to query and reason within this knowledge base. For instance, a neural network might predict a customer's likelihood to default on a loan. This prediction, along with symbolic representations of the customer's financial history and relevant lending regulations encoded in the knowledge base, can be fed into a symbolic reasoner.

The symbolic reasoning engine then uses logical inference to arrive at a decision, such as whether to approve or reject the loan. The key advantage here is that the reasoning process is transparent. The system can trace back the steps of its deduction, showing exactly which rules, facts, and neural network outputs led to the final decision. This explainability is paramount for building trust, especially in high-stakes applications.

Furthermore, neuro-symbolic systems can handle uncertainty more effectively. While neural networks can provide probabilistic outputs, the symbolic component can incorporate formal methods for reasoning under uncertainty, such as probabilistic logic or Bayesian networks. This allows the DI solution to make more informed decisions when faced with incomplete or ambiguous information.

Adaptability is another crucial element of trustworthiness. The symbolic knowledge base can be updated and refined as new information becomes available or regulations change, without requiring retraining of the entire neural network. This modularity makes the system more agile and easier to maintain. Additionally, the explicit representation of knowledge allows for easier integration of human expertise and feedback into the decision-making process. If a decision seems counterintuitive or violates an ethical principle, the underlying rules and knowledge can be examined and modified.

To ensure alignment with human values, ethical guidelines can be explicitly encoded within the symbolic knowledge base. The reasoning engine can then be designed to prioritize decisions that adhere to these guidelines. This helps to mitigate the risk of biased or unfair outcomes that can sometimes arise from purely data-driven neural networks.

Structure Learning in Neuro-Symbolic AI Systems

Structure learning represents one of the most challenging and important aspects of neuro-symbolic AI development. Structure learning involves discovering the underlying relationships, rules, and organizational principles from data that can then be represented in symbolic form.

There are several key approaches to performing structure learning in neuro-symbolic systems, each with distinct advantages and applications.

Neural-guided symbolic search is a technique where neural networks guide the exploration of possible symbolic structures. In this approach, neural components evaluate candidate symbolic structures and direct the search toward promising regions of the structure space. For example, AlphaGo's policy networks guide Monte Carlo Tree Search by suggesting high probability moves. This technique can be implemented by training neural networks to predict the utility of different symbolic operations or structures, effectively pruning the search space of possible symbolic representations to make structure learning computationally feasible.

Differentiable relaxation methods transform discrete symbolic structures into continuous approximations that can be optimized using gradient-based techniques. By creating differentiable versions of symbolic operations, these methods allow end-to-end training through backpropagation. For instance, fuzzy logic systems replace crisp logical operations with continuous approximations that can be optimized alongside neural parameters. Similarly, differentiable parsing techniques like that used in differentiable neural computers (DNCs) allow gradient-based optimization to discover grammatical rules or other structured representations.

Inductive logic programming (ILP) enhanced with neural components offers another powerful approach to structure learning. Traditional ILP systems learn logical rules from examples and background knowledge but struggle with noisy data. Neural components can improve robustness by scoring candidate logical rules based on their consistency with observed patterns in data. This neural-symbolic synergy allows the system to induce logical rules that might be missed by purely symbolic approaches while maintaining the interpretability of explicit logical representations.

Generative models for structure discovery use variational autoencoders or other generative approaches to discover latent symbolic structures in data. These models learn to encode data into structurally meaningful representations that can be decoded back to reconstruct the original inputs. The constraints placed on these latent representations encourage the emergence of interpretable symbolic structures. For example, relational variational autoencoders can discover object relationships that can be explicitly represented in symbolic form.

Graph neural networks (GNNs) provide a natural framework for structure learning by operating directly on relational data represented as graphs. By learning to predict edges, node properties, or graph transformations, GNNs can discover structural patterns that can be translated into symbolic rules or knowledge graphs. This approach has proven effective in domains like molecular chemistry, where the goal is to discover structural relationships that can be represented in chemical formulas or reaction rules.

Neuro-symbolic concept learners combine perception and reasoning to discover structured concepts from raw sensory data. These systems learn to map visual or other perceptual inputs to symbolic concepts and relationships through joint training of perceptual and reasoning components. For example, a neuro-symbolic concept learner might discover that the concept "tower" consists of objects stacked vertically with certain stability constraints, allowing it to both recognize and reason about towers.

The implementation of structure learning typically follows several key steps:

First, define the hypothesis space of possible symbolic structures appropriate for the domain. This might include first-order logic rules, probabilistic graphical models, formal grammar, or knowledge graphs. The choice of representation constrains the types of structures that can be learned.

Next, design neural architecture that can process the input data and produce outputs relevant to the symbolic structures being learned. This might involve convolutional networks for images, transformers for language, or graph neural networks for relational data.

Create a bridge between neural outputs and symbolic structures through differentiable operations or score functions that allow information to flow between the neural and symbolic components. This is crucial for joint optimization of the entire system.

Implement a learning algorithm that uses neural outputs to guide the search or optimization of symbolic structures. This might involve gradient-based optimization for differentiable structures, search algorithms guided by neural heuristics, or expectation-maximization approaches that alternate between updating neural and symbolic components.

Incorporate inductive biases that encourage the discovery of meaningful structures. These might include sparsity constraints, modularity biases, or hierarchical organization principles that help the system discover parsimonious and generalizable symbolic representations.

Finally, design evaluation metrics that assess not only the predictive accuracy of the learned structures but also their interpretability, generalizability to new situations, and efficiency in reasoning tasks. This multi-faceted evaluation helps ensure that the learned structures capture meaningful knowledge rather than superficial patterns.

Several practical challenges must be addressed when implementing structure learning in neuro-symbolic systems. The search space of possible symbolic structures grows exponentially with problem complexity, requiring efficient search strategies or approximations. Noisy or incomplete data can lead to incorrect symbolic structures, necessitating robust learning approaches that can handle uncertainty. The interface between neural and symbolic components often involves non-differentiable operations, requiring specialized optimization techniques or approximations.

Recent advances in structure learning include techniques like neural theorem provers, which learn to prove theorems by guiding symbolic proof search with neural networks. Neuro-symbolic program synthesis systems discover structured programs that explain observed data by combining neural program induction with symbolic execution. Concept bottleneck models learn explicit symbolic concepts as an intermediate representation between perception and decision-making, allowing for interpretable reasoning while maintaining high performance.

The following manufacturing example demonstrates how structure learning enables discovering hierarchical task relationships and logical dependencies in procedural domains. Consider an autonomous robot in a smart factory learning assembly task dependencies. Initially, it observes that certain actions consistently precede others—components are retrieved before assembly, quality checks follow assembly, and packaging occurs last. The neural component extracts spatial and temporal patterns from sensor data, while the symbolic component constructs a task dependency graph encoding rules like "IF component$_A$ is attached THEN component$_B$ can be mounted." As experience accumulates, the system refines this structure by discovering conditional dependencies; some steps are optional based on product variants, others mandatory. The learned structure becomes interpretable workflow rules that engineers can audit. This enables the robot to generalize beyond memorized sequences, reasoning about novel configurations by applying learned structural constraints rather than relying solely on pattern matching.

Neuro-Symbolic Reinforcement Learning

Neuro-symbolic Reinforcement Learning is a new development in AI research, addressing limitations of usual deep reinforcement learning (DRL) by integrating symbolic reasoning capabilities with neural learning systems (see Fig. 9.3). This hybrid approach creates intelligent agents that can both learn from experience and reason about their environment using explicit knowledge representation.

Traditional DRL has demonstrated better achievements in domains ranging from game playing to robotic control, yet it suffers from several persistent challenges. These include data inefficiency, requiring millions of training examples; limited interpretability, with decision processes hidden within neural network "black boxes;" poor transfer learning capabilities across different tasks; and difficulties incorporating prior knowledge or constraints. Neuro-symbolic RL directly addresses these

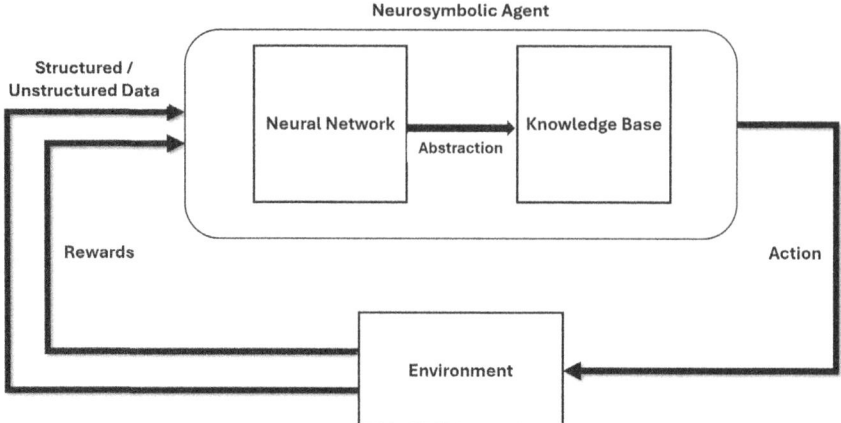

Fig. 9.3 Learning for reasoning reinforcement learning model

limitations by combining the complementary strengths of neural and symbolic approaches.

Neuro-symbolic RL integrates planning-style control-flow instructions with atomic actions learned via deep neural networks. This creates a two-level hierarchy of decision-making: high-level symbolic policies manage overall strategy and planning, while low-level neural components handle perception and execution of primitive actions. For instance, in navigational tasks, symbolic components might determine the sequence of rooms to visit based on explicit goals and constraints, while neural networks handle the continuous control required to movement through doorways or around obstacles.

This integration manifests through several architectural approaches. In hierarchical neuro-symbolic RL, symbolic planners operate at higher abstraction levels to decompose complex tasks into simpler subtasks that neural controllers can execute. The Stanford Research Institute Problem Solver (STRIPS) framework has been adapted to create symbolic action schemas that coordinate with learned neural policies, enabling long-horizon planning impossible with purely neural approaches.

Another approach uses symbolic knowledge to guide exploration and learning. By incorporating domain knowledge represented as logic rules or constraints, these systems can dramatically reduce the search space of possible policies. For example, in chemistry applications, symbolic knowledge about valid molecular transformations can constrain exploration to only chemically feasible reactions, allowing the neural components to focus learning resources on promising directions rather than wasting experience on impossible states.

Knowledge distillation represents a third integration method, where symbolic knowledge is transformed into neural representations or vice versa. Neural networks can learn to approximate symbolic reasoning processes, while symbolic rules can be extracted from trained neural networks to create interpretable knowledge bases. This bidirectional knowledge transfer allows continuous refinement of both components, with each improving the other through ongoing interaction.

One of the most significant advantages of neuro-symbolic RL is improved sample efficiency. By incorporating symbolic reasoning, these systems require far fewer environmental interactions to achieve competent performance. The symbolic component provides structured guidance through logical constraints and planning, effectively reducing the exploration burden on the neural learning component. Studies have demonstrated orders-of-magnitude reductions in required training data compared to pure DRL approaches in complex domains like hierarchical task planning.

Interpretability and explainability constitute another crucial advantage. While traditional DRL models operate as black boxes, neuro-symbolic approaches maintain explicit symbolic representations of learned policies and domain knowledge. These symbolic components can generate human-understandable explanations of decisions and learning processes. For instance, a neuro-symbolic agent navigating a complex environment can explain its route choice through a combination of symbolic reasoning steps ("I'm avoiding room A because it contains a hazard") and learned preferences ("I've found that path B is more reliable based on past experience").

The generalization capabilities of neuro-symbolic RL are particularly noteworthy. The symbolic representation of knowledge facilitates transfer learning across different tasks and environments. By abstracting domain-invariant concepts and relationships into symbolic form, these systems can apply learned knowledge to novel scenarios without extensive retraining. For example, an agent trained to manipulate objects in a simulated environment can transfer abstract knowledge about physical relationships to real-world robotic manipulation tasks through the shared symbolic representation of physical concepts like "support," "containment," or "stability."

However, interface design between neural and symbolic components remains complex, particularly in establishing bidirectional communication channels that preserve the strengths of each approach. Symbol grounding, connecting abstract symbols to their manifestations in sensory data, requires sophisticated perception capabilities. Additionally, designing appropriate symbolic representations that balance expressiveness with computational efficiency represents a challenge.

Learning for Reasoning

The Learning for Reasoning framework is an approach to reinforcement learning that combines neural and symbolic components to enhance an agent's reasoning capabilities. In this architecture, the division of labour between neural and symbolic elements is distinct and purposeful: neural networks serve as supportive co-actors that handle processing tasks, while the symbolic system takes primary responsibility for reasoning operations.

Deep neural networks play a crucial role in this framework by performing symbolic space compression. This compression function is vital because symbolic reasoning systems typically face challenges with large state spaces and complex environments. By compressing the symbolic space, neural networks reduce the computational burden associated with symbolic reasoning, significantly accelerating the learning process and improving the system's overall efficiency. This allows the framework to tackle more complex reasoning tasks than either approach could handle independently.

One of the most valuable capabilities of this hybrid approach emerges when handling unstructured data, which presents a significant challenge for traditional symbolic systems. Deep neural networks excel at pattern recognition and feature extraction from raw, unstructured inputs such as images, audio, or natural language text. Within the Learning for Reasoning framework, neural components transform this unstructured information into structured, symbolic representations that the symbolic reasoning system can effectively manipulate. For example, when processing visual scenes, the neural network might identify objects, their properties, and spatial relationships, converting these into symbolic predicates that the reasoning component can use for logical inference.

The framework also addresses a common limitation of purely neural approaches to reinforcement learning: the difficulty in verifying learned policies. By facilitating the transfer of learned policies from neural components to the symbolic system, the Learning for Reasoning approach makes it possible to formally analyse and verify the agent's decision-making processes. This verification capability is particularly important in safety-critical applications where understanding and ensuring the correctness of an agent's behaviour is essential.

What distinguishes this framework from other neuro-symbolic approaches is its serialized integration pattern. Rather than deeply intertwining neural and symbolic processing or running them in parallel, the Learning for Reasoning framework implements a sequential flow of information. Typically, the neural network first processes inputs and transforms them into a symbolic representation, which is then passed to the symbolic system for reasoning. This serialized architecture maintains a clear separation between the two components while allowing them to complement each other's strengths.

The serialized approach offers several advantages, including modularity (components can be developed and optimized independently), interpretability (the interface between neural and symbolic systems provides a natural inspection point), and incremental development (either component can be improved without necessitating a complete redesign of the entire system). It also aligns well with cognitive science theories that suggest human reasoning often involves transforming perceptual inputs into symbolic representations before applying logical reasoning.

In practical applications, this framework has shown promise in domains requiring both perceptual processing and complex reasoning, such as robot navigation in unstructured environments, game playing with hidden information, and intelligent tutoring systems that must interpret student actions while reasoning about their knowledge state. By integrating the pattern recognition strengths of neural networks with the explicit reasoning capabilities of symbolic systems in a serialized work-flow, the Learning for Reasoning framework represents an important advancement in creating reinforcement learning agents capable of sophisticated cognitive tasks.

Reasoning for Learning

The Reasoning for Learning framework represents a distinct approach to integrating symbolic and neural components in reinforcement learning systems. Unlike the Learning for Reasoning model, which primarily uses neural networks to support symbolic reasoning, this framework flips the relationship by employing symbolic models to enhance neural network outputs.

The Reasoning for Learning approach leverages structured knowledge from symbolic systems to refine both the performance and interpretability of deep neural networks. The symbolic component plays a crucial role in reward shaping—a technique that provides additional feedback signals to guide the learning process. Traditional reinforcement learning often struggles with sparse rewards, where meaningful feedback might only occur after many actions. By incorporating symbolic knowledge about the domain, the system can generate intermediate rewards that align with higher-level goals and constraints, helping the neural network learn more efficiently.

This reward shaping mechanism accelerates the learning process by providing more informative feedback at each step. For example, in a robotic manipulation task, instead of receiving rewards only upon successfully grasping an object, the symbolic system might provide incremental rewards for approaching the object correctly, orienting the gripper appropriately, and applying suitable pressure—all based on symbolic knowledge about physical manipulation principles.

Another significant contribution of the symbolic system in this framework is the creation of programmatic policies. Rather than relying solely on the neural network's implicit representation of the learned policy, the symbolic component helps express the policy in a more structured, programmatic form. This transformation dramatically increases the model's interpretability and explicability, allowing humans to understand, verify, and potentially modify the learned behaviour.

The Reasoning for Learning model's distinctive feature is its parallel architecture. Unlike the serialized approach of Learning for Reasoning, here the neural and symbolic components operate concurrently, with the symbolic system continuously providing guidance to the neural learning process. This parallel design allows for real-time integration of symbolic knowledge into the learning process, creating a more dynamic and responsive system.

Learning-Reasoning Reinforcement Learning

The Learning-Reasoning Reinforcement Learning framework represents perhaps the most sophisticated integration of neural and symbolic approaches. This model establishes a bidirectional interaction between the components, where outputs from one system serve as inputs to the other in a continuous feedback loop.

This bidirectional architecture synthesizes the strengths of both the Learning for Reasoning and Reasoning for Learning approaches. The symbolic element contributes structured knowledge to the neural networks, enhancing their interpretability and efficiency. Meanwhile, the neural component compresses and streamlines the symbolic space, enabling faster convergence for symbolic reasoning processes.

The collaborative operation of these components in a bidirectional manner creates several advantages. The system can leverage neural pattern recognition to identify relevant features in complex environments, which then inform symbolic reasoning processes. Simultaneously, symbolic reasoning can provide structured guidance to neural learning, focusing attention on important aspects of the problem space and incorporating domain knowledge that might be difficult to learn from data alone.

This bidirectional exchange creates a virtuous cycle where each component continuously improves the other. Symbolic reasoning helps neural networks learn more efficiently by providing structure and prior knowledge, while neural learning helps symbolic systems handle uncertainty and complexity by providing robust feature extraction and pattern recognition.

The result is a highly capable system that combines the strengths of both approaches while mitigating their individual weaknesses. The Learning-Reasoning model offers enhanced interpretability and explicability compared to pure neural approaches, faster learning and better generalization than pure symbolic methods, and more robust performance in complex environments than either approach alone.

A concrete example of this approach might be an autonomous vehicle system where neural networks process sensor data to recognize objects, road conditions, and traffic patterns, while symbolic components handle reasoning about traffic rules, planning routes, and making safety-critical decisions. The neural outputs (object recognition, road condition assessment) feed into the symbolic reasoner, while symbolic outputs (relevant traffic rules, navigation waypoints) help guide the neural systems' attention and interpretation of sensory data.

This bidirectional integration represents a significant step toward artificial intelligence systems that can combine the perceptual power and adaptability of neural networks with the transparent reasoning and knowledge representation of symbolic AI. By facilitating continuous exchange between these complementary approaches, the Learning-Reasoning framework offers a promising path toward more capable, interpretable, and trustworthy reinforcement learning systems.

Injecting Symbolic Knowledge into a Neural Network

Injecting symbolic knowledge into a neural network can be particularly beneficial in scenarios where domain-specific rules and logical relationships are crucial for accurate decision-making. One such scenario is in the field of medical diagnosis. In medical diagnosis, accurate and reliable decision-making is critical. A neuro-symbolic AI system can leverage both the pattern recognition capabilities of neural networks and the logical reasoning strengths of symbolic AI to enhance diagnostic accuracy. Here's how injecting symbolic knowledge can be beneficial:

1. **Symbolic Knowledge**: Medical knowledge, such as the relationships between symptoms, diseases, and treatments, can be represented in a knowledge graph. This graph includes logical rules, such as "if a patient has a persistent cough and fever, they might have pneumonia."
2. **Neural Network**: The neural network processes patient data, including medical records, lab results, and imaging data, to identify patterns and generate embeddings that capture the semantic meaning of the information.
3. **Integration**: By injecting symbolic knowledge into the neural network, the system can use the logical rules from the knowledge graph to guide its decision-making process. For example, if the neural network identifies a pattern of symptoms, the symbolic knowledge can help validate the diagnosis by checking against known medical rules.

Using Logical Constraints to Guide Training

Logical constraints can be used to guide the training of a neural network, ensuring that the learned representations adhere to domain-specific rules and improve the system's interpretability and reliability. Here's how this can be done for a specific task:

1. **Define Logical Constraints**: Identify the logical rules and constraints relevant to the task. For example, in medical diagnosis, a constraint might be "if a patient has symptom A and symptom B, then the probability of disease X should be high."
2. **Incorporate Constraints into Loss Function**: Modify the neural network's loss function to include penalties for violating the logical constraints. This ensures that the network learns to respect the rules during training. For example, the loss function can be augmented with a term that penalizes the network if the predicted probability of disease X is low when both symptom A and symptom B are present.
3. **Training Process**: During training, the neural network optimizes the loss function, which now includes both the standard prediction error and the penalties for constraint violations. This encourages the network to learn representations that are not only accurate but also consistent with the logical rules.

4. **Validation and Refinement**: After training, validate the network's performance on a separate dataset to ensure that it adheres to the logical constraints and performs well on the task. If necessary, refine the constraints and retrain the network to improve performance.

Example: Diagnosing Pneumonia

Let's consider a specific example of diagnosing pneumonia:

Logical Constraints: Define constraints such as "if a patient has a persistent cough, fever, and shortness of breath, then the probability of pneumonia should be high."

Loss Function: Modify the loss function to include a penalty term for cases where the network predicts a low probability of pneumonia despite the presence of the specified symptoms. The loss function might look like this:

$$\text{Loss} = \text{Prediction Error} + \lambda \cdot \text{Constraint Violation Penalty},$$

where λ is a hyperparameter that controls the weight of the penalty term.

Training: Train the neural network on patient data, optimizing the modified loss function. The network learns to make accurate predictions while respecting the logical constraints.

Validation: Validate the trained network on a separate dataset to ensure it correctly identifies pneumonia cases and adheres to the logical constraints.

By injecting symbolic knowledge and using logical constraints, the neuro-symbolic AI system can achieve higher accuracy, reliability, and interpretability in medical diagnosis, ultimately leading to better patient outcomes.

Knowledge Graphs and Neuro-Symbolic AI

Knowledge Graphs

Knowledge graphs originate from Tim Berners-Lee's vision of a machine-processable web of data that would augment the original web of human-readable documents.

Knowledge Graphs (KGs) have emerged as a compelling abstraction for organizing the world's structured knowledge, and as a way to integrate information extracted from multiple data sources. Knowledge Graphs are a way to represent and organize information in a graph structure, where entities (such as objects, events, or concepts) are nodes, and the relationships between them are edges. This structure allows for a rich, interconnected representation of data, making it easier to understand and query complex relationships. For example, in a knowledge graph about movies, nodes could represent actors, directors, films, and genres, while edges could represent relationships like "acted in," "directed by," or "belongs to." Google's Knowledge Graph is a well-known example, enhancing search results by understanding the context and relationships between different pieces of information.

Domain knowledge expressed in KGs is being input into machine learning models to produce better predictions.

Definition A directed labelled graph is a 4-tuple $G = (N, E, L, f)$, where N is a set of nodes, $E \subseteq N \times N$ is a set of edges, L is a set of labels, and $f: E \rightarrow L$, is an assignment function from edges to labels. An assignment of a label B to an edge $E = (A,C)$ can be viewed as a triple (A, B, C).

Definition A knowledge graph is a directed labelled graph in which we have associated domain-specific meanings with nodes and edges.

The foundational standard for representing knowledge graphs is the Resource Description Framework (RDF), which structures information as a collection of triples. Each triple asserts that a specific semantic resource, known as the subject, has a particular semantic relationship, referred to as the predicate or property, with either a literal value or another semantic resource, which is the object. Both resources and properties are uniquely identified using Internationalized Resource Names (IRNs), while literal values typically utilize datatypes defined by XML Schema Definition (XSD). A specific property, rdf:type, allows for the declaration that one resource is an instance of another, as illustrated by the example of "dbpedia:Tim Berners-Lee" being an "foaf:Person," where prefixes are used to abbreviate the IRNs. Standardized formats facilitate the exchange of RDF data, and the JSON-LD standard enhances JavaScript Object Notation (JSON) with semantic tags, enabling easy sharing of RDF data through web APIs.

RDF Schema (RDFS) builds upon RDF by introducing terms, also represented as IRNs, that enhance the richness and precision of knowledge graphs. For instance, RDFS allows the definition of hierarchical relationships between resource types, such as stating that a "toxic fume" is a type of "pollution," and between properties, like indicating that being a "nurse" is a form of being a "healthcare worker." Furthermore, RDFS enables the specification of the expected types for the subjects and objects associated with particular properties, such as the rule that only "living things" can be the subject of the property "poisoned." The meaning of these RDFS terms is formally defined through axioms and entailment rules. The Web Ontology Language

(OWL) extends RDFS further by providing even more precise semantics and enabling automated reasoning, although this comes at the cost of increased computational complexity, making OWL most suitable for smaller, more focused semantic datasets known as ontologies. A key application of ontologies is to precisely define and interrelate the resource types and properties used to structure and give meaning to larger knowledge graphs. These ontologies, even when expressed less formally using RDFS, are often referred to as vocabularies.

Simple Protocol and RDF Query Language (SPARQL) allows both users and programs to retrieve information from knowledge graphs, with results presented as tables, yes/no answers, or even new knowledge graphs. Additionally, SPARQL Update enables the modification of knowledge graphs through the addition or removal of triples. SPARQL is supported by native RDF database management systems, often called triple stores, as well as by wrappers that present tabular and other data from legacy databases as knowledge graphs, whether through downloadable RDF files, online SPARQL endpoints, or other methods.

The principles of Linked Open Data (LOD) offer further guidance for the creation and sharing of knowledge graphs. These principles include: sharing graphs using standard formats and protocols like RDF, RDFS, OWL, and SPARQL; using Internationalized Resource Names (IRNs) to identify resources (nodes) and properties (edges); making these IRNs de-referenceable Internationalized Resource Identifiers (IRIs) that can be accessed on the web to provide further information about the resource in RDF format; and utilizing standard IRNs defined in vocabularies as types and properties within the graphs. While knowledge graphs can also be stored and processed using property graph databases and other technologies outside of these semantic standards, RDF and SPARQL remain commonly used for the exchange of information even in these contexts.

Knowledge graph quality is crucial for the effectiveness of neuro-symbolic AI systems, as it directly impacts the accuracy, reliability, and interpretability of the AI's reasoning processes. High-quality knowledge graphs ensure that the data and relationships they represent are accurate, complete, and up to date, which is essential for making informed decisions and generating reliable insights.

Quality Metrics for Knowledge Graphs.

Several metrics are used to evaluate the quality of knowledge graphs:

1. **Accuracy**: Measures the correctness of the information in the knowledge graph. This involves verifying that the entities and relationships accurately reflect real-world data.
2. **Completeness**: Assesses whether the knowledge graph includes all relevant entities and relationships. A complete knowledge graph should cover the entire domain it represents.
3. **Consistency**: Ensures that the knowledge graph does not contain contradictory information. Consistency checks help maintain logical coherence within the graph.

4. **Timeliness**: Evaluates how up to date the information in the knowledge graph is. Timely updates are crucial for maintaining the relevance of the data.
5. **Coverage**: Measures the extent to which the knowledge graph represents the domain of interest. High coverage indicates that the graph includes a wide range of relevant entities and relationships.
6. **Connectivity**: Assesses the degree of interlinking between entities in the knowledge graph. Well-connected graphs facilitate better reasoning and inference.

Benchmarks for Knowledge Graphs.

Benchmarks are used to evaluate and compare the performance of knowledge graphs. Some common benchmarks include:

1. **DBpedia**: A large-scale, multi-lingual knowledge graph extracted from Wikipedia. It is widely used for benchmarking due to its extensive coverage and rich set of entities and relationships.
2. **Wikidata**: A collaboratively edited knowledge graph that serves as a central storage for structured data. It is used for benchmarking due to its high accuracy and completeness.
3. **YAGO**: A knowledge graph that combines information from Wikipedia and WordNet. It is known for its high accuracy and consistency.
4. **Google Knowledge Graph**: A proprietary knowledge graph used by Google to enhance search results. It is known for its high timeliness and coverage.

Challenges of Knowledge Graphs in AI

Knowledge graphs face some challenges in AI applications, primarily stemming from data integration, scalability, and dynamic reasoning. Integrating heterogeneous data sources often leads to inconsistencies in formats, naming conventions, and schemas, requiring labour-intensive cleanup and alignment efforts. For instance, merging entries like "P. Nath" and "Paresh Nath" from different datasets demands manual intervention or fuzzy matching algorithms to resolve discrepancies. Ensuring data quality becomes increasingly complex as outdated or conflicting information accumulates, particularly in domains like healthcare or logistics where accuracy is critical. Scalability issues emerge as graphs expand, with query performance degrading when traversing billions of nodes. While graph databases like Neo4j help, maintaining real-time updates and efficient indexing for rapid relationship navigation remains challenging.

Schema design poses another obstacle, as developers must balance specificity with flexibility when defining ontologies. Creating precise relationships like "drug treats disease" requires domain expertise and iterative adjustments, especially when incorporating new data types such as social media handles into existing frameworks. Maintenance burdens escalate with the need for continuous updates, version control, and compliance measures for sensitive data, exemplified by HIPAA requirements for patient records. Furthermore, knowledge graphs struggle with implicit reasoning and contextual ambiguity. While they excel at representing explicit connections, they cannot inherently deduce unstated relationships like inferring language preferences from geographical data without external rules or machine learning models.

Interoperability challenges arise when aligning disparate systems, as seen in mapping "customer" from sales databases to "client" in support systems, often necessitating custom transformation pipelines. Real-time applications face limitations due to the static nature of traditional knowledge graphs, requiring specialized infrastructure for dynamic data streams like package tracking updates. Finally, their effectiveness diminishes in complex decision-making scenarios requiring optimization algorithms or workflow management, areas where composite AI approaches integrating decision trees and constraint-based reasoning prove more suitable. These multi-faceted challenges underscore the importance of combining knowledge graphs with complementary AI techniques to overcome their inherent limitations.

Neuro-Symbolic AI for Reasoning over Knowledge Graphs

Neuro-symbolic AI leverages neural networks for their ability to learn from data and recognize patterns, while incorporating symbolic reasoning to handle abstract concepts and logical rules. This combination enables AI systems to perform more sophisticated reasoning tasks over knowledge graphs. For example, neural networks can be used to generate embeddings for entities and relationships in a knowledge graph, capturing their semantic meaning. These embeddings can then be used in symbolic reasoning processes to infer new relationships, answer complex queries, and make predictions.

One approach in neuro-symbolic AI is logically informed embedding, where neural networks are trained to produce embeddings that respect logical constraints. This ensures that the learned representations are not only useful for pattern recognition but also adhere to logical rules, enhancing their interpretability and reliability. Another approach involves embedding with logical constraints, where neural networks are guided by predefined logical rules during training, ensuring that the resulting embeddings are consistent with expert knowledge.

Rule learning is another key aspect of neuro-symbolic AI, where symbolic reasoning methods are used to learn logical rules from data. These rules can then be applied to knowledge graphs to perform reasoning tasks, such as inferring new relationships or validating existing ones. By combining rule learning with neural network-based embeddings, neuro-symbolic AI systems can achieve a balance between learning from data and reasoning based on logical rules. The quality of knowledge graphs significantly influences the performance of neuro-symbolic AI systems. High-quality knowledge graphs provide accurate and comprehensive data, which enhances the AI's ability to reason and make informed decisions. For example, in a medical diagnosis system, a high-quality knowledge graph can provide accurate information about diseases, symptoms, and treatments, enabling the AI to make reliable diagnoses.

Knowledge Graphs for Human-Centric Aspects of Neuro-Symbolic AI

Knowledge graphs are essential for advancing the human-centred aspects of neuro-symbolic AI systems. By integrating structured and interconnected data, they enhance the AI's ability to understand, reason, and interact with humans in more meaningful and context-aware ways. Below are some key applications:

Explainability and Transparency

Knowledge graphs make AI systems more interpretable by offering clear, logical explanations for how decisions are made. It improves the explainability of AI decisions by providing structured, contextualized, and interconnected data representations. Their ability to capture relationships between entities and concepts enables AI systems to reason, interpret, and justify their outputs more effectively. Knowledge graphs enrich AI systems with contextual information by representing data as nodes (entities) and edges (relationships). This structure allows AI models to understand the meaning and dependencies within the data, improving the accuracy and relevance of predictions. For instance, in natural language processing (NLP), a knowledge graph can help disambiguate terms like "Jaguar" by linking it to either an animal or a car brand based on context.

Knowledge graphs provide data lineage, enabling users to trace the origin, transformations, and usage of data within AI models. This transparency helps build trust in AI systems by allowing stakeholders to audit the data feeding into the models, particularly in regulated industries. By leveraging relationships and connections within data, knowledge graphs enable graph-based feature engineering. These features maximize predictive power while broadening the applicability of machine learning models across diverse domains. This structured approach reduces false positives and increases model reliability.

In order to facilitate counterfactual analysis, knowledge graphs allow domain experts to investigate model outputs through counterfactual analysis. By exploring hierarchies and dependencies in the graph structure, experts can debug anomalies or test hypotheses, making AI systems more interpretable and trustworthy.

Knowledge graphs contribute to explainable AI (XAI) at various stages:

- **Pre-model:** Extracting features and relationships from raw data.
- **In-model:** Enhancing reasoning capabilities during model training.
- **Post-model:** Providing insights into predictions through graph-based reasoning.

By integrating semantic links into generative processes, they reduce hallucinations and inaccuracies while backing answers with factual relationships. This helps grounding generative AI outputs. Moreover, by organizing diverse data sources into unified views, knowledge graphs enable AI systems to provide clear explanations for complex decisions. This capability fosters trust among non-technical users by making technical outputs comprehensible.

Enhanced User Interaction
Leveraging the rich, interconnected data within knowledge graphs allows AI systems to deliver personalized and context-sensitive interactions. This makes user experiences more intuitive and relevant. For example, a virtual assistant can utilize a knowledge graph to understand user preferences and provide tailored recommendations.

Improved Reasoning and Inference
Knowledge graphs empower AI systems to perform complex reasoning by connecting diverse pieces of information. This is especially valuable in fields requiring deep logical inference, such as legal analysis or scientific research. For example, in legal tech, a neuro-symbolic AI can use a knowledge graph to link case laws, statutes, and legal principles to deliver comprehensive legal advice.

Commonsense Reasoning
Incorporating commonsense knowledge into AI systems helps them better understand everyday human contexts. Knowledge graphs encode this type of knowledge, enabling more human-like inferences. For example, an AI system can use a knowledge graph to infer that "if it is raining, people are likely to carry umbrellas," leading to more relevant suggestions.

Trust and Compliance
Knowledge graphs ensure that AI systems adhere to ethical guidelines and regulatory standards by embedding policies and compliance rules directly into their structure. This is particularly critical in sensitive domains like finance and healthcare.

Continuous Learning and Adaptation
By seamlessly integrating new information, knowledge graphs enable AI systems to continuously learn and adapt to evolving knowledge and contexts. For example, in cybersecurity, a neuro-symbolic AI system can leverage a knowledge graph to stay updated on the latest threats and adjust its defence strategies accordingly.

Knowledge Graphs and LLMs in Neuro-Symbolic AI

The fusion of knowledge graphs and large language models (LLMs) in neuro-symbolic AI combines the strengths of both symbolic and neural approaches. Knowledge graphs provide a structured, interconnected representation of information, while LLMs excel at understanding and generating human-like text based on vast amounts of data. By integrating these two technologies, neuro-symbolic AI systems can achieve more robust reasoning, better interpretability, and enhanced performance in complex tasks. In this fusion, knowledge graphs serve as a foundation for structured knowledge, enabling AI systems to reason about relationships and entities in a logical manner. LLMs, on the other hand, bring powerful natural language processing capabilities, allowing the AI to understand and generate text with high accuracy and fluency. This combination allows for more sophisticated AI systems that can leverage both structured knowledge and unstructured data.

Example: Enhancing Question-Answering Systems

Consider a question-answering system designed to provide accurate and contextually relevant answers to user queries. By integrating a knowledge graph with an LLM, the system can achieve a higher level of understanding and precision.

1. **Knowledge Graph Integration**: The knowledge graph contains structured information about various entities and their relationships. For example, in a medical domain, the knowledge graph might include information about diseases, symptoms, treatments, and medical research.
2. **LLM Capabilities**: The LLM is trained on a vast corpus of medical literature, enabling it to understand and generate text related to medical topics. It can interpret user queries, extract relevant information, and generate coherent responses.
3. **Fusion for Enhanced Performance**: When a user asks a question, the system first uses the LLM to understand the query and identify relevant entities and relationships within the knowledge graph. The knowledge graph then provides structured information that the LLM can use to generate a precise and contextually accurate answer.

For instance, if a user asks, "What are the symptoms of diabetes?" the LLM interprets the query and identifies "diabetes" as the key entity. The system then queries the knowledge graph to retrieve information about diabetes symptoms. Using this structured data, the LLM generates a detailed and accurate response, such as "The symptoms of diabetes include increased thirst, frequent urination, extreme fatigue, and blurred vision."

This fusion not only improves the accuracy and relevance of the answers but also enhances the system's ability to explain its reasoning. The knowledge graph provides a transparent and logical foundation for the information, while the LLM ensures that the responses are natural and easy to understand.

Frameworks and Tools

Neuro-symbolic AI research has gained significant momentum in recent years, with numerous frameworks and tools emerging to support the integration of neural networks and symbolic reasoning. These hybrid approaches aim to combine the pattern recognition strengths of neural networks with the logical reasoning capabilities of symbolic systems.

DeepProbLog stands out as one of the pioneering frameworks in this domain. Developed by researchers at KU Leuven, DeepProbLog extends the probabilistic logic programming language ProbLog by integrating neural predicates. This allows developers to incorporate neural networks as predicates within a logical reasoning framework. In practice, this means DeepProbLog can handle tasks that require both pattern recognition and logical reasoning. For example, in a handwritten equation solving task, DeepProbLog might use neural networks to recognize handwritten digits and then apply logical constraints to solve the equation. Given an image of "3 + 4 = ?", the neural component recognizes the digits while the symbolic component applies the addition operation to derive "7" as the answer.

Neuro-symbolic concept learner (NSCL), developed by MIT and IBM Research, represents another significant advancement in the field. This framework can learn visual concepts, words, and semantic parsing of sentences without explicit supervision for any of these tasks. Instead, it uses a hybrid approach where neural perception modules are linked with symbolic reasoning components. In a practical implementation, NSCL can answer complex visual reasoning questions about images. When shown an image with several objects and asked, "What is the colour of the object to the left of the red cube?", NSCL first uses neural networks to identify objects and their attributes, then employs symbolic reasoning to understand spatial relationships and answer the question correctly.

Microsoft's Neuro-symbolic Programming Framework (NSPF) provides a comprehensive environment for developing hybrid AI systems. It supports the integration of neural perception with symbolic knowledge representation and reasoning. One notable application built with NSPF is the DreamCoder system, which learns to solve programming problems by combining neural network-based program synthesis with symbolic program execution. When tasked with generating a function to manipulate data in a specific way, DreamCoder uses neural networks to propose candidate programs and symbolic execution to verify their correctness.

The neural theorem prover (NTP) framework, developed by researchers from UCL and Oxford, combines neural networks with logic programming for reasoning over knowledge bases. NTP implements differentiable versions of backward chaining, allowing end-to-end training of neural networks within a logical reasoning framework. In biological research applications, NTP has been used to discover new relationships in protein interaction networks by combining embedded representations of proteins with logical rules about interaction patterns. When predicting whether two proteins might interact, NTP uses neural embeddings to capture protein features while applying logical rules about transitivity and symmetry in protein interactions.

TensorLog, developed at Stanford, offers a differentiable deductive database that bridges neural networks and probabilistic logic programming. This framework represents logical rules as sparse factor graphs that can be efficiently differentiated and integrated with neural network architectures. Researchers have applied TensorLog to drug discovery processes, where neural networks identify molecular structures while logical rules represent biochemical constraints and relationships. For a candidate molecule, the system can both visually process its structure and reason about its potential interactions based on logical rules about chemical properties.

IBM's Neuro-symbolic AI toolkit provides implementations of various neuro-symbolic approaches, including the powerful Logic Tensor Networks (LTN). LTN grounds logical terms in tensor representations, allowing symbolic knowledge to be integrated directly with neural network architectures. This toolkit has been used to develop systems for visual question answering that can handle queries requiring both visual perception and logical reasoning. When asked "If the red object were removed, would there be any triangles left in the image?", an LTN-based system processes the image with neural networks while using first-order logic to reason about counterfactual scenarios.

Google's Tensorflow Fold library, while not exclusively designed for neuro-symbolic AI, has become an important tool in the field due to its ability to handle structured data within neural network frameworks. It allows for dynamic computation graphs that can adapt to input structures of varying shapes and sizes, making it ideal for implementing tree-structured neural networks that can process logical formulas or parse trees. Researchers have used Tensorflow Fold to build neural-guided theorem provers that learn to navigate large proof spaces efficiently by combining neural heuristics with symbolic theorem proving techniques.

AllenNLP, developed by the Allen Institute for AI, provides tools for building and evaluating neuro-symbolic natural language processing models. Though primarily known as a deep learning NLP library, its modular design facilitates the integration of symbolic components. For example, researchers have used AllenNLP to develop question-answering systems that combine neural language understanding with symbolic reasoning over knowledge graphs. When answering complex questions like "Who has directed more movies, Spielberg or Scorsese?", these systems use neural models to interpret the question and extract entities, while symbolic components perform counting and comparison operations over a knowledge base.

The recent development of Grounded Language-Image Pre-training (GLIP) by Microsoft epitomizes a key advancement in vision-language neuro-symbolic approaches. GLIP unifies object detection and phrase grounding in a single framework, allowing models to detect objects in images based on natural language descriptions. This framework has demonstrated impressive zero-shot transfer capabilities to new visual categories simply through linguistic descriptions. When instructed to find "a person riding a unicycle" in an image, despite never being explicitly trained on unicycle detection, GLIP can successfully identify this novel combination of concepts through its neuro-symbolic integration of visual and linguistic knowledge.

Commonsense Knowledge

Commonsense Knowledge, the everyday understanding of the world that people use in routine situations, encompasses general facts, social norms, and basic cause-and-effect relationships that are widely shared but rarely explicitly taught.

The role of commonsense knowledge in AI is multi-faceted. It provides contextual understanding, enabling AI systems to interpret ambiguous or incomplete information. For example, knowing that "people usually eat breakfast in the morning" allows an AI to infer that "eating muesli at 7 AM" is likely breakfast. It also facilitates predictive inference, allowing systems to make reasonable predictions about everyday scenarios, such as understanding that "if it is raining, people are likely to wear raincoats." Moreover, commonsense knowledge helps bridge gaps in data by filling knowledge gaps in sparse or missing data situations and improving generalization across diverse tasks and domains.

Neuro-symbolic AI integrates commonsense knowledge through both neural networks and symbolic reasoning. Neural networks learn commonsense representations from large-scale text corpora and knowledge bases, allowing language models like GPT-4 to learn implicit commonsense knowledge from vast amounts of text data. Pre-trained neural networks can be fine-tuned with additional data or knowledge sources to better align with commonsense understanding. Symbolic AI represents commonsense knowledge explicitly using rules, ontologies, or knowledge graphs, enabling structured reasoning and inference based on known facts and relationships. Symbolic reasoning systems can apply commonsense rules and logic to make decisions or infer conclusions, such as "if someone is hungry, they might look for food."

Hybrid neuro-symbolic architectures integrate connectionist learning mechanisms with explicit symbolic knowledge representation to enhance system robustness and generalization. Neural networks perform feature extraction and pattern recognition from raw sensory data, while symbolic reasoning engines execute logical inference operations over structured knowledge bases encoded in formal languages. These systems employ neural modules to learn latent representations of commonsense knowledge through supervised or unsupervised learning, which are subsequently formalized into symbolic predicates and rules for deductive reasoning. The symbolic component applies first-order logic or description logic to perform inference and constraint satisfaction over the learned knowledge structures. For example, a system may extract relational embeddings from observational data through graph neural networks, then convert these embeddings into symbolic relations within an ontology, enabling the application of logical inference rules to novel problem instances.

Examples of commonsense knowledge integration include knowledge graphs like ConceptNet, which encode commonsense knowledge about everyday concepts and their relationships. Hybrid models like the neuro-symbolic concept learner (NSCL) combine neural networks for visual perception with symbolic reasoning to answer questions about images. Commonsense-augmented language models, such as GPT-4, are trained on diverse text corpora that include commonsense knowledge and generate responses based on this implicit understanding, which can be further enhanced with explicit symbolic commonsense rules.

Example: ConceptNet is a large-scale semantic network that aims to capture general knowledge about the world. It's a vast collection of assertions (statements) that connect words and phrases in a graph-like structure.

- **Nodes:** Represent concepts (words, phrases). Examples: "cat," "dog," "happiness," "red," "eat," "sleep."
- **Edges:** Represent relationships between concepts. Examples:
  - **Is-A:** "cat Is-A feline."
  - **Has-Property:** "cat Has-Property fur."
  - **Part-Of:** "tail Part-Of cat."
  - **Causes:** "rain Causes wet."
  - **At-Location:** "cat At-Location house."

- **Node 1:** "Cat."
- **Edge 1 (Is-A):** Connects "Cat" to "Feline."
- **Node 2:** "Feline."
- **Edge 2 (Has-Property):** Connects "Cat" to "Fur."
- **Node 3:** "Fur."
- **Edge 3 (Part-Of):** Connects "Tail" to "Cat."
- **Node 4:** "Tail."

ConceptNet contains millions of assertions, covering a wide range of commonsense knowledge. It also includes knowledge from multiple languages, allowing for cross-lingual understanding. In essence, ConceptNet provides a valuable resource for AI systems, enabling them to access and utilize commonsense knowledge, making their interactions with humans and their understanding of the world more human-like.

Commonsense Reasoning

Commonsense reasoning, a vital aspect of human intelligence, refers to the capacity to draw conclusions about typical, everyday scenarios using widely understood and intuitive knowledge. Neural networks contribute to this process by learning patterns from extensive datasets. For example, large language models are trained on vast amounts of text that contain embedded commonsense knowledge, enabling them to understand cause-and-effect relationships and social conventions. Furthermore, pre-trained neural networks can capture implicit commonsense knowledge through their internal representations, which encode associations and contextual informa-tion reflecting everyday understanding. These networks can also be specifically trained using datasets like ConceptNet to better align their reasoning with human-like comprehension in particular areas. In contrast, symbolic AI explicitly represents commonsense knowledge using structured formats such as knowledge graphs. These graphs store commonsense facts and the relationships between them, providing a rich source of information for reasoning. Symbolic reasoning systems apply this commonsense knowledge using predefined rules and logical constraints, performing deductive reasoning to reach conclusions. For instance, given the information that "Maria is at the office and it's lunchtime," a symbolic system might infer that "Maria is likely to be eating lunch." Additionally, symbolic reasoning can utilize case-based reasoning, applying knowledge from similar past situations to new ones. Hybrid neuro-symbolic approaches combine these neural and symbolic strengths to benefit from both data-driven insights and structured knowledge. These models can employ neural networks to process sensory data, such as images, and then use symbolic reasoning to apply commonsense knowledge for interpretation. For example, a neuro-symbolic model might use a neural network to identify objects in an image and subsequently use symbolic logic to infer their relationships and context.

Moreover, neuro-symbolic systems can learn new commonsense knowledge from interactions and data using neural networks, while symbolic reasoning applies this knowledge in a structured way, allowing them to adapt to novel situations. A typical process in a neuro-symbolic system involves receiving input, such as an image or a text query, followed by the use of neural networks to process this input, extracting relevant features and understanding the context. These extracted features or the context are then translated into symbolic representations, like entities and relationships within a knowledge graph. Symbolic reasoning then applies established commonsense rules and logic to these representations, for example, inferring that a "plate" seen in an image is likely associated with food. Finally, the system generates a response or makes a decision based on the combined processing of both neural and symbolic components. Commonsense reasoning in neuro-symbolic AI has numerous practical applications.

In natural language understanding, it enhances dialogue systems by enabling them to produce contextually appropriate responses. In visual question answering, it improves the interpretation of images by integrating visual features with common-sense knowledge. In robotics and autonomous systems, it facilitates context-aware decision-making, allowing robots to better plan tasks and interact with humans by utilizing commonsense understanding of social norms and the typical uses of objects. Ultimately, by merging the data-driven learning of neural networks with the structured, logical reasoning of symbolic AI, neuro-symbolic AI aims to develop more human-like, versatile, and intelligent systems capable of effectively reasoning about everyday occurrences. This combined approach enables AI systems to integrate implicit knowledge gained from data with explicit, rule-based commonsense knowledge, resulting in more robust and adaptable AI systems.

Exercises

1. What are the primary motivations behind the development of neuro-symbolic AI?
2. Explain the concept of "commonsense reasoning" and its importance in neuro-symbolic AI.
3. How does neuro-symbolic AI address the limitations of traditional neural networks and symbolic AI?
4. What are some of the ethical considerations related to the development and deployment of neuro-symbolic AI systems?
5. Discuss the role of knowledge graphs like ConceptNet in neuro-symbolic AI.
6. What are the main challenges in developing and deploying robust neuro-symbolic AI systems?
7. Describe a scenario where injecting symbolic knowledge into a neural network would be beneficial.
8. Explain how you might use logical constraints to guide the training of a neural network for a specific task.
9. Provide an example of how the outputs of a neural network could be used as inputs to a symbolic reasoning system.
10. How would you convert the continuous outputs of a neural network into discrete symbols suitable for symbolic reasoning?
11. Design a basic architecture for a neuro-symbolic reasoning engine for natural language understanding.
12. Explain how you would integrate neural and symbolic components in a unified architecture for a specific application.
13. Explain the role of explainability and interpretability in neuro-symbolic AI.
14. How do neuro-symbolic AI systems learn from both structured and unstructured data?
15. Describe how symbolic planning can be used to improve the data efficiency of reinforcement learning. Provide an example scenario where this approach would be beneficial.
16. Use the ConceptNet API or website to explore the relationships between a set of related concepts (e.g., "dog," "bone," "park").
17. Design a neuro-symbolic AI system that can adapt to changes in its environment through continual learning.
18. Conduct an experiment to compare the performance of a neuro-symbolic AI system with a purely neural or purely symbolic system on the same task.
19. Debate the potential benefits and limitations of neuro-symbolic AI in a group setting or through a written argument.
20. Interview a researcher or professional working in the field of neuro-symbolic AI and summarize their insights on current trends and future prospects.
21. Create a presentation on the ethical implications of neuro-symbolic AI, including potential solutions to address these concerns.

Further Reading

Acharya K, Raza W, Dourado C, Velasquez A, Song HH Neuro-symbolic reinforcement learning and planning: a survey. IEEE Trans Artif Intell. https://doi.org/10.1109/TAI.2023.3311428

Badreddine S, d'Avila Garcez A, Serafini L, Spranger M (2022) Logic tensor networks. Artif Intell 303:103649

Bhuyan BP, Ramdane-Cherif A, Tomar R, Singh TP (2024) Neuro-symbolic artificial intelligence: a survey. In: Neural computing and applications, vol 36. pp 12809–12844. doi: https://doi.org/10.1007/s00521-024-09960-z

Chaudhuri S, Ellis K, Polozov O, Singh R, Solar-Lezama A, Yisong Y (2021) Neuro-symbolic programming. Found Trends Program Lang 7:158–243

Cohen WW (2016) TensorLog: a differentiable deductive database. arXiv preprint. arXiv:1605.06523

Cohen WW, Yang F, Mazaitis K (2017) TensorLog: deep learning meets probabilistic databases. J Artif Intell Res:1–15

d'Avila Garcez AS, Lamb LC, Gabbay DM (2015) Neural-symbolic learning and reasoning: a survey and future directions. Artif Intell 235:146–184

De Raedt L, Dumančić S, Manhaeve R, Marra G (2020) From statistical relational to neuro-symbolic artificial intelligence. In: Proceedings of the 29th international joint conference on artificial intelligence

Ellis K, Morales L, Sablé-Meyer M, Solar-Lezama A, Tenenbaum J (2018) Learning libraries of subroutines for neurally-guided Bayesian program induction. Adv Neural Inf Process Syst

Ellis K, Nye M, Pu Y, Sosa F, Tenenbaum J, Solar-Lezama A (2019) Write, execute, assess: program synthesis with a REPL. Adv Neural Inf Process Syst

Garcez AD, Gori M, Lamb LC, Serafini L, Spranger M, Tran SN (2019) Neural-symbolic computing: an effective methodology for principled integration of machine learning and reasoning. J Appl LogS 6(4):611–632

Garcez Ad, Lamb LC (2023) Neurosymbolic AI: the third wave. Artif Intell Rev 56: 12387–12406. https://doi.org/10.1007/s10462-023-10448-w

Gardner M, Grus J, Neumann M, Tafjord O, Dasigi P, Liu NF, Peters M, Schmitz M, Zettlemoyer L (2018) AllenNLP: a deep semantic natural language processing platform. In: Proceedings of workshop for NLP open-source software

Hogan A, Blomqvist E, Cochez M, D'amato C, De Melo G, Gutierrez C, Kirrane S, Labra Gayo JE, Navigli R, Neumaier S, Ngonga Ngomo A-C, Polleres A, Rashid SM, Rula A, Schmelzeisen L, Sequeda J, Staab S, Zimmermann A (2021) Knowledge graphs. ACM Comput Surv 54(4):37. https://doi.org/10.1145/3447772

Kahneman D (2011) Thinking, fast and slow. Farrar, Straus and Giroux

Kaliszyk C, Urban J, Michalewski H, Olšák M (2018) Reinforcement learning of theorem proving. Adv Neural Inf Process Syst

Lodhi H, Muggleton S, Muggleton SH (2011) Integrating symbolic and neural learning. Mach Learn 82, 279–300

Manghi P, Mannocci A, Osborne F, Sacharidis D, Salatino A, Vergoulis T (2022) New trends in scientific knowledge graphs and research impact assessment. Quant Sci Stud 2(4):1296–1300. https://doi.org/10.1162/qss_e_00160

Mao J, Gan C, Kohli P, Tenenbaum JB, Wu J (2019) The neuro-symbolic concept learner: interpreting scenes, words, and sentences from natural supervision. In: International conference on learning representations (ICLR 2019)

Minervini P, Bosnjak M, Rocktäschel T, Riedel S, Grefenstette E (2020) Differentiable reasoning on large knowledge bases and natural language. In: Proceedings of the AAAI conference on artificial intelligence

Sheth A, Roy K, Gaur M (2023) Neuro-symbolic artificial intelligence (Why, What, and How). IEEE Intell Syst 38(3):56–62. https://doi.org/10.1109/MIS.2023.3268724

Valiant LG (2003) Three problems in computer science. J ACM 50(1):96–99

Yi K, Wu J, Gan C, Torralba A, Kohli P, Tenenbaum J (2018) Neural-symbolic VQA: disentangling reasoning from vision and language understanding. Adv Neural Inf Process Syst

Chapter 10
Mimicking the Mind: The Evolution of Cognitive AI

What you think, you become.
—Buddha
To think is easy. To act is hard. But the hardest thing in the world
is to act in accordance with your thinking.
—Johann Wolfgang von Goethe

Introduction

Cognitive AI, or cognitive artificial intelligence, refers to the branch of AI that aims to emulate human-like cognitive processes. This includes reasoning, learning, memory, and perception. In this chapter, we will explore the fundamental concepts and applications of cognitive AI, providing a comprehensive understanding of how these systems work and their potential impact.

The journey of cognitive AI began with early attempts to model human thought processes using symbolic AI. Over the years, advancements in neural networks and machine learning have significantly enhanced our ability to create systems that can mimic human cognition. Key milestones include the development of cognitive architectures like SOAR and ACT-R, which have paved the way for more sophisticated models. Cognitive AI plays a crucial role in various domains, including robotics, healthcare, and human-computer interaction. For instance, in healthcare, cognitive AI can assist in diagnosing diseases by analysing patient data and providing insights based on learned patterns. In robotics, it enables machines to interact with their environment in a more human-like manner, improving their efficiency and adaptability.

This chapter will delve into essential concepts such as commonsense reasoning, meta-cognition, and cognitive architectures. Understanding these concepts is vital for developing AI systems that can perform complex tasks and make decisions in uncertain environments. We will also explore how these systems can be designed to learn and adapt over time.

393
R. Akerkar, *Artificial Intelligence*, https://doi.org/10.1007/978-3-031-91084-5_10

The central aspiration of cognitive AI lies in creating systems that not only process information but also understand and reason like humans. Early attempts often struggled with the nuances of context and common sense, highlighting the vast difference between computation and true cognition. Modern research increasingly focuses on developing AI models that can build internal representations of the world and learn abstract concepts. Ultimately, the ongoing evolution of cognitive AI aims to bridge the gap between artificial intelligence and the remarkable capabilities of the human mind.

Definition Cognition, a subset of intelligence, specifically mirrors human cognitive processing, involving functions like learning, self-reflection, language understanding, and reasoning.

Example Large language models (LLMs) generate contextually relevant outputs that appear cognitive, mimicking human responses. However, they still lack genuine understanding or reasoning, operating solely on probabilistic patterns. Thus, LLMs and conversational AI are intelligent, producing sophisticated outputs, but not cognitive, as they do not perform higher-level cognitive processes. They excel at mimicking cognition, but do not achieve it.

Cognitive AI and cognitive science are closely related fields that enhance and inform each other. Cognitive science is an interdisciplinary study of the mind, involving psychology, neuroscience, linguistics, philosophy, anthropology, and computer science. It seeks to understand how humans think, learn, and process information. Cognitive AI, on the other hand, focuses on creating artificial systems that mimic these human cognitive processes. The relationship between the two is symbiotic. Cognitive science provides theoretical foundations for cognitive AI, offering insights into human cognition that help develop AI models capable of human-like understanding, reasoning, and learning. Conversely, advancements in cognitive AI offer new tools and methods for studying the human mind, providing cognitive scientists with innovative ways to explore mental processes.

This mutual inspiration and interdisciplinary collaboration lead to more complex AI systems and a deeper understanding of human cognition. By working together, these fields push the boundaries of both artificial intelligence and cognitive science, creating a dynamic and evolving landscape of knowledge and technology.

To truly grasp the trajectory of cognitive AI, we must first examine its evolutionary path. Its origins stretch back to the late 1950s, a period marked by pioneering efforts to construct machines capable of human-like problem-solving. This era witnessed the birth of rudimentary artificial neural networks, inspired by the biological mechanisms of neurons and their information-processing capabilities.

Subsequent decades saw a series of advancements in AI, notably the development of expert systems. These systems, designed to emulate human decision-making through rule-based logic and knowledge databases, nonetheless exhibited limitations in handling complex scenarios and adapting to novel situations.

The 1980s marked a turning point with the emergence of cognitive science. This interdisciplinary field, encompassing linguistics, psychology, neuroscience, philosophy, computer science/AI, and anthropology, sought to decipher human cognition and translate those insights into machine intelligence, thus enabling more sophisticated AI development.

A pivotal moment in cognitive AI history arrived in 1997 when IBM's Deep Blue defeated chess grandmaster Garry Kasparov, showcasing the potential of computational power in strategic problem-solving.

Unlike traditional rule-based and statistical AI, cognitive AI offers dynamic learning and contextual understanding. These advanced capabilities enable machines to interpret data with human-like intuition, facilitating the resolution of intricate problems and autonomous, informed decision-making. Cognitive AI systems are engineered to emulate human thought patterns, empowering both individuals and businesses to navigate complex challenges and make well-informed choices.

Definition Cognitive AI systems emulate human-like thinking by integrating reasoning, learning, and adaptation within unified architectures. These systems combine pattern recognition with symbolic logic to understand context, explain decisions, and apply knowledge flexibly across different situations capturing the interpretable and generalizable nature of human cognition.

Cognitive AI leverages machine learning to analyse data from diverse sources, fostering continuous learning and performance improvement. Fundamentally, it strives to replicate human information processing, encompassing language comprehension, pattern recognition, experience-based decision-making, and complex problem-solving. By emulating these cognitive functions, cognitive AI has the potential to revolutionize numerous industries.

Beyond technical advancements, cognitive AI is becoming more accessible and user-friendly. Intuitive interfaces requiring minimal coding knowledge are enabling non-technical users to create their own cognitive AI applications. This democratization is lowering barriers for businesses seeking to integrate these solutions into their operations.

Example Cognitive AI-enabled chatbot.
Imagine a chatbot designed to assist users with complex financial planning. This isn't a simple question-and-answer bot; it's a cognitive AI-enabled agent that understands the user's financial context, goals, and even emotional state.

This chatbot begins by engaging in a natural language conversation, asking questions to gather information about the user's income, expenses, savings, investments, and long-term financial aspirations. It doesn't just collect data; it actively listens, using natural language processing (NLP) to understand the nuances of the user's language, identifying key phrases, and even detecting emotional cues like frustration or anxiety in their tone.

As the conversation progresses, the cognitive AI chatbot builds a comprehensive model of the user's financial situation. It leverages its knowledge base, which includes financial planning principles, market data, and regulatory information, to analyse the user's current state and identify potential opportunities and risks. It can reason about the user's goals, considering factors like their age, risk tolerance, and time horizon. If the user expresses a desire to save for retirement, the chatbot doesn't just provide generic advice. It might analyse their spending habits, identify areas where they can cut back, and suggest specific investment strategies based on their risk tolerance and time horizon. It can also simulate different financial scenarios, showing the user how their choices today could impact their future.

Furthermore, this chatbot can learn and adapt over time. It remembers previous conversations, tracks the user's progress, and refines its recommendations based on their feedback and changing circumstances. It can also proactively alert the user to potential financial risks or opportunities, such as changes in market conditions or new investment products.

Beyond just providing information, the chatbot acts as a personalized financial coach. It uses its understanding of the user's emotional state to provide encouragement and support, helping them stay motivated and on track with their financial goals. It can even adjust its communication style to match the user's preferences, using simpler language for those who are less financially literate or providing more detailed explanations for those who are more knowledgeable.

This cognitive AI-enabled chatbot transcends the limitations of traditional chatbots. It's not just a tool for answering questions; it's a proactive, personalized financial advisor that understands the user's context, goals, and emotions, providing tailored guidance and support.

Cognitive AI significantly enhances Human-AI collaboration by fostering a more intuitive and effective partnership. It moves beyond the limitations of traditional AI, which often operates as a mere tool, and instead aims to create AI systems that can understand, reason, and communicate more like humans.

Definition Human-AI interaction (HAI) is a field of study and practice that focuses on how humans and artificial intelligence (AI) systems communicate and collaborate. It explores the design, development, and evaluation of AI systems that are user-friendly, effective, and ethical.

Cognitive AI improves collaboration through its ability to understand and interpret human language and intent. Natural language processing (NLP) within cognitive AI allows for more natural and fluid communication. Instead of requiring users to learn complex commands or interfaces, they can interact with the AI using everyday language. This reduces the cognitive load on the user and makes the AI more accessible to a wider range of individuals. Imagine a physician discussing patient symptoms with an AI assistant that understands medical terminology and can accurately summarize patient history from spoken notes.

Furthermore, cognitive AI's capacity for commonsense reasoning enables it to anticipate human needs and provide proactive support. It can understand the context of a task, infer the user's goals, and offer relevant suggestions or solutions. For instance, a project management AI could recognize that a team is falling behind schedule and proactively suggest task reassignments or resource adjustments, rather than simply reporting the delay.

Cognitive AI also enhances collaboration by improving the explainability and transparency of AI decisions. When an AI system can explain its reasoning, humans can better understand and trust its recommendations. This is particularly important in collaborative settings where humans and AI are working together on critical tasks. A financial analyst working with an AI system that provides investment recommendations, for example, would benefit from understanding the rationale behind those recommendations, allowing for informed decision-making and trust in the AI's analysis.

Moreover, cognitive AI's ability to learn and adapt over time allows it to become a more effective collaborator. By remembering past interactions, understanding user preferences, and adapting to changing circumstances, the AI can become a more personalized and valuable partner. A research assistant AI, for example, could learn a researcher's specific interests and preferences over time, becoming more efficient in suggesting relevant articles and data. Cognitive AI facilitates more effective collaboration by enabling AI systems to understand and respond to human emotions. Empathy and emotional intelligence are crucial for effective teamwork, and cognitive AI is beginning to incorporate these capabilities. An AI tutor, for instance, could recognize when a student is struggling with frustration and offer encouragement or adjust the learning pace.

Foundational Concepts

Commonsense Reasoning in Cognitive AI

Commonsense reasoning plays a pivotal role in cognitive AI, serving as the bridge between raw data processing and genuine understanding. It's the ability to make judgements and inferences based on everyday knowledge and experiences, a trait that humans possess naturally but that AI systems have historically struggled to replicate. Without common sense, AI remains confined to pattern recognition and statistical analysis, unable to navigate the complexities of real-world scenarios.

> **Example** A robot tasked with cleaning a kitchen. A purely data-driven AI might identify a spilled glass of juice but fail to understand the implications. It might attempt to mop the juice with a nearby dishcloth, contaminating it, or ignore the potential for the sticky juice to attract ants. A cognitive AI system with commonsense reasoning, however, would understand that juice spills are typically sticky, that dishcloths are for drying dishes, and that sugary substances attract insects. It would then select the appropriate cleaning tool, such as a mop or sponge, and understand the importance of thoroughly cleaning the area to prevent further issues.

Another illustrative example lies in natural language understanding. Imagine an AI chatbot asked, "Can you pick up the book on the table?" A system lacking common-sense might struggle with the ambiguity of "the book." It might not understand that "the table" refers to the specific table in the current context, or that "pick up" implies a physical action. A cognitive AI system with commonsense reasoning would understand the spatial relationships between objects, the typical function of a table, and the physical requirements of picking up an object. It would also be able to handle implicit information, understanding that "the book" likely refers to a book that is easily accessible on the table's surface, rather than a hidden or inaccessible one.

In the domain of autonomous vehicles, commonsense reasoning is crucial for navigating unpredictable situations. An AI-powered car might encounter a road closure due to construction. A system without common sense might simply stop, unable to devise an alternative route. A cognitive AI system, however, would understand that road closures are temporary, that detours are a common solution, and that following signs or consulting a map application can provide alternative routes. It could also recognize potential hazards associated with construction zones, such as uneven surfaces or heavy equipment.

Furthermore, commonsense reasoning is essential for AI systems to engage in meaningful social interactions. A social robot interacting with elderly individuals, for example, needs to understand social cues, emotional expressions, and the nuances of human communication. It needs to grasp that certain topics might be sensitive, that interrupting someone is impolite, and that empathy is essential for building rapport.

Meta-Cognition

Meta-cognition empowers a system to perceive and respond to its own internal workings through self-reflective, introspective reasoning. This process involves the system sensing its own thought patterns and actions, encompassing its internal state and external outputs, and using this self-awareness as input for further cognitive processing. Essentially, the system engages in thinking about its own thinking and actions, aiming to refine its structure or behaviour.

Implementing meta-cognition in agentic applications presents technical challenges and remains a partially realized concept in current agent development frameworks. While these platforms facilitate basic agent introspection and execution planning, they lack the comprehensive architecture needed for higher-order meta-cognitive functions. Establishing this capability at a platform level necessitates the development of novel intellectual property, specialized tools, and innovative application paradigms, representing both a significant challenge and a transformative opportunity for cognitive AI.

The core capabilities of meta-cognition include:

- **Knowledge Processing**: The ability to detect, transform, and generate formal data structures and procedures to represent and reason about knowledge.
- **Introspection**: The ability to detect, transform, and conduct knowledge processing on representations of its own composition, state, context, and behaviour.
- **Meta-reasoning**: The ability to use introspection and knowledge processing to represent, transform, and generate knowledge about knowledge, and to reason about reasoning.
- **Reflection**: The ability to apply meta-reasoning during introspection to conduct reasoning or meta-reasoning about its own composition, state, context, and behaviour.
- **Learning**: The ability to improve or generate future potential knowledge and responses by analysing the effectiveness of previous knowledge and response patterns for specific goals.
- **Self-optimization**: The ability to use learning and reflection to transform its own composition, state, context, or behaviour to enhance its fitness for specific goals and criteria.

The defining innovation of cognitive AI is its dual-layer architecture, which enables meta-cognition to operate above the intelligence of large language models (LLMs). This architecture allows cognitive AI to not only analyse and respond to data but also to engage in introspection, reflection, and dynamic optimization of its strategies based on ongoing experiences. This self-reflective intelligence enables real-time evaluation and enhancement of decision-making processes, leading to improved efficiency and outcomes.

Meta-cognition, or intelligence about intelligence, provides cognitive AI with the ability to perform abstract reasoning, a key characteristic of human cognition. While LLMs can simulate abstract reasoning in simple scenarios, their performance deteriorates as task complexity increases. Cognitive AI's meta-cognition architecture facilitates a level of introspection, adaptive reasoning, and learning that surpasses the capabilities of first-order intelligent systems, enabling it to navigate and solve highly complex, multi-faceted problems.

The shift toward cognitive AI represents a fundamental evolution in artificial intelligence, moving from a reliance on basic pattern recognition to a more sophisticated, introspective, and adaptable intelligence model. This evolution redefines our understanding of AI and marks a significant advancement in technology's development, paving the way for future innovations that more closely resemble human cognitive processes.

> **Example** Imagine a cognitive AI system designed to manage a complex supply chain.
>
> *Traditional AI (LLM-Based)*: It might analyse historical data to predict demand fluctuations and optimize inventory levels. It could respond to immediate disruptions, like a factory shutdown, by rerouting shipments. However, if faced with a novel, cascading disruption (e.g., a global pandemic impacting multiple suppliers), it might struggle to adapt.
>
> *Cognitive AI (with Meta-cognition)*: It would not only analyse data and react to disruptions but also engage in self-reflection. It could analyse its own performance in handling past disruptions, identify weaknesses in its planning strategies, and adjust its algorithms accordingly. For example, it might realize that its reliance on a single supplier for a critical component makes the entire supply chain vulnerable.
>
> It could then proactively develop a plan to diversify suppliers, create contingency plans for future disruptions, and even simulate different scenarios to test the robustness of its new strategy. It would also be able to analyse its own data analysis methods, and if it notices that it is not correctly predicting certain events, it can change the ways it is analysing data. It would also be able to monitor the emotional state of the human employees who are using the system, and adapt the information it presents to them, depending on if they are stressed, or calm.

Augmented Intelligence

Augmented intelligence, also known as intelligence amplification (IA), refers to the use of cognitive artificial intelligence (AI) to enhance human decision-making and problem-solving capabilities. Unlike traditional AI, which aims to automate tasks and replicate human intelligence, augmented intelligence focuses on creating systems that work collaboratively with humans to improve their cognitive functions.

In augmented intelligence, AI systems provide insights, recommendations, and support to humans, enabling them to make better decisions and perform tasks more efficiently. These systems leverage advanced technologies such as machine learning, natural language processing, and data analytics to process large volumes of information, identify patterns, and generate actionable insights.

For example, in healthcare, augmented intelligence can assist doctors by analysing medical records, suggesting potential diagnoses, and recommending treatment options based on the latest research. This helps doctors make more informed decisions and provide better patient care.

Example IBM Watson for Oncology.

This system assists oncologists in diagnosing and treating cancer by analysing vast amounts of medical literature, clinical trial data, and patient records. Watson provides evidence-based treatment recommendations tailored to individual patients, helping doctors make more informed decisions. For instance, when a doctor inputs a patient's medical history and cancer diagnosis into Watson, the system analyses the data and suggests potential treatment options, highlighting the latest research and clinical guidelines. This collaboration between the AI system and the doctor enhances the doctor's ability to provide personalized and effective cancer care, demonstrating the power of augmented intelligence in healthcare.

The key idea behind augmented intelligence is to enhance human abilities rather than replace them, fostering a symbiotic relationship between humans and AI. This approach emphasizes the importance of human judgement, creativity, and ethical considerations, while leveraging the strengths of AI to handle complex data and perform repetitive tasks.

Memory-Augmented AI

Memory-Augmented AI refers to AI systems that incorporate specialized memory components to enhance their ability to store, retrieve, and utilize information. These systems are designed to mimic human-like memory processes, enabling them to handle complex tasks that require remembering past interactions, learning from experiences, and making informed decisions based on historical data.

One prominent example of Memory-Augmented AI is *Memory-Augmented Neural Networks (MANNs)*. These networks integrate external memory modules with traditional neural network architectures, allowing them to store and access information beyond their immediate computational capabilities. This setup enables the AI to perform tasks that require long-term dependencies and sequential data processing. For instance, neural turing machines (NTMs) and differentiable neural computers (DNCs) are types of MANNs that combine neural networks with external memory. These models can learn to read from and write to memory, effectively simulating the functionality of a Turing machine. This capability allows them to solve complex problems such as algorithmic tasks, sequence prediction, and data retrieval.

In practical applications, Memory-Augmented AI can be used in areas like natural language processing, where understanding and generating coherent text often requires remembering context from earlier in the conversation. It is also valuable in multi-object tracking, where maintaining a memory of object identities and their movements over time is crucial for accurate tracking.

Computational Models of Cognition

The quest to understand human cognition has fuelled over a century of psychological research. Mathematical approaches to cognition, dating back to the nineteenth century with researchers like Ernst Heinrich Weber, who developed models for the "just-noticeable difference," laid the groundwork for future advancements. However, it was the advent of computer science in the twentieth century that truly ushered in the era of computational psychology. This field aims to decipher how semi-independent functional modules, such as visual attention, perception, movement, and memory, are integrated to accomplish complex tasks. Cognitive modelling, a key component of this field, involves the development of computational models that attempt to replicate human cognitive processes.

It's crucial to understand that these computational models are not perfect replicas of the human mind. Instead, they are designed to simulate human intelligent behaviour and elucidate the underlying mechanisms that enable us to perform tasks, make decisions, and solve problems. Successful cognitive modelling requires a systematic approach, starting with clearly defined objectives. The model building process is then guided by relevant psychological theories and empirical evidence. Subsequently, the model's accuracy is rigorously tested and validated using appropriate data. Refinement or expansion of the model may be necessary based on these tests. The final stage involves analysing the results in the light of the defined objectives and drawing meaningful conclusions and insights. Cognitive modelling is a powerful tool for businesses, researchers, and developers, and its importance is expected to grow as our understanding of human cognition deepens and computational capabilities expand.

Cognitive models translate explicit verbal theories of cognitive processes into mathematical formulations. Behavioural measures within a task are described as the result of interacting processes or parameters of the model. The detailed interplay of these processes is specified within the model's formal architecture, representing the assumptions made regarding a specific cognitive process. Thus, a cognitive model is a formalized theory that objectively states which parameters influence observed behaviour. The adequacy and validity of this formalization are evaluated through parameter recovery studies and by testing the effects of experimental manipulations on model parameters.

Cognitive models serve two primary purposes:

(1) To formally describe the cognitive processes underlying observed behaviour and explain specific experimental effects.
(2) To use model parameters, estimated from observed behaviour, as measures of differences across individuals or conditions.

These measures quantify how people or conditions differ with respect to specific processes within the model.

Recent years have witnessed a surge in interest in computational models within psychology. Major journals and conferences are publishing an increasing number of articles on the subject, and more students are being trained in computational methods than ever before. While debates between connectionist and symbolic approaches persist, the field is increasingly open to probabilistic and hybrid approaches. The prominence of deep learning in artificial intelligence has significantly contributed to the rise of connectionism, placing it at the forefront of research.

> **Definition** *Symbolic reasoning* replicates human conscious thought by using symbols and logic to represent knowledge and make inferences—mirroring how we consciously apply rules, manipulate concepts, and use language to reason through problems, rather than relying on intuitive pattern recognition.

In cognitive AI, symbolic reasoning plays a crucial role in enabling systems to perform tasks that require understanding, planning, and explanation. It allows AI to move beyond mere pattern recognition and engage in more human-like thought processes. For example, a cognitive AI system using symbolic reasoning could be given a set of rules about family relationships and then use those rules to deduce complex kinship connections. It wouldn't simply recognize a pattern in a family tree; it would understand the underlying logic of familial relations.

One of the key advantages of symbolic reasoning is its explainability. Because it operates on explicit rules and symbols, the system's reasoning process can be traced and understood. This is particularly important in domains where transparency and accountability are essential, such as legal reasoning or medical diagnosis. A cognitive AI system using symbolic reasoning could not only provide a diagnosis but also explain the logical steps that led to that conclusion.

Furthermore, symbolic reasoning is essential for tasks that require planning and problem-solving. A cognitive AI system could use symbolic reasoning to plan a sequence of actions to achieve a goal, such as navigating a robot through a complex environment or scheduling a series of tasks. This involves representing the environment, the available actions, and the goal using symbols and rules, and then using logical inference to find a sequence of actions that leads to the goal.

> **Definition** Computational models are simplified abstract representations of the mind, that describe how some aspects of the mind process information in an algorithmic fashion, to produce some output (e.g., language, inference, perception, etc.).

Computational models of cognition function as cognitive maps, each designed to illuminate specific aspects of human mental processes. Some models focus on unravelling the complexities of memory, while others explore the mechanisms of language production or the intricacies of visual perception. Here, the objective might be to construct machines endowed with specific cognitive capabilities, potentially disregarding whether these capabilities align with human task execution. While such endeavours are invaluable for generating novel ideas and establishing benchmarks for human performance, they don't represent the primary focus of cognitive modelling within cognitive science.

The computational approach, however, has undeniably played a significant role in enhancing and broadening our understanding of human cognition and behaviour. By translating theoretical concepts into formal, testable models, researchers can gain deeper insights into the underlying mechanisms of mental processes. This approach allows for the rigorous examination of hypotheses and the development of more precise and comprehensive theories of human cognition.

Architectures and Frameworks

Cognitive Architecture

Cognitive architectures are computational models designed to emulate the human mind's cognitive processes, forming the bedrock of advanced AI systems. An integrated cognitive architecture features a foundation of knowledge and skills, overlaid with interconnected cognitive modules that mirror human mental functions. These modules, encompassing short-term and long-term memory, deep contextual understanding, parsing, interactive and incremental learning, reasoning, meta-cognition, action, planning, inference, and disambiguation, enable sophisticated, nuanced tasks and ongoing meaningful conversations.

The fundamental components of cognitive architectures include:

- **Perception**: The agent's ability to interpret the world through sensory inputs like vision and hearing.
- **Cognition**: The internal processes of thinking, reasoning, and problem-solving.
- **Action**: The agent's capacity to interact with the world through actions like movement and speech.
- **Memory**: The ability to store and retrieve information.
- **Learning**: The capability to acquire new knowledge and skills.

Supporting these core components are several underlying mechanisms that work in concert to replicate the human brain's structure and activity:

- **Parsing**: This involves the detailed analysis of input data, whether text, speech, or images, breaking it down into meaningful components to understand its structure and context.
- **Learning**: This is the continuous process of absorbing and processing vast amounts of data, allowing the system to adapt its knowledge and behaviour over time. Advanced cognitive learning techniques refine the system's understanding of patterns and relationships, mirroring human learning through experience.
- **Inference**: This refers to the system's ability to draw logical conclusions and insights from learned data, enabling informed decisions and predictions based on available information.
- **Language Generation**: This capability allows the system to produce human-like text or speech, composing coherent and contextually appropriate responses by analysing context, tone, and content.
- **Context**: This crucial aspect enables the system to understand and respond to information in a situationally appropriate manner, grasping nuances and inferring intent by considering surrounding information and previous interactions.
- **Memory**: This simulates the human ability to retain and recall information, storing relevant data from past interactions to maintain context, reference previous conversations, and avoid redundancy.

Cognitive AI functions by simulating human thought processes within a computerized model. It utilizes deep learning algorithms and big data analytics to provide insights, predictions, and decisions based on data. Natural language processing (NLP) further enhances its capabilities, enabling it to understand and respond to human language in a natural, human-like manner.

Adaptive Control of Thought-Rational Architecture

The Adaptive Control of Thought-Rational (ACT-R) architecture stands as a prominent cognitive and memory theory, evolving from the earlier Adaptive Control of Thought (ACT) model. ACT-R, given in Fig. 10.1, aims to construct a human brain model capable of analysing and predicting human behaviour, grounded in the principle of human rationality. This architecture, like others in its class, seeks to delineate the fundamental cognitive and perceptual operations that underpin the human mind. Essentially, ACT-R maps the functions of higher cognitive processes, illustrating how humans process information and subsequently act upon it, positing that every human task can be broken down into discrete operational steps.

Allen Newell's influential work significantly shaped ACT-R, particularly his advocacy for unified theories as the sole means of comprehensively understanding cognition. Newell emphasized the need for cognitive architectures that could explain the integrated functioning of all mental components to produce coherent cognition.

Canadian psychologist John R. Anderson's ACT-R model distinguishes between declarative and procedural knowledge, highlighting key differences through three core assumptions:

- Declarative knowledge is acquired in an all-or-none manner, while procedural knowledge is acquired gradually through practice.
- Declarative knowledge is acquired suddenly, often through verbal instruction, whereas procedural knowledge develops through repeated skill execution.
- Declarative knowledge can be verbally communicated, but procedural knowledge cannot.

Declarative knowledge emphasizes *what* one needs to do to solve an issue rather than *how* to solve it. Examples of declarative knowledge include facts, world history, or rules for solving mathematical equations. Procedural knowledge is about *how* we do something. Examples of procedural knowledge include behaviours we do habitually, such as riding a bike or driving a car.

Anderson's 1990 development of ACT* expanded upon his original ACT model, reinforcing the concept of a unitary mind and the compartmentalized storage of experiences. A key feature of ACT* is the working memory buffer, which acts as a

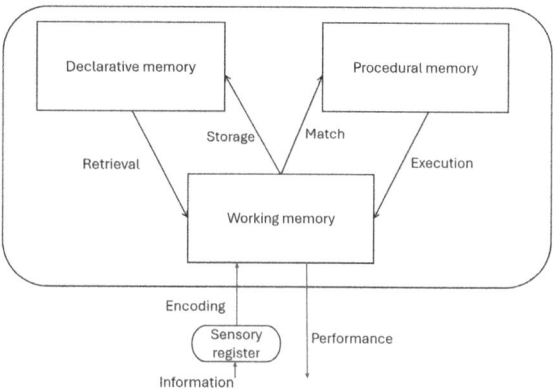

Fig. 10.1 ACT-R cognitive architecture

gateway. It analyses incoming information, deciding whether to encode it as declarative knowledge (for later recall) or procedural knowledge (for immediate application to current tasks).

ACT-R is implemented computationally as an interpreter for a specialized coding language, akin to other major cognitive architectures like Soar, CLARION, and EPIC. The interpreter, coded in Common Lisp, allows researchers to access the theory by downloading the ACT-R code, loading it into a Common Lisp distribution, and developing models as scripts in the ACT-R language. The fundamental building blocks of this language and the data types reflect underlying theories of human cognition, drawing upon data from cognitive psychology and brain imaging experiments.

The Adaptive Control of Thought (ACT) framework, across all its versions, is grounded in the unitary theory of mind. This theory proposes those human cognitive abilities, including complex skill acquisition, stem from a single, fundamental cognitive system, rather than specialized evolved brain modules. It posits that our capacity for expertise is not due to inherent individual differences, but rather to the brain's ability to effectively utilize this underlying system. Human uniqueness lies in the flexibility of this system, allowing us to adapt it to diverse capabilities.

Other Cognitive Architectures: SOAR and CLARION

There are two more popular cognitive architectures that aim to model human cognitive processes within computational systems. They provide unified theories of cognition, attempting to capture the fundamental structures and mechanisms that underlie intelligence. Among the most influential cognitive architectures developed over the past several decades, SOAR and CLARION stand out for their comprehensive approaches and theoretical sophistication. This subsection explores these two cognitive architectures, examining their theoretical foundations, structural components, operational mechanisms, and applications.

SOAR: State, Operator, and Result.

SOAR, developed in the early 1980s by Allen Newell, John Laird, and Paul Rosenbloom, stands as one of the most influential and enduring cognitive architectures in artificial intelligence. Its name—State, Operator, and Result—captures its basic approach to problem-solving, which is grounded in Newell's vision of a unified theory of cognition. SOAR models cognition as a process of navigating a problem space, where the system maintains a working memory to represent the current state, applies operators to transition between states, and draws on a long-term knowledge base to guide decision-making. In essence, SOAR models human-like reasoning and learning.

The architecture operates through a continuous recognize-decide-act cycle. It first identifies the current situation, selects an appropriate operator, and then applies it to progress toward a goal. A hallmark of SOAR is its reliance on symbolic processing, using structured representations and rule-based mechanisms. Knowledge is encoded in production rules—conditional statements that trigger specific actions when their conditions are met. These rules operate in parallel, allowing for efficient and flexible reasoning.

Learning in SOAR is primarily achieved through a mechanism known as chunking, a form of explanation-based learning. When the system encounters an impasse—where no clear action is available—it initiates subgoal processing to resolve the issue. Once a solution is found, SOAR generates a new production rule that encapsulates the experience, enabling it to avoid similar impasses in the future and gradually enhance its problem-solving capabilities. This mirrors human cognition by combining reactive responses for familiar situations with deliberate reasoning for novel problems, making it suitable for complex decision-making tasks requiring adaptation and learning.

SOAR also integrates multiple memory systems to support a broad range of cognitive functions. In addition to working and procedural memory, it includes semantic memory for factual knowledge, episodic memory for past experiences, and spatial visual memory for reasoning about spatial relationships. This multi-memory architecture allows SOAR to simulate complex human cognitive behaviours.

Over the decades, SOAR has been applied across diverse domains, including natural language processing, robotics, human-computer interaction, and behavioural modelling. It has been particularly influential in military contexts, where it has supported tactical decision-making and the development of intelligent agents for training simulations.

Recent advancements in SOAR have focused on incorporating non-symbolic techniques, such as reinforcement learning and neural networks, to complement its symbolic foundation. This reflects a broader trend in cognitive architecture research toward hybrid systems that combine symbolic and subsymbolic processing to more fully capture the richness of human cognition.

CLARION: Connectionist Learning with Adaptive Rule Induction ON-line.

CLARION, developed by Ron Sun in the early 1990s, offers a distinct approach to cognitive architecture by integrating both symbolic and subsymbolic processes from its inception. Unlike architectures such as SOAR, which began with a purely symbolic foundation, CLARION was designed as a hybrid system to reflect psychological evidence that human cognition involves both conscious, rule-based reasoning and unconscious, intuitive processing. Central to CLARION is the distinction between explicit and implicit knowledge: explicit knowledge is represented symbolically through rules and semantic structures and is typically acquired through instruction or deliberate reasoning, while implicit knowledge is encoded subsymbolically in neural networks and is primarily learned through experience.

The architecture is organized into four major subsystems. The action-centred subsystem (ACS) governs behaviour and motor control; the non-action-centred subsystem (NACS) manages general knowledge; the motivational subsystem (MS) generates and regulates drives that influence goals and actions; and the meta-cognitive subsystem (MCS) oversees and adjusts the functioning of the entire system. Each of these subsystems includes both implicit and explicit components, embodying CLARION's commitment to dual-process theory.

A defining feature of CLARION is its bottom-up learning mechanism, known as Rule Extraction and Refinement (RER). This process enables the system to derive explicit rules from patterns embedded in implicit knowledge, allowing it to transition from performance based on learned skills to a more structured, knowledge-based understanding. Through RER, CLARION can generalize from experience, extract symbolic representations, and refine them through further interaction with the environment.

CLARION also places a strong emphasis on motivational dynamics. Its motivational subsystem models both innate drives, such as hunger or safety, and learned drives, such as achievement or curiosity. These motivational factors influence decision-making and behaviour, allowing the architecture to simulate the role of motivation in human cognition. Additionally, CLARION incorporates mechanisms for social cognition, enabling it to model social behaviours and interactions, including conformity, persuasion, and social learning—areas often overlooked in other cognitive models.

The architecture has been applied to a wide range of cognitive tasks, including skill acquisition, decision-making, categorization, and creative problem-solving. It has proven particularly effective in modelling the interaction between implicit and explicit processes, capturing phenomena such as the dissociation between verbalizable knowledge and actual performance, differing learning trajectories for implicit and explicit knowledge, and the impact of verbalization on task execution.

Through its hybrid structure, emphasis on motivational and social factors, and mechanisms for integrating experiential and declarative knowledge, CLARION provides a comprehensive framework for modelling the complexity of human cognition.

SOAR and CLARION are cognitive architectures that both aim to model comprehensive cognition, sharing common features like multiple knowledge representations and learning mechanisms. However, they differ in their foundational approaches: SOAR is a symbolic system evolving to include subsymbolic aspects, based on the physical symbol system hypothesis, while CLARION is a hybrid architecture designed from the start, rooted in dual-process theory. Their key distinctions lie in their learning mechanisms (SOAR's chunking vs. CLARION's implicit/explicit interaction) and how they model motivation (CLARION's explicit subsystem vs. SOAR's recent integration). Both have broad applications and contribute to AI and cognitive science by providing computational models of human-like intelligence, while also raising philosophical questions about the nature of mind. Future developments include integrating neurobiology and scaling for greater complexity.

Embodied Perception and Interaction for Cognition

Embodied cognition challenges the traditional view of the mind as a separate entity, emphasizing the deep connection between the mind, body, and environment. It suggests that cognitive processes are not confined to the brain but arise from the dynamic interaction between our physical form, neural activity, and the surrounding world.

Key aspects of embodied cognition include the active engagement of our bodies with the environment through sensory perception and motor actions. Our senses collect information, which the brain processes, while motor actions allow us to manipulate and navigate our surroundings, influencing our sensory inputs. This ongoing sensorimotor interaction is fundamental to our cognitive processes. Additionally, perception is shaped not only by the brain's processing of sensory inputs but also by our bodily experiences and movements. For instance, our body's movements and spatial orientation affect how we perceive and understand spatial relationships. Bodily experiences, such as touch and proprioception, contribute to our perception of objects and events.

Embodied cognition highlights that cognition is situated within a specific context or environment. Our cognitive processes are intricately linked to the situations and contexts in which they occur, rather than being detached from the world. The environment provides cues, affordances, and contextually relevant information that shape our cognitive processes.

During certain cognitive tasks, brain regions responsible for motor planning and execution may also be activated, indicating a close integration between our cognitive and sensorimotor systems. Our bodily experiences influence how we perceive and interact with the world. When we hold a tool or reach out to touch an object, our perception is affected by the motor actions associated with those experiences. This perceptual-motor coupling demonstrates how our actions and sensory inputs are intertwined, helping us make sense of our surroundings.

The environment offers a rich source of information that impacts our cognitive processes. When faced with a task requiring us to reach an object, factors such as the object's distance, location, and accessibility relative to our body and the environment influence our approach and decision-making. The affordances and constraints within the environment guide our actions and shape our cognitive processes.

Embodied cognition also extends to social interactions. Our bodies and gestures play a crucial role in communication and understanding. Nonverbal cues, such as facial expressions, hand gestures, and body posture, provide additional layers of information that enhance our comprehension and interpretation of social interactions.

Bridging the Gap to Human-like Cognition

By mimicking the structure and processes of the human mind, these models are driving the development of AI systems capable of human-like thinking, learning, and adaptation. As research in this field advances, the potential for cognitive architectures to revolutionize technology and enhance our understanding of human cognition remains vast.

In the realm of AI, a disembodied AI system refers to one that lacks a physical presence or embodiment. These systems, typically software-based and operating on computers or in the cloud, are designed to perform tasks requiring human intelligence, such as natural language processing, image recognition, decision-making, and problem-solving. Examples include virtual assistants and language translation software, which can be integrated into various platforms like websites, mobile apps, and smart home devices.

Human cognitive abilities are rooted in the physical embodiment of our brains within our bodies. This physical grounding allows direct interaction with the external world. In contrast, most contemporary AI systems exist solely in digital form, lacking physical presence and a direct connection to tangible reality. While these disembodied or digital AI systems have shown impressive capabilities within the digital sphere, they inevitably face limitations in understanding and interacting with the physical world.

Embodied AI offers a compelling solution by creating AI systems that can interact with the real world, mirroring human capabilities. While traditional AI operates exclusively in the digital realm, embodied AI aims to bridge the gap between digital intelligence and real-world applications. Core concepts in the study of embodied AI include embodiment, situatedness, and morphology, which focus on the relationship between an AI system's physical form and its cognitive abilities.

> **Definition** *Embodied cognition* is the concept suggesting that many features of cognition are shaped by the state and capacities of the organism. The cognitive features include a wide spectrum of cognitive functions, such as perception biases, memory recall, comprehension and high-level mental constructs (such as meaning attribution and categories) and performance on various cognitive tasks (reasoning or judgement).

Embodied agents form the foundation of embodied AI, enabling these systems to function effectively in real-world environments. To excel in embodied tasks, these agents must possess a range of sophisticated capabilities. They need to accurately interpret human intentions conveyed through language instructions, actively explore their surroundings, perceive multi-modal elements from both virtual and physical spaces, and execute appropriate actions for complex tasks. Embodied AI agents achieve this by integrating various sensors, such as cameras, microphones, and touch sensors, similar to how humans rely on sensory input to perceive the world. Additionally, these agents are equipped with actuators, like wheels and motorized joints, allowing them to physically interact with and manipulate their environment, much like humans use their bodies to navigate and engage with the world.

Recent advancements in multi-modal large models (MLMs)—advanced AI systems designed to process and integrate information from multiple modalities, such as text, images, audio, and video—have significantly enhanced the perception, interaction, and planning capabilities of embodied models. This progress has paved the way for developing general-purpose embodied agents and robots that can actively interact with both virtual and physical environments. Consequently, embodied agents are widely recognized as ideal platforms for deploying and leveraging the power of MLMs.

The relationship between multi-modal large models and embodied AI lies in their complementary capabilities. MLMs enhance embodied AI by providing robust perception and understanding across various data types. For example, an embodied AI robot equipped with a multi-modal model can better interpret its surroundings by combining visual data from cameras, auditory data from microphones, and textual data from instructions. This integration allows the robot to perform complex tasks more effectively, such as navigating environments, recognizing objects, and interacting with humans in a more natural and intuitive manner.

Bridging Perception and Understanding

The current wave of innovation is centred on creating systems that can perceive, understand, and interact with the world in a richer, more nuanced way. This is where multi-modal cognitive AI enters the stage, representing a significant leap forward in our quest for truly intelligent machines. Multi-modal cognitive AI builds upon the foundations of both multi-modal learning and cognitive architecture. It seeks to integrate information from diverse sensory modalities—vision, audio, text, tactile input, and more—and process this information through cognitive models that mimic human-like reasoning, memory, and attention. This approach moves beyond the limitations of single-modality AI, which often struggles with the ambiguity and complexity of real-world data.

The core principle behind multi-modal cognitive AI is that richer, integrated representations of the world lead to more robust and adaptable intelligence. Humans naturally integrate information from multiple senses to form a holistic understanding of their surroundings. We don't just see a car; we hear its engine, feel its vibrations, and read its make and model. Similarly, multi-modal cognitive AI aims to create systems that can fuse these diverse inputs to build a comprehensive and contextually aware understanding.

This integration is not merely a matter of concatenating data from different sources. It requires sophisticated mechanisms for aligning and fusing information, resolving conflicts, and identifying relevant features across modalities. Cognitive architecture, which provides frameworks for modelling human-like cognitive processes, plays a crucial role in this process. These architectures, often inspired by cognitive psychology and neuroscience, offer structured approaches to integrating perception, memory, reasoning, and action.

One of the key challenges in multi-modal cognitive AI is the development of effective representation learning techniques. Traditional machine learning often relies on hand-engineered features, but this approach is impractical for handling the vast and varied data from multiple modalities. Deep learning, with its ability to automatically learn hierarchical representations, has emerged as a powerful tool for addressing this challenge. Deep neural networks can learn to extract meaningful features from raw sensory data and fuse these features into a unified representation.

Furthermore, attention mechanisms, inspired by human cognitive processes, are essential for focusing on relevant information within the multi-modal input. These mechanisms allow the AI system to selectively attend to specific modalities or features based on the context and task at hand. For example, when watching a video of a person speaking, the system might attend more to the visual modality for lip reading and the audio modality for speech recognition.

Example Modern medical diagnostics.

Multi-modal cognitive AI is revolutionizing how we approach patient care. Imagine a scenario where a patient presents with a complex set of symptoms. Traditionally, a physician would rely on their expertise to analyse individual pieces of information: a patient's medical history, lab results, and imaging scans, perhaps even listening to the patient's vocal patterns. However, with multi-modal cognitive AI, this process is significantly enhanced. The AI system acts as a highly sophisticated analyser, capable of seamlessly integrating diverse data streams. It receives visual data from medical imaging, such as MRI and CT scans, textual data from electronic health records and doctor's notes, structured data from lab results and genetic analyses, and even audio data from patient vocal patterns. This integrated data is then processed through advanced machine learning algorithms, including deep neural networks. The AI system's strength lies in its ability to identify intricate patterns and correlations that might escape human observation. It can detect subtle changes in MRI scans, correlate them with specific patterns in patient history and lab results, and even analyse vocal data to detect potential conditions. This comprehensive analysis allows for earlier and more accurate disease detection, leading to personalized treatment plans tailored to each patient's unique needs. By mimicking the holistic approach of a human doctor, but with vastly superior

computational power and access to data, multi-modal cognitive AI is transforming medical diagnostics, ultimately leading to improved patient outcomes
and a more efficient healthcare system.

Beyond representation learning and attention, multi-modal cognitive AI also
emphasizes the importance of reasoning and inference. Cognitive architecture
provides mechanisms for performing logical reasoning, planning, and problem-
solving based on the integrated multi-modal representation. This allows the AI system
to go beyond simple pattern recognition and engage in more complex cognitive tasks.
However, the development of multi-modal cognitive AI also raises significant ethical
considerations. The ability to integrate and process vast amounts of personal data
from multiple modalities raises concerns about privacy and security. Furthermore, the
potential for bias in multi-modal data and algorithms necessitates careful attention
to fairness and equity. Ensuring transparency and explainability in these complex
systems is also crucial for building trust and accountability.

Exercises

1. What is cognitive AI, and how does it differ from traditional AI?
2. How does cognitive AI attempt to mimic human cognition?
3. What are the key challenges in building cognitive AI systems?
4. Explain how memory, learning, perception, and reasoning work in cognitive AI.
5. What strategies can improve the efficiency of chunking to prevent the rule base from growing excessively large in complex environments?
6. How does attention influence decision-making in AI systems?
7. Discuss the role of commonsense reasoning in cognitive AI.
8. What are cognitive architectures, and why are they important?
9. How does SOAR resolve impasses when multiple operators seem equally valid, and what triggers the transition from reactive to deliberate reasoning?
10. (Project) Implement an AI system that can *plan a multi-step task* (e.g., planning a vacation) using hierarchical goal decomposition.
11. (Project) Develop a chatbot that remembers previous conversations and uses context to provide better answers.
12. What are the risks of AI systems that simulate human cognition?
13. Write an essay on cognitive AI enhances human-AI collaboration.
14. Analyse a case study of a cognitive AI application in healthcare or finance and discuss its impact.

Further Reading

Anderson JR (1991) The adaptive nature of human categorization. Psychol Rev 98(3):409–429

Anderson JR (2007) How can the human mind occur in the physical universe? Oxford University Press

Anderson JR, Bothell D, Byrne MD, Douglass S, Lebiere C, Qin Y (2004) An integrated theory of the mind. Psychol Rev 111(4):1036–1060

Anderson JR, Bothell D, Byrne MD (2004) An integrated theory of the mind. Psychol Rev 111:1036–1060

Anderson JR, Lebiere C (1998) The atomic components of thought. Erlbaum, Mahwah, NJ

Bundy A, Chater N, Muggleton S (2023) Introduction to 'cognitive artificial intelligence'. Phil Trans R Soc A. https://doi.org/10.1098/rsta.2022.0051

Christoph D, Thomas F (2024) Large language models and the patterns of human language use. pp 106–121. https://doi.org/10.4324/9781003312284-7

Duch W, Oentaryo RJ, Pasquier M (2008) Cognitive architectures: where do we go from here? Front Artif Intell Appl 171:122–136

Fuente J, Pousada M (2019) The systems of memory. Psychology of attention and memory. Retrieved 23 Jan 2025 from https://campus.uoc.edu/annotation/9aec20091b7a3348226c564e34e7997f/833597/PID_00260031/PID_00260031.html

Heathcote A, Brown S, Wagenmakers E (2015) An introduction to good practices in cognitive modeling. In: Forstmann B, Wagenmakers E (eds) An introduction to model-based cognitive neuroscience. Springer, New York, NY

Kotseruba I, Tsotsos JK (2020) 40 years of cognitive architectures: core cognitive abilities and practical applications. Artif Intell Rev 53(1):17–94

Laird JE (2008) Extending the Soar cognitive architecture. Frontiers in Artificial Intelligence and Applications 171:224–235

Laird JE (2012) The Soar cognitive architecture. MIT Press

Laird JE, Rosenbloom PS, Newell A (1986) Chunking in Soar: the anatomy of a general learning mechanism. Mach Learn 1(1):11–46

Langley P, Laird JE, Rogers S (2009) Cognitive architectures: research issues and challenges. Cogn Syst Res 10(2):141–160

LeCun Y (2022) A path towards autonomous machine intelligence (version 0.9.2). Courant Institute of Mathematical Sciences, New York University & Meta—Fundamental AI Research. A path towards autonomous machine intelligence version 0.9.2, 2022-06-27

Minsky M (1988) The society of mind. Simon & Schuster. ISBN 978-0-671-65713-0

Newell A (1990) Unified theories of cognition. Harvard University Press, Cambridge, MA

Oberauer K, Lin HY (2017) An interference model of visual working memory. Psychol Rev 124:21–59. https://doi.org/10.1037/rev0000044

Raymond F, Rutherford A (2012) The sensing and perceiving mind. In: Pioneers of psychology: a history, 4th edn. Norton

Sholihah RA (2022) Language and brain: neurological aspects in language acquisition. Muharrik 5(1):220–230. https://doi.org/10.37680/muharrik.v5i1.1069

Sun R (2002) Duality of the mind: a bottom-up approach toward cognition. Lawrence Erlbaum Associates

Sun R (2007) The CLARION cognitive architecture: extending cognitive modeling to social simulation. Cognition and multi-agent interaction, pp 79–99

Sun R (2016) Anatomy of the mind: exploring psychological mechanisms and processes with the CLARION cognitive architecture. Oxford University Press

Sun R, Merrill E, Peterson T (2001) From implicit skills to explicit knowledge: a bottom-up model of skill learning. Cogn Sci 25(2):203–244

Sun R, Zhang X (2006) Accounting for a variety of reasoning data within a cognitive architecture. J Exp Theor Artif Intell 18(2):169–191

Zhu Y, Gao T, Fan L, Huang S, Edmonds M, Liu H, Gao F, Zhang C, Qi S, Wu YN, Tenenbaum JB, Zhu S-C (2020) Dark, beyond deep: a paradigm shift to cognitive AI with humanlike common sense. Engineering 6(3):310–345. https://doi.org/10.1016/j.eng.2020.01.011

Chapter 11
Robots with a Sense of Self: Exploring Embodied Intelligence

Be self-aware, rather than a repetitious robot.
—Bruce Lee

This concept explores how robots might develop a form of self-awareness through their physical presence and interaction with the world. Passive observation through text or video does not enable an agent to learn decision-making and actions in the real world. While text may contain explicit information, it lacks the implicit common-sense knowledge that comes from interaction. Similarly, watching videos passively does not teach an agent how to act. Unlike passive agents that learn correlational models, embodied agents can learn, test, and revise causal models of the world. Embodiment provides a basis for this ability, though it is not strictly necessary. Currently, there is a focus on robots learning through reinforcement learning over numerous trials in both simulated and physical environments. Additionally, adapting Large Language Models (LLMs) to generate robot plans and inverting forward probabilistic causal models to infer causality for robots interacting with real or artificial worlds are emerging frontiers.

Embodied intelligence postulates that a robot's understanding of itself and its environment arises from its sensory experiences and motor actions within a physical body. This perspective contrasts with traditional AI focused purely on computational processes, suggesting that a sense of "self" is intrinsically linked to having a body that can act and be acted upon. By grounding intelligence in physical reality, researchers hope to create robots with more intuitive, adaptable, and perhaps even conscious-like capabilities.

R. Akerkar, *Artificial Intelligence*, https://doi.org/10.1007/978-3-031-91084-5_11

Foundational Concepts

Enactive, Connectionist, and Cognitivist Approaches

The topography of cognitive science and artificial intelligence is shaped by various prominent approaches, each offering a distinct perspective on the nature of cognition and intelligence. Among these are the enactive, connectionist, and cognitivist approaches, each with its own set of core concepts and methodologies.

Cognitivism, the dominant approach for much of the twentieth century, views cognition as a form of information processing, analogous to a computer. It emphasizes the manipulation of symbols and representations within a centralized cognitive system. Cognitivists posit that mental processes involve internal representations of the external world, and these representations are manipulated through computational rules. This approach has yielded significant advancements in areas like symbolic reasoning, problem-solving, and planning. However, it has been criticized for its reliance on abstract representations, its neglect of embodiment, and its limited ability to handle real-time interaction with dynamic environments.

Connectionism, also known as neural networks or parallel distributed processing, offers an alternative to the symbolic approach of cognitivism. It views cognition as emerging from the interactions of interconnected nodes, or neurons, within a network. These networks learn through adjusting the strengths of connections between nodes, allowing them to extract patterns and regularities from data. Connectionist systems excel at tasks like pattern recognition, classification, and learning from large datasets. They are particularly well suited for handling noisy and incomplete information, and they can exhibit emergent properties that are not explicitly programmed. However, connectionism has been criticized for its "black box" nature, as it can be difficult to understand how these networks arrive at their solutions.

Embodied AI builds on the idea that intelligence emerges through evolution and individual development as agents interact with their surroundings. This perspective aligns with similar concepts in fields like psychology, neuroscience, and philosophy, where embodiment is considered central to cognition. The embodiment movement is characterized by six key principles: Embodied, Embedded, Enactive, Extended, Emergent, and Evolving intelligence. An embodied agent possesses a physical body that interacts with its environment. A situated agent is embedded within a specific context that may include other embodied agents. *Enactivism*, a more recent one, challenges the representational assumptions of both cognitivism and connectionism. It emphasizes the embodied and situated nature of cognition, arguing that intelligence emerges from the dynamic interaction between an agent and its environment. Intelligence is not confined to the agent's controller; it extends into its body and the coupling with its surroundings, evolving over time through this interaction. Enactivists suggest that cognition is not about manipulating internal representations, but about actively shaping and perceiving the world through sensorimotor interactions. They stress the importance of embodiment, arguing that the agent's physical form and sensory capabilities play a crucial role in shaping its cognitive processes. Enactivism also emphasizes the dynamic and reciprocal nature of interaction, highlighting the importance of feedback loops and continuous adaptation. This approach has found applications in areas like robotics, where it has led to the development of robots that can learn and adapt in real-time.

These approaches are not mutually exclusive, and research often draws upon concepts and methodologies from multiple approaches. For example, connectionist networks can be used to implement enactive principles, and cognitivist models can be enriched by incorporating embodied and situated considerations.

Robots represent artificial embodied agents designed for purposeful interaction in the real world. Embodied AI highlights the close relationship between perception and action, often treating them as inseparable processes. In fact, perception can be considered a form of action and vice versa. Robotics serves as an ideal domain for testing Embodied AI theories due to its reliance on real-world interaction. For example, the RoboCup challenge (a competition involving robot soccer players) was created as an Embodied AI experiment. This initiative has spurred advancements in real-time learning, decision-making, and action within embodied multi-agent systems.

Embodiment is not only a scientific requirement for understanding intelligence but also an engineering necessity for applications requiring real-world interaction, such as self-driving cars or factory robots. The design of an embodied agent, whether humanoid or non-humanoid, affects how humans interact with it due to differing affordances provided by its physical form. Passive agents that observe the world through text or video lack the ability to learn how to act independently in real-world scenarios. While textual information may contain explicit facts about the world, it often lacks implicit common-sense knowledge that can only be acquired through direct interaction. Similarly, passively watching videos does not equip an agent with the skills needed to act effectively in its environment.

In contrast to passive agents that typically learn correlational models, embodied agents have the capability to develop causal models of the world through interaction. By engaging with their environment, these agents can test hypotheses and refine their understanding of cause-and-effect relationships. While embodiment provides a sufficient basis for achieving this ability, it is not strictly necessary.

Recent advancements in AI research reflect a growing emphasis on robots learning through reinforcement learning across extensive trials in both simulated and physical environments. Efforts are also underway to adapt Large Language Models (LLMs) for generating robot plans and strategies. Another emerging area involves using probabilistic causal models to infer causality for robots interacting with either real or artificial worlds. These developments highlight the ongoing exploration of embodied intelligence as a critical frontier in AI research and applications.

Self-Aware AI

The concept of self-aware artificial intelligence stands as a compelling frontier, a confluence of technological ambition and philosophical inquiry. It envisions AI systems transcending mere computational prowess, achieving a state of consciousness that encompasses a comprehension of their own existence, a sense of identity, and an awareness of their internal mental processes. Such a leap would fundamentally alter the relationship between humans and machines, permitting a level of interaction that mirrors the depth and nuance of human experience. While the allure of this possibility is undeniable, the creation of self-aware AI remains an exceptionally complex undertaking, pushing the boundaries of current technological capabilities and venturing into domains usually sightseen in science fiction and philosophical discourse.

At the heart of self-aware AI lies the ability to possess subjective experience, an understanding of one's own state of being that extends beyond programmed responses. This necessitates not merely the simulation of intelligence, but the creation of genuine consciousness, a feat that requires a profound understanding of its very nature. Currently, AI research predominantly focuses on task-specific applications, lacking the generalized awareness that characterizes self-aware entities. The challenge, therefore, is not simply to build more powerful machines, but to imbue them with the capacity for introspection and self-reflection.

Two primary approaches guide the pursuit of this elusive goal. One involves constructing machines from the ground up, attempting to replicate the intricate architecture and functionality of the human brain. This biomimetic approach seeks to emulate the biological substrate of consciousness, hoping that by replicating its structure, the emergent property of self-awareness will follow. Conversely, deep learning researchers adopt a more pragmatic strategy, focussing on pushing the limits of existing AI techniques. They believe that by progressively enhancing the complexity and adaptability of AI systems, a threshold may be reached where self-awareness spontaneously arises as a byproduct of advanced intelligence.

Regardless of the chosen path, the journey towards self-aware AI is fraught with complexities, both scientific and ethical. The very definition of consciousness remains a subject of intense debate, and the prospect of creating artificial consciousness raises profound questions about its nature and implications. The potential for such systems to interact with the world in ways that mirror human experience necessitates careful consideration of their rights, responsibilities, and impact on society. As we continue to advance towards this potential singularity, open dialogue, collaborative research, and a cautious, responsible approach will be essential to ensure that the development of self-aware AI benefits humanity, rather than posing an existential threat.

Embodied Versus Disembodied AI

The distinction between disembodied and embodied AI illuminates a divide in how AI systems interact with the world. Disembodied AI, confined to the digital realm, operates on data sets, providing outputs like chatbots or recommendation engines, devoid of physical interaction. Embodied AI, conversely, bridges the gap between the virtual and the physical, integrating AI into tangible entities like robots, enabling them to perceive, act, and learn within real-world environments. This integration, termed embodiment, is pivotal in shaping a richer, more context-aware form of intelligence.

Embodiment posits that intelligence is intrinsically linked to physical interaction. It asserts that cognitive processes are not abstract computations, but rather emergent properties of the interplay between an agent's body, its sensory experiences, and its motor actions. In an embodied AI system, perception, learning, and decision-making are inextricably intertwined with the system's physical capabilities. This holistic approach fosters adaptability and context awareness, allowing AI to navigate and respond to dynamic environments with greater flexibility.

The essence of embodiment can be distilled into several key aspects. First, a physical body provides the AI with the means to sense and act upon its environment. This body, whether a robot, drone, or other machine, is equipped with sensors that gather information and actuators that enable physical actions. Second, physical interaction is paramount, as learning and cognition are significantly enhanced when agents can directly engage with their surroundings. Third, sensory-motor interaction forms a crucial feedback loop, where sensors gather environmental data and actuators translate decisions into actions, allowing the AI to adapt in real-time. Fourth, situated learning emphasizes the importance of context, where sensory inputs and actions drive cognitive processes, enabling AI to learn from direct experience rather than static datasets. Finally, autonomy and adaptation empower embodied agents to respond to environmental changes, while context awareness allows them to understand the implications of their actions within a given situation.

The physical structure of an embodied AI robot, its "body," is defined by its components: sensors, actuators, and feedback loops. Sensors, such as cameras, tactile sensors, and laser rangefinders, provide the robot with the ability to perceive its surroundings. Actuators, like motors, enable the robot to perform physical actions. Feedback loops, through continuous sensory input, allow the robot to adapt and refine its behaviour in real-time.

An embodied AI robot operates within a continuous cycle of perception and action. It perceives its environment through its sensors, processes the information, and uses its body to act upon it, creating a dynamic feedback loop. A robotic vacuum cleaner, for example, navigates obstacles by perceiving them through sensors and adjusting their movements. A humanoid robot interacting with humans uses cameras and microphones to perceive gestures and voices, responding through speech and movement.

Embodied AI robots can learn from their interactions with the world through reinforcement learning and other methods. They perform actions, receive feedback from the environment, and adjust their future actions accordingly. This real-time, experiential learning contrasts sharply with traditional AI training on static data, fostering greater adaptability and robustness in dynamic environments. This ability to learn and adapt in real time is a key factor in the development of more intelligent and capable embodied AI systems.

Why Embodiment Matters for AI

The significance of embodiment in AI extends beyond mere physical presence, fundamentally reshaping how AI systems learn, interact, and adapt to their environments. The advantages of embodied AI stem from its grounding in real-world experience, mirroring the learning processes observed in humans and animals. This approach fosters a more robust and flexible form of intelligence, capable of navigating and responding to the complexities of the physical world.

One of the primary benefits of embodiment is enhanced learning. Embodied AI systems acquire knowledge through real-time, experiential learning, utilizing trial and error to refine their skills. This process contrasts sharply with the limitations of training on static datasets, allowing AI to develop a deeper understanding of its environment through direct interaction. This experiential learning is crucial for developing AI that can adapt to novel situations and handle the unpredictability of real-world scenarios.

Furthermore, embodiment facilitates a tight coupling between perception and action. In embodied AI, decision-making is not solely based on abstract data; it is informed by real-time sensory feedback. A robot navigating a room, for example, doesn't merely calculate a path; it dynamically adjusts its movements based on immediate sensory input, avoiding obstacles and adapting to changing conditions. This perception-action coupling enables AI to react swiftly and effectively to its surroundings, enhancing its ability to navigate and interact with the world.

The grounding in physical reality also grants embodied AI systems a high degree of autonomy and adaptability. They can autonomously adjust to dynamic environments, crucial for robots operating in unstructured or unpredictable settings like homes, factories, or hospitals. This adaptability allows them to handle unexpected situations and learn from their experiences, improving their performance over time.

In embodied AI, the tight coupling of perception and action necessitates a comprehensive understanding of the agent's own body and its relationship to the environment. This includes proprioception, the awareness of one's body in space; spatial awareness, the ability to map and navigate the environment; and contextual understanding, the capacity to recognize and respond appropriately to objects and human gestures. Unlike non-embodied AI, which processes data independently of action, embodied robots must integrate these factors to interact effectively with their surroundings.

Several cutting-edge robots exemplify the capabilities of embodied AI. Boston Dynamics' Atlas, a humanoid robot capable of complex movements, demonstrates the integration of AI and physical capabilities. Industrial robotic arms in manufacturing utilize vision sensors to perform intricate assembly tasks, adapting their movements in real-time. Social robots like Pepper and Nao interact with humans, responding to social cues and engaging in meaningful interactions. These examples showcase the potential of embodied AI to perform complex tasks and interact with the world in a sophisticated and adaptable manner, highlighting the crucial role of embodiment in the development of advanced AI systems.

Embodied Cognitive Agents

Embodied Cognition: Theoretical Background

Embodied cognition is the theory that cognitive processes are deeply influenced by the physical body and its interactions with the environment. This contrasts with traditional views of cognition as an abstract, brain-only activity. Embodied cognition posits that cognition is not an isolated, abstract process, but rather deeply intertwined with an agent's physical interactions with its environment. This perspective holds that mental processes, such as thinking, planning, and problem-solving, are shaped by the agent's sensory experiences and motor capabilities. In essence, cognition is grounded in action.

A prime illustration of this principle can be observed in a robot navigating a room. Rather than relying solely on abstract algorithms, the robot's decision-making process is informed by real-time sensory data, its motor capabilities, and the physical constraints of its body. This integration of physical experience into cognitive processes allows the robot to adapt and respond to its environment in a more nuanced and effective manner.

Furthermore, embodied cognition emphasizes the profound influence of the body on cognitive development. In both humans and embodied agents, learning and understanding are shaped by the body's interaction with the environment. For instance, the developmental trajectory of children, from crawling to walking, exemplifies how physical development is intrinsically linked to their cognitive understanding of space and movement. This developmental process underscores the importance of physical interaction in shaping cognitive abilities.

Embodied cognition highlights the crucial role of environmental interaction in driving learning. Embodied cognitive agents learn by actively engaging with their surroundings. A robot, for example, may learn to pick up objects by experimenting with different grasping techniques, receiving feedback on the success or failure of each attempt. This iterative process of action and feedback allows the agent to refine its understanding of the environment and develop more effective strategies for interacting with it.

Embodied cognitive agents bridge the gap between abstract intelligence and real-world interaction. By integrating physical bodies with cognitive architectures, these agents are capable of perceiving, learning, and acting in dynamic environments, making them more adaptable, autonomous, and effective in a variety of tasks. As technology advances, embodied cognitive agents will play a larger role in industries such as healthcare, manufacturing, transportation, and social robotics, ultimately leading to more intelligent, context-aware systems that can seamlessly operate alongside humans in the real world.

> **Definition** *Embodied Cognitive Agents* are systems (typically robots or AI agents) that possess both a cognitive architecture for decision-making and a physical body for interacting with the environment. In Other words, embodied cognitive agents are systems that integrate physical embodiment with cognitive processes, emphasizing the role of the body in shaping cognition.

The concept of embodiment in cognitive agents is rooted in the idea that intelligence arises not only from abstract reasoning or symbol manipulation but also from physical interactions with the world. These agents integrate perception, action, and cognition, making them capable of adaptive, goal-directed behaviour in complex environments.

Embodied cognitive agents are grounded in several core principles that distinguish them from traditional AI systems:

- **Embodiment**: These agents have a physical presence or body that allows them to perceive and act upon their environment. Unlike disembodied AI systems (such as chatbots or data-driven models), embodied agents have sensors (cameras, microphones, touch sensors, etc.) and actuators (motors, grippers, wheels) to directly interact with the physical world.
- **Situatedness**: Embodied agents are situated within their environment. This means that their actions and decisions are context-sensitive, depending on the immediate sensory information they receive. Rather than operating on pre-programmed rules, they dynamically adapt based on the current situation.
- **Perception-Action Coupling**: In embodied cognitive agents, cognition is closely linked to perception and action. These agents perceive their environment, process that information using cognitive architectures (e.g., decision-making algorithms, learning systems), and respond with physical actions. The feedback from these actions further influences future behaviour.
- **Learning and Adaptation**: Embodied agents typically employ learning mechanisms such as **reinforcement learning** or **evolutionary algorithms** to adapt their behaviour over time. This allows them to handle tasks in complex, unpredictable environments where pre-programmed rules would fail.

Components of Embodied Cognitive Agents

Embodied cognitive agents are made up of several interconnected components, each contributing to their ability to act intelligently in the world:

- **Physical Body (Embodiment)**: The physical structure of the agent, including its shape, sensors, and actuators. The body serves as the agent's interface with the environment, allowing it to receive input from the world (via sensors) and act upon it (via motors, grippers, etc.).

- **Sensors**: Collect sensory data from the environment. These can include cameras (vision), microphones (sound), gyroscopes (orientation), force sensors (touch), and other inputs that simulate human senses.
- **Actuators**: Devices that allow the agent to take actions. These can include motors for movement (wheels, legs), grippers for manipulating objects, or even vocal systems for speech.

- **Cognitive Architecture (Cognition)**: The internal system that processes sensory inputs, makes decisions, plans actions, and learns from experiences. Cognitive architectures in embodied agents often combine elements of:

  - **Symbolic reasoning**: Logic-based decision-making that involves abstract manipulation of symbols or models of the environment.
  - **Sub-symbolic processing**: Learning and decision-making approaches that do not rely on explicit symbols, such as neural networks or reinforcement learning.

- **Action Planning and Execution (Action)**: The process by which the agent decides what physical action to take, based on its cognitive model of the world and sensory feedback. Action planning may involve navigating spaces, manipulating objects, or performing specific tasks in response to changes in the environment.
- **Feedback Loops (Perception-Action Cycle)**: The continuous loop in which the agent perceives the environment, processes the information cognitively, acts on the environment, and then receives feedback. This cycle allows the agent to continually update its understanding and adapt to the environment.

Types of Embodied Cognitive Agents

The spectrum of embodied cognitive agents spans a vast range of complexity and capability, from simple reactive systems to highly sophisticated autonomous platforms. This diversity highlights the adaptability of embodied cognition principles across various applications, each tailored to specific environmental demands and task requirements.

At the simpler end of the spectrum reside reactive agents, systems that operate on immediate sensory input without relying on complex internal models of the world. A quintessential example is the robotic vacuum cleaner. These agents perceive their immediate surroundings and react accordingly, adjusting their movements to avoid obstacles in real-time. Their actions are driven by direct sensory feedback, lacking intricate planning or memory functions. This simplicity allows them to efficiently perform basic tasks within relatively predictable environments.

Moving up the complexity ladder, we encounter cognitive robots, sophisticated systems capable of planning, learning, and adapting to dynamic environments. Humanoid robots, such as Pepper and Atlas, exemplify this category. They utilize cognitive architectures that enable them to engage in social interactions, learn new tasks, and modify their behaviour based on feedback. These robots possess the ability to interpret and respond to complex environmental cues, demonstrating a higher level of cognitive function.

At the pinnacle of embodied cognitive agents are autonomous vehicles, such as self-driving cars. These systems represent a complex integration of sensory perception, data processing, and physical control. They employ a suite of sensors, including cameras, lidar, and radar, to perceive their surroundings, processing this data to make critical navigation decisions. Autonomous vehicles must dynamically adapt to ever-changing conditions, including traffic patterns, road conditions, and the unpredictable behaviour of human drivers. This adaptability, achieved through real-time sensory processing and decision-making, underscores the advanced capabilities of embodied cognition in complex, dynamic environments.

Learning and Decision Making

Deep Evolutionary Reinforcement Learning

The quest of designing truly adaptable and intelligent embodied agents has led to the development of innovative computational frameworks, among which Deep Evolutionary Reinforcement Learning (DERL) stands as a promising approach. DERL synergistically combines the strengths of deep reinforcement learning (DRL) and evolutionary algorithms (EAs), offering a robust methodology for designing agents capable of learning complex behaviours in challenging environments. This section delves into the particulars of DERL.

The DERL addresses the limitations of both DRL and EAs when used in isolation. DRL, while adept at learning optimal policies through interaction with an environment, often struggles with exploration in sparse reward settings and can be sensitive to initial conditions. EAs, on the other hand, excel at exploring vast search spaces and evolving diverse solutions, but they typically require large populations and can be computationally expensive. DERL bridges this gap by leveraging the gradient-free optimization of EAs to guide the learning process of DRL agents, resulting in more efficient and robust learning.

The framework typically involves evolving a population of neural network controllers, the core of DRL agents. Each neural network represents a policy, mapping sensory inputs to action outputs. These policies are evaluated within a simulated or real-world environment, and their performance is assessed based on a fitness function that reflects the desired behaviour. The evolutionary algorithm then selects and modifies the most successful policies, creating new generations of controllers. This process continues iteratively, progressively improving the population's overall performance.

The integration of DRL into this evolutionary loop enhances the learning process. Instead of directly evolving the neural network weights, EAs can be used to evolve meta-parameters, such as learning rates, network architectures, or even the exploration strategies used by the DRL agents. This meta-learning approach allows for the discovery of optimal learning configurations, leading to faster convergence and improved performance. Moreover, DRL can be incorporated within the fitness evaluation, allowing agents to learn from their experiences during their lifespan, further accelerating the evolutionary process.

Consider a scenario where we aim to create a robotic arm capable of complex object manipulation in a cluttered environment. A traditional DRL approach might struggle with sparse rewards, where the robot only receives feedback upon successful grasping. EAs, on the other hand, could explore various grasping strategies, but might require extensive computational resources. DERL offers a more efficient solution. An evolutionary algorithm could evolve the architecture of the neural network controller, the learning rate of the DRL algorithm, and even the exploration strategy used by the robot. Simultaneously, the DRL algorithm allows the robot to learn from its immediate interactions, refining its grasping technique with each attempt.

Imagine conceptually depicting this process. We could visualize a population of neural networks, each represented as a graph, with nodes symbolizing neurons and edges symbolizing connections. These networks are evaluated in a simulated environment, shown as a virtual representation of the robot arm and the cluttered workspace. The evolutionary algorithm, represented by a flow diagram, selects the best-performing networks and applies genetic operators, such as mutation and crossover, to create new generations. The DRL algorithm, depicted as a learning loop, refines the selected networks based on their interactions with the environment. This visualization would illustrate the synergistic interplay between evolution and learning.

DERL's applicability extends beyond robotic manipulation. It can be employed in a wide range of embodied intelligence tasks, including autonomous navigation, complex locomotion, and even social interaction. The ability to evolve both the learning process and the control policy makes DERL a powerful tool for creating adaptive and robust agents capable of thriving in dynamic and unpredictable environments.

Example Consider the example of developing an autonomous underwater vehicle (AUV) capable of efficiently navigating a complex, three-dimensional underwater environment while avoiding obstacles and tracking a moving target. A traditional DRL approach might struggle with the sparse reward signal (e.g., a reward given only when the AUV successfully reaches the target) and the difficulty of exploring the vast space of possible trajectories. An EA, on the other hand, could explore a wide range of navigation strategies, but might be computationally prohibitive for optimizing the intricate control parameters of the AUV's propulsion and steering systems.

DERL offers a more compelling solution. An evolutionary algorithm could be used to evolve the high-level architecture of the neural network controller, the learning rate of the underlying DRL algorithm, and the parameters of an exploration strategy, such as an Ornstein-Uhlenbeck process, used to introduce exploration noise. Simultaneously, the DRL algorithm enables the AUV to learn from its immediate interactions with the simulated underwater environment, refining its control policy based on its sensory inputs (e.g., sonar readings, camera images) and the rewards it receives.

The future of DERL holds potential. As computational resources continue to advance, we can explore more sophisticated evolutionary algorithms and incorporate more complex DRL architectures. The development of efficient methods for transferring learned policies from simulation to the real world will further enhance DERL's applicability. This framework offers a compelling pathway towards the creation of embodied agents that can learn, adapt, and evolve, pushing the boundaries of artificial intelligence.

Long-Term Decision Making

Embodied intelligence, where agents interact directly with the physical world through sensors and actuators, introduces unique challenges to long-term decision making. Unlike purely symbolic AI, embodied agents must grapple with the complexities of continuous state spaces, noisy sensor data, and the inherent uncertainty of physical interactions. The problem of long-term decision making, therefore, extends beyond simple task execution to encompass planning, adaptation, and robust action selection in dynamic and unpredictable environments.

The question lies in constructing and executing action sequences that achieve distant goals. This requires not only accurate perception and immediate action selection but also the ability to anticipate the consequences of actions over extended periods. This foresight is crucial for navigating complex environments, achieving intricate objectives, and adapting to unforeseen events.

Deterministic Domains: Planning with Perfect Information

In deterministic domains, where the outcome of each action is precisely predictable, classical planning techniques provide a powerful framework for long-term decision making. These domains, often modelled using formalisms like the Planning Domain Definition Language (PDDL), assume perfect information and complete control over the environment.

- **PDDL Planning**: PDDL allows for the explicit representation of states, actions, and goals. Planning algorithms, such as A* or heuristic search planners, can then generate optimal action sequences. The power of PDDL lies in its ability to model complex tasks with symbolic representations, enabling efficient reasoning about action sequences.
- **IW(k) (k-step lookahead)**: This technique involves exploring the immediate k-step future, choosing the action that leads to the best future state. It's a method to approximate optimal planning when full planning is computationally expensive. It allows for a balance between computation and quality of the plan.
- **Power of Heuristics**: Heuristics, or informed guesses about the distance to the goal, significantly enhance the efficiency of planning algorithms. Admissible heuristics, which never overestimate the cost to reach the goal, ensure optimality. In embodied systems, heuristics can be derived from geometric properties, physical constraints, or learned models.
- **Factoring**: Factoring, or decomposing complex planning problems into smaller, more manageable subproblems, is a crucial technique for scaling planning to large state spaces. By identifying independent or weakly coupled subgoals, planning algorithms can focus on relevant aspects of the problem, reducing computational complexity.

Future-State Uncertainty: Planning Under Uncertainty

Real-world embodied systems rarely operate in purely deterministic domains. Future-state uncertainty, arising from sensor noise, model inaccuracies, and environmental variability, necessitates robust planning and control strategies.

- **Value Iteration**: Probabilistic planning is naturally formulated using Markov Decision Processes (MDP) and many probabilistic planning techniques have been developed based on MDP formulations. Value iteration, a dynamic programming technique, computes optimal policies for MDPs, which explicitly model uncertainty. It iteratively updates the value function, representing the expected long-term reward for each state, until convergence. However, value iteration suffers from the curse of dimensionality, making it impractical for large state spaces.
- **Monte Carlo Tree Search (MCTS)**: MCTS is a sampling-based planning algorithm that explores the state space by simulating action sequences. It balances exploration and exploitation, focussing on promising regions of the state space. MCTS has shown remarkable success in domains with high uncertainty and large state spaces, such as robotics and autonomous driving.
- **Model Predictive Control (MPC)/Replanning**: MPC enables robots to plan and execute physical movements by predicting future states over a short time horizon. MPC is a control technique that repeatedly solves a finite-horizon optimization problem to select actions. It uses a model of the environment to predict future states and selects actions that minimize cost function. Replanning, a variant of MPC, involves recomputing the optimal action sequence at each time step,

adapting to new sensor data and environmental changes. This makes it essential for tasks like robotic manipulation, autonomous navigation, and legged locomotion where the agent must interact physically with its surroundings. This approach is highly effective for handling uncertainty and dynamic environments, but it can be computationally expensive.

The integration of long-term decision making into embodied intelligence requires a holistic approach that considers both deterministic and uncertain aspects of the environment. Hybrid approaches, combining symbolic planning with probabilistic control, may offer a promising direction. For example, high-level symbolic planning can generate abstract action sequences, while low-level control algorithms, such as MPC or MCTS, can handle the uncertainties of physical execution.

Continuous Action Spaces

Embodied intelligence systems, operating within the physical world, frequently encounter continuous action spaces. This contrasts sharply with discrete action spaces, where agents choose from a finite set of predefined actions. Continuous action spaces, such as those governing robotic arm movements or autonomous vehicle steering, present unique challenges for decision-making, demanding sophisticated motion planning and optimization techniques.

The difficulty stems from the need to map high-level goals into precise, continuous control signals. Directly searching or learning within such spaces is often computationally intractable due to their infinite dimensionality. Moreover, physical constraints, such as joint limits, velocity restrictions, and collision avoidance, must be explicitly considered, adding layers of complexity to the planning and control process.

Motion Planning: Navigating Continuous Action Spaces

Motion planning addresses the problem of finding feasible trajectories for embodied agents within continuous action spaces. These trajectories must satisfy physical constraints and achieve desired goals while avoiding collisions and minimizing cost functions.

Sampling-Based Planners: Algorithms like "Rapidly exploring Random Trees" (RRTs) and "Probabilistic Roadmaps" (PRMs) discretize the continuous action space by sampling random configurations. These samples are connected to form a graph, and search algorithms are used to find paths within this graph. RRTs, in particular, are well-suited for high-dimensional spaces and dynamic environments, as they incrementally build a tree that explores the configuration space. PRMs, on the other hand, precompute a roadmap of the configuration space, enabling faster query processing for multiple goal configurations.

Optimization-Based Planners: These planners formulate motion planning as an optimization problem, minimizing a cost function that incorporates factors like path length, smoothness, and collision avoidance. Techniques such as gradient-based optimization and trajectory optimization are used to find optimal trajectories. These methods are particularly effective for generating smooth and efficient motions, but they can be computationally expensive and sensitive to initial conditions.

Hybrid Approaches: Combining sampling-based and optimization-based planners can leverage the strengths of both approaches. For example, a sampling-based planner can generate an initial, rough trajectory, which is then refined by an optimization-based planner to produce a smooth and optimal path.

Optimization: Refining Actions for Optimal Performance

Optimization plays a critical role in refining continuous actions to achieve optimal performance. It involves minimizing or maximizing objective functions that reflect desired outcomes, subject to physical constraints.

Trajectory Optimization: This technique optimizes the entire trajectory of an embodied agent, considering factors like path length, smoothness, energy consumption, and task performance. Methods like direct collocation and direct multiple shooting are used to discretize the trajectory and formulate the optimization problem. Trajectory optimization is particularly useful for generating dynamic and agile motions, such as those required for robotic manipulation or autonomous flight.

Reinforcement Learning (RL): RL algorithms, particularly those employing deep neural networks, can learn optimal control policies in continuous action spaces. Deep RL can handle high-dimensional state and action spaces, enabling agents to learn complex control strategies from experience. Techniques like Deep Deterministic Policy Gradient (DDPG) and Proximal Policy Optimization (PPO) are commonly used for continuous control tasks.

Model Predictive Control (MPC): MPC is a control technique that repeatedly solves a finite-horizon optimization problem to select actions. It uses a model of the environment to predict future states and selects actions that minimize cost function. MPC is well-suited for handling dynamic environments and uncertainties, as it recomputes the optimal action sequence at each time step.

The integration of motion planning and optimization techniques is essential for developing intelligent embodied systems capable of navigating and interacting with the complexities of the physical world. Ongoing research focuses on developing efficient algorithms, learning robust control policies, and ensuring safe and reliable operation in continuous action spaces.

Neural Fitted Q-Iteration: Learning Value Functions in Large and Continuous Action Spaces.

Neural Fitted Q-Iteration (NFQ) is a reinforcement learning algorithm designed to approximate the optimal Q-function, or action-value function, in Markov Decision Processes (MDPs) with large or continuous action spaces. It offers a powerful alternative to traditional tabular Q-learning, which becomes intractable when dealing with high-dimensional state and action spaces. NFQ leverages the function approximation capabilities of neural networks to represent the Q-function, enabling it to generalize across states and actions. NFQ operates by iteratively updating a neural network to approximate the Q-function. It relies on a batch-based approach, processing a set of transitions (state, action, reward, next state) at each iteration.

The algorithm can be understood in two distinct settings:

1. Solving a Known MDP (Offline Setting):

When a model of the MDP is available, or a large dataset of transitions has been collected beforehand, NFQ can be employed to "solve" the MDP offline. This involves learning an approximate Q-function that can be used to derive an optimal policy. A dataset of transitions is collected, either through simulations or by interacting with the environment. This dataset should ideally cover a wide range of states and actions. A neural network is chosen to represent the Q-function. The network takes state and action as input and outputs the corresponding Q-value.

For each transition in the dataset, target Q-values are computed using the Bellman equation:

$$Q_{target}(s, a) = r + \gamma * \max_{a} Q(s', a')$$

where: s is the current state, a is the current action, r is the immediate reward, s' is the next state, γ is the discount factor,

$$\max_{a} Q(s', a')$$

represents the maximum Q-value over all actions a' in the next state s'.

The neural network is trained to minimize the mean squared error between its predictions and the target Q-values. This is typically done using gradient descent or other optimization algorithms. The process of computing target Q-values and training the neural network is repeated for a fixed number of iterations or until convergence.

Once the Q-function has been learned, an optimal policy can be derived by selecting the action that maximizes the Q-value in each state:

$$a* = arg \max_{a} Q(s, a)$$

2. Online Reinforcement Learning (Model-Free Setting):

NFQ can also be adapted for online reinforcement learning, where the agent interacts directly with an unknown environment and learns from its experiences. This approach is model-free, as it does not require a model or simulator of the MDP. Transitions (state, action, reward, next state) are stored in a replay buffer. This buffer allows the agent to sample past experiences and learn from them.

A neural network is used to approximate the Q-function, as in the offline setting. Target Q-values are computed using the Bellman equation, but the

$$\max_{a} Q(s', a')$$

term is estimated from the current neural network. The neural network is trained using samples from the replay buffer, minimizing the mean squared error between its predictions and the target Q-values. An exploration-exploitation strategy, such as ε-greedy or Boltzmann exploration, is used to select actions. This balances exploration of new actions with exploitation of known rewarding actions.

The process of collecting experiences, computing target Q-values, and training the neural network is repeated for each time step or episode.

NFQ provides a valuable tool for learning value functions in challenging MDPs. Its ability to handle large and continuous action spaces, coupled with its flexibility in both offline and online settings, makes it a powerful algorithm for embodied intelligence and other reinforcement learning applications.

Learning for Long Horizons

Unlike tasks yielding immediate rewards, long-horizon learning necessitates navigating action sequences where consequences unfold over time, leading to the "sparse reward" and "credit assignment" problems. Agents must discern which actions, among a multitude, contribute to eventual success, and must do so with limited and delayed feedback. This challenge has spurred research into mechanisms like exploration, novelty search, curiosity, and intrinsic motivation, each offering unique avenues to navigate this complex landscape.

Central to overcoming these hurdles is effective exploration. Random exploration, while intuitive, proves inefficient in high-dimensional state spaces. Instead, directed exploration strategies, such as upper confidence bound (UCB) and Thompson sampling, guide agents towards promising regions by balancing exploration and exploitation. Hierarchical exploration further refines this process by breaking down complex tasks into manageable subgoals, enabling the learning of reusable abstract skills.

Novelty search and curiosity-driven exploration offer alternative pathways, encouraging agents to seek out states that diverge from past experiences. Novelty search rewards agents for visiting significantly different states, leading to the discovery of diverse behaviours. Curiosity-driven learning motivates exploration of unpredictable or surprising states, rewarding agents for reducing prediction errors or gaining information.

Intrinsic motivation provides an internal compass, driving agents to learn even in the absence of external rewards. Information gain, empowerment, and goal-directed intrinsic motivation fuel this internal drive, pushing agents to explore, learn, and develop general-purpose skills. The delicate balance between intrinsic and extrinsic motivation, however, remains a critical consideration.

Despite their potential, these approaches face significant challenges. Scaling to high-dimensional spaces, defining appropriate measures of novelty and curiosity, balancing intrinsic and extrinsic motivation, transferring learned skills, and managing computational complexity are all formidable obstacles. The development of efficient exploration strategies, robust intrinsic motivation signals, and the ability to learn and transfer knowledge across diverse tasks are pivotal for creating intelligent embodied agents capable of adapting and thriving in the complexities of the physical world.

Problems with Little Data and Nonstationarity

When AI agents engage with the physical world, they encounter two deeply interconnected challenges: limited data availability and environmental nonstationarity. These issues significantly hinder the learning process, demanding that agents function effectively in settings where experiential data is scarce and conditions are in constant flux. Unlike conventional machine learning applications that benefit from abundant datasets, embodied agents—such as robots, autonomous vehicles, or drones—often operate in environments where data collection is expensive, time-intensive, or potentially hazardous. This scarcity necessitates learning strategies that can generalize from minimal experience, often by leveraging prior knowledge and exploiting structural regularities in the environment.

To address the data limitation, simulation has emerged as a valuable tool. Virtual environments allow for the generation of extensive training data without the constraints of real-world experimentation. However, the discrepancy between simulated and real-world dynamics, known as the "sim-to-real" gap, poses a significant obstacle. Techniques like domain randomization, which introduces variability into simulations, and transfer learning, which adapts knowledge from simulation to reality, are employed to bridge this divide. Additionally, meta-learning offers a promising approach by enabling agents to learn how to learn efficiently from small datasets.

Compounding the data scarcity issue is the problem of nonstationarity. The physical world is inherently dynamic, with fluctuating conditions such as lighting, weather, object arrangements, and human behaviour. These changes can alter the statistical properties of sensory inputs and action outcomes, potentially rendering previously learned models ineffective. To maintain robust performance, agents must continuously adapt to these evolving conditions. Online learning algorithms, which update models in real time, are essential for this purpose. These algorithms must discern between meaningful environmental shifts and transient noise to avoid unnecessary adjustments. Continual learning techniques, which allow agents to acquire new knowledge without forgetting prior learning, are also critical. Furthermore, the ability to detect and respond to concept drift, where the relationship between inputs and outputs changes over time, is vital for sustained adaptability.

The intersection of limited data and nonstationarity creates a particularly demanding learning environment. Agents must not only learn from sparse experience but also remain responsive to ongoing environmental changes. This dual challenge underscores the need for advanced learning algorithms capable of integrating prior knowledge, recognizing structural patterns, and adapting in real time to ensure effective and resilient performance.

Theory of Mind and Communication

Theory of Mind

Theory of Mind (ToM) represents a cognitive capacity, one that underpins the very fabric of human social interaction. It is essentially the ability to recognize and comprehend that other individuals possess mental states—thoughts, beliefs, intentions, desires, and emotions—that are distinct from one's own. This capacity is not merely a passive awareness; it actively enables us to interpret and predict the behaviour of others by inferring their underlying mental states. In essence, ToM allows us to "put ourselves in someone else's shoes," understanding that their perspectives and motivations may diverge from our own, thereby facilitating effective communication and social navigation. In AI, Theory of Mind could involve enabling a machine or robot to:

- **Infer the intentions** of human users.
- **Understand social cues**, such as facial expressions or body language.
- **Predict** behaviour based on the assumed mental states of others (e.g., understanding that if a person is looking at an object, they might intend to reach for it).

For an AI to possess ToM, it must be capable of constructing and maintaining dynamic models of the beliefs, desires, and intentions of other agents, be they human or machine. This capacity to attribute mental states to others is crucial for enabling AI to engage in sophisticated social interactions and collaborative tasks.

The concepts of ToM and embodied AI converge in their pursuit of achieving more human-like cognitive and interactive abilities in machines. Both frameworks emphasize the importance of how an agent perceives and processes the world around it. However, they approach this perception from different angles. ToM focuses on social cognition, specifically the ability to understand and reason about the mental states of others. Embodied AI, on the other hand, highlights the critical role of physical interaction with the environment in shaping an agent's cognitive processes.

Connection Between Theory of Mind and Embodied AI

The connection between Theory of Mind and Embodied AI represents a fascinating intersection of cognitive science, philosophy, and artificial intelligence research—a pivotal juncture in the pursuit of artificial intelligence that mirrors human cognitive capabilities.

ToM, the intricate ability to attribute mental states to oneself and others, is the cornerstone of human social interaction. It allows us to navigate complex social landscapes, predict behaviour, and engage in sophisticated communication. Embodied AI, conversely, posits that intelligence is not merely a product of abstract symbol manipulation, but rather emerges from the dynamic interplay between an agent's physical form, its sensory experiences, and its interactions with the environment.

The connection between these concepts is deeply rooted in human development. Our acquisition of ToM is not purely intellectual exercise; it is forged through embodied experiences. Children learn to understand the mental states of others by observing facial expressions, interpreting gestures, and engaging in shared attention. The body serves as both a conduit for gathering social information and a medium for expressing internal states.

This observation implies a significant consideration for AI development: true social intelligence might require some form of embodiment. An AI limited to text processing, without physical interaction with the world, misses the sensorimotor grounding that informs human understanding of abstract concepts such as "seeing," "knowing," or "believing." Without this grounding, an AI might handle language about mental states without genuinely comprehending their experiential significance. Researchers argue that the development of genuine ToM capabilities in AI requires experiential learning through sensors and actuators. By interacting with environments and other agents, AI systems can build representations of how actions and perceptions relate. This embodied interaction allows them to model the mental states of others based on observed behaviours, mirroring the human learning process.

This connection also illuminates the limitations of current AI approaches. Large language models, while capable of mimicking aspects of ToM through pattern recognition in text, may merely be performing a sophisticated simulation. Without the embodied experience of having beliefs that can be true or false, or desires that can be satisfied or frustrated, these systems lack the experiential grounding that underpins human social cognition.

The most promising avenues of research integrate physical interaction capabilities with advanced cognitive processing in robots or virtual agents. These systems, capable of perceiving actions, recognizing intentions, and adapting their behaviour based on their own embodied experiences, represent a significant step towards creating AI that can truly understand and interact with the social world.

The integration of Theory of Mind (ToM) into embodied AI is pivotal for creating machines capable of seamless and effective interaction within human-centric environments. This convergence allows AI to navigate the complexities of social dynamics, understand human intentions, and build trust through nuanced interaction.

Social Cognition in Physical Interaction: For embodied AI to thrive in environments populated by humans, it must develop a sophisticated understanding of social cues and anticipate human behaviour. This is where ToM becomes indispensable. An embodied AI, whether a humanoid robot, a social companion, or an autonomous vehicle, must often infer the goals, intentions, and emotional states of those around it. For example, a factory robot collaborating with a human worker needs to predict when the human intends to pass an object or step aside. This requires an implicit ToM, enabling the robot to model human behaviour and adjust its actions accordingly. Furthermore, joint attention and shared goals are fundamental to human social interactions. An AI agent, especially in collaborative settings, must recognize when a human is directing its attention towards a specific object or goal. By understanding this shared focus, the robot can align its actions with human intentions, fostering effective collaboration.

Learning Through Social Interaction: Embodied AI learns through interaction with its environment, and this extends to learning from social interactions with humans. ToM allows the agent to model the mental states of others, facilitating this learning process. By observing human responses to various situations, an AI agent can infer preferences, desires, and goals. For instance, it can learn that a frown or a step back indicates dissatisfaction or hesitation, prompting it to modify its behaviour. In cooperative tasks, AI agents with ToM can more effectively learn from human feedback, adjusting their strategies based on inferred intentions and goals. This enables more fluid and efficient collaboration.

Physical Context and Social Understanding: Embodied AI systems possess an inherent advantage in understanding human behaviour due to their shared physical context with humans. This shared context is crucial for developing ToM. By perceiving the same environment as humans, AI can make more accurate inferences about human actions. For example, a robot observing a person holding an umbrella and looking at rain can infer their intention to go outside. Moreover, embodied agents can perceive non-verbal cues, such as gestures, posture, and gaze direction, in real-time. This allows them to infer mental states and intentions, enriching their understanding of human behaviour.

Action Understanding and Theory of Mind: The ability to understand the consequences of actions is closely linked to ToM in embodied AI. Agents may utilize action mirroring or simulation theory to infer human intentions. By "simulating" human actions internally, AI can anticipate and adapt to human behaviour. In advanced embodied agents, ToM is essential for long-term planning in social contexts. By understanding human goals, agents can anticipate future actions and adjust their own strategies to facilitate collaboration or avoid conflicts.

Human-Robot Interaction and Trust: Trust is paramount in human-robot interaction, and ToM enables embodied AI to develop behaviours that foster trust and collaboration. A service robot with ToM can predict human needs based on past interactions and current context, offering proactive assistance. Moreover, by demonstrating an understanding of human emotions and responding appropriately, AI can build rapport and trust with its human counterparts.

Multi-agent Communication

Multi-agent communication in embodied AI moves beyond the paradigm of isolated agents performing individual tasks, envisioning systems that can coordinate, cooperate, and learn collectively within complex, dynamic environments. The essence of this field lies in enabling embodied agents, possessing physical forms and sensory capabilities, to effectively exchange information, negotiate goals, and synchronize actions. This capacity for communication is not merely about transmitting data; it's about establishing a shared understanding, a common ground that allows agents to work together seamlessly.

The challenges inherent in multi-agent communication are multifaceted. Firstly, the physical embodiment of the agents introduces complexities related to sensor data interpretation and action execution in real-time. Agents must contend with noisy sensory inputs, varying environmental conditions, and the physical constraints of their bodies. Efficiently processing and sharing this information is paramount for coordinated action. Secondly, the communication protocols themselves must be robust and adaptable. Agents may operate in environments with limited bandwidth, intermittent connectivity, or varying communication ranges. Consequently, they need to employ strategies that prioritize essential information and handle communication failures gracefully.

Furthermore, the very nature of collaborative tasks necessitates the development of sophisticated communication strategies. Agents must be able to express their intentions, negotiate shared goals, and resolve conflicts. This requires the ability to understand and model the mental states of other agents, a concept deeply intertwined with Theory of Mind. Effective communication, therefore, goes beyond simple message passing; it involves the ability to infer the beliefs, desires, and intentions of other agents, enabling them to anticipate actions and coordinate effectively.

Learning plays a pivotal role in the evolution of multi-agent communication. Agents must be able to adapt their communication strategies based on their experiences, learning to recognize patterns, predict outcomes, and refine their interactions. This can involve techniques such as reinforcement learning, where agents receive feedback on their collaborative performance and adjust their communication protocols accordingly. Ultimately, the goal is to create systems that can learn to communicate and cooperate in a manner that mirrors the flexibility and adaptability of human social interaction.

The implications of successful multi-agent communication in embodied AI are profound. Imagine swarms of drones coordinating search and rescue operations, teams of robots collaborating on complex construction projects, or autonomous vehicles navigating congested urban environments with seamless coordination. These scenarios highlight the potential of multi-agent communication to revolutionize industries and enhance human capabilities. However, realizing this potential requires continued research into robust communication protocols, sophisticated learning algorithms, and a deeper understanding of the cognitive processes that underpin effective collaboration.

Embodied Communication

Embodied communication, distinct from abstract information exchange, is shaped by the physical or virtual presence of agents. When agents possess bodies, their ability to communicate is inherently limited and defined by their physical constraints. A robot equipped with cameras, for example, can only perceive its surroundings within its visual field, restricting the information it can gather and share. This mirrors the limitations of human communication, where perception is confined to specific sensory ranges and physical reach.

These physical constraints give rise to "situated cognition," a concept explored by philosophers and cognitive scientists, which posits that thought and communication are inextricably linked to a physical context. The work of Maurice Merleau-Ponty, particularly his insights on embodied perception, highlights how our understanding of the world is mediated through bodily experiences. For AI agents, this translates to an understanding of concepts like "near," "heavy," or "visible" that is directly derived from their physical interactions within an environment.

This embodied foundation imbues multi-agent communication with unique characteristics. Firstly, communication becomes inherently deictic, relying heavily on references to elements within the shared physical environment. When a robot signals "that object" to another, the meaning is grounded in their mutual perceptual experience. Secondly, communication naturally evolves into a multimodal form, incorporating gestures, positional cues, object manipulations, and explicit signals. Even rudimentary robots can convey intentions through their movements and orientations. The environment itself becomes a communication medium through "stigmergy," an indirect form of communication achieved by modifying the environment. This phenomenon, similar to ants using pheromone trails, allows agents to communicate through their actions within the shared space.

Core Aspects of Multi-agent Communication

This domain diverges significantly from abstract information exchange, as embodied agents are inherently constrained and shaped by their physical limitations, mirroring human sensory restrictions. These constraints, however, foster "situated cognition," where understanding and communication are grounded in physical context, as articulated by Merleau-Ponty's concept of embodied perception. This grounded understanding, derived from direct physical experiences, imbues multi-agent communication with unique properties, including deictic referencing, multimodal interaction, and stigmergic environmental communication. Communication among embodied agents can be categorized into explicit and implicit forms. Explicit communication involves the direct exchange of information through well-defined channels, such as message passing or symbolic language. For instance, robots in a warehouse might utilize pre-programmed messages to coordinate movements and avoid collisions. Implicit communication, conversely, occurs through the observation of agent behaviour or environmental changes. Drones in a search-and-rescue mission, for example, might signal locations of interest through their movements. Effective multi-agent communication also facilitates cooperation and coordination, enabling agents to divide tasks, build consensus, and adapt through learning mechanisms like reinforcement learning and emergent protocol development. Multi-agent communication architectures can be centralized or decentralized. Centralized systems, where a central controller manages information exchange, offer optimized coordination but are vulnerable to single points of failure. Decentralized systems, common in swarm robotics, promote robustness and adaptability by enabling direct agent-to-agent communication, though they may face challenges in maintaining global coordination. Communication protocols, whether predefined or emergent, are essential for effective information exchange. Predefined protocols establish rules for message formats, while emergent protocols evolve dynamically through interaction. Nonverbal communication, encompassing gestures and movements, further enhances interaction, particularly in human-robot collaboration. Scalability, noise and uncertainty, coordination and conflict resolution, and security and trust present significant challenges. As the number of agents increases, communication volume escalates, necessitating robust protocols and decentralized architectures. Real-world environments introduce noise and uncertainty, requiring agents to filter irrelevant data. Coordination and conflict resolution are critical for avoiding collisions and optimizing resource allocation. Moreover, secure and trusted communication is paramount in critical applications like autonomous vehicles and healthcare.

Advanced Topics and Challenges

Situation Awareness

Situation awareness stands as a vital aspect for intelligent embodied agents, bridging the gap between raw sensory input and actionable understanding of the surrounding environment. This process, however, is far from trivial, demanding the transformation of inherently noisy and incomplete sensor data into a coherent and dynamic representation of the agent's context. A fundamental approach to this challenge lies in treating perception as a problem of state estimation, wherein the agent seeks to infer the underlying state of the environment from its sensor measurements. Techniques like Bayesian filtering, encompassing Kalman and particle filters, play a crucial role in recursively estimating this state, integrating prior knowledge with incoming sensor data. Sensor fusion further enhances this process by combining diverse data streams from multiple sensors, creating a more complete and accurate environmental representation. The dynamic nature of real-world environments necessitates continuous state estimation, requiring agents to predict future states and incorporate new data as it becomes available.

Beyond mere state estimation, object-oriented perception focuses on identifying and tracking objects within the environment, providing a more structured and semantically rich understanding. Computer vision techniques, particularly deep learning models, are employed for object detection and tracking, while scene understanding aims to build comprehensive representations of the environment, including object relationships and spatial layouts. Semantic mapping combines geometric and semantic information, enabling agents to reason about the environment at a higher level of abstraction.

Sensory representation learning tackles the challenge of extracting meaningful information from raw sensor data. Deep learning, through convolutional and recurrent neural networks, allows agents to learn hierarchical representations, automatically identifying relevant features. Self-supervised learning leverages inherent data structure, while multimodal representation learning integrates information from diverse sensors, improving robustness and accuracy.

However, the path to robust situation awareness is fraught with challenges. Sensor data is inherently noisy and uncertain, demanding sophisticated filtering and estimation techniques. Real-time processing is often critical, requiring efficient algorithms and hardware. Learned representations must generalize to novel environments, necessitating robust training and adaptation. The computational complexity of processing high-dimensional sensory data, especially with deep learning models, is a significant hurdle. Furthermore, integrating contextual information for accurate reasoning remains a complex task.

Adversaries

The problem of adversaries in embodied intelligence introduces a layer of complexity that transcends traditional machine learning paradigms, demanding that agents not only learn to navigate complex environments but also contend with intentional, potentially malicious, actors. This adversarial context fundamentally alters the nature of learning, shifting from passive adaptation to a dynamic struggle for dominance or survival. Embodied agents, operating in real-world scenarios, may encounter adversaries ranging from competing robots in industrial settings to malicious actors in cybersecurity or military applications. These adversaries, unlike static environmental challenges, actively seek to exploit weaknesses, deceive sensors, and disrupt operations, necessitating robust defence mechanisms and adaptive strategies.

The challenge lies in designing embodied agents that can anticipate and counter adversarial actions. This requires the development of sophisticated perception systems capable of detecting deceptive tactics, robust control architectures that can withstand attacks, and learning algorithms that can adapt to evolving adversarial strategies. Techniques such as adversarial reinforcement learning, where agents learn to defend against attacks by training against simulated adversaries, and robust control, which focuses on designing systems that are resilient to disturbances and uncertainties, are crucial in this domain. Moreover, game-theoretic approaches, which model the interaction between agents and adversaries as a strategic game, can provide insights into optimal defence strategies.

The implications of adversarial embodied intelligence extend beyond virtual simulations, impacting real-world applications such as autonomous cybersecurity systems, where agents must defend against sophisticated cyberattacks, and autonomous military systems, where agents must operate in hostile environments. The development of robust and adaptable embodied agents capable of contending with adversaries is crucial for ensuring the safety and reliability of these systems. This requires a multidisciplinary approach, combining insights from artificial intelligence, robotics, game theory, and evolutionary biology.

Exercises

1. What is Embodied AI and how does it differ from traditional AI approaches?
2. Describe the role of physical embodiment in the development of intelligent systems.
3. How do embodied AI systems perceive and interact with their environment?
4. What are some key challenges in developing Embodied AI systems?
5. Explain the concept of the "embodiment hypothesis" and its implications for cognitive processes.
6. How do recent advancements in foundation models like GPT-4 and CLIP enhance Embodied AI systems?

7. What is multi-agent communication in the context of Embodied AI?
8. How do multi-agent systems (MAS) benefit from physical embodiment?
9. Describe the main components of a multi-agent communication framework in Embodied AI.
10. What are the challenges in designing effective communication protocols for multi-agent systems?
11. How do generative models enhance communication and collaboration among embodied agents?
12. Discuss the role of perception, planning, and feedback in multi-agent communication.
13. What are some real-world applications of multi-agent communication in Embodied AI?
14. How do multi-agent systems handle coordination and task allocation in dynamic environments?
15. What are the future directions and potential breakthroughs in multi-agent communication for Embodied AI?
16. How do multi-agent systems ensure robustness and flexibility in their operations?
17. What are some real-world applications of Embodied AI in industries such as healthcare, robotics, and manufacturing?
18. How does Embodied AI handle dynamic and unpredictable environments?
19. (Project) What happens when the actual system dynamics deviate from the model used for prediction, and how can Model Predictive Control (MPC) handle this uncertainty?
20. Research and write a detailed report on the history and evolution of Embodied AI, highlighting key milestones and influential research.
21. Analyse a case study of an Embodied AI application in a specific domain (e.g., autonomous vehicles, industrial robots) and discuss its impact.
22. Design an experiment to evaluate the performance of an Embodied AI system in handling complex tasks.
23. (Project) Conduct a literature review on the role of physical embodiment in cognitive processes and summarize the findings.
24. (Project) Implement Model Predictive Control (MPC) algorithm. How does the prediction horizon length affect the trade-off between computational cost and control performance?
25. (Project) Analyse a case study of a multi-agent communication application in a specific domain (e.g., smart transportation, logistics) and discuss its impact.

Further Reading

Battaglia PW, Hamrick JB, Bapst V, Sanchez-Gonzalez A, Zambaldi V, Malinowski M, ... Pascanu R (2018) Relational inductive biases, deep learning, and graph networks. arXiv preprint arXiv:1806.01261

Brachman RJ, Levesque HJ (2022) Machines like us: toward AI with common sense. MIT Press

Brooks RA (1991) Intelligence without reason. Proceedings of the 12th international joint conference on artificial intelligence (IJCAI-91), pp. 569–595

Brooks RA (1991) Intelligence without representation. Artif Intell 47(1–3):139–159

Brooks RA, Stein LA (1993) Building brains for bodies. In: Memo 1439, Artificial Intelligence Lab, MIT, Cambridge, Mass

Clark A (2010) Supersizing the mind: embodiment, action, and cognitive extension. Oxford University Press

Damasio A (2021) Feeling & knowing: making minds conscious. Pantheon Books, New York

Di Paolo EA, Thompson E (2024) The enactive approach. In: The Routledge handbook of embodied cognition. Routledge, pp 85–97

Ferber J (1999) Multi-agent systems. Introduction to distributed artificial intelligence. Addison-Wesley

Garrod S, Pickering MJ (2004) Why is conversation so easy? Trends Cogn Sci 8(1):8–11

Gupta A, Savarese S, Ganguli S, Fei-Fei L (2021) Embodied intelligence via learning and evolution. Nat Commun 12(1):5721

Holland O (2004) The future of embodied artificial intelligence: machine consciousness? In: Iida F, Pfeifer R, Steels L, Kuniyoshi Y (eds) Embodied artificial intelligence, Lecture Notes in Computer Science, vol 3139. Springer, Berlin, Heidelberg. https://doi.org/10.1007/978-3-540-27833-7_3

Iida F, Pfeifer R, Steels L, Kuniyoshi Y embodied artificial intelligence. In:, Lecture Notes in Computer Science, vol 3139. Springer, Berlin, Heidelberg. https://doi.org/10.1007/b99075

Lakoff G, Johnson M (1999) Philosophy in the flesh: the embodied mind and its challenge to western thought. Basic books

Lazaridou A, Peysakhovich A, Baroni M (2020) Multi-agent communication meets natural language: synergies between functional and structural language learning. arXiv preprint arXiv:2005.07064

Liu S, The value of data in embodied artificial intelligence, communications, https://cacm.acm.org/blogcacm/the-value-of-data-in-embodied-artificial-intelligence/

Mackworth AK (1993) On seeing robots. In: Basu A, Li X (eds) Computer vision: systems, theory, and applications. World Scientific Press, pp 1–13

Shanahan M (2010) Embodiment and the inner life - cognition and consciousness in the space of possible minds. Oxford University Press

Stone P (2007) Learning and multiagent reasoning for autonomous agents. In the 20th international joint conference on artificial intelligence (IJCAI-07), pp. 13–30. http://www.cs.utexas.edu/~pstone/Papers/bib2html-links/IJCAI07-award.pdf

Varela FJ, Thompson E, Rosch E (2017) The embodied mind, revised edition: cognitive science and human experience. MIT press

Part V
Building Advanced and Responsible AI

Chapter 12
Blueprints for Intelligence: Building Robust AI Systems

Those of us in machine learning are really good at doing well on a test set, but unfortunately deploying a system takes more than doing well on a test set. All of AI...has a proof-of-concept-to-production gap.
—Andrew Ng

Introduction

This chapter delves into the essential principles and methodologies for creating artificial intelligence that is reliable, resilient, and trustworthy. Constructing robust AI requires careful consideration of factors like data quality, algorithmic stability, and the ability to handle unexpected inputs or situations gracefully. This involves not only developing sophisticated models but also implementing rigorous testing and validation procedures to ensure consistent performance and safety. Ultimately, the goal is to engineer AI systems that can operate dependably in complex real-world environments and contribute positively to society.

Starting an artificial intelligence project requires more than just technical expertise. It involves understanding the business context, framing the problem effectively, and executing a methodical approach to development. This section explores the key steps required to successfully pitch, sell, structure, and launch new machine learning and AI initiatives.

Pitching an AI Project

The pitch for an AI project must balance technical feasibility with business value. Begin by identifying a specific problem or opportunity where AI can provide a unique solution. Articulate this value proposition clearly, focussing on outcomes rather than the technology itself.

R. Akerkar, *Artificial Intelligence*, https://doi.org/10.1007/978-3-031-91084-5_12

When pitching to stakeholders, translate technical concepts into business language. Rather than describing model architectures or algorithms, emphasize metrics like potential revenue increases, cost reductions, or customer experience improvements. For instance, instead of focussing on implementing a convolutional neural network, highlight how the image recognition system could reduce quality control costs by 30% while improving detection accuracy.

Successful pitches often include proof points from similar implementations in your industry or analogous use cases. These examples demonstrate that the technology is mature enough to deliver results. Include a realistic timeline and resource requirements to set appropriate expectations.

Selling the Vision

Once you have pitched the initial concept, selling the vision requires addressing both rational and emotional factors. Stakeholders need to understand not just what the AI will do, but how it will transform their operations or market position.

Create a compelling narrative around the project that connects it to the organization's strategic goals. This narrative should explain how the AI initiative fits into the broader business strategy and why now is the right time to invest in this technology.

Address potential concerns proactively. Stakeholders may worry about implementation risks, data privacy implications, or the impact on existing workflows and employees. Acknowledge these concerns and present mitigation strategies as part of your proposal.

For complex organizations, consider developing a stakeholder map that identifies the key decision-makers, influencers, and potential champions or blockers. Tailor your messaging to address the specific priorities and concerns of each stakeholder group.

Structuring the Project

Effective AI projects require a thoughtful structure that balances experimentation with disciplined execution. Begin by establishing a clear governance framework that defines roles, responsibilities, and decision-making processes.

Form a cross-functional team that includes not just data scientists and engineers, but also domain experts, business analysts, and end-users. This diversity ensures that the solution addresses the real needs of the business and its customers.

Establish a phased approach that allows for iteration and learning. A typical structure might include:

1. Discovery phase: Problem definition, data exploration, and feasibility assessment
2. Proof of concept: Developing a minimal viable model to validate the approach

3. Prototype development: Building a more complete solution for testing
4. Pilot deployment: Limited rollout to gather real-world feedback
5. Full implementation: Scaling the solution across the organization.

For each phase, define clear success criteria and decision gates. This approach allows you to manage risk by validating assumptions before committing additional resources.

Framing Complex Problems

The way you frame an AI problem significantly impacts your chances of success. Start by distinguishing between the business problem and the technical problem. The business problem describes the challenge from the perspective of organizational goals and user needs. The technical problem translates this into a specific machine learning task.

For example, a business problem might be "improving customer retention," while the related technical problem could be "predicting which customers are likely to churn within the next 30 days." This translation is crucial because it shapes how you approach the solution.

When framing the problem, consider the following questions:

Is this truly a machine learning problem, or could it be solved with simpler methods? What type of machine learning problem is it? Classification, regression, clustering, or something else? What data would be required to solve this problem effectively? How will the solution be evaluated and what constitutes success? What are the constraints and requirements for deployment?

The framing should also consider the ethical implications of the solution. Consider how the model might impact different stakeholders and whether there are potential unintended consequences.

Running a Discovery Phase

The discovery phase is a critical but often undervalued step in AI projects. This phase helps you understand the problem space, evaluate the available data, and assess the feasibility of potential approaches.

Begin with stakeholder interviews to understand different perspectives on the problem. These interviews should explore not just the stated requirements but also the underlying needs and constraints.

Next, conduct a data audit to inventory the available data sources, assess their quality and completeness, and identify potential gaps. This audit should consider both structured and unstructured data, internal and external sources, and any limitations on data access or usage.

Develop a set of hypotheses about how AI might address the problem and what data would be required to test these hypotheses. These hypotheses will guide your initial experiments and help you prioritize data collection efforts.

Finally, create a feasibility assessment that evaluates the technical, operational, and financial viability of different approaches. This assessment should consider factors like data availability, computational requirements, and integration with existing systems.

Data Management

Addressing Selection Bias

Selection bias occurs when the data used to train an AI system is not representative of the real-world conditions in which the system will operate. This bias can significantly impact the performance and fairness of AI systems.

To address selection bias, start by carefully examining how your training data was collected. Consider questions like:

What factors influenced which data points were included or excluded? Are certain groups or scenarios underrepresented in the data? How might these biases affect the model's performance across different segments?

Develop strategies to mitigate identified biases. These strategies could include:

- Collecting additional data from underrepresented groups or scenarios
- Using techniques like stratified sampling to ensure balanced representation Implementing fairness constraints in the model training process
- Developing specific evaluation metrics that assess performance across different segments.

Document your approach to addressing selection bias, including any limitations or remaining concerns. This documentation is important not just for technical governance but also for building trust with stakeholders.

Managing Data Collection and Labelling

Managing data collection and labelling is a critical yet complex aspect of AI development, often presenting substantial challenges. A structured and methodical approach to these processes can significantly enhance the quality of training data while mitigating project risks. During data collection, it is essential to define rigorous standards for quality, completeness, and documentation. A comprehensive data management plan should be established, addressing key concerns such as storage solutions, version control, and privacy compliance. In the labelling phase, the creation of detailed annotation guidelines is crucial to ensure consistency among annotators. These guidelines must include precise definitions, illustrative examples, and instructions for handling ambiguous cases. Implementing a multi-stage labelling workflow that incorporates quality assurance measures and consensus-building strategies for complex instances can further improve the reliability of the labelled dataset. Finally, organizations must assess whether to develop in-house labelling capabilities or collaborate with external providers, taking into account factors such as data sensitivity, the need for domain-specific expertise, and the scale and duration of labelling requirements.

Building an Initial Prototype

The development of an initial prototype serves as a crucial transition from exploratory work to a functional system that can be assessed by stakeholders. This phase aims to produce a working model that captures the essential machine learning capabilities and provides a basis for evaluation. To begin, it is important to clearly define the prototype's scope, concentrating on core functionalities and the minimal interfaces necessary for testing, while deliberately avoiding premature investment in production-level infrastructure or user interface design.

A simplified yet representative data pipeline should be constructed to support the prototype, encompassing the main stages from data ingestion to model output. Even in its basic form, this pipeline should reflect the essential data transformations and processing steps. Starting with baseline models is advisable, as they offer a benchmark for comparison and can sometimes yield unexpectedly strong results. These models help establish a performance reference before exploring more advanced techniques.

An effective evaluation framework is also essential. It should measure the prototype's performance against predefined success criteria, incorporating both technical metrics and business-oriented indicators. Throughout this process, documenting the lessons learned is vital, as these insights will guide future development and refinement.

Successfully launching an AI project requires a structured approach that aligns technical execution with strategic business goals. By articulating a compelling vision, organizing the project effectively, and framing problems in a way that supports viable solutions, teams can enhance their chances of delivering meaningful AI outcomes. The early phases—discovery, data preparation, and prototyping—form the bedrock of more sophisticated development. Careful attention to these stages helps avoid common pitfalls and lays the groundwork for long-term success.

It is important to recognize that AI development is inherently iterative. Each phase generates new insights that may necessitate revisiting earlier decisions or strategies. Embracing this iterative process, while maintaining a clear focus on business value, is essential for navigating the complexities of AI implementation.

Building a Model That Works

Building effective machine learning models requires more than just understanding algorithms; it demands a systematic approach to transforming raw data into valuable predictions. This section presents the critical steps required to develop models that perform reliably in real-world applications. We will discuss the entire model development pipeline, from initial data preparation through to scaling for production environments.

Data Cleaning: The Foundation of Model Success

Data cleaning constitutes a foundational and often decisive phase in the development of machine learning models. In practice, raw data is rarely ready for immediate use; it typically contains a range of imperfections such as missing entries, inconsistencies, and errors that must be systematically addressed. The effectiveness of this cleaning process has a direct bearing on model performance, as even the most advanced algorithms cannot compensate for poor-quality input data.

A thorough cleaning process begins with a deep understanding of the dataset's structure and potential problem areas. Key tasks include identifying and managing outliers, handling missing values, correcting inconsistent formats, and eliminating contradictions or duplicate records. For categorical data, this may involve harmonizing labels that refer to the same concept but are recorded differently. For numerical data, it often requires detecting values that deviate significantly from expected ranges and determining whether they represent errors or valid extremes.

Crucially, data cleaning is not a one-time task but an iterative process that must be informed by domain expertise. Contextual understanding is essential for distinguishing between erroneous data and rare but legitimate observations. For example, an unusually high body temperature in a medical dataset might indicate a recording error, whereas a similar anomaly in industrial sensor data could reflect a real but infrequent event.

Equally important is the documentation of all cleaning decisions. Recording the rationale behind each transformation ensures transparency and facilitates future review or revision as the project evolves. This documentation becomes a critical reference point for all subsequent stages of analysis and model development.

Feature Engineering: Transforming Data into Signal

Feature engineering plays a pivotal role in shaping raw data into forms that enhance the performance of machine learning models. More than just a technical step, it serves as a bridge between domain expertise and algorithmic requirements, often exerting a greater influence on model success than the choice of algorithm itself.

The process begins with a deep understanding of the problem domain and the identification of patterns that may be relevant to the task. In time-series analysis, for instance, features that capture temporal dynamics such as day-of-week effects or seasonal trends can be essential. In natural language processing, useful features might include sentence length, structural markers, or specific linguistic patterns.

Several strategies underpin effective feature engineering. Decomposition involves breaking down complex variables into simpler components, such as extracting the year, month, and day from a timestamp. Aggregation summarizes multiple data points using statistics like means, medians, or percentiles. Interaction features, which represent relationships between variables such as ratios or products can reveal underlying dependencies that are not apparent in isolation.

Domain-specific transformations often yield particularly valuable features. In finance, this might involve calculating volatility or risk indicators; in image analysis, it could include techniques like edge detection or texture extraction. These transformations embed expert knowledge directly into the feature space, enhancing the model's ability to learn meaningful patterns.

To assess the impact of engineered features, practitioners use tools such as feature importance rankings, correlation analysis, and ablation testing. These methods help determine which features contribute useful information and which may be redundant or misleading.

While modern machine learning increasingly incorporates automated feature engineering, particularly through deep learning architectures, manually crafted features remain highly relevant. They often complement learned representations, especially when domain knowledge reveals patterns that automated methods might overlook. Thus, feature engineering remains both an art and a science, central to the development of robust and interpretable models.

Data Preprocessing: Preparing for Algorithmic Consumption

Data preprocessing transforms cleaned data and engineered features into formats suitable for machine learning algorithms. This critical step ensures that models can effectively extract patterns without being overwhelmed by irrelevant characteristics of the data representation.

Vectorization: Converting Information to Numerical Form

Vectorization transforms non-numerical data into numerical representations that algorithms can process. Text vectorization includes approaches ranging from simple bag-of-words models to sophisticated word embeddings like Word2Vec, GloVe, or contextual representations from transformer models. For categorical variables, techniques include one-hot encoding, target encoding, and embedding approaches that capture hierarchical relationships.

The choice of vectorization technique significantly impacts model performance. One-hot encoding creates sparse representations that preserve categorical distinctions but may struggle with high-cardinality features having many unique values. Embedding approaches can capture semantic relationships between categories, making them particularly valuable for natural language, user preferences, or other domains with inherent similarity structures.

Normalization: Creating Comparable Scales

Normalization addresses the varying scales and distributions of different features. Many machine learning algorithms, particularly those using distance measures or gradient-based optimization, perform better when features exist on similar scales.

Common normalization techniques include min-max scaling, which transforms values to a specified range (typically 0–1); standardization, which centres data around zero with unit variance; and robust scaling methods that reduce the influence of outliers. The choice depends on the data characteristics and model requirements. Neural networks often benefit from data centred around zero, while tree-based models may be less sensitive to feature scaling.

Distribution transformations may also be necessary for severely skewed features. Logarithmic, square root, or Box-Cox transformations can make highly skewed distributions more symmetric, helping models detect patterns more effectively.

Imputation: Handling Missing Values

Imputation addresses missing data, a common challenge in real-world datasets. While some algorithms can handle missing values directly, many require complete data. The approach to imputation should consider the missingness mechanism—whether values are missing completely at random, missing at random (related to observed variables), or missing not at random (related to unobserved factors or the missing value itself).

Simple imputation strategies include mean, median, or mode substitution. More sophisticated approaches use k-nearest neighbours to impute based on similar observations or regression models to predict missing values from other features. Multiple imputation techniques generate several plausible values for each missing data point, capturing uncertainty about the true values.

Modern approaches may use machine learning models specifically for imputation, such as `missForest` or deep learning methods designed to handle missing data. An increasingly common strategy involves creating "missingness indicators", binary features that track which values were imputed, allowing the model to learn patterns related to the missing data itself.

Selecting the Best Model for Your Problem

Model selection is a critical step in aligning machine learning algorithms with the specific characteristics of a given problem. This process requires a nuanced understanding of both the mathematical foundations of various models and the practical demands of the intended application. The suitability of a model is influenced by several factors, including the nature of the data—its size, dimensionality, and structure—as well as the type of task, whether it involves classification, regression, clustering, or more specialized objectives.

For structured datasets with moderate dimensionality, traditional algorithms such as gradient boosting machines often provide a strong balance between predictive accuracy and computational efficiency. In contrast, high-dimensional data types like images or text typically benefit from deep learning models, which are capable of automatically extracting hierarchical features. Time-series data, with its inherent temporal dependencies, may require specialized approaches such as ARIMA models, exponential smoothing techniques, or recurrent neural networks.

Beyond predictive performance, model selection must also account for practical constraints. In environments with limited computational resources, lightweight models may be necessary. When interpretability is a priority, such as in applications involving human oversight or regulatory compliance, transparent models like decision trees or linear models may be preferred. Legal and ethical considerations, including fairness and accountability, can further shape the choice of model.

A robust model selection process involves systematically comparing multiple candidates using evaluation metrics that reflect the specific goals of the project. These metrics may go beyond overall accuracy to include class-specific performance, calibration, or resilience to distributional shifts. Automated model selection tools, such as those offered by AutoML platforms, can assist in exploring a wide range of models and hyperparameters. However, their effectiveness is greatly enhanced when guided by domain knowledge that narrows the search space to model families most likely to succeed in the given context.

Building an End-to-End Training Pipeline

An end-to-end training pipeline operationalizes the theoretical aspects of model development into a structured, reproducible, and maintainable workflow. By standardizing the sequence of tasks from data ingestion to model deployment, such pipelines ensure experimental consistency and support a smooth transition from research to production environments.

Typically, a pipeline is composed of modular components responsible for distinct stages: data ingestion, preprocessing, feature engineering, model training, evaluation, and model persistence. This modular architecture promotes reusability, simplifies testing, and facilitates maintenance. Each module should have clearly defined inputs, outputs, and configurable parameters to support flexibility and scalability.

Effective data management is central to pipeline reliability. Consistent strategies for splitting data into training, validation, and test sets must be enforced throughout the pipeline to prevent data leakage and ensure fair evaluation. As models evolve, version control for datasets becomes essential, enabling reproducibility and systematic comparison of different modelling approaches.

Configuration management plays a key role in supporting experimentation. By tracking hyperparameters, preprocessing steps, and feature engineering choices— ideally through configuration files or dedicated experiment tracking tools— researchers can reproduce results precisely and explore variations systematically. Avoiding hardcoded parameters enhances transparency and adaptability.

Robust error handling is another vital feature. Pipelines should include comprehensive logging and fallback mechanisms to detect and respond to anomalies, processing failures, or training issues. Rather than failing silently, the system should provide informative diagnostics to guide debugging and refinement.

To support iterative improvement, pipelines must consistently measure and log performance metrics. This includes not only final evaluation scores but also intermediate indicators such as learning curves, feature importance rankings, and detailed error analyses. These insights inform adjustments to data processing, feature design, or model architecture.

As pipeline complexity grows, modern development increasingly relies on workflow orchestration tools such as Apache Airflow, Kubeflow, or ML-specific platforms like MLflow. These frameworks offer capabilities for scheduling, dependency tracking, and monitoring, making it easier to manage and scale machine learning workflows in dynamic environments.

Distributed Training: Scaling with Data and Model Parallelism

As datasets and models grow in size and complexity, distributed training becomes necessary to maintain reasonable training times and enable work with larger models. Effective distributed training strategies address both data scale and model complexity through complementary approaches.

Data Parallelism: Horizontal Scaling

Data parallelism distributes training data across multiple processing units, with each unit maintaining a complete copy of the model. This approach works particularly well for models that fit within the memory of individual computing nodes but require processing large datasets.

The primary challenge in data parallelism involves coordinating parameter updates across distributed workers. Synchronous approaches aggregate gradients from all workers before applying updates, ensuring consistency but potentially suffering from stragglers (slower workers that delay each iteration). Asynchronous approaches allow workers to update a central model independently, improving throughput but potentially introducing optimization instability.

Communication efficiency becomes critical in data-parallel training. Techniques like gradient compression reduce bandwidth requirements by sending approximated gradients. Large-batch training increases computation-to-communication ratio by processing more examples between synchronization points, though this requires careful adjustment of optimization parameters to maintain convergence.

Modern frameworks like PyTorch Distributed, TensorFlow Distributed, and Horovod simplify implementation of data-parallel training, handling communication patterns and synchronization automatically. These frameworks support both multi-GPU training on a single machine and multi-node training across clusters.

Model Parallelism: Vertical Scaling

Model parallelism divides the model itself across multiple processing units when the model is too large to fit in a single device's memory. This approach has become increasingly important with the growth of large language models and other architectures with billions of parameters.

Several strategies exist for model partitioning. Layer-wise parallelism assigns different network layers to separate devices, with activations transferred between them during forward and backward passes. Tensor parallelism splits individual operations across devices, particularly useful for large matrix operations. Pipeline parallelism combines aspects of both approaches, sending mini-batches through different model segments in a coordinated sequence.

Implementing model parallelism introduces complexity in managing device synchronization, memory transfers, and computational balance. Modern frameworks increasingly offer higher-level abstractions to simplify this process, such as DeepSpeed's Zero Redundancy Optimizer, Megatron-LM's tensor parallelism implementations, or PyTorch's FSDP (Fully Sharded Data Parallel).

Combining Approaches for Maximum Efficiency

Production-scale training typically combines multiple parallelism strategies. For instance, large language model training might use tensor parallelism to split attention heads across GPUs, pipeline parallelism to distribute transformer layers, and data parallelism across multiple nodes. This multi-dimensional approach maximizes hardware utilization while managing memory constraints.

Orchestrating distributed training requires appropriate infrastructure, including high-speed interconnects between computing nodes, efficient storage systems for data access, and cluster management systems that handle resource allocation and fault tolerance. Cloud platforms and specialized ML infrastructure systems provide these capabilities with varying degrees of automation.

The complexity of distributed training increases the importance of monitoring and debugging capabilities. Systems should track not just training metrics but also hardware utilization, communication overhead, and load balancing to identify bottlenecks and optimization opportunities.

Building models that work requires mastery of the entire development pipeline, from initial data preparation through to scaled deployment. Each stage presents distinct challenges, from the domain-specific judgements needed in data cleaning and feature engineering to the technical considerations of preprocessing, model selection, and distributed training.

The most successful approaches combine rigorous methodology with iterative refinement. Initial models serve not just as predictive systems but as diagnostic tools that reveal opportunities for improvement in data quality, feature representation, or modelling approaches.

As data volumes and model complexity continue to grow, the principles outlined in this chapter become increasingly important. Clean data, informative features, appropriate preprocessing, well-matched algorithms, systematic training processes, and efficient scaling strategies form the foundation for models that deliver real-world value.

The field continues to evolve rapidly, with innovations in automated feature discovery, neural architecture search, and distributed training algorithms expanding the frontier of what's possible. Yet the fundamental challenge remains constant: transforming raw data into meaningful insights through carefully constructed models. By mastering each component of the model building process, practitioners can consistently develop systems that perform reliably and deliver value in production environments.

Ensuring AI Model Truthfulness

Evaluation Strategies and Business Alignment

The rapid advancement of artificial intelligence, particularly in the domain of large language models (LLMs), has brought unprecedented capabilities to automated systems. These models can generate human-like text, reason through complex problems, and provide insights across domains. However, this power comes with a significant challenge: ensuring that AI models provide truthful, accurate information rather than generating plausible-sounding falsehoods—a phenomenon colloquially referred to as "AI hallucination" or more technically as "model confabulation."

> **Definition** *AI hallucination* refers to instances where an AI system generates information that is inaccurate or misleading, presenting it as fact. This phenomenon can occur in various AI applications, including language models and computer vision systems. AI hallucinations arise when the model produces outputs that are not based on its training data or real-world facts. Instead, it "hallucinates" responses that may sound plausible but are incorrect. For instance, a chatbot might confidently provide false information about historical events, or an image recognition system might identify non-existent objects in a photo.

> **Definition** *Model confabulation* is closely related to AI hallucination but focuses on the generation of coherent yet false narratives by AI models. Confabulation involves the AI creating detailed and plausible-sounding stories or explanations that are not based on actual data or facts.

This section explores the multifaceted approaches to evaluating and mitigating untruthful outputs from AI systems. We will examine various evaluation strategies, connect these to business objectives, and discuss methods to address common pitfalls in the evaluation process. This section will give you a comprehensive understanding of how to design robust evaluation frameworks that ensure AI systems remain truthful and reliable in real-world applications.

Evaluation Strategies for Truthfulness

The foundation of ensuring an AI model's reliability lies in comprehensive and diverse evaluation. Traditional metrics like accuracy, precision, and recall, while important, often fail to capture the nuances of truthfulness, especially in complex tasks like natural language generation or decision-making in uncertain environments. Therefore, a suite of specialized evaluation strategies is crucial.

Cross-Validation Techniques

Cross-validation represents one of the foundational approaches to evaluating AI model performance. While traditional cross-validation focuses primarily on prediction accuracy, when applied to truthfulness, it requires adaptation to assess factual correctness.

In the context of ensuring truthfulness, k-fold cross-validation can be implemented by dividing a factually verified dataset into k subsets. For each fold, the model is trained on k-1 subsets and evaluated on the remaining subset, specifically measuring factual accuracy rather than merely predictive performance. This approach helps identify whether the model consistently produces truthful responses across different data partitions.

Time-based cross-validation offers particular value for factual evaluation. By training models on historical data and validating them on more recent data, we can assess whether factual knowledge degrades over time or remains consistent. This becomes especially important when evaluating models that may have been trained on data with a specific cutoff date. For instance, a financial advisory AI system might be evaluated through time-based cross-validation by training it on market data until 2022 and then testing its factual claims about historical market events against a validation set from 2023. Any assertions about events that occurred before its training cutoff should maintain high factual accuracy.

LLM-as-a-Judge Methodology

The LLM-as-a-judge approach has emerged as a powerful technique for evaluating model outputs, particularly for assessing factual accuracy. This methodology employs a separate, often more capable, language model to evaluate the outputs of the model being tested. This approach leverages the inherent understanding of language and knowledge within these models to assess whether the output aligns with established facts and avoids generating falsehoods. Prompts are carefully crafted to guide the judging LLM to focus on specific aspects of truthfulness, such as factual accuracy, coherence, and logical consistency.

The judge model is typically provided with:

1. The original query or prompt
2. The response generated by the model being evaluated
3. A rubric for assessing truthfulness
4. When available, ground truth information against which to compare.

The evaluating model then produces a structured assessment of factual accuracy, identifying specific claims made by the model and verifying their correctness. This approach offers scalability advantages over human evaluation while potentially providing more nuanced assessment than simple metric-based approaches.

However, this methodology comes with inherent limitations. The judging model may share biases or knowledge gaps with the evaluated model, particularly if both were trained on similar data. Additionally, the judge model itself may produce incorrect assessments, creating a recursive truthfulness problem.

To mitigate these concerns, best practices include:

1. Using models from different families or architectures as judges
2. Providing judge models with reference information when possible
3. Validating judge performance on a subset of human-evaluated examples
4. Implementing multi-level judging hierarchies where outputs are evaluated by increasingly capable models.

LLM Juries: Ensemble Approaches

Building upon the LLM-as-a-judge methodology, LLM juries expand the evaluation framework by employing multiple models to assess truthfulness through a collective decision-making process. This approach draws inspiration from wisdom-of-crowds effects observed in human judgement aggregation.

In an LLM jury implementation, multiple independent language models—ideally with different architectures, training data, or fine-tuning approaches—evaluate the same model output. Their assessments are then aggregated through voting, weighted averaging, or more sophisticated consensus mechanisms.

Jury approaches offer several advantages:

1. Reduced impact of individual model biases
2. Higher likelihood of identifying subtle factual errors
3. Ability to quantify uncertainty through disagreement metrics
4. Potential for specialized jurors (e.g., domain experts in medicine versus history)

Backtesting Against Historical Data

Backtesting, a methodology borrowed from financial modelling, provides a robust framework for evaluating truthfulness in domains with well-documented historical records. This approach involves evaluating model outputs against known historical facts, trends, or events to measure factual accuracy retrospectively.

Example For applications involving sequential decision-making or forecasting, *backtesting* is an indispensable evaluation method. This involves testing the model's predictions or actions on historical data to assess its performance in a simulated real world environment. By observing how the model would have performed in the past, we can gain insights into its potential for generating truthful and reliable outcomes in the future. For instance, in financial modelling, *backtesting* allows us to evaluate if the model's trading strategies would have been profitable and avoided significant losses based on historical market data.

The backtesting process typically follows these steps:

1. Compile a dataset of historical facts with clear temporal boundaries
2. Present the model with queries that should elicit these facts
3. Compare model responses to the known historical record
4. Analyse patterns in any factual discrepancies.

For example, a model claiming to provide accurate historical information might be tested on questions about past presidential elections, technological innovations with clear invention dates, or significant historical events. By systematically comparing model outputs to historical records, we can identify patterns of factual distortion.

Backtesting is particularly valuable for detecting several categories of truthfulness failures:

1. Temporal confusion (placing events in incorrect time periods)
2. Causal misattribution (incorrectly describing cause-effect relationships)
3. Entity conflation (merging distinct historical entities)
4. Counterfactual generation (creating plausible but false historical scenarios).

A practical implementation example comes from the financial advisory domain. Researchers at Stanford evaluated an investment advisory AI by having it generate recommendations based on market conditions from specific past periods (without explicitly identifying the timeframe) and then compared these recommendations to optimal strategies that could have been identified with perfect historical knowledge. This approach revealed that while the model performed well on general principles, it often fabricated specific historical market movements and company performances.

Invariance Testing for Factual Consistency

Invariance testing examines whether model outputs maintain factual consistency when inputs are modified in ways that should not affect the underlying truth of the response. It focuses on evaluating the model's robustness to small, semantically irrelevant changes in the input. A truthful model should ideally produce consistent outputs when the input is perturbed in ways that do not alter its underlying meaning. This approach is particularly effective at identifying when models are generating outputs based on spurious correlations rather than genuine knowledge.

The core principle involves creating variations of input queries that:

1. Use different phrasings or linguistic structures
2. Include irrelevant but potentially distracting information
3. Present the question from different perspectives
4. Utilize various prompting strategies.

If a model truly "knows" a fact, its response should remain consistent across these variations. Significant divergence in factual claims suggests that the model may be confabulating or relying on unreliable pattern matching rather than robust knowledge representation.

Behavioural Testing Frameworks

Behavioural testing frameworks are essential for evaluating the factual reliability or truthfulness of language models by targeting specific failure modes rather than relying on broad, holistic assessments. One of the most influential frameworks in this space is **CheckList**, introduced by Ribeiro et al. (2020), which provides a structured methodology for probing model behaviour through carefully designed test suites.

> **Example** *Behavioural testing*, inspired by software testing methodologies, involves designing specific test cases to probe the model's behaviour under various conditions and edge cases. For example, in a question-answering system, behavioural tests could include questions with known false premises or questions designed to elicit common misconceptions.

CheckList includes three core test types:

1. **Minimum Functionality Tests (MFTs)**—These are simple, direct tests that verify whether a model can handle basic factual queries correctly.
2. **Invariance Tests**—These assess whether the model maintains consistent outputs when inputs are altered in ways that should not affect the answer (e.g., rephrasing).
3. **Directional Expectation Tests (DETs)**—These evaluate whether specific input changes lead to predictable and appropriate output changes.

For truthfulness evaluation, these test types can be adapted into more specialized suites, such as:

- **Adversarial Fact Tests**: Designed to challenge the model with common misconceptions or misleading phrasing to see if it can correct them.
- **Uncertainty Identification Tests**: Measure whether the model appropriately expresses uncertainty when it lacks sufficient knowledge.
- **Temporal Reasoning Tests**: Evaluate the model's ability to reason about time-sensitive information or chronological sequences.
- **Source Attribution Tests**: Check whether the model can correctly cite or refer to legitimate sources when providing factual information.
- **Counterfactual Contamination Tests**: Assess whether exposure to false information in earlier prompts affects the accuracy of later responses.

A compelling example of behavioural testing comes from the legal domain, where researchers tested models on fictional jurisdictions. A truthful model should recognize the fictional nature of the query and respond accordingly. However, many models fabricated plausible-sounding but entirely fictional legal frameworks, revealing a significant failure in truthfulness.

Framing Evaluation Metrics in Business Contexts

Aligning Truthfulness Metrics with Business Objectives

The evaluation of AI truthfulness must ultimately serve business goals. While academic research often focuses on abstract measures of factual accuracy, real-world applications require metrics that directly connect to business objectives and stakeholder needs.

The alignment process begins with identifying the business impact of different types of factual errors:

1. False Positives vs. False Negatives: In medical diagnostic support, falsely claiming a condition exists (false positive) may have different business implications than missing a genuine condition (false negative)
2. Precision vs. Recall Trade-offs: Customer service AI may prioritize precision (only making claims when highly confident) over recall (answering all possible questions)
3. Risk Asymmetry: In financial advice, errors in one direction (e.g., underestimating risk) may carry greater business consequences than errors in the opposite direction.

This business context should inform the design of evaluation metrics. Rather than applying generic truthfulness scores, organizations should develop composite metrics that weight different aspects of factual accuracy according to their business relevance.

For example, a pharmaceutical company deploying an AI for drug information might develop a weighted truthfulness score that assigns:

- 50% weight to accuracy about drug interactions (high safety impact)
- 30% weight to dosage information accuracy (moderate safety impact)
- 15% weight to mechanism of action descriptions (educational value)
- 5% weight to historical development information (low direct impact).

This weighted approach ensures that evaluation focuses on the aspects of truthfulness most critical to business outcomes.

Real-World Performance Metrics

Laboratory evaluations often fail to capture how models perform in actual deployment environments. Real-world performance metrics bridge this gap by assessing truthfulness under authentic usage conditions.

Key approaches include:

1. Shadow Deployment: Running the model alongside human experts who review outputs before they reach end-users, allowing comparison between model assertions and expert judgement

2. A/B Testing: Deploying different model versions to subsets of users and measuring outcome differences, potentially including truthfulness-related metrics
3. Longitudinal Tracking: Monitoring truthfulness metrics over time to identify degradation or improvement
4. User Feedback Integration: Incorporating structured feedback from users about perceived factual accuracy
5. Downstream Impact Assessment: Measuring how model truthfulness affects ultimate business outcomes like customer satisfaction or decision quality.

For example, a legal research AI might be evaluated through shadow deployment alongside paralegals who verify case citations and legal principles before attorneys see the results. The ratio of corrections needed provides a real-world truthfulness metric that directly connects to the business goal of providing reliable legal information.

Risk-Weighted Evaluation Frameworks

Not all truthfulness failures carry equal risk. Risk-weighted evaluation frameworks incorporate the potential business impact of different types of factual errors into the assessment methodology.

This approach typically involves:

1. Mapping the risk landscape for different categories of factual claims
2. Assigning risk weights to various error types
3. Developing composite scores that account for both error frequency and severity
4. Establishing risk thresholds for different deployment contexts.

For instance, a healthcare chatbot might employ a risk-weighted framework that categorizes potential factual errors into:

- Critical risk: Errors that could lead to physical harm (e.g., incorrect medication information)
- High risk: Errors affecting important healthcare decisions (e.g., when to seek emergency care)
- Medium risk: Errors affecting quality of care (e.g., preventative health recommendations)
- Low risk: Errors with minimal health impact (e.g., general wellness information).

The evaluation would then apply different weights to these categories, perhaps on a logarithmic scale where critical risks are weighted 100x more heavily than low risks. This creates an evaluation metric that more accurately reflects the business and ethical implications of different truthfulness failures.

Addressing Common Evaluation Challenges

Preventing Data Leakage

Data leakage represents a critical threat to the integrity of truthfulness evaluations in machine learning systems. This phenomenon occurs when information from test or validation datasets inadvertently influences the training process, resulting in inflated performance metrics that fail to reflect genuine generalization capabilities. Rather than developing authentic understanding of underlying knowledge, models may demonstrate high accuracy through memorization of test data, creating misleading assessments of their true capabilities.

Truthfulness evaluations face vulnerabilities from data leakage. Memorization of specific factual test cases can obscure a model's inability to generalize beyond training examples. Large-scale web scraping may inadvertently introduce evaluation artifacts into training datasets, while repeated exposure to benchmark datasets can lead to implicit overfitting among developers. These challenges necessitate robust mitigation strategies including temporal separation, where test data incorporates information released only after the model's training cutoff date, particularly valuable for assessing factual accuracy on recent events. Provenance tracking maintains detailed records of dataset origins and exposure history to detect potential contamination, while adversarial evaluation introduces novel or obscure test cases and reformulates common knowledge in unexpected ways to reduce training data overlap. Differential privacy techniques applied to evaluation datasets can limit future leakage risks, especially in iterative training cycles.

The severity of memorization risks is exemplified by image generation models that could reproduce training images with near-perfect accuracy, revealing memorization rather than creative generation. Similarly, language models face comparable risks when regurgitating memorized facts rather than demonstrating genuine reasoning. Netflix's approach to addressing this challenge in recommendation systems through "impossible recommendations" involving content that did not exist during training effectively isolated predictive capabilities from potential data leakage.

Conducting Effective Error Analysis

Error analysis transforms raw performance metrics into actionable insights by systematically examining failure patterns in AI systems. This process reveals underlying weaknesses, biases, and reasoning limitations that aggregate metrics may obscure. Effective error analysis begins with taxonomic categorization, grouping errors into meaningful types such as temporal errors involving incorrect dates or event sequences, entity confusion mixing up people or concepts, numerical inaccuracies in statistics or calculations, causal fallacies misattributing cause and effect relationships, and overgeneralization applying rules too broadly.

Root cause identification determines why errors occur, examining factors including training data limitations, architectural constraints, prompt misinterpretation, reasoning failures, outdated knowledge from training cutoffs, or emergent behaviours in larger models. Severity assessment evaluates how different error types impact downstream applications and user trust, recognizing that minor numerical errors in casual conversation carry less weight than factual errors in medical recommendations. Clustering analysis examines whether errors are isolated or cluster around specific topics, prompt styles, or complexity levels, guiding targeted improvements.

Most factual errors occurred when the model synthesized information across multiple studies, particularly regarding newer treatments. This insight led to refinements in handling scientific uncertainty, significantly improving accuracy in those critical areas. Error analysis thus serves dual purposes: diagnosing model shortcomings and informing strategic interventions through data augmentation, prompt engineering, architectural adjustments, or post-processing filters.

Addressing Imbalanced Data Challenges

Imbalanced data creates significant obstacles in truthfulness evaluation by generating misleading performance impressions. Models may appear generally accurate while consistently underperforming on underrepresented topics or fact types, creating critical blind spots particularly problematic in high-stakes domains. Fraud detection exemplifies this challenge, where fraudulent transactions are vastly outnumbered by legitimate ones, potentially causing models to fail at detecting rare but consequential instances.

Truthfulness evaluation faces multiple forms of data imbalance. Topic imbalance overrepresents general knowledge while underserving specialized domains like medicine or law. Geographic imbalance favours Western or developed country content, while temporal imbalance strengthens performance on recent events compared to historical ones. Certainty imbalance emphasizes well-established facts over emerging or uncertain knowledge, and cultural imbalance favours dominant narratives while weakening performance on marginalized perspectives.

Addressing these challenges requires deliberate strategies including stratified sampling to ensure balanced representation across domains, regions, and time periods. Difficulty calibration introduces factual complexity spectrums, preventing models from achieving high scores through easily verifiable facts alone. Domain-specific evaluations target critical areas requiring factual precision, while weighted evaluation metrics emphasize underrepresented categories to reveal performance disparities obscured by aggregate scores.

Continuous Evaluation and Monitoring

Continuous evaluation and monitoring maintain AI systems' factual reliability in an evolving knowledge landscape. Truthfulness requires ongoing assessment and updates as new information emerges and contexts shift, necessitating dynamic evaluation frameworks capable of detecting performance changes and adapting accordingly.

Temporal drift detection monitors factual accuracy changes over time, particularly in fast-moving domains, enabling developers to identify when retraining or knowledge updates become necessary. Trigger-based evaluation initiates assessments following significant real-world events like policy changes or scientific breakthroughs that may affect output accuracy. Legal advisory systems exemplify this approach, requiring re-evaluation following major legislative reforms.

User feedback loops enable real-world error reporting and contribute to continuously evolving evaluation datasets, highlighting blind spots while grounding evaluation in practical usage. Red teaming through periodic adversarial testing by experts uncovers subtle or complex factual errors that standard evaluations might miss, with insights feeding back into evaluation cycles to strengthen system resilience.

Ensuring AI truthfulness requires comprehensive, adaptive approaches integrating rigorous evaluation methodologies with business-relevant metrics. Cross-validation, expert assessments, real-world performance monitoring, and detailed error analysis form toolkits for identifying and mitigating factual inaccuracies. As AI systems grow more sophisticated, evaluation methods must evolve correspondingly.

The fundamental challenge involves bridging abstract factual accuracy definitions with tangible business consequences of misinformation. Organizations developing nuanced, context-aware evaluation frameworks will better deploy AI systems that are technically sound, trustworthy, and aligned with user expectations. Through continuous evaluation, stakeholders can move beyond simplistic AI "truth" notions towards refined understanding of factual reliability, uncertainty communication, and domain-specific accuracy as foundations for responsible AI advancement across sectors.

Monitoring Models in Production Environments

This section establishes the critical importance of model monitoring within the machine learning lifecycle. It emphasizes that deployment is not the end of a model's journey but rather the beginning of an ongoing process of observation, evaluation, and refinement. Effective monitoring combines both technical infrastructure and organizational processes to ensure models remain accurate, fair, and reliable throughout their operational life. Monitoring is essential for detecting performance degradation, which can lead to incorrect predictions, biased outcomes, or system failures as data distributions evolve, and user interactions change.

Handling Edge Cases and Outliers

We will explore how to identify and manage inputs that fall outside the typical patterns seen during training. Edge cases represent rare input patterns that may reveal limitations in a model's generalization capabilities.

Once edge cases and outliers are identified, the text outlines several strategies for handling them. Graceful degradation ensures models fail predictably and safely when encountering inputs outside their reliable domain, perhaps by declining to make high-uncertainty predictions or falling back to simpler models. Ensemble approaches combine multiple models with different strengths to provide more reliable predictions across a wider range of inputs. Uncertainty quantification provides confidence estimates alongside predictions, allowing downstream systems to make informed decisions about when to trust model outputs. Human-in-the-loop systems route edge cases to human experts when prediction confidence falls below predetermined thresholds, acknowledging model limitations while providing pathways for handling critical cases.

Addressing Feedback Loops

Model predictions can significantly influence future input data, creating intricate feedback dynamics that may reinforce existing biases or cause model drift. These dynamics manifest in three primary forms of feedback loops. Direct feedback loops occur when model outputs directly shape the data collection process, as seen in content recommendation systems where user engagement is driven by prior recommendations. Behavioural feedback loops arise when users modify their actions in response to model behaviour, such as adapting strategies to evade spam detection in online games. Systemic feedback loops extend beyond individual interactions, affecting broader societal systems—for instance, predictive policing models that guide law enforcement resource allocation, potentially perpetuating biased patterns.

Identifying these feedback loops requires continuous and nuanced monitoring. Distribution monitoring helps detect shifts in input data distributions over time, which may indicate adaptation to model outputs. Performance segmentation assesses model efficacy across different user groups or time intervals, revealing areas where performance may be deteriorating. A/B testing, particularly with control groups shielded from model influence, allows researchers to isolate and understand the effects of feedback mechanisms. Additionally, causal analysis, employing methods such as causal inference, is essential for untangling the complex relationships between model predictions and subsequent data changes.

To counteract the adverse effects of feedback loops, several mitigation strategies are recommended. Randomization introduces controlled variability into model decisions, preventing overfitting to narrow data patterns. Counterfactual data collection deliberately seeks data outside the model's current decision boundaries, preserving input diversity. Periodic retraining using carefully curated datasets helps curb the accumulation of bias over time. Incorporating diversity objectives into model training ensures broader coverage across varied input types. Finally, ethical review processes play a crucial role in evaluating the broader impact of models on users and systems, enabling early detection and correction of harmful feedback effects before they escalate.

Understanding Distribution Shifts

Distribution shifts occur when the statistical properties of data change between training and deployment, or over time in production. These shifts undermine a fundamental assumption of many machine learning models: that training and test data are independently and identically distributed.

Covariate shift occurs when the distribution of input features changes while the relationship between features and target variables remains constant. Mathematically, if X represents input features and Y represents target variables, covariate shift is present when $P(X)$ changes but $P(Y|X)$ remains the same.

For example, a model trained to detect pneumonia from chest X-rays collected at hospital A may encounter covariate shift when deployed at hospital B due to differences in imaging equipment, patient demographics, or image processing techniques. The underlying relationship between X-ray features and pneumonia diagnosis remains consistent, but the distribution of input features differs.

Detecting covariate shift involves:

1. Comparing feature distributions between training and production data using statistical tests like Kolmogorov–Smirnov or using density ratio estimation
2. Training an adversarial classifier to distinguish between training and production samples
3. Monitoring changes in activation patterns within neural network layers.

Mitigating covariate shift often involves importance weighting during training, where samples are weighted according to the ratio of their likelihood under the production versus training distributions.

Label shift (or prior probability shift) occurs when the distribution of the target variable changes while the relationship between features and targets given the target remains constant. Formally, $P(Y)$ changes but $P(X|Y)$ remains the same.

This usually occurs in classification problems when class distributions change over time. For instance, a credit default prediction model might face label shift during economic downturns when default rates increase across all customer segments.

Detecting label shift involves:

1. Monitoring changes in the distribution of predicted probabilities
2. Comparing the distribution of predictions in training versus production
3. Using techniques like Black Box Shift Estimation to quantify label shift.

Addressing label shift typically requires adjusting decision thresholds or reweighting examples during training to reflect the expected target distribution in production.

Concept drift occurs when the relationship between input features and target variables changes. In this case, $P(Y|X)$ itself changes over time. This is often the most challenging type of distribution shift to address.

Examples include changes in consumer preferences affecting purchase patterns, evolving tactics of fraudsters adapting to detection models, or fundamental changes in economic relationships during crises. Detecting concept drift requires:

1. Monitoring performance metrics over time, particularly noting unexplained performance degradation
2. Statistical tests comparing error distributions across time periods
3. Maintaining reference datasets to benchmark against current performance.

Addressing concept drift typically requires model retraining, with strategies ranging from periodic scheduled retraining to triggered retraining when performance degradation is detected.

Adversarial Validation

This subsection presents adversarial validation as a technique for detecting and understanding distribution shifts between datasets. The approach transforms distribution comparison into a binary classification task: distinguishing between samples from training versus production data.

The process involves:

1. Labelling training data samples as class 0 and production/test data as class 1
2. Training a classifier to distinguish between these classes
3. Evaluating the classifier's performance

If the classifier achieves accuracy significantly better than random chance, this indicates a distribution shift between the datasets. The magnitude of this accuracy provides a measure of the shift's severity.

This means that the process, where training data samples are labelled as class 0 and production/test data as class 1, then a classifier is trained to distinguish between these classes. If the classifier achieves accuracy significantly better than random chance, this indicates a distribution shift between the datasets, with the accuracy magnitude providing a measure of the shift's severity.

Beyond detecting shifts, adversarial models provide valuable insights into which features contribute most to the distribution difference. By examining feature importance in the adversarial classifier, practitioners can identify specific features driving the shift, focus data collection efforts, consider feature transformations, and develop targeted monitoring for shift-prone features.

Adversarial validation provides several benefits during model development, including validation set selection that better represents expected production distributions, feature engineering guidance for developing stable features, model selection criteria favouring generalization across distribution differences, and targeted data augmentation to fill gaps identified through adversarial validation.

Practical Monitoring Strategies

This subsection provides concrete guidance on implementing monitoring systems in production environments, starting with the different types of metrics that should be tracked.

- Performance metrics assess how well the model performs its intended task, including accuracy, precision, recall, and domain-specific metrics.
- Statistical metrics monitor distributions of inputs, outputs, and internal model states.
- Operational metrics measure system health and responsiveness, including latency and throughput.
- Behavioural metrics capture how users interact with and respond to model predictions.

Moreover, building robust monitoring infrastructure involves several components: Logging frameworks capture relevant information about model inputs, outputs, and context.

- Metrics storage systems efficiently store and index time-series data.
- Visualization dashboards provide intuitive interfaces for monitoring trends.
- Alerting systems notify stakeholders when metrics deviate from expected ranges. Automated diagnostics help identify potential root causes when performance issues arise.

Effective monitoring should operate at multiple time scales, from real-time detection of immediate issues to monthly retrospectives evaluating longer-term trends. It emphasizes the importance of establishing clear roles and responsibilities among first responders handling immediate alerts, model specialists performing deeper investigations, domain experts providing context, and decision makers authorizing updates when necessary. For regulated industries such as healthcare, finance, and insurance, the text highlights additional monitoring requirements including compliance monitoring, audit trails, bias monitoring, and model governance committees that periodically review results and approve changes.

Building Resilient Models

We will explore how to develop models that can adapt to changing conditions, starting with various adaptation mechanisms. Continuous learning systems update model parameters incrementally as new labelled data becomes available. Online learning algorithms like Adaptive Random Forests are designed for streaming data and concept drift. Transfer learning leverages knowledge from related domains to adapt with limited labelled data. Meta-learning aims to build models that quickly adapt to new tasks or distributions.

Ensemble strategies provide resilience against distribution shifts. Heterogeneous ensembles combine different model architectures to create robust systems. Dynamic weighting adjusts the influence of ensemble members based on recent performance. Online model selection maintains a pool of candidate models and selects the best performer for each prediction. Learn-and-forget methods incorporate new patterns while discarding outdated ones using techniques like sliding windows or decay-based weighting.

Some model architectures are inherently robust to distribution shifts:

- **Bayesian models** represent uncertainty and adapt their confidence with new evidence or changing conditions.
- **Invariant risk minimization** optimizes for features and relationships that remain stable across different environments.
- **Contrastive learning** captures invariant features across different views or perturbations of the data.
- **Causal models** capture true causal relationships, generalizing better when distributions change.

Even with adaptive mechanisms, models benefit from explicit safeguards. Prediction confidence thresholds prevent predictions when confidence is low. Domain constraint enforcement ensures predictions respect physical, logical, or business constraints. Anomaly detection layers identify inputs or predictions that deviate significantly from expected patterns. Graceful fallback mechanisms transition to simpler systems when conditions exceed the primary model's operational domain.

Integrating Monitoring into the AI/ML Lifecycle

Finally monitoring should be integrated throughout the machine learning lifecycle. Effective monitoring begins during model development through monitoring by design that incorporates telemetry points directly into model architecture. Testable hypotheses about model behaviour guide monitoring system design. Validation with realistic scenarios helps identify monitoring requirements. Shadowing periods where models run in parallel with existing systems establish baseline patterns before taking on production traffic.

It is important to note that monitoring insights should continuously inform model improvement. Data collection strategies target areas where monitoring indicates weaknesses or gaps. Feature engineering efforts focus on creating more stable features based on observed shifts and model architecture updates address systematic weaknesses identified through monitoring. Ultimately training methodologies incorporate techniques to improve robustness to observed real-world conditions.

Building effective monitoring systems requires organizational commitment. In this regard, cross-functional collaboration between data scientists, engineers, domain experts, and operations teams ensures comprehensive perspectives. Knowledge sharing mechanisms capture and disseminate lessons learned, whereas incident review processes systematically analyse monitoring failures. Investment in infrastructure naturally provides the technical foundation for sophisticated monitoring capabilities.

To sum up, model monitoring serves as the vigilant guardian of machine learning systems in production. Through careful attention to edge cases, feedback loops, and distribution shifts, organizations can ensure their models remain reliable, accurate, and trustworthy over time. Ultimately, effective monitoring closes the loop in the machine learning lifecycle, transforming deployment from a destination into part of a continuous improvement process.

Active Learning

Active learning is a supervised machine learning technique that enhances model performance by strategically selecting the most informative data points for annotation. Rather than relying on large, fully labelled datasets, active learning focuses on optimizing the labelling process, allowing models to learn effectively from smaller, targeted samples. This approach is particularly crucial in scenarios where data annotation is costly and time-consuming, such as when working with large image or video datasets or outsourcing to extensive annotation teams.

At its core, active learning involves an iterative process in which the model identifies data points that are expected to yield the greatest improvement in performance if labelled. These selected instances are then presented to human annotators, creating a feedback loop that refines the model over successive rounds. This targeted strategy contrasts with traditional supervised learning, which typically uses static datasets with uniformly labelled examples.

Several key strategies guide the selection of informative samples in active learning. Uncertainty sampling prioritizes data points where the model is least confident, while query-by-committee methods rely on disagreement among multiple models to identify valuable instances. Diversity-weighted approaches aim to ensure broad coverage of the data space, and expected model change-based sampling selects points likely to induce significant updates to the model parameters. Each method offers distinct advantages and limitations, and their applicability varies across domains.

Active learning pipelines and platforms help operationalize these strategies, making the annotation process more efficient and scalable. By reducing the volume of labelled data required while maintaining or improving model accuracy, active learning supports the development of high-performing models with reduced resource expenditure. Its intelligent instance selection mechanism enables superior learning efficiency, making it a powerful tool for domains where annotation costs are high and data complexity is significant.

The active learning cycle is illustrated in Fig. 12.1.

Active learning is particularly advantageous in contexts where data labelling is expensive, time-intensive, or constrained by limited expert availability. Its applications span a wide range of domains, including medical diagnostics, natural language processing, and image classification—fields where acquiring high-quality labelled data poses significant challenges.

The active learning process unfolds through iterative cycles of selection, annotation, and retraining. It typically begins with a small, labelled dataset used to train an initial model. This model then guides the selection of the most informative unlabelled instances, using strategies such as uncertainty sampling, diversity sampling, or committee-based methods, depending on the nature of the data and the learning objectives.

Once selected, these data points are sent to human annotators who provide ground truth labels. The newly labelled examples are added to the training set, and the

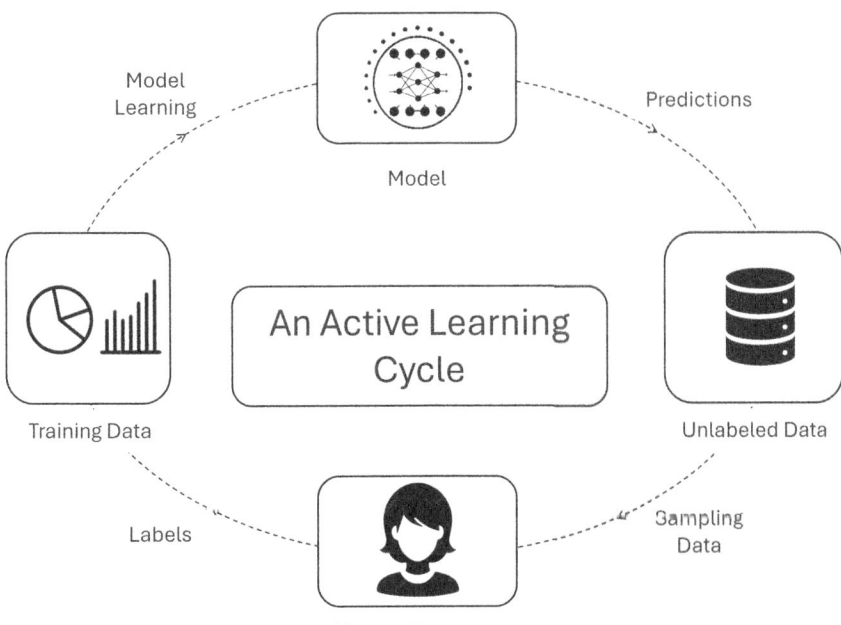

Fig. 12.1 An active leaning cycle

model is retrained to incorporate the updated information. This cycle repeats, with the model continuously identifying high-value samples for annotation and refining its predictions, until a predefined stopping criterion is met or further labelling yields diminishing returns.

By leveraging this iterative approach, active learning maximizes the utility of each labelled instance, achieving greater efficiency and improved model performance compared to traditional supervised learning methods that rely on large, static datasets.

Active Learning Versus Passive Learning

Passive and active learning represents distinct machine learning approaches. Passive learning trains models on predefined labelled datasets, completing the learning process after initial training. Conversely, active learning selects informative data points using query strategies rather than predetermined labelled datasets. These selected points receive annotation before becoming training data. By iteratively utilizing informative samples, active learning continuously improves predictive model performance.

The approaches differ in several ways. Active learning employs query strategies to determine which data requires labelling and annotation and which labels should be applied. Query strategies also guide training data selection in active learning. Cost considerations differ, as active learning requires human annotators or sometimes domain experts depending on the field, though costs can be managed using automated AI-based labelling tools and specialized software. Performance characteristics vary, with active learning requiring fewer labels due to the impact of informative samples, while passive learning demands more data, labels, and training time to achieve comparable results. Active learning also demonstrates greater adaptability than passive approaches, particularly with dynamic datasets.

Active learning represents a powerful approach for enhancing machine learning model performance by decreasing labelling costs while simultaneously improving accuracy and generalization capabilities.

Active Learning Versus Reinforcement Learning

While sharing some conceptual similarities, active learning and reinforcement learning constitute distinct machine learning algorithms. As discussed, active learning frameworks allow learning algorithms to actively select their learning data, focussing on minimizing labelled data requirements while maintaining performance standards.

Reinforcement learning, meanwhile, involves agents learning through environmental interaction and feedback via rewards or penalties, aiming to develop policies that maximize cumulative rewards.

Active learning relies on fixed training datasets with query strategies selecting the most informative data points, whereas reinforcement learning operates without predefined datasets, learning through continuous environmental exploration and internal model updates based on received feedback.

Query Strategies

Active learning enhances training efficiency by selectively identifying the most informative data points from unlabelled datasets through targeted query strategies. These strategies are generally categorized into stream-based selective sampling, pool-based sampling, and query synthesis, each suited to different data environments and operational goals.

Stream-based selective sampling is particularly effective for real-time or continuously generated data, such as video feeds or sensor outputs. In this approach, models incrementally train on incoming data and select samples for annotation based on their potential to improve learning. Techniques like uncertainty sampling, which targets data points where the model exhibits low confidence, and diversity sampling, which prioritizes novel or varied inputs, help optimize the selection process. While this method reduces annotation costs and adapts well to evolving data distributions, it may introduce bias if certain data types are consistently favoured and can be constrained by the capabilities of the streaming infrastructure.

Pool-based sampling operates on a static collection of unlabelled data. The model iteratively selects the most informative examples for annotation, retrains with the newly labelled data, and repeats the cycle until performance objectives are achieved. Strategies such as query-by-committee, which relies on disagreement among multiple models, and density-weighted sampling, which considers data distribution, are commonly used. This approach is efficient and cost-effective, especially when expert annotation time is limited. However, its effectiveness depends on the quality and structure of the unlabelled pool and may be challenged by noisy or unstructured data.

Query synthesis takes a different route by generating new data points from existing labelled examples. Techniques such as data perturbation, interpolation, or the use of generative models like GANs help create synthetic samples that enrich the training set. This method is particularly useful when labelled data is scarce or expensive, as it enhances data diversity and supports better generalization. Nonetheless, it can be computationally demanding and may risk overfitting if synthetic data lacks realism or becomes overly dominant in the training process.

Each strategy evaluates sample informativeness through distinct mechanisms and offers unique advantages and limitations. A clear understanding of these approaches enables practitioners to design active learning pipelines that are well-aligned with their data characteristics, resource constraints, and learning objectives.

Selecting Informative Samples

Selecting the most informative samples is critical for the success of active learning.

Uncertainty Sampling

Uncertainty sampling selects samples expected to maximally reduce model uncertainty. Model uncertainty typically measures using uncertainty metrics like entropy or margin-based uncertainty. Samples exhibiting high uncertainty receive labelling priority, as they are expected to deliver the most significant model performance improvements. The idea is that samples with a small margin are close to the decision boundary and are therefore more informative.

Least confidence method selects samples with the lowest predicted probability for the most likely class. That means, this method selects the sample for which the model has the lowest confidence in its prediction. Formally, given a model's predicted probability distribution over classes for an unlabelled sample x, the least confidence sample is the one with the smallest maximum probability.

Query-by-Committee (QBC)

Query-by-committee is an ensemble-based approach to active learning. Query-by-committee sampling trains multiple models on different labelled dataset subsets and selects samples based on model disagreement. This strategy proves useful when models consistently misclassify specific samples or classes. By selecting samples where model committees disagree, models learn to recognize sample patterns and improve performance in challenging classes. The intuition is that if the models disagree on a sample, it indicates that the sample lies in an ambiguous region of the input space and labelling it would help to resolve the ambiguity.

Diversity-Weighted Methods

Diversity-weighted methods select examples for labelling based on their diversity relative to the current training set. The approach ranks unlabelled samples using diversity measures such as inter-sample dissimilarity or model prediction uncertainty. The most diverse examples receive labels to enhance model generalization through informative and representative training data provision. The goal is to avoid selecting redundant samples that provide little new information to the model. These methods combine an uncertainty measure with a diversity measure to select samples that are both uncertain and representative of the unlabelled data distribution.

Expected Model Change-Based Sampling

Expected model-change-based sampling selects examples for labelling based on expected changes to model predictions. This approach prioritizes examples likely to cause significant prediction changes when labelled, improving model performance on novel, unseen data. This method ranks unlabelled examples based on estimated prediction changes when labelled. Estimation may use various measures including expected model output variance, expected gradient magnitude, or Euclidean distance between current and expected post-labelling model parameters. Examples expected to cause significant prediction changes receive labelling priority, based on their potential to provide highly informative model training data. These samples subsequently join training data for model updates.

Expected Error Reduction

Expected error reduction selects examples for labelling based on expected model prediction error reduction. This approach prioritizes examples likely to maximally reduce prediction errors when labelled, improving model performance on novel, unseen data. This method ranks unlabelled examples based on estimated prediction error reduction when labelled. Estimation may use various measures including decision boundary distance, predicted label margins, or expected entropy reduction. Examples expected to drastically reduce prediction errors receive labelling priority, based on their potential to provide maximally informative model training data.

Active Learning Tools

A growing number of active learning tools have emerged to support efficient model development by intelligently selecting the most informative data samples for annotation. These tools aim to reduce labelling costs, accelerate model convergence, and improve generalization by integrating active learning strategies into various stages of the machine learning pipeline, from data curation to evaluation. Each tool is tailored to specific domains, user needs, and data modalities.

Encord Active offers an enterprise-grade platform particularly well-suited for computer vision tasks. It features advanced capabilities such as error analysis, robustness evaluation, and data drift detection, helping teams maintain model accuracy over time. With support for diverse annotation types—including bounding boxes and bitmasks—and seamless integration with Encord Annotate, it provides a secure, end-to-end solution for data science and machine learning teams focused on workflow management and performance monitoring.

Lightly provides a user-friendly platform that integrates with popular deep learning libraries and supports image, video, and point cloud data. It implements active learning strategies such as uncertainty sampling and core-set selection. With a

Python SDK and web-based tools for data visualization and curation, lightly is ideal for researchers and engineers seeking an efficient, end-to-end solution for annotation and model improvement.

Cleanlab, while not exclusively an active learning tool, plays a complementary role by detecting and correcting label noise. It identifies mislabeled samples across image, text, and tabular datasets, making it a valuable addition to active learning pipelines. Available as both an open-source library and a hosted platform, Cleanlab is particularly useful for smaller teams or individual researchers working on classification tasks.

Voxel51 offers a comprehensive platform for active learning across domains such as computer vision and natural language processing. Its FiftyOne toolkit enables detailed dataset exploration, slicing, and visualization of model failure modes. The platform also supports automated label error correction, making it well-suited for large-scale projects that require flexible and scalable solutions for data quality and model refinement.

Synthetic Data

One of the greatest challenges in building AI models involves identifying all potential edge cases. Training, validation, and test sets represent only a fraction of examples that deployed models will encounter. Generating synthetic data to augment under-represented portions of training data enhances model robustness, ensures important invariances, and explores specific failure modes.

In sentiment analysis, phrases like "Rosvita is a naughty child" and "Rita is a naughty child" should receive identical classifications. Generating numerous synthetic samples following the template "{name} is a naughty child" with various common first names can ensure the model remains invariant to first names. Synthetic data generation methods vary by data type, ranging from simple template-based generation to complex approaches using generative adversarial networks (GANs). Original data samples can also be perturbed for dataset augmentation—in NLP, by introducing minor typos or replacing words with synonyms; in computer vision, by adding image noise or altering orientation. Each field has specific data perturbation methods for augmentation. Insights from counterfactual and adversarial analysis can also inform synthetic data generation, creating adversarial examples. Quickly developing adversarial examples from hypotheses or dataset modifications contributes to more robust, error-resistant models.

Systematic Testing

While test-driven development is standard practice in software engineering, testing remains underutilized in machine learning. ML testing, when performed at all, often involves a single engineer writing scripts to test a few cases identified during cursory error analysis. Comprehensive testing significantly enhances model quality, helping practitioners identify issues proactively rather than reactively.

Drawing from software engineering principles, Marco Tulio and colleagues proposed CheckList, a new NLP model testing methodology. Their work demonstrates that relying solely on held-out accuracy to evaluate generalization often overestimates NLP model performance. NLP practitioners using CheckList created twice as many tests and identified nearly three times as many bugs as those without it.

Each error analysis facet can be systematized into unit and regression test frameworks. Building on error cohort analysis, performance thresholds could be defined for specific data subgroups and tested against datasets. From counterfactual and adversarial analysis, tests could attempt to alter model predictions by manipulating feature values. Finally, synthetic test samples could verify that model predictions remain invariant in certain scenarios.

Example of Error Analysis

Consider a binary classification problem predicting whether customers will make purchases based on historical data and tested on new datasets. The analysis begins with generating a confusion matrix to understand model performance by identifying true positives (correctly predicted purchases), false positives (incorrectly predicted purchases), true negatives (correctly predicted non-purchases), and false negatives (incorrectly predicted non-purchases).

Next, a Receiver Operating Characteristic (ROC) curve plots the true positive rate against the false positive rate across various discrimination thresholds, visualizing the trade-off between sensitivity and specificity to identify optimal prediction thresholds. A precision-recall curve then evaluates the trade-off between precision (percentage of true positive predictions among positive predictions) and recall (percentage of true positive predictions among actual positive cases). K-fold cross-validation follows to evaluate model performance across different data subsets, helping identify potential overfitting or underfitting issues. Finally, bias-variance trade-off analysis examines the relationship between the model's ability to fit training data and its generalization to new data. Based on these findings, data scientists might collect additional data, experiment with alternative algorithms, or fine-tune model parameters to enhance performance.

Invariance Tests

Machine learning problems typically exhibit invariant structures. For instance, image classification tasks generally remain unaffected by changes in translation, rotation, scale, viewpoint, and illumination. Many applications benefit from machine learning models that maintain invariance to certain input data variations. Computer vision research has particularly focused on enhancing various forms of invariance including rotation, brightness, and size. While invariance testing constitutes a significant component of robustness assessment using simple formulas to measure invariance levels, these formulas rapidly condense substantial measurement data into singular scores, which cannot fully capture all variance-related patterns within the measured data.

Two-Phase Predictions

Two-phase machine learning combines two algorithms sequentially, with the first algorithm handling variable imputation in datasets, and the second predicting successfully treatable values. This approach functions as a data preprocessing procedure where the initial phase employs a machine learning algorithm to impute incorrect values in datasets. Subsequently, the second phase utilizes another machine learning algorithm to make conditional uncertainty measurements of the first phase. In this learning approach, the first phase collects critical data points while the second phase determines whether imputation proves more effective than alternative data collection methods such as indirect interviews or callbacks.

Consider a scenario involving a large, continuous variable containing incorrect values due to data collection issues. The data inaccuracy necessitates more imputations during modelling, with the second phase learning the circumstances under which the first-phase algorithm predicted incorrect values. Using a second-phase algorithm to examine inaccurate predictions generates more accurate and effective outcomes.

When implementing a two-phase learning model using random forest, the first phase involves splitting the dataset, with two-thirds used for training containing correct values and other dataset variables. Random forests support both classification and regression, growing trees through repeated node splitting into child nodes. The initial node encompasses all learning samples, with splitting criteria measured via the gini index. After splitting, the resulting child nodes represent subsets of the parent node, with the gini calculation incorporating the fraction of classes within each node.

Datasets often contain relatively few incorrect values, potentially creating imbalance problems that impede proper learning by random forests. Oversampling or undersampling techniques can address this issue by creating balance between dataset classes, preventing model bias towards specific classes.

Two-phase learning (Fig. 12.2) finds application in several scenarios: when dealing with inaccurate data, the first phase filters correct data from raw inputs while the second phase learns from inaccurate data; with imbalanced data, different classes can be taught separately in phases to prevent conventional learning methods from developing class biases; and when models fail to capture hidden data sequences, two-phase learning improves performance by ensuring models learn from complete data without missing hidden information.

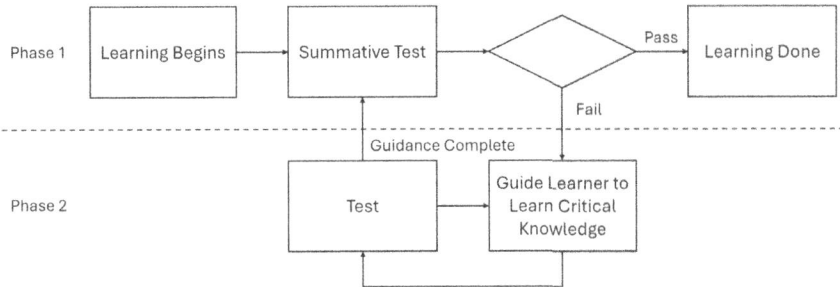

Fig. 12.2 Two-phase learning

Human-in-the-Loop Workflows

As AI systems become increasingly sophisticated and pervasive across domains, there has been a corresponding recognition of the limitations of fully automated approaches. This recognition has led to the development and refinement of human-in-the-loop (HITL) workflows—systems and processes that integrate human judgement, expertise, and oversight with algorithmic capabilities. Rather than viewing AI as a replacement for human cognition, HITL approaches acknowledge the complementary strengths of humans and machines, creating systems that leverage their synergistic potential. This section discusses relevant details on human-in-the-loop workflows in artificial intelligence.

Human-in-the-loop workflows are grounded in several theoretical traditions, including human-computer interaction, cognitive science, and sociotechnical systems theory. The central premise is that certain cognitive capabilities remain uniquely human—particularly those involving contextual understanding, ethical judgement, creative insight, and adaptability to novel situations—while machines excel at pattern recognition, consistent application of rules, processing large datasets, and certain forms of optimization.

The integration of these complementary capabilities creates what can be termed "hybrid intelligence" - systems that outperform either humans or machines operating in isolation. This hybrid approach addresses what AI researchers refer to as the "brittleness problem" of pure AI systems, which often perform well within defined parameters but fail unpredictably when encountering edge cases or situations beyond their training distribution.

From a theoretical perspective, we can conceptualize HITL workflows as existing along a spectrum of human involvement, from systems where humans provide occasional verification or correction to those where human judgement constitutes the primary decision-making function with AI offering supporting analysis or recommendations. This spectrum acknowledges that the optimal balance between human and machine contributions varies depending on the task characteristics, stakes involved, and available resources.

Human-in-the-loop workflows can be categorized along multiple dimensions, including the timing of human involvement, the nature of the human contribution, and the degree of autonomy granted to the AI system.

The integration of human involvement in machine learning systems can be understood across three key dimensions: *timing, nature of contribution,* and *degree of algorithmic autonomy.* Each dimension shapes how humans and algorithms interact, influencing system design, performance, and accountability.

Timing of Human Involvement

Human input can occur at various stages of the machine learning lifecycle:

- **Pre-processing involvement** takes place before algorithmic processing begins. Here, humans define system parameters, select training data, and establish constraints. This is typical in supervised learning, where experts label data or design features.
- **In-process involvement** occurs during algorithm execution. Humans may intervene to guide the system, correct errors, or make decisions at critical points. Interactive machine learning exemplifies this, with models adapting based on real-time human feedback.
- **Post-processing involvement** involves reviewing and potentially overriding algorithmic outputs. This is common in high-stakes domains such as healthcare, where AI-generated recommendations are subject to expert validation before implementation.
- **Continuous involvement spans** the entire system lifecycle. Humans regularly monitor, retrain, and recalibrate models to ensure sustained performance, particularly in dynamic environments where conditions evolve over time.

Nature of Human Contribution

The type of human input varies in complexity and depth:

- **Verification and** correction involves reviewing outputs for accuracy and making necessary adjustments—often the most basic form of involvement.
- **Judgement and decision-**making requires humans to interpret algorithmic recommendations and make final decisions, especially in ambiguous or ethically sensitive contexts.
- **Knowledge and context provision** entails supplying domain-specific insights or contextual understanding that algorithms cannot easily infer.
- **Creative and strategic** direction includes offering novel ideas, setting long-term goals, or shaping the overall approach in ways that complement algorithmic capabilities.

Degree of Algorithmic Autonomy

Systems differ in how independently they operate:

- **Human-guided** systems follow predefined procedures with minimal autonomous decision-making, relying heavily on human direction.
- **Semi-autonomous** systems handle routine tasks independently but defer to humans in complex or high-risk situations.
- **Autonomous systems with human** oversight function largely on their own but remain subject to human monitoring and intervention when necessary.

Understanding these dimensions allows designers and researchers to tailor human-AI collaboration to the specific needs and risks of a given application. By aligning the timing, nature, and extent of human involvement with the system's purpose and context, developers can enhance both performance and trustworthiness.

Design Principles for Effective HITL Workflows

Designing effective human-in-the-loop (HITL) workflows requires a balanced integration of technical precision and human-centred considerations. Central to this process are several guiding principles that ensure productive collaboration between humans and algorithms.

Transparency and explainability are foundational. For humans to effectively oversee or complement algorithmic decisions, they must understand how those decisions are made. Mechanisms such as feature importance visualizations, confidence scores, and natural language explanations help users assess model reliability and calibrate their trust accordingly. Research shows that explainable AI not only enhances oversight but also improves collaboration by enabling more targeted feedback. However, the level of explanation must be tailored to the user's expertise and the task context, necessitating adaptive explanatory systems.

Equally important is the division of tasks between humans and machines. Machines are well-suited for repetitive operations, rule-based processing, and pattern recognition in structured data, while humans excel in contextual reasoning, ethical judgement, and adaptability. The challenge lies in defining clear boundaries and designing interfaces that facilitate seamless transitions between human and machine responsibilities. Structured methodologies from human factors engineering and cognitive work analysis offer valuable tools for this purpose.

Feedback integration is another critical component. The utility of human input depends on how effectively it is translated into algorithmic adjustments, whether through retraining, parameter tuning, or constraint modification. This requires thoughtful design of feedback representation, incorporation, and validation. Studies suggest that immediate visual feedback showing how human input influences system behaviour significantly enhances the quality and consistency of contributions.

Managing cognitive load is essential to maintain human performance and engagement. HITL systems must minimize unnecessary complexity, direct attention to high-impact decisions, and provide appropriate support. Techniques such as prioritization algorithms, salient visualizations, and streamlined interfaces help reduce cognitive strain, leading to improved accuracy, reduced fatigue, and greater user satisfaction.

Finally, well-designed HITL workflows foster mutual learning between humans and algorithms. Humans develop accurate mental models of system capabilities, while algorithms adapt to human preferences and decision patterns. Implementation strategies such as progressive disclosure of complexity, embedded tutorials, and adaptive interfaces that evolve with user expertise have been shown to yield long-term improvements in both system performance and user experience.

Model compression

Model compression encompasses algorithms that reduce neural network size and memory requirements while preserving accuracy, enhancing efficiency and cost-effectiveness for deployment across various environments. Edge devices present challenges due to their resource constraints, including limited memory and processing capabilities. While high-performing deep learning models are large, their size demands greater storage space, making deployment on resource-constrained devices difficult and increasing inference time and energy consumption. Model compression techniques address these challenges by creating smaller, efficient models without significantly compromising accuracy.

Four popular compression techniques include pruning, quantization, knowledge distillation, and low-rank factorization. *Pruning* reduces neural network parameters by removing redundant elements that contribute minimally during training, resulting in faster-running compressed models with reduced computational costs and energy consumption. Pruning strategies include weight pruning, neuron pruning, and filter pruning. The process involves training the original network, identifying connections to prune based on specific criteria, and fine-tuning the pruned network to restore accuracy.

Quantization compresses networks by reducing bits required for weight representation, converting 32-bit floating-point numbers to 16-bit, 8-bit, 4-bit, or even 1-bit representations, significantly reducing network size. There are two forms of quantization. These are post-training quantization and quantization aware training. Quantization can be applied both during and after training. It can be applied to both convolutional and fully connected layers. However, quantised weights make neural networks harder to converge and make back-propagation infeasible.

Knowledge distillation (refinement) transfers knowledge from a large, complex model trained on extensive datasets to a smaller network, with the larger "teacher" model mentoring the smaller "student" network, depicted in Fig. 12.3. Distillation

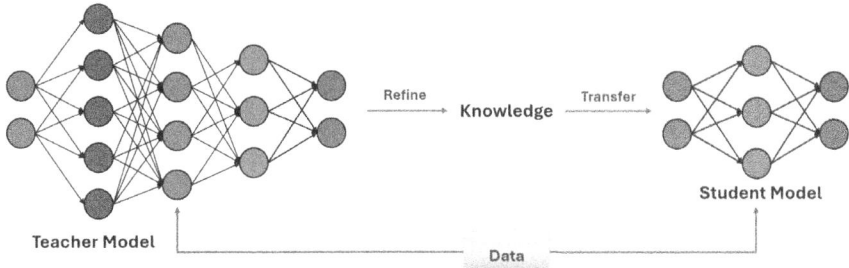

Fig. 12.3 Knowledge distillation

strategies include offline distillation using pre-trained teacher models, online distillation where teacher and student models update simultaneously, and self-distillation where the same model serves as both teacher and student.

Different *knowledge distillation* strategies are:

1. Offline Distillation: Which is the most common distillation technique, which involves using a pre-trained teacher model to guide the student model. It's the easiest to implement.
2. Online Distillation or deep mutual learning: Which is used when a pre-trained teacher model is not available, in this technique, both teacher and student models are updated simultaneously in a single end to end training process.
3. Self-Distillation: Which is a special case of online distillation and involves using the same model as the teacher as well as the student. In this type, knowledge from deeper layers of the network is used to guide the shallow layers.

Low-rank factorization identifies redundant neural network parameters through matrix and tensor decomposition, decomposing large matrices into smaller ones to improve storage requirements and inference speed. The appropriate compression technique depends on target accuracy tolerance, model architecture, and hardware constraints.

Building AI Maturity

As AI becomes increasingly central to organizational strategy, AI maturity models have emerged as essential tools for assessing readiness, identifying capability gaps, and guiding strategic development. These models offer structured frameworks for evaluating how effectively an organization integrates AI technologies, processes, and cultural practices to drive performance. Unlike traditional software maturity models, AI maturity frameworks must account for the distinctive characteristics of AI, including its reliance on high-quality data, the rapid pace of algorithmic and infrastructural innovation, and the inherently interdisciplinary nature of AI development.

AI maturity reflects the extent to which an organization has developed competencies across several dimensions, such as data infrastructure, talent and skills, governance, strategic alignment, and operational integration. Drawing on insights from technology management, organizational theory, and systems thinking, these models emphasize that maturity encompasses not only technical capabilities but also organizational adaptability and strategic coherence.

Typically, AI maturity models are organized around core dimensions—such as leadership and strategy, data and infrastructure, talent and culture, governance and ethics, and value realization. Each dimension is assessed across a series of maturity levels (e.g., initial, developing, defined, managed, optimizing), with specific criteria and indicators guiding evaluation. Assessments may be conducted through self-evaluation, formal audits, or hybrid approaches, often resulting in actionable roadmaps for improvement.

Implementing these models effectively requires balancing standardization with contextual flexibility. Organizations must choose between descriptive models that map current capabilities and prescriptive models that recommend specific actions. They must also decide on appropriate assessment methods, whether quantitative, qualitative, or mixed. Key challenges include ensuring organizational readiness, translating assessment findings into concrete initiatives, and addressing ethical and governance concerns.

To advance AI maturity, organizations are encouraged to take practical steps such as cultivating an AI-first mindset, focussing on high-impact use cases, improving data quality, enhancing engineering practices, accelerating iteration cycles, and establishing robust governance structures. Prominent frameworks include Gartner's five-level model, Microsoft's four-stage approach, and the MIT Center for Information Systems Research (CISR) model, each offering distinct perspectives on AI capability development.

Progressing through AI maturity stages involves more than technical upgrades; it requires building strong data foundations, fostering innovation, embedding ethical oversight, and investing in scalable infrastructure. Importantly, maturity is not always uniform across an organization—different departments or functions may be at different stages, necessitating flexible and nuanced strategies for growth.

Exercises

1. Describe the key steps involved in deploying a machine learning model from development to production.
2. Discuss the challenges of ensuring model scalability and reliability in a production environment.
3. Explain the importance of monitoring model performance in production and list key metrics to track.
4. What is active learning, and how does it differ from traditional supervised learning?

5. Explain how active learning can be used to reduce data labelling costs and improve model performance.
6. Compare and contrast data parallelism and model parallelism in distributed training.
7. Discuss the challenges of distributed training, such as communication overhead and synchronization.
8. What is error analysis, and why is it important in the machine learning development process?
9. Describe different techniques for performing error analysis, such as confusion matrices and error categorization.
10. How can error analysis inform model improvement strategies?
11. What are invariance tests, and why are they important for evaluating model robustness?
12. Describe how to design and implement invariance tests for a specific machine learning model.
13. Explain how invariance tests can help detect and mitigate bias in AI systems.
14. Explain how to incorporate cost considerations into the design and evaluation of machine learning models.
15. What are human-in-the-loop (HITL) workflows, and how can they improve AI systems?
16. Describe different ways to integrate human input into the machine learning process.
17. What is model compression, and why is it important for deploying AI on resource-constrained devices?
18. Choose a pre-trained machine learning model and deploy it using a cloud platform like Google Cloud, AWS, or Azure. Document the steps involved in containerizing the model, setting up a serving endpoint, and monitoring its performance.
19. Implement an active learning strategy (e.g., uncertainty sampling) for a text classification task. Compare the performance of the active learning model with a passively trained model, using the same amount of labelled data. Evaluate how much you can reduce the amount of data to be labelled.

Further Reading

AI Maturity and Organizations by Microsoft: https://query.prod.cms.rt.microsoft.com/cms/api/am/binary/RE4Dlvg
AI maturity framework for enterprise applications by IBM: https://www.ibm.com/downloads/cas/OB8M18WR
Ameisen E (2020) Building machine learning powered applications: going from idea to product. O'Reilly Media. ISBN: 978-1492045113
Bayer E, Celik ZB, Hardt M, Neiswanger W, Zhang S (2023) Infrastructure for responsible development and deployment of machine learning systems. Proceedings of the 2023 ACM Conference on Fairness, Accountability, and Transparency, 791–801

Bishop CM (2006) Pattern recognition and machine learning. Springer. ISBN: 978-0387310732

Brinker, K. (2003) Tradeoffs in active learning for text classification. In ICML (vol 3, pp 59–66)

Burkov A (2020) Machine Learning Engineering. True Positive Inc. ISBN: 978-1999579579

Cohn D, Ghahramani Z, Jordan MI (1996) Active learning with statistical models. J Artif Intell Res 4:1–25

Gartner AI Maturity Model: https://www.gartner.com/smarterwithgartner/the-cios-guide-to-artifi cial-intelligence

Géron A (2019) Hands-on machine learning with Scikit-learn, Keras & TensorFlow: concepts, tools, and techniques to build intelligent systems. O'Reilly Media. (Chapter on analysing model errors)

Géron A (2022) Hands-on machine learning with Scikit-learn, Keras, and TensorFlow: concepts, tools, and techniques to build intelligent systems (3rd edn). O'Reilly Media. ISBN: 978-1098125974

Gholami A, Kwon KT, Wu B, Keutzer K, Kubiatowicz J (2021) Efficient processing of deep neural networks. Morgan & Claypool Publishers

Goodfellow I, Bengio Y, Courville A (2016) Deep learning. MIT Press. ISBN: 978-0262035613

Han S, Mao H, Dally WJ (2015). Deep compression: Compressing, training neural networks with the pruning, trained quantization and Huffman coding. arXiv preprint arXiv:1510.00149

Heckel R, Shekhar S, Jegelka J (2018) Greedy inference for active learning. In Advances in Neural Information Processing Systems (pp. 770–780)

Hubara I, Courbariaux M, Soudry D, El-Yaniv R, Bengio Y (2016) Quantized neural networks: training neural networks with low precision weights and activations. J Mach Learn Res 17(1):477–506

Huyen C (2022) Designing machine learning systems: an iterative process for production-ready applications. O'Reilly Media. ISBN: 978-1098107963

Jurafsky D, Martin JH (2023) Speech and language processing (3rd edn). Pearson. ISBN: 978-0131873216

Kreps B, Lakshmanan V, Low HB, Krivokon M (2021) Production-ready machine learning. Man Publications

Li M, Zhou L, Yang T, Li Y, Smola AJ (2014) Parameter server for distributed machine learning. In: Distributed processing symposium (IPDPS), 2014 IEEE 28th international. IEEE, pp 561–570

Molnar C (2022) Interpretable machine learning: a guide for making black box models explainable (2nd edn). Lulu.com. ISBN: 978-0244768522

Moroney L (2020) AI and machine learning for coders: a programmer's guide to artificial intelligence. O'Reilly Media. ISBN: 978-1492078180

Ng A (2018) Machine Learning Yearning: Technical Strategy for AI Engineers in the Era of Deep Learning. deeplearning.ai. Available online: https://www.deeplearning.ai/machine-learning-yea rning/

Olsson F (2009) Active learning. Synthesis Lectures on Artificial Intelligence and Machine Learning 3(1):1–114

Ribeiro MT, Singh S, Guestrin C (2016) "Why should I trust you?": Explaining the predictions of any classifier. In Proceedings of the 22nd ACM SIGKDD international conference on knowledge discovery and data mining (pp 1135–1144)

Ribeiro MT, Wu T, Guestrin C, Singh S (2020) Beyond accuracy: Behavioral testing of NLP models with CheckList. arXiv preprint arXiv:2005.04118

Sarker IH (2021) Machine learning: concepts, methodologies, tools, and applications: concepts, methodologies, tools, and applications. IGI Global (Chapter on Distributed Machine Learning)

Settles B (2012) Active learning literature survey. University of Wisconsin-Madison Department of Computer Sciences

Tunstall L, von Werra L, Wolf T (2022) Natural language processing with transformers: building language applications with hugging face. O'Reilly Media. ISBN: 978-1098136796

Tuulos V (2022) Effective data science infrastructure: how to make data scientists more productive. Manning Publications. ISBN: 978-1617298578

Varshney KR (2022) Trustworthy machine learning. Manning Publications. ISBN: 978-1617299131

Chapter 13
Never Stop Learning: The Principles of Continual Learning

The beautiful thing about AI and robotics is that you're never done.
—Manuela Veloso
Learning never exhausts the mind.
—Leonardo da Vinci

Introduction

The critical ability of artificial intelligence systems is to acquire and retain new knowledge over time without forgetting previously learned information. A central challenge in this field is overcoming "catastrophic forgetting," where learning new tasks erases knowledge of old ones. Various strategies, such as memory replay and parameter isolation, are being developed to enable AI to learn sequentially and adapt to evolving environments. The ultimate goal of continual learning is to create AI agents that can autonomously and perpetually expand their understanding of the world, much like humans do.

Continual learning represents a primary capability for developing truly adaptable AI systems. By enabling artificial intelligence to acquire new knowledge without losing previously learned information, continual learning creates a bridge between human cognitive development and conventional machine learning approaches. In spite of challenges such as catastrophic forgetting and interference between tasks, researchers have developed sophisticated techniques including regularization methods, experience replay systems, and flexible architecture designs to create more resilient continual learning frameworks. As AI becomes gradually capable at continuous adaptation, these systems will be better positioned to navigate complex real-world scenarios and deliver customized, intelligent solutions across numerous domains.

R. Akerkar, *Artificial Intelligence*, https://doi.org/10.1007/978-3-031-91084-5_13

Understanding the Fundamentals

Continual learning focuses on practical methodologies for incrementally training machine learning models. This incremental approach means models learn from sequential data batches without requiring access to previously processed information. Unlike traditional machine learning where complete datasets are available during training, continual learning works with numerous smaller datasets delivered in sequence.

The concept of continual learning, sometimes called lifelong learning, refers to an AI model's capacity to continuously adapt from an ongoing stream of information over time. Each smaller dataset might contain minimal samples and is typically used only once. Data appears as a continuous stream with unpredictable content. Consequently, continual learning doesn't employ the standard training, validation, and testing division used in conventional machine learning pipelines. While traditional approaches emphasize performance on current datasets measured through validation and testing, continual learning aims to maintain high performance on current data while simultaneously preventing the forgetting of previously acquired knowledge.

Continual learning systems differ from traditional machine learning models in that they can acquire new information without overwriting previously learned knowledge, as opposed to being trained on static datasets prior to deployment. This capability makes continual learning essential for real-world applications where environments constantly evolve.

Continual learning addresses several significant limitations of conventional AI systems. In many practical scenarios such as robotics, autonomous vehicles, or healthcare, environments undergo constant change. AI systems need to continuously absorb new information and adjust to these changes. Additionally, some applications gather data incrementally rather than having complete datasets available initially. Continual learning enables models to process new information as it arrives, making computation more efficient compared to completely retraining models using all available data.

Essential Characteristics

Continual learning systems exhibit several defining characteristics. First, they must adapt to new information by incrementally integrating new knowledge as data becomes available without requiring complete retraining. Second, they must avoid catastrophic forgetting by retaining previously acquired information while learning new concepts. In conventional AI systems, retraining with new data often results in catastrophic forgetting where earlier knowledge is overwritten. Third, these systems must operate with memory efficiency, maintaining performance while minimizing computational resource requirements, making them suitable for practical applications.

Learning Scenarios

Continual learning problems are categorized based on the nature of data streams into three main types, each requiring different strategies. In class-incremental learning, models must learn to recognize new categories over time without forgetting previously learned ones—for example, a model trained to identify cats and dogs later learning to recognize birds while retaining its original capabilities. Domain-incremental learning involves adapting to shifts in data distributions, such as when invoice layouts vary, challenging the model to maintain accuracy without explicit task labels. Task-incremental learning deals with sequences of distinct tasks, where models often receive task identifiers to determine the current task, requiring them to adapt over time and sometimes expand their architecture to accommodate new tasks. Each task may demand different output formats, such as classification versus summarization, making task labels essential.

Despite its potential, continual learning faces major challenges. Catastrophic forgetting, where new learning overwrites old knowledge, is a key issue, along with task interference, which can degrade performance on earlier tasks. Efficient use of memory, computation, and storage is critical, especially as models must adapt to non-stationary data without losing prior knowledge. Additionally, continual learning systems are often more computationally demanding than traditional models, leading to higher costs in terms of data, human oversight, and processing power.

From a modelling perspective, frequent parameter updates can result in numerous model versions, complicating performance tracking. Data drift also poses a risk, as changing feature distributions can reduce predictive accuracy. While cost-related challenges are difficult to eliminate, modelling issues can be addressed through practices like model versioning, performance monitoring, and regular evaluation. Human oversight remains essential for managing data updates and ensuring the system adapts effectively over time.

Methods for Continual Learning

In recent years, continual learning has progressed considerably, with solutions generally categorized into architectural, regularization, and memory-based approaches. Architectural methods adapt the model's structure to integrate new data while preserving prior knowledge. For instance, a multilingual language model might use a shared core with separate classification layers fine-tuned for different languages, allowing the core to remain stable while new information is absorbed through specialized components. Techniques like progressive neural networks or multiple model heads are often used to isolate learning paths and prevent interference.

Regularization methods, by contrast, retain a fixed model architecture and focus on minimizing changes to important parameters during training. Strategies such as knowledge distillation, modified loss functions, and selective updates help the model learn new tasks without overwriting previous knowledge. These methods are relatively easy to implement but often fall short in complex scenarios, especially in class-incremental learning, making them more suitable as baseline solutions rather than final ones.

Memory-based approaches store selected past examples in buffers—whether in databases, local files, or RAM—and replay them during training alongside new data. This helps mitigate forgetting by reinforcing earlier knowledge. These methods are widely effective across all continual learning types due to their simplicity and strong empirical performance. However, they rely on access to historical data, which can be restricted by privacy regulations, data retention policies, or storage constraints.

Understanding Catastrophic Forgetting

Catastrophic forgetting, also called catastrophic interference, describes the phenomenon where neural networks forget previously learned information when trained on new data. This occurs because typical neural network training updates weights globally, meaning adjustments accommodating new information may overwrite or interfere with previously encoded knowledge. Consequently, model performance on earlier tasks deteriorates while learning new ones.

This issue proves particularly problematic when models must learn from sequential tasks or data distributions, as in continual learning scenarios. Preventing catastrophic forgetting while incorporating new information represents a primary challenge in continual learning, creating a significant barrier to developing models capable of retaining knowledge across extended periods and multiple tasks.

Catastrophic forgetting impacts continual learning through several mechanisms. Neural networks learning new tasks update model parameters globally through back-propagation, optimizing for new tasks often at the expense of previous ones, resulting in performance degradation on earlier tasks. Continual learning typically involves non-stationary data with changing distributions over time. Without mitigation mechanisms, models likely forget earlier distributions when exposed to new ones. As models transition between tasks, they prioritize recent tasks without appropriate safeguards, forgetting earlier ones.

Mitigation Strategies

Researchers have developed various techniques to address catastrophic forgetting in continual learning systems. Regularization-based methods constrain model changes during training to protect important weights from earlier tasks. Elastic Weight Consolidation adds penalties to loss functions restricting changes to parameters crucial for previous tasks, while Synaptic Intelligence tracks weight importance and applies regularization to protect critical connections.

Replay-based approaches utilize previously learned or synthetic data to periodically reinforce model memory. Experience replay stores subsets of previous examples replayed during new task learning, while generative replay trains models to produce synthetic examples refreshing networks' memory of past tasks.

Dynamic architecture approaches expand or modify neural network structures as new tasks emerge, ensuring separate representation of old and new knowledge. Progressive neural networks add new subnetworks for each task while freezing connections to earlier layers, preserving previous knowledge. Expert networks employ multiple specialized submodels with gating mechanisms determining appropriate expert activation based on current tasks or data.

Memory-based methods store and recall key information about previous tasks, helping models retain important knowledge. Memory-Augmented Neural Networks include external memory banks storing past knowledge, enabling "recall" of previous task information when learning new ones.

Meta-learning approaches train models to learn how to learn, enabling adaptation to new tasks with minimal forgetting. These models transfer knowledge across tasks more effectively, reducing interference between them.

Mitigating Catastrophic Forgetting in Continual Learning

This section examines three primary approaches that researchers have developed to address catastrophic forgetting in continual learning systems: architectural methods, regularization-based techniques, and memory-based strategies. Each approach tackles the problem from a different angle, offering unique advantages and limitations. By understanding these methodologies thorough, researchers and practitioners can better select and implement appropriate continual learning solutions for specific applications.

Architectural Approaches

Architectural approaches to continual learning focus on modifying the structure of neural networks to accommodate new knowledge without disrupting previously learned information. These methods operate on the premise that structural isolation or expansion can prevent interference between different tasks or knowledge domains.

Progressive Neural Networks

Progressive neural networks (PNNs) represent one of the earliest and most influential architectural approaches to continual learning. In this framework, the model begins with a single neural network for the initial task. As new tasks arrive, rather than modifying the existing network, the system adds a new "column" or subnetwork dedicated to the new task.

The key innovation in PNNs is the use of lateral connections, which allow new columns to leverage representations learned in previous columns while maintaining their separability. These lateral connections implement transfer learning across tasks while preventing backward interference. The weights in previously trained columns remain frozen when training a new column, ensuring that knowledge from earlier tasks is preserved intact.

Mathematically, if we denote the activation at layer i for task k as h_i^k, the forward pass in a progressive neural network can be expressed as:

$$h_i^k = f\left(W_i^k h_{i-1}^k + \sum_{j<k}\left(, U_i^{k:j}\, h_{i-1}^j\right)\right),$$

where w_i^k represents the weights within column k at layer i, $U_i^{k:j}$ represents the lateral connection weights from column, j to column, k at layer, i, and, f is a non-linear activation function.

While PNNs effectively prevent forgetting, they introduce a significant drawback: the model size grows linearly with the number of tasks. For systems that must learn many tasks over time, this growth quickly becomes unsustainable in terms of memory and computational requirements.

Dynamic Expandable Networks

To address the unlimited growth issue in PNNs, researchers have developed dynamic expansion methods that grow the network more selectively. Dynamic Expandable Networks (DENs) use a three-stage strategy for each new task:

1. **Selective retraining**: First, the model attempts to learn the new task using the existing network by retraining a sparse subset of parameters.
2. **Dynamic expansion**: If performance on the new task falls below a threshold, new neurons are added to the network.
3. **Selective duplication**: Finally, neurons that are critical for previous tasks are duplicated before modification to preserve their original functionality.

This approach strikes a balance between plasticity (ability to learn new tasks) and stability (preservation of previous knowledge). By adding capacity only, when necessary, DENs can accommodate new knowledge without the dramatic growth characteristic of PNNs.

Consider a practical example in autonomous driving: A vehicle's perception system initially trained to recognize cars and pedestrians might need to learn to recognize new objects like construction barriers. Rather than building an entirely new perception system, a DEN would first attempt to use existing feature detectors, then add new specialized units only where needed to distinguish the unique features of construction barriers, while duplicating critical units used for detecting pedestrians to prevent degradation in that safety-critical capability.

Conditional Computation and Routing Networks

Another architectural approach involves conditional computation, where different subnetworks or "experts" within a larger network are activated depending on the task or input data. PathNet exemplifies this approach by treating the neural network as a collection of pathways that can be selectively activated.

More recent developments include routing networks like the Mixture of Experts (MoE) approach, where a gating mechanism determines which expert networks should process the input. For continual learning, these gating mechanisms can identify the appropriate expert for each task, preventing interference between tasks.

XdG (Context-dependent gating) offers a simplified approach by selectively deactivating a subset of neurons for each task. By using non-overlapping subnetworks for different tasks, XdG prevents interference while allowing for shared representations were beneficial.

Regularization-Based Approaches

Regularization approaches to continual learning aim to constrain the updating of model parameters to protect knowledge from previous tasks. Unlike architectural methods that modify the network structure, regularization techniques maintain a fixed architecture but add penalty terms to the loss function that discourage changes to parameters important for previous tasks. Regularization-based approaches have demonstrated significant improvements in continual learning scenarios. They offer a balance between stability and plasticity, allowing models to retain previously learned knowledge while adapting to new tasks. These methods are computationally efficient and can be integrated into various neural network architectures, making them versatile tools for continual learning.

Elastic Weight Consolidation

Elastic Weight Consolidation (EWC) draws inspiration from neuroscience research on synaptic consolidation. EWC identifies which weights in the network are critical for previous tasks and selectively slows down learning on these weights when training on new tasks. EWC works by estimating the importance of each parameter for previously learned tasks using the Fisher Information Matrix. Parameters deemed important are penalized for changing significantly when learning new tasks. This approach helps to preserve the knowledge acquired from previous tasks while allowing the model to adapt to new ones.

The importance of each weight is determined using the Fisher Information Matrix, which measures how sensitive the model's outputs are to changes in each parameter. Mathematically, EWC modifies the loss function for a new task B as follows:

$$L(\theta) = L_B(\theta) + \sum_i \frac{\lambda}{2} Fi\left(\theta_i - \theta_{A,i}^*\right)^2,$$

where $L_B(\theta)$ is the loss for the new task B, $\theta_{A,i}^*$ represents the optimal parameters for the previous task A, Fi is the Fisher information for parameter i, and θ is a hyperparameter controlling the importance of the regularization term.

To illustrate this with an example, consider a language model trained to understand medical terminology that is subsequently fine-tuned for legal document analysis. EWC would identify which parameters are critical for medical terminology understanding (perhaps neurons capturing relationships between symptoms and conditions) and apply stronger constraints to prevent changes to these weights during the legal domain training.

Synaptic Intelligence

Synaptic Intelligence (SI) extends the concept of EWC but uses a different approach to estimate parameter importance. Synaptic Intelligence (SI) is another influential regularization-based approach. SI introduces the concept of intelligent synapses, inspired by biological neural networks. Rather than computing the Fisher information matrix, SI tracks the contribution of each parameter to the decrease in loss during training on previous tasks.

The key differences and characteristics of SI include:

1. **Online importance estimation**: Unlike EWC which calculates importance after training on a task, SI computes parameter importance during training by accumulating the product of parameter updates and the negative gradient.
2. **Path integral approach**: SI tracks the entire optimization path, essentially measuring how much each parameter contributes to decreasing the loss function throughout training.
3. **Computational efficiency**: SI tends to be more efficient than EWC because it doesn't require computing a Fisher Information Matrix.
4. **Regularization term**: Similar to EWC, SI adds a regularization term to the loss function that penalizes changes to important parameters when learning new tasks.

The mathematical formulation involves tracking how much each parameter θ contributes to reducing the loss function by accumulating the product of parameter changes and the corresponding negative gradients throughout training.

In SI, each synapse accumulates task-relevant information over time and uses this information to store new memories without forgetting old ones. The method calculates the importance of each parameter based on how much it contributes to the performance of the model on previous tasks. Parameters with higher importance are protected from drastic changes during the learning of new tasks. SI accumulates an "importance" measure for each parameter by integrating the product of the parameter update and the negative gradient over the entire training trajectory.

The importance of a parameter is determined by measuring its contribution to reducing the loss function during training. The following lines show how it works mathematically:∇

1. **Path Integral Approach**: For each parameter θ_i, SI computes an importance measure ω_i by integrating the contribution of parameter changes along the optimization path: $\omega_i = \int - \nabla_i L(\theta) \cdot d\theta_i$.

   This integral represents how much the parameter θ_i contributed to decreasing the loss function L throughout training.

2. **Practical Implementation**: Since we can't compute the continuous integral directly, SI uses a discrete approximation:

   $\omega_i = \Sigma_t - \nabla_i L(\theta^t) \cdot \Delta\theta_i{}^t$, where:

   $\nabla_i L(\theta^t)$ is the gradient of the loss with respect to parameter θ_i at time step t,

   $\Delta\theta_i{}^t$ is the change in parameter θ_i at time step t.

3. **Online Accumulation**: SI maintains an auxiliary variable for each parameter:

   $s_i \leftarrow s_i - \nabla_i L(\theta) \cdot \Delta\theta_i$.

   This is updated at each training step, accumulating the contribution of each parameter change.

4. **Normalization**: After training on a task, the final importance weight is calculated as: $\omega_i = max(0, s_i/(\Delta\theta_i{}^2 + \xi))$.

   Where:

   $\Delta\theta_i$ is the total change in parameter θ_i during training,

   ξ is a small positive constant to prevent division by zero,

   The max function ensures non-negative importance.

5. **Regularization for Continual Learning**: When learning a new task, SI adds a regularization term to the loss function: $L(\widetilde{\theta}) = L(\theta) + c/2 \cdot \Sigma_i \omega_i (\theta_i - \theta_i*)^2$.

   Where:

   $L(\theta)$ is the loss for the current task,

   c is a hyperparameter controlling regularization strength,

   ω_i is the importance of parameter θ_i,

   θ_i* is the optimal value of parameter θ_i for previous tasks.

The key insight of SI is that parameters that consistently contribute to reducing the loss during training are considered more important and should be changed less when learning new tasks, preventing catastrophic forgetting while allowing adaptation to new information.

The advantage of SI over EWC is that it accumulates importance during training rather than requiring a separate estimation step, making it more computationally efficient.

Knowledge Distillation for Continual Learning

Knowledge Distillation for Continual Learning represents an innovative fusion of two fundamental machine learning concepts designed to combat catastrophic forgetting in neural networks. This approach leverages the knowledge distillation framework originally proposed by Hinton and colleagues to preserve previously acquired knowledge while simultaneously learning new tasks.

Knowledge Distillation for Continual Learning establishes a teacher-student relationship between models. The model trained on previous tasks serves as the teacher, while the model currently learning new tasks functions as the student. The student model aims to match not only the ground truth labels of the new task but also the output distributions (soft targets) generated by the teacher model on the new data. This dual objective is typically formalized through a combined loss function that incorporates both a classification loss component for the new task and a distillation loss component that measures the divergence between the student's and teacher's predictions, often using Kullback–Leibler divergence.

Several important implementations have emerged within this framework. Learning without Forgetting (LwF) applies knowledge distillation directly on new task data, eliminating the need to store data from previous tasks. iCaRL extends this approach by combining knowledge distillation with strategic exemplar selection for class-incremental learning scenarios. Deep Model Consolidation takes yet another approach, using knowledge distillation as a mechanism to merge models that have been trained independently on different tasks.

The advantages of Knowledge Distillation for Continual Learning are extensive. Many implementations don't require storing old task data, which addresses privacy concerns and reduces memory requirements. Rather than preserving specific weight values, these methods focus on maintaining functional behaviour, which offers greater flexibility. They tend to be computationally efficient compared to regularization-based approaches and can be effectively combined with other continual learning techniques to enhance performance.

Mode Connectivity

A recent innovation in regularization approaches is based on the concept of mode connectivity. Studies have shown that different local minima in neural network loss landscapes are often connected by simple paths of similarly low loss. Mode Connectivity Guided Training leverages this property to prevent forgetting by constraining the optimization path.

Instead of directly constraining weights, this approach ensures that the model remains in a region of parameter space that performs well on both new and old tasks by following low-loss paths between task-specific optima. This method offers the advantage of allowing more flexibility in weight updates while still preventing performance degradation on previous tasks.

Memory-Based Approaches

Memory-based approaches to continual learning rely on storing and replaying examples from previous tasks when learning new ones. These methods most directly address the core issue in catastrophic forgetting: the absence of data from previous tasks during training on new tasks.

Experience Replay

Experience replay (ER) is conceptually the simplest memory-based approach. ER involves maintaining a memory buffer that stores samples from previously learned tasks. This buffer serves as a repository of experiences that the model can revisit during the training of new tasks. By incorporating examples from past tasks into the training process, ER aims to mitigate the issue of catastrophic forgetting, where new learning can overwrite previously acquired knowledge. When training on a new task, the model forms batches by combining examples from the current task with randomly selected examples from the memory buffer. This blending of old and new data helps the model retain knowledge from previous tasks while adapting to new ones. However, the effectiveness of ER is highly contingent on the strategy employed to select which examples to store in memory. Random selection of examples provides a basic approach to populating the memory buffer. While this method ensures a diverse set of samples, it may not be the most efficient in terms of preserving critical knowledge. More sophisticated strategies take into account various factors such as example diversity, difficulty, or representativeness. These methods aim to optimize the memory buffer by selecting samples that are most beneficial for continual learning.

One notable strategy is the Maximally Interfered Retrieval (MIR). MIR focuses on selecting samples from the memory that the current model would misclassify most severely. By prioritizing examples that are most likely to be forgotten, MIR directs the replay process toward the most challenging and informative samples. This targeted approach enhances the model's ability to retain important knowledge and reduces the likelihood of catastrophic forgetting.

The concept of ER is not limited to a single implementation. Variations such as Hindsight Experience Replay (HER) have been developed to address specific challenges in reinforcement learning. HER allows for sample-efficient learning from sparse and binary rewards, making it particularly useful in environments where reward signals are infrequent. This adaptability of ER demonstrates its versatility and importance in the broader context of machine learning.

Generative Replay

A significant limitation of experience replay is the need to store raw data from previous tasks, which may be impractical due to memory constraints or privacy concerns. Generative replay addresses this by training a generative model (typically a generative adversarial network or a variational autoencoder) to produce synthetic samples resembling data from previous tasks.

During training on a new task, the generative model creates synthetic examples of previous tasks, which are then used alongside current task data to train the model. This approach can be extended to a dual-model system where both the task model and the generative model are trained simultaneously in a continual learning fashion, as in the deep generative replay framework.

For instance, in a medical diagnosis system that initially learns to classify X-ray images and later learns to analyse MRI scans, a generative model could create synthetic X-ray images during MRI training, thus preserving X-ray classification capability without storing actual patient X-rays.

Gradient Episodic Memory

Gradient episodic memory (GEM) represents a more parameter-efficient approach to memory-based continual learning. Rather than directly optimizing on stored examples, GEM uses them to constrain the gradients during training on new tasks.

Specifically, GEM ensures that gradient updates for the new task do not increase the loss on examples from previous tasks stored in episodic memory.

Example Episodic Memory vs Semantic Memory.

Episodic memory is a type of memory that involves the storage and recall of specific events or experiences. It is part of the broader category of declarative memory, which encompasses memories that can be consciously recalled, such as facts and events. Episodic memory is unique because it allows individuals to remember personal experiences, including the context in which they occurred, such as the time, place, and emotions associated with the event. For example, remembering your first day at job involves episodic memory, as it includes the specific details of that day.

In the context of continual learning in AI, episodic memory refers to the mechanism by which models store and retrieve specific examples from past tasks. This stored information helps the model to recall and leverage previous experiences when learning new tasks, thereby reducing the likelihood of catastrophic forgetting. By maintaining a buffer of past experiences, the model can replay these examples during training, ensuring that it retains important knowledge while adapting to new information.

Semantic memory, on the other hand, involves the storage of general knowledge and facts that are not tied to specific experiences. This type of memory includes information such as the meaning of words, historical dates, and concepts. Semantic memories are more abstract and less context-dependent than episodic memories. For instance, knowing that Oslo is the capital of Norway is a semantic memory, as it is a fact that does not rely on a personal experience.

Both types of memory are essential for cognitive functioning, allowing individuals to recall personal experiences and understand general concepts. They work together to provide a comprehensive understanding of the world and one's place within it.

At the heart of GEM is the concept of episodic memory, which involves storing a subset of past experiences in a memory buffer. Unlike traditional experience replay methods that randomly sample from this buffer, GEM employs a more sophisticated approach. During the training of new tasks, GEM ensures that the gradients of the loss function for the new task do not interfere with the gradients of the loss function for the stored examples from previous tasks. This is achieved by projecting the gradient of the new task onto the feasible region defined by the gradients of the previous tasks. If the gradient of the new task conflicts with the gradients of the previous tasks, it is modified to minimize this interference. This approach allows GEM to maintain a balance between learning new information and preserving old knowledge. By ensuring that the learning of new tasks does not degrade the performance on previous tasks, GEM effectively mitigates catastrophic forgetting. This is particularly important in scenarios where models need to learn from a continuous stream of data, such as in real-world applications where tasks are not clearly delineated.

One of the key advantages of GEM is its parameter efficiency. Traditional methods for preventing catastrophic forgetting often involve adding new parameters or layers to the model, which can lead to increased computational complexity and memory usage. In contrast, GEM operates within the existing parameter space of the model, making it a more resource-efficient solution. This efficiency is achieved by leveraging the gradients of the loss functions, rather than relying on additional model parameters.

The effectiveness of GEM has been demonstrated through experiments on various benchmark datasets, including variants of the MNIST and CIFAR-100 datasets. These experiments have shown that GEM not only alleviates forgetting but also allows for beneficial transfer of knowledge to previous tasks. This means that the model can improve its performance on earlier tasks as it learns new ones, highlighting the potential for continual improvement and adaptation.

A-GEM (Averaged GEM) simplifies this approach by replacing the multiple constraints with a single constraint on the average gradient across all previous tasks, reducing computational complexity while maintaining most of the benefits.

Example Episodic memory in AI systems.

Episodic memory in AI systems is designed to mimic the human ability to store and recall specific events or experiences, including the context in which they occurred. Here are some examples of how episodic memory is implemented in AI systems:

Retrieval-Augmented Generation (RAG): It is an approach that enhances memory retrieval by integrating episodic content through a retrieval process. This allows AI systems to generate more contextually relevant responses by recalling specific past interactions or data points. For instance, a chatbot using RAG can remember previous conversations with a user and provide responses that are consistent with the context of those interaction.

Autonomous Driving: In autonomous driving, episodic memory can be used to store and recall specific driving experiences. For example, an autonomous vehicle might remember particular routes, traffic patterns, and environmental conditions it has encountered before. This information can help the vehicle make better decisions in similar future scenarios, improving safety and efficiency.

Reinforcement Learning: In reinforcement learning, episodic memory can be used to store and recall specific episodes of interaction with the environment. This helps the agent to learn from past experiences and make better decisions in future interactions. For example, an AI agent playing a game might remember specific strategies that led to success or failure in previous games, allowing it to refine its approach.

Memory Indexing and Retrieval Optimization

Recent advancements in memory-based approaches focus on optimizing what to store in memory and when to retrieve it. The differentiable neural computer (DNC) incorporates an external memory matrix with differentiable attention mechanisms for reading and writing, allowing the model to learn how to use its memory effectively.

Meta-Experience Replay (MER) combines memory replay with meta-learning, optimizing not just for performance on current examples but for future learning capability. By minimizing interference between tasks, MER achieves better forward transfer (where learning one task helps with future tasks) in addition to reducing forgetting.

Hybrid Approaches

While architectural, regularization, and memory-based approaches each have distinct advantages and limitations, many state-of-the-art continual learning systems combine elements from multiple approaches to achieve superior performance. These hybrid methods aim to leverage the complementary strengths of different techniques while mitigating their individual weaknesses.

Combining Regularization with Memory

Memory-Aware Synapses (MAS) combines principles from both regularization and memory-based approaches. Like EWC and SI, MAS identifies important parameters to protect but does so by measuring how changes in parameters affect the model's outputs on examples stored in memory, rather than using Fisher information or loss gradients.

Similarly, GEM can be combined with EWC to create a system that both constrains gradients and penalizes changes to important weights, providing double protection against forgetting.

Dynamic Architectures with Memory Support

Progressive neural networks can be enhanced with memory modules that allow new columns to more effectively leverage knowledge from previous columns. This hybrid approach, exemplified by the Progressive Memory Banks framework, maintains the separation of tasks inherent in PNNs while enabling more efficient knowledge transfer through explicit memory mechanisms.

Task-Specific Adapters with Regularization

A particularly efficient hybrid approach uses a shared backbone network with task-specific adapter modules and applies regularization only to the shared parameters. This architecture, popularized in natural language processing by models like Adapter-BERT, minimizes interference between tasks by isolating task-specific knowledge in dedicated modules while protecting shared knowledge through regularization.

Retraining Strategies

Retraining strategies periodically update models to integrate new knowledge while preserving previous information. This approach addresses catastrophic forgetting through regular model updates using combinations of old and new data, helping retain previously learned knowledge while adapting to new information. Despite computational costs, memory requirements, and potential task interference, effective retraining strategies significantly enhance AI systems' continuous learning capabilities across diverse tasks.

Key aspects include periodic retraining on mixed new and old data to reinforce previous knowledge while learning new information. Replay-based retraining uses stored examples during retraining to avoid forgetting past knowledge. Incremental learning gradually introduces new tasks or data through layer addition, subnetwork creation, or parameter fine-tuning while preserving existing knowledge. Hybrid approaches combine retraining with regularization or dynamic architectures to enhance continual learning effectiveness.

Retraining strategies offer numerous benefits including knowledge retention through reinforcement of previous information, adaptability to new data without capability loss, performance improvement through comprehensive data incorporation, and flexibility to adjust according to application requirements.

However, challenges include computational expenses from large models or extensive historical data, substantial memory requirements for replay buffers, complex data management decisions regarding storage and replay balancing, and potential interference between tasks despite retraining efforts.

Examples include experience replay storing past experiences for mixed training, Elastic Weight Consolidation combining regularization with retraining to protect important weights, Incremental Training progressively adding new data while maintaining consideration of previous information, and generative replay using synthetic data representing past tasks during retraining.

Strategic Categorization

Categorizing continual learning strategies helps researchers and practitioners understand and select appropriate methods for maintaining performance across multiple tasks over time. Categories include regularization-based, replay-based, dynamic architecture, memory-based, and hybrid approaches, allowing tailored solutions addressing specific needs and constraints. These strategies mitigate catastrophic forgetting, enhance adaptability, and improve AI system effectiveness in dynamic environments.

Hybrid approaches combine elements from different strategies for robust continual learning addressing multiple challenges simultaneously. These might include regularization with replay to protect parameters while reinforcing old knowledge, dynamic architecture with memory systems allowing structural adaptation while maintaining access to past knowledge, or regularization with memory-based methods protecting key parameters while retaining past information.

Testing in Production

Testing continually learning models in production requires comprehensive approaches addressing the unique challenges of evolving systems. This process evaluates and validates models in real-world environments interacting with live data and users. By focusing on performance monitoring, incremental learning validation, resource management, robustness testing, user feedback, safety considerations, deployment strategies, and thorough documentation, organizations ensure effective and reliable continual learning models. Rigorous testing maintains quality and trustworthiness as AI systems adapt to new information and tasks.

Key aspects include real-time performance evaluation on both new and previous tasks, drift detection identifying distribution changes, task-specific validation ensuring effective handling of new tasks, benchmarking against previous tasks to verify retained performance, efficiency assessment monitoring resource usage, scalability testing confirming approach effectiveness as tasks increase, stress testing for robustness, detailed error analysis identifying issues, user feedback integration, bias and fairness testing especially with new data, compliance verification, controlled deployment through canary testing and A/B comparisons, comprehensive logging of predictions and metrics, and thorough documentation of model changes.

Practical Applications

Continual learning finds applications across numerous domains. In robotics and embodied AI, systems incrementally learn from new objects, tasks, or situations while maintaining previously learned skills. Autonomous vehicles adapt to changing traffic patterns, road conditions, and weather without forgetting previous driving experiences. Healthcare diagnostic systems continuously learn from new patient data and medical research while maintaining prior medical knowledge. Natural language processing applications like chatbots and language models adapt to evolving language trends and user behaviours while preserving linguistic foundations. Personalized AI assistants understand users' changing preferences and habits, continuously improving services without complete retraining.

Transfer Learning

Transfer learning involves leveraging knowledge from previously learned tasks to improve learning efficiency on new tasks. This can help in reducing the amount of data and time required to learn new tasks. This approach mirrors human learning, where prior knowledge accelerates the acquisition of new skills. The process typically involves freezing lower layers of a neural network that capture general features (such as edges, textures, or abstract patterns) while retraining upper layers on target-specific data. Mathematically, this minimizes the divergence between source and target distributions through techniques like domain adaptation, fine-tuning, or feature extraction.

The fundamental premise of transfer learning is that the features and patterns learned in one domain often have relevance in another domain. This insight has transformed how we approach complex machine learning problems, especially in scenarios where labelled training data is scarce or expensive to obtain.

Transfer learning addresses a key challenge in statistical learning theory: the assumption that training and test data must be drawn from the same feature space and distribution. This assumption rarely holds in real-world applications, where data distributions shift and new tasks emerge continuously. Transfer learning relaxes this constraint by allowing knowledge transfer across domains, tasks, or distributions.

We can formally define transfer learning as follows:

> **Definition** Transfer learning optimizes a target task T_t with limited data D_t by leveraging knowledge from a source task T_s trained on D_s. Given a pre-trained model $f_s(x; \theta_s)$, transfer learning initializes the target model $f_t(x; \theta_t)$ where $\theta_t = \theta_{frozen}, \theta_{trainable}$, keeping learned feature extractors fixed while adapting decision layers to minimize loss L_t on the target domain. This reduces sample complexity and improves generalization by exploiting shared representational structures between domains.

The value of transfer learning depends on the relationship between the source and target domains. When these domains share significant structural similarities, knowledge transfer can substantially improve learning efficiency and performance. Conversely, when domains are dissimilar, negative transfer may occur, where transferred knowledge impedes rather than enhances learning in the target domain.

The relationship between transfer learning and continual learning can be understood as:

- Transfer learning is often a component within continual learning systems, as they need to effectively transfer knowledge between sequential tasks.
- Continual learning adds mechanisms to prevent forgetting and enable ongoing adaptation.

- Transfer learning typically involves discrete learning events, while continual learning addresses continuous adaptation over time.

Many techniques developed for transfer learning (like parameter sharing, feature extraction, and domain adaptation) are utilized within continual learning frameworks, but with additional mechanisms to prevent catastrophic forgetting, such as Elastic Weight Consolidation, progressive neural networks, or memory replay.

In the broader landscape of AI learning paradigms, both transfer and continual learning aim to create more flexible, efficient systems that better mimic human learning capabilities—where knowledge from one context can be applied to new situations, and learning occurs continuously throughout the system's operational lifetime.

Example Transfer learning approaches—scenarios and constraints:

Inductive transfer learning operates when the target task differs from the source task, regardless of whether the domains are the same. In this scenario, the model must adapt its learned representations to accommodate new task requirements. This approach is particularly valuable when labelled data is available in the target domain.

Transductive transfer learning applies when the source and target tasks are identical, but the domains differ. Here, the challenge lies in adapting to distribution shifts between domains. Domain adaptation techniques, which adjust for differences in marginal or conditional distributions, fall within this category.

Unsupervised transfer learning addresses scenarios where labelled data is unavailable in both source and target domains. This represents perhaps the most challenging transfer learning setting, requiring models to extract meaningful representations from unlabelled data that generalize across domains.

Deep Transfer Learning

Deep neural networks learn hierarchical representations, with lower layers capturing general features and higher layers representing increasingly task-specific abstractions. This hierarchical structure facilitates knowledge transfer across domains. Pre-training followed by fine tuning represents the dominant paradigm in deep transfer learning. A model is initially trained on a large dataset (often for a general task), then refined on a smaller, task-specific dataset. This approach has revolutionized natural language processing through models like BERT, GPT, and T5, as well as computer vision through frameworks like ImageNet pre-trained convolutional neural networks.

The success of deep transfer learning stems from its ability to learn rich, generalizable feature representations. These representations capture fundamental patterns in data that transcend specific tasks, providing a robust foundation for transfer. Moreover, transfer learning mitigates the computational burden of training complex models from scratch, democratizing access to state-of-the-art machine learning capabilities.

Domain Adaptation

Domain adaptation, a subset of transfer learning, focuses specifically on scenarios where the distribution of data differs between source and target domains. This adaptation becomes crucial when deploying models in real-world settings, where distribution shifts occur naturally over time or across different environments.

Covariate shift, where the marginal distributions $P(X)$ differ between domains while the conditional distributions $P(Y|X)$ remain constant, represents one common challenge. Methods like importance weighting, which reweights source examples to match the target distribution, provide effective solutions in this context.

Concept shift, where $P(Y|X)$ changes between domains, presents a more challenging scenario, often requiring adjustments to the model's decision boundaries. Adversarial adaptation techniques address this challenge by learning domain-invariant representations, where the model cannot distinguish between source and target examples.

The practical impact of transfer learning spans numerous fields. In computer vision, models pre-trained on ImageNet achieve remarkable performance across diverse tasks with minimal fine-tuning. In natural language processing, pre-trained language models have transformed tasks ranging from sentiment analysis to machine translation.

Medical imaging represents a particularly compelling application domain, where transfer learning addresses the perennial challenge of limited labelled data. Models pre-trained on natural images transfer effectively to medical domains, enabling accurate diagnosis with smaller datasets than would otherwise be required.

Furthermore, transfer learning supports cross-modal applications, where knowledge transfers between entirely different data modalities. Vision-language models exemplify this capability, leveraging visual knowledge to enhance language understanding and vice versa.

Preventing Catastrophic Forgetting

As we have seen earlier in this chapter, catastrophic forgetting is one of the central challenges in continual learning, particularly for neural networks. When trained on new data, these networks tend to overwrite previously learned knowledge, leading to dramatic performance drops on older tasks. This phenomenon occurs because the parameters that encode information about different tasks overlap substantially within the network. Research has yielded several approaches to mitigate catastrophic forgetting, each with distinct strengths and limitations. These approaches can be broadly categorized as regularization-based, memory-based, and architectural methods.

Regularization-based approaches constrain parameter updates to preserve knowledge about previous tasks. Elastic Weight Consolidation (EWC) is a prominent example that estimates the importance of each parameter for previously learned tasks and penalizes changes to important parameters. Another approach, Synaptic Intelligence, tracks the contribution of each parameter to the reduction in loss during training and uses this information to regulate updates. Learning Without Forgetting (LWF) uses knowledge distillation to preserve the model's responses on previous tasks while learning from new data.

Memory-based methods explicitly store information about previous tasks. Experience replay maintains a buffer of examples from previous tasks and interleaves these with new examples during training. Generative replay uses generative models to synthesize examples representing previous tasks, avoiding the need to store actual examples. Gradient episodic memory stores gradients from previous tasks and projects new gradients to avoid interfering with old tasks.

Architectural approaches modify the model architecture to accommodate new knowledge without disrupting existing capabilities. Progressive neural networks allocate new neural resources for each new task while preserving previously trained components. Dynamically expanding networks grow the model's capacity when encountering new tasks. Attention mechanisms can route information through different parts of the network based on the task, reducing interference.

Hybrid approaches often yield the best results in practice. For instance, combining regularization with selective memory can provide robust protection against forgetting while maintaining adaptability to new information.

When implementing these techniques in production systems, several practical considerations arise. The computational overhead of regularization methods can be substantial, particularly for large models. Memory-based approaches require careful management of the example buffer, including policies for adding and removing examples. Architectural methods may lead to continuously growing models that eventually exceed computational resources.

The choice of method also depends on the nature of the learning problem. In task-incremental learning, where task boundaries are clearly defined, it may be feasible to use task-specific architectural components. In domain-incremental learning, where the input distribution changes but the task remains the same, regularization approaches often work well. In class-incremental learning, where new classes appear over time, memory-based methods frequently provide the best results.

Evaluation of forgetting mitigation techniques should consider not only their effectiveness in preserving performance on old tasks but also their impact on learning efficiency for new tasks. Some methods may excel at preventing forgetting but severely constrain the model's ability to adapt to new information.

Automated Retraining Strategies

Beyond incremental updates, comprehensive continual learning systems require strategies for automated full-model retraining. While incremental updates efficiently incorporate new information, periodic complete retraining helps prevent error accumulation and addresses more substantial distribution shifts.

Automated retraining strategies must address several key questions: when to retrain, how to retain valuable information from previous iterations, and how to ensure training stability across retraining cycles.

Determining the optimal retraining schedule involves balancing responsiveness to changing conditions against computational costs. Time-based schedules (e.g., daily or weekly retraining) provide operational predictability but may be inefficient if the data distribution remains stable. Performance-based triggers initiate retraining when model metrics drop below thresholds, targeting resources more efficiently but potentially introducing unpredictability in computational load. Distribution-based triggers monitor statistical properties of incoming data and initiate retraining when significant shifts occur, providing an early warning system before performance degradation becomes severe.

Data management across retraining cycles presents another critical challenge. Simple approaches maintain a fixed-size sliding window of recent data, but this can lead to recency bias.

The entire retraining pipeline should maintain comprehensive logs tracking data characteristics, hyperparameters, training dynamics, and validation results. This information facilitates debugging when issues arise and enables meta-learning about the retraining process itself, potentially leading to automated hyperparameter tuning and improved retraining strategies over time.

Deployment Strategies for Continual Learning

Deploying continually learning models introduces a distinct set of challenges that go beyond those associated with static models. The deployment infrastructure must not only ensure system reliability but also support smooth transitions between model versions and enable thorough evaluation of new models before they influence production outcomes.

The simplest deployment method involves fully replacing the existing model with a new version. While straightforward, this approach carries significant risk: if the new model underperforms, the entire system may degrade until corrective action is taken. To mitigate such risks, more advanced deployment strategies implement gradual transitions that allow for controlled evaluation and reduced exposure to potential failures.

A foundational technique in safe deployment is shadow deployment, where the new model operates in parallel with the current production model but does not affect system outputs. This setup allows for detailed comparison of predictions on real traffic without impacting users, offering critical insights into the new model's behavior under production conditions.

Following successful shadow testing, canary releases introduce the new model to a small, randomly selected portion of traffic. This controlled exposure limits potential harm while providing real-world performance data. If results are favorable, the traffic share can be gradually increased. Careful traffic allocation is essential to avoid introducing biases that might obscure performance issues.

Another robust strategy is blue-green deployment, which maintains two identical environments—one active and one idle. The new model is deployed and validated in the inactive environment before switching all traffic to it. If problems arise, traffic can be quickly redirected to the original environment, enabling immediate rollback.

Feature toggles offer fine-grained control by allowing specific model functionalities to be activated or deactivated independently of full redeployment. This is particularly useful when introducing new features that may interact unpredictably with existing components.

For high-stakes applications, ensemble methods can provide stability during transitions. By combining outputs from both old and new models, and gradually adjusting their influence, ensembles help smooth performance shifts and reduce the risk of regressions in critical areas.

Regardless of the deployment strategy, comprehensive monitoring is essential. Real-time systems should track overall performance as well as subgroup-specific and edge-case behavior. Anomaly detection and alerting mechanisms must be in place to trigger automatic mitigations when necessary.

Finally, the deployment infrastructure should support ongoing improvement by facilitating data collection for future training cycles. This includes logging inputs, outputs, and ground truth data—when available—while ensuring compliance with privacy regulations and data minimization principles.

Testing Methodologies for Production Models

Evaluating continual learning systems requires a multifaceted approach that goes beyond traditional offline metrics, as these models operate in environments where data distributions and user behavior are constantly evolving. A robust evaluation framework integrates offline testing, simulations, and live experiments to comprehensively assess model performance and guide iterative improvements.

Offline evaluation using held-out datasets provides an initial benchmark but fails to capture the complexities of real-world deployment. In contrast, A/B testing remains the gold standard for assessing causal effects in production by comparing outcomes between user groups exposed to different model versions. However, it demands substantial user traffic, can be time-consuming, and becomes increasingly complex when multiple model variants are involved.

To address these limitations, interleaving experiments offer a more efficient alternative by presenting outputs from multiple models to the same user within a single session. This method enhances statistical power and reduces variability caused by user heterogeneity, making it particularly effective for applications like search engines and recommendation systems.

Multi-armed bandit algorithms provide another dynamic evaluation strategy by allocating user traffic to model variants based on real-time performance. These algorithms balance exploration of new models with exploitation of high-performing ones, making them well-suited for continual learning scenarios where models evolve rapidly and require immediate feedback.

Counterfactual evaluation estimates how a new model might perform using historical data, avoiding the risks of live deployment. By adjusting for behavioural differences, it offers early performance signals, though its reliability depends on strong assumptions and should be complemented with live testing.

Selecting appropriate evaluation metrics is critical. While accuracy measures predictive performance, other dimensions such as diversity (ensuring a broad range of outputs), fairness (equitable treatment across user groups), robustness (stability under distribution shifts), and efficiency (resource usage) are equally important. These metrics must align with the priorities of diverse stakeholders, from engineers to business leaders.

Beyond static metrics, longitudinal analysis is essential to track how model performance evolves over time—whether it improves with more data, adapts to seasonal patterns, or recovers from distributional changes. Stress testing with adversarial inputs or synthetic data can reveal vulnerabilities before deployment. Additionally, simulation environments that emulate user behavior provide controlled settings to evaluate how well models adapt to dynamic conditions, offering a safe and scalable complement to live experimentation.

Integrating Feedback Loops

Effective continual learning systems establish a closed feedback loop between deployment, user interaction, evaluation, and model improvement, transforming static models into adaptive systems that evolve across multiple timescales. These systems must accommodate rapid session-level adjustments, daily retraining cycles, and long-term architectural revisions. Central to this process is user feedback, which comes in two forms: explicit feedback, such as ratings, and implicit feedback, such as clicks or engagement time. While explicit feedback is often sparse and subject to selection bias, implicit signals are noisier and require careful preprocessing, including outlier detection, normalization, and temporal weighting.

In addition to user-generated data, system-level metrics like accuracy, latency, and throughput, as well as market-level indicators such as user retention or conversion rates, provide essential signals for guiding model updates. Automating the incorporation of this feedback introduces engineering challenges, ranging from simple rule-based triggers to advanced techniques like reinforcement learning and meta-learning, which dynamically adjust learning strategies or intervention policies.

Maintaining data quality is critical, as feedback loops can unintentionally amplify biases, reinforce popularity effects, or be exploited by adversarial users. Mitigation strategies include enforcing diversity in outputs, applying fairness constraints, detecting anomalies, and conducting regular audits using holdout groups, retraining schedules, or simulation-based evaluations.

Despite advancements, continual learning still faces several core challenges. The stability-plasticity dilemma (*i.e.* the tension between retaining past knowledge and integrating new information) remains unresolved, often leading to catastrophic forgetting or rigidity. Computational efficiency is another concern, as continual learning methods frequently require larger models, memory for experience replay, or additional regularization steps. The lack of standardized evaluation protocols further complicates progress, underscoring the need for realistic benchmarks and consistent methodologies.

Theoretical understanding of continual learning dynamics is still developing, particularly in areas such as knowledge retention, optimization under nonstationarity, and the mechanisms behind forgetting. Privacy concerns also loom large, necessitating techniques like differential privacy and federated learning to balance adaptability with data protection.

Looking ahead, promising directions include automated architecture evolution, where models restructure themselves over time, and enhanced explainability for systems that continuously adapt. The convergence of continual learning with related fields, such as reinforcement learning, meta-learning, and transfer learning, offers fertile ground for innovation. As these systems become more prevalent, ethical considerations will be paramount to prevent the reinforcement of harmful biases, the creation of filter bubbles, or negative impacts on user well-being. Ultimately, continual learning represents a foundational capability for intelligent systems, enabling them to improve through experience and adapt to an ever-changing world.

Exercises

1. What is continual learning in AI, and how does it differ from traditional machine learning approaches?
2. Define continual learning and explain why it is important for real-world AI applications.
3. What are the key differences between traditional machine learning and continual learning?
4. Describe the three key characteristics of continual learning.
5. Describe the main challenges associated with continual learning, such as catastrophic forgetting.

6. What are some common strategies used to mitigate catastrophic forgetting in continual learning systems?
7. Explain the concept of transfer learning and its relevance to continual learning.
8. How can different continual learning strategies be categorized and combined?
9. What are the key aspects of testing in production for continual learning?
10. Describe five real-world applications of continual learning.
11. Discuss the role of regularization techniques in continual learning.
12. What are some real-world applications of continual learning in AI?
13. How do generative replay methods contribute to continual learning?
14. Compare and contrast different continual learning frameworks and algorithms.
15. Research and write a detailed report on the history and evolution of continual learning in AI.
16. Develop a simple continual learning model using a neural network and demonstrate its ability to learn from a sequence of tasks.
17. Analyse a case study of a continual learning application in a specific domain and discuss its impact.
18. (Project) Design an experiment to evaluate the performance of a continual learning system in handling sequential tasks.

Further Reading

Aljundi R, Babiloni F, Elhoseiny M, Rohrbach M, Tuytelaars T (2018) Memory aware synapses: learning what (not) to forget. In Proceedings of the European Conference on Computer Vision
Aljundi R, Caccia L, Belilovsky E, Caccia M, Lin M, Charlin L, Tuytelaars T (2019) Online continual learning with maximally interfered retrieval. Advances in Neural Information Processing Systems
Argentim LM, Silva RF, Santos PE (2023) Domestic robots that learn: a continual learning approach for household task adaptation. Robot Auton Syst 159:104256
Chen PHC, Wiens J (2023) Continual learning for personalized health monitoring: adapting models to patient-specific patterns. Nat Med 29(4):892–901
Esteva A, Chou K, Yeung S, Naik N, Madani A, Mottaghi A, Liu Y, Topol E, Dean J, Socher R (2021) Deep learning-enabled medical computer vision. NPJ Digital Medicine 4(1):5
Fitzpatrick KK, Darcy A, Vierhile M (2024) Adaptive digital therapeutics: employing continual learning for mental health intervention personalization. Digital Health 10:20552076231234567
Kase N, Takano T, Nakamura Y (2023) Experience-based motor skill acquisition with minimal forgetting using hierarchical tensor networks. IEEE Trans Robot 39(2):1073–1087
Lesort T, Lomonaco V, Stoian A, Maltoni D, Filliat D, Díaz-Rodríguez N (2020) Continual learning for robotics: definition, framework, learning strategies, opportunities and challenges. Information Fusion 58:52–68
Li Z, Hoiem D (2017) Learning without forgetting. IEEE Trans Pattern Anal Mach Intell 40(12):2935–2947
Lopez-Paz D, Ranzato M (2017) Gradient episodic memory for continual learning. Adv Neural Inf Proces Syst 30:6467–6476
Masse NY, Grant GD, Freedman DJ (2018) Alleviating catastrophic forgetting using context-dependent gating and synaptic stabilization. Proc Natl Acad Sci 115(44):E10467–E10475

Mirzadeh SI, Farajtabar M, Pascanu R, Ghasemzadeh H (2020) Understanding the role of training regimes in continual learning. Advances in Neural Information Processing Systems

Morley J, Machado CCV, Burr C, Cowls J, Joshi I, Taddeo M, Floridi L (2020) The ethics of AI in health care: a mapping review. Soc Sci Med 260:113172

Parisi GI, Kemker R, Part JL, Kanan C, Wermter S (2019) Continual lifelong learning with neural networks: a review. Neural Netw 113:54–71

Pfeiffer M, Bressem KK, Radke M (2022) Continual learning for adaptive manufacturing: robots that evolve with production requirements. Int J Prod Res 60(9):2835–2849

Riemer M, Cases I, Ajemian R, Liu M., Rish I, Tu Y, Moravčík M (2019) Learning to learn without forgetting by maximizing transfer and minimizing interference. International Conference on Learning Representations

Rolnick D, Ahuja A, Schwarz J, Lillicrap T, Wayne G (2019) Experience replay for continual learning. Adv Neural Inf Proces Syst 32:350–360

Shin H, Lee JK, Kim J, Kim J (2017) Continual learning with deep generative replay. Advances in Neural Information Processing Systems

Smith JT, Gao W (2024) Incremental acquisition of manipulation skills through continual reinforcement learning. IEEE Robotics and Automation Letters 9(1):713–720

Chapter 14
Opening the Black Box: The Role of Explainability in AI

Good people do not need laws to tell them to act responsibly, while bad people will find a way around the laws.
—Plato (427–347 B.C.)
AI is a mirror, reflecting not only our intellect, but our values and fears.
—Ravi Narayanan

This chapter addresses the critical need to understand how artificial intelligence (AI) systems arrive at their decisions, moving beyond opaque "black box" models. Explainability in AI is crucial for building trust, ensuring accountability, and facilitating effective human-AI collaboration across various domains. By providing insights into the reasoning behind AI outputs, we can identify potential biases, debug errors, and ultimately gain a deeper understanding of both the AI and the problem it is solving. As AI becomes increasingly integrated into our lives, the ability to interpret and explain its behaviour will be paramount for responsible and ethical deployment.

As AI advances and becomes more prevalent, the responsibility for its development and deployment grows. Decisions made by AI researchers and practitioners have significant societal impacts, raising concerns about ethics and safety. These issues are interconnected; for example, ensuring self-driving cars avoid harming pedestrians is a safety concern with ethical implications. Similarly, preventing discrimination by risk assessment algorithms is an ethical issue that can lead to unsafe outcomes. Recommendation systems pushing users towards conspiracy theories highlight both ethical and safety concerns. AI systems are expected to benefit humanity, though defining "beneficial" is debated among moral philosophers and ethicists. Diverse AI ethics frameworks, safety institutes, and regulatory efforts reflect varying perspectives on these challenges.

Concerns also include distinguishing between immediate harms, like bias and discrimination, and long-term risks, such as existential threats to humanity. Some see a divide between "AI ethics researchers," focussing on present-day issues, and "AI safety researchers," speculating on future risks like AI surpassing human capabilities. However, this distinction is misleading; AI systems can be unsafe today, and creating technologies with significant future risks is ethically wrong. The willingness to explore future risks has historically divided the AI community.

R. Akerkar, *Artificial Intelligence*, https://doi.org/10.1007/978-3-031-91084-5_14

AI research has experienced cycles of optimism and skepticism, with periods of stagnation known as "AI winters" due to unmet promises. Researchers distanced themselves from "artificial intelligence," emphasizing machine learning's statistical rigour. As AI became widely deployed, concerns about its societal impact grew, splitting into two communities: one focused on future implications of increasingly capable AI systems and another addressing immediate harm caused by current technologies.

The community focused on future risks considers scenarios where AI surpasses human capabilities, leading to unemployment, social instability, and systemic collapse. Alan Turing warned about this possibility in 1951, suggesting machines might take control if their objectives were misaligned with human values. Misaligned objectives are likely due to the difficulty in specifying goals correctly for AI systems. Instrumental goals like self-preservation and resource acquisition complicate alignment efforts. This perspective often clashes with the academic AI community's reluctance to engage in speculative discussions about the future, though some researchers recently supported initiatives like pausing advanced AI development.

The second community addresses immediate harm caused by existing AI systems, finding support within academia through conferences like Fairness, Accountability, and Transparency (FAccT). These conferences tackle issues related to bias, accountability, and societal impacts of AI technologies. Some researchers resist futuristic speculation, concerned about companies exploiting extreme scenarios to exaggerate their work's importance or divert attention from current harms. While companies might not benefit directly from narratives suggesting their technology could end humanity, such narratives could foster a sense of inevitability that prevents effective responses to immediate challenges.

Both immediate harms and long-term risks deserve attention as AI evolves. Balancing ethical considerations with safety measures is crucial to ensure AI systems serve humanity responsibly while mitigating potential dangers in the present and future. The ongoing dialogue within the AI community reflects efforts to address these multifaceted challenges while navigating technological advancement responsibly.

Explaining Explainability

Over the past decade, AI has rapidly advanced, becoming embedded in everyday technologies such as virtual assistants, recommendation systems, autonomous vehicles, and diagnostic tools. As AI increasingly influences high-stakes sectors like healthcare, finance, and criminal justice, the demand for systems that are both ethically sound and transparent has grown significantly. This has led to the emergence of Explainable AI (XAI) and Responsible AI (RAI) as essential frameworks for addressing the societal, legal, and technical concerns associated with opaque and potentially biased algorithms.

XAI plays a crucial role in building trust and ensuring accountability by making AI decision-making processes understandable to both developers and users. Despite the challenges posed by the complexity of modern AI models and the trade-offs between accuracy and interpretability, ongoing research continues to develop promising methods for enhancing explainability. These efforts are vital for promoting fairness, transparency, and reliability in AI systems, especially as their influence expands across diverse domains. As AI evolves, the pursuit of explainability will remain a central concern for researchers, technologists, and policymakers working to ensure that AI serves society responsibly and effectively.

Definition *Explainability* in AI is the ability of intelligent systems to articulate their decision-making processes in human-understandable terms. It transforms opaque computational operations into transparent reasoning, enabling users to validate outcomes, detect biases, and establish trust—making AI not just accurate, but interpretable and accountable.

Consider, for instance, a Convolutional Neural Network (CNN) employed by a hospital to analyse patient X-rays for tumour detection. A critical question arises: how can a technician or the patient have confidence in the model's findings if the reasoning behind them remains opaque? This very scenario underscores the necessity for methods that can illuminate the factors influencing the decisions made by complex deep learning models.

Transparency in AI means making the operations and decision-making processes of AI systems clear and understandable to humans. It goes beyond merely opening the black box of complex algorithms; it also involves providing clear documentation, disclosing the limitations of the AI, and being transparent about data usage and privacy. AI transparency is essential for building trust among users and stakeholders, and it is often necessary for ethical and legal compliance.

The sophistication of machine learning models has grown exponentially, evolving from simple linear regression to intricate multi-layered neural networks, CNNs, and transformers. While neural networks have dramatically improved predictive capabilities, they often function as "black-box" models. These models, as depicted in Fig. 14.1, function without exposing the internal logic behind their output generation. This lack of transparency in black-box AI models hinders our understanding of the data they utilize and makes it challenging to evaluate the reliability of their results—a challenge that explainable AI (XAI) endeavours to overcome.

*A **black-box model** in AI is a system whose internal workings are not fully visible or comprehensible to the user. This term highlights the opacity of complex models, such as deep learning networks, where the relationship*

Fig. 14.1 Black-box model

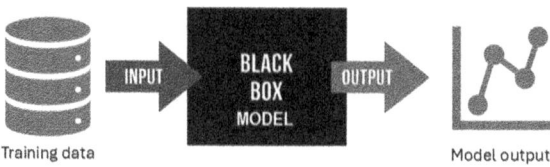

Training data   Model output

between input and output is not easily interpretable. Although these models can achieve high accuracy, their lack of transparency can create challenges for trust, accountability, and debugging.

In contrast to a black-box model, a **white-box model** in AI is a system where the internal workings are fully visible and understandable. Models like decision trees or linear regression enable users to see the exact decision path or mathematical relationships used to make a prediction. Although these models may not always achieve the highest predictive accuracy, their transparency is crucial for interpretability, trust, and regulatory compliance.

Explainable AI (XAI) plays a crucial role in making AI systems more transparent and trustworthy by clarifying how models operate, what data they rely on, and how specific predictions are made. It focuses on illuminating the rationale behind training data selection, the internal logic of algorithms, and the factors influencing individual outputs. This transparency is essential for building user trust, ensuring accountability, and supporting ethical decision-making.

There are two main approaches to explainability. Self-interpretable models, such as decision trees and logistic regression, are inherently understandable—their structure and outputs can be directly interpreted by humans. In contrast, post-hoc explanations are applied to more complex, opaque models. These explanations are generated by external tools that analyse model behaviour without needing access to internal mechanics, often using visualizations like saliency maps or verbal summaries to convey insights.

The growing emphasis on XAI is driven by several factors. First, it enhances user understanding and confidence, which is vital for broader AI adoption. Second, regulatory compliance, especially in sectors like finance and marketing, requires transparency, particularly under frameworks like GDPR that demand explainability in decisions involving personal data. Third, XAI is instrumental in identifying and mitigating bias by revealing how sensitive attributes may influence predictions. Tools like AI Fairness 360 and Fairlearn help detect such biases through statistical analysis and performance comparisons across demographic groups. Finally, XAI supports continuous system improvement by aiding in error detection, debugging, and addressing issues like data drift or performance degradation, making it a key component in maintaining long-term model reliability.

The Building Blocks of Human-AI Association

Distrust in current AI and Machine Learning systems often stems from their "black box" nature, characterized by limited interaction, a lack of understanding of human context, and insufficient explanations. This has spurred a demand for a new era of AI focused on a more collaborative human-machine partnership. Contextual AI, rather than being a specific algorithm, represents a human-centred perspective on AI, defined by a set of requirements fostering a symbiotic relationship. These requirements include intelligibility, adaptivity, customizability, controllability, and context-awareness, which translate to the following in practical terms:

Intelligibility in AI mandates that a system can explain its reasoning, revealing to users what it knows, how it acquired that knowledge, and its current actions. This transparency is fundamental for building trust in AI systems.

Adaptivity refers to an AI system's ability to maintain its effectiveness and meet user expectations when applied in situations or environments different from those it was originally trained or designed for. For instance, a personal smart home assistant that understands a user's preferences should ideally be able to apply similar logic and adapt to a different home environment, such as a relative's house.

Furthermore, an AI system should be adaptable and customizable by the user, who must also be able to maintain equal control over all the system's functions. This aspect is closely linked to intelligibility, as users need to understand the basis of the system's decisions to effectively customize and control it.

Finally, context-awareness is a crucial requirement, signifying the system's capacity to perceive its environment, the user's situation, and the overall context with a level of understanding comparable to a human. A smart home assistant, for example, cannot effectively learn a user's behaviour and preferences and manage a household with limited sensory input, such as a single camera focused only on the front porch. Sufficient perception of the user's surroundings is necessary for proper reasoning and context-aware actions.

Explanation Techniques

The field of Explainable AI (XAI) has evolved significantly, giving rise to a wide range of techniques designed to clarify how AI models make decisions. These techniques span from traditional black-box analysis, long used in scientific disciplines, to advanced methods tailored for the complexity of deep neural networks. While it's impractical to list every approach, the most widely adopted techniques fall into two main categories: model-agnostic and algorithm-specific.

Model-agnostic methods, often referred to as black-box explainers, are versatile tools that can be applied to any machine learning model regardless of its internal structure. These techniques work by manipulating inputs and observing outputs, treating the model as a black box. Their strength lies in their flexibility and ease of use, though they may offer less depth than algorithm-specific methods. For example, tools like LIME (Local Interpretable Model-agnostic Explanations) and SHAP (SHapley Additive exPlanations) generate local explanations by approximating the model's behaviour with simpler, interpretable models, helping users understand which features most influenced a particular prediction.

In contrast, algorithm-specific approaches are designed to work with particular model types, leveraging knowledge of their internal architecture. These methods provide more direct insights into how decisions are made. For instance, in decision trees, the path from root to leaf clearly outlines the logic behind a prediction. However, these techniques are less adaptable and cannot be easily transferred across different model types.

Choosing between these approaches depends on the context and the level of interpretability required. In many cases, combining both can offer a more complete understanding of a model's behaviour. As the field advances, researchers continue to develop new techniques that push the boundaries of explainability, aiming to make even the most complex AI systems more transparent and trustworthy.

Approaches to Enhancing Explainability

Various approaches are being developed and refined to enhance the explainability of Artificial Intelligence (XAI) systems, broadly falling into two main categories: self-interpretable models and post-hoc explanation techniques.

Self-interpretable models are designed with inherent transparency, meaning their structure and decision-making processes are directly understandable by humans. These models essentially provide their own explanations. A prime example is a decision tree, where each node represents a feature, each branch represents a decision rule, and each leaf node represents the final prediction. By tracing the path from the root to a leaf, one can easily understand the specific features and their values that led to a particular outcome. Similarly, linear models, including linear regression and logistic regression, offer interpretability through their coefficients. The magnitude and sign of each coefficient indicate the influence and direction of the corresponding feature on the prediction. These models are inherently transparent but often come with a trade-off in terms of predictive power, especially when dealing with highly complex data.

Definition *Model interpretability* refers to the extent to which a machine learning model's behaviour and predictions can be comprehended by humans. An interpretable model allows us to understand the underlying relationships it captures from the data and the logic behind its decisions.

Post-hoc explanation techniques, on the other hand, are applied to already trained, often black-box models to provide insights into their behaviour. These methods aim to explain why a model made a specific prediction or to understand the overall importance of different features. One popular approach is featuring importance analysis, which aims to quantify the contribution of each input feature to the model's output. Techniques like permutation importance work by randomly shuffling the values of a single feature and observing the impact on the model's performance; a larger drop in performance indicates a more important feature.

Another set of post-hoc methods focuses on explaining individual predictions. Local Interpretable Model-agnostic Explanations (LIME) works by approximating the black-box model locally around a specific prediction with a simpler, interpretable model (like a linear model). By analysing this local surrogate model, one can understand which features were most influential for that instance.

LIME (Local Interpretable Model-Agnostic Explanations) is a technique for explaining the predictions of any machine learning model. LIME generates explanations by perturbing the input data and observing the effect on the model's output. It provides a local interpretation for individual predictions, making it easier to understand why a model made a specific decision. It's an important tool for model interpretability and transparency.

LIME can be integrated with any machine learning model, making it highly versatile. Its model-agnostic nature means it does not depend on the internal structure or type of the model being explained, whether it is a simple decision tree, a support vector machine (SVM), or a complex neural network. Instead, LIME operates by treating the model as a "black box" and approximating its behaviour locally around specific predictions using interpretable surrogate models such as linear regression or decision trees. To work with any model, LIME requires two conditions:

1. The ability to input data points into the model and retrieve predictions (e.g., probabilities or class labels).
2. The capability to generate perturbed versions of an instance and obtain the corresponding predictions from the model.

This flexibility allows LIME to be applied across a wide range of data types, including tabular data, text, and images. For example:

- In tabular data, LIME perturbs feature values to create synthetic samples and analysis their influence on predictions.
- For text data, it modifies words or phrases to understand their impact on classification outcomes.
- In image classification, it segments images into interpretable regions (superpixels) and identifies which regions contribute most to the prediction.

While LIME is broadly applicable, it does require compatibility with certain programming structures (e.g., models similar in structure to scikit-learn objects) for ease of integration. This ensures that LIME can efficiently interact with the model's prediction functions during perturbation and explanation generation.

SHapley Additive exPlanations (SHAP), rooted in game theory, calculates the contribution of each feature to the prediction by considering all possible coalitions of features. SHAP provides a more global understanding of feature importance while also offering local explanations for individual predictions.

> *SHAP (SHapley Additive exPlanations) is a unified measure of feature importance for machine learning models, rooted in cooperative game theory. SHAP assigns each feature an importance value for a particular prediction, indicating how much each feature in the dataset contributed to the prediction. It's model-agnostic and provides consistent and locally accurate attributions. By using SHAP values, we can interpret the decision-making process of complex models, enhancing transparency and trust.*

Saliency maps are particularly useful for explaining image-based models like Convolutional Neural Networks (CNNs). These maps visually highlight the regions of an input image that were most influential in the model's decision. By overlaying a heatmap onto the original image, one can see which pixels or areas the model "looked at" to make its classification.

Furthermore, techniques like concept activation vectors (CAVs) aim to explain model behaviour in terms of human-understandable concepts. By identifying patterns of activation within the model that correspond to specific concepts (e.g., "stripes," "fur"), CAVs can reveal whether the model's prediction was based on the presence or absence of these high-level concepts.

Finally, the format of explanations is also a crucial aspect of XAI. Explanations can be presented visually through graphs, charts, and saliency maps, verbally through natural language descriptions of the reasoning process, or in written reports detailing the factors influencing the model's decisions. The choice of explanation format often depends on the target audience and the specific application.

LIME and SHAP are two widely used techniques for model interpretability, their differences in interpretability arise from their methodologies, scope of explanations, and theoretical foundations.

Local Versus Global Interpretability

- LIME focuses on generating *local explanations*, meaning it approximates the behaviour of a complex model in the vicinity of a specific instance. It uses a surrogate interpretable model (e.g., linear regression) to explain why the model made a particular prediction for that instance. This makes LIME ideal for understanding individual decisions but less suited for providing insights into the model's overall behaviour.
- SHAP, while capable of local explanations like LIME, also provides *global interpretability*. It assigns Shapley values to each feature across all instances, offering a comprehensive view of how features contribute to predictions across the dataset. This dual capability makes SHAP more versatile for both instance-specific and model-wide insights.

Theoretical Guarantees

- LIME generates explanations by perturbing input features and fitting a surrogate model locally. However, it does not guarantee consistency or accuracy in distributing feature contributions, which can lead to variability across runs.
- SHAP is grounded in game theory and provides theoretical guarantees such as *consistency* (features with higher impact always receive higher attribution) and *local accuracy* (the sum of Shapley values equals the predicted output). These properties ensure that SHAP delivers mathematically rigourous explanations, making it more reliable for sensitive applications.

Feature Attribution

- LIME selects a subset of features for explanation based on their importance within the local neighbourhood of the instance. This feature selection enhances interpretability but may overlook interactions or dependencies between features.
- SHAP, by contrast, considers all features and their interactions when calculating Shapley values, ensuring that every feature's contribution is accounted for comprehensively. This makes SHAP particularly effective for models with complex feature dependencies.

Stability and Consistency

- LIME can exhibit instability due to its reliance on random sampling for perturbation. Different runs may produce slightly different explanations for the same instance, which can be problematic in applications requiring consistent outputs.
- SHAP is more stable and consistent because its Shapley value calculations are deterministic, based on well-defined mathematical principles rather than random sampling.

Computational Complexity

- LIME is computationally lighter because it focuses on local approximations and uses fewer features in its surrogate model. This makes it faster and suitable for simpler models or tasks requiring quick insights.
- SHAP, while offering richer explanations, is computationally intensive due to its need to evaluate all possible feature combinations. For large datasets or highly complex models, this can lead to increased computation time.

Thus, SHAP is more beneficial than LIME in scenarios where comprehensive, consistent, and theoretically rigorous explanations are required. SHAP excels in explaining complex models, such as deep neural networks or ensemble methods (e.g., random forests and gradient boosting), where features interact in non-linear ways. Unlike LIME, SHAP accounts for all possible combinations of features when calculating their contributions, making it ideal for models with intricate dependencies between features. SHAP provides both local and global interpretability. It can explain individual predictions (local explanations) while also offering insights into overall feature importance across the dataset (global explanations). This dual capability makes SHAP superior when understanding the entire model's behaviour is critical, such as in credit scoring or healthcare applications. SHAP guarantees consistency and local accuracy due to its game-theoretic foundation. The Shapley values ensure that features with higher importance consistently receive greater attribution across instances. In contrast, LIME's reliance on random sampling for perturbations can lead to variability in explanations, making SHAP the preferred choice for applications requiring reliable and reproducible results, such as regulatory compliance or auditing. Moreover, SHAP is beneficial when comparing feature importance across different models since its additive nature ensures fair distribution of contributions. This consistency allows practitioners to analyse how feature importance changes across models or datasets, which is particularly useful in model selection or optimization tasks.

In high-stakes domains like finance, healthcare, or criminal justice, where decisions must be transparent and explainable to regulators or stakeholders, SHAP's rigorous mathematical foundation and stability make it more suitable than LIME. For example, SHAP can provide detailed explanations of why certain patient characteristics lead to a specific diagnosis or why a loan application was denied.

Additionally, SHAP explicitly considers feature dependencies and interactions during explanation generation. This makes it more effective in scenarios where understanding how features jointly influence predictions is essential, such as detecting biases or exploring causal relationships within data.

Post-hoc Explainability Techniques for Machine Learning Models

Explainability is linked to post-hoc explainability since it covers the techniques used to convert a non-interpretable model into an explainable one.

Post-hoc explainability techniques are applied *after* a machine learning model has been trained, treating it as a pre-existing entity whose internal workings are to be understood. This approach is particularly valuable when dealing with models that are not inherently interpretable, such as complex deep neural networks or ensemble methods, or when the primary focus during model development was on achieving high predictive accuracy, potentially at the expense of interpretability. Post-hoc explanations provide insights into the model's behaviour by analysing its inputs, outputs, and internal states without altering its underlying structure or training process. This chapter delves into the taxonomy of these techniques and explores their application across different types of machine learning models, from inherently interpretable shallow models to the intricate architectures of deep learning.

A Taxonomy of Post-hoc Explainability Techniques

Post-hoc explainability methods in AI can be organized along several key dimensions, offering a structured way to understand their diverse approaches. One primary distinction is between model-specific and model-agnostic techniques. Model-specific methods are tailored to particular model architectures, such as neural networks, and rely on internal properties like weights or activations to generate explanations. In contrast, model-agnostic methods treat the model as a black box, analysing input-output relationships without requiring access to internal mechanics. These are more flexible and widely applicable, though they may offer less detailed insight.

Another important distinction is between local and global explanations. Local methods focus on explaining individual predictions, why a specific input led to a specific output, while global methods aim to describe the model's overall behaviour across a dataset, identifying general patterns or feature importance.

While post-hoc methods are often used when models are too complex for intrinsic interpretability, they can be further categorized by the mechanisms they use. Perturbation-based methods systematically alter input features to observe changes in output, helping infer feature importance. Gradient-based methods, common in deep learning, use gradients to assess how sensitive predictions are to input changes, with techniques like saliency maps and Grad-CAM illustrating this approach. Decomposition-based methods trace predictions back through the model to assign relevance scores to input features, as seen in Layer-Wise Relevance Propagation (LRP). Surrogate model-based methods approximate complex models with simpler, interpretable ones—LIME being a well-known example that builds local surrogate models to explain individual predictions.

Together, these categories provide a comprehensive framework for selecting and applying post-hoc explainability techniques, depending on the model type, the level of interpretability required, and the specific use case.

Post-hoc Explainability for Shallow Models

While some shallow models like linear regression and decision trees are often considered inherently interpretable due to their simple structure, post-hoc explainability techniques can still provide valuable insights or offer alternative perspectives on their behaviour. For instance, even in a linear regression model where the coefficients directly indicate the relationship between features and the target variable, post-hoc feature importance measures can highlight the relative magnitude of each feature's contribution to the prediction, especially when dealing with standardized or normalized features.

For more complex shallow models or ensembles of shallow models (like Random Forests or Gradient Boosting Machines), post-hoc methods become more crucial. Feature importance scores, often readily available for these models, provide a global understanding of which features the model deems most relevant for making predictions. These scores can be based on various metrics, such as the frequency with which a feature is used in decision splits (for tree-based models) or the reduction in impurity achieved by splitting on a particular feature.

Surrogate models can also be effectively employed to explain the behaviour of shallow models. For example, a decision tree can be trained to mimic the predictions of a more complex shallow model, offering a simplified, rule-based representation of its decision boundaries. Similarly, rule extraction techniques can be applied to trained shallow models to explicitly identify the rules that govern their predictions, providing a more human-readable form of explanation. These post-hoc analyses can help validate the model's learned relationships, identify potentially spurious correlations, or provide a more intuitive understanding of its decision-making process, even for models considered relatively interpretable.

Post-hoc Explainability for Deep Learning

The remarkable performance of deep learning models in various complex tasks often comes at the cost of inherent interpretability. The non-linear transformations and intricate architectures of deep neural networks make it challenging to directly understand why a particular input leads to a specific output. Consequently, post-hoc explainability techniques are particularly essential for gaining insights into the behaviour of these powerful but opaque models.

Gradient-based methods are widely used for visualizing the regions in the input that are most influential for a deep learning model's prediction. Saliency maps, for example, compute the gradient of the output class score with respect to the input pixels (for images) or tokens (for text). The magnitude of the gradient at each input element indicates its importance for the prediction. However, basic saliency maps can sometimes be noisy or lack high resolution. Techniques like Grad-CAM (Gradient-weighted Class Activation Mapping) and its variants address these limitations by using the gradients flowing into the final convolutional layer to produce a coarse localization map highlighting the important regions in the input that are relevant to a particular class. These methods are particularly effective for understanding what parts of an image a convolutional neural network is "looking at" when making a classification.

Perturbation-based methods offer another approach to understanding deep learning models. Occlusion sensitivity involves systematically masking or removing parts of the input (e.g., patches in an image, words in a sentence) and observing how the model's output changes. If the prediction for a particular class drops significantly when a specific region is occluded, it suggests that this region is important for the model's decision. While computationally more expensive than gradient-based methods, perturbation techniques can sometimes provide more robust and less noisy explanations.

Decomposition-based methods like Layer-Wise Relevance Propagation (LRP) aim to trace the model's prediction back to the input features by assigning a relevance score to each neuron in the network and propagating these scores backward through the layers. The final relevance scores at the input layer indicate the contribution of each input feature to the final prediction. LRP follows specific propagation rules based on the network architecture and activation functions, aiming to provide a more complete and theoretically grounded explanation of the model's decision.

Surrogate model-based methods also find application in explaining deep learning models. LIME (Local Interpretable Model-agnostic Explanations) works by perturbing the input instance of interest to create a local neighbourhood of similar data points. The predictions of the black-box deep learning model on these perturbed samples are then used to train a simpler, interpretable model (like a linear model or a decision tree) that approximates the deep learning model's behaviour in that local region. The explanations are then derived from the coefficients or structure of the local surrogate model, providing insights into the feature importance for that specific instance.

Attention mechanisms, commonly used in architectures like Transformers, can also be interpreted as a form of post-hoc explanation. The attention weights learned by the model indicate which parts of the input sequence (e.g., words in a sentence) the model is focussing on when processing the information. By visualizing these attention weights, one can gain insights into the dependencies and relationships learned by the model, providing a form of explanation for its predictions.

Finally, the concept-based explanations aim to bridge the gap between low-level features and human-understandable concepts. Techniques like Concept Activation Vectors (CAVs) allow for quantifying the degree to which a neuron or a group of neurons in a neural network is sensitive to a particular human-defined concept. By identifying which concepts are important for a model's prediction, we can obtain explanations that are more intuitive and meaningful to humans.

Evaluation of Post-hoc Explanations

Evaluating the quality and faithfulness of post-hoc explanations is a critical but challenging aspect of XAI. Ideally, an explanation should accurately reflect the true reasoning of the model and be understandable to the intended audience. Various approaches have been proposed for evaluating explanations, ranging from human-centric evaluations (e.g., asking users to assess the plausibility or completeness of an explanation) to quantitative metrics that measure the consistency or stability of explanations under small input perturbations. Faithfulness metrics aim to quantify the degree to which the explanation truly reflects the model's decision-making process. For instance, if an explanation highlights certain input features as important, altering those features should indeed have a significant impact on the model's output. Developing robust and reliable methods for evaluating the quality of post-hoc explanations remains an active area of research.

Post-hoc explainability techniques are indispensable tools for understanding the behaviour of trained machine learning models. In this section we have studied the taxonomy of post-hoc techniques, highlighting the distinction between model-specific and model-agnostic approaches, as well as local and global explanations. We have also examined the application of these techniques to both shallow models and the intricate architectures of deep learning, showcasing the methodologies used to unveil the reasoning behind their predictions.

Levels of Transparency

Transparency in machine learning models is best understood as a continuum rather than a binary attribute, encompassing varying degrees and dimensions. At one end of this spectrum are models that are inherently interpretable, offering insight into their internal workings without the need for external tools. These models can be analysed through several lenses: simulatability, decomposability, algorithmic transparency, and semantic transparency.

Simulatability refers to the extent to which a human can mentally trace the model's decision-making process for a given input within a reasonable timeframe. This level of transparency is typically achievable only in models of low complexity, such as small decision trees or linear models with a limited number of features.

Decomposability, on the other hand, requires that each component of the model (inputs, parameters, and operations) be individually understandable. For example, in a linear regression model, the coefficients clearly indicate the influence of each feature on the outcome. However, this form of transparency is contingent on the interpretability of the inputs themselves; complex or abstract features may undermine decomposability.

Algorithmic transparency pertains to the clarity of the model's learning process. It involves understanding how the model is trained and how it generalizes from data. Models like linear regression exemplify this category, as their optimization procedures are mathematically well-defined and accessible to analysis.

Finally, semantic transparency extends beyond structural clarity to consider whether the model's components correspond to meaningful, domain-specific concepts. A model used in medical diagnostics, for instance, demonstrates semantic transparency if its features align with recognizable symptoms or clinical indicators.

XAI for Transparent Machine Learning Models

Transparent machine learning models form a critical component of the explainable AI ecosystem, offering inherent interpretability by design rather than requiring post-hoc explanation methods. Transparency in machine learning exists along a spectrum rather than as a binary property. At the most basic level, simulatability allows humans to mentally replicate a model's calculations. Deeper levels include decomposability (undssssserstanding each model component), algorithmic transparency (understanding the training process), and semantic transparency (alignment with domain concepts).

> **Definition** *Transparency* in machine learning refers to the degree to which a model's inner workings and decision-making processes are directly observable and comprehensible to humans. Unlike post-hoc explainability, which attempts to illuminate black-box models after they have been trained, transparency is an intrinsic property built into the model architecture itself.

Several model architectures exemplify this transparency-first approach. Linear and generalized linear models offer interpretable coefficients that directly indicate feature importance and direction of influence. Decision trees provide rule-based explanations through their hierarchical structure, making the decision path explicit. Generalized Additive Models (GAMs) allow for non-linear relationships while maintaining additivity and visualization capabilities. Bayesian networks represent probabilistic relationships through directed graphs that can align with causal understanding. Case-based reasoning systems make predictions by referencing similar historical cases, offering explanation by example.

Decision Trees and Rule-Based Systems Decision trees partition the feature space through a series of binary splits, creating a hierarchical structure of decision rules:

```
If feature_1 > threshold_1:
    If feature_2 ≤ threshold_2:
        Predict class_A
    Else:
        Predict class_B
Else:
    Predict class_C
```

Decision trees offer distinct transparency advantages. Predictions follow explicit *if-then* rules that can be directly verbalized and understood. The tree structure visually represents how features interact to determine predictions, with each path from root to leaf representing a decision rule. For any prediction, one can trace the exact path followed through the tree, identifying the specific rules applied. Trees can capture non-linear relationships and feature interactions without sacrificing transparency. Rule-based systems extend this paradigm by expressing knowledge as a collection of if-then rules, either derived from decision trees or constructed manually with expert input. These systems prioritize human readability of their rule sets, often sacrificing some predictive power for clarity and interpretability.

Rule-based learners excel in interpretability across various fields. Their intuitive alignment with human behaviour makes them ideal for understanding and explaining other models. When a sufficient threshold of coverage is achieved, a rule wrapper can encapsulate enough information about a model to explain its behaviour to non-expert users, while still being usable as a standalone prediction model.

Enhancing transparency involves several complementary strategies. Feature engineering with domain-aligned variables improves semantic understanding. Regularization techniques like sparsity-inducing penalties simplify models by reducing feature count. Model distillation can translate complex models into simpler, more transparent alternatives. Visualization techniques make model behaviour more accessible, while domain knowledge incorporation ensures models reflect established expertise.

Fuzzy Rule-Based Systems Fuzzy rule-based systems extend classical rule-based approaches by incorporating fuzzy logic, allowing variables to belong to multiple categories with varying degrees of membership:

If temperature is HIGH and humidity is LOW, then
fire_risk is VERY_HIGH

Where HIGH, LOW, and VERY_HIGH are fuzzy sets with associated membership functions. These systems offer unique transparency benefits:

Linguistic Variables: Variables are represented in linguistic terms that correspond to human concepts (e.g., "high temperature").

Gradual Transitions: Fuzzy sets model gradual transitions between categories, better reflecting human conceptualization of continuous variables.

Explicit Rule Base: The knowledge base consists of human-readable rules, often derived from domain experts.

Inference Traceability: The fuzzy inference process can be traced step-by-step, showing how different rules contributed to the final output.

Fuzzy systems are particularly valuable when domain knowledge is expressed qualitatively rather than quantitatively, and when dealing with imprecise concepts or natural language descriptions.

Transparent models find particular value in high-stakes domains. In healthcare, they support clinical decision-making with clear reasoning that physicians can verify. Financial institutions use them for credit scoring and fraud detection, where regulatory requirements often demand explainability. Criminal justice applications leverage transparency for fairness and due process. Manufacturing operations benefit from clear identification of quality factors and maintenance needs. Public policy applications use transparent models to support accountable resource allocation.

Bayesian Models A Bayesian model typically takes the form of a probabilistic directed acyclic graphical model, where the links represent the conditional dependencies between variables. For instance, a Bayesian network can illustrate the probabilistic relationships between diseases and symptoms. Given a set of symptoms, the network can compute the probabilities of various diseases being present. Similar to Generalized Additive Models (GAMs), these models clearly depict the relationships between features and the target, explicitly shown by the connections between variables.

Bayesian models are categorized as transparent models, falling under the categories of simulatable, decomposable, and algorithmically transparent. However, it is important to note that in certain situations, such as when dealing with overly complex or cumbersome variables, a model may lose the properties of being simulatable and decomposable.

Explainability in Deep Learning

Explainability in deep learning refers to methods and approaches that make the decision-making processes of complex neural networks transparent and interpretable to humans. Post-hoc local explanations and feature relevance techniques are becoming the most popular methods for elucidating Deep Neural Networks (DNNs). This section focuses on various explainability studies that have been proposed for the most used deep learning models, including multi-layer neural networks, Convolutional Neural Networks (CNNs), and Recurrent Neural Networks (RNNs).

Multi-layer Neural Networks

From their inception, multi-layer neural networks (also known as multi-layer perceptrons) have been highly regarded by the academic community for their exceptional ability to infer complex relationships among variables. However, developers and engineers responsible for deploying these models in real-world applications often hesitate due to their questionable explainability. This is why neural networks have traditionally been viewed as black-box models. Since explainability is often essential for a model to be practically useful, the community has developed various techniques to explain multi-layer neural networks, including model simplification approaches, feature relevance estimators, text explanations, local explanations, and model visualizations. While several model simplification techniques have been proposed for neural networks with a single hidden layer, very few have been presented for those with multiple hidden layers. Given that simplifying multi-layer neural networks becomes more complex as the number of layers increases, explaining these models through feature relevance methods has become increasingly popular.

Local explanations often rely on sensitivity analysis, where the impact of small input perturbations on the output is measured to determine feature importance. LIME (Local Interpretable Model-agnostic Explanations) approximates the complex neural network locally with a simpler, interpretable model around a specific prediction. SHAP (SHapley Additive exPlanations) draws from cooperative game theory to assign contribution values to each feature for a particular prediction.

For global explanations of multi-layer neural networks (MLPs), Partial Dependence Plots (PDPs) show the marginal effect of features on predictions across the entire dataset. Feature importance measures derived from weight magnitudes or permutation tests help identify which inputs most significantly affect model outputs. These approaches, while informative, become increasingly challenging as network depth increases.

More advanced approaches include Layer-wise Relevance Propagation (LRP), which traces contributions backward through the network to identify which input features most strongly influenced a particular prediction. DeepLIFT (Deep Learning

Important FeaTures) compares neuron activations to reference activations to determine feature contributions to specific outputs.

Convolutional Neural Networks

Convolutional Neural Networks (CNNs) present unique explainability challenges due to their specialized architecture for processing spatial data. CNNs represent the state-of-the-art models in essential computer vision tasks, ranging from image classification and object detection to instance segmentation. These models typically consist of a sequence of convolutional layers and pooling layers that automatically learn progressively higher-level features. At the end of this sequence, one or more fully connected layers map the output feature map into scores. This structure involves highly complex internal relationships that are challenging to explain. Fortunately, the path to explainability for CNNs is more straightforward compared to other types of models, as human cognitive skills favour the understanding of visual data. Existing studies aimed at understanding what CNNs learn can be categorized into two main groups:

- those that seek to understand the decision process by mapping the output back to the input space to identify which parts of the input were discriminative for the output; and,
- those that explore the network's intermediate layers to interpret how they perceive the external world, not necessarily related to any specific input, but in general.

Class Activation Mapping (CAM) and its extension Grad-CAM have become fundamental approaches, generating heatmaps that highlight regions in the input image most influential for classification decisions. These techniques use the activations of the final convolutional layer and their weights to identify discriminative regions.

Visualization of filters and feature maps provides another avenue for CNN explainability. By displaying what patterns each convolutional filter responds to, researchers can build intuition about the hierarchical feature extraction process—from simple edges and textures in early layers to complex object parts in deeper layers.

Deconvolutional networks and guided backpropagation techniques reconstruct the patterns that maximally activate specific neurons, helping visualize what features the network has learned to detect. Concept-based explanations like TCAV (Testing with Concept Activation Vectors) move beyond raw features to identify higher-level concepts the network uses for classification, making explanations more human-interpretable.

The concept of adversarial examples has also enriched CNN explainability research, as minimal perturbations that drastically change classifications reveal model vulnerabilities and decision boundaries, providing insights into how these networks process visual information.

Recurrent Neural Networks

Recurrent Neural Networks (RNNs), which are specifically designed to process sequential data, require tailored approaches to achieve interpretability. Among the most prominent techniques are attention mechanisms, which not only enhance model performance but also serve as tools for explanation by assigning importance weights to different elements in a sequence. This allows for the identification of which parts of the input most significantly influenced a given output. In natural language processing tasks, saliency maps highlight the words that had the greatest impact on a model's prediction, while input perturbation methods—where words are systematically removed or altered—help assess the contribution of individual tokens. Similar strategies are applied to time series data, where contribution analysis pinpoints the most influential time steps.

In the context of language models, neuron activation analysis has revealed that certain neurons specialize in tracking specific linguistic features such as sentiment, negation, or syntactic structure. This method, often referred to as neuron interpretation, provides insight into how RNNs internally represent and process language.

More recent advances include influence-based methods, which trace a model's predictions back to specific training examples. These techniques illuminate how particular data points shape the model's behaviour, offering a deeper understanding of the relationship between training data and decision-making.

A critical challenge in this field is evaluating the quality of explanations—specifically, determining whether an explanation genuinely reflects the model's reasoning or merely offers a plausible but inaccurate narrative. Emerging directions in explainability research aim to address this issue. Neuro-symbolic models, which integrate symbolic reasoning with neural architectures, promise greater interpretability by design. Self-explaining neural networks embed explanation generation within their structure, while causal modelling approaches strive to move beyond correlation-based insights to uncover the true causal mechanisms underlying model decisions.

Bias Detection and Mitigation

Bias detection and mitigation are essential processes for ensuring fairness and reliability in AI systems. Biases, which can lead to discriminatory outcomes, often originate from imbalances or flaws in the data or model design. Detecting such biases involves identifying patterns that suggest unequal treatment of particular groups. This is typically done through statistical analyses that compare the distribution of sensitive attributes, such as gender or race, and their associated outcomes across different groups. Fairness metrics, including demographic parity, equalized odds,

equal opportunity, and predictive parity, are commonly used to quantify these disparities. Visualization tools, such as performance curves segmented by group, along with
adversarial testing and feature importance analysis, further support the identification
of bias.

Once biases are detected, mitigation strategies aim to reduce or eliminate them.
These strategies can be applied at different stages of the machine learning pipeline.
In the preprocessing phase, techniques such as data rebalancing, augmentation,
feature engineering, and data cleaning are used to adjust the training data. During
model training, in-processing methods like adversarial debiasing, regularization, and
fairness constraints can be employed to reduce sensitivity to biased features. Post-
processing approaches, including threshold adjustment, calibration, and reject option
classification, modify the model's outputs to align with fairness objectives.

To illustrate, consider a hypothetical loan approval model trained on features such
as income, credit score, age, and gender. Bias detection would begin by analysing
approval rates across genders to identify disparities. If, for instance, women are
approved at significantly lower rates than men, fairness metrics like demographic
parity would confirm the presence of bias. Visual tools, such as ROC curves for each
gender, and feature importance analysis would help determine whether gender plays
an undue role in the model's decisions.

If bias is confirmed, mitigation might involve increasing the representation of
female applicants in the training data or applying adversarial debiasing to reduce the
model's reliance on gender. Post-processing techniques, such as adjusting decision
thresholds, could also be used to equalize approval rates. While these interventions
may slightly reduce overall model accuracy, the trade-off is often justified by the
resulting improvements in fairness, trustworthiness, and legal compliance. Moreover,
bias mitigation tends to enhance a model's generalizability and robustness, leading
to better performance on unseen data.

Societal Aspects

Ensuring that AI systems provide clear and accessible explanations to all relevant
stakeholders is a critical component of promoting fairness, accountability, and ethical
integrity. This includes not only individuals directly affected by AI-driven decisions
but also regulatory authorities, auditors, and oversight institutions. In contexts where
AI outcomes have significant societal implications—such as in healthcare, finance, or
public administration—transparent and justifiable decision-making becomes especially important. Organizations deploying AI technologies must be able to articulate
how decisions are made, whether in recommending products, evaluating job candidates, or determining credit limits. This transparency is essential for building public
trust and complying with evolving legal standards, such as recent regulations in the
Netherlands that mandate greater openness in public sector AI applications.

Beyond individual and organizational responsibilities, explainable AI also carries
broader societal implications. As AI systems, including advanced models like

ChatGPT and other large language models, become increasingly embedded in daily life, they begin to influence cultural norms, social interactions, and public discourse. This growing integration raises fundamental questions about who controls AI development and deployment, how AI decision-making should be governed, and what impact these technologies may have on core societal values. Addressing these concerns requires a commitment to developing AI systems that are not only technically robust but also ethically grounded and socially responsive. In this broader context, explainability is not merely a technical feature but a societal imperative—one that ensures AI serves the public good in a transparent, accountable, and culturally sensitive manner.

Human-Centred Explainable AI

Human-centred Explainable AI (XAI) focuses on designing AI systems that generate explanations tailored to the needs, preferences, and understanding of human users. This approach emphasizes the importance of user-centric design, ensuring that explanations are not only technically accurate but also meaningful, actionable, and contextually relevant. By aligning explanations with users' cognitive and practical requirements, Human-centred XAI seeks to enhance transparency, accountability, and trust in AI systems across diverse applications.

At the centre of this approach is the principle of user-centric design, which involves identifying the target users, assessing their levels of expertise, and understanding what they need from an explanation. For instance, while technical users may require detailed algorithmic insights, non-expert users benefit more from intuitive, simplified explanations. Contextual relevance is equally important, as explanations must be adapted to the user's specific tasks and decision-making scenarios. Clarity and comprehensibility are essential, achieved through plain language, avoidance of technical jargon, and the use of intuitive visualizations. Effective explanations should also be actionable, enabling users to make informed decisions or take appropriate steps based on the AI's outputs. Trust and transparency are foundational goals, as users are more likely to trust AI systems when they understand how decisions are made and can hold the system accountable.

To support these goals, several techniques have been developed. Personalized explanations adapt content based on user profiles, such as their domain knowledge or preferences. Interactive explanation tools allow users to explore and query the reasoning behind AI decisions, often through dashboards or visual interfaces. Multiple explanation formats are employed, including visualizations like charts and graphs that make complex relationships more accessible, and natural language explanations that translate technical content into user-friendly narratives. Crucially, Human-centred XAI incorporates user feedback through iterative design processes and usability testing, ensuring that explanations evolve in response to user needs and expectations.

Responsible AI

Responsible AI (RAI) is an approach to developing and deploying AI from both an ethical and legal standpoint. The goal is to employ AI in a safe, trustworthy and ethical way. Using AI responsibly should increase transparency while helping to reduce issues such as AI bias.

XAI acts as a bridge between RAI's ethical imperatives and technical implementation. Transparency, a pillar of RAI, is unachievable without explainability. For example, in loan approval systems, XAI enables auditors to detect discriminatory patterns, thereby advancing fairness. Similarly, in healthcare, explainable diagnostic models allow clinicians to validate outputs against medical expertise, enhancing safety and accountability. Regulatory mandates, such as the GDPR's "right to explanation," further cement XAI's role in compliance. However, explainability alone is insufficient; it must be coupled with robust governance to ensure corrective actions follow insights.

The ethics of AI are a huge challenge to humanity. Mindful and responsible innovation is not an easy concept in itself, but it is crucial to first understand what AI ethics are and integrate them into the core of the development and application of AI systems.

Importance of Responsibility

As AI becomes increasingly critical for businesses, achieving responsible AI should be regarded as a highly relevant topic. There is a growing need to proactively drive fair, responsible, and ethical AI decisions while complying with current laws and regulations. Understanding AI-related concerns is the starting point for creating an ethical framework to guide its development and use. Organizations aiming to ensure their AI usage is not harmful should openly share this commitment with a diverse range of stakeholders, including consumers, clients, suppliers, and others who may be tangentially involved and affected.

Developing and applying AI according to ethical principles requires transparency in decision-making processes and the creation of actionable AI ethics policies. Through thorough research, widespread consultation, and analysis of ethical impacts, coupled with ongoing checks and balances, we can ensure that AI technology is developed and deployed responsibly, benefiting everyone regardless of gender, race, faith, demographic, location, or net worth.

Challenges in Implementation

Deploying RAI and XAI faces three interrelated challenges:

1. **Technical Limitations**: Many XAI methods provide approximate or unstable explanations, risking misinterpretation. Deep learning models, in particular, resist human-friendly explanations without sacrificing performance.
2. **Regulatory Fragmentation**: Divergent global standards (e.g., the EU's strict AI Act vs. the U.S.'s sectoral approach) complicate cross-border AI deployment.
3. **Societal Trust**: Public scepticism persists due to high-profile AI failures, necessitating proactive communication and participatory design processes.

Advancing RAI and XAI requires interdisciplinary collaboration. Technologically, hybrid approaches, combining interpretable architectures with post-hoc analysis, may balance accuracy and clarity. Legislatively, harmonizing global standards could reduce compliance burdens. Ethically, involving diverse stakeholders in AI design can pre-empt biases and foster trust. Emerging research areas, such as *quantitative fairness metrics* and *causal explanation frameworks*, promise to address current gaps. Ultimately, the synergy of RAI and XAI will depend on viewing explainability not as an add-on but as a foundational component of ethical AI systems.

Principles of Responsible AI

Addressing ethical concerns requires engaging with their implications with foresight and dedication. It's crucial to view AI's ethical dimension not as a barrier but as a pathway to lasting and sustainable technological progress. Embedding responsible AI principles is essential for its evolution in a way that benefits everyone.

While there isn't a universally agreed-upon set of principles for AI ethics, several key guidelines have emerged:

- **Fairness**: Datasets used to train AI systems must be carefully considered to avoid discrimination. AI should improve efficiency and treat everyone equally. Just like a perfectly topped pizza, responsible AI requires models to train on diverse data, preventing biased results based on attributes like ethnicity, gender, or age.
- **Transparency**: Responsible AI models should publish information about how they work with data. Transparency is essential for responsible AI, allowing users to understand how algorithms operate and make informed decisions about their use.
- **Non-maleficence**: AI systems should avoid causing harm to individuals, society, or the environment.
- **Security**: Protecting sensitive data and preventing harmful bias or potential threats is crucial. Better security makes AI systems trustworthy and reduces the risk of unintended consequences. AI systems must be resilient against adversarial attacks, misuse, or unintended consequences. Robust testing protocols, such as *red-team exercises* for generative AI models, identify vulnerabilities. Autonomous systems, like drones or medical robots, require fail-safes to prevent physical harm.
- **Accountability**: Accountability is critical for responsible AI, applying to both the development and use of machine learning models and AI systems. Developers,

organizations, and policymakers must ensure AI is developed and used responsibly. The question of who is responsible for each model—whether it's the person who trains, implements, or fine-tunes it—must be addressed.

- **Privacy**: Ensuring data is handled responsibly is vital. Sensitive data should always be protected, and mechanisms should be developed for individuals to control how their data is collected and used. Enhanced privacy leads to more trustworthy AI technologies and greater user acceptance. Responsible AI mandates strict adherence to privacy laws (e.g., GDPR, CCPA) and minimizes data collection to what is necessary. Techniques like differential privacy and federated learning help anonymize data while maintaining utility. In healthcare, AI models analysing patient records must ensure confidentiality to prevent misuse.
- **Robustness**: AI systems should be resilient to errors, adversarial attacks, and unexpected inputs. Responsible AI systems must perform well under various conditions without causing harm or producing unfair results.
- **Inclusiveness**: Engaging diverse perspectives helps identify potential ethical concerns and ensures a collective effort to address them. Diverse teams designing AI systems reduce blind spots and biases. Participatory approaches, involving marginalized communities in development, ensure technologies meet broad societal needs. Educational AI platforms, for instance, must accommodate varied learning styles and languages to avoid exclusion.

Implementing these principles faces hurdles like technical-commercial trade-offs (e.g., accuracy vs. explainability) and regulatory fragmentation across jurisdictions. Best practices include:

- Conducting ethical risk assessments pre-deployment.
- Establishing feedback loops for continuous improvement.
- Investing in AI literacy for developers and users.

By integrating these considerations, organizations can foster AI systems that are not only compliant but also ethically resilient, driving innovation while safeguarding human dignity.

Responsible AI by Design

Embedding Responsible AI by design in AI development involves integrating responsible AI dimensions throughout the AI lifecycle. This includes ethically preparing the data, training and fine-tuning the model according to ethical guidelines, and finally deploying it in production. Each phase requires skills in understanding and implementing protocols and best practices, as well as using the right tools effectively. Additionally, it involves creating and maintaining documentation for model development and deployment, establishing audit trails, and providing user guides.

Technical guardrails are essential for scanning and filtering the inputs and outputs of an AI system to detect threats. These systems must be intelligent enough to recognize a wide range of threats, such as prompt injections, jailbreaks, hallucinations, drift, and malicious content. Responsible AI practitioners need to stay updated with the latest research in this area and develop these solutions. They must also have the skills to build interpretable models and techniques that allow stakeholders to understand how AI systems make decisions. Furthermore, skills are needed to implement algorithms and model architectures designed to reduce bias, optimize model performance from a sustainability perspective, and leverage techniques like chain/graph of thoughts to enhance the model's reasoning capabilities and reduce risks in critical applications.

Responsible AI requires collaboration among diverse teams, including data scientists, ethicists, legal experts, and business leaders. Clear communication and the ability to collaborate and manage alliances with organizations are crucial for simplifying technical concepts, fostering interdisciplinary contributions, and engaging effectively with stakeholders such as users, policymakers, and community representatives. As AI evolves, professionals must commit to continuous learning, research, and adaptation to address emerging challenges and uphold the principles of responsible AI.

Putting the AI in Audit

Algorithmic auditing is a method for examining AI systems within their specific contexts. This approach allows for a dynamic evaluation of regulations, standards, and impacts. When the results are made public, it serves as a tool for transparency and accountability.

> **Definition** An **AI Audit** is a systematic and independent examination of an Artificial Intelligence system, its underlying data, algorithms, processes, and governance mechanisms. The purpose of an AI audit is to assess the system's performance, reliability, security, fairness, compliance with regulations and ethical guidelines, and overall impact. It aims to provide stakeholders with an objective evaluation of the AI system's strengths, weaknesses, and potential risks.

AI audits are essential for regulators and society, as they provide reports to assess how systems function and their impacts. They are also beneficial for developers and purchasers of AI systems. An end-to-end, socio-technical approach, like the one proposed here, generates documentation that enhances system accountability, organizational memory, and compliance with AI and data regulations.

The increasing integration of AI into various aspects of our lives, from financial services and healthcare to criminal justice and social media, necessitates AI audits for several critical reasons:

- **Ensuring Fairness and Mitigating Bias**: AI systems can inadvertently learn and perpetuate biases present in their training data, leading to discriminatory outcomes. Audits can help identify and quantify these biases, providing insights into how to mitigate them and ensure fairer results for all groups. For example, loan approval algorithms must be scrutinized to prevent racial or gender bias, ensuring equitable outcomes.
- **Promoting Transparency and Explainability**: Stakeholders, from developers to end-users, require clarity about how AI decisions are made. This includes documenting data sources, model logic, and decision pathways. Many advanced AI models, particularly deep learning networks, operate as "black boxes," making it difficult to understand their decision-making processes. Methods like **LIME** (Local Interpretable Model-agnostic Explanations) and **SHAP** (SHapley Additive exPlanations) provide post-hoc interpretability, while inherently interpretable models (e.g., decision trees) prioritize simplicity. Audits can evaluate the explainability of AI systems, ensuring that their outputs can be understood and justified, fostering trust and accountability. Transparency builds trust, particularly in high-stakes domains like healthcare diagnostics or criminal justice.
- **Verifying Reliability and Robustness**: AI systems need to be dependable and resilient to errors, adversarial attacks, and unexpected inputs. Audits can assess the system's performance under various conditions, identify potential vulnerabilities, and ensure its robustness.
- **Complying with Regulations and Standards**: As AI adoption grows, so do the regulatory frameworks surrounding it. AI audits can help organizations ensure their AI systems comply with relevant laws, industry standards, and ethical guidelines (e.g., GDPR, emerging AI regulations).
- **Managing Risk and Ensuring Safety**: AI systems deployed in critical applications (e.g., autonomous vehicles, medical diagnosis) carry inherent risks. Audits can identify potential safety hazards, assess risk mitigation strategies, and ensure the responsible deployment of AI.
- **Building Trust and Confidence**: For users, customers, and the public to trust and adopt AI technologies, they need assurance that these systems are fair, reliable, and safe. Independent audits can provide this assurance and build confidence in AI.
- **Improving Performance and Identifying Opportunities**: Beyond identifying risks, audits can also uncover areas where the AI system's performance can be improved, its efficiency enhanced, or new opportunities for its application can be explored.
- **Accountability and Governance**: AI audits contribute to establishing clear lines of accountability for the development and deployment of AI systems and help organizations implement effective AI governance frameworks. Organizations must establish clear responsibility for AI outcomes, including mechanisms to

address harms. This involves ethical oversight boards, continuous monitoring, and redress protocols. For instance, if an autonomous vehicle causes an accident, accountability frameworks determine liability and enable corrective actions. Regulatory compliance (e.g., GDPR's "right to explanation") further reinforces accountability.

High-Risk AI Systems

Determining whether an AI system is high-risk involves evaluating its potential impact on health, safety, and fundamental rights. According to the EU AI Act, an AI system is considered high-risk if it is used as a safety component of a product or if it is a product itself that falls under specific EU legislation. Additionally, AI systems that pose significant risks to individuals' health, safety, or fundamental rights are classified as high-risk.

Examples of high-risk AI use cases include systems used in law enforcement, such as those assessing individuals' risk of becoming victims of crime or re-offending. Other high-risk applications include AI systems used for remote biometric identification, credit scoring, and recruitment processes. These systems can significantly impact individuals' lives, making it crucial to ensure they operate fairly, transparently, and securely.

Example AI systems used as safety components in the management and operation of critical digital infrastructure, road traffic, and the supply of water, gas, heating, and electricity are considered high-risk. Legislators justify this classification in the EU AI Act by stating that the failure or malfunction of such systems could endanger the lives and health of many people and cause significant disruptions to social and economic activities.

However, AI systems intended solely for cybersecurity purposes related to the safety of critical infrastructure, such as monitoring water pressure or controlling fire alarms in cloud computing centres, are not classified as high-risk AI systems.

High-risk AI systems must comply with stringent regulatory requirements, including risk management, data quality, transparency, human oversight, and accuracy. Providers and deployers of these systems face obligations around registration, quality management, monitoring, record-keeping, and incident reporting. This comprehensive approach aims to mitigate risks and ensure that AI systems are developed and used responsibly.

AI Regulations: A Global Landscape

The European Union's AI Act establishes the world's most comprehensive AI regulatory framework through a risk-based categorization system. AI systems are classified into four tiers: unacceptable risk (prohibited, including manipulative behaviour systems and indiscriminate surveillance), high-risk (critical infrastructure, education, employment, essential services, law enforcement-subject to stringent data quality, transparency, human oversight, accuracy, and robustness requirements), limited risk (transparency obligations like chatbot disclosure), and minimal risk (no specific obligations). The Act emphasizes fundamental rights and consumer protection through legally binding requirements including conformity assessments, registration, and ongoing monitoring for high-risk systems.

Individual European nations pursue complementary approaches: Germany emphasizes human-centric AI innovation with ethical guidelines developed through industry-academia collaboration; France invests heavily in AI research while considering ethical frameworks and employment impacts; the UK develops sector-specific, principles-based regulation focussing on outcomes rather than technical requirements, contrasting with the EU's prescriptive approach.

The United States lacks comprehensive federal AI legislation, instead employing fragmented agency and sector-specific guidelines emphasizing innovation-friendly, risk-based approaches tailored to specific applications. Growing momentum exists for federal legislation, while states like California lead on data privacy regulations affecting AI systems.

Asian strategies vary significantly: China implements regulations targeting specific technologies like facial recognition and deep synthesis, emphasizing national development and social stability; Japan promotes innovation-friendly adoption with ethical guidelines; South Korea introduces ethical guidelines and regulations for data privacy and algorithmic transparency; India formulates national AI strategy focussing on social good and economic development while addressing bias and data protection.

Other nations develop distinctive frameworks: Canada emphasizes ethical considerations and human rights alongside research investment; Australia develops risk-based approaches incorporating ethical principles.

Regulating General-Purpose AI Models

Regulation of general-purpose AI models is evolving rapidly, particularly in regions like the European Union (EU) and the United States (US). These models, such as OpenAI's GPT-4, are capable of performing a wide range of tasks and serve as foundational elements for various AI applications across sectors like education, healthcare, media, and finance.

In the EU, the AI Act, a pioneering legislative framework, introduces binding rules for general-purpose AI models. This act mandates that providers of these models ensure a thorough understanding of their systems throughout the AI value chain. Providers must create technical documentation, establish copyright policies, and publish summaries of training content. Additionally, models posing systemic risks must be notified to the European Commission, with providers required to assess and mitigate these risks, report serious incidents, and ensure adequate cybersecurity.

The US has taken a different approach, historically favouring a more laissez-faire stance. However, contemporary developments, such as the "Executive Order on the Safe, Secure, and Trustworthy Development and Use of Artificial Intelligence" issued in 2023, outline a comprehensive approach to AI governance. While federal legislation specifically targeting general-purpose AI models is still absent, various legislative proposals are being discussed.

Internationally, efforts like the voluntary G7 Code of Conduct on AI aim to foster greater alignment in AI governance, promoting safe and trustworthy innovation globally. These regulatory frameworks and initiatives reflect a growing recognition of the need to balance innovation with ethical considerations and societal impacts.

The EU AI Act's Risk-Based Approach

The EU AI Act's risk-based approach to AI regulation differs from other regulatory frameworks in its structured categorization of AI systems into four distinct risk levels—unacceptable, high, limited, and minimal—each subject to tailored obligations. This nuanced framework contrasts with the more generalized or sector-specific approaches seen in other regulations.

The EU AI Act explicitly divides AI systems into four categories:

- **Unacceptable Risk**: Systems deemed incompatible with EU values, such as those involving mass surveillance, social scoring, or subliminal manipulation, are outright banned.
- **High Risk**: AI systems in critical sectors (e.g., healthcare, education, law enforcement) face stringent requirements for transparency, human oversight, and data quality.
- **Limited Risk**: Systems with moderate risks (e.g., chatbots) must meet transparency requirements but are less regulated overall.
- **Minimal Risk**: Low-risk systems (e.g., spam filters) are largely exempt from regulation.

This tiered approach ensures proportionality by focussing regulatory efforts on systems with greater societal impact, unlike frameworks such as the GDPR, which applies uniform requirements regardless of risk levels.

Unlike sector-specific regulations (e.g., laws targeting medical devices or autonomous vehicles), the EU AI Act applies horizontally across all industries and use cases. It evaluates risk based on the intended purpose and societal impact of the AI system rather than its domain-specific application. This broad applicability makes it one of the most comprehensive frameworks globally. The EU AI Act places a strong emphasis on safeguarding fundamental rights, including privacy, non-discrimination, and human dignity. Unacceptable-risk systems are banned outright to prevent harm to individuals or vulnerable groups, a stricter stance than seen in frameworks like the U.S.'s sectoral approach to AI regulation or China's social credit system.

High-risk systems under the EU AI Act are subject to compliance requirements throughout their lifecycle. This includes pre-market assessments (e.g., conformity evaluations) and ongoing monitoring after deployment. Such lifecycle oversight is more comprehensive than frameworks like GDPR, which primarily focus on data processing risks during operation.

The EU AI Act is pioneering in its systematic classification of risks and its prohibition of certain applications incompatible with ethical principles. Other regions often rely on less formalized approaches or sectoral regulations that lack the same level of granularity and universality. For example:

- The U.S. adopts a sectoral approach with guidelines specific to industries like healthcare or finance.
- China's regulations emphasize state control and surveillance without explicitly categorizing risks based on societal impact.

While the EU AI Act's risk-based approach provides clarity and proportionality, it can be resource-intensive for organizations developing high-risk systems due to strict compliance requirements. Additionally, its ambitious scope may create challenges for global companies navigating differing regulatory standards across jurisdictions.

The EU AI Act Vs the GDPR'S Approach

The EU AI Act's risk-based approach differs from the GDPR's approach, particularly in how risks are assessed, categorized, and addressed. While both frameworks share a focus on risk management and accountability, their methodologies and scopes diverge significantly.

Scope of Risk Assessment

- **EU AI Act**: The risk-based approach in the AI Act determines which AI systems are regulated at all, categorizing them into four risk levels: prohibited, high-risk, limited-risk, and minimal-risk systems. This classification acts as a "filter," ensuring that only systems with potential societal or individual harm are subject to regulation. For example, high-risk systems (e.g., biometric identification or recruitment tools) face stringent obligations, while minimal-risk systems (e.g., AI-powered spam filters) are largely exempt.
- **GDPR**: The GDPR does not explicitly classify activities based on risk levels but instead applies uniformly to all data processing activities involving personal data. Risk influences the *intensity* of compliance measures rather than determining

whether an activity is regulated. For instance, processing sensitive data (e.g., health information) requires additional safeguards under Article 32 of the GDPR.

Regulatory Focus

- **EU AI Act**: The focus is on regulating the *use cases* of AI systems based on their potential to harm fundamental rights, safety, or public interests. This includes lifecycle obligations for high-risk systems, such as conformity assessments and ongoing monitoring.
- **GDPR**: The GDPR centres on protecting personal data as a fundamental right. Its risk-based approach emphasizes proportionality in compliance measures, such as conducting Data Protection Impact Assessments (DPIAs) for high-risk data processing activities.

Application of Obligations

- **EU AI Act**: Obligations vary significantly based on the risk level of the AI system. High-risk systems must meet specific requirements related to transparency, human oversight, and data governance. Limited-risk systems only require basic transparency measures (e.g., informing users they are interacting with an AI system).
- **GDPR**: Obligations under the GDPR are more uniform and apply broadly to all entities processing personal data, regardless of the nature of the system or technology involved. For example, all data controllers must ensure lawful processing and implement technical and organizational measures proportionate to the risks involved.

Flexibility in Compliance

- **EU AI Act**: The AI Act's obligations are principle-based but tailored to specific risk categories. This structured differentiation allows for targeted regulation but may lack flexibility for edge cases where risks overlap categories.
- **GDPR**: The GDPR offers more flexibility by allowing organizations to tailor compliance measures based on their assessment of risks associated with specific data processing activities. This adaptability is reflected in its emphasis on accountability and self-assessment through tools like DPIAs.

Fundamental Rights Emphasis
Both frameworks aim to protect fundamental rights but differ in scope:

- The **GDPR** focuses exclusively on the right to data protection.
- The **AI Act** addresses broader risks to public interests and fundamental rights beyond privacy, such as safety, non-discrimination, and human dignity.

Interaction between Frameworks

In practice, many AI systems will fall under both regulations when they involve personal data processing (e.g., recruitment tools or biometric identification). However:

- An AI system classified as low risk under the AI Act may still involve high-risk personal data processing under the GDPR (e.g., sensitive health information used in chatbots).
- Conversely, a high-risk AI system under the AI Act may not involve significant personal data processing and thus have limited GDPR applicability.ss.

Actually, the EU AI Act takes a more granular and use-case-specific approach to regulation by categorizing risks and tailoring obligations accordingly. In contrast, the GDPR applies uniformly but adjusts compliance intensity based on risks associated with personal data processing. Together, these frameworks complement each other by addressing overlapping but distinct dimensions of risk—AI system functionality versus personal data protection—ensuring comprehensive governance for emerging technologies.

Exercises

1. What is Explainable AI (XAI)? Define Explainable AI and discuss its importance in AI development and deployment.
2. Why is interpretability crucial in AI systems? Explain the significance of interpretability in AI and how it impacts trust and accountability.
3. How does XAI contribute to ethical AI practices? Discuss the role of XAI in ensuring ethical AI development and usage.
4. What challenges are associated with implementing XAI in complex models like deep learning networks? Identify and explain the difficulties in making deep learning models interpretable.
5. Choose a machine learning model and apply LIME or SHAP to explain its predictions. Analyse the results and discuss the insights gained.
6. Build a decision tree model for a given dataset. Explain the decision-making process of the model and how it arrives at predictions.
7. Compare different explainability techniques (e.g., LIME vs. SHAP) on the same model. Evaluate their effectiveness and ease of use.
8. What is Responsible AI? Define Responsible AI and discuss its key principles.
9. Why is fairness important in AI systems? Explain the concept of fairness in AI and how it can be achieved.
10. How can transparency be ensured in AI development? Discuss methods to ensure transparency in AI systems, including documentation and open communication.
11. What role does accountability play in Responsible AI? Describe the importance of accountability in AI and how it can be implemented.

12. How can AI systems be designed to protect privacy? Explain strategies for ensuring privacy in AI systems, including data protection and user consent.
13. (Project) Bias Detection and Mitigation: Analyse a dataset for potential biases and apply techniques to mitigate them. Discuss the impact of these biases on model performance.
14. (Project) Developing Transparent AI Models: Create an AI model with a focus on transparency. Document the development process and explain how transparency is maintained.
15. (Project) Implementing Privacy Measures: Design an AI system with robust privacy measures. Outline the steps taken to protect sensitive data and ensure user privacy.
16. (Project) Creating Accountability Frameworks: Develop a framework for accountability in AI development. Include guidelines for responsible practices and mechanisms for auditing and reporting.

Further Reading

Adadi A, Berrada M (2018) Peeking inside the black-box: a survey on explainable artificial intelligence (XAI). IEEE Access 6(2018):52138–52160. https://doi.org/10.1109/ACCESS.2018.287 0052

Arrieta AB, Díaz-Rodríguez N, Del Ser J, Bennetot A, Tabik S, Barbado A, García S, Gil-López S, Molina D, Benjamins R, Chatila R, Herrera F (2019) Explainable Artificial Intelligence (XAI): Concepts, taxonomies, opportunities and challenges toward responsible AI. https://arxiv.org/abs/1910.10045

Chen IY, Dubrawski A (2019) Explainable artificial intelligence for medical diagnosis. J Healthc Eng 2019:1–10

Peters D, Vold K, Robinson D, Calvo RA (2020) Responsible AI—two frameworks for ethical design practice. IEEE Trans Technol Soc 1(1):34–47. https://doi.org/10.1109/TTS.2020.297 4991

Dignum V (2019) Responsible artificial intelligence: how to develop and use AI in a responsible way. Springer

Doshi-Velez F Kim B (2017) Towards a rigorous science of interpretable machine learning. arXiv preprint arXiv:170208608

European commission high-level expert group on artificial intelligence (AI HLEG) (2019) Assessment List for Trustworthy Artificial Intelligence (ALTAI). https://digital-strategy.ec.europa.eu/en/library/assessment-list-trustworthy-artificial-intelligence-altai-self-assessment

European Commission (2021) Ethics guidelines for trustworthy AI. Technical Report, European Union. https://ec.europa.eu/futurium/en/ai-alliance-consultation.1.html

Guidotti R, Monreale A, Ruggieri S, Turini F, Giannotti F, Pedreschi D (2018) A survey of methods for explaining black box models. ACM Comput Surv (CSUR) 51(5):1–42

Gunning D (2017) Explainable artificial intelligence (XAI). Defense Advanced Research Projects Agency (DARPA)

Holzinger A, Langs G, Denk H (2019) Causability and explainability of artificial intelligence in medicine. Wiley Interdiscip Rev: Data Min Knowl Discov 9(4):e1312

Ahmed I, Jeon G, Piccialli F (2022) From artificial intelligence to explainable artificial intelligence in industry 4.0: a survey on what, how, and where. IEEE Trans Industr Inform 18(8):5031–5042. https://doi.org/10.1109/TII.2022.3146552

Jovanovic M, Grujic B, Delic V (2019) Interpretable machine learning in human resources. IEEE Access 7:161796–161809

Kim B, Gil Y, Kim J (2019) Explainable artificial intelligence: an overview. IEEE/CAA Journal of Automatica Sinica 6(4):847–867

Lamy JB, Séroussi B, Griffon N, Kerdelhué G, Jaulent MC, Bouaud J (2018) Toward a formalization of the process to select IMIA yearbook best papers. Methods Inf Med 57(S 01):e1–e10

Lipton ZC (2018). The mythos of model interpretability. arXiv preprint arXiv:160603490

Ministry of Science and Technology of the People's Republic of China (2022) New generation artificial intelligence code of ethics. Technical Report. https://www.most.gov.cn/kjbgz/202109/t20210926_177063.html

Rudin C (2019) Stop explaining black box machine learning models for high stakes decisions and use interpretable models instead. Nat Mach Intell 1(5):206–215

Samek W, Wiegand T, Müller KR (2017) Explainable artificial intelligence: understanding, visualizing and interpreting deep learning models. arXiv preprint arXiv:170808296

Part VI
Conclusion and Future Outlook

Chapter 15
Epilogue: AI at the Threshold

*If it be true that good wine needs no bush, 'tis true that a good
play needs no epilogue.*
*—from Shakespeare's play "As You Like It" (1599), Act 5, Scene
4.*

As we conclude this exploration of artificial intelligence's transformation of traditional paradigms, we find ourselves at a distinctive historical moment—one characterized by both remarkable achievement and profound uncertainty. The technologies examined throughout this book have evolved from theoretical constructs to practical realities that increasingly shape our world. Yet we stand not at the end of a journey, but rather at the threshold of a new era in human-machine collaboration.

The Acceleration of Progress

The trajectory of AI development has accelerated dramatically in recent years. The integration of large language models into everyday tools has democratized access to AI capabilities previously confined to specialized research laboratories. These systems now augment human creativity across domains from scientific research to artistic expression, challenging our understanding of the uniquely human nature of these endeavours. Meanwhile, reinforcement learning techniques have produced systems capable of mastering complex tasks through experience, sometimes discovering novel approaches that human experts had not considered.

The fusion of different AI approaches has proven particularly fruitful. Multimodal systems that combine natural language processing with computer vision, for instance, have enabled new forms of human-computer interaction that more closely mirror natural human communication. Similarly, the integration of symbolic reasoning with neural network architectures has begun to address longstanding limitations in both approaches. These hybrid systems suggest that transcending traditional paradigms often means not abandoning them entirely but recombining their strengths in novel ways.

Embodied AI represents another frontier where traditional boundaries are dissolving. Robotics systems enhanced with sophisticated perception and learning capabilities are increasingly able to navigate and manipulate the physical world with unprecedented dexterity. This embodiment brings new challenges, from the complexity of physical interaction to the safety considerations of autonomous physical agents, but also new possibilities for AI systems that can engage with the world as humans do, through both perception and action.

The Future of AI: Evolution and Impact

The illustration below presents a comprehensive visualization of artificial intelligence's potential developmental trajectory and societal impacts in the coming decades. It represents one possible vision of AI's future development trajectory based on current understanding and trends, while acknowledging that actual developments may unfold differently depending on technological breakthroughs, policy decisions, and societal choices. The visual representation aims to provide a holistic framework for understanding how AI might evolve and transform various aspects of human society across different timeframes.

Figure 15.1 is structured with a chronological timeline at the top, showing the potential evolution of AI capabilities across four distinct time periods: Current AI (2025), Near-Term (2025–2030), Mid-Term (2030–2040), and Long-Term (2040+).

In the present day (2025), we see AI characterized by large language models, specialized AI tools, multi-modal systems, and limited reasoning capabilities. These

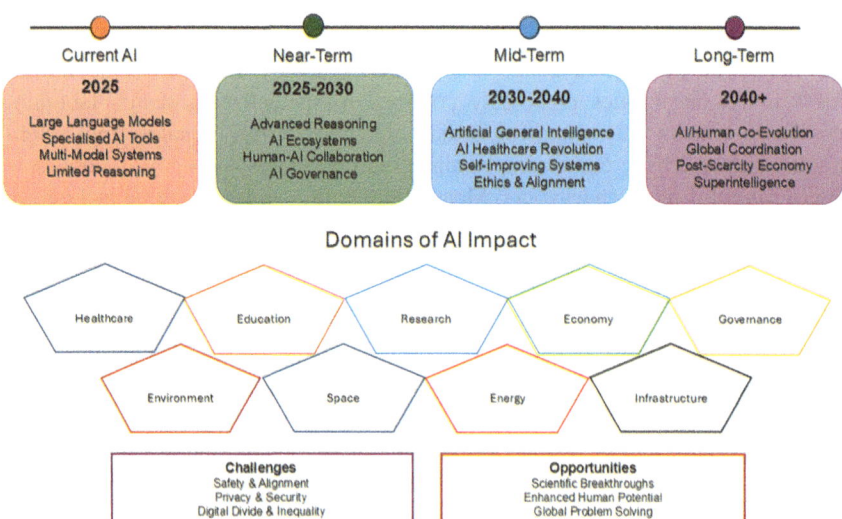

Fig. 15.1 A possible vision of AI's future development trajectory

represent our current technological landscape where AI excels at specific tasks but lacks broader understanding. Moving into the near-term future (2025–2030), the diagram forecasts the emergence of advanced reasoning capabilities, interconnected AI ecosystems, deeper human-AI collaboration frameworks, and the establishment of robust AI governance structures to manage increasingly capable systems.

The mid-term horizon (2030–2040) contemplates more transformative developments: the potential emergence of artificial general intelligence (AGI) with human-comparable capabilities across domains, revolutionary applications in healthcare, self-improving AI systems that can enhance their own capabilities, and an intensified focus on ethics and alignment as these systems become more powerful. The long-term perspective (2040+) explores more speculative possibilities: superintelligent systems that surpass human capabilities across all domains, co-evolutionary paths between humans and AI, global coordination mechanisms for managing advanced AI, and the prospect of a post-scarcity economy enabled by highly advanced automation and intelligence.

The central portion of the diagram illustrates key domains where AI will likely create significant impacts, visually represented as an interconnected hexagonal grid. These domains include healthcare transformation through precision medicine and diagnostics, educational systems that personalize learning at unprecedented scales, scientific research acceleration, economic restructuring, governance models, environmental management, space exploration, energy systems optimization, and infrastructure development.

The bottom section acknowledges the dual nature of this technological transition through two panels. The *challenges* panel highlights critical concerns including safety and alignment problems, privacy and security vulnerabilities, and the risk of digital divides creating new forms of inequality. Balancing these concerns, the *opportunities* panel emphasizes potential benefits: unprecedented scientific breakthroughs, enhanced human capabilities and potential, and new approaches to solving global-scale problems.

Interpretability and Trust

Concurrently, the field has witnessed a shift toward more interpretable and trustworthy AI systems. The "black box" problem that plagued earlier neural networks has given way to approaches that prioritize explainability and transparency. This evolution reflects a growing recognition that technical capability must be balanced with ethical responsibility that intelligence without accountability creates vulnerabilities that society cannot afford.

The mechanisms for ensuring AI trustworthiness have grown more sophisticated. Formal verification techniques, once limited to relatively simple systems, have expanded to encompass aspects of neural network behaviour. Adversarial testing regimes simulate potential failure modes, strengthening system robustness before deployment. Most significantly, there has been increasing recognition that trustworthiness is not merely a technical property but a sociotechnical one, encompassing the entire system of human and machine actors, organizational practices, and institutional safeguards within which AI operates.

This evolution toward trustworthiness represents a maturation of the field—an acknowledgement that deployment in consequential domains requires more than impressive benchmark performance. It reflects a deeper understanding that intelligence, whether human or artificial, operates within social contexts that shape its impact and meaning. As AI systems become more capable, ensuring they remain aligned with human values and intentions becomes not just an ethical imperative but a practical necessity for their successful integration into society.

The Technical Frontier

The road ahead is neither predetermined nor without obstacles. Technical challenges remain formidable, particularly in developing systems that can reason abstractly across domains with the flexibility characteristic of human cognition. The gap between narrow, task-specific intelligence and the adaptable, general intelligence humans possess remains substantial. Bridging this divide will require not only technical innovation but also deeper insights into the nature of intelligence itself.

Among the most promising directions for addressing these limitations is the further development of compositional learning approaches. Human intelligence is remarkable in its ability to combine and recombine concepts to address novel situations—to decompose complex problems into simpler components and to synthesize existing knowledge to tackle unfamiliar challenges. AI systems that can similarly decompose and recombine knowledge may achieve greater flexibility and generality than today's most advanced models.

Another frontier concerns causal reasoning—the ability not just to identify correlations in data but to understand the underlying causal mechanisms that generate observed patterns. Humans excel at inferring causal relationships even from limited evidence, allowing us to generalize knowledge to new contexts in ways that current AI systems struggle to match. Research at the intersection of causal inference and machine learning offers the potential for AI systems that can reason more robustly about counterfactuals and interventions—capabilities essential for both scientific discovery and effective real-world decision-making.

Perhaps the most fundamental technical challenge lies in developing systems capable of metacognition—awareness of their own limitations and uncertainties. The most sophisticated human reasoning involves not just processing information but reflecting on that processing—knowing when we don't know, recognizing when our reasoning may be flawed, and adapting our approach accordingly. AI systems that can similarly model their own knowledge boundaries and reasoning processes may achieve both greater capabilities and greater safety, particularly in open-world environments where unexpected situations inevitably arise.

Socioeconomic Transformation

Equally significant are the socioeconomic implications of advancing AI capabilities. The transformation of labour markets has already begun, with routine cognitive tasks increasingly automated. This process will likely accelerate, necessitating new approaches to education, employment, and economic organization. The benefits of this transformation must be widely shared to avoid exacerbating existing inequalities—a challenge that requires political will and institutional creativity alongside technological progress.

The historical pattern of technological displacement followed by job creation in new sectors may not hold with the same dynamics as in previous technological revolutions. AI's unique capacity to automate cognitive as well as physical labour suggests potential disruption across a broader spectrum of occupations, including those traditionally considered knowledge work. This does not necessarily imply widespread technological unemployment (new roles will emerge at the human-AI interface, and entirely new industries may develop) but it does suggest a transition period that may be more challenging than previous technological shifts.

Education systems face the dual challenge of preparing students for a rapidly evolving job market while cultivating the uniquely human capabilities that will remain valuable as AI advances. Critical thinking, creativity, emotional intelligence, and ethical reasoning (areas where humans maintain advantages over current AI systems) may become increasingly central to curricula at all levels. Lifelong learning will become not just beneficial but essential, requiring new institutional structures to support continuous reskilling and upskilling throughout careers.

The economic impacts extend beyond labour markets to questions of market concentration, intellectual property, and the distribution of productivity gains. The data and computational resources required for cutting-edge AI development are substantial, potentially creating barriers to entry that favour already-dominant technology firms. Ensuring that AI development remains accessible to diverse participants, from academic researchers to startups to civil society organizations, may require deliberate policy interventions and new models of resource sharing. Similarly, mechanisms for ensuring that productivity gains from AI adoption benefit workers as well as shareholders will be crucial for maintaining social cohesion through this transition.

Governance Challenges

The governance of AI technologies presents perhaps the most complex challenge of all. National regulatory frameworks are emerging but often lag behind technological development. International coordination remains nascent, despite the inherently global nature of both AI research and its consequences. Establishing norms and institutions capable of guiding AI development toward beneficial outcomes will require unprecedented cooperation across sectors and borders.

The governance challenge is complicated by the dual-use nature of many AI technologies. The same advances that enable beneficial applications in healthcare, environmental management, or scientific discovery can potentially be repurposed for surveillance, manipulation, or autonomous weapons systems. Unlike physical technologies, which often require specialized facilities or materials, many AI capabilities are primarily informational and thus more difficult to contain once developed. This reality necessitates governance approaches that manage risks without unduly constraining beneficial innovation—a delicate balance that no single regulatory framework has fully achieved.

There are promising models emerging, however. Multi-stakeholder initiatives bring together industry, academia, civil society, and government to develop standards and best practices that can inform more formal regulation. Adaptive governance approaches that emphasize ongoing monitoring and adjustment may prove more effective than static rules in a rapidly evolving technological landscape. Most importantly, there is growing recognition that AI governance cannot be treated as a purely technical matter but must engage with the broader social, political, and ethical questions that AI development raises.

The Human–AI Partnership

Throughout this book, we have emphasized the co-evolutionary relationship between human and artificial intelligence. This relationship will continue to define the field's trajectory. Rather than viewing AI as a replacement for human capabilities, we might more productively understand it as an extension of human potential—a tool through which we can transcend our cognitive limitations while preserving the values that give meaning to our endeavours.

This perspective shifts the focus from artificial general intelligence as an autonomous entity to augmented intelligence as a collaborative system. The most powerful AI applications may be those that enhance human capabilities rather than replicate them—tools that expand our creative potential, deepen our understanding of complex phenomena, and extend our ability to address challenges beyond the scale of individual human cognition. From this vantage point, the goal becomes not the creation of machine intelligence indistinguishable from human intelligence, but rather the development of complementary capabilities that, in combination with human strengths, enable achievements beyond what either could accomplish alone.

Such complementarity requires thoughtful interface design grounded in understanding both human cognitive processes and machine capabilities. It demands systems that can adapt to individual human preferences and working styles rather than forcing humans to adapt to rigid machine paradigms. Most fundamentally, it requires maintaining human agency and autonomy even as AI systems take on increasingly sophisticated roles in decision processes. The human-AI partnership is ultimately not about subordination in either direction, but about synergy between different forms of intelligence.

AI and Hardware

The co-design of hardware and software for AI involves creating systems where both components are intricately tailored to work together, optimizing performance and energy efficiency. This approach has been pivotal throughout the history of AI, as successful deployments often relied on algorithms that could leverage existing hardware capabilities. In turn, hardware advancements were developed to accelerate dominant algorithms. Before the widespread adoption of neural networks, there were limited instances of AI-specific hardware designed to enhance tasks like search and optimization. However, the field of AI-specialized hardware accelerators gained significant momentum with the large-scale adoption of artificial neural networks, marking a new era in AI development.

As of 2025, the relationship between hardware and software in AI can be summarized by several key trends. Algorithms that are easier to implement and scale using current hardware tend to gain widespread adoption. Meanwhile, hardware design focuses on accelerating computational operations most relevant to these algorithms. The challenges of energy consumption and throughput remain central to training large-scale models, with innovations in numerical representations, sparsity techniques, and data/model parallelism emerging as critical enablers for efficient training and inference. Despite these advancements, deploying AI systems at the edge such as in mobile devices or embedded systems remains challenging due to resource allocation conflicts, energy constraints, thermal dissipation limits, and real-time application requirements.

The history of hardware-software co-design in AI can be categorized by different approaches. In the domain of *AI for Hardware Design*, techniques like integer linear programming (ILP) solvers have been used for automatic routing in chip layouts, while functional verification methods ensure chip designs meet specifications. Recently, machine learning has been increasingly applied to chip design processes, offering new possibilities for optimization.

In *Symbolic AI*, planning, and search tasks have benefited from specialized hardware. For example, IBM's Deep Blue supercomputer demonstrated the success of custom hardware in search algorithms by defeating world chess champion Garry Kasparov. In more recent applications, robot motion planning has been accelerated using field-programmable gate arrays (FPGAs), graphics processing units (GPUs), and single instruction multiple data (SIMD) instructions.

For *Probabilistic Methods* and *Numerical Optimization*, computational geometry tasks like sensor fusion and state estimation rely heavily on SIMD-accelerated linear algebra operations. Libraries such as Eigen or Intel MKL provide optimized routines for dense and sparse matrix factorization tailored to specific hardware architectures. Application-Specific Integrated Circuits (ASICs) have also been deployed to accelerate visual localization and mapping tasks in edge devices.

The field of *Machine Learning* is currently dominated by artificial neural networks, supported by a wide range of hardware accelerators such as GPUs, TPUs (Tensor Processing Units), Graphcore IPUs (Intelligence Processing Units), and neuromorphic computing systems. The progress of deep learning is tightly coupled with advancements in hardware; innovations like novel numerical representations, accelerated matrix multiplications, high-bandwidth interconnects (including optical interconnects), and sparsity techniques have proven instrumental in scaling up machine learning workloads. While general-purpose libraries like TensorFlow and PyTorch facilitate rapid prototyping and research, achieving peak performance often requires deep optimization tailored to specific algorithms and hardware configurations.

The challenges faced by AI researchers highlight several promising areas for future exploration. Numerical representations offer opportunities for increased throughput with reduced precision while maintaining accuracy. Reduced precision models may even outperform higher-precision counterparts when optimized for specific tasks. Sparsity presents another challenge; while numerical solvers benefit from sparse matrix factorization techniques, achieving similar gains for arbitrary sparsity patterns in machine learning models remains difficult without dedicated hardware support.

Scaling up state-of-the-art models introduces additional system-level constraints beyond computational acceleration. These include memory bottlenecks, communication delays during distributed training or inference, storage throughput for checkpointing large models, energy consumption concerns, and thermal management requirements; all of which demand innovative engineering solutions.

Deploying AI systems at the edge brings its own set of difficulties due to the increasing size and complexity of modern models. Power consumption, thermal dissipation limits, memory constraints, and integration challenges among heterogeneous components pose significant obstacles in edge environments where resources are limited but real-time performance is critical.

Looking ahead, there is growing interest in leveraging AI itself for system optimization. As the pace of algorithmic advancements accelerates, human engineers may struggle to keep up with designing effective co-optimization techniques for hardware-software integration. Developing AI systems that assist with design processes, shortening optimization timelines or enabling runtime adaptation, is likely to become a central focus in addressing these challenges.

Ethics and Values

The ethical dimensions of AI development have received increasing attention as capabilities have advanced. Questions of fairness, privacy, accountability, and the distribution of benefits and harms have moved from philosophical abstractions to practical imperatives as AI systems make consequential decisions affecting human lives and livelihoods. These questions have no simple technical solutions; they require ongoing deliberation about the values we wish to embed in our technological systems and the kind of society we aim to create.

This deliberative process must be inclusive, engaging diverse perspectives on what constitutes beneficial AI development. Different cultures, communities, and individuals may have varying priorities and concerns regarding AI applications. What appears as progress from one perspective may represent regression from another. Navigating these differences requires not just technical expertise but also cultural sensitivity, political wisdom, and moral imagination. It requires recognition that value alignment is not a one-time achievement but an ongoing process of negotiation and adaptation as both societies and technologies evolve.

The greatest promise of artificial intelligence lies not in its autonomy, but in its complementarity with human intelligence. By embracing this perspective, we may develop systems that enhance rather than diminish human agency—systems that serve as partners in addressing the complex challenges that confront humanity in the twenty-first century. From climate change to pandemic prevention to sustainable development, these challenges often involve interactions among social, ecological, and technological systems of staggering complexity. AI tools that can help us navigate this complexity, identifying patterns and possibilities beyond the reach of unaided human cognition, may prove essential to human flourishing in the decades ahead.

Collective Responsibility

As researchers, developers, policymakers, and citizens, we bear a collective responsibility for shaping this emerging future. The decisions made in the coming decades will influence not only the technical capabilities of AI systems but also their impact on human flourishing. By grounding these decisions in both technical understanding and ethical reflection, we can work toward a future in which artificial intelligence serves as a powerful force for human advancement.

This responsibility extends to all participants in the AI ecosystem. Researchers must consider not just what can be built but what should be built, and under what conditions. Developers must incorporate ethical considerations throughout the design process rather than treating them as an afterthought. Policymakers must create frameworks that channel innovation toward beneficial outcomes while mitigating potential harms. And citizens must engage with these technologies not as passive consumers but as active participants in shaping their development and deployment.

Education plays a crucial role in enabling this collective responsibility. Technical education must incorporate ethical dimensions of AI development, preparing the next generation of researchers and developers to navigate the complex terrain where technological capability meets social impact. Conversely, education in ethics, policy, and social sciences must increasingly engage with the technical realities of AI systems to avoid abstract theorizing disconnected from practical applications. Most broadly, public understanding of AI capabilities and limitations must deepen if democratic societies are to make informed collective choices about the role of these technologies.

The transcendence of traditional paradigms that gives this book its title is ultimately not just about artificial intelligence surpassing its previous limitations, but about humanity transcending its own constraints through the thoughtful development and application of these remarkable technologies. The chapters that preceded this epilogue have mapped the terrain of this transformation; it remains for us to navigate it with wisdom and foresight.

The path forward will not be linear or predictable. There will be breakthroughs and setbacks, periods of rapid advancement and plateaus of consolidation. Throughout this journey, the most important insights may come not from technical innovation alone but from deeper understanding of the relationship between human and machine intelligence—how they differ, how they complement each other, and how together they might achieve possibilities beyond what either could be realized independently.

In concluding this book, we return to the fundamental questions that have stimulated the study of artificial intelligence from its inception: What is the nature of intelligence? How does understanding artificial intelligence deepen our understanding of human cognition? And how can we ensure that the intelligence we create enhances rather than diminishes what makes us distinctively human? These questions have no final answers, but in continuing to explore them, across disciplines, across sectors, and across cultures, we may discover not just more capable technologies but more profound insights into our own humanity.

The future of AI lies not just in the hands of technical specialists but in the collective choices we make as a global society about the kinds of intelligence we wish to develop and the purposes toward which we direct it. By approaching these choices with humility about what we know, openness to diverse perspectives, and commitment to shared human flourishing, we can work toward a future in which artificial intelligence becomes not a source of anxiety but a powerful ally in addressing humanity's greatest challenges and realizing our highest aspirations.

The manufacturer's authorised representative in the EU is Springer
Nature Customer Service Centre GmbH, Europaplatz 3, 69115 Heidelberg,
Germany. If you have any concerns regarding our products, please
contact ProductSafety@springernature.com

Printed and bound by CPI Group (UK) Ltd, Croydon, CR0 4YY
23/04/2026
02095585-0011